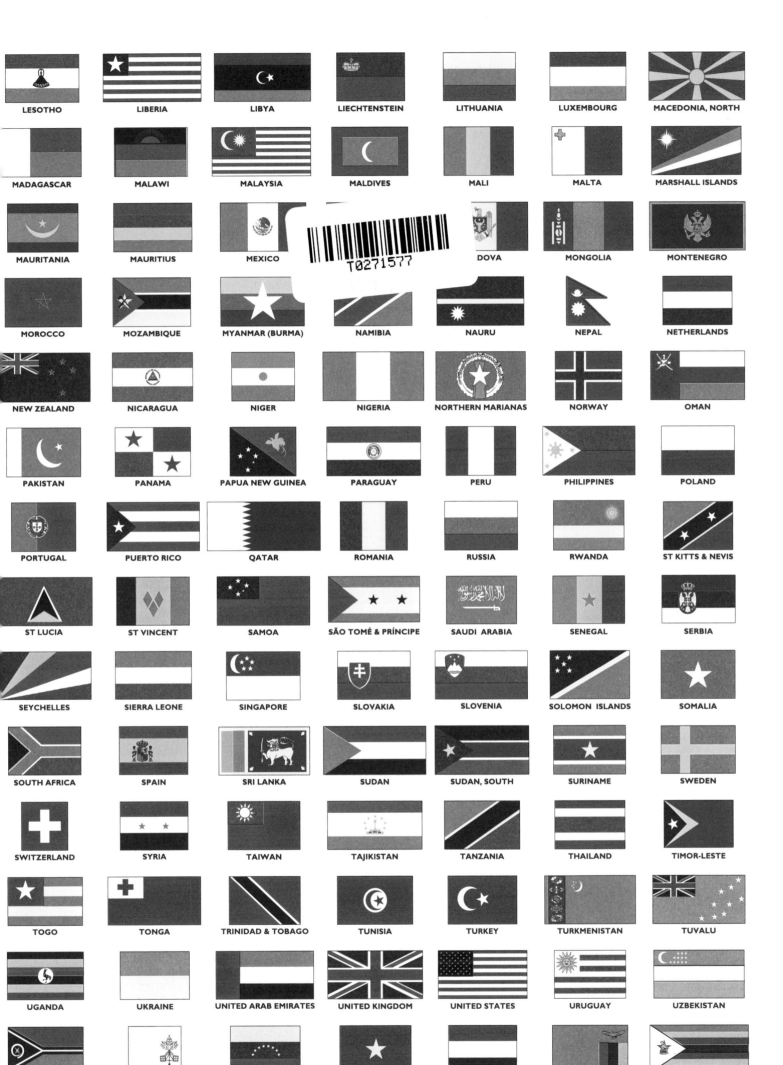

LESOTHO	LIBERIA	LIBYA	LIECHTENSTEIN	LITHUANIA	LUXEMBOURG	MACEDONIA, NORTH
MADAGASCAR	MALAWI	MALAYSIA	MALDIVES	MALI	MALTA	MARSHALL ISLANDS
MAURITANIA	MAURITIUS	MEXICO		DOVA	MONGOLIA	MONTENEGRO
MOROCCO	MOZAMBIQUE	MYANMAR (BURMA)	NAMIBIA	NAURU	NEPAL	NETHERLANDS
NEW ZEALAND	NICARAGUA	NIGER	NIGERIA	NORTHERN MARIANAS	NORWAY	OMAN
PAKISTAN	PANAMA	PAPUA NEW GUINEA	PARAGUAY	PERU	PHILIPPINES	POLAND
PORTUGAL	PUERTO RICO	QATAR	ROMANIA	RUSSIA	RWANDA	ST KITTS & NEVIS
ST LUCIA	ST VINCENT	SAMOA	SÃO TOMÉ & PRÍNCIPE	SAUDI ARABIA	SENEGAL	SERBIA
SEYCHELLES	SIERRA LEONE	SINGAPORE	SLOVAKIA	SLOVENIA	SOLOMON ISLANDS	SOMALIA
SOUTH AFRICA	SPAIN	SRI LANKA	SUDAN	SUDAN, SOUTH	SURINAME	SWEDEN
SWITZERLAND	SYRIA	TAIWAN	TAJIKISTAN	TANZANIA	THAILAND	TIMOR-LESTE
TOGO	TONGA	TRINIDAD & TOBAGO	TUNISIA	TURKEY	TURKMENISTAN	TUVALU
UGANDA	UKRAINE	UNITED ARAB EMIRATES	UNITED KINGDOM	UNITED STATES	URUGUAY	UZBEKISTAN
VANUATU	VATICAN CITY	VENEZUELA	VIETNAM	YEMEN	ZAMBIA	ZIMBABWE

PHILIP'S

AGES 14–18

KEY STAGE 4, GCSE & A-LEVEL

Royal Geographical Society with IBG

MODERN
SCHOOL ATLAS

Agriculture 38, 136–7
Airports 142
Air travel 42, 142
Alternative energy 139

Balance of trade 140
Biomes 58, 74, 92, 100, 106, 118, 134–5
BRICS countries 151
Bush fires 101

Carbon dioxide emissions 37, 130
Children's Climate Risk Index (CCRI) 130
Climate 34–5, 58, 74, 92, 100,
106, 118, 128–9, 132–3
Climate change 35, 130–1
Climate statistics 132–3
Coal 101, 138
Commonwealth 151
Conservation 37
Container ports 141
Continental drift 124
Covid-19 cases 153
Crime rate 48

Deforestation 131
Desertification 131
Drought 101
Drug traffic 153

Earthquakes 11, 81, 83, 115, 125
Education 48, 145
Electricity generation 41, 139
El Niño 129
Employment 39, 80, 140
Energy 40–1, 101, 138
European Union (EU) 60
Eurozone 60
Exports 39, 141

Family size 149
Fishing 38, 136–7
Flood risk 36

Food production 38, 136–7
Forestry 136–7
Fuel 40–1, 138

Gender Inequality Index (GII) 145
Geology 32, 124
Global Peace Index (GPI) 152
Global warming 35, 61, 130
Greenhouse gases 37, 130
Gross National Income (GNI) 144
Group of Seven (G7) 151

Hadley Cell 128
Health care 145
Heatwaves 101
Human Development Index (HDI) 144
Hurricanes 116
Hydroelectricity 41, 80, 101, 139

Illiteracy 145
Imports 39
Industry 39, 80, 140
Infant mortality 149
Inter-tropical convergence zone (ITCZ) .. 127–8

Languages 59, 150
La Niña 129
Latitude and longitude 6
LEDCs 146
Life expectancy 149

Malnutrition 137
Manufacturing 39, 80, 141
Map projections 7–8
MEDCs 146
Migration 47, 152
Minerals 101, 139
Monsoon 85

National parks 37
Natural vegetation 37, 134–5
Nuclear power 11, 41, 139

Ocean conveyor belt 126
Ocean currents 126
Oil and gas 40–1, 88, 101, 138

Plate tectonics 124–5
Population 46–7, 59, 75, 93, 101,
107, 119, 146–9

Religions 150
Remittances 152
Remote sensing 9–17
Renewable energy 41, 139

Satellite imagery 9–17
Scale 5
Services 39, 140
Shale gas 41
Soils 37, 134–5
Standards of living 48, 61, 144

Terrorism 153
Time zones 142
Tourism 43, 61, 113, 143
Trade 39, 141
Transport 42
Travel 36, 42–3, 142
Tsunamis 11, 81, 83

Unemployment 48, 61
United Nations (UN) 151
Urban population 148
Urban regeneration 14–15

Volcanoes 81, 115, 125

Waste recycling 36
Water supply 36, 88, 144
Wealth 48, 61, 144
Wind power 41
World Heritage Sites 37, 143

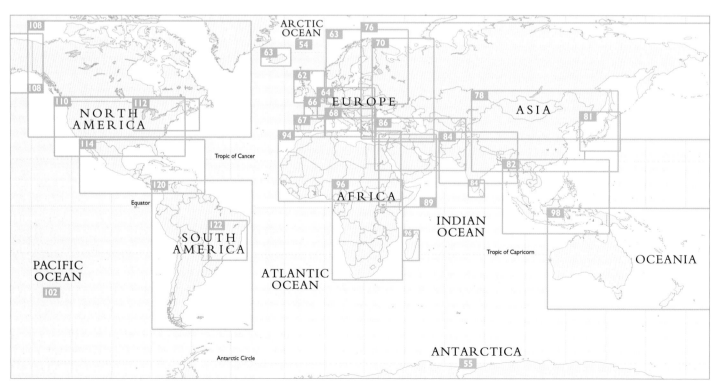

MAP SYMBOLS..4
SCALE...5
LATITUDE AND LONGITUDE.....................................6
MAP PROJECTIONS..7–8
GEOGRAPHICAL INFORMATION SYSTEMS....................8

REMOTE SENSING   9–17

INTRODUCTION 10–11
ENVIRONMENTAL MONITORING 11
COLOUR COMPOSITES 12
VEGETATION AND LANDFORMS 13
URBAN REGENERATION 14–15
GEOLOGICAL INTERPRETATION 16

UNITED KINGDOM AND IRELAND   17–48

IRELAND: NORTH 18–19
    SOUTH 20–21
NORTHERN SCOTLAND 22–23
SOUTHERN SCOTLAND 24–25
NORTHERN ENGLAND 26–27
WALES AND SOUTH-WEST ENGLAND.............28–29
SOUTH AND SOUTH-EAST ENGLAND...........30–31
UK AND IRELAND: GEOLOGY 32
    RELIEF OF LAND 33
    CLIMATE..34–35
    ENVIRONMENT 36–37
    AGRICULTURE, INDUSTRY AND TRADE 38–39
    ENERGY 40–41
    TRANSPORT AND TOURISM 42–43
    COUNTIES AND REGIONS 44–45
    POPULATION TRENDS 46–47
    STANDARDS OF LIVING 48

THE WORLD   49–122

THE WORLD: RELIEF OF LAND 50–51
    COUNTRIES 52–53
ARCTIC OCEAN AND ANTARCTICA 54–55
EUROPE: RELIEF OF LAND 56
    COUNTRIES 57
    CLIMATE AND BIOMES 58
    POPULATION 59
EUROPEAN UNION/EUROPE 60–61
UK AND IRELAND 62
SCANDINAVIA AND THE BALTIC LANDS 63
CENTRAL EUROPE 64–65
FRANCE 66
SPAIN AND PORTUGAL 67
ITALY AND THE BALKAN STATES 68–69
EASTERN EUROPE AND TURKEY 70–71
ASIA: RELIEF OF LAND 72
    COUNTRIES 73
    CLIMATE AND BIOMES 74
    POPULATION AND WEALTH 75
RUSSIA AND NORTHERN ASIA 76–77
CHINA AND THE FAR EAST 78–79
CHINA: INDUSTRY AND HYDROELECTRICITY 80
JAPAN 81
SOUTH-EAST ASIA 82–83
SOUTH ASIA 84–85
THE MIDDLE EAST 86–87
    OIL AND WATER 88
ARABIA AND THE HORN OF AFRICA 89
AFRICA: RELIEF OF LAND 90
    COUNTRIES 91
    CLIMATE AND BIOMES 92
    POPULATION AND WEALTH 93
NORTHERN AFRICA 94–95
CENTRAL AND SOUTHERN AFRICA 96–97

OCEANIA...98–99
    CLIMATE AND POPULATION 100–101
PACIFIC OCEAN 102–103
NORTH AMERICA: RELIEF OF LAND 104
    COUNTRIES 105
    CLIMATE AND BIOMES 106
    POPULATION AND WEALTH 107
CANADA 108–109
UNITED STATES 110–111
NORTH-EAST UNITED STATES AND THE ST LAWRENCE ...112–113
MEXICO, CENTRAL AMERICA AND THE CARIBBEAN 114–115
CARIBBEAN: HURRICANES 116
SOUTH AMERICA: RELIEF OF LAND 117
    CLIMATE AND BIOMES 118
    POPULATION AND WEALTH 119
SOUTH AMERICA 120–121
SOUTH-EAST BRAZIL 122

WORLD THEMES   123–160

THE WORLD: VOLCANOES AND EARTHQUAKES 124–125
    TEMPERATURE AND OCEAN CURRENTS 126
    PRESSURE, WINDS AND PRECIPITATION 127
    CLIMATE 128–129
    CLIMATE CHANGE 130–131
    CLIMATE STATISTICS 132–133
    BIOMES 134–135
    AGRICULTURE AND FOOD 136–137
    ENERGY AND MINERALS 138–139
    INDUSTRY AND TRADE 140–141
    TRAVEL AND TOURISM 142–143
    STANDARDS OF LIVING 144–145
    POPULATION DISTRIBUTION 146–147
    POPULATION TRENDS 148–149
    LANGUAGES AND RELIGION 150
    INTERNATIONAL ORGANIZATIONS 151
    HUMAN CONCERNS 152–153
    SOCIAL AND ECONOMIC STATISTICS ...154–159
    PHYSICAL DIMENSIONS 160

INDEX   161–184

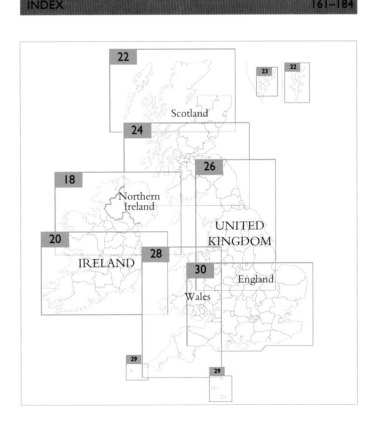

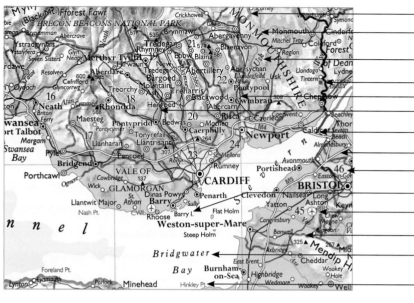

- National park boundary
- Administrative area name
- River name
- Place of interest
- Road
- Perennial river
- Railway tunnel
- Motorway
- Built-up area
- Island name
- Airport
- Administrative boundary
- Sea feature name
- Cape name

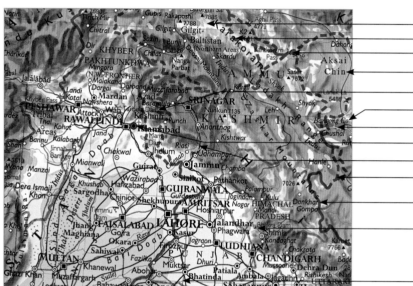

- Permanent ice and glacier
- Mountain range name
- Mountain pass (m)
- Regional name
- Dam name
- Lake name
- Perennial lake
- Capital city
- Railway under construction
- Disputed international boundary
- International boundary
- Dam
- Canal

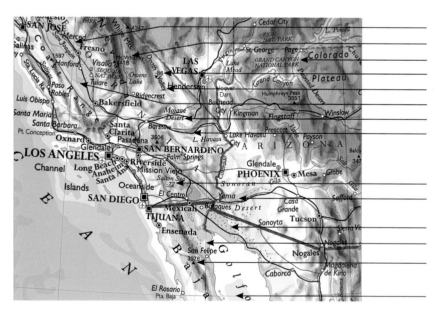

- Aqueduct
- Mountain peak name
- National park name
- Depth (m)
- Valley name
- Intermittent lake
- Desert name
- Railway
- Height of lake surface (m)
- Intermittent river
- Sand desert
- Line of longitude
- Elevation (m)
- Line of latitude

Settlement symbols and type styles vary according to the scale of each map and indicate the relative importance of towns rather than specific population figures

The scale of a map is the relationship of the distance between any two points shown on the map and the distance between the same two points on the Earth's surface. For instance, 1 inch on the map represents 1 mile on the ground, or 10 kilometres on the ground is represented by 1 centimetre on the map.

Instead of saying 1 centimetre represents 10 kilometres, we could say that 1 centimetre represents 1 000 000 centimetres on the map. If the scale is stated so that the same unit of measurement is used on both the map and the ground, then the proportion will hold for any unit of measurement. Therefore, the scale is usually written 1:1 000 000. This is called a 'representative fraction' and usually appears at the top of the map page, above the scale bar.

Calculations can easily be made in centimetres and kilometres by dividing the second figure in the representative fraction by 100 000 (i.e. by deleting the last five zeros). Thus at a scale of 1:5 000 000, 1 cm on the map represents 50 km on the ground. This is called a 'scale statement'. The calculation for inches and miles is more laborious, but 1 000 000 divided by 63 360 (the number of inches in a mile) shows that 1:1 000 000 can be stated as 1 inch on the map represents approximately 16 miles on the ground.

Many of the maps in this atlas feature a scale bar. This is a bar divided into the units of the map – miles and kilometres – so that a map distance can be measured with a ruler, dividers or a piece of paper, then placed along the scale bar, and the distance read off. To the left of the zero on the scale bar there are usually more divisions. By placing the ruler or dividers on the nearest rounded figure to the right of the zero, the smaller units can be counted off to the left.

The map extracts below show Los Angeles and its surrounding area at six different scales. The representative fraction, scale statement and scale bar are positioned above each map. Map 1 is at 1:27 000 and is the largest scale extract shown. Many of the individual buildings are identified and most of the streets are named, but at this scale only part of central Los Angeles can be shown within the given area. Map 2 is much smaller in scale at 1:250 000. Only a few important buildings and streets can be named, but the whole of central Los Angeles is shown. Maps 3, 4 and 5 show how greater areas can be depicted as the map scale decreases, down to Map 6 at 1:35 000 000. At this small scale, the entire Los Angeles conurbation is depicted by a single town symbol and a large part of the south-western USA and part of Mexico is shown.

The scales of maps must be used with care since large distances on small-scale maps can be represented by one or two centimetres. On certain projections scale is only correct along certain lines, parallels or meridians. As a general rule, the larger the map scale, the more accurate and reliable will be the distance measured.

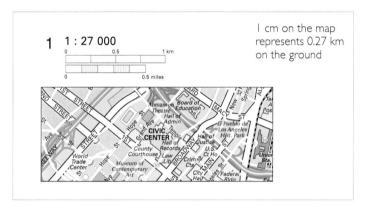

1 1 : 27 000

1 cm on the map represents 0.27 km on the ground

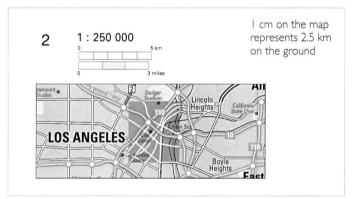

2 1 : 250 000

1 cm on the map represents 2.5 km on the ground

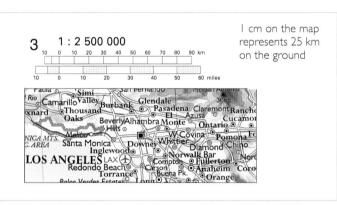

3 1 : 2 500 000

1 cm on the map represents 25 km on the ground

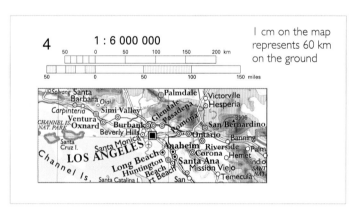

4 1 : 6 000 000

1 cm on the map represents 60 km on the ground

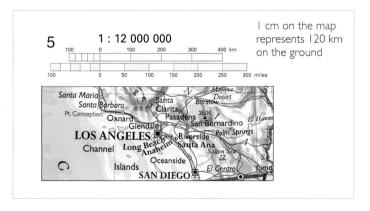

5 1 : 12 000 000

1 cm on the map represents 120 km on the ground

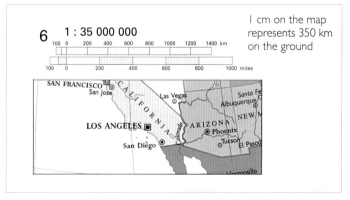

6 1 : 35 000 000

1 cm on the map represents 350 km on the ground

Accurate positioning of individual points on the Earth's surface is made possible by reference to the geometric system of latitude and longitude.

Latitude is the distance of a point north or south of the Equator measured at an angle with the centre of the Earth, whereby the Equator is latitude 0 degrees, the North Pole is 90 degrees north and the South Pole 90 degrees south. Latitude parallels are drawn west–east around the Earth, parallel to the Equator, decreasing in diameter from the Equator until they become a point at the poles. On the maps in this atlas the lines of latitude are represented by blue lines running across the map in smooth curves, with the degree figures in blue at the sides of the maps. The degree interval depends on the scale of the map.

Lines of longitude are meridians drawn north–south, cutting the lines of latitude at right angles on the Earth's surface and intersecting with one another at the poles. Longitude is measured by an angle at the centre of the Earth from the prime meridian (0 degrees), which passes through Greenwich in London. It is given as a measurement east or west of the Greenwich Meridian from 0 to 180 degrees. The meridians are normally drawn north–south vertically down the map, with the degree figures in blue in the top and bottom margins of the map.

In the index each place name is followed by its map page number, its letter-figure grid reference, and then its latitude and longitude. The unit of measurement is the degree, which is subdivided into 60 minutes. An index entry states the position of a place in degrees and minutes. The latitude is followed by N(orth) or S(outh) and the longitude E(ast) or W(est).

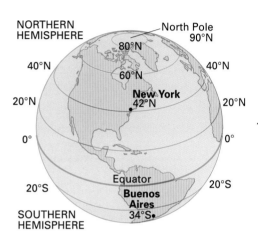

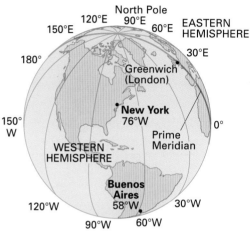

Latitude

Lines of latitude cross the atlas maps from east to west. The Equator is at 0°. All other lines of latitude are either north or south of the Equator. Line 40°N is almost halfway towards the North Pole. The North Pole is at 90°N.

Longitude

Lines of longitude run from north to south. These lines meet at the North Pole and the South Pole. Longitude 0° passes through Greenwich. This line is also called the Prime Meridian. Lines of longitude are either east of 0° or west of 0°. There are 180 degrees of longitude both east and west of 0°.

Using latitude and longitude

Latitude and longitude lines make a grid that can be printed on a map. You can find a place if you know its latitude and longitude. The degree of latitude is either north or south of the Equator. The longitude number is either east or west of the Greenwich Meridian.

HOW TO LOCATE A PLACE OR FEATURE

The two diagrams (right) show how to estimate the required distance from the nearest line of latitude or longitude on the map page, in order to locate a place or feature listed in the index (such as Helston in the UK and Mount McKinley in the USA, as detailed in the above example).

In the left-hand diagram there are 30 minutes between the lines and so to find the position of Helston an estimate has to be made: 7 parts of the 30 minutes north of the 50°0N latitude line, and 17 parts of the 30 minutes west of the 5°0W longitude line.

In the right-hand diagram it is more difficult to estimate because there is an interval of 10 degrees between the lines. In the example of Mount McKinley, the reader has to estimate 3 degrees 4 minutes north of 60°0N and 1 degree west of 150°0W.

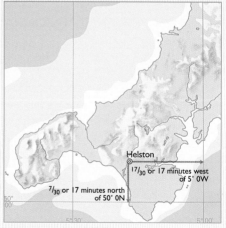

Helston, U.K. 29 G3 50°7N 5°17W
Helston is on map page 29, in grid square G3, and is 50 degrees 7 minutes north of the Equator and 5 degrees 17 minutes west of Greenwich.

Mt. McKinley, U.S.A. 108 C4 63°4N 151°0W
Mount McKinley is on map page 108, in grid square C4, and is 63 degrees 4 minutes north of the Equator and 151 degrees west of Greenwich.

A map projection is the systematic depiction of the imaginary grid of lines of latitude and longitude from a globe on to a flat surface. The grid of lines is called the 'graticule' and it can be constructed either by graphical means or by mathematical formulae to form the basis of a map. As a globe is three dimensional, it is not possible to depict its surface on a flat map without some form of distortion. Preservation of one of the basic properties listed below can only be secured at the expense of the others and thus the choice of projection is often a compromise solution.

Correct area

In these projections the areas from the globe are to scale on the map. This is particularly useful in the mapping of densities and distributions. Projections with this property are termed 'equal area', 'equivalent' or 'homolographic'.

Correct distance

In these projections the scale is correct along the meridians, or, in the case of the 'azimuthal equidistant', scale is true along any line drawn from the centre of the projection. They are called 'equidistant'.

Correct shape

This property can only be true within small areas as it is achieved only by having a uniform scale distortion along both the 'x' and 'y' axes of the projection. The projections are called 'conformal' or 'orthomorphic'.

Map projections can be divided into three broad categories – **'azimuthal'**, **'conic'** and **'cylindrical'**. Cartographers use different projections from these categories depending on the map scale, the size of the area to be mapped, and what they want the map to show.

AZIMUTHAL OR ZENITHAL PROJECTIONS

These are constructed by the projection of part of the graticule from the globe on to a plane tangential to any single point on it. This plane may be tangential to the equator (equatorial case), the poles (polar case) or any other point (oblique case). Any straight line drawn from the point at which the plane touches the globe is the shortest distance from that point and is known as a 'great circle'. In its 'gnomonic' construction any straight line on the map is a great circle, but there is great exaggeration towards the edges and this reduces its general uses. There are five different ways of transferring the graticule on to the plane and these are shown below. The diagrams below also show how the graticules vary, using the polar case as the example.

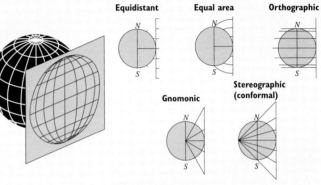

Polar case

The polar case is the simplest to construct and the diagram on the right shows the differing effects of all five methods of construction, comparing their coverage, distortion, etc, using North America as the example.

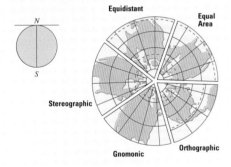

Oblique case

The plane touches the globe at any point between the Equator and poles. The oblique orthographic uses the distortion in azimuthal projections away from the centre to give a graphic depiction of the Earth as seen from any desired point in space.

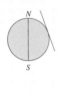

Equatorial case

The example shown here is Lambert's Equivalent Azimuthal. It is the only projection which is both equal area and where bearing is true from the centre.

CONICAL PROJECTIONS

These use the projection of the graticule from the globe on to a cone which is tangential to a line of latitude (termed the 'standard parallel'). This line is always an arc and scale is always true along it. Because of its method of construction, it is used mainly for depicting the temperate latitudes around the standard parallel, i.e. where there is least distortion. To reduce the distortion and include a larger range of latitudes, the projection may be constructed with the cone bisecting the surface of the globe so that there are two standard parallels, each of which is true to scale. The distortion is thus spread more evenly between the two chosen parallels.

Simple conical with one standard parallel

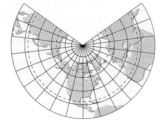

Bonne

This is a modification of the simple conic, whereby the true scale along the meridians is sacrificed to enable the accurate representation of areas. However, scale is true along each parallel but shapes are distorted at the edges.

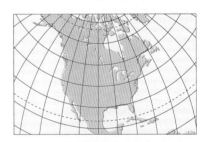

Albers Conical Equal Area

This projection uses two standard parallels. The selection of these relative to the land area to be mapped is very important. It is equal area and is especially useful for large land masses oriented east–west, such as the USA.

CYLINDRICAL AND OTHER WORLD PROJECTIONS

This group of projections are those which permit the whole of the Earth's surface to be depicted on one map. They are a very large group of projections and the following are only a few of them. Cylindrical projections are constructed by the projection of the graticule from the globe on to a cylinder tangential to the globe. Although cylindrical projections can depict all the main land masses, there is considerable distortion of shape and area towards the poles. One cylindrical projection, Mercator, overcomes this shortcoming by possessing the unique navigational property that any straight line drawn on it is a line of constant bearing ('loxodrome'). It is used for maps and charts between 15° either side of the Equator. Beyond this, enlargement of area is a serious drawback, although it is used for navigational charts at all latitudes.

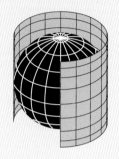

Simple cylindrical

Cylindrical with two standard parallels

Mercator

Eckert IV (pseudocylindrical equal area)

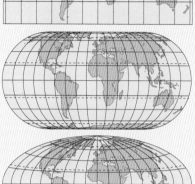

Hammer (polyconic equal area)

GEOGRAPHIC INFORMATION SYSTEMS

A Geographic Information System (GIS) enables any available geospatial data to be compiled, presented and analysed using specialized computer software.

Many aspects of our lives now benefit from the use of GIS – from the management and maintenance of the networks of pipelines and cables that supply our homes, to the exploitation or protection of the natural resources that we use. Much of this is at a regional or national scale and the data collected from satellites form an important part of our interpretation and understanding of the world around us.

GIS systems are used for many aspects of central planning and modern life, such as defence, land use, reclamation, telecommunications and the deployment of emergency services. Commercial companies can use demographic and infrastructure data within a GIS to plan marketing strategies, identifying where their services would be most needed, and thus decide where best to locate their businesses. Insurance companies use GIS to determine premiums based on population distribution, crime figures and the likelihood of natural disasters, such as flooding or subsidence.

Whatever the application, all the relevant data can be prepared in a GIS so that a user can extract and display the information of particular interest on a map, or compare it with other material in order to help analyse and resolve a specific problem. From analysis of the data that has been acquired, it is often possible to use a GIS to create a computer 'model' of possible future situations and see what impact various actions may have. A GIS can also monitor change over time, aiding the interpretation of long-term trends.

A GIS may also use satellite data to extract useful information and map large areas, which would otherwise take many man-years using other methods. For applications such as hydrocarbon and mineral exploration, forestry, agriculture, environmental monitoring and urban development, these developments have made it possible to undertake projects on a global scale unheard of before.

To find out more about how GIS works and how it affects our lives, why not go the Ordnance Survey's Mapzone website at: https://www.ordnancesurvey.co.uk/mapzone/gis-zone

Examples of the type of information that can be added to a GIS

relief

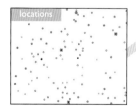
drainage

boundaries

locations

names

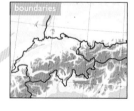
transport

GIS

REMOTE SENSING

The first satellite to monitor our environment systematically was launched as long ago as April 1961. It was called TIROS-1 and was designed specifically to record atmospheric change. The first of the generation of Earth resources satellites was Landsat-1, launched in July 1972. The succeeding decades have seen a revolution in our ability to survey and map our environment. Digital sensors mounted on satellites now scan vast areas of the Earth's surface day and night and at a range of resolutions from 0.3 m to several kms depending on the type of satellite. At any one time, up to 50 satellites may be in orbit. They collect and relay back to Earth huge volumes of geographical data, which is processed and stored by computers.

Satellite imagery and remote sensing

An ability to collect data of large areas at high resolution and the freedom from national access restrictions, have meant that sensors on these satellite platforms are increasingly replacing surface and airborne data-gathering techniques. Twenty-four hours a day, satellites are scanning the Earth's surface and atmosphere, adding to an ever-expanding range of geographic and geophysical data available to help us understand and manage our human and physical environments. Remote sensing is the science of extracting information from such images.

Satellite orbits

Most high resolution Earth-observation satellites are in a nearpolar, Sun-synchronous orbit (*see diagram below right*). At altitudes of between 400–900 km the satellites revolve around the Earth approximately every 100 minutes and on each orbit cross the equator at a similar local (solar) time, usually late morning. This helps ensure the sun is at a high elevation yet atmospheric moisture, which commonly increases throughout the day in warm climates, is relatively low. High resolution sensors can be pointed sideways from the orbital path, resulting in a 1–3 day interval, or 'revisit' time, between imaging opportunities.

Exceptions to these Sun-synchronous orbits include the geostationary meteorological satellites, such as the European Meteosat, American GOES and Russian Elektro satellites. These have an approximate 36,000 km high orbit and rotate around the Earth every 24 hours, thus remaining above the same point on the Equator. These satellites acquire frequent images showing cloud and atmospheric moisture movements for almost a full hemisphere.

In addition, there are constellations of global navigation satellite systems, each comprising 20–30 satellites, such as the American Global Positioning System (GPS), Russian GLONASS and, under

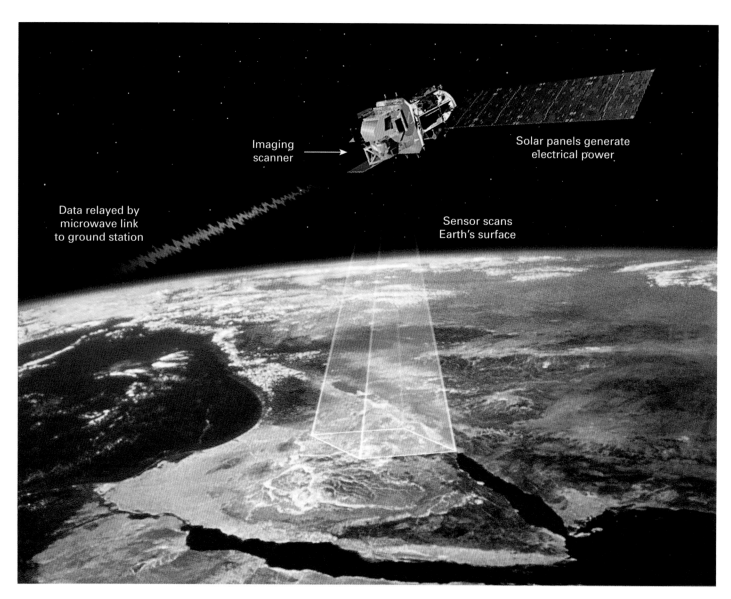

Imaging scanner

Solar panels generate electrical power

Data relayed by microwave link to ground station

Sensor scans Earth's surface

Landsat-8

This is the latest addition to the Landsat Earth-observation satellite programme, orbiting at 710 km above the Earth. With onboard recorders, the satellite can store data until it passes within range of a ground station. Basic geometric and radiometric corrections are then applied before distribution of the imagery to users.

development, the European Galileo system. These satellites circle the Earth at a height of 20,200 km in different orbital planes, enabling us to fix our position on the Earth's surface to an accuracy of a few centimetres. Although initially developed for military use, these systems now assist everyday life used by smart phones and in-car navigation systems. More precise corrections to location accuracy improves both terrestrial and aerial surveys, aircraft and marine navigation as well as guidance for precision agriculture.

Digital sensors
Early satellite designs involved images being exposed to photographic film and returned to Earth by capsule for processing. However, even the first commercial satellite imagery, from Landsat-1, used digital imaging sensors and transmitted the data back to ground stations (see *diagram opposite*).

Optical, or passive, sensors record the radiation reflected from the Earth for specific wavebands. Radar, or active, sensors transmit their own microwave radiation, which is reflected from the Earth's surface back to the satellite and recorded. This allows this type of sensor to operate twenty-four hours a day and in all weather. Synthetic Aperture Radar (SAR) images are examples of the latter.

Whichever scanning method is used, each satellite records image data of constant width but potentially several thousand kilometres in length. Once the data has been received on Earth, it may be split into approximately square sections or 'scenes' for distribution or, increasingly, customers provide a polygon of their 'Area of Interest' which is extracted from the full image strip.

Spectral resolution, wavebands and false-colour composites
Satellites can record data from many sections of the electromagnetic spectrum (wavebands) simultaneously. Since we can only see images made from the three primary colours (red, green and blue), a selection of any three wavebands needs to be made in order to form a picture that will enable visual interpretation of the scene to be made. When any combination other than the visible bands are used, such as near or middle infrared, the resulting image is termed a 'false-colour composite'.

The selection of these wavebands depends on the purpose of the final image – geology, hydrology, agronomy and environmental needs each have their own optimum waveband combinations.

ENVIRONMENTAL MONITORING

Fukushima Nuclear Power Station, Japan
This image was captured by the GeoEye-1 satellite, travelling at 6 km/sec and 680 km above the Earth. In front of the pylons, in the centre of the image, the damaged reactors in the heart of the irradiated area can be seen, following the March 2011 Japanese earthquake and tsunami. It allowed initial assessment of a very dangerous area to take place with minimum risk to human life. *(©DigitalGlobe, Inc. All Rights Reserved)*

Natural-colour and false-colour composites

These images show the salt ponds at the southern end of San Francisco Bay, which now form the San Francisco Bay National Wildlife Refuge. They demonstrate the difference between 'natural colour' (top) and 'false colour' (bottom) composites.

The top image is made from visible red, green and blue wavelengths. The colours correspond closely to those one would observe from an aircraft. The salt ponds appear green or orange-red due to the colour of the sediments they contain. The urban areas appear grey and vegetation is either dark green (trees) or light brown (dry grass).

The bottom image is made up of near-infrared, visible red and visible green wavelengths. These wavebands are represented here in red, green and blue, respectively. Since chlorophyll in healthy vegetation strongly reflects near-infrared light, this is clearly visible as red in the image.

False-colour composite imagery is therefore very sensitive to the presence of healthy vegetation. The bottom image thus shows better discrimination between the 'leafy' residential urban areas, such as Palo Alto (south-west of the Bay), and other urban areas by the 'redness' of the trees. The high chlorophyll content of watered urban grass areas shows as bright red, contrasting with the dark red of trees and the brown of natural, dry grass. *(USGS)*

Nishino-shima, Japan

This small volcanic island, in the Ogasawara chain, erupted into the world at the end of 2013 in the western Pacific Ocean some 1,000 km south of Tokyo. This natural-colour image was captured by Landsat 8 in August 2014 and shows the long white plume of volcanic gases. The continuing flowing out of lava on the eastern side of the island makes this a dangerous island to approach until conditions settle. (NASA)

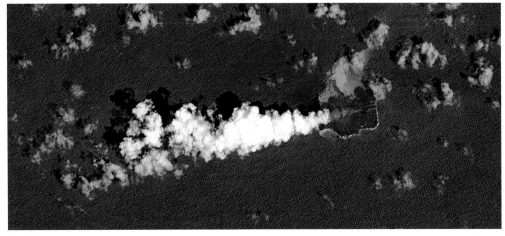

Piqiang Fault, China

By recording and processing the amount of energy reflected or emitted from the Earth in different ways, satellite images can help scientists see patterns in landforms that otherwise might be hard to make out with the naked eye. The colours assigned here clearly show the movement of the bands of sedimentary rocks along the fault line. The land has moved by about 3km along the fault. (NASA)

Kazakhstan/China

The startling contrast in land-use across the international border between Kazakstan, to the west, and China, to the east, is made clear in this Landsat 8 image. There is huge pressure on China to extract the maximum agricultural output from any suitable land, even when it requires irrigation. In the corresponding area of Kazakhstan, there is less need for intensive agriculture and therefore no irrigation. (NASA)

Niger Delta, West Africa

The River Niger is the third longest river in Africa after the Nile and Congo, and this false-colour image shows the different vegetation types. Deltas are by nature constantly evolving sedimentary features and often contain many ecosystems within them. In the case of the Niger Delta, there are also vast hydrocarbon reserves beneath it with associated wells and pipelines. Satellite imagery helps to plan activity and monitor this fragile and changing environment. (USGS)

West India Docks, 1983

This vertical image shows the derelict site of the West India Docks, which were built between 1802 and 1870, as part of the London Docks which eventually stretched from Tower Bridge downstream to Beckton in the east.

The most successful year for the London Docks, in terms of tonnage handled, was 1961. However, by the 1970s they could no longer compete with coastal ports due to the containerisation of cargo and increased size of ships. This resulted in their rapid closure, consequent high unemployment and the economic decline in the area.

By 1981 the docks had closed. These images were taken as part of an aerial survey for the London Docklands Development Corporation, a new government Enterprise Zone covering all of the London Docks. Planning regulations were relaxed, transport infrastructure (the Docklands Light Railway) was constructed and financial incentives offered to attract businesses and property developers.

In this mosaic, made up of eight separate images and taken in 1983, the three docks making up the West India group can be seen. In the south dock empty Thames lighters, once used to move cargo from larger ships, are still visible. The warehouse at the western end of the middle spur was called 'Canary Wharf', where ships from the Canary Islands unloaded cargo, principally bananas and tomatoes. The name was subsequently adopted for the whole area. The building in the northeast corner, with the visible external roof supports, is Billingsgate Fish Market which moved from the City of London into this new building in 1982.

Aerial surveys from aircraft are still used by organisations such as the Ordnance Survey since they are efficient for large areas, provide higher resolution imagery than satellites and can be more flexible in areas such as the UK, where cloud cover often limits imaging opportunities. (©Tower Hamlets Local History Library and Archives)

Canary Wharf, 2014

Regeneration of the West India Docks site started in 1988. The whole 39 hectare area was renamed 'Canary Wharf' by the developers. The rapid construction of buildings such as One Canada Square (Canary Wharf Tower, the highest building in the area), and the extension of the Jubilee tube line from Green Park to Stratford attracted many companies to relocate from the City of London and elsewhere.

The satellite image, dating from 2014, shows how much the area has been developed. Over 100,000 people now work there, primarily in the financial and insurance sectors. To support these businesses, many others work in IT, retail and the legal profession.

Very little of what can be seen in the top image, in 1983, is visible here, with the newer buildings being constructed over parts of the North Dock. Billingsgate still occupies its place and is still London's fish market, most of its produce arriving by road from all over the country. In the northwest, the roofs of a group of the original former warehouses can be seen in both images. These are the earliest buildings on the site, dating from the early nineteenth century, and now partially house the Museum of London Docklands. The long shadows cast by the new buildings show how high they are.

Future developments include the planned opening of Crossrail in 2018 and the construction of more residential property, to the east of the main business centre, as well as the further commercial development of high-rise offices.

Satellite imagery is most useful for mapping areas in remote or inaccessible areas of the world, particularly where cloud cover is not too persistent. The ability to revisit and monitor small sites without the high cost of aircraft mobilisation is another benefit. (NPA Satellite Mapping, CGG)

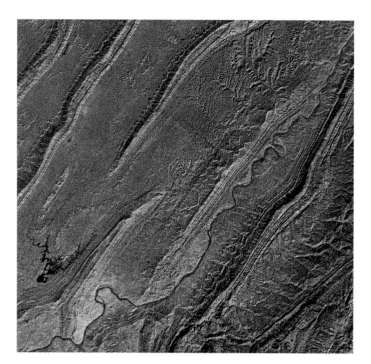

Sichuan Basin, China

The north-east/south-west trending ridges in this image are anticlinal folds developed in the Earth's crust as a result of plate collision and compression. Geologists map these folds and the lowlands between them formed by synclinal folds, as they are often the areas where oil or gas are found in commercial quantities. The river shown in this image is the Yangtse, near Chongqing. *(China RSGS)*

Pingualuit Crater, Canada

The circular feature is a meteorite crater in the Ungava Peninsula, Québec, formed by an impact over 1.4 million years ago. It is 3.4 km wide and 264 m deep. The lake within has no link to any water sources and has been formed only by rain and snow. Thus the water is among the world's clearest and least saline. Sediments in the lake have been unaffected by ice sheets and are important for scientific research. *(NPA Satellite Mapping, CGG)*

Wadi Hadramaut, Yemen

Yemen is extremely arid – however, in the past it was more humid and wet, enabling large river systems to carve out the deep and spectacular gorges and dried-out river beds (*wadis*) seen in this image. The erosion has revealed many contrasting rock types. The image has been processed to exaggerate this effect, producing many shades of red, pink and purple, which make geological mapping easier and more cost-effective. *(USGS)*

Zagros Mountains, Iran

These mountains were formed as Arabia collided with Southern Eurasia. The upper half of this colour-enhanced image shows an anti-cline that runs east–west. The dark grey features are called diapirs, which are bodies of viscous rock salt that are very buoyant and some-times rise to the surface, spilling and spreading out like a glacier. The presence of salt in the region is important as it stops oil escaping to the surface. *(USGS)*

UNITED KINGDOM AND IRELAND

1:1 000 000

SHETLAND ISLANDS on same scale

FOULA a on same scale

ST. KILDA b on same scale

ft m

3000 1000
2250 750
1500 500
1200 400
600 200
300 100
0 0

m ft
20 60
50 150
100 300
200 600

A T L A N T I C
O C E A N

Muckle Flugga
Herma Ness
▲285 Haroldswick
Bluemull Sd.
Baltasound Balta
Cullivoe Unst
Gutcher Uyeasound Mu Ness
Belmont
Ramna Stacks Hascosay
Pt. of Fethaland Fetlar
Isbister Mid Yell The Snap
North Roe Ulsta Burravoe
Ronas Hill ▲453 Yell Colgrave Sd.
The Faither
Esha Ness Out Skerries
Hillswick Sullom Lunna Ness
Brae
St. Magnus Bay S H E T L A N D Skaw Taing
Muckle Roe Vidlin Whalsay
Papa Stour Voe Symbister
Papa Aith South Nesting B.
Sd. of Papa Sandness Dury Voe
Walls Score Hd.
Vaila Easter Bressay
Gruting Voe Skeld Lerwick I. of Noss
Scalloway Bard Hd.
Hamnavoe
West Burra 293 Bressay Sd.
Kettla Ness Helli Ness
Hoswick Mousa
St. Ninian's I. Northpunds
Scousburgh
Boddam
Fitful Hd.
B. of Quendale JARLSHOF PREHISTORIC SITE
Sumburgh Sumburgh Hd.

Foula ▲418

217 ▲ Fair Isle

Boreray ▲384
Soay ▲376 St. Kilda
▲376

Butt of Lewis (Rubha Robhanais)
South Dell Port of Ness (Port Nis)
Borve Ness Cellar Hd.
Barvas (Barabhas)
Shawbost North Tolsta Tolsta Hd.
Carloway (Carlabhagh) Back Broad Bay
Great Bernera Ben Mholach ▲291 Tiumpan Hd.
Gallan Hd. Uig Newmarket Portnaguran
Callanish Stornoway (Steòrnabhaigh) Eye Peninsula
L. Roag Gorynahine Melbost Bayble
Aird Brenish Balallan L. Erisort Chicken Hd.
▲575 L E W I S (Leodhais)
Gisla Cromore
Scarp L. Langavat Kintarvie Gravir L. Shell
North Kebock Hd.
Harris Beinn Mhor Lemreway
Gasker Husinish Pt. Ardvourlie ▲799
Husinish (Huisinis) Clisham EILEAN
West L. Tarbert Adhaisig SIAR
Taransay Tarbert (Tairbeart)
Sd. of Taransay East L. Tarbert
Toe Hd. Scarastavore Scalpay
South Harris Sd. of Shiant
Pabbay (Na Hearadh) Shiant Is.
Leverburgh (An t-Ob) Fladda-chuain
Sd. of Pabbay Rodel (Roghadal) Eilean Trodday
Berneray Renish Pt. Rubha Hunish
(WESTERN ISLES)
Haskeir Is. Kilmaluag
Griminish Pt. Vaternish Pt. Staffin
Sollas Ascrib Is. Uig
North Uist (Uibhist a Tuath) Lochmaddy (Loch Nam Madadh)
Paible L. Maddy L. Snizort
Monach Is. Clachan Dunvegan Hd. Isay Stein Trotternish
Sound of Monach Carinish L. Eport Milovaig Lusta The Storr 719
Baleshare Eaval ▲347 Neist Pt. Lephin DUNVEGAN CASTLE Carbost
Grimsay Ronay Dunvegan Portree
Benbecula (Beinn na Faoghla) Roskhill Raasay
Creagony Wiay Healaval Bheag ▲488 Brocadale
Ardivachar Pt. Bagh nam Coillore Sconser
L. Bee Faoileann Wiay I. Harport Sligachan
Rubh'an Fernilea Scalpay
Howmore Dunan Carbost 775
Hecla ▲605 Glenbrittle Minginish
South Uist Ben Mhor Cuillin Hills Elgol
(Uibhist a Deas) ▲620 Soay Sd. Bla Bheinn ▲928
L. Eynort Soay 992
Daliburgh Lochboisdale
(Loch Boghasdail) L. Boisdale
Kilbride
Sd. of Eriskay
Sound of Barra Eriskay Canna
Greian Hd. Sanday
Barra (Bharraigh) Rum (Rhum)
Castlebay Heaval ▲384 Bruernish Pt. Kinloch 810
Vatersay Sd. of Canna Sd. of Rum
Sandray Muck
Pabbay Sorisdale
Mingulay
Barra Hd. Berneray 268
Coll
Clabhach
Arinagour Caliach Pt.
Tobermory
Drimnin

North Minch
Handa I.
Eddrachillis Bay
Pt. of Stoer Oldany I.
Drumbeg
Assynt
Stoer
Enard B.
Rubha Coigeach 167
Reiff
Summer Is. Achiltibuie L. Lurgainn
Priest I. Coigach
Greenstone Pt. Grunard B.
Gruinard Mellon L. Broom
An Teallach ▲1062
INVEREWE GARDEN Poolewe L. na Sealga
Longa I. 179 L. Gairloch W e s t e r
Gairloch Port Henderson Kerrysdale
Red Point Talladale ▲981
Rona Diabaig Slioch
L. Torridon Kinlochewe
Liathach Fasag Torridon ▲1053
Shieldaig Achnashellach
Applecross Forest Coulags H I G H
Applecross 1052
Toscaig L. Kishorn
Stromemore Lochcarron
Crowlin Is. Plockton Stromeferry
Narrows L. Carron
Kyle of Lochalsh
Kyleakin Auchtertyre
Breakish L. Alsh EILEAN DONAN CASTLE
Broadford Kylerhea Dornie
Glenelg Five Sisters ▲1068
Eilean Iarmain Shiel Bridge The Saddle 1012
Teangue Glen Shiel
Sd. of Sleat L. Hourn
Armadale Ladhar Bheinn ▲1019
Ardvasar Knoydart L. Quoich
Pt. of Sleat Inverie
Sanday L. Nevis 1040
Sgurr na Ciche
Mallaig
Morar Tarbet L. Arka
▲983 Culvain
L. Morar
Arisaig Glenfinnan
310 L. Shiel Kinlocheil
LOCHAILORT CAMH CHARN
Rhois-Bheinn ▲882 L. Ell
Moidart Kinlochmoidart Fort Wil
Shona I. L. Moidart
Ardnamurchan Mingary Ben Hiant ▲527 Sunart Strontian Ardgour
Kilchoan Acharacle Salen L. Sunart 888
Pt. of Ardnamurchan Corran Oh
Sorisdale L. Leven

Projection : Conical with two standard parallels
West from Greenwich

ORKNEY ISLANDS
on same scale

NORTH SEA

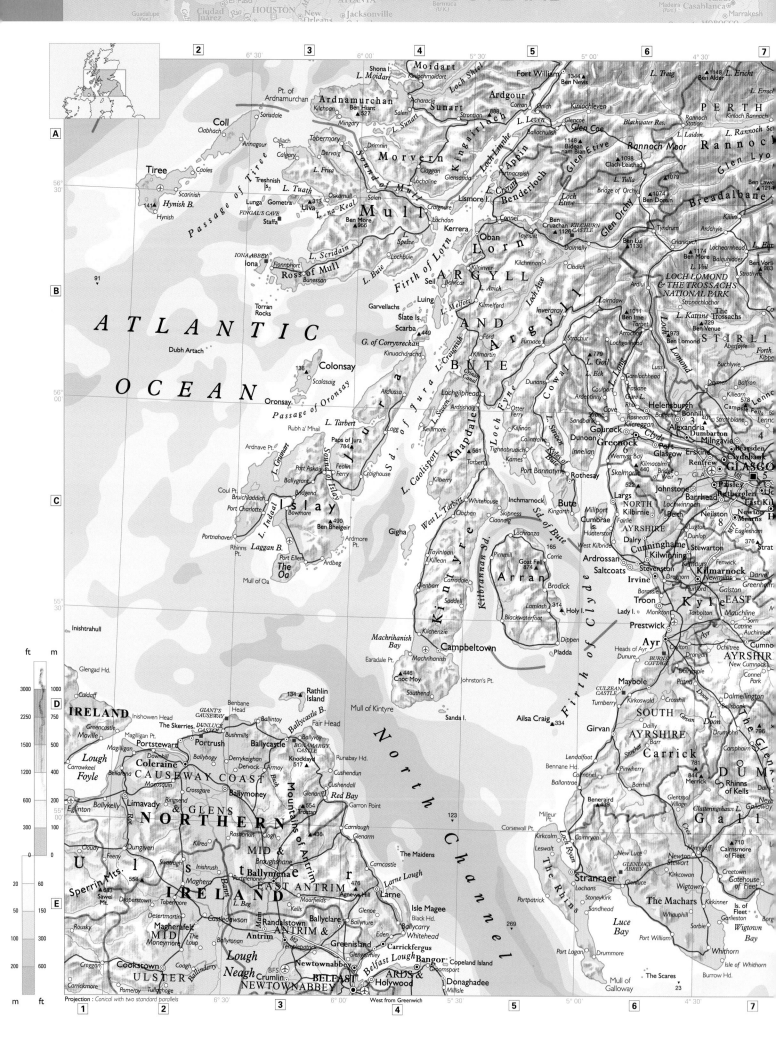

Key to Scottish unitary authorities on map
2 DUNDEE CITY
3 WEST DUNBARTONSHIRE
4 EAST DUNBARTONSHIRE
5 CITY OF GLASGOW
6 INVERCLYDE
7 RENFREWSHIRE
8 EAST RENFREWSHIRE
9 NORTH LANARKSHIRE
10 FALKIRK
11 CLACKMANNANSHIRE
12 WEST LOTHIAN
13 CITY OF EDINBURGH
14 MIDLOTHIAN

NORTH SEA

ANGUS

Montrose
Arbroath
Carnoustie
Dundee
Firth of Tay
St. Andrews
FIFE
Kirkcaldy
Firth of Forth
Dunfermline
EDINBURGH
Musselburgh
LOTHIAN
Haddington
Dunbar
Berwick-upon-Tweed
Lammermuir Hills
Merse
SCOTTISH BORDERS
Galashiels
Kelso
Peebles
Selkirk
Hawick
Jedburgh
Cheviot Hills
The Cheviot 816
NORTHUMBERLAND NATIONAL PARK
NORTHUMBERLAND
Kielder Res.
Alnwick
Morpeth
Blyth
NEWCASTLE UPON TYNE
TYNE & WEAR
Sunderland
Gateshead
South Shields
Tynemouth
Whitley Bay
Hexham
Washington
Chester-le-Street
Durham
Hartlepool
& GALLOWAY
Dumfries
Annan
Gretna
Carlisle
CUMBERLAND
WESTMORLAND
& FURNESS
Penrith
DURHAM
Weardale
Teesdale
Teesside
Middlesbrough
Redcar
Workington
Cockermouth

1:1 000 000

COPYRIGHT PHILIP'S

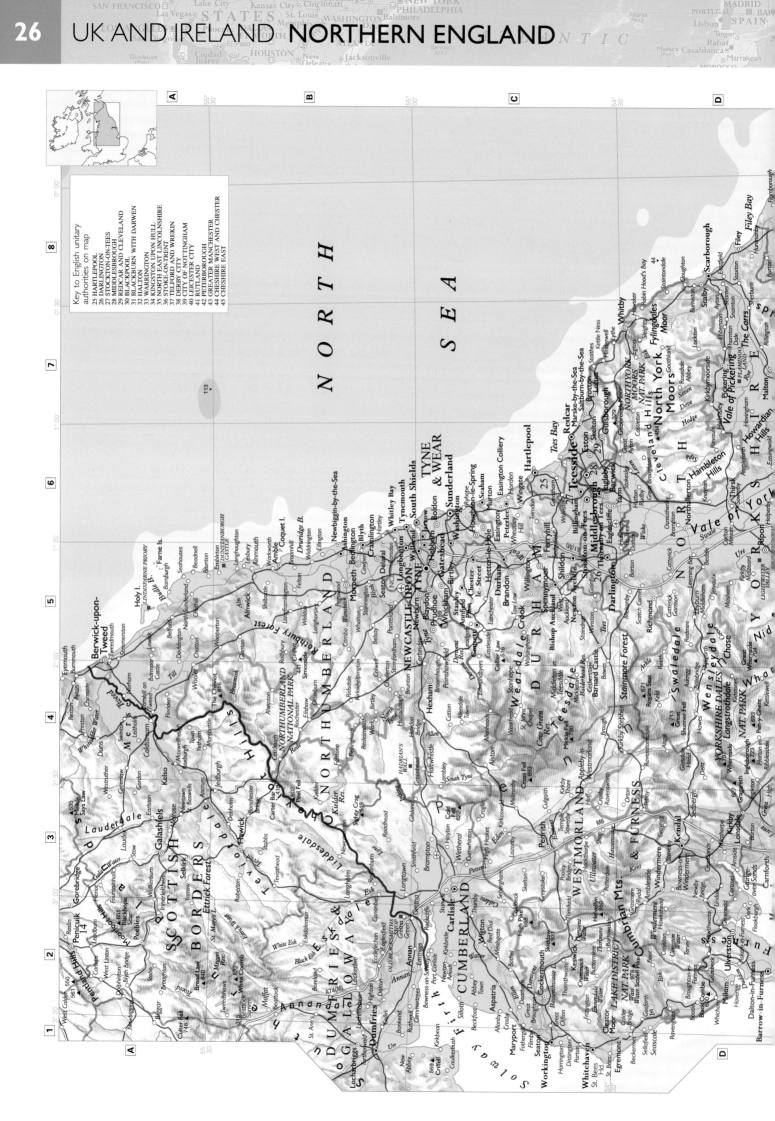

NORTH

SEA

1:1 000 000

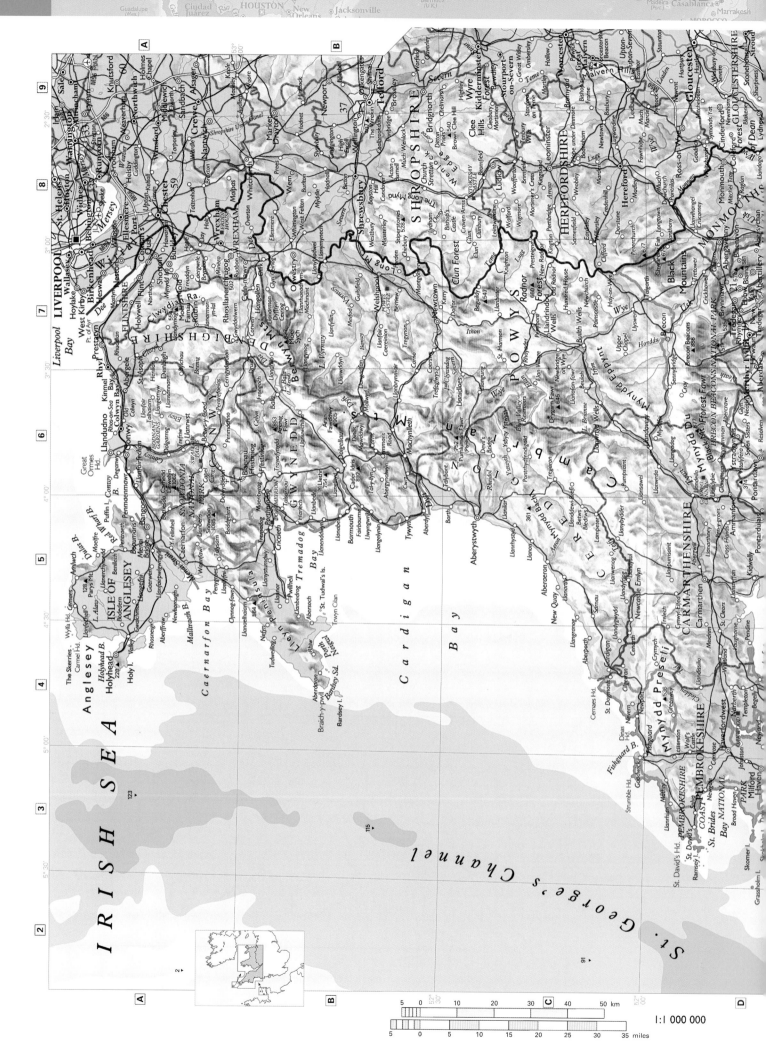

1:1 000 000

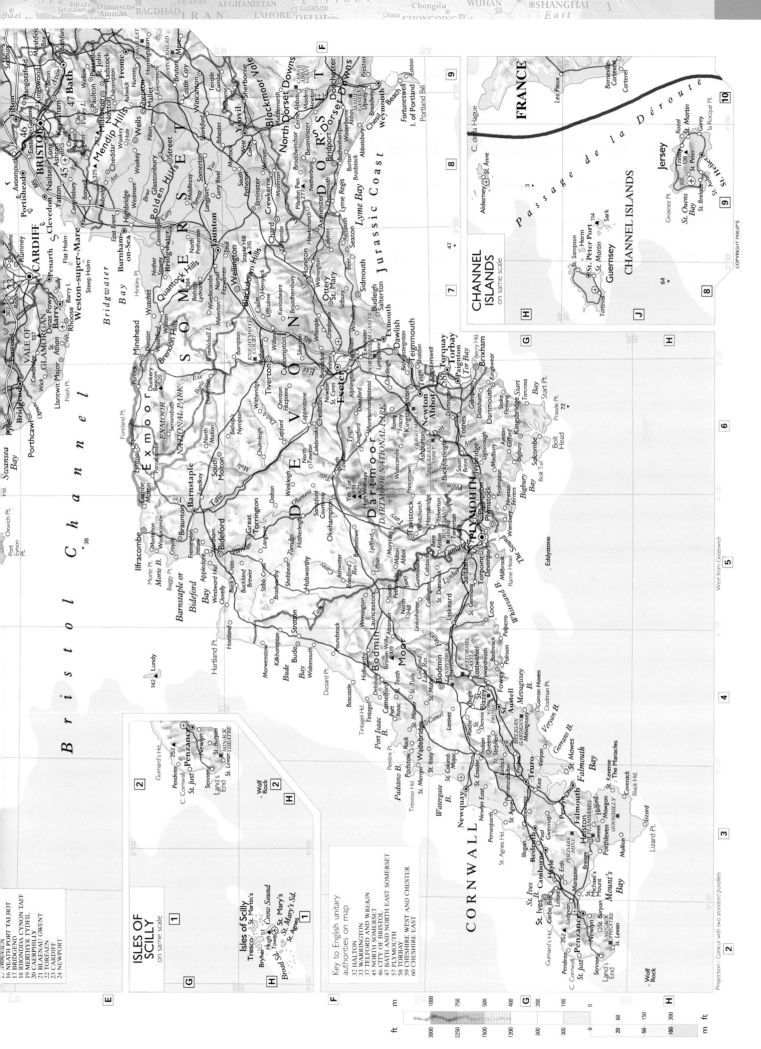

FRANCE

CHANNEL ISLANDS
on same scale

Jersey

Guernsey

CHANNEL ISLANDS

Passage de la Déroute

Bristol Channel

Swansea Bay

CARDIFF

VALE OF GLAMORGAN

Porthcawl

Bridgend

Barnstaple or Bideford Bay

EXMOOR NATIONAL PARK

Minehead

Barnstaple

Bideford

Ilfracombe

SOMERSET

BRISTOL

Weston-super-Mare

Bridgwater Bay

Mendip Hills

Wells

Glastonbury

Taunton

Quantock Hills

Blackdown Hills

DEVON

Exeter

DARTMOOR NATIONAL PARK

Okehampton

Tiverton

Crediton

Plymouth

Torquay Torbay
Paignton

Newton Abbot

Dartmouth

CORNWALL

Bodmin Moor

Truro

Falmouth Bay

Penzance

Newquay

St. Ives

Land's End

Jurassic Coast

Lyme Bay

DORSET

North Dorset Downs

Dorchester

Weymouth

I. of Portland

Portland Bill

Bournemouth

ISLES OF SCILLY
on same scale

Isles of Scilly

Tresco
Bryher
St. Martin's
St. Mary's
St. Agnes

Wolf Rock

Key to English unitary authorities on map

16 NEATH PORT TALBOT
17 BRIDGEND
18 RHONDDA CYNON TAFF
19 MERTHYR TYDFIL
20 CAERPHILLY
21 BLAENAU GWENT
22 TORFAEN
23 CARDIFF
24 NEWPORT

32 HALTON
33 WARRINGTON
37 TELFORD AND WREKIN
45 NORTH SOMERSET
46 CITY OF BRISTOL
47 BATH AND NORTH EAST SOMERSET
57 PLYMOUTH
58 TORBAY
59 CHESHIRE WEST AND CHESTER
60 CHESHIRE EAST

Projection: Conical with two standard parallels

West from Greenwich

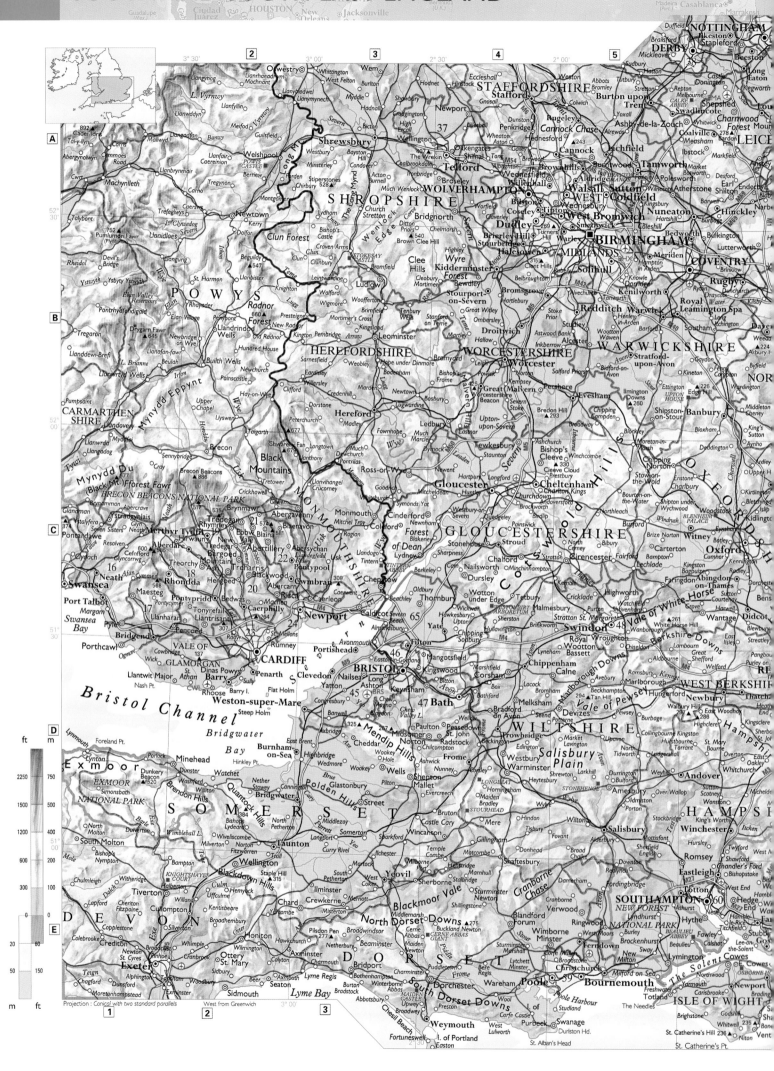

Key to English unitary
authorities on map

37 TELFORD AND WREKIN
38 DERBY CITY
39 CITY OF NOTTINGHAM
40 LEICESTER CITY
41 RUTLAND
42 PETERBOROUGH
43 MILTON KEYNES
44 LUTON
45 NORTH SOMERSET
46 CITY OF BRISTOL
47 BATH AND NORTH EAST SOMERSET
48 SWINDON
49 READING
50 WOKINGHAM
51 WINDSOR AND MAIDENHEAD
52 SLOUGH
53 BRACKNELL FOREST
54 THURROCK
55 SOUTHEND-ON-SEA
56 MEDWAY
59 BOURNEMOUTH, CHRISTCHURCH
   AND POOLE
60 SOUTHAMPTON
61 PORTSMOUTH
62 BRIGHTON AND HOVE
63 BEDFORD
64 CENTRAL BEDFORDSHIRE
65 SOUTH GLOUCESTERSHIRE

Key to Welsh unitary
authorities on map

16 NEATH PORT TALBOT
17 BRIDGEND
18 RHONDDA CYNON TAFF
19 MERTHYR TYDFIL
20 CAERPHILLY
21 BLAENAU GWENT
22 TORFAEN
23 CARDIFF
24 NEWPORT

1:1 000 000

COPYRIGHT PHILIP'S

CENOZOIC (Tertiary)
Pliocene, Oligocene & Eocene

MESOZOIC (Secondary)

Cretaceous
- Chalk
- Upper Greensand & Gault
- Lower Greensand & Speeton Clay
- Wealden Clay
- Hastings Beds

Jurassic
- Upper
- Middle
- Liassic

Trias
- Keuper Marl & Sandstone
- Bunter Sandstone

PALAEOZOIC (Primary)

Permian
- Sandstone & Marls
- Magnesium Limestone

Carboniferous
- Coal Measures
- Millstone Grit & Culm Measures
- Carboniferous Limestone

Old Red Sandstone (Devonian)

Silurian

Ordovician

Cambrian

PRE-CAMBRIAN
Torridonian, Charnian, etc.

Schists & Gneisses (Metamorphic)

Igneous
- Volcanic: Basalt, etc.
- Intrusive Rocks

Alluvium

For geological time scale refer to page 124 in the World Section

SOUTHERN LIMITS OF QUATERNARY ICE SHEETS

Devensian (94 000 – 10 000 years ago) ————
Wolstonian (175 000 – 128 000 years ago) — — —
Anglian (660 000 – 420 000 years ago) - - - - - - -
(after Lowe and Walker)

The last period of geological time, the Quaternary, can be subdivided into two epochs; the Pleistocene, which began around two million years ago and ended with the final decay of the last (Devensian) ice sheet 10 000 years ago, and the Holocene which represents the last 10 000 years of warmer climatic conditions.

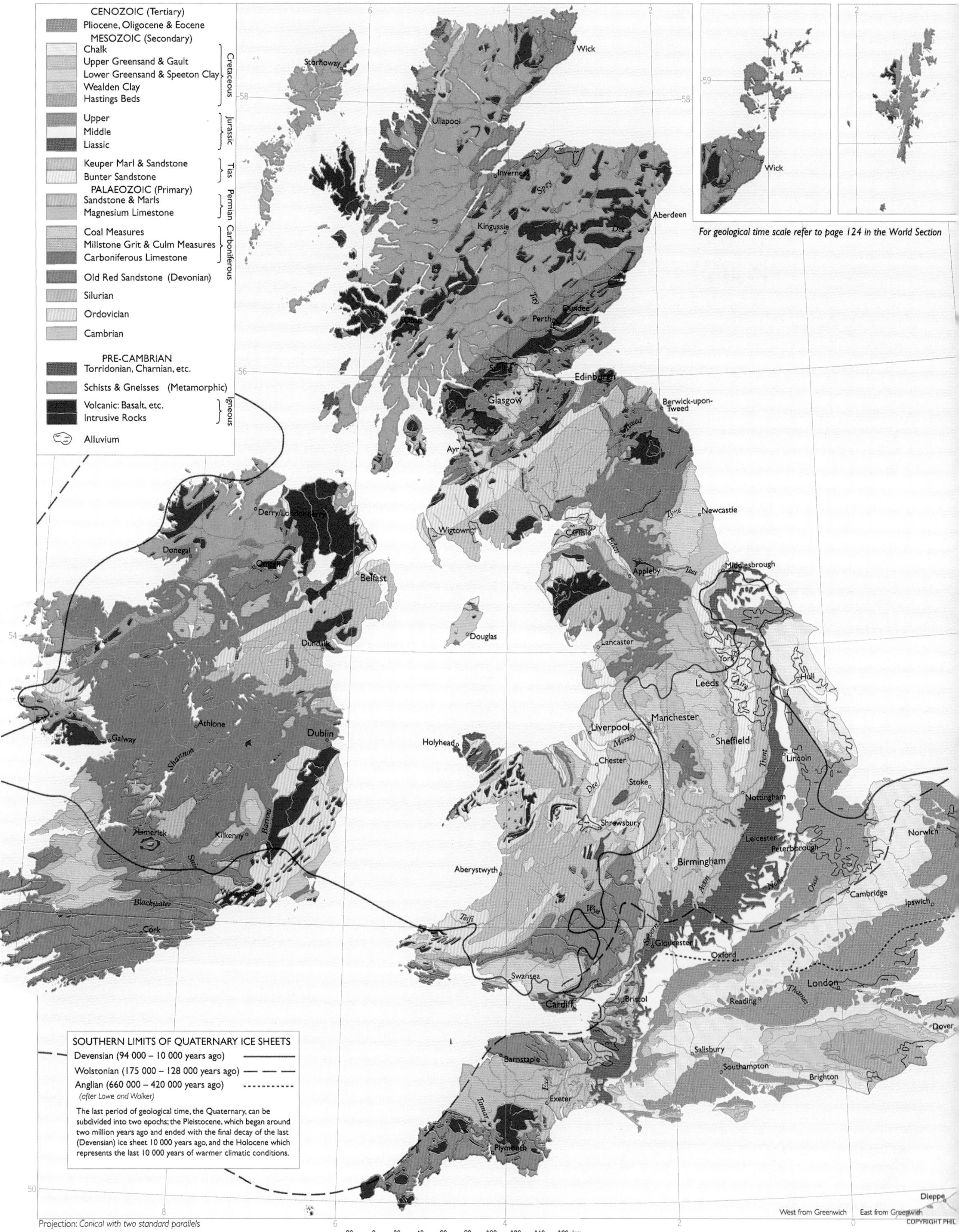

Projection: *Conical with two standard parallels*

20 0 20 40 60 80 100 120 140 160 km
20 0 20 40 60 80 100 miles

1:4 000 000

West from Greenwich   East from Greenwich

COPYRIGHT PHIL

Map labels (selected): Stornoway, Wick, Ullapool, Inverness, Spey, Kingussie, Aberdeen, Dee, Tay, Perth, Dundee, Edinburgh, Berwick-upon-Tweed, Tweed, Glasgow, Ayr, Wigtown, Carlisle, Newcastle, Tyne, Appleby, Tees, Middlesbrough, Derry/Londonderry, Donegal, Belfast, Dundalk, Douglas, Lancaster, York, Ouse, Hull, Leeds, Aire, Manchester, Liverpool, Mersey, Sheffield, Trent, Lincoln, Chester, Dee, Stoke, Nottingham, Holyhead, Shrewsbury, Leicester, Peterborough, Norwich, Athlone, Dublin, Shannon, Galway, Birmingham, Avon, Cambridge, Ipswich, Limerick, Kilkenny, Barrow, Aberystwyth, Teifi, Wexford, Severn, Gloucester, Oxford, Blackwater, Cork, Swansea, Bristol, Thames, Reading, London, Cardiff, Salisbury, Southampton, Brighton, Dover, Barnstaple, Exe, Exeter, Tamar, Plymouth, Dieppe

ATLANTIC

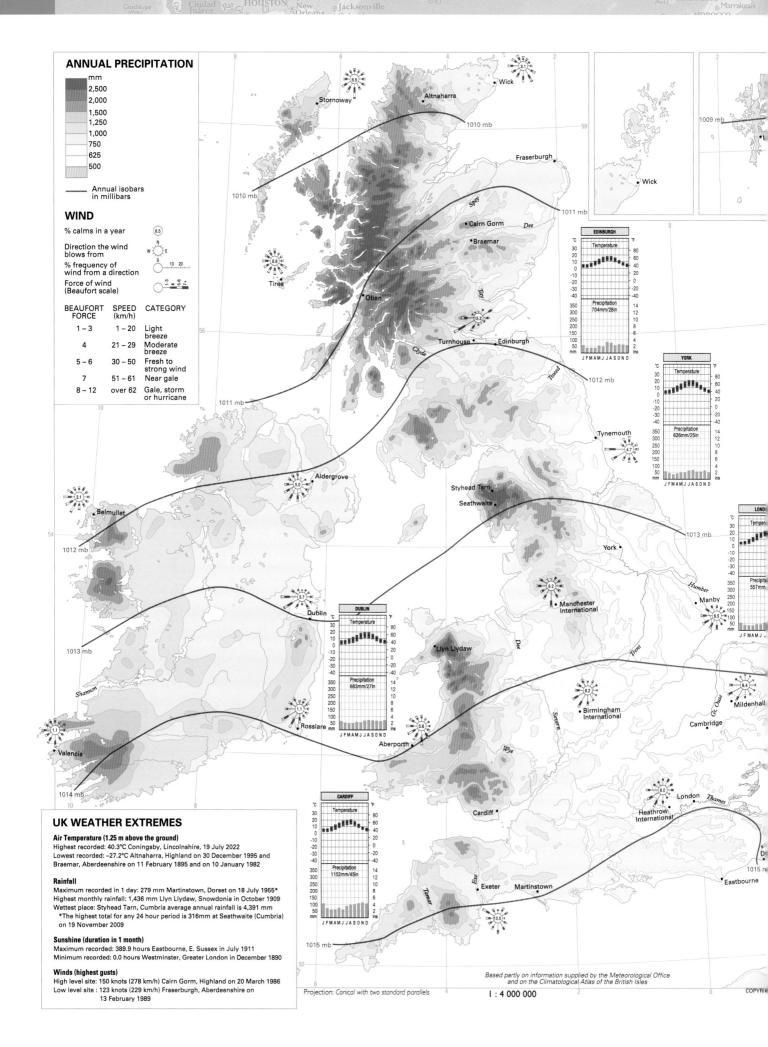

ANNUAL PRECIPITATION

mm
2,500
2,000
1,500
1,250
1,000
750
625
500

—— Annual isobars in millibars

WIND

% calms in a year

Direction the wind blows from

% frequency of wind from a direction

Force of wind (Beaufort scale)

BEAUFORT FORCE	SPEED (km/h)	CATEGORY
1 – 3	1 – 20	Light breeze
4	21 – 29	Moderate breeze
5 – 6	30 – 50	Fresh to strong wind
7	51 – 61	Near gale
8 – 12	over 62	Gale, storm or hurricane

UK WEATHER EXTREMES

Air Temperature (1.25 m above the ground)
Highest recorded: 40.3°C Coningsby, Lincolnshire, 19 July 2022
Lowest recorded: –27.2°C Altnaharra, Highland on 30 December 1995 and Braemar, Aberdeenshire on 11 February 1895 and on 10 January 1982

Rainfall
Maximum recorded in 1 day: 279 mm Martinstown, Dorset on 18 July 1955*
Highest monthly rainfall: 1,436 mm Llyn Llydaw, Snowdonia in October 1909
Wettest place: Styhead Tarn, Cumbria average annual rainfall is 4,391 mm
    *The highest total for any 24 hour period is 316mm at Seathwaite (Cumbria) on 19 November 2009

Sunshine (duration in 1 month)
Maximum recorded: 389.9 hours Eastbourne, E. Sussex in July 1911
Minimum recorded: 0.0 hours Westminster, Greater London in December 1890

Winds (highest gusts)
High level site: 150 knots (278 km/h) Cairn Gorm, Highland on 20 March 1986
Low level site : 123 knots (229 km/h) Fraserburgh, Aberdeenshire on 13 February 1989

Projection: Conical with two standard parallels

1 : 4 000 000

Based partly on information supplied by the Meteorological Office and on the Climatological Atlas of the British Isles

EDINBURGH
Temperature
Precipitation 704mm/28in

YORK
Temperature
Precipitation 626mm/25in

DUBLIN
Temperature
Precipitation 683mm/27in

CARDIFF
Temperature
Precipitation 1152mm/45in

LONDON
Temperature
Precipitation 557mm

JANUARY TEMPERATURE
Actual surface temperature

°C
7
6
5
4
3
2
1
0

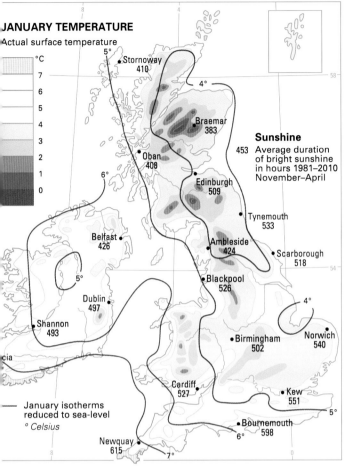

Sunshine
453 Average duration of bright sunshine in hours 1981–2010 November–April

— January isotherms reduced to sea-level
° Celsius

Stornoway 410
Braemar 383
Oban 408
Edinburgh 509
Tynemouth 533
Belfast 426
Ambleside 424
Scarborough 518
Blackpool 526
Dublin 497
Shannon 493
Birmingham 502
Norwich 540
Cardiff 527
Kew 551
Bournemouth 598
Newquay 615

CHANGES IN UK RAINFALL PATTERNS
Annual percentage change in precipitation, 1914-2007

- Over 10% increase
- 0 – 10% increase
- 0 – 2.5% decrease
- 2.5 – 5% decrease
- Over 5% decrease

Seasonal percentage change in precipitation, 1914-2007

region
increase
decrease

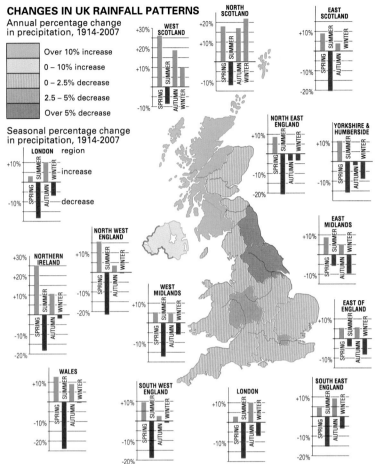

WEST SCOTLAND
NORTH SCOTLAND
EAST SCOTLAND
NORTH EAST ENGLAND
YORKSHIRE & HUMBERSIDE
LONDON
NORTH WEST ENGLAND
EAST MIDLANDS
NORTHERN IRELAND
WEST MIDLANDS
EAST OF ENGLAND
WALES
SOUTH WEST ENGLAND
LONDON
SOUTH EAST ENGLAND

JULY TEMPERATURE
Actual surface temperature

°C
17
16
15
14
13
12
11
10

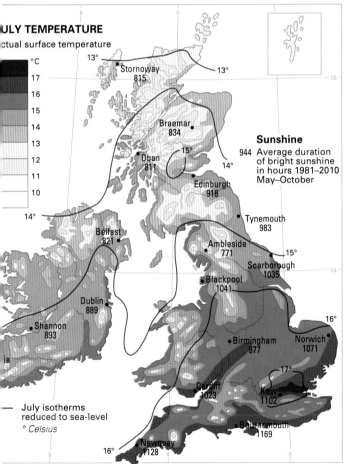

Sunshine
944 Average duration of bright sunshine in hours 1981–2010 May–October

— July isotherms reduced to sea-level
° Celsius

Stornoway 815
Braemar 834
Oban 811
Edinburgh 918
Tynemouth 983
Belfast 821
Ambleside 771
Scarborough 1035
Blackpool 1041
Dublin 889
Shannon 893
Birmingham 977
Norwich 1071
Cardiff 1023
Kew 1102
Bournemouth 1169
Newquay 1128

COPYRIGHT PHILIP'S

CHANGES IN SUMMER AND WINTER RAINFALL 1870–2010

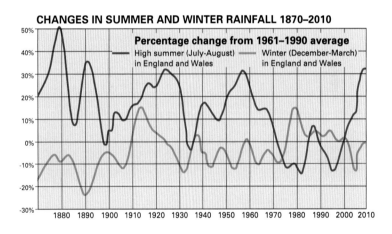

Percentage change from 1961–1990 average
— High summer (July-August) in England and Wales
— Winter (December-March) in England and Wales

CHANGES IN AVERAGE SURFACE TEMPERATURE 1850–2010

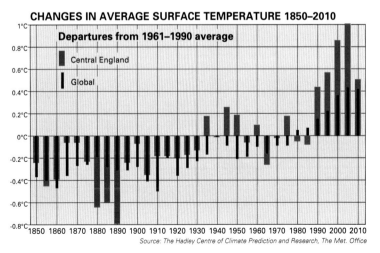

Departures from 1961–1990 average
■ Central England
| Global

Source: The Hadley Centre of Climate Prediction and Research, The Met. Office

WATER SUPPLY

Regions of reliably high rainfall (more than 1,250 mm in at least 70% of the years)

③ Major reservoirs (capacity over 20 million cubic metres, see list opposite for details)

→ Existing inter-regional transfers of water (by pipeline and river)

→ Proposed inter-regional transfers of water (by pipeline and river)

☐ Proposed estuary storage site

▽ Proposed groundwater storage site

Principal sources of groundwater (porous and jointed aquifers)

THAMES WATER Water supply and sewerage companies in the UK

MAJOR RESERVOIRS
(with capacity in million m³)

England

1	Kielder Reservoir	198
2	Rutland Water	123
3	Haweswater	85
4	Grafham Water	59
5	Cow Green Reservoir	41
6	Thirlmere	41
7	Carsington Reservoir	36
8	Roadford Reservoir	35
9	Bewl Water Reservoir	31
10	Colliford Lake	29
11	Ladybower Reservoir	28
12	Hanningfield Reservoir	27
13	Abberton Reservoir	25
14	Draycote Water	23
15	Derwent Reservoir	22
16	Grimwith Reservoir	22
17	Wimbleball Lake	21
18	Chew Valley Lake	20
19	Balderhead Reservoir	20
20	Thames Valley (linked reservoirs)	
21	Lea Valley (linked reservoirs)	
22	Longendale (linked reservoirs)	

Wales

23	Elan Valley
24	Llyn Celyn
25	Llyn Brianne
26	Llyn Brenig
27	Llyn Vyrnwy
28	Llyn Clywedog
29	Llandegfedd Reservoir

Scotland

30	Loch Lomond
31	Loch Katrine
32	Megget Reservoir
33	Loch Ness
34	Blackwater Reservoir
35	Daer Reservoir
36	Carron Valley Reservoir

Ireland

37	Poulaphouca Reservoir
38	Inishcarra Reservoir
39	Carrigadrohid Reservoir

Kielder Water in Northumberland is the largest reservoir in the British Isles.

WASTE RECYCLING

The percentage of total household waste recycled in 2020/21

Over 50%
45 – 50%
40 – 45%
35 – 40%
Under 35%

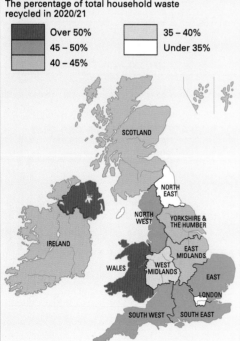

JOURNEY TO SCHOOL IN THE UK

Mode of travel to school by children aged 5–16 in 2022/23

Other mode
Walking
Bus
Car

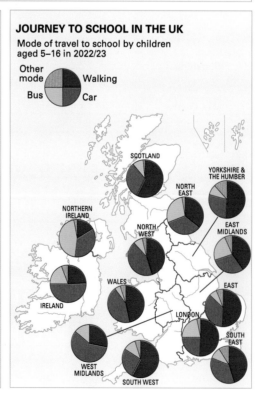

FLOOD RISK IN ENGLAND AND WALES

Areas at greatest risk from flooding (as designated by the Environment Agency)

...ILS

- Calcareous brown earth
- Brown earth
- Acid brown earth
- Podsol
- Peaty podsol
- Grey-brown podsol
- Gley
- Basin peat and alluvial gleys
- Peaty gley and blanket peat

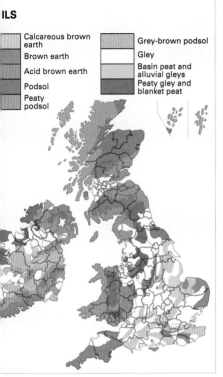

NATURAL VEGETATION

The plant cover associated with a particular environment if it was unaffected by human activity

- Oak
- Beech and oak
- Ash and oak
- Birch and oakwood
- Scots pine
- Heath, moorland, water meadows, fen, bog and marsh

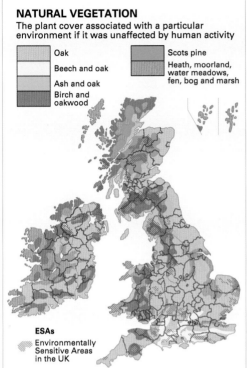

ESAs
Environmentally Sensitive Areas in the UK

GREENHOUSE GAS EMISSIONS

CO$_2$ emissions in tonnes per capita 2021

- Over 20
- 12 – 20
- 10 – 12
- 8 – 10
- 6 – 8
- Under 6

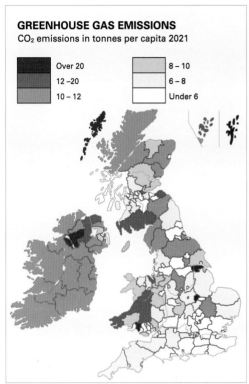

...D HERITAGE SITES

...ttlement of Skara Brae is part of Neolithic ...

...ns of basalt form the Giant's Causeway on the ...oast of Northern Ireland.

...ed in the 6th century, Canterbury Cathedral has ...nlarged and rebuilt, mainly in the Gothic style.

CONSERVATION

- National Parks
- National Landscapes
- National Scenic Areas (NSAs)
- Forest Parks, Regional Parks in Scotland and Special Protection Areas (SPAs)
- Green Belts (and the urban areas they surround)
- Heritage Coast (England and Wales)

* World Heritage Sites in the UK and Ireland

Other designated UK sites not shown:
St. Kilda, Atlantic Ocean
Henderson I., Pacific Ocean
Gough I. and Inaccessible I., Atlantic Ocean
St. George, Bermuda
Gorham's Cave Complex, Gibraltar

TYPES OF FARM

- Dairy cattle
- Beef cattle
- Sheep
- Pigs and/or poultry
- Mixed farming
- Market gardening (fruit and vegetables)
- Cereals
- Other crops (mainly potatoes, sugar beet)
- Northern limit of 9 month growing season
- Forests
- Built-up areas
- Areas with over 1,000 mm rainfall per year

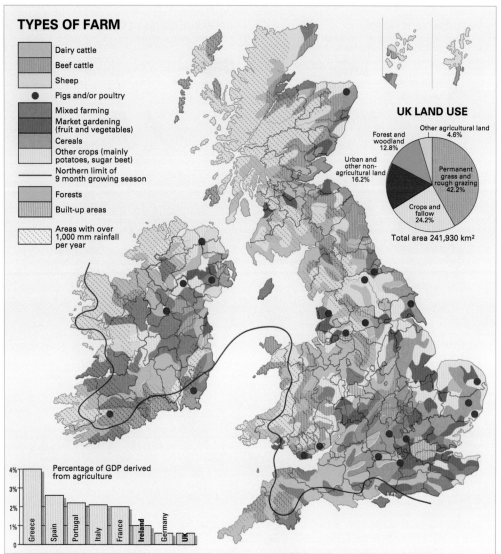

Percentage of GDP derived from agriculture

Greece, Spain, Portugal, Italy, France, Ireland, Germany, UK

UK LAND USE

- Other agricultural land 4.6%
- Forest and woodland 12.8%
- Urban and other non-agricultural land 16.2%
- Permanent grass and rough grazing 42.2%
- Crops and fallow 24.2%

Total area 241,930 km²

CEREAL FARMING

The percentage of the total farmland used for growing cereals in 2022

- Over 40
- 25 – 40
- 10 – 25
- 5 – 10
- 0 – 5

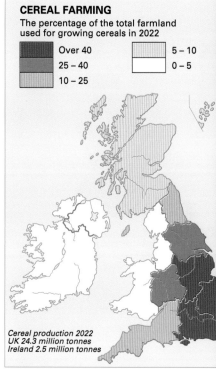

Cereal production 2022
UK 24.3 million tonnes
Ireland 2.5 million tonnes

DAIRY FARMING

The number of dairy cows per 100 hectares of farmland in 2022

- Over 30
- 20 – 30
- 10 – 20
- 0 – 10

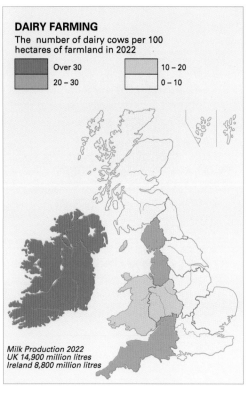

Milk Production 2022
UK 14,900 million litres
Ireland 8,800 million litres

LIVESTOCK FARMING

The number of beef cattle, sheep and pigs per 100 hectares of farmland in 2022

- Over 500
- 400 – 500
- 300 – 400
- 200 – 300
- Under 200

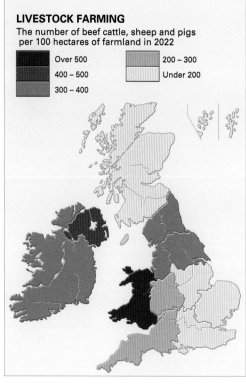

West of Scotland and Rockall 81,500 tonnes
North Sea 396,400 to
Irish Sea 27,300 tonnes
Bristol Channel and Celtic Sea 20,500 tonnes
English Channel 54,400 tonnes
West Ireland and Sole Bank 10,600 tonnes

Ports: Cullivoe, Scalloway, Le, Scrabster, Kinlochbervie, Ullapool, Fraserburg, Peterh, Killybegs, Belfast, Ardglass, Kilkeel, Bridlington, H, Grimsby, Castletownbere, Leig on-S, Whitsta, Shore, Brixham, Plymouth, Newlyn

FISHING

Major fishing ports by size of catch landed

- Demersal e.g. cod (Deep sea fish)
- Pelagic e.g. mackerel (Shallow sea fish)
- Shellfish e.g. lobster

The most impor inshore fishing

North Sea 396,400 tonne

Total amount caugh each fishing region UK vessels

1000 500 200 100 50 m   Depth of sea in metres

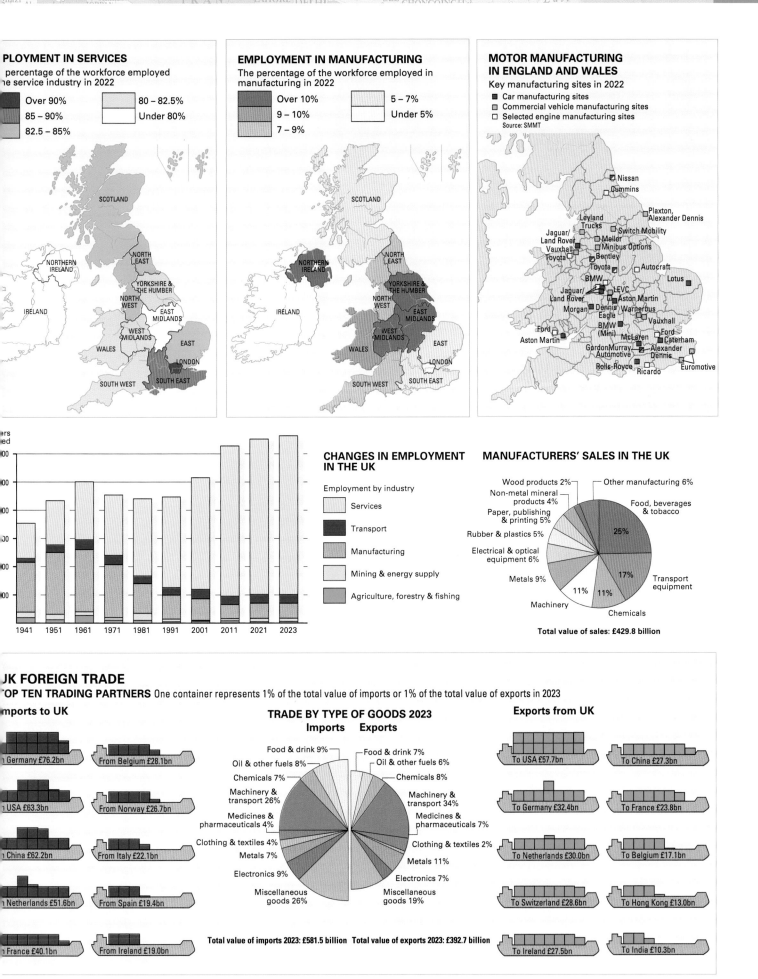

[EM]PLOYMENT IN SERVICES

[The] percentage of the workforce employed [in th]e service industry in 2022

- Over 90%
- 85 – 90%
- 82.5 – 85%
- 80 – 82.5%
- Under 80%

EMPLOYMENT IN MANUFACTURING

The percentage of the workforce employed in manufacturing in 2022

- Over 10%
- 9 – 10%
- 7 – 9%
- 5 – 7%
- Under 5%

MOTOR MANUFACTURING IN ENGLAND AND WALES

Key manufacturing sites in 2022

- Car manufacturing sites
- Commercial vehicle manufacturing sites
- Selected engine manufacturing sites

Source: SMMT

Site labels: Nissan, Cummins, Plaxton, Alexander Dennis, Leyland Trucks, Switch Mobility, Jaguar/Land Rover, Mellor, Minibus Options, Vauxhall, Bentley, Toyota, Toyota, Autocraft, BMW, Lotus, Jaguar/Land Rover, LEVC, Aston Martin, Morgan, Dennis, Warnerbus, Eagle, Vauxhall, Ford, BMW (Mini), McLaren, Ford, Aston Martin, Caterham, Gordon Murray Automotive, Alexander Dennis, Rolls-Royce, Ricardo, Euromotive

CHANGES IN EMPLOYMENT IN THE UK

Employment by industry

- Services
- Transport
- Manufacturing
- Mining & energy supply
- Agriculture, forestry & fishing

1941 1951 1961 1971 1981 1991 2001 2011 2021 2023

MANUFACTURERS' SALES IN THE UK

- Wood products 2%
- Non-metal mineral products 4%
- Paper, publishing & printing 5%
- Rubber & plastics 5%
- Electrical & optical equipment 6%
- Metals 9%
- Machinery 11%
- Chemicals 11%
- Transport equipment 17%
- Food, beverages & tobacco 25%
- Other manufacturing 6%

Total value of sales: £429.8 billion

UK FOREIGN TRADE

TOP TEN TRADING PARTNERS One container represents 1% of the total value of imports or 1% of the total value of exports in 2023

Imports to UK

- Germany £76.2bn
- From Belgium £28.1bn
- USA £63.3bn
- From Norway £26.7bn
- China £62.2bn
- From Italy £22.1bn
- Netherlands £51.6bn
- From Spain £19.4bn
- France £40.1bn
- From Ireland £19.0bn

TRADE BY TYPE OF GOODS 2023

Imports
- Food & drink 9%
- Oil & other fuels 8%
- Chemicals 7%
- Machinery & transport 26%
- Medicines & pharmaceuticals 4%
- Clothing & textiles 4%
- Metals 7%
- Electronics 9%
- Miscellaneous goods 26%

Exports
- Food & drink 7%
- Oil & other fuels 6%
- Chemicals 8%
- Machinery & transport 34%
- Medicines & pharmaceuticals 7%
- Clothing & textiles 2%
- Metals 11%
- Electronics 7%
- Miscellaneous goods 19%

Total value of imports 2023: £581.5 billion   Total value of exports 2023: £392.7 billion

Exports from UK

- To USA £57.7bn
- To China £27.3bn
- To Germany £32.4bn
- To France £23.8bn
- To Netherlands £30.0bn
- To Belgium £17.1bn
- To Switzerland £28.6bn
- To Hong Kong £13.0bn
- To Ireland £27.5bn
- To India £10.3bn

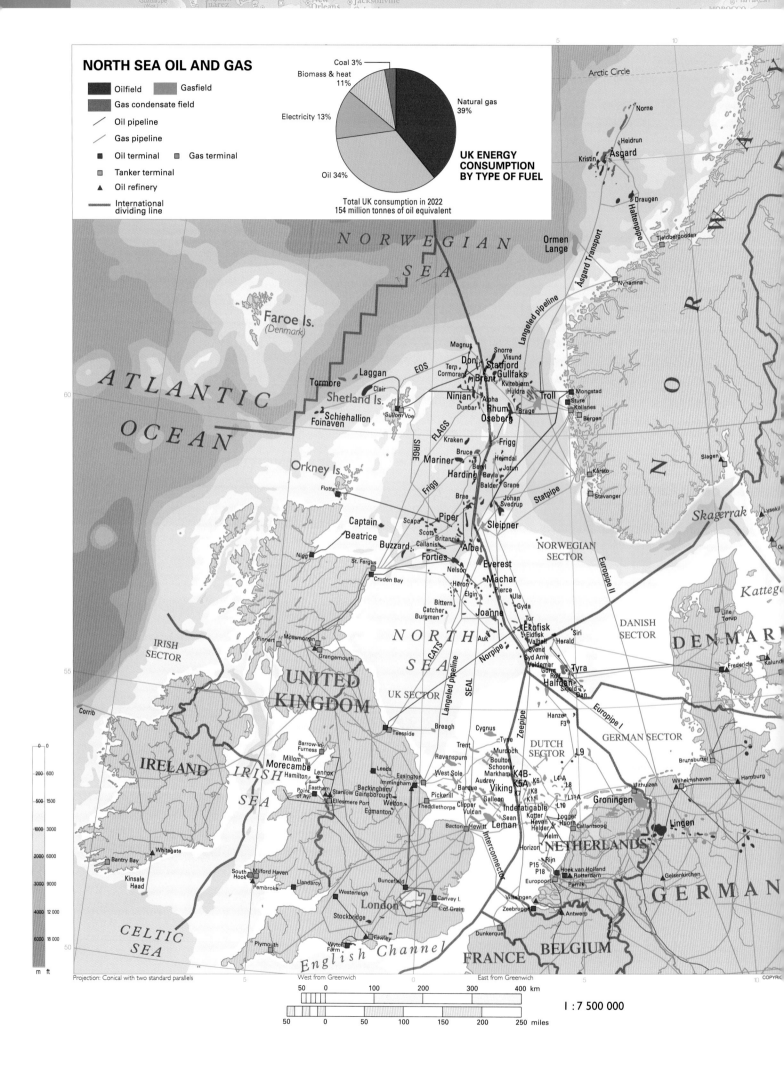

NORTH SEA OIL AND GAS

- Oilfield
- Gasfield
- Gas condensate field
- Oil pipeline
- Gas pipeline
- Oil terminal
- Gas terminal
- Tanker terminal
- Oil refinery
- International dividing line

UK ENERGY CONSUMPTION BY TYPE OF FUEL

- Natural gas 39%
- Oil 34%
- Electricity 13%
- Biomass & heat 11%
- Coal 3%

Total UK consumption in 2022
154 million tonnes of oil equivalent

Projection: Conical with two standard parallels

West from Greenwich   East from Greenwich

50 0 100 200 300 400 km

50 0 50 100 150 200 250 miles

1 : 7 500 000

PRODUCTION OF PRIMARY FUELS IN THE UK 1980–2022

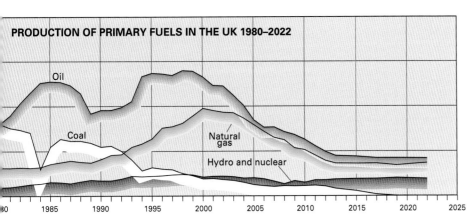

Oil

Coal

Natural gas

Hydro and nuclear

1985 1990 1995 2000 2005 2010 2015 2020 2025

ENERGY IMPORTS

Percentage of each type of fuel imported by the UK, 2022

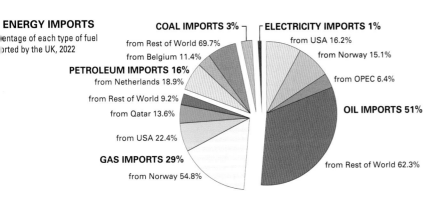

COAL IMPORTS 3%
from Rest of World 69.7%
from Belgium 11.4%

ELECTRICITY IMPORTS 1%
from USA 16.2%
from Norway 15.1%
from OPEC 6.4%

OIL IMPORTS 51%
from Rest of World 62.3%

PETROLEUM IMPORTS 16%
from Netherlands 18.9%
from Rest of World 9.2%
from Qatar 13.6%
from USA 22.4%

GAS IMPORTS 29%
from Norway 54.8%

Total U.K. imports 2022: 181.1 million tonnes of oil equivalent

PROSPECTING FOR SHALE GAS IN GREAT BRITAIN

☐ Areas where licenses have been granted to prospect for shale gas

Rock outcrops where shale gas may occur
Kimmeridge Clay
Oxford Clay
Liassic outcrops
Millstone Grit
Cambrian outcrops

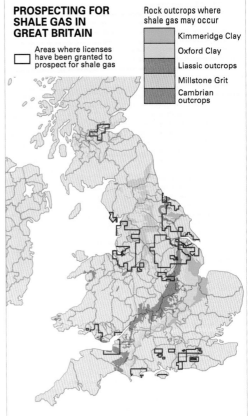

RENEWABLE ENERGY IN THE UK

The amount of energy generated from renewable sources in gigawatt hours, 2022

Over 25,000
20,000 – 25,000
10,000 – 20,000
5,000 – 10,000
Under 5,000
Possible sites for tidal power generation

Major wind farm
Major solar farm
Possible site for wave power farm

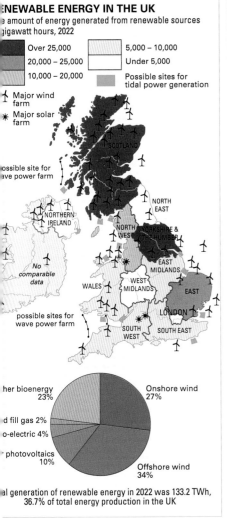

SCOTLAND
NORTHERN IRELAND
NORTH EAST
NORTH YORKSHIRE & WEST THE HUMBER
No comparable data
EAST MIDLANDS
WALES
WEST MIDLANDS
EAST
LONDON
SOUTH WEST
SOUTH EAST

possible sites for wave power farm

Other bioenergy 23%
Onshore wind 27%
Land fill gas 2%
Hydro-electric 4%
Solar photovoltaics 10%
Offshore wind 34%

Total generation of renewable energy in 2022 was 133.2 TWh, 36.7% of total energy production in the UK

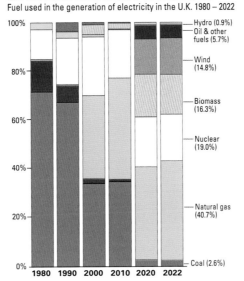

Wind farm at Royd Moor, South Yorkshire. The turbines are 35m high to the hub and have a rotor diameter of 37m. They generate enough electricity to power 3300 homes over a year.

CHANGES IN ELECTRICITY GENERATION

Fuel used in the generation of electricity in the U.K. 1980 – 2022

Hydro (0.9%)
Oil & other fuels (5.7%)
Wind (14.8%)
Biomass (16.3%)
Nuclear (19.0%)
Natural gas (40.7%)
Coal (2.6%)

100%
80%
60%
40%
20%
0%
1980 1990 2000 2010 2020 2022

ELECTRICITY GENERATION

Power Stations (with capacity)
☐ Coal-fired (over 1,000 MW)
■ Peat-fired (over 100 MW)
■ Oil-fired (over 500 MW)
☐ Combined cycle gas turbine (over 1,000 MW)
☐ Nuclear (over 1,000 MW)
☐ Proposed nuclear sites
▲ Pumped storage scheme
■ Hydro-electric (over 40 MW)
☐ Solar (over 60MW)
■ Biomass

Fasnakyle Foyers Peterhead
Glendoe
Rannoch Errochty
Cruachan Clunie
Clachan Lochay
Sloy
Torness
Lynemouth
Hartlepool
VPI Immingham
Heysham Saltend
Drax S. Humber
Edenderry Shotwick Bank
Moneypoint Dinorwig Connahs West Burton B
Turlough Hill Ffestiniog Quay Staythorpe
Ardnacrusha Rheidol Sizewell B
Pembroke Didcot B
Seabank Grain
Hinkley Point C (opening delayed)

It is important to generate electricity in a number of different ways to ensure a constant supply. Reliance on coal has decreased dramatically and renewable sources are becoming more important.

ROADS AND FERRIES

- M6 — Motorways
- —— Other main roads
- ·········· Principal car ferry routes
- – – – Channel Tunnel

RAILWAYS

- —— Electrified lines
- —— Other main lines
- **——** High-speed rail link London to Lille, Brussels and Paris
- – – – High Speed 2 (HS2) rail link (under con.) London to Birmingham

CHANNEL TUNNEL AND HIGH-SPEED RAIL LINKS IN EUROPE

Estimated journey times between London and other selected European cities

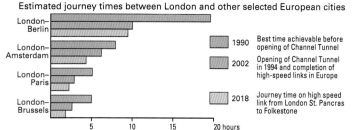

- 1990 — Best time achievable before opening of Channel Tunnel
- 2002 — Opening of Channel Tunnel in 1994 and completion of high-speed links in Europe
- 2018 — Journey time on high speed link from London St. Pancras to Folkestone

MEANS OF TRANSPORTATION WITHIN THE UK

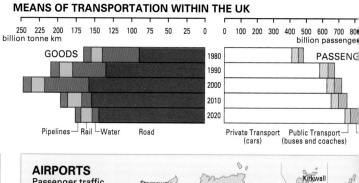

GOODS — billion tonne km — Pipelines, Rail, Water, Road

PASSENGER — billion passenger — Private Transport (cars), Public Transport (buses and coaches)

SEAPORTS

Goods traffic by port in million tonnes

60,000
10,000
1,000
5,000
30,000

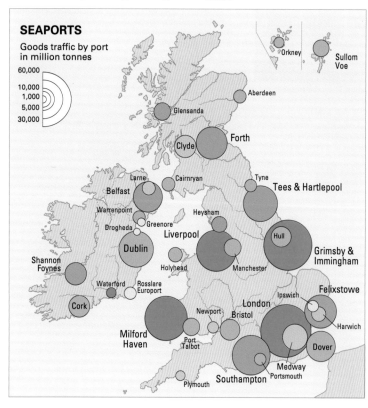

AIRPORTS

Passenger traffic in millions

80,000
20,000
5,000
1,000
10,000
40,000

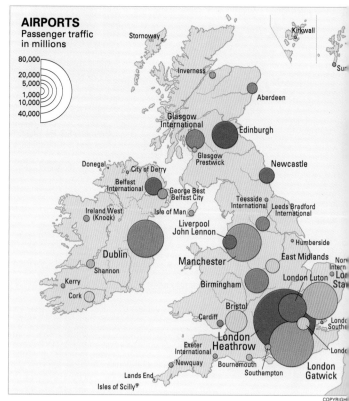

COPYRIGH

...SURE (LEISURE)

- National Parks
- National Landscapes
- National Scenic Areas
- Built-up areas
- Long distance footpaths
- Main tourist resorts
- Other tourist attractions

TRAVEL

- Motorways
- Other important roads
- Main railways
- Main ferry routes
- Channel Tunnel
- ⊕ Main airports
- ○ Ports and other towns

TOP UK TOURIST ATTRACTIONS

- ● Museum or gallery
- ● Historic Property
- ○ Other attraction

		Visitors in millions (2022)
1.	Windsor Great Park	5.6
2.	Natural History Museum, London	4.7
3.	British Museum, London	4.1
4.	Tate Modern, London	3.9
5.	Southbank Centre, London	2.9
6.	National Gallery, London	2.7
7.	Victoria & Albert Museum, London	2.4
8.	Somerset House, London	2.3
9.	Science Museum, London	2.3
10.	Tower of London	2.0
11.	National Museum of Scotland, Edinburgh	2.0
12.	Royal Botanic Gardens, Kew	2.0
13.	Royal Museums, Greenwich	1.6
14.	RHS Garden, Wisley	1.5
15.	Royal Albert Hall, London	1.4
16.	Edinburgh Castle	1.3
17.	Scottish National Gallery, Edinburgh	1.3
18.	St Paul's Cathedral, London	1.2
19.	Riverside Museum, Glasgow	1.2
20.	British Library, London	1.1

Windsor Great Park, Berkshire, England, was the most visited tourist attraction in the UK in 2022.

TOP IRELAND TOURIST ATTRACTIONS

- ● Museum or gallery
- ● Historic Property
- ○ Other attraction

		Visitors in millions (2022)
1.	Phoenix Park Visitor Centre, Dublin	2.0
2.	Kilkenny Castle Parklands	1.4
3.	Dublin Zoo	1.2
4.	Cliffs of Moher Visitor Experience, Clare	1.1
5.	Guinness Storehouse, Dublin	1.1
6.	Castletown House Parklands, Kildare	1.0
7.	Book of Kells, Dublin	0.8
8.	National Gallery of Ireland, Dublin	0.8
9.	Emerald Park, Meath	0.8
10.	St Patrick's Cathedral, Dublin	0.4

ORIGIN OF VISITORS TO THE UK

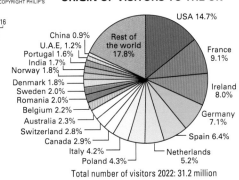

- USA 14.7%
- France 9.1%
- Ireland 8.0%
- Germany 7.1%
- Spain 6.4%
- Netherlands 5.2%
- Poland 4.3%
- Italy 4.2%
- Canada 2.9%
- Switzerland 2.8%
- Australia 2.3%
- Belgium 2.2%
- Romania 2.0%
- Sweden 2.0%
- Denmark 1.8%
- Norway 1.8%
- India 1.7%
- Portugal 1.6%
- U.A.E. 1.2%
- China 0.9%
- Rest of the world 17.8%

Total number of visitors 2022: 31.2 million

VISITS ABROAD BY UK RESIDENTS

Millions of visitors from UK (2022)

0 1 2 3 4 5 6 7 8 9 10 11 12 13 14 15 16

- Spain
- France
- Italy
- Greece
- Portugal
- U.S.A.
- Rep. of Ireland
- Turkey
- Poland
- Netherlands
- Germany

Total number of UK tourists 2022: 71 million

...TRAL ...DON (CENTRAL LONDON)

REGENTS PARK
British Library
British Museum
Holborn
St Paul's Cathedral
City of London
West End
National Portrait Gallery
Somerset House
...ENSINGTON GARDENS
HYDE PARK
Royal Academy
National Gallery
Tate Modern
Tower of London
Royal Albert Hall
Buckingham Palace
Southbank Centre
Southwark
...ral History ...useum (Natural History Museum)
Victoria and Albert Museum
Westminster
Westminster Abbey
Houses of Parliament
Tate Britain
...sington (Kensington)

COPYRIGHT PHILIP'S

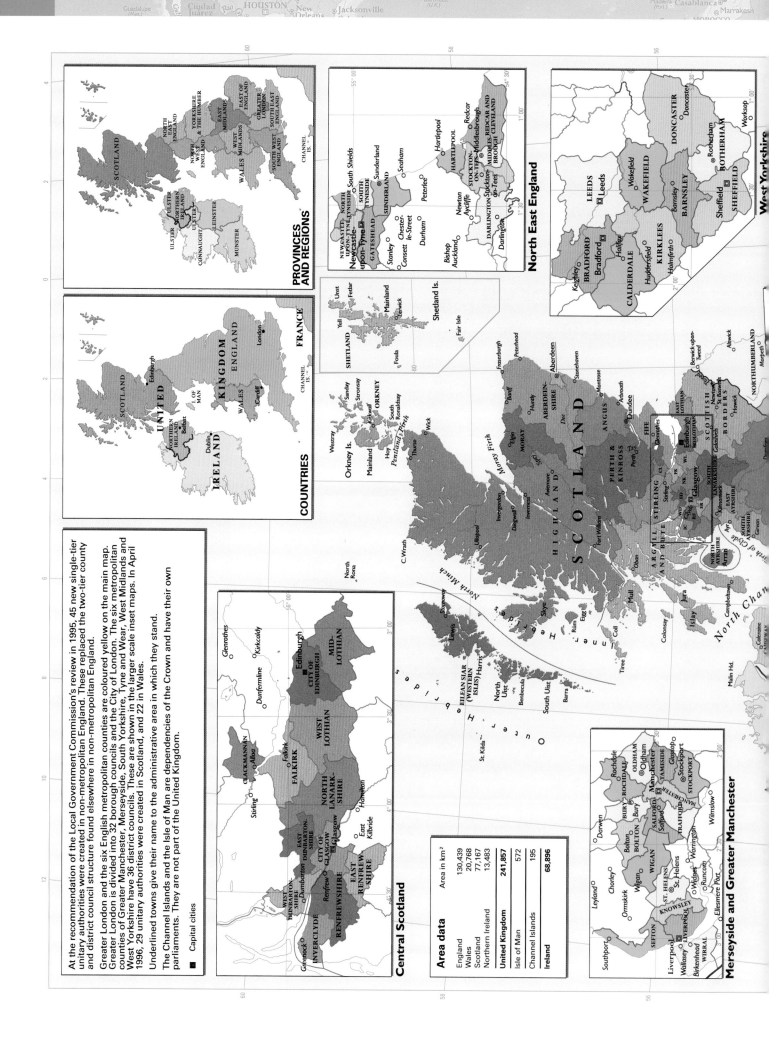

At the recommendation of the Local Government Commission's review in 1995, 45 new single-tier unitary authorities were created in non-metropolitan England. These replaced the two-tier county and district council structure found elsewhere in non-metropolitan England.

Greater London and the six English metropolitan counties are coloured yellow on the main map. Greater London is divided into 32 borough councils and the City of London. The six metropolitan counties of Greater Manchester, Merseyside, South Yorkshire, Tyne and Wear, West Midlands and West Yorkshire have 36 district councils. These are shown in the larger scale inset maps. In April 1996, 29 unitary authorities were created in Scotland, and 22 in Wales.

Underlined towns give their name to the administrative area in which they stand.

The Channel Islands and the Isle of Man are dependencies of the Crown and have their own parliaments. They are not part of the United Kingdom.

■ Capital cities

PROVINCES AND REGIONS

COUNTRIES

North East England

West Yorkshire

Central Scotland

Area data

	Area in km²
England	130,439
Wales	20,768
Scotland	77,167
Northern Ireland	13,483
United Kingdom	**241,857**
Isle of Man	572
Channel Islands	195
Ireland	**68,896**

Merseyside and Greater Manchester

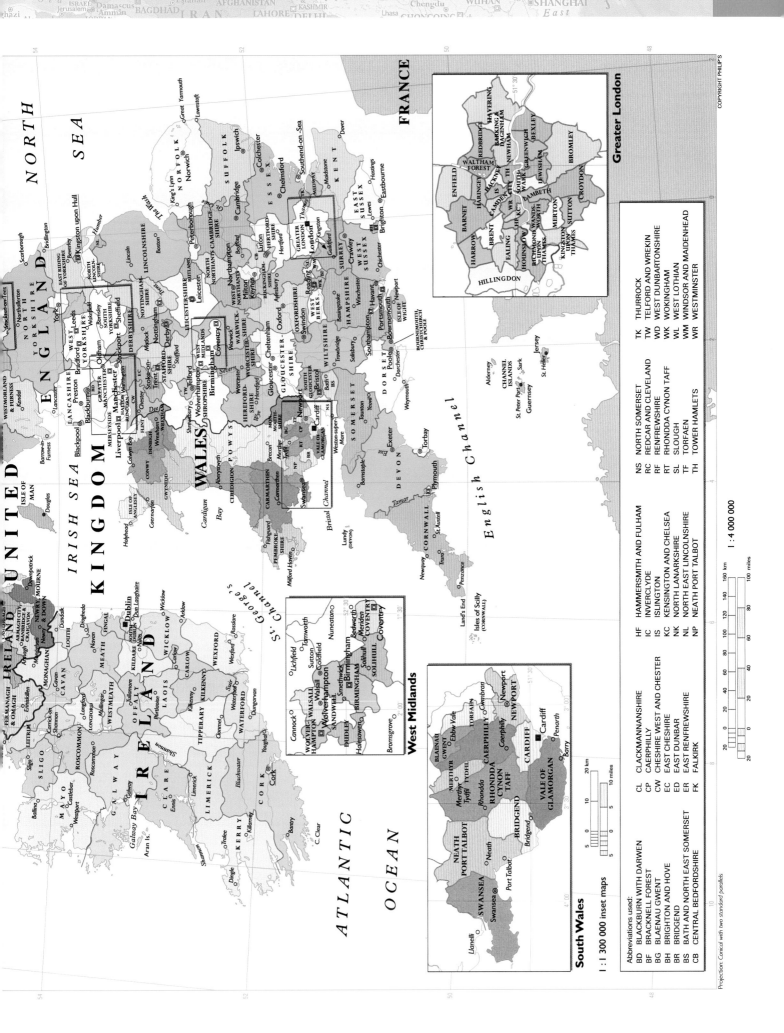

POPULATION DENSITY
Persons per sq km (2022)

- Over 5,000
- 2,000 – 5,000
- 1,000 – 2,000
- 500 – 1,000
- 200 – 500
- 100 – 200
- 50 – 100
- Under 50

POPULATION DATA (2022)	Population ('000s)	Density (persons per sq km)
England	57,106	438
Wales	3,132	151
Scotland	5,437	70
Northern Ireland	1,911	139
United Kingdom	**67,585**	**278**
Ireland	**5,149**	**76**

Projection: Conical with two standard parallels

1 : 4 000 000

POPULATION DENSITY IN 1891

Persons per sq km

- Over 1,000
- 500 – 1,000
- 200 – 500
- 100 – 200
- 50 – 100
- 25 – 50
- Under 25

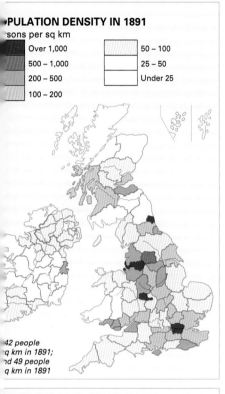

...42 people
...q km in 1891;
...nd 49 people
...q km in 1891

NATIONALITY

Non-British as a percentage of total population

- Over 10%
- 7.5 – 10%
- 5 – 7.5%
- 0 – 5%

340 000 Total number of non-British people in each region

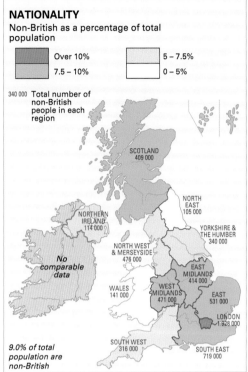

SCOTLAND 409 000

NORTHERN IRELAND 114 000

NORTH EAST 105 000

YORKSHIRE & THE HUMBER 340 000

NORTH WEST & MERSEYSIDE 476 000

EAST MIDLANDS 414 000

No comparable data

WALES 141 000

WEST MIDLANDS 471 000

EAST 531 000

LONDON 1 928 000

SOUTH WEST 316 000

SOUTH EAST 719 000

9.0% of total population are non-British

INTERNAL MIGRATION

The difference between the number moving in and the number moving away per 1,000 inhabitants*

- Over 5 moved in
- 1 – 5 moved in
- 0 – 1 moved in
- 0 – 1 moved away
- 1 – 5 moved away
- Over 5 moved away

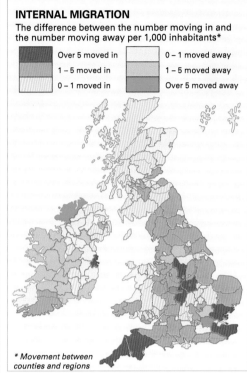

* Movement between counties and regions

NATURAL POPULATION CHANGE

...difference between the number of births and the number of deaths per thousand inhabitants

- Over 5 more births
- 2.5 – 5 more births
- 1 – 2.5 more births
- 0 – 1 more births
- 0 – 2 more deaths
- Over 2 more deaths

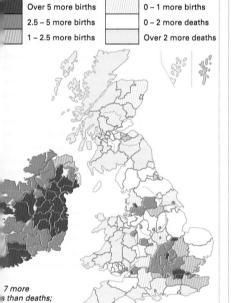

...7 more
...s than deaths;
...d 7.5 more
...s than deaths

YOUNG PEOPLE

The percentage of the population under 15 years old

- Over 21%
- 19 – 21%
- 17 – 19%
- Under 17%

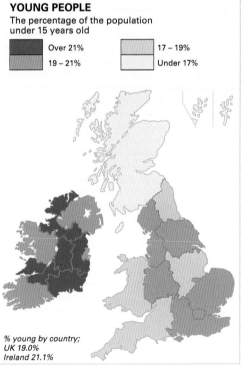

% young by country;
UK 19.0%
Ireland 21.1%

OLDER PEOPLE

The percentage of the population aged 65 and over

- Over 22%
- 20 – 22%
- 18 – 20%
- 16 – 18%
- 14 – 16%
- Under 14%

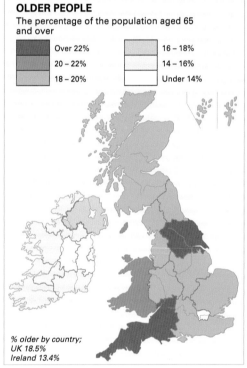

% older by country;
UK 18.5%
Ireland 13.4%

VITAL STATISTICS (1920–2022)

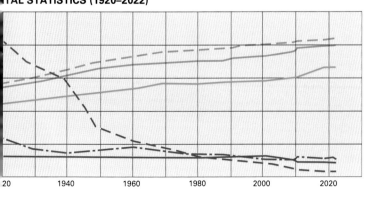

- Total population (in millions)
- Infant mortality (deaths per 1,000 live births)
- Birth rate (births per 1,000 of the population)
- Death rate (deaths per 1,000 of the population)
- Male life expectancy (in years)
- Female life expectancy (in years)

20   1940   1960   1980   2000   2020

AGE STRUCTURE OF THE UK

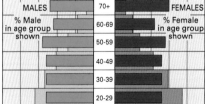

1901   2022   Age   1901   2022

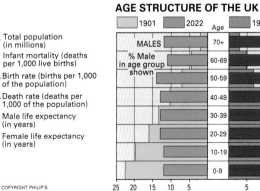

MALES

% Male in age group shown

FEMALES

% Female in age group shown

70+
60-69
50-59
40-49
30-39
20-29
10-19
0-9

25 20 15 10 5   5 10 15 20 25

HOUSE PRICES
Annual change in house prices
2022-2023

Over 10%		6 – 7%	
8 – 10%		4 – 6%	
7 – 8%		Under 4%	

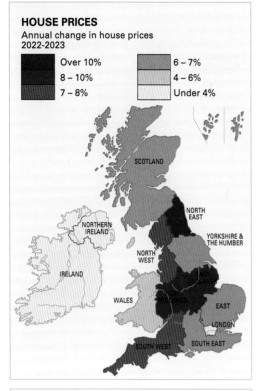

UNEMPLOYMENT
The percentage of the workforce
unemployed in 2023

Over 5%		3 – 4%	
4 – 5%		Under 3%	

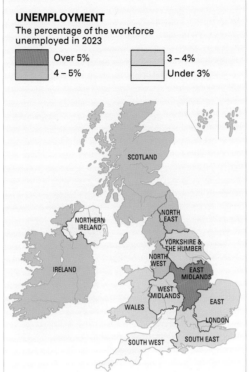

INCOME
The average gross weekly earnings of males
and females in full employment in 2023

Over £800		£650 – £675	
£700 – £800		£625 – £650	
£675 – £700		£600 – £625	

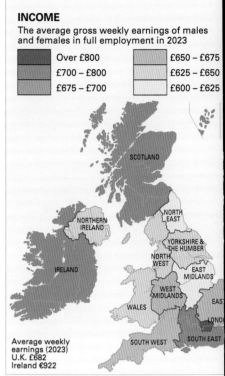

Average weekly
earnings (2023)
U.K. £682
Ireland €922

EDUCATION
The percentage of pupils achieving the equivalent of
grade 5 in 7 subjects at GCSE level in 2022/23

Over 50%		40 – 45%	
45 – 50%		Under 40%	

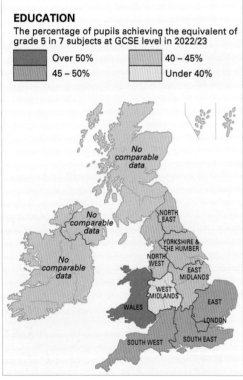

CRIME RATE
Total recorded crimes per
1,000 people in 2023

Over 110		50 – 70	
90 – 110		Under 50	
70 – 90			

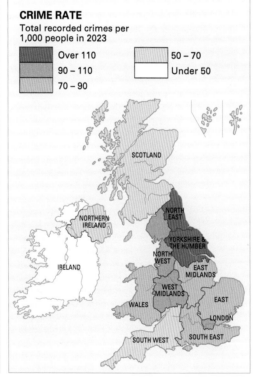

GOVERNMENT EXPENDITURE ON SERVIC
Expenditure per head on services such as health
recreation, education etc. in 2021/22

Over £14,000		£11,000 – £1	
£13,000 – £14,000		Under £11,00	
£12,000 – £13,000			

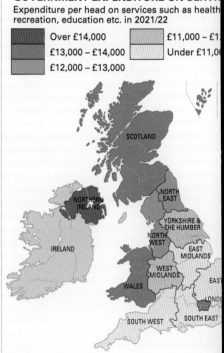

COMPARISON OF HOUSEHOLD EXPENDITURE

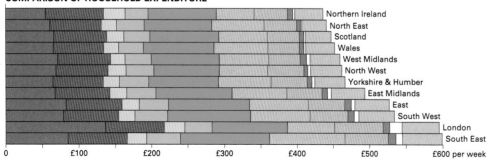

Northern Ireland
North East
Scotland
Wales
West Midlands
North West
Yorkshire & Humber
East Midlands
East
South West
London
South East

0   £100   £200   £300   £400   £500   £600 per week

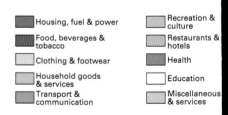

Housing, fuel & power		Recreation & culture	
Food, beverages & tobacco		Restaurants & hotels	
Clothing & footwear		Health	
Household goods & services		Education	
Transport & communication		Miscellaneous & services	

Average household expenditure per week in UK in 2022

THE WORLD

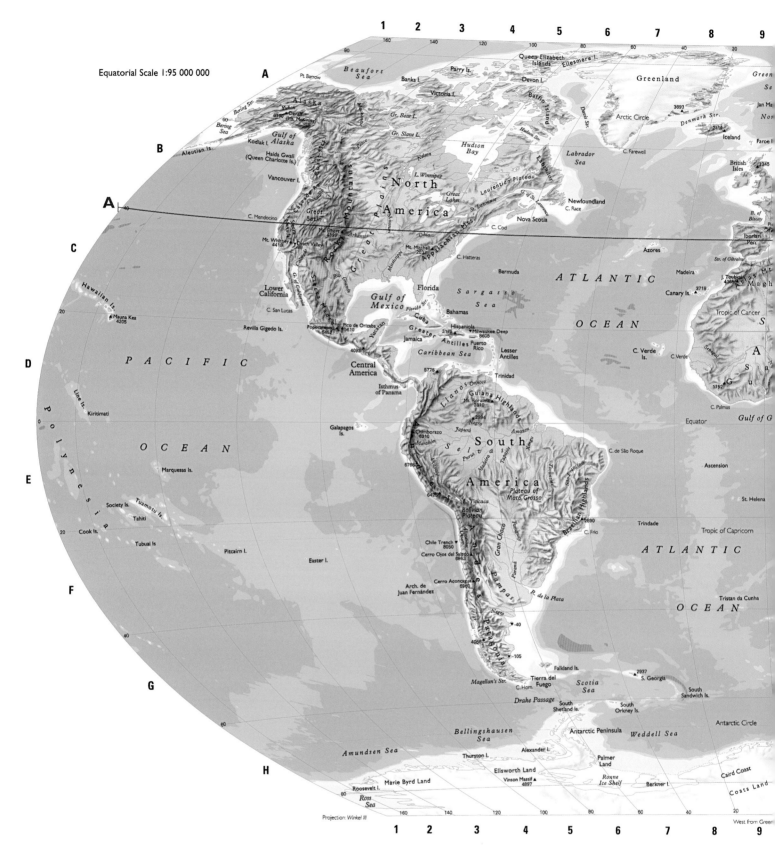

Equatorial Scale 1:95 000 000

Projection: Winkel III

West from Green

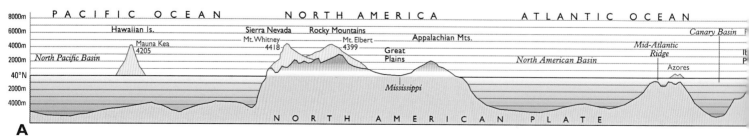

| 8000m | PACIFIC OCEAN | NORTH AMERICA | ATLANTIC OCEAN |

6000m — Hawaiian Is. · Sierra Nevada · Rocky Mountains · Canary Basin

4000m — Mauna Kea 4205 · Mt. Whitney 4418 · Mt. Elbert 4399 · Appalachian Mts. · Mid-Atlantic Ridge

2000m — North Pacific Basin · Great Plains · North American Basin · Azores

40°N

2000m — Mississippi

4000m

NORTH AMERICAN PLATE

A

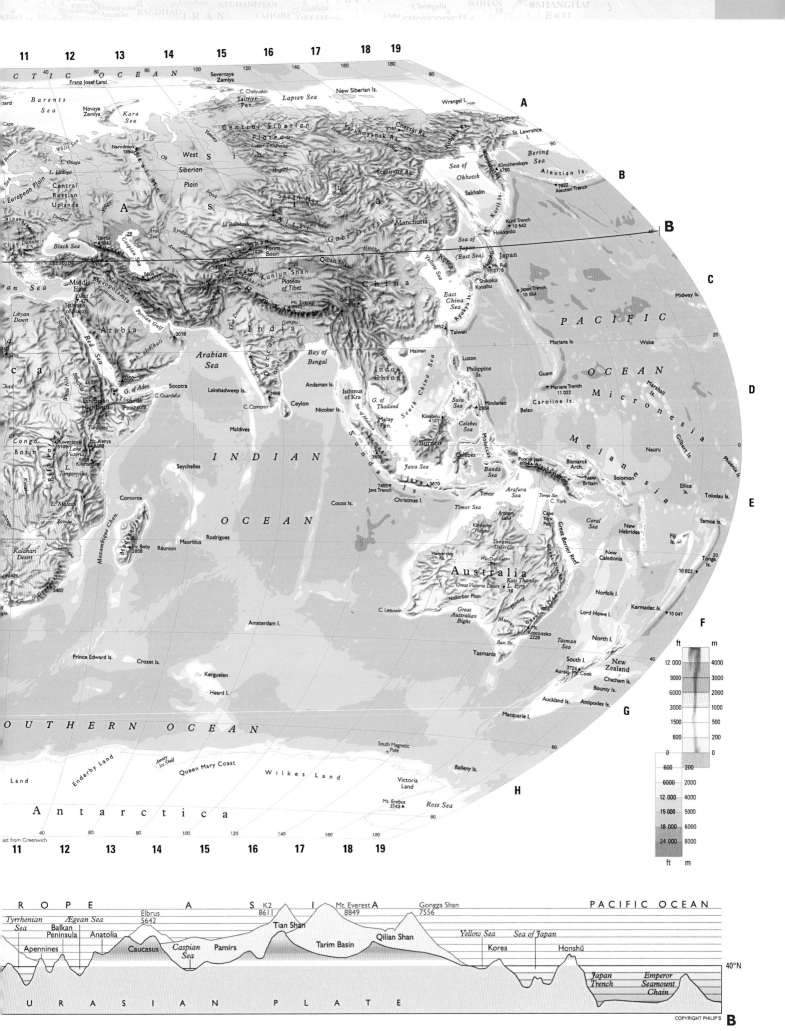

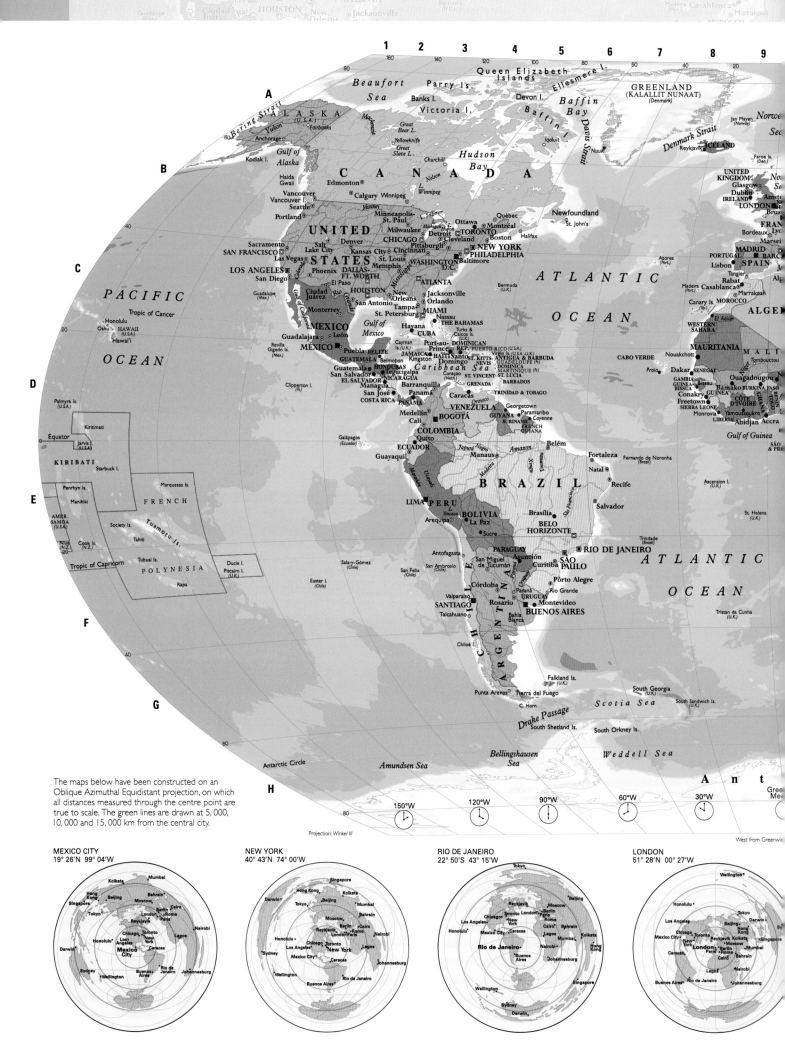

1 2 3 4 5 6 7 8 9

Queen Elizabeth Islands
Beaufort Sea Parry Is. Devon I. Ellesmere I. GREENLAND (KALALLIT NUNAAT) (Denmark)
Banks I. Victoria I. *Baffin Bay* Jan Mayen (Norway) Norw

A

Bering Strait ALASKA (U.S.A.) Fairbanks Great Bear L. *Baffin I.* Denmark Strait ICELAND
Yukon Anchorage Mackenzie Yellowknife Great Slave L. Nuuk Reykjavik
Kodiak I. Gulf of Alaska Churchill Iqaluit Faroe Is. (Den.)

B

Haida Gwaii Edmonton *Hudson Bay* Newfoundland UNITED KINGDOM No
Vancouver Calgary Winnipeg St. John's Glasgow Se
Vancouver I. L. Winnipeg Dublin IRELAND LONDON Brus
Seattle C A N A D A Nelson Québec FRAN
Portland Minneapolis-St. Paul Ottawa Montréal Bordeaux Ly
Milwaukee Detroit TORONTO Halifax Marsei
UNITED CHICAGO Cleveland Boston MADRID BARC
Sacramento Denver Pittsburgh NEW YORK PORTUGAL SPAIN
SAN FRANCISCO Salt Lake City STATES Cincinnati PHILADELPHIA Lisbon M
Las Vegas Kansas City St. Louis WASHINGTON ATLANTIC Tangier
LOS ANGELES Phoenix DALLAS- Memphis D.C. Baltimore Rabat
San Diego FT. WORTH ATLANTA Bermuda Madeira (Port.) Casablanca
El Paso HOUSTON (U.K.) OCEAN Canary Is. (Sp.) MOROCCO ALGE
Guadalupe (Mex.) Ciudad New Jacksonville WESTERN El Aaiún
Juárez Orleans Orlando SAHARA
Revilla Gigedo Is. (Mex.) San Antonio Tampa MIAMI MAURITANIA MALI
Monterrey St. Petersburg Nassau CABO VERDE Nouakchott Tombouctou
MEXICO THE BAHAMAS Praia Dakar SENEGAL Niger Ouagadougou
Guadalajara León Gulf of Havana Turks & GAMBIA Bamako BURKINA FASO
MÉXICO Mexico CUBA Caicos Is. GUINEA- Bissau GUINEA Conakry CÔTE
Puebla BELIZE Cayman Is. Port-au- DOMINICAN PUERTO RICO (U.S.A.) SIERRA LEONE Freetown D'IVOIRE
GUATEMALA Belmopan (U.K.) Prince REP. Virgin Is. (U.S.A.-U.K.) Monrovia Yamoussoukro
Guatemala HONDURAS JAMAICA Santo ST. KITTS ANTIGUA & BARBUDA LIBERIA Abidjan Accra
San Salvador Tegucigalpa Kingston HAITI Domingo NEVIS GUADELOUPE (Fr) Gulf of Guinea
EL SALVADOR NICARAGUA Caribbean Sea DOMINICA MARTINIQUE (Fr) SÃO
Managua Curaçao ST. VINCENT ST. LUCIA & PRÍ
COSTA RICA Barranquilla (Neth.) GRENADA BARBADOS
San José Panamá Caracas TRINIDAD & TOBAGO
PANAMA Medellín VENEZUELA Georgetown
Cali BOGOTÁ GUYANA Paramaribo
COLOMBIA SURINAME Cayenne
Galápagos (Ecuador) Quito FRENCH GUIANA
ECUADOR Japurá Negro Belém Fernando de Noronha (Brazil)
Guayaquil Amazon Manaus Fortaleza
Madeira Xingu Natal
Marañón B R A Z I L Recife Ascension I. (U.K.)
LIMA PERU Ucayali São Francisco Salvador
Titicaca BOLIVIA Brasília St. Helena (U.K.)
Arequipa La Paz BELO Trindade (Brazil)
Sucre HORIZONTE
Antofagasta PARAGUAY Asunción RIO DE JANEIRO ATLANTIC
San Miguel SÃO OCEAN
de Tucumán Paraná Curitiba PAULO
Córdoba Pôrto Alegre Tristan da Cunha (U.K.)
Valparaíso Paraná Rio Grande
SANTIAGO Rosario URUGUAY Montevideo
Talcahuano Bahía BUENOS AIRES
Chiloé I. Blanca
ARGENTINA Falkland Is. (U.K.) South Georgia (U.K.)
Punta Arenas Tierra del Fuego South Sandwich Is. (U.K.)
C. Horn *Scotia Sea*
Drake Passage South Shetland Is. South Orkney Is.

PACIFIC Tropic of Cancer Honolulu
Oahu HAWAII (U.S.A.)
OCEAN Hawai'i
Palmyra Is. (U.S.A.)
Kiritimati
Equator Jarvis I. (U.S.A.)
KIRIBATI Starbuck I.
Penrhyn Is. Marquesas Is.
Manihiki FRENCH
AMER. SAMOA (U.S.A.) Society Is. Tuamotu Is.
Niue (N.Z.) Cook Is. (N.Z.) Tahiti
Tropic of Capricorn Tubuai Is. Ducie I.
POLYNESIA Pitcairn I. (U.K.)
Rapa
Sala-y-Gómez (Chile)
Easter I. (Chile) San Félix (Chile) San Ambrosio (Chile)
Clipperton I. (Fr)

C
D
E
F
G
H

Bellingshausen Sea *Weddell Sea*
Antarctic Circle *Amundsen Sea* A n t
Gree
Me

The maps below have been constructed on an Oblique Azimuthal Equidistant projection, on which all distances measured through the centre point are true to scale. The green lines are drawn at 5, 000, 10, 000 and 15, 000 km from the central city.

150°W 120°W 90°W 60°W 30°W

Projection: Winkel III

West from Greenwic

MEXICO CITY
19° 26'N 99° 04'W

NEW YORK
40° 43'N 74° 00'W

RIO DE JANEIRO
22° 50'S 43° 15'W

LONDON
51° 28'N 00° 27'W

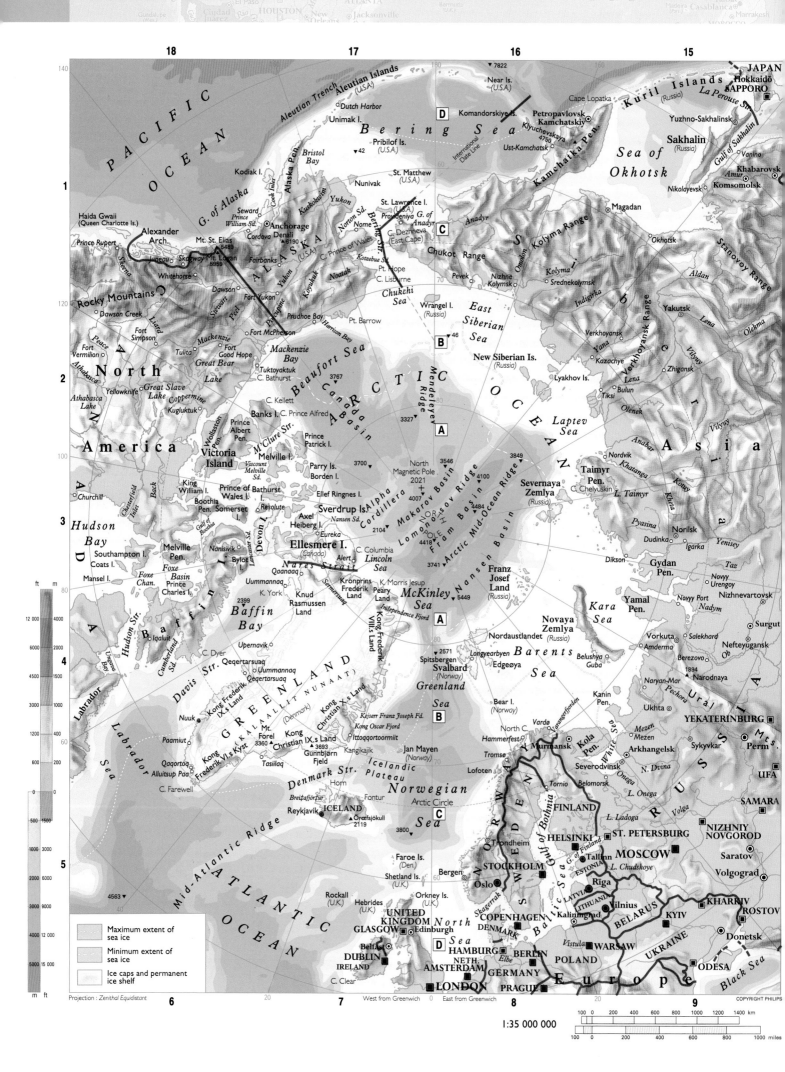

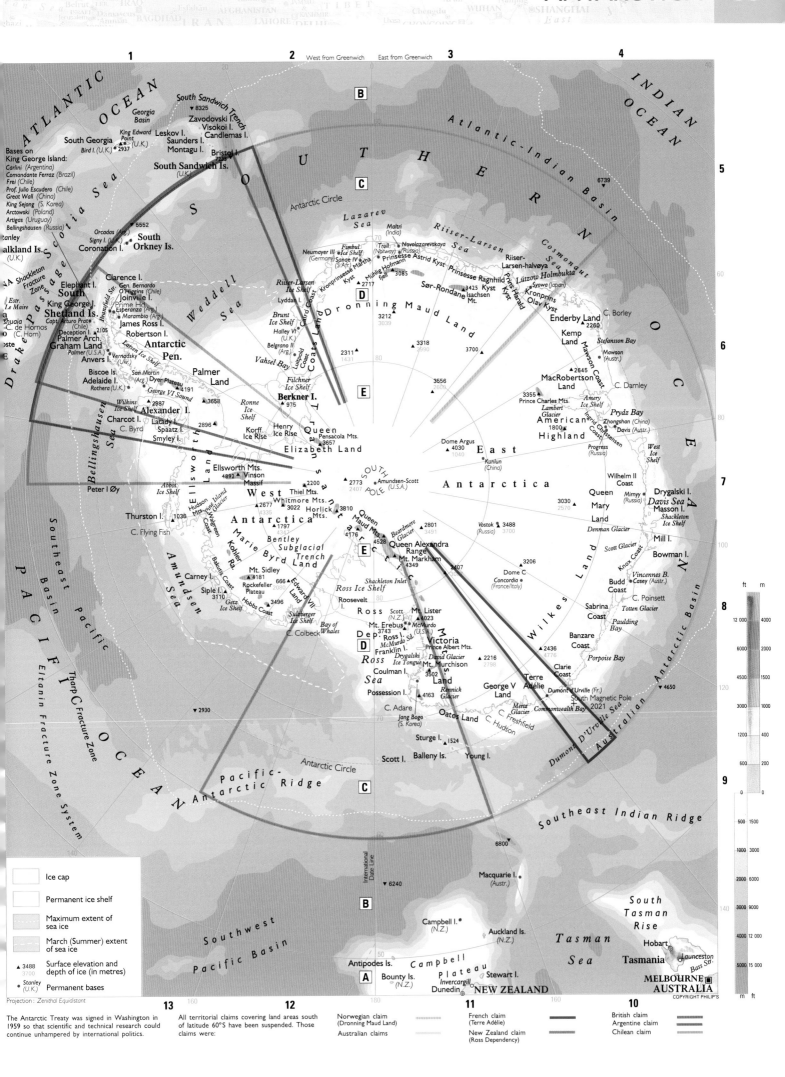

ATLANTIC OCEAN

Georgia Basin

South Sandwich Trench ▾ 8325

South Georgia
Bird I. (U.K.) ● 2937
King Edward Point (U.K.)

Zavodovski I.
Visokoi I.
Candlemas I.

Leskov I.
Saunders I.
Montagu I.

Bristol I.
7235 ▾

Bases on King George Island:
Carlini (Argentina)
Comandante Ferraz (Brazil)
Frei (Chile)
Prof. Julio Escudero (Chile)
Great Wall (China)
King Sejong (S. Korea)
Arctowski (Poland)
Artigas (Uruguay)
Bellingshausen (Russia)

South Sandwich Is. (U.K.)

SOUTHERN

B

Atlantic-Indian Basin

INDIAN OCEAN

5

6739

Stanley

Falkland Is. (U.K.)

Scotia Sea

Orcadas (Arg.) ● 5552
Signy I. (U.K.)
Coronation I.   South Orkney Is.

C

Antarctic Circle

Lazarev Sea

Maitri (India)

Neumayer III (Germany)
Sanae IV (S.Afr.)
Fimbul Ice Shelf
Troll (Norway)
Novolazarevskaya (Russia)
Syowa (Japan)

Prinsesse Astrid Kyst
Prinsesse Ragnhild Kyst

Riiser-Larsen Sea

Cosmonaut Sea

Lützow Holmbukta

Enderby Land   C. Borley
2260

Kemp Land

Stefansson Bay

Mawson (Austr.)

MacRobertson Land

C. Darnley

6

Drake Passage

N Shackleton Fracture Zone
Estr.
Le Maire
shuaia
C. de Hornos
(C. Horn)
oste

Elephant I.
Clarence I.
Gen. Bernardo O'Higgins (Chile)
Joinville I.
Esperanza (Arg.)
Marambio (Arg.)
Capt. Arturo Prat (Chile)
Deception I. (Chile) ● 2105

South Shetland Is.
King George I.

James Ross I.
Robertson I.

Brunsfield Str.
Prime Hd.

Palmer Arch.
Graham Land
Palmer (U.S.A.)
Anvers I.
Vernadsky (Ukr.)

Antarctic Pen.

Weddell Sea

Coats Land
Caird Coast

Riiser-Larsen Ice Shelf

Kronprinsesse Märtha Kyst

Mühlig Hofmann fjell 3085

2717 ▲

Isachsen Mt. 3425

Sør-Rondane

Prins Harald Kyst

Kronprins Olav Kyst

3212

Lyddan I.

Dronning Maud Land

3318

3039

3700

Prince Charles Mts.
Lambert Glacier
Amery Ice Shelf

Zhongshan (China)
Davis (Austr.)

Prydz Bay

American Highland

Ingrid Christensen Coast

Progress (Russia)

West Ice Shelf

7

Biscoe Is.
Adelaide I.
Rothera (U.K.)

San Martín (Arg.)
Dyer Plateau

Palmer Land

2896 ▲

Halley VI (U.K.)

Belgrano II (Arg.)

Filchner Ice Shelf

Berkner I.
975

Queen Elizabeth Land

3556
2600

3355
2600

1800

Vinson Massif 4892 ▲

Ellsworth Mts.

2200

2773

South Pole

Amundsen-Scott (U.S.A.) 2407

East Antarctica

Dome Argus 4030
1040

Kunlun (China)

3030
2570

Queen Mary Land

Mirnyy (Russia)

Drygalski I.

Davis Sea
Masson I.
Shackleton Ice Shelf

8

Bellingshausen Sea

Charcot I.
C. Byrd

Alexander I.
Latady I.
Spaatz I.
Smyley I.

2987 ▲

George VI Sound 4191

Ronne Ice Shelf

Korff Ice Rise

Henry Ice Rise

3658 ▲

Pensacola Mts.
3657

West Antarctica

Thiel Mts.

Whitmore Mts.
3022

Horlick Mts.
3810

Vostok 3488
(Russia) 3700

Dome C
Concordia
(France/Italy)

3206

Wilhelm II Coast

Wilkes

Vincennes B.
Casey (Austr.)

Budd Coast

C. Poinsett

Bowman I.

9

Peter I Øy

Abbot Ice Shelf

Hudson Mts.
Walgreen Coast

Thurston I.   1036

C. Flying Fish

Ellsworth Land

1797

2677
4335

Bentley Subglacial Trench

Queen Maud Mts.
4176

Beardmore Glacier
4528
2801
3491

Queen Alexandra Range
Mt. Markham 4349

2407
200

Scott Glacier

Denman Glacier

Mill I.

Totten Glacier

Sabrina Coast

Paulding Bay

Banzare Coast

Porpoise Bay

Southeast Pacific Basin

Eltanin Fracture Zone System

Tharp C Fracture Zone

Amundsen Sea

Carney I.

Siple I.
3110

Marie Byrd Land

Bakutis Coast

Getz Ice Shelf

Mt. Sidley 4181

Rockefeller Plateau

Koettlitz Ra.

666 ▲ 2080

Edward VII Land
Sulzberger Ice Shelf

3496

Bay of Whales

Shackleton Inlet

Ross Ice Shelf

Roosevelt I.

Ross Sea

2436
4776

Clarie Coast

2216
2798

George V Land

Terre Adélie

Dumont d'Urville (Fr.)

4650

South Magnetic Pole 2021

PACIFIC OCEAN

D

Bay of Whales

C. Colbeck

Ross Dep.

Ross Sea

Scott (N.Z.)
Mt. Lister 4023

McMurdo Sd.
McMurdo (U.S.A.)
Mt. Erebus 3743
Ross I.
Franklin I.
Drygalski Ice Tongue

Victoria Land

Prince Albert Mts.
David Glacier
Mt. Murchison 3502

Coulman I.

Possession I.

C. Adare

Jang Bogo (S. Korea)

4163

Rennick Glacier

Mertz Glacier
Commonwealth Bay

Oates Land

C. Freshfield
C. Hudson

Dumont D'Urville Sea

Australian Antarctic Basin

ft   m
12 000   4000
6000   2000
4500   1500
3000   1000
1200   400
600   200

0   0

500   1500
1000   3000
2000   6000
3000   9000
4000   12 000
5000   15 000
m   ft

2930 ▾

Pacific-Antarctic Ridge

70

Antarctic Circle

Sturge I. 1524

Scott I.

Balleny Is.

Young I.

Southeast Indian Ridge

6800 ▾

Macquarie I. (Austr.)

South Tasman Rise

B

Southwest Pacific Basin

6240 ▾

International Date Line

Campbell I. (N.Z.)

Auckland Is. (N.Z.)

Tasman Sea

Hobart

Launceston Bass Str.

Tasmania

South Tasman Rise

MELBOURNE
AUSTRALIA
COPYRIGHT PHILIP'S

A

Antipodes Is.

Bounty Is. (N.Z.)

Campbell Plateau

Stewart I.

Dunedin   Invercargill   NEW ZEALAND

50

Legend

☐ Ice cap

☐ Permanent ice shelf

☐ Maximum extent of sea ice

☐ March (Summer) extent of sea ice

▲ 3488 / 3700   Surface elevation and depth of ice (in metres)

● Stanley (U.K.)   Permanent bases

Projection: Zenithal Equidistant

The Antarctic Treaty was signed in Washington in 1959 so that scientific and technical research could continue unhampered by international politics.

All territorial claims covering land areas south of latitude 60°S have been suspended. Those claims were:

Norwegian claim (Dronning Maud Land)

Australian claims

········· French claim (Terre Adélie)

New Zealand claim (Ross Dependency)

British claim

Argentine claim

Chilean claim

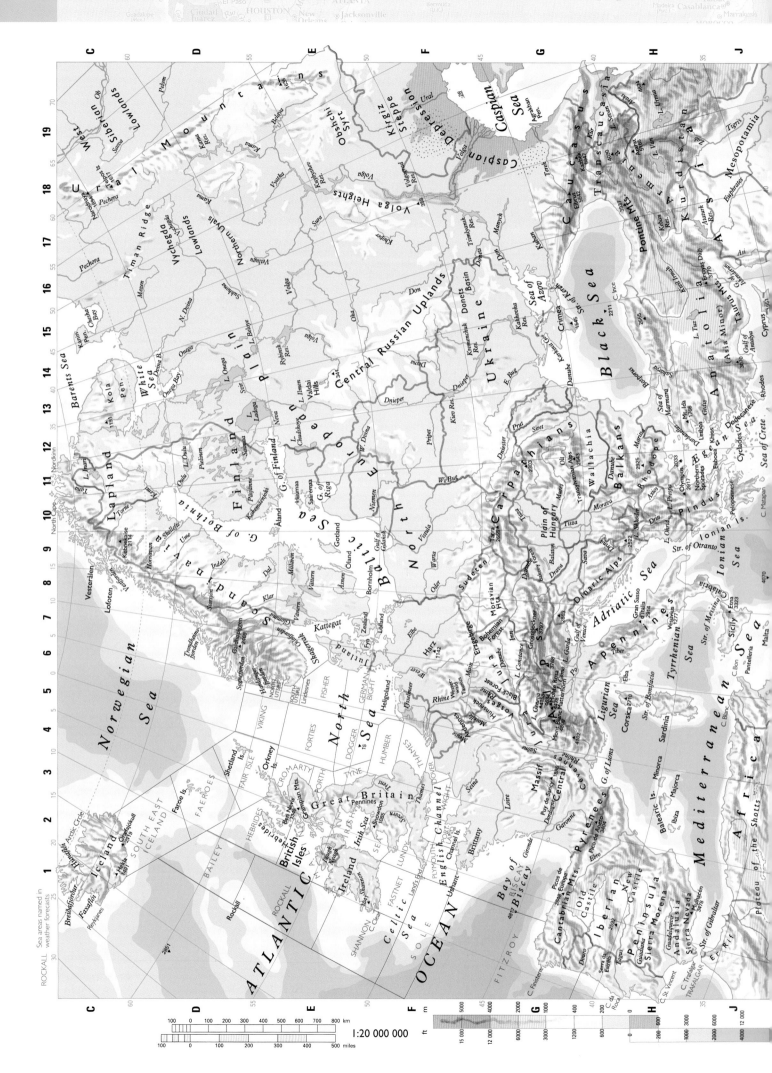

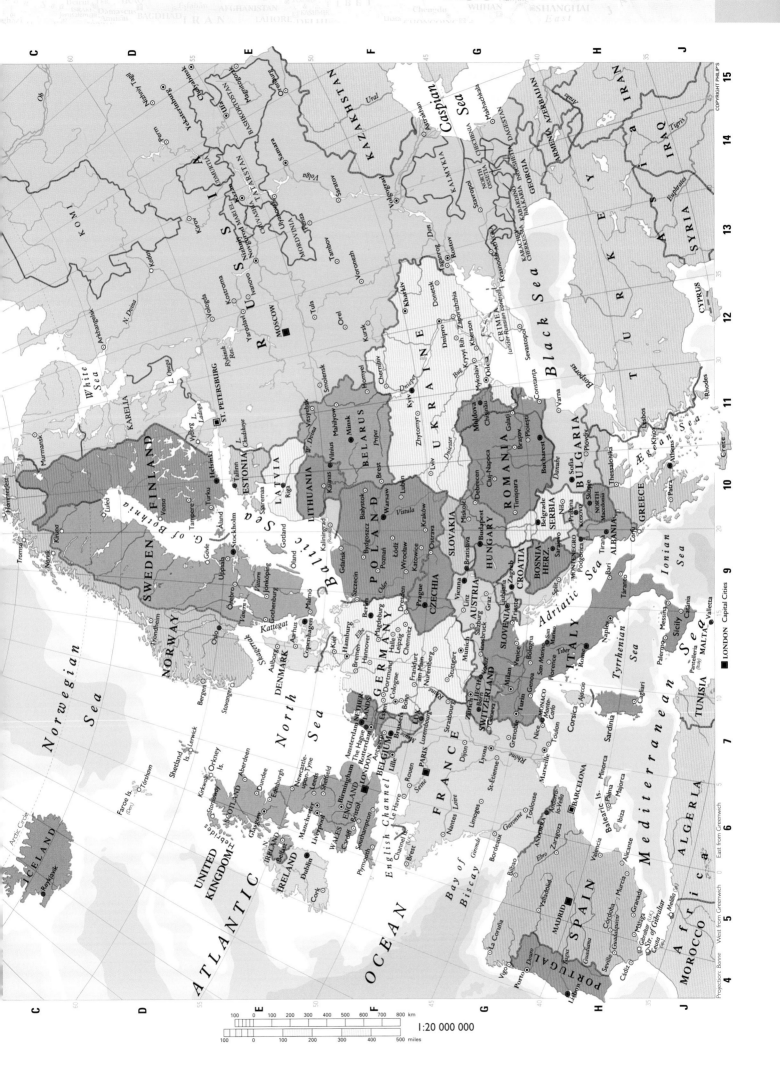

Projection: Bonne   West from Greenwich   0   East from Greenwich

COPYRIGHT PHILIP'S

■ LONDON Capital Cities

1:20 000 000

100   0   100   200   300   400   500   600   700   800 km

100   0   100   200   300   400   500 miles

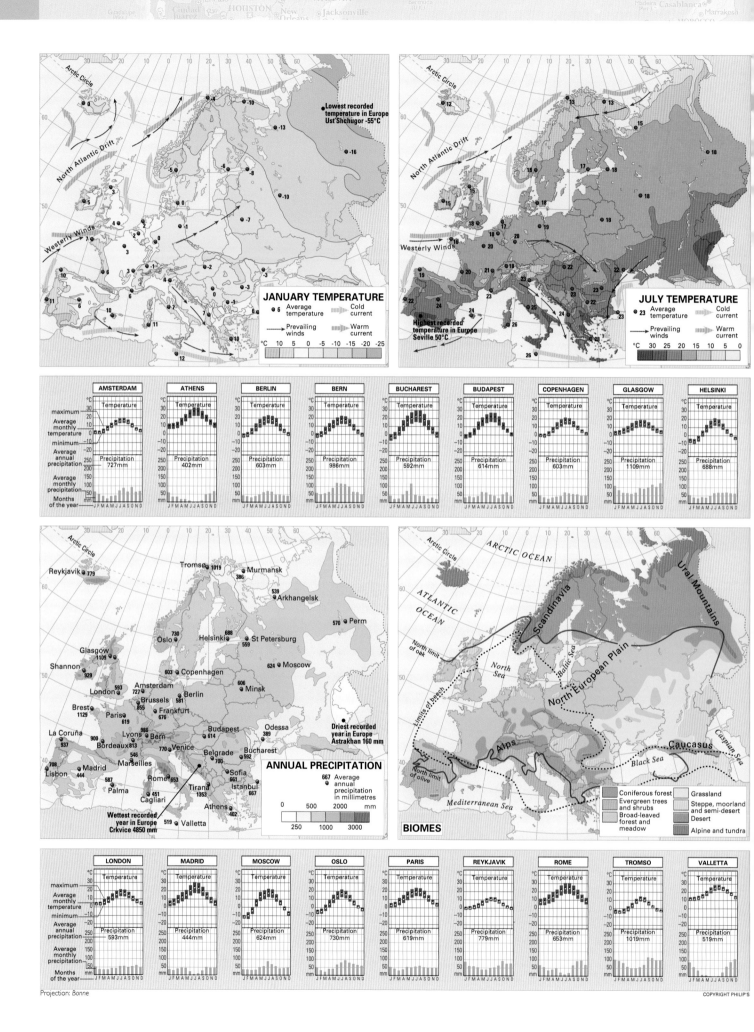

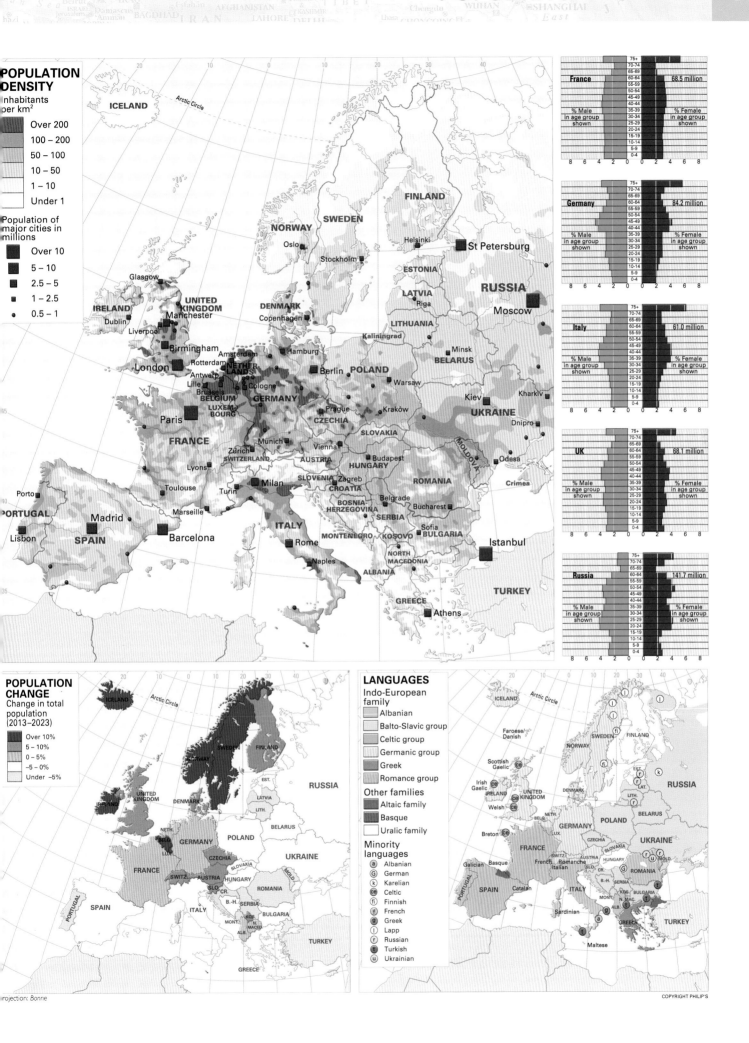

POPULATION DENSITY
Inhabitants per km²

- Over 200
- 100 – 200
- 50 – 100
- 10 – 50
- 1 – 10
- Under 1

Population of major cities in millions

- Over 10
- 5 – 10
- 2.5 – 5
- 1 – 2.5
- 0.5 – 1

France 68.5 million
% Male in age group shown | % Female in age group shown

Germany 84.2 million

Italy 61.0 million

UK 68.1 million

Russia 141.7 million

POPULATION CHANGE
Change in total population (2013–2023)

- Over 10%
- 5 – 10%
- 0 – 5%
- –5 – 0%
- Under –5%

LANGUAGES
Indo-European family
- Albanian
- Balto-Slavic group
- Celtic group
- Germanic group
- Greek
- Romance group

Other families
- Altaic family
- Basque
- Uralic family

Minority languages
- (a) Albanian
- (G) German
- (k) Karelian
- (ce) Celtic
- (fi) Finnish
- (fr) French
- (g) Greek
- (l) Lapp
- (r) Russian
- (t) Turkish
- (u) Ukrainian

Projection: Bonne

COPYRIGHT PHILIP'S

GROWTH OF THE EU

€ Euro-zone ○ EU headquarters

- Founder members (Treaty of Rome 1957)
- Admission in 1973
- Admission in 1981
- Admission in 1986
- Admission in 1990 (German unification)
- Admission in 1995
- Admission in 2004
- Admission in 2007
- Admission in 2013

The UK was a member from 1973 to 2020

EU COUNTRY COMPARISONS	Population (thousands)	Annual Income (US$ per capita)
Germany	84,220	54,030
France	68,522	45,290
Italy	61,021	38,200
Spain	47,223	32,090
Poland	37,992	18,900
Romania	18,326	15,570
Netherlands	17,464	60,230
Belgium	11,914	53,890
Czechia	10,706	26,100
Sweden	10,536	63,500
Greece	10,498	21,810
Portugal	10,223	25,950
Hungary	9,670	19,010
Ireland	9,670	79,300
Austria	8,941	55,720
Bulgaria	6,828	13,350
Denmark	5,947	73,520
Finland	5,615	54,930
Slovakia	5,425	35,260
Croatia	4,169	19,600
Lithuania	2,656	23,870
Slovenia	2,100	29,590
Latvia	1,822	21,850
Cyprus	1,308	31,520
Estonia	1,203	27,120
Luxembourg	661	89,200
Malta	467	32,860
Total EU 2023 (27 countries)	**455,127**	**39,343**

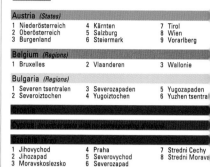

REGIONS OF THE EU

Austria (States)
1 Niederösterreich
2 Oberösterreich
3 Burgenland
4 Kärnten
5 Salzburg
6 Steiermark
7 Tirol
8 Wien
9 Vorarlberg

Belgium (Regions)
1 Bruxelles
2 Vlaanderen
3 Wallonie

Bulgaria (Regions)
1 Severen tsentralen
2 Severoiztochen
3 Severozapaden
4 Yugoiztochen
5 Yugozapaden
6 Yuzhen tsentra

Croatia

Cyprus (member state with no corresponding division)

Czechia (Kraj)
1 Jihovychod
2 Jihozapad
3 Moravskoslezsko
4 Praha
5 Severovychod
6 Severozapad
7 Stredni Cechy
8 Stredni Morave

Denmark (member state with no corresponding division)

Estonia (member state with no corresponding division)

Finland (Provinces)
1 Åland
2 Itä-Suomi
3 Väli-Suomi
4 Pohjois-Suomi
5 Etelä-Suomi

France (Regions)
1 Alsace
2 Aquitaine
3 Auvergne
4 Bourgogne
5 Bretagne
6 Centre
7 Champagne-Ardenne
8 Corse
9 Franche-Comté
10 Ile-de-France
11 Languedoc-Roussillon
12 Limousin
13 Loire (Pays de la)
14 Lorraine
15 Midi-Pyrénées
16 Nord-Pas-de-Calais
17 Normandie (Ba
18 Normandie (Ha
19 Picardie
20 Poitou-Charent
21 Provence-Alpes Côte d'Azur
22 Rhône-Alpes

Germany (Länder)
1 Baden-Württemberg
2 Niedersachsen
3 Bayern
4 Berlin
5 Brandenburg
6 Bremen
7 Hamburg
8 Hessen
9 Mecklenburg-Vorpommern
10 Nordrhein-Westfalen
11 Rheinland-Pfalz
12 Saarland
13 Sachsen
14 Sachsen-Anhalt
15 Schleswig-Hols
16 Thüringen

Greece (Regions)
1 Anatoliki Makedonia kai Thraki
2 Kriti
3 Voreio Aigaio
4 Notio Aigaio
5 Epiros
6 Attiki
7 Sterea Ellas
8 Dytiki Ellas
9 Ionioi Nisoi
10 Dytiki Makedon
11 Kentriki Makede
12 Peloponnese
13 Thessaly

Hungary (Megyék)
1 Del-Alfold
2 Del-Dunantul
3 Eszak-Alfold
4 Eszak-Magyarszag
5 Kozep-Dunantul
6 Kozep-Magyarorszag
7 Nyugat-Dunant

Ireland (Regions)
1 Border, Midland & Western
2 Southern & Eastern

Italy (Regions)
1 Abruzzo
2 Basilicata
3 Calábria
4 Campánia
5 Emilia-Romagna
6 Friuli-Venézia Giulia
7 Lazio
8 Liguria
9 Lombardia
10 Marche
11 Molise
12 Umbria
13 Piemonte
14 Puglia
15 Sardegna
16 Sicilia
17 Toscana
18 Trentino-Alto A Südtirol
19 Valle d'Aosta
20 Véneto

Latvia (member state with no corresponding division)

Lithuania (member state with no corresponding division)

Luxembourg (member state with no corresponding division)

Malta (member state with no corresponding division)

Netherlands (Regions)
1 Noord-Nederland
2 Oost-Nederland
3 West-Nederland
4 Zuid-Nederland

Poland (Voivodships)
1 Dolnošlaskie
2 Kujawsko-Pomorskie
3 Łódzkie
4 Lubelskie
5 Lubuskie
6 Mafopolskie
7 Mazowieckie
8 Opolskie
9 Podkarpackie
10 Podlaskie
11 Pomorskie
12 Šląskie
13 Swietokrzyskie
14 Warmiňsko-Ma
15 Wielkopolskie
16 Zachodniopomo

Portugal (Autonomous regions)
1 Alentejo
2 Algarve
3 Centro
4 Lisboa
5 Norte

Romania (Regions)
1 Bucureşti-Ilfov
2 Centru
3 Nord-Est
4 Nord-Vest
5 Sud
6 Sud-Est
7 Sud-Vest
8 Vest

Slovakia (Kraj)
1 Bratislavsky Kraj
2 Stredne Slovensko
3 Vychodne Slovensko
4 Zapadne Slovensko

Slovenia (member state with no corresponding division)

Spain (Autonomous communities)
1 Andalucía
2 Aragon
3 Asturias
4 Islas Baleares
5 País Vasco
6 Islas Canarias
7 Cantabria
8 Castilla y Léon
9 Castilla-La Mancha
10 Cataluña
11 Extremadura
12 Galicia
13 Madrid
14 Murcia
15 Navarra
16 Rioja (La)
17 Valencia

Sweden (Regions)
1 Stockholm
2 Östra Mellansverige
3 Sydsverige
4 Västsverige
5 Norra Mellansverige
6 Mellersta Norrland
7 Övre Norrland
8 Småland med ö

Projection: Bonne

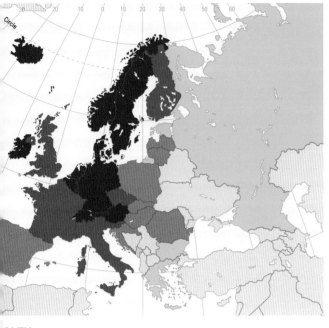

ALTH

value of total production divided
opulation (US$ per person 2022)

- Over $50,000
- $40,000 – $50,000
- $30,000 – $40,000
- $20,000 – $30,000
- Under $20,000

Richest countries
Norway US$ 95,520
Switzerland US$ 95,490
Luxembourg US$ 89,200

Poorest countries
Ukraine US$ 4,260
Moldova US$ 5,500
Kosovo US$ 5,660

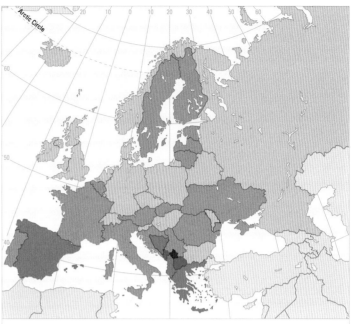

UNEMPLOYMENT
The percentage of the labour force without jobs (2022)

- Over 20%
- 15 – 20%
- 10 – 15%
- 5 – 10%
- Under 5%

Highest unemployment
Kosovo 30.5%
North Macedonia 16.2%
Montenegro 15.3%

Lowest unemployment
Moldova 0.9%
Liechtenstein 2.0%
Czechia 2.2%

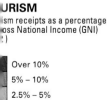

URISM

sm receipts as a percentage
oss National Income (GNI)
)

- Over 10%
- 5% – 10%
- 2.5% – 5%
- Under 2.5%

Tourist destinations

- ◼ Cultural & historical centres
- ◻ Coastal resorts
- ◻ Ski resorts
- ◼ Centres of entertainment
- ◼ Places of pilgrimage
- ◼ Places of great natural beauty

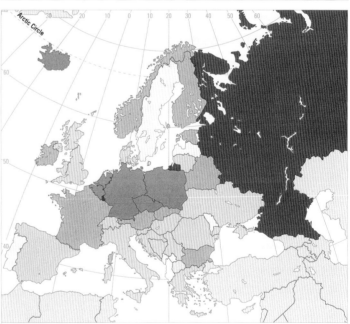

GLOBAL WARMING
Carbon dioxide emissions in tonnes per capita (2021)

- Over 10
- 8 – 10
- 6 – 8
- 4 – 6
- 2 – 4
- Under 2

Highest emissions (tonnes per capita)
Luxembourg 13.1
Russia 12.1
Czechia 9.2

Lowest emissions (tonnes per capita)
Albania 1.6
Moldova 1.8
Montenegro 2.8

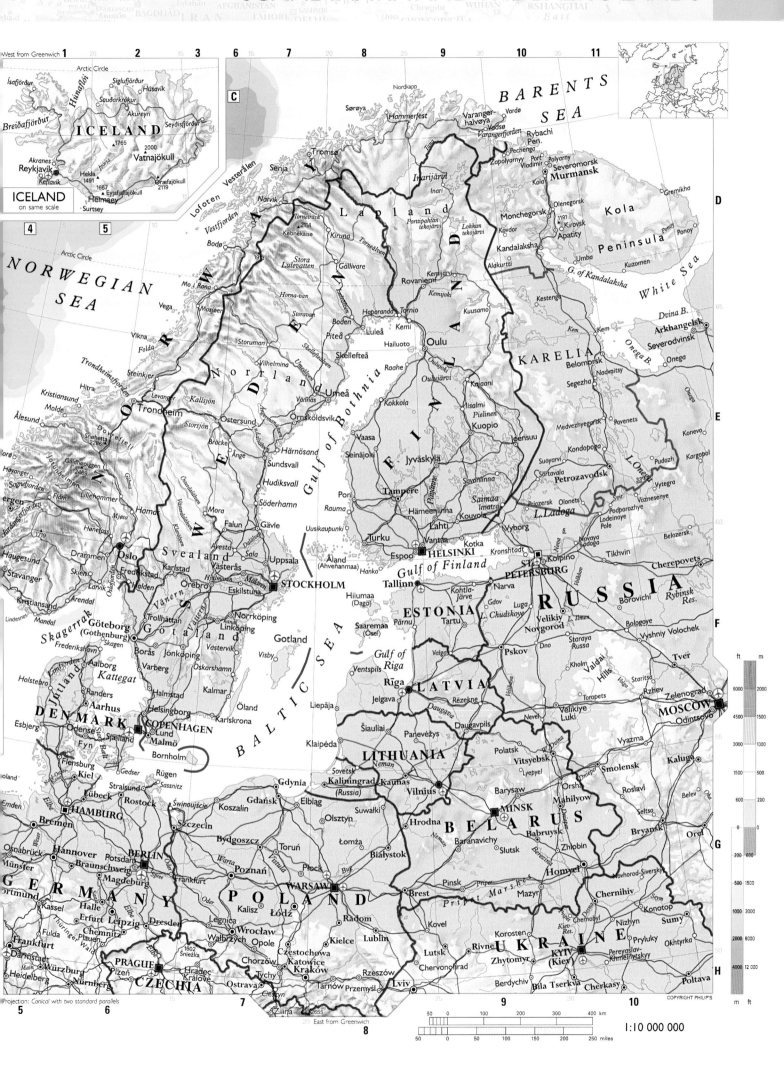

ICELAND

ICELAND
on same scale

BARENTS SEA

NORWEGIAN SEA

NORWAY

SWEDEN

FINLAND

Lapland

KARELIA

Kola Peninsula

White Sea

RUSSIA

ESTONIA

LATVIA

LITHUANIA

BALTIC SEA

Gulf of Bothnia

Gulf of Finland

Gulf of Riga

DENMARK

Kattegat

Skagerrak

Gotland

GERMANY

POLAND

BELARUS

UKRAINE

CZECHIA

STOCKHOLM

HELSINKI

COPENHAGEN

MOSCOW

ST. PETERSBURG

WARSAW

BERLIN

HAMBURG

MINSK

PRAGUE

KYIV (KIEV)

Projection: Conical with two standard parallels

1:10 000 000

COPYRIGHT PHILIP'S

Projection: Conical with two standard parallels

1:5 000 000

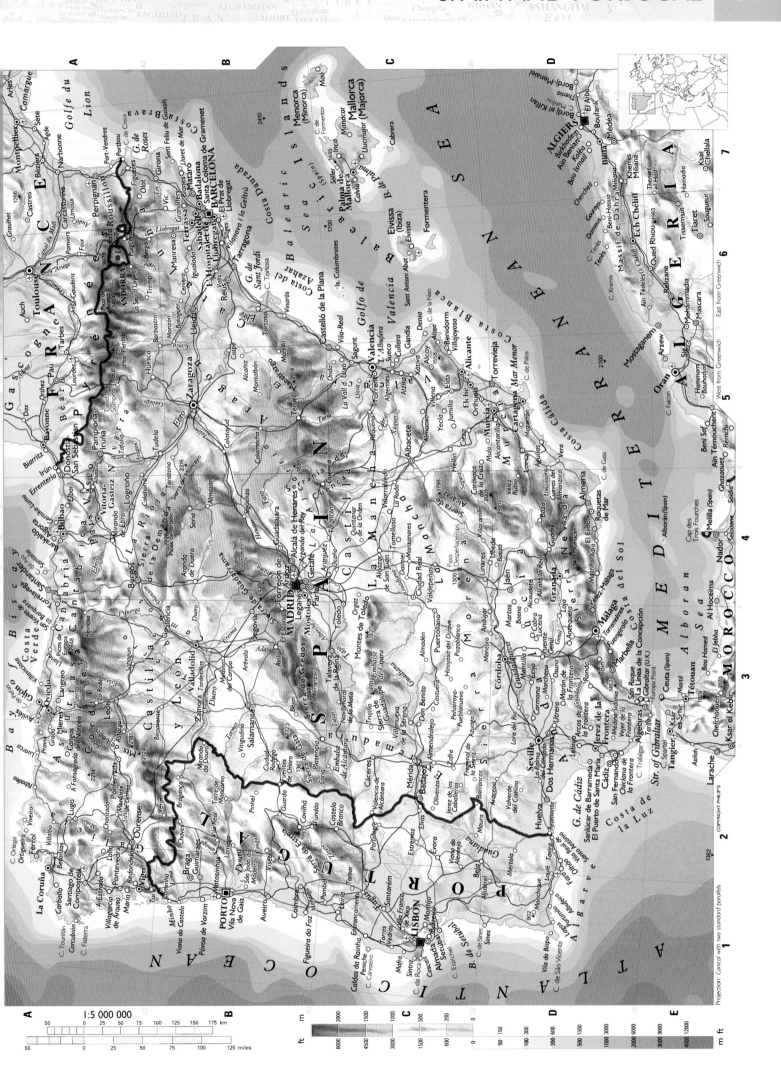

ISTANBUL ARM AZER Bakı TURK Saharganid Tashkent SINKIANG Taiyuan Dalian SEOUL TOKYO
GREECE Ankara TURK Yerevan Ashkhabad Tibilisi Tashkent Lanzhou WUHAN SHANGHAI
CYPRS SYRIA IRAQ TEHRAN Mashhad KABUL Iskanbad TIBET Chengdu WUHAN East
Beirut Damascus BAGDAD IRAN Isfahan AFGHANISTAN JAMMU KASHMIR Lhasa SHANGHAI
Jerusalem Amman BAGDAD IRAN LAHORE DELHI

C H I N A

1:5 000 000

Projection: Conical with two standard parallels   East from Greenwich

COPYRIGHT PHILIPS

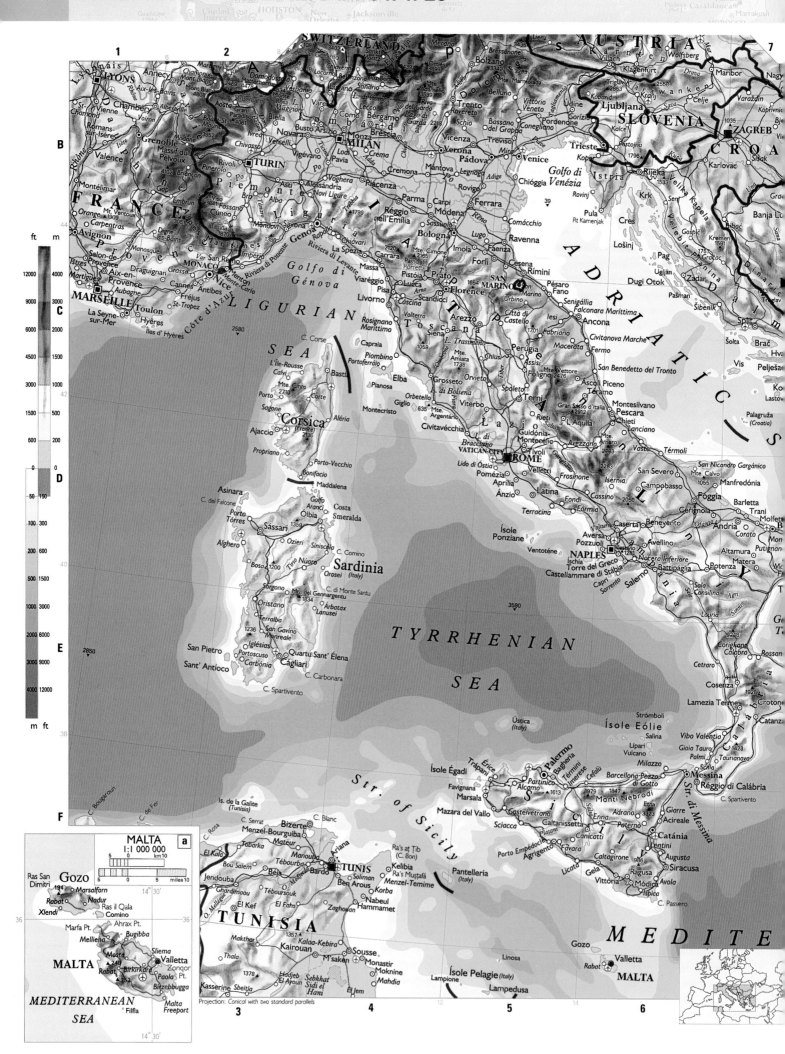

SWITZERLAND
AUSTRIA
SLOVENIA
ZAGREB
CROA

FRANCE
MILAN
TURIN
Venice
Golfo di
Venézia
Trieste
Ljubljana

MONACO
Genoa
Bologna
San Marino
ADRIATIC

MARSEILLE
LIGURIAN
SEA
Florence
Toscana

Corsica
(France)
ROME
VATICAN CITY

Sardinia
(Italy)
Cágliari

TYRRHENIAN
SEA

NAPLES

Str. of Sicily
Palermo
Messina
Réggio di Calábria

MALTA
1:1 000 000

Gozo
Comino

TUNIS

MALTA
Valletta

TUNISIA

MEDITERRANEAN
SEA

Projection: Conical with two standard parallels

MEDITE

MALTA
Valletta

1:10 000 000

50   0   100   200   300   400 km

50   0   50   100   150   200   250 miles

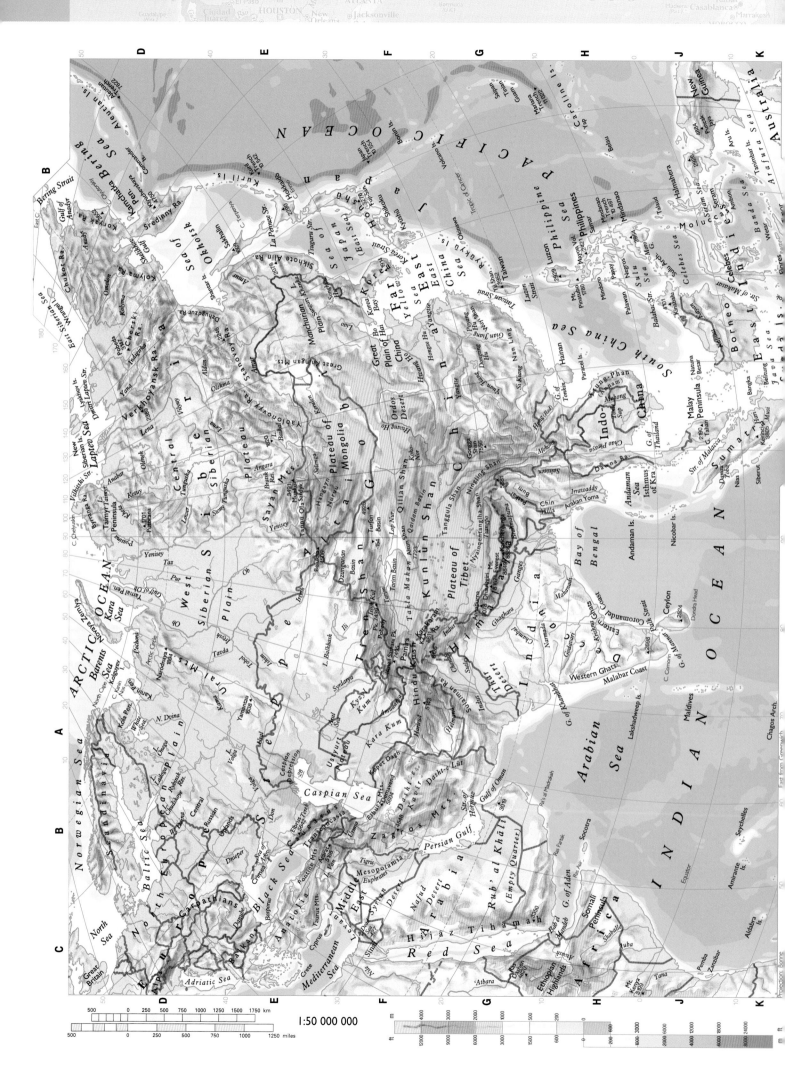

1:50 000 000

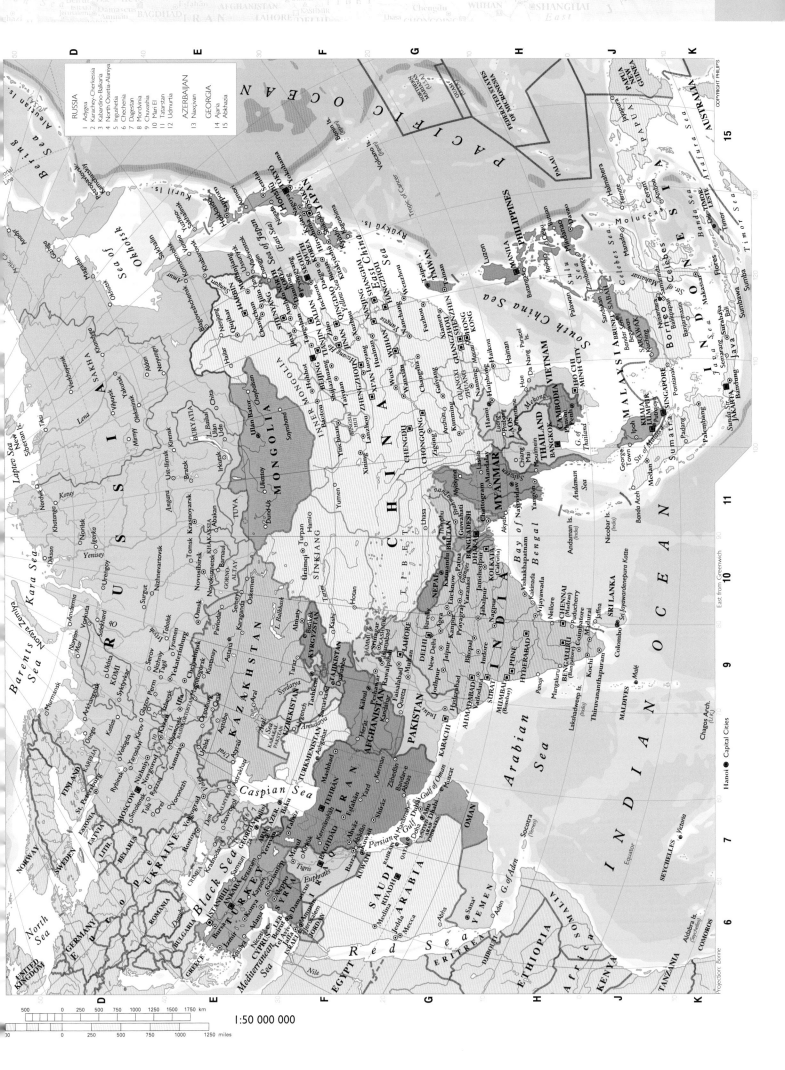

RUSSIA
1 Adygea
2 Karachey-Cherkessia
3 Kabardino-Balkaria
4 North Ossetia-Alanya
5 Ingushetia
6 Chechenia
7 Dagestan
8 Mordvinia
9 Chuvashia
10 Mari El
11 Tatarstan
12 Udmurtia

AZERBAIJAN
13 Naxçivan

GEORGIA
14 Ajaria
15 Abkhazia

Hanoi ● Capital Cities

East from Greenwich

Projection: Bonne

500 0 250 500 750 1000 1250 1500 1750 km

0 250 500 750 1000 1250 miles

1:50 000 000

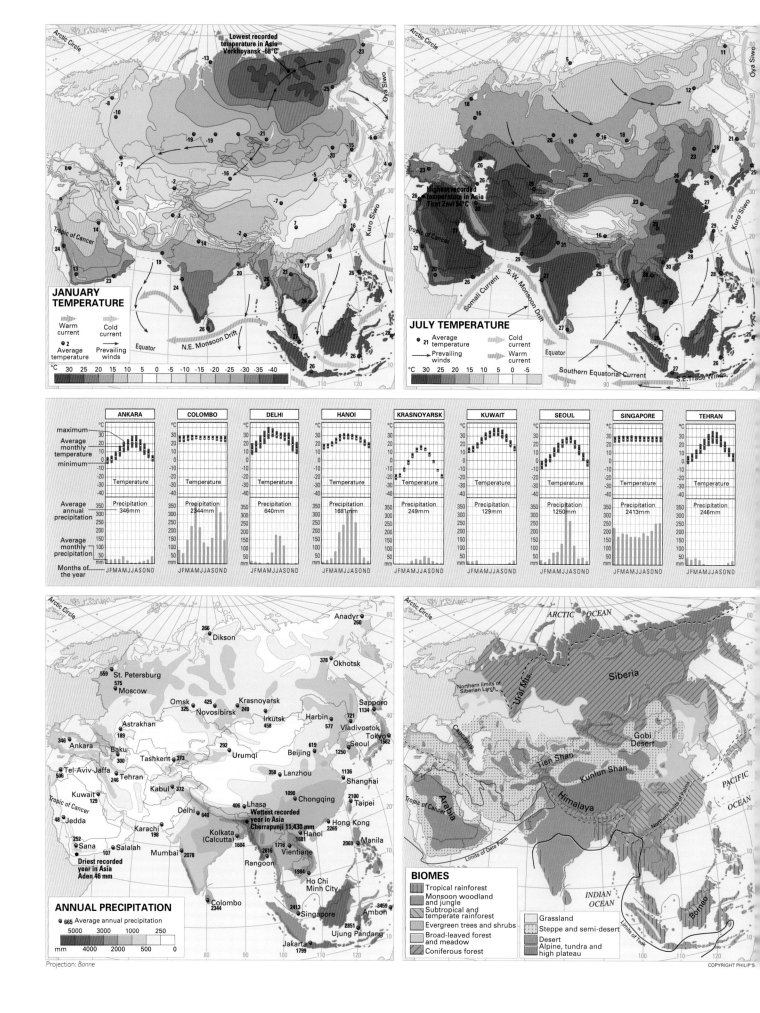

JANUARY TEMPERATURE

Warm current
Cold current
● 2 Average temperature
Prevailing winds

°C 30 25 20 15 10 5 0 -5 -10 -15 -20 -25 -30 -35 -40

Lowest recorded temperature in Asia Verkhoyansk -68°C

N.E. Monsoon Drift

JULY TEMPERATURE

● 21 Average temperature
Cold current
Prevailing winds
Warm current

°C 30 25 20 15 10 5 0 -5

Highest recorded temperature in Asia Tirat Zevi 54°C

Somali Current
S.W. Monsoon Drift
Southern Equatorial Current
S.E. Trade Winds

Climate graphs

ANKARA	COLOMBO	DELHI	HANOI	KRASNOYARSK	KUWAIT	SEOUL	SINGAPORE	TEHRAN

maximum
Average monthly temperature
minimum

Temperature

Average annual precipitation

Average monthly precipitation

Months of the year

City	Precipitation
ANKARA	346mm
COLOMBO	2344mm
DELHI	640mm
HANOI	1681mm
KRASNOYARSK	249mm
KUWAIT	129mm
SEOUL	1250mm
SINGAPORE	2413mm
TEHRAN	246mm

ANNUAL PRECIPITATION

● 665 Average annual precipitation

mm 5000 4000 3000 2000 1000 500 250 0

Anadyr 260
Dikson 266
Okhotsk 378
St. Petersburg 559
Moscow 575
Sapporo 1134
Omsk 425
Krasnoyarsk 249
Novosibirsk 325
Harbin 721
Astrakhan 189
Irkutsk 458
Vladivostok 577
Tokyo 1562
Ankara 346
Seoul 1250
Baku
Tashkent 373
Urumqi 292
Beijing 619
Tel-Aviv-Jaffa 506
Tehran 246
Lanzhou 358
Shanghai 1136
Kabul 372
Lhasa 406
Chongqing 1090
Taipei 2100
Kuwait 129
Delhi 640
Hong Kong 2265
Jedda 48
Wettest recorded year in Asia Cherrapunji 11,430 mm
Hanoi 1681
Manila 2069
Karachi 198
Kolkata (Calcutta) 1604
Vientiane 1716
Sana 107
Mumbai 2078
Rangoon 2616
Salalah
Ho Chi Minh City 1984
Driest recorded year in Asia Aden 46 mm
Colombo 2344
Singapore 2413
Ambon 3459
Ujung Pandang 2851
Jakarta 1799

Projection: Bonne

BIOMES

Tropical rainforest
Monsoon woodland and jungle
Subtropical and temperate rainforest
Evergreen trees and shrubs
Broad-leaved forest and meadow
Coniferous forest
Grassland
Steppe and semi-desert
Desert
Alpine, tundra and high plateau

ARCTIC OCEAN
Northern limits of Siberian Larch
Ural Mts.
Siberia
Caucasus
Gobi Desert
Tien Shan
Arabia
Kunlun Shan
Himalaya
Tropic of Cancer
Northern limits of Palms
PACIFIC OCEAN
Limits of Date Palm
INDIAN OCEAN
Limits of Teak
Borneo

COPYRIGHT PHILIP'S

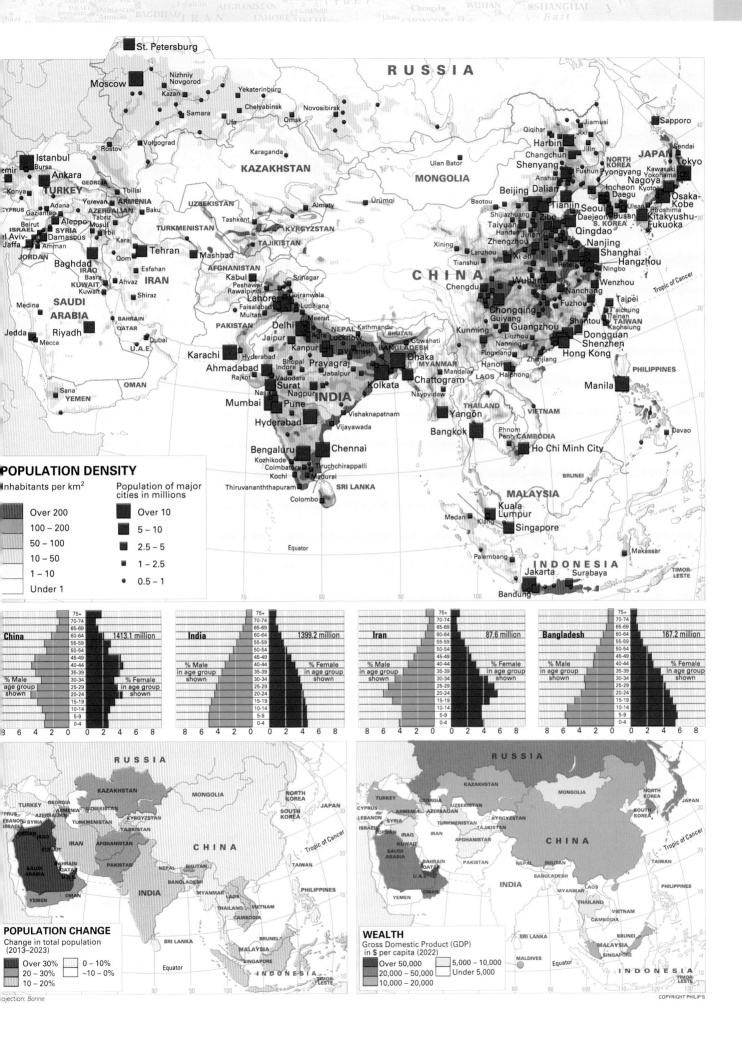

POPULATION DENSITY

Inhabitants per km²

- Over 200
- 100 – 200
- 50 – 100
- 10 – 50
- 1 – 10
- Under 1

Population of major cities in millions

- Over 10
- 5 – 10
- 2.5 – 5
- 1 – 2.5
- 0.5 – 1

China 1413.1 million

% Male in age group shown

% Female in age group shown

75+
70-74
65-69
60-64
55-59
50-54
45-49
40-44
35-39
30-34
25-29
20-24
15-19
10-14
5-9
0-4

India 1399.2 million

% Male in age group shown

% Female in age group shown

Iran 87.6 million

% Male in age group shown

% Female in age group shown

Bangladesh 167.2 million

% Male in age group shown

% Female in age group shown

POPULATION CHANGE

Change in total population (2013–2023)

- Over 30%
- 20 – 30%
- 10 – 20%
- 0 – 10%
- –10 – 0%

WEALTH

Gross Domestic Product (GDP) in $ per capita (2022)

- Over 50,000
- 20,000 – 50,000
- 10,000 – 20,000
- 5,000 – 10,000
- Under 5,000

Projection: Bonne

COPYRIGHT PHILIP'S

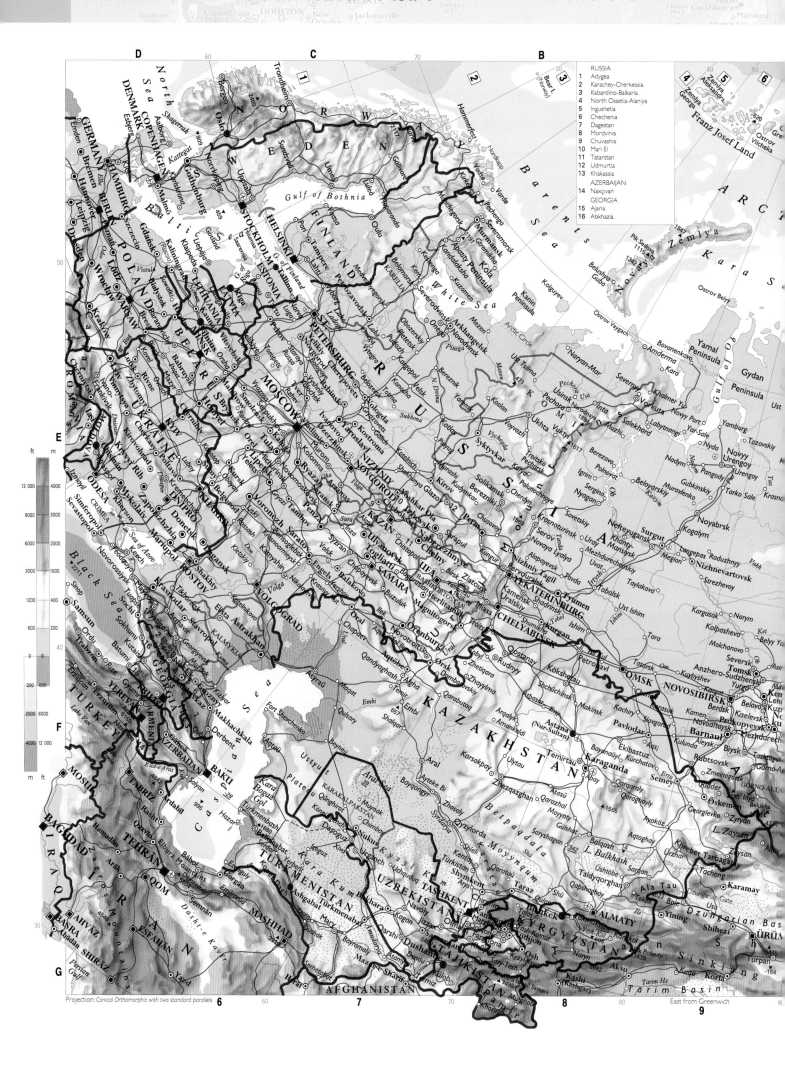

East from Greenwich

RUSSIA
1 Adygea
2 Karachey-Cherkessia
3 Kabardino-Balkaria
4 North Ossetia-Alaniya
5 Ingushetia
6 Chechenia
7 Dagestan
8 Mordvinia
9 Chuvashia
10 Mari El
11 Tatarstan
12 Udmurtia
13 Khakassia
AZERBAIJAN
14 Naxçivan
GEORGIA
15 Ajaria
16 Abkhazia

A | B | C | D | E | F

9 10 15 16 17 18 19

OCEAN

Severnaya Zemlya

Ostrov Komsomolets
Ostrov Oktyabrskoy Revolyutsii
Ostrov Bolshevik

Byrranga Ra.
Taimyr Peninsula
L. Taimyr
Nordvik

New Siberian Islands

Laptev Sea

East Siberian Sea

Wrangel I.

Chukot Range

Chukchi Sea

C. Dezhneva (East C.)
Gulf of Anadyr
St. Lawrence I. (USA)

Koryak Range

Sredinnyy

Kamchatka Peninsula

Bering Sea

R U S S I A

Verkhoyansk Range

Chersky Range

S A K H A

Yakutsk

Sea of Okhotsk

Sakhalin

Kuril Islands

Stanovoy Range

Tablonovyy Range

Yablonovyy Range

Sikhote Alin Ra.

ULAN BATOR

MONGOLIA

Gobi Desert

Altai

Ch'ngjin

Sea of Japan (East Sea)

Hokkaidō
SAPPORO
Hakodate

Honshū

JAPAN
KYOTO
KOBE
OSAKA

CHINA

BEIJING
TANGSHAN
DALIAN

HARBIN
CHANGCHUN
SHENYANG

Manchuria

NORTH KOREA
PYONGYANG

SEOUL
SOUTH KOREA
DAEJEON
DAEGU
BUSAN
GWANGJU
INCHEON

Arctic Circle

100 0 100 200 300 400 500 600 700 800 km

1:20 000 000

100 0 100 200 300 400 500 miles

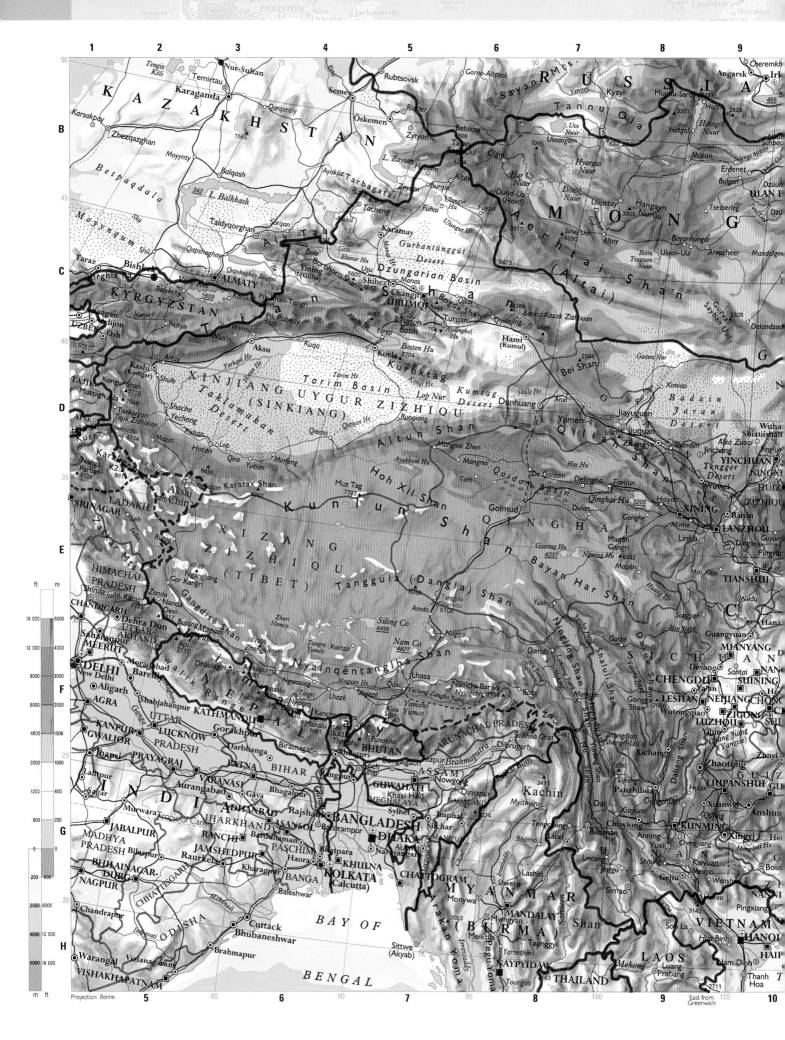

1:15 000 000

HONG KONG, MACAU AND SHENZHEN
1:1 000 000

EMPLOYMENT IN INDUSTRY

Income by province - the value of total production divided by the population in US$

XINJIANG

GANSU

TIBET

QINGHAI

HEILONGJIANG

JILIN

INNER MONGOLIA

LIAONING

BEIJING

TIANJIN

HEBEI

NINGXIA HUI

SHANXI

SHANDONG

SHAANXI

HENAN

JIANGSU

SICHUAN

HUBEI

ANHUI

SHANGHAI

CHONGQING

ZHEJIANG

HUNAN

JIANGXI

GUIZHOU

YUNNAN

FUJIAN

GUANGXI ZHUANGZU

GUANGDONG

HONG KONG
MACAU

HAINAN

GDP per capita (US$)

- Over $15,000
- $9,000 – $15,000
- $7,000 – $9,000
- Under $7,000

CHINA'S SHARE OF WORLD MANUFACTURING
(for selected goods)

Hydroelectricity — China 27%, Brazil 8%, USA 8%, Canada 6%, India 4%
World total: 1,308 billion kWh

Paper — China 26%, USA 18%, Germany 6%, Japan 6%, S. Korea 3%
World total: 410,000,000 tonnes

Cement — China 56%, India 8%, Indonesia 2%, USA 2%, Vietnam 2%
World total: 4,100,000,000 tonnes

Coal — China 48%, Indonesia 9%, USA 9%, Australia 8%, India 8%
World total: 4,002,600,000 tOe

tOe = tonnes of oil equivalent

Aluminium — China 57%, India 6%, Russia 6%, Canada 5%, UAE 4%
World total: 65,200,000 tonnes

Steel — China 53%, India 6%, Japan 5%, USA 5%, Russia 4%, S. Korea
World total: 1,900,000,000 tonnes

Motor vehicles — China 28%, USA 12%, Japan 11%, Germany 5%, Mexico 4%
World total: 92,000,000 vehicles

Computer Devices — China 46%, Mexico 9%, Netherlands 8%, USA 7%
World total: 368.4 billion US$

INDUSTRIAL DEVELOPMENT

Core regions

- Industrial regions
- ● Major centres for industry and services
- ●• Other industrial centres
- ⊙ Centres for iron and steel and chemicals
- ▨ Rapidly developing coastal regions
- ▪ Special Economic Zones (SEZ)
- ▽ Special Administrative Regions (SAR) 'One country, two systems'

Peripheral regions

- Densely populated and industrialized peripheral region
- Peripheral region with traditional heavy industry
- Remote undeveloped region
- ← Direction of future growth
- — Important rail links

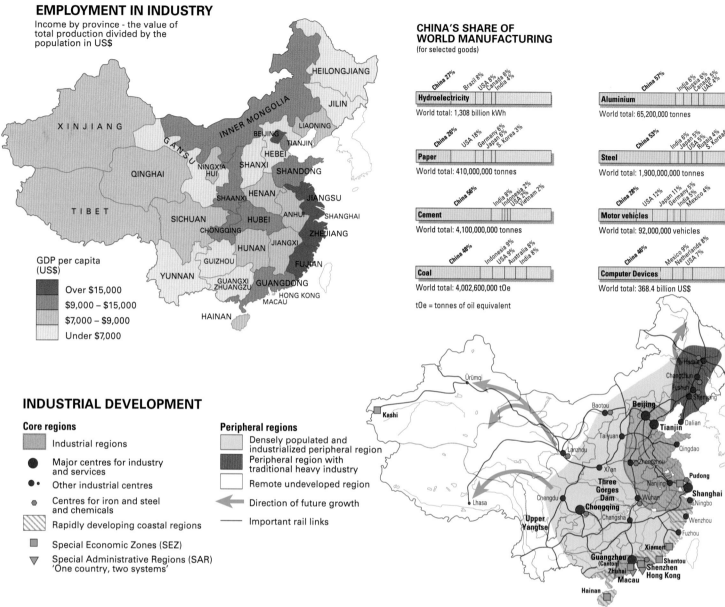

Ürümqi
Kashi
Baotou
Beijing
Tianjin
Dalian
Taiyuan
Lanzhou
Qingdao
Xi'an
Zhengzhou
Pudong
Three Gorges Dam
Nanjing
Shanghai
Chengdu
Wuhan
Ningbo
Chongqing
Changsha
Wenzhou
Lhasa
Fuzhou
Upper Yangtse
Xiamen
Guangzhou (Canton)
Zhuhai
Shantou
Shenzhen
Macau
Hong Kong
Hainan
Harbin
Changchun
Fushun
Shenyang

HYDROELECTRIC POWER ON THE UPPER YANGTSE
1: 7 000 000

(1988) Year of completion

Twelve new dams are either planned or under construction on the upper reaches of China's longest river, the Yangtse. The total power generated by these dams will far exceed that produced by the massive Three Gorges Dam. Hydroelectricity is seen as an important alternative to coal, which provides nearly 70% of China's energy needs.

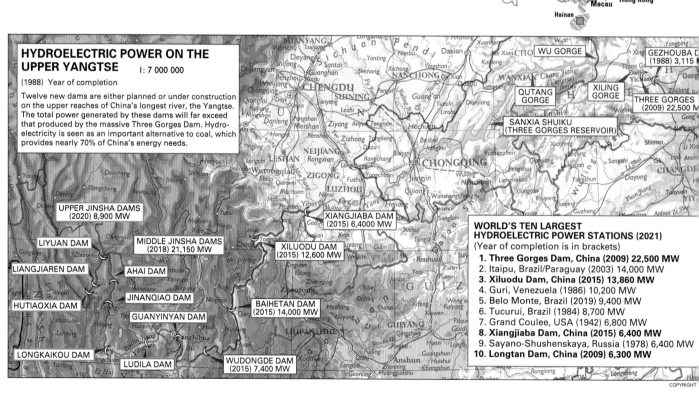

WU GORGE

GEZHOUBA D (1988) 3,115

QUTANG GORGE

XILING GORGE

THREE GORGES (2009) 22,500 M

SANXIA SHUIKU (THREE GORGES RESERVOIR)

UPPER JINSHA DAMS (2020) 8,900 MW

LIYUAN DAM

MIDDLE JINSHA DAMS (2018) 21,150 MW

XIANGJIABA DAM (2015) 6,4000 MW

LIANGJIAREN DAM

AHAI DAM

XILUODU DAM (2015) 12,600 MW

HUTIAOXIA DAM

JINANQIAO DAM

BAIHETAN DAM (2015) 14,000 MW

GUANYINYAN DAM

LONGKAIKOU DAM

LUDILA DAM

WUDONGDE DAM (2015) 7,400 MW

WORLD'S TEN LARGEST HYDROELECTRIC POWER STATIONS (2021)
(Year of completion is in brackets)

1. **Three Gorges Dam, China (2009) 22,500 MW**
2. Itaipu, Brazil/Paraguay (2003) 14,000 MW
3. **Xiluodu Dam, China (2015) 13,860 MW**
4. Guri, Venezuela (1986) 10,200 MW
5. Belo Monte, Brazil (2019) 9,400 MW
6. Tucuruí, Brazil (1984) 8,700 MW
7. Grand Coulee, USA (1942) 6,800 MW
8. **Xiangjiaba Dam, China (2015) 6,400 MW**
9. Sayano-Shushenskaya, Russia (1978) 6,400 MW
10. **Longtan Dam, China (2009) 6,300 MW**

SAN FRANCISCO   Lake City   Kansas City   St. Louis   Cincinnati   PHILADELPHIA   PORTUGAL   MADRID
Las Vegas   STATES   Memphis   WASHINGTON   Baltimore   Lisbon   SPAIN
    ATLANTA   D.C.   A T L A N T I C   Azores   Rabat
HOUSTON   New   Jacksonville   Madeira Casablanca   Marrakesh
    Orleans

1   **2**   **3**   **4**   **5**

Letpadan   Thoen   Vientiane   Nong Khai   Ba Don
Tharrawady   (Viangchan)   Nakhon   Dong Hoi
MYANMAR   Uttaradit   Loei   Udon Thani   Phanom   Thakhek
Insein   Thaton   Sawankhalok   701   Quang Tri
A   YANGON   Mae Sot   Phitsanulok   Sakon Nakhon   Savannakhet   Hue
Maubin   G. of   Mawlamyine   THAILAND   Phetchabun   Khon Kaen   Da Nang
Pyapon   Mottama   Kyaikkami   Chaiyaphum   Roi Et   Hoi An   VIETNAM
(BURMA)   Ye   Nakhon Sawan   Nakhon   Mun   Ubon   Saravan   Binh Son   Quang Ngai
Natkyitzin   Phra Nakhon   Ratchasima   Buriram   Ratchathani   Sisaket   Pakxe   2598   An Nhon
15   Dawei   Si Ayutthaya   Saraburi   Khu Khan   Cheom Ksan   Plateau du   Qui Nhon
Moscos   Kanchanaburi   BANGKOK   Aranyaprathet   Kulen   Stoeng Treng   Kon Tum   Song Cau
Is.   2075   Samut Prakan   Sisophon   Siemreab   ANGKOR   Mei Ku   A Yun Pa   Mui Nay
Mali Kyun   Phet Buri   Chon Buri   Battambang   Tonle Sap   CAMBODIA   Buon Me Thuot
B   Kadan   Sattahip   Pattaya   Rayong   1813   Kracheh   Senmonorom   2405   Nha Trang
Kyun   Mergui   Chanthaburi   Kampong Chhnang   Kampong Cham   Cam Ranh
Letsok-   Prachuap   Ko Chang   Kampong   Pouthisat   Thom   Da Lat
aw Kyun   Khiri Khan   Ko Kut   PHNOM PENH   Preah   4424
Tanintharyi   Hua Hin   Krong   Svay Rieng   Bien Hoa   Phan Rang
Mergui   Bang Saphan   Koh Kong   Takeo   Long   My Tho   Phan Thiet
Lanbi Kyun   Bokpyin   Chumphon   Chaak Kampong Saom   Kampot   Xuyen   HO CHI MINH CITY   Mui Dinh
Arch.   Maliwun   Isthmus   Kampong Saom   Hon Chong   Sa Dec   Vung Tau   Nanshan I.
Zadetkyi Kyun   Ranong   of Kra   Dao Phu Quoc   Rach Gia   CAN THO   Loaita I.
10   Ko Phangan   Soc Trang   Itu Aba I.
Thailand   Ko Samui   Bac Lieu   Con Son   Sin Cowe I.
Phangnga   Surat Thani   Ca Mau   Spratly Is.
1835   Nakhon Si Thammarat   Mui Ca Mau
Phuket   Pak Phanang   Spratly I.   C. Buliluyan
Ko Phi Phi   Thung Song   Amboyna Cay   Balaba
Trang   Phatthalung   Phattalung
C   Ban Kantang   Thale Luang   Malay   S O U T H   Kudat
We   Songkhla   Peninsula   Langkon   Langkok
Sabang   Hat Yai   Pattani   Kota Belud   Gunung
Banda Aceh   Satun   Yala   Narathiwat   C H I N A   Kinabalu
Sigli   P. Langkawi   Tumpat   4101   Kota Kinabalu
Meureudu   Alor Setar   Kota Bharu   S E A   SABA
Bireuen   George Town   Sungai   Kep. Perhentian   Bandar Labuan   Beaufort   Papar   Tenom
Lhokseumawe   Butterworth   Petani   P. Redang   LABUAN   Melalap
Idi   Kuala   Kuala Terengganu   Bandar Seri Begawan   Menumbok
Langsa   Taiping   Pasir Mas   BRUNEI   Lawas
5   Peureulak   Sepetang   Dungen   Kuala Belait   Miri   Limbang
Takengon   IPOH   Gunung Tahan   M A L A Y S I A   Seria
Pangkalanbrandan   Kampar   2190   P. Tenggol   Niah   2988
3381   Kuala Kubu   Kemaman   Tutong   Marudi
Meulaboh   Langsa   Teluk   Bharu   PENINSULAR   Laut   Bintulu
Ujung Raja   Belawan   Intan   Kuala Lipis   MALAYSIA   Kepulauan   Telukbutun   Mukah   SARAWAK
Tapaktuan   MEDAN   KLANG   Mentakab   Natura   1035   Natuna   Oya
Binjai   Tebingtinggi   KUALA LUMPUR   Kuantan   Besar   Binjai   Besar   Sibu   Kanowit   Tanjungselor
Kabanjahe   Putrajaya   Bintangau   Sarikei   Kapit
Pematangsiantar   Klang   Serdang   Matak   Sarikei   Longnawan
Danau Toba   Port Dickson   P. Tioman   Siantan   2988   2988
D   Simeulue   Prapat   Tanjungbalai   Mersing   Kuching   Saratok   Longnawan
Sinabang   Musala   Bagansiapiapi   Segamat   Kepulauan   Midai   Bau   Betong   Sri Aman   2240
Parapat   Rupat   Muar   Kluang   Anambas   Kepulauan   Serasan   Niut   Pegunungan
Kepulauan   Tarutung   Dumai   Batu   (Indonesia)   Natuna   Tanjung   1701   Tebekang   Lanjak
Banyak   886   Bengkalis   Pahat   Selatan   Lunou
Lahewa   Gunungsitoli   JOHOR BAHRU   Sambas   Ngabang   Putussibau
Nias   Padangsidempuan   SINGAPORE   Kota Tinggi   Singkawang   Sanggau   Sintang   Kapuas Hulu
Siaksriindrapura   BATAM   Tanjungpinang   Lingga   Kepulauan   Mempawah   G. Saran   Nangapinoh   Muarajuloi   Longiram   Tenggarong
Pekanbaru   Bintan   Badas   1758   Pegunungan   Muar
Telukdalem   Bangkinang   Kepulauan   PONTIANAK   Nangatayan   Schwaner   Purukcahu   Muaratewe
Pini   Lubuksikaping   Riau   Sukadana   2278   Kualakurun   San
Tanahmasa   Kepulauan   Ketapang   Sukamara
Kepulauan Batu   Bukittinggi   Payakumbuh   Rengat   Berhala   Nangataman   Kumai   Palangkaraya   Tanjung
Tanahbala   Pasirkuning   Selat   Singkep   Sukaraja   Kalakapuas   Amuntai   Barabai
0   Padangpanjang   Sawahlunto   Muaratebo   Karimata   Kendawangan   Kualajelai   Pangkalanbuun   Semuda   1892   Kandangan
Siberut   Solok   Belinyu   Kualapembuang   Sampit   Martapura   Kotabaru
Padang   Muarabungo   Han   Sungailiat   Kepulauan   Martapura   Pelaihari   Sebuku
Sungaipenuh   3805 Kerinci   Jambi   Pangkalpinang   Karimata   BANJARMASIN   Pagatan   Karamb
E   Pulau   Bangko   Muaratembesi   Bangka   Dendang   Pelaihari   Jorong   Pulau Lau
Pagai Utara   Sipura   Muaro   Tanjungpandan   Belitung   Satui
Pulau   Mukomuko   Sarolangun   Muntok   Belinting   Tanjung Puting   Kepulauan
Pagai Selatan   PALEMBANG   Belitung   Teluk   Laut Kecil
Lubuklinggau   Sungaigerong   Manggar   Sampit   Tg. Selatan
Curup   Sekayu   Toboali   Kepulauan
Tebingtinggi   Tanjung Lumut   J A V A   Karimunjawa   Kepulauan
Bengkulu   Lahat   Muarenim   Bawean   Sangkapura   Masalembo
Dempo   G r e a t e r   S u n d a   I s l a   Kepulauan
3159   Perabumulih   S E A   Kangean
F   Baturaja   Menggala   Tanjung Sambar   Kepulauan
Manna   Kotabumi   Bandar   Karimunjawa   Madura
Enggano   Lampung   Bawean   Sampang
I N D I A N   6073   Kalianda   Tegal   Semarang   Gresik   Singaraja
Kotaagung   Serang   Merak   Pekalongan   Tuban   Bangkalan   Madura
O C E A N   JAKARTA   Pemalang   Bojonegoro   SURABAYA   F
Bogor   Cirebon   Kendal   Pasuruan   Less
Sukabumi   Purwakarta   Jatibarang   Tegal   Madiun   Probolinggo
BANDUNG   Garut   Slamet   Magelang   3265   Kediri   Jember   Singaraja   3142
Tasikmalaya   Cilacap   Kebumen   Yogyakarta   Surakarta   3670   Malang   Blitar   Banyuwangi   Rinjani   3726
Teluk Pelabuhan   Semeru   Denpasar   Bali   3726
Java Trench   6650   J a v a   Tulungagung   Penida   Lombok
    Mataram   Provo   Taliwa

Projection: Mercator   East from Greenwich

1   100   **2**   105   **3**   110   **4**   115   **5**

100   0   100   200   300   400   500 km
100   0   50   100   150   200   250   300   350 miles

1:12 500 000

ft   m
12 000   4000
9000   3000
6000   2000
4500   1500
3000   1000
1200   400
600   200
0   0
200   600
2000   6000
4000   12 000
6000   18 000
8000   24 000
m   ft

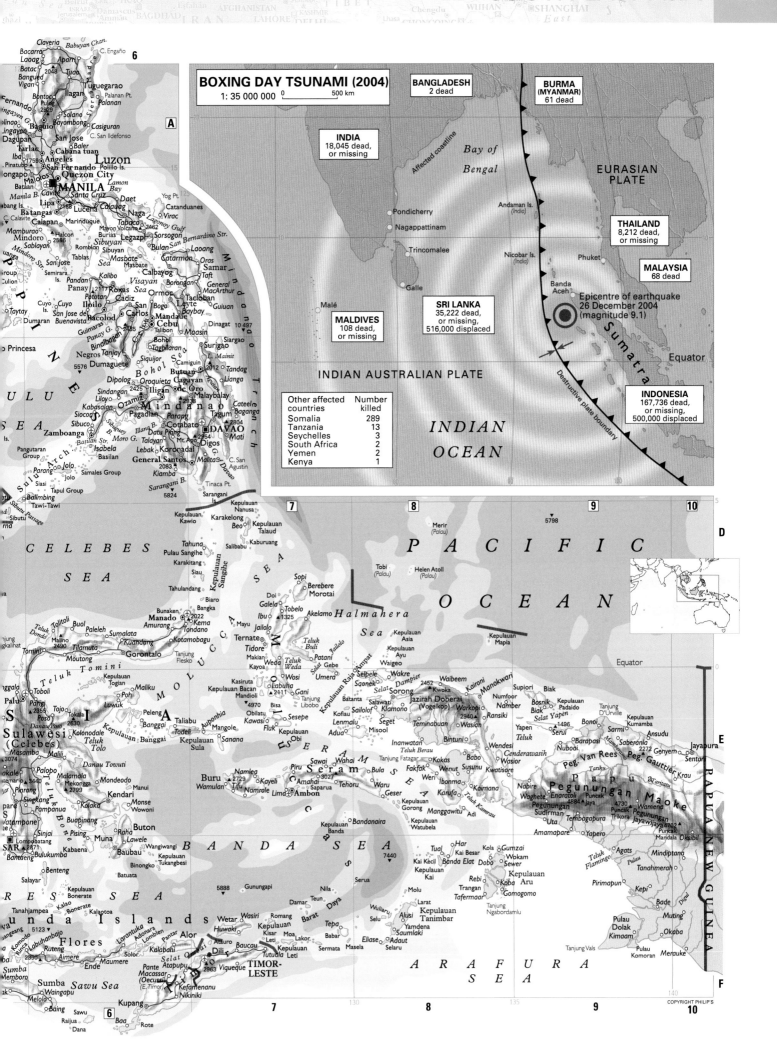

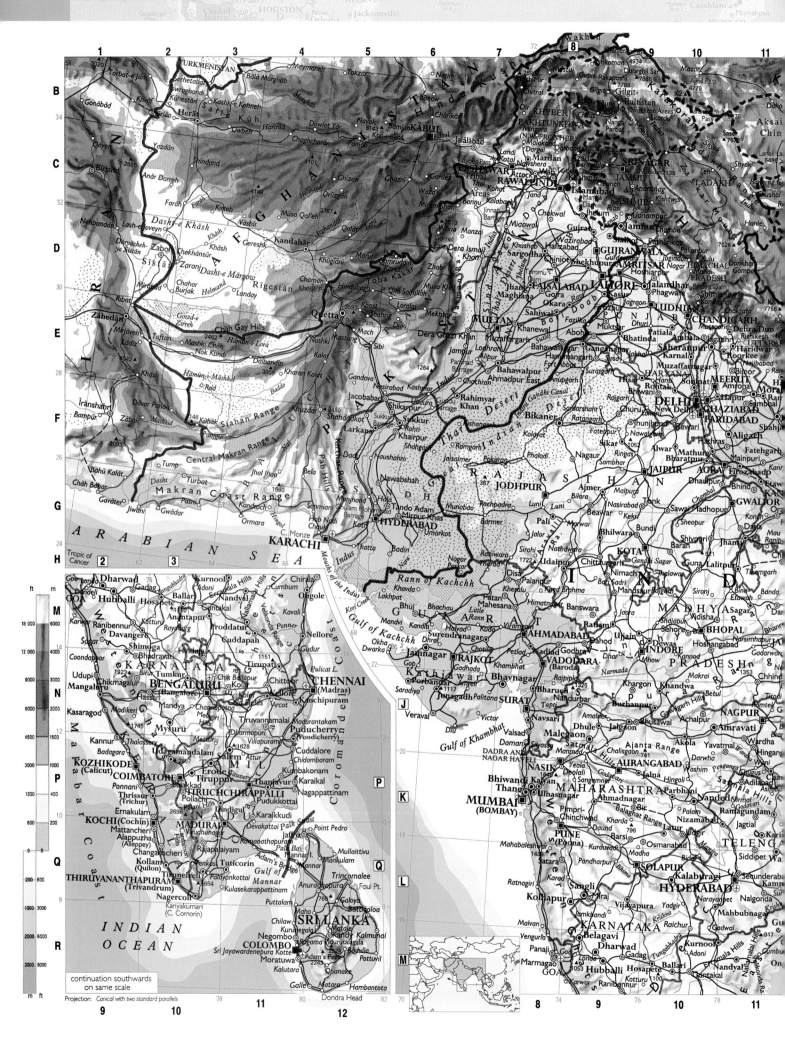

continuation southwards
on same scale

Projection: Conical with two standard parallels

THE MONSOON 1:100 000 000

13

Monthly rainfall

mm		mm	
400		50	
200		25	
100		0	

→ Wind direction

ITCZ (intertropical convergence zone)

In early March, which normally marks the end of the subcontinent's cool season and the start of the hot season, winds blow outwards from the mainland. But as the overhead sun and the ITCZ move northwards, the land is intensely heated, and a low-pressure system develops. The south-east trade winds, which are drawn across the Equator, change direction and are sucked into the interior to become south-westerly winds, bringing heavy rain. By November, the overhead sun and the ITCZ have again moved southwards and the wind directions are again reversed. Cool winds blow from the Asian interior to the sea, losing any moisture on the Himalayas before descending to the coast.

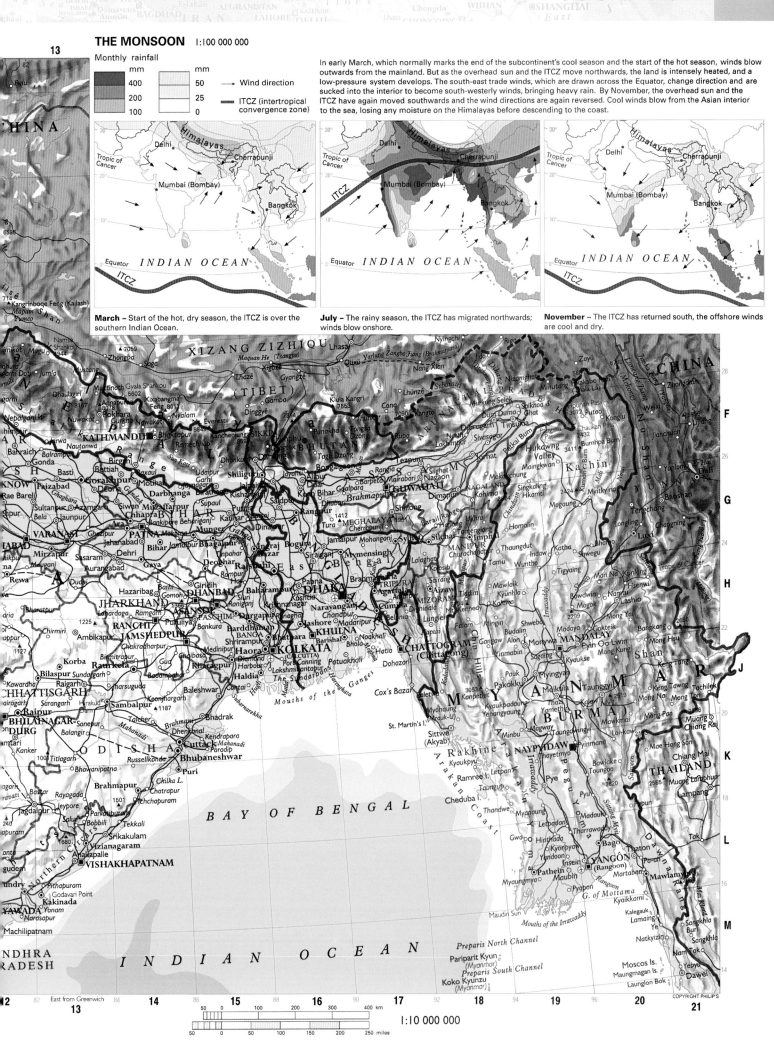

March – Start of the hot, dry season, the ITCZ is over the southern Indian Ocean.

July – The rainy season, the ITCZ has migrated northwards; winds blow onshore.

November – The ITCZ has returned south, the offshore winds are cool and dry.

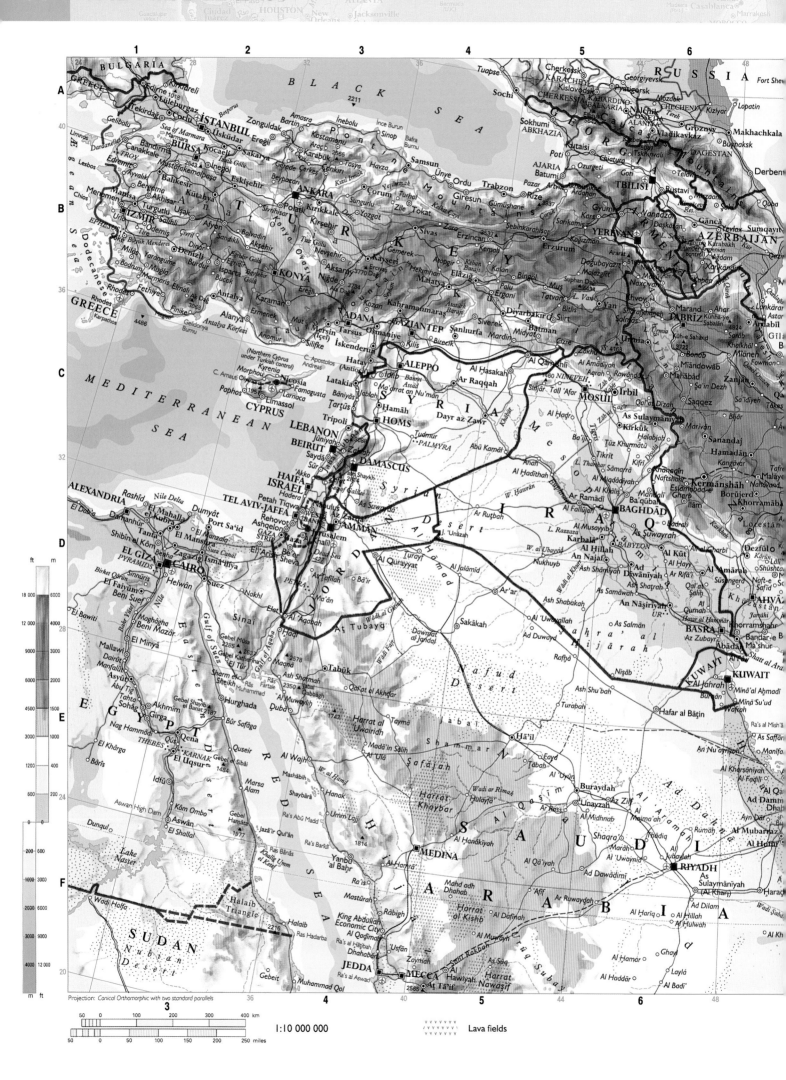

Projection: Conical Orthomorphic with two standard parallels

1:10 000 000

Lava fields

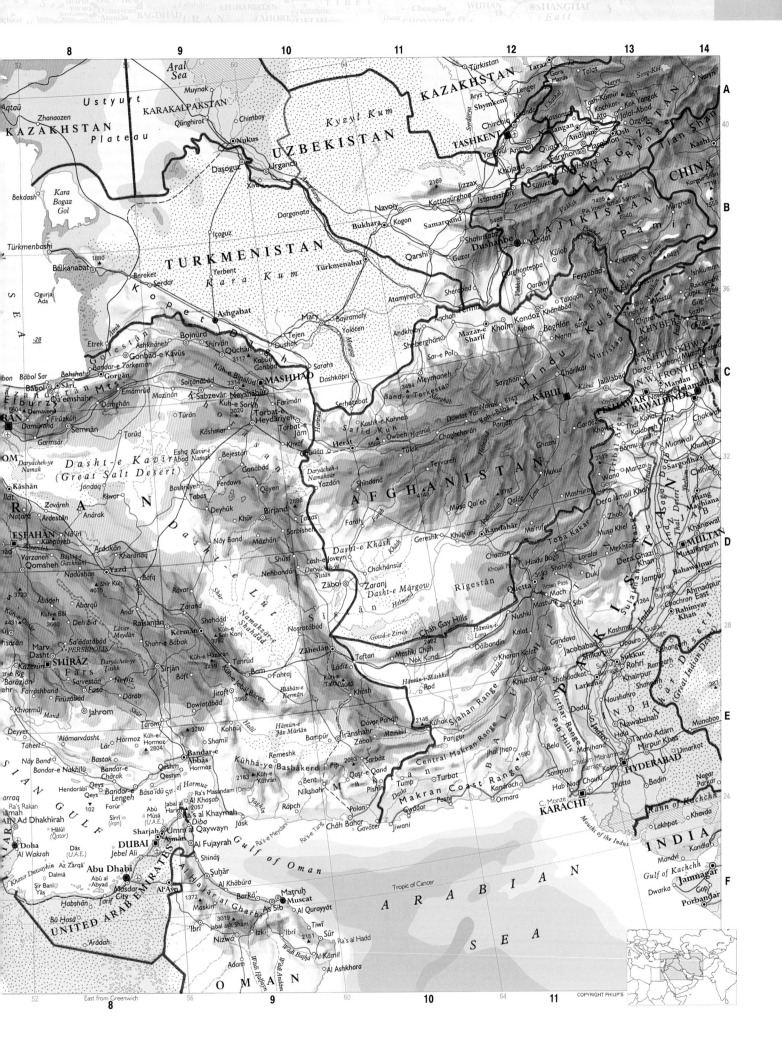

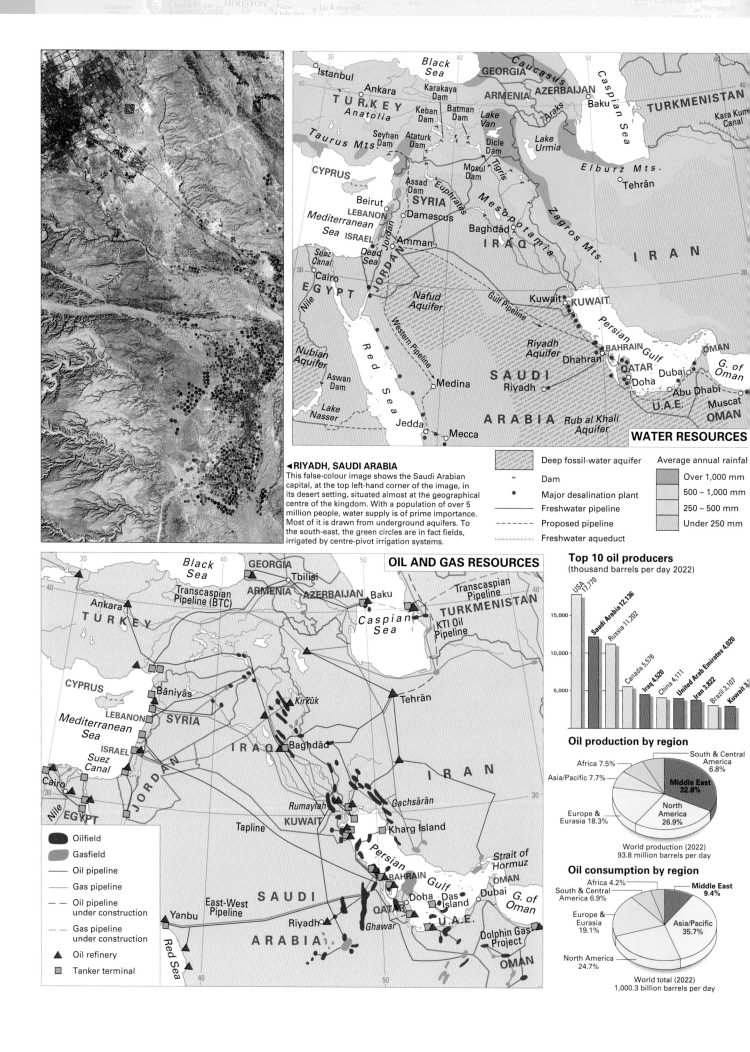

◄ **RIYADH, SAUDI ARABIA**
This false-colour image shows the Saudi Arabian capital, at the top left-hand corner of the image, in its desert setting, situated almost at the geographical centre of the kingdom. With a population of over 5 million people, water supply is of prime importance. Most of it is drawn from underground aquifers. To the south-east, the green circles are in fact fields, irrigated by centre-pivot irrigation systems.

WATER RESOURCES

- Deep fossil-water aquifer
- ˘ Dam
- ● Major desalination plant
- ——— Freshwater pipeline
- – – – – Proposed pipeline
- ·········· Freshwater aqueduct

Average annual rainfall
- Over 1,000 mm
- 500 – 1,000 mm
- 250 – 500 mm
- Under 250 mm

OIL AND GAS RESOURCES

- ● Oilfield
- ● Gasfield
- ——— Oil pipeline
- ——— Gas pipeline
- – – Oil pipeline under construction
- – – Gas pipeline under construction
- ▲ Oil refinery
- ■ Tanker terminal

Top 10 oil producers
(thousand barrels per day 2022)

USA 17,770
Saudi Arabia 12,136
Russia 11,202
Canada 5,576
Iraq 4,520
China 4,111
United Arab Emirates 4,020
Iran 3,822
Brazil 3,107
Kuwait 3

Oil production by region

- Africa 7.5%
- Asia/Pacific 7.7%
- Europe & Eurasia 18.3%
- South & Central America 6.8%
- Middle East 32.8%
- North America 26.9%

World production (2022)
93.8 million barrels per day

Oil consumption by region

- Africa 4.2%
- South & Central America 6.9%
- Europe & Eurasia 19.1%
- North America 24.7%
- Middle East 9.4%
- Asia/Pacific 35.7%

World total (2022)
1,000.3 billion barrels per day

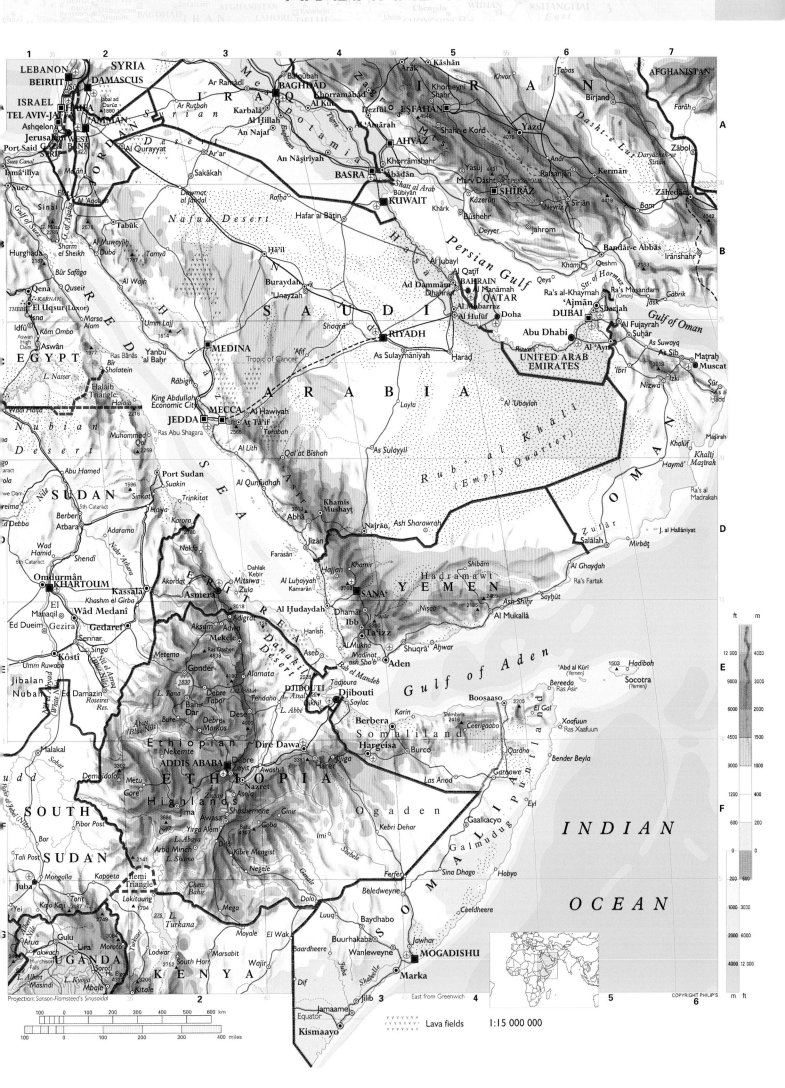

Projection: Sanson-Flamsteed's Sinusoidal

| 100 | 0 | 100 | 200 | 300 | 400 | 500 | 600 km |
| 100 | 0 | 100 | 200 | 300 | 400 miles |

v v v v v v   Lava fields   1:15 000 000

COPYRIGHT PHILIP'S

ft   m
12 000   4000
9000   3000
6000   2000
4500   1500
3000   1000
1200   400
600   200
0   0
200   600
1000   3000
2000   6000
4000   12 000
m   ft

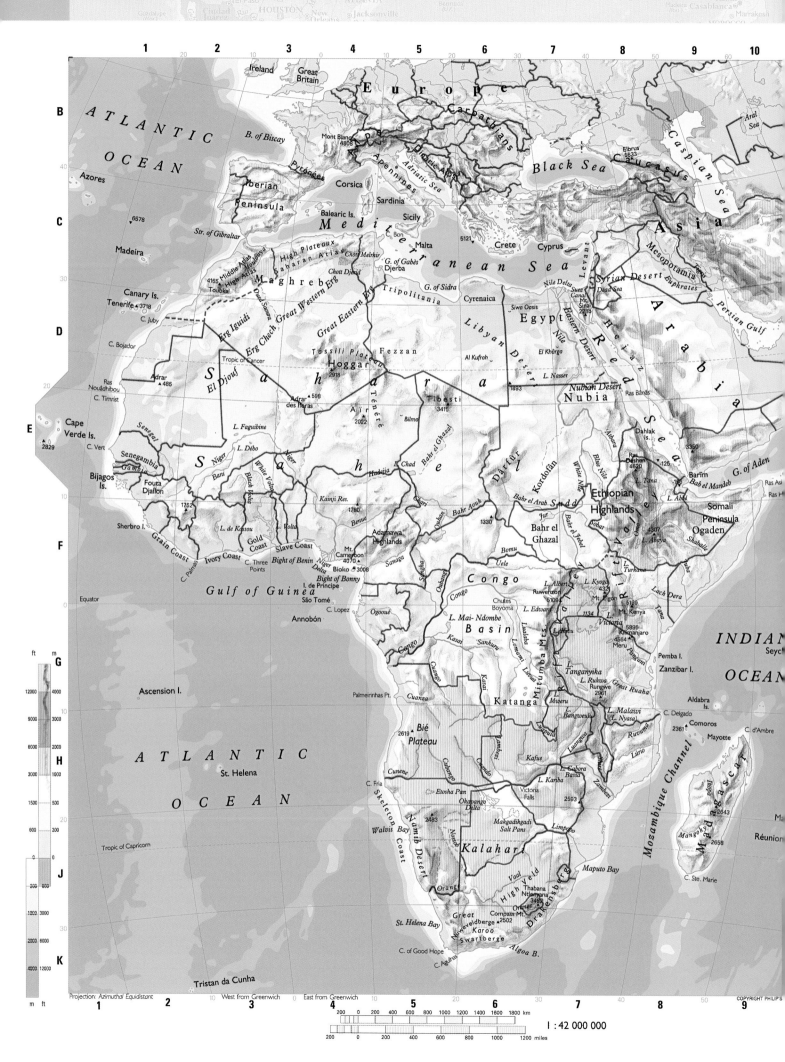

SAN FRANCISCO · Lake City · Kansas City · Cincinnati · PHILADELPHIA · Azores · PORTUGAL · MADRID · BAR
Las Vegas · St. Louis · WASHINGTON, D.C. · Baltimore · Lisbon · SPAIN
S T A T E S · NEW YORK · Rabat · Tangier · Casablanca
HOUSTON · Madeira · MOROCCO · Marrakesh
New Orleans · Jacksonville

A T L A N T I C

B

A T L A N T I C
O C E A N

Azores

Madeira

Canary Is.
Tenerife ▲3718
C. Juby

Ras
Nouâdhibou
C. Timrist

Cape
Verde Is.
▲2829
C. Vert

Bijagos
Is.

Sherbro I.

Ireland
Great
Britain

B. of Biscay

Iberian
Peninsula
Str. of Gibraltar

▲6578

E u r o p e
Carpathians

Alps
Mont Blanc
4808
Pyrénées
Apennines
Corsica

Sardinia

Balearic Is.
Sicily

M e d i t e

Dinaric Alps
Adriatic Sea

C. Bon

Malta
5121

Crete

Caspian
Sea

Elbrus
5633
Black Sea
Caucasus

Cyprus

Aral
Sea

A s i a

Mesopotamia

Tigris

C

D

Middle Atlas
High Atlas
4165
Toubkal
Oued Saoura

High Plateaux
Saharan Atlas
Maghreb

Chott Melrhir
Chott Djerid
Djerba

r r a n e a n S e a

G. of Gabès

G. of Sidra

Tripolitania

Cyrenaica

Nile Delta
Suez
Canal

Levant

Syrian Desert Euphrates

Dead Sea
Mt.
Sinai
2285

Persian Gulf

A r a b i a

Erg Iguidi
Erg Chech
Great Western Erg

Great Eastern Erg

E g y p t

Hejaz

Tropic of Cancer

Adrar ▲485

S a
El Djouf

Adrar ▲598
des Iforas

Tassili Plateau
Hoggar
2918

Fezzan

h
a
Ténéré

Aïr
▲2022

Bilma

Libyan Desert

Al Kufrah

r
Tibesti
3415

Al Khârga

Nile

El Nasser

L. Nasser

Siwa Oasis

Eastern Desert

1893

Nubian Desert

Nubia

Ras Bânâs

Dahlak Is.

Red
Sea

3350

E

S
Senegal
Niger
L. Faguibine

Senegambia
Gambia
Fouta
Djallon

White Volta

Niger

Ban

a

L. Débo

Bani

Black Volta

Hadejia

L. Chad

Bahr el Ghazal

Darfur

Kordofan

White Nile
Blue Nile

L. Tana

Ras
Dashen
4620

-125

Barim
Bab el Mandeb

G. of Aden

Ras As

Ras

Athara

F

1752

Grain Coast

Kainji Res.

L. de Kassou

Ivory Coast

Gold
Coast

Slave Coast

1780

L. Volta

Benue

Mt.
Cameroon
4070
Bioko ▲3008

C. Palmas
C. Three
Points

Bight of Benin
Niger
Delta

Bight of Bonny
I. de Príncipe

Adamawa
Highlands

Sanaga

1330

Chari

Sénué

Bahr Aouk

Bomu

Uele

Bahr el Arab

Bahr el
Ghazal

Jur

Bahr el Jebel

Sudd

Congo

Sobat

Ethiopian
Highlands

L. Abbé

▲4307

Somali
Peninsula
Ogaden

Shabelle

Juba

G

Ascension I.

Equator

Gulf of Guinea

São Tomé

C. Lopez

Annobón

Ogooué

Palmeirinhas Pt.

L. Mai-Ndombe

Oubangi

Congo

B a s i n

Kasai

Sankuru

Lomami

Lualaba

Congo

Lukuga

Chutes
Boyoma

L. Albert
Ruwenzori
5109
L. Edward

L. Kyoga
4321 Mt. Elgon
5199 Mt. Kenya

1134

Lukou
Victoria
5895
Kilimanjaro
4564 Meru

Rift Valley

L. Turkana

Lach Dera

Tana

Pangani

Pemba I.

I N D I A N

Seyc

H

A T L A N T I C

St. Helena

O C E A N

2619

Bié
Plateau

Cuanza

Kwango

Kasai

Kwilu

Katanga

Mitumba Mts.

L. Tanganyika

L. Rukwa
Rungwe
2961

L. Mweru

L. Bangweulu

Great Ruaha

Zanzibar I.

Ruvuma

C. Delgado

2361 Comoros

Mayotte

Aldabra
Is.

O C E A N

C. d'Ambre

J

K

St. Helena Bay

Cunene
C. Fria
Skeleton Coast

Walvis Bay

Namib Desert

Etosha Pan

Okavango
Delta

Okavango

2483

Nossob

Cubango

Makgadikgadi
Salt Pans

Cuando

Zambezi

Kafue

L. Kariba

Victoria
Falls

2593

Limpopo

K a l a h a r i

Vaal

Orange

High Veld

Thabana
Ntlenyana
3482

Orange
Compass Mt.
▲2502

Great
Nieuveldberge
Karoo
Swartberge

C. of Good Hope

C. Agulhas

Algoa B.

Maputo Bay

Drakensberg

L. Malawi
(L. Nyasa)

L. Gabora
Bassa

Luangwa

Luapula

Lulonga

Mozambique Channel

Madagascar

2643

Mangoky

2658

Maromokotra

C. Ste. Marie

M

Réunion

ft   m
12000 4000
9000   3000
6000   2000
3000   1000
1500   500
600   200
0   0
200   600
1000   3000
2000   6000
4000   12000
m   ft

200 0 200 400 600 800 1000 1200 1400 1600 1800 km

200 0   200   400   600   800   1000   1200 miles

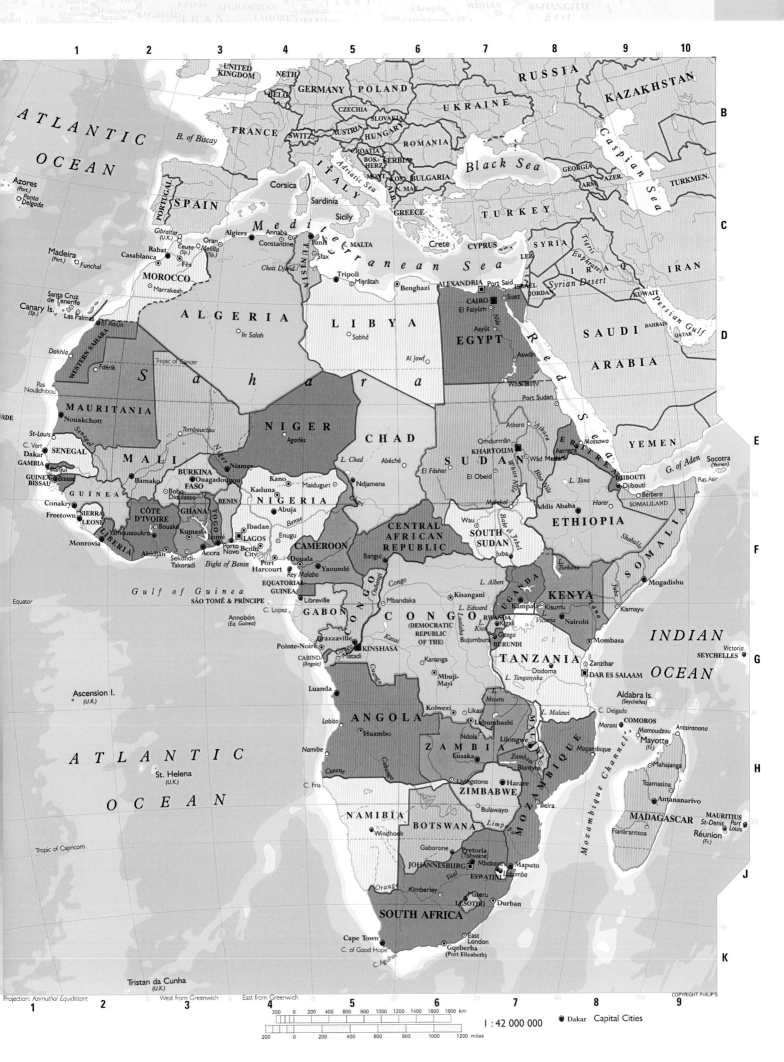

1 : 42 000 000   ● Dakar   Capital Cities

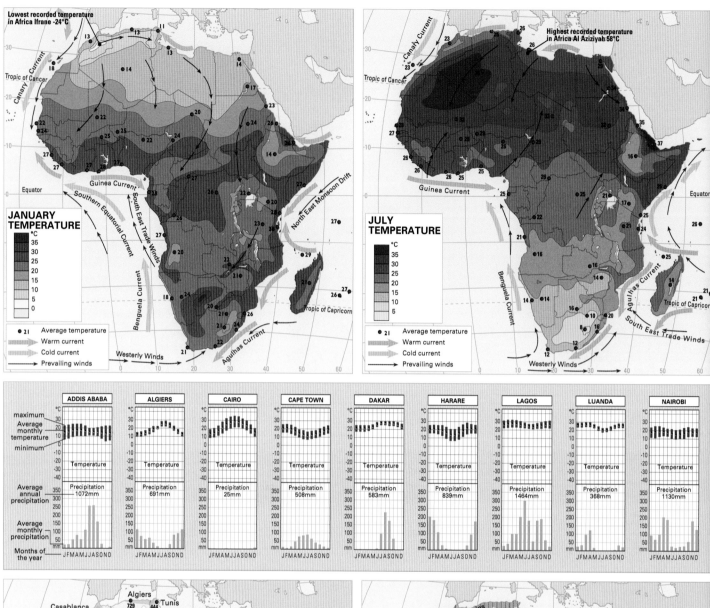

JANUARY TEMPERATURE

Lowest recorded temperature in Africa Ifrane -24°C

°C
35
30
25
20
15
10
5
0

• 21 Average temperature
Warm current
Cold current
Prevailing winds

JULY TEMPERATURE

Highest recorded temperature in Africa Al Aziziyah 58°C

°C
35
30
25
20
15
10
5

• 21 Average temperature
Warm current
Cold current
Prevailing winds

ADDIS ABABA — Temperature — Precipitation 1072mm

ALGIERS — Temperature — Precipitation 691mm

CAIRO — Temperature — Precipitation 25mm

CAPE TOWN — Temperature — Precipitation 508mm

DAKAR — Temperature — Precipitation 583mm

HARARE — Temperature — Precipitation 839mm

LAGOS — Temperature — Precipitation 1464mm

LUANDA — Temperature — Precipitation 368mm

NAIROBI — Temperature — Precipitation 1130mm

maximum
Average monthly temperature
minimum

Average annual precipitation

Average monthly precipitation

Months of the year

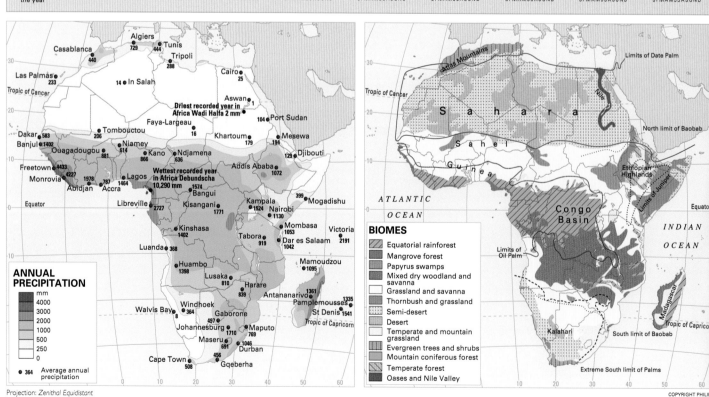

ANNUAL PRECIPITATION

mm
4000
3000
2000
1000
500
250
0

• 364 Average annual precipitation

Casablanca 440
Algiers 729
Tunis 444
Tripoli 288
Las Palmas 233
In Salah 14
Cairo 25
Aswan 1
Driest recorded year in Africa Wadi Halfa 2 mm
Faya-Largeau 16
Port Sudan 104
Tombouctou 206
Khartoum 179
Mesewa 194
Dakar 583
Niamey 614
Ndjamena 636
Djibouti 129
Banjul 1402
Ouagadougou 881
Kano 866
Addis Ababa 1072
Freetown 4433
Monrovia 4227
Abidjan 1978
Accra 787
Lagos 1464
Wettest recorded year in Africa Debundscha 10,290 mm
Bangui 1574
Kampala 1524
Mogadishu 399
Libreville 2727
Kisangani 1771
Nairobi 1130
Kinshasa 1402
Mombasa 1053
Victoria 2191
Tabora 919
Dar es Salaam 1042
Luanda 368
Mamoudzou 1095
Huambo 1398
Lusaka 810
Harare 839
Antananarivo 1361
Pamplemousses 1335
Walvis Bay 8
Windhoek 364
Gaborone 497
St Denis 1541
Johannesburg 709
Maputo 769
Maseru 1046
Durban 1710
Cape Town 508
Gqeberha 456

Projection: Zenithal Equidistant

BIOMES

Equatorial rainforest
Mangrove forest
Papyrus swamps
Mixed dry woodland and savanna
Grassland and savanna
Thornbush and grassland
Semi-desert
Desert
Temperate and mountain grassland
Evergreen trees and shrubs
Mountain coniferous forest
Temperate forest
Oases and Nile Valley

Atlas Mountains
Limits of Date Palm
Sahara
North limit of Baobab
Sahel
Guinea
Ethiopian Highlands
Limits of Juniper
ATLANTIC OCEAN
Congo Basin
Equator
INDIAN OCEAN
Limits of Oil Palm
Kalahari
South limit of Baobab
Madagascar
Tropic of Capricorn
Extreme South limit of Palms

COPYRIGHT PHILIP'S

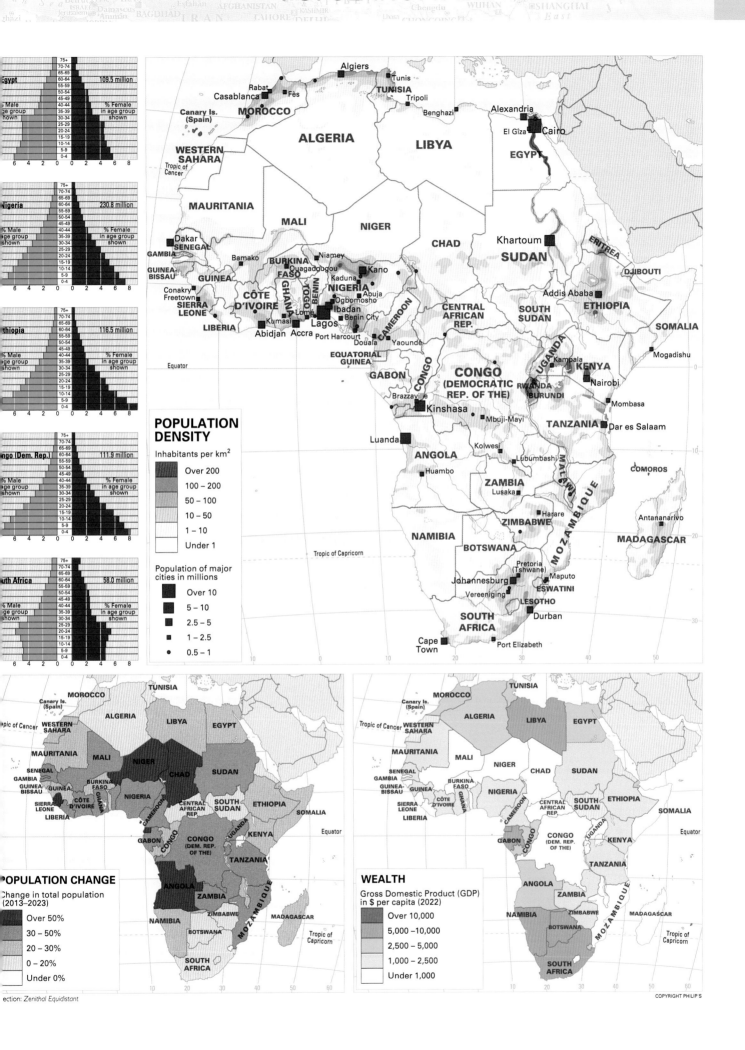

Egypt 109.5 million
% Male age group shown / % Female in age group shown

Nigeria 230.8 million

Ethiopia 116.5 million

Congo (Dem. Rep.) 111.9 million

South Africa 58.0 million

POPULATION DENSITY

Inhabitants per km²
- Over 200
- 100 – 200
- 50 – 100
- 10 – 50
- 1 – 10
- Under 1

Population of major cities in millions
- Over 10
- 5 – 10
- 2.5 – 5
- 1 – 2.5
- 0.5 – 1

POPULATION CHANGE

Change in total population (2013–2023)
- Over 50%
- 30 – 50%
- 20 – 30%
- 0 – 20%
- Under 0%

Projection: Zenithal Equidistant

WEALTH

Gross Domestic Product (GDP) in $ per capita (2022)
- Over 10,000
- 5,000 –10,000
- 2,500 – 5,000
- 1,000 – 2,500
- Under 1,000

COPYRIGHT PHILIP'S

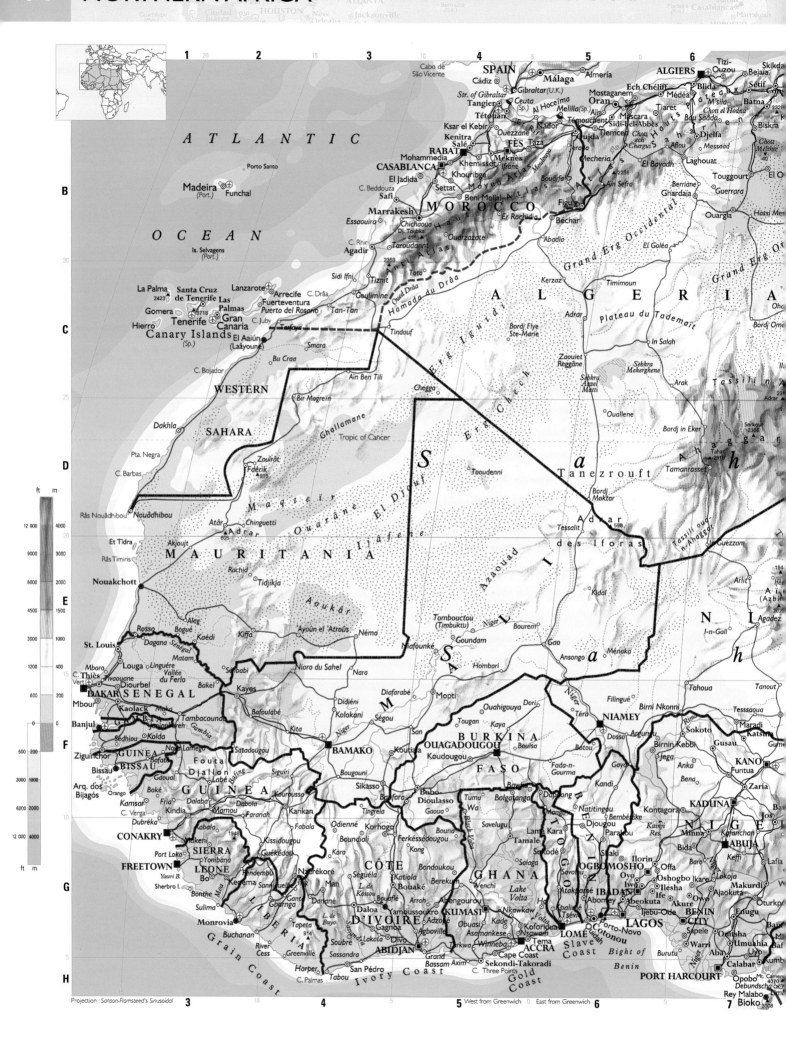

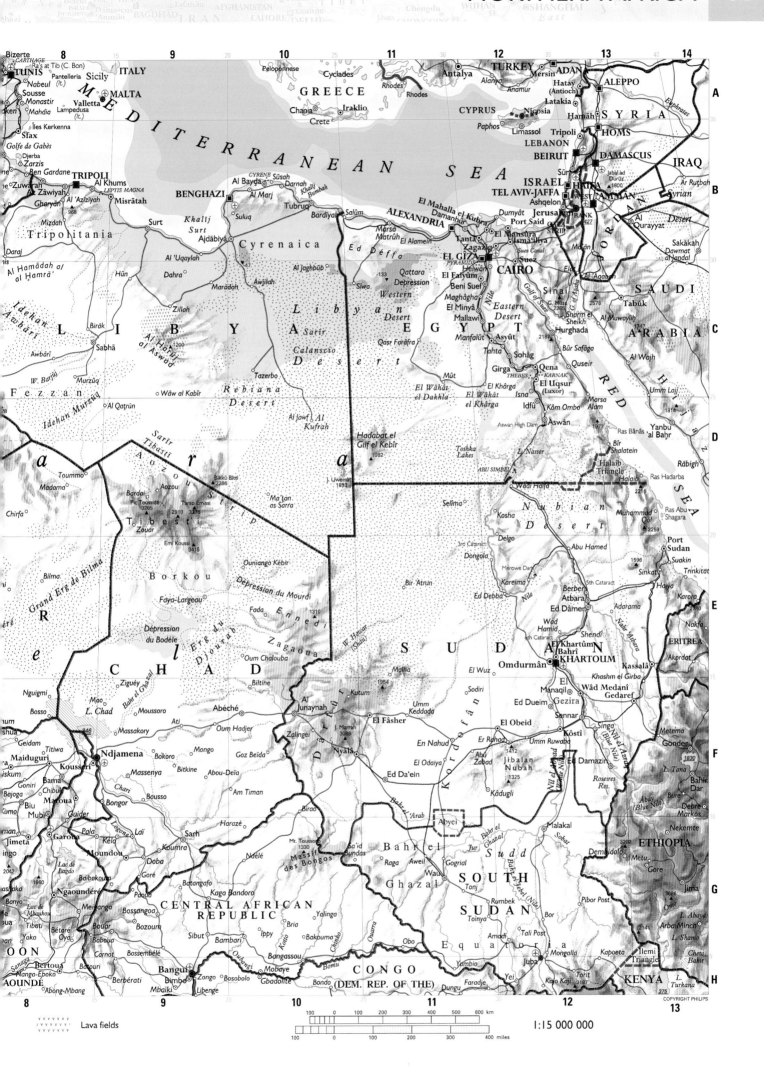

Lava fields

100 0 100 200 300 400 500 600 km

100 0 100 200 300 400 miles

1:15 000 000

COPYRIGHT PHILIPS

INDIAN OCEAN

MADAGASCAR
on same scale
as main map

COPYRIGHT PHILIP'S

INDIAN OCEAN

ATLANTIC OCEAN

SOUTH AFRICA

NAMIBIA

BOTSWANA

ZIMBABWE

ZAMBIA

Kalahari

Namib Desert

Skeleton Coast

Tropic of Capricorn

Projection : Sanson-Flamsteen's Sinusoidal

1:15 000 000

East from Greenwich

SAN FRANCISCO · Lake City · Kansas City · Cincinnati · PHILADELPHIA · PORTUGAL · MADRID · SPAIN
STATES · Las Vegas · St. Louis · WASHINGTON D.C. · Baltimore · NEW YORK · Lisbon · Azores · Tangier
Phoenix · DALLAS · Memphis · Rabat · Casablanca
El Paso · FT. WORTH · ATLANTA · Madeira · Marrakesh
Ciudad Juárez · HOUSTON · New Orleans · Jacksonville · Bermuda · A T L A N T I C · MOROCCO
Guadalupe

3 120 · **4** 125 · 130 · **5** · **6** 135 · 140 · **7** 145 · **8** 150 · **9**

Waigeo · Biak
Sorong · Vogelkop · Yapen · Jayapura · Bismarck Sea · Bismarck Archipelago · Kaveng · Ire
2452 · Peninsula · Wewak · Madang · Bismarck · 1481
Palu · Maluku (Moluccas) · Misool · Fakfak · Papua · Pegunungan Maoke · PAPUA NEW GUINEA · Koko · 2438 · Brit
2490 · Equator · Kep. Sula · Puncak Jaya · 4884 · 4072 · 3993 · New · Mount Hagen · Mt. Wilhelm · 4508 · Lae · 4121 · Sol
Sulawesi (Celebes) · Seram Sea · Buru · Seram (Ceram) · 3019 · Guinea · 2027 · New Britain
Mamuju · 2799 · 2736 · Ambon · Kep. Aru · Owen Stanley Range · 3989
Palopo · 3440 · Kendari · Weber 7260 · Kep. Kai · Kep. Aru · Fly · Gulf of Papua · Port Moresby · D'Entrec · Island
Parepare · Watampone · Butung · Banda Sea · Basin · 3350 · Pulau Dolak · Louisiade Archipela
MAKASSAR (Ujung Pandang) · Kep. Tanimbar · Torres Strait · Coral Sea
Flores Sea · Wetar · Leti · Babar · Arafura Sea · Badu I. · Moa I. · Basin · Cora
Sumbawa · 5123 · Flores · Alor · Dili · 2963 · 3310 · Prince of Wales I. · C. York
Raba · 2821 · Timor · TIMOR-LESTE · C. Croker · Weipa · Cape York · Great
Sumba · 2350 · Ende · Kupang · Timor Sea · Melville I. · Cobourg Pen. · C. Arnhem · Peninsula
Roti · Savu Sea · Bathurst I. · Arnhem · Groote · Weipa · Cairns
North Australian Basin · Darwin · Land · Eylandt · Gulf of Carpentaria · Queensland Plateau
Ashmore and Cartier Is. · Katherine · Wellesley Is. · Cooktown · Great Barrier Reef
C. Londonderry · Joseph Bonaparte Gulf · Latrimah · Normanton · 1622 · Cairns · ISL
Bonaparte Archipelago · Wyndham · Kununurra · Daly Waters · Bartle Frere · Cor
Kimberley · L. Argyle · Barkly Tableland · Forsayth · Charters Towers · Townsville · Whitsunday Is. · TER
970 · Derby · Halls Creek · Tennant Creek · Kajabbi · Mitchell · L. Dalrymple · Mackay
Broome · NORTHERN · Tanami Desert · Mount Isa · Cloncurry · Hughenden · Winton · Rockhampt
Great Sandy Desert · TERRITORY · MacDonnell Ranges · Alice Springs · Dajarra · QUEENSLAND · Emerald · Gladsto
Port Hedland · L. Mackay · 1531 · Mt. Zeil · Longreach · 1312
Dampier · Karratha · Lake Disappointment · Gibson Desert · 1126 · 867 · Mt. Woodroffe · Simpson Desert · Yaraka · Charleville · Roma · Maryborough
N.W. Cape · Pannawonica · Newman · AUSTRALIA · Uluru (Ayers Rock) · 1435 · Sturt Stony Desert · 216 · Quilpie · Cunnamulla · Toowoomba · Gympie
Mt. Meharry · Hamersley Range · WESTERN · Musgrave Ranges · SOUTH · Cooper Creek · Thargomindah · Dirranbandi · BRI
Pilbara · Paraburdoo · L. Carnegie · Great Victoria Desert · -16 · Kati Thanda-Lake Eyre · Warrego · Moree
Carnarvon · Gascoyne · AUSTRALIA · Coober Pedy · AUSTRALIA · Bourke · Walgett
Shark Bay · Meekatharra · Leonora · Marree · Paroo · Darling · NEW SOUTH · Tamworth · Round
Mount Magnet · Murchison · Lake Barlee · Lake Torrens · St. · Flinders Ranges · Broken Hill · Cobar · WALES · 1585 · Dubbo
Geraldton · Kalgoorlie-Boulder · Tarcoola · 1168 · Mary Pk. · Newcastle
INDIAN OCEAN · Nullarbor Plain · Penong · Lake Gairdner · Port Augusta · Mildura · Orange · Bathurst · Gosfo
Perth · Northam · Norseman · Whyalla · Port Pirie · Murray · Hay · Griffith · Wagga Wagga · SYDN
Rockingham · Esperance · Eyre Pen. · Yorke Pen. · ADELAIDE · Murrumbidgee · Canberra A.C.T. · Wollon
Bunbury · 1052 · Great Australian Bight · Port Lincoln · Spencer Gulf · Murray Bridge · Swan Hill · Mt. Kosciuszko 2228 · Albury · Bombala
Naturaliste Plateau · C. Leeuwin · Augusta · Albany · 5632 · Kangaroo I. · Gulf St. Vincent · Bendigo · Shepparton · Wodonga · Snowy Mts. · C. Howe
Encounter B. · VICTORIA · Horsham · Ballarat · MELBOURNE · Sale
South Australian Basin · Mount Gambier · Geelong · Wilsons Promontory
Warrnambool · Bass Strait · Flinders I.
King I. · Furneaux Group · Tasman Aby
S O U T H E R N   O C E A N · Burnie · Devonport · Launceston · 1617 · Mt. Ossa · TASMANIA · Hobart · S.E. Cape
South Tasman Plateau

Elevation scale (ft / m): 6000 / 2000 · 4500 / 1500 · 3000 / 1000 · 1200 / 400 · 600 / 200 · 0 / 0 · 200 / 600 · 2000 / 6000 · 4000 / 12 000 · 6000 / 18 000 · m / ft

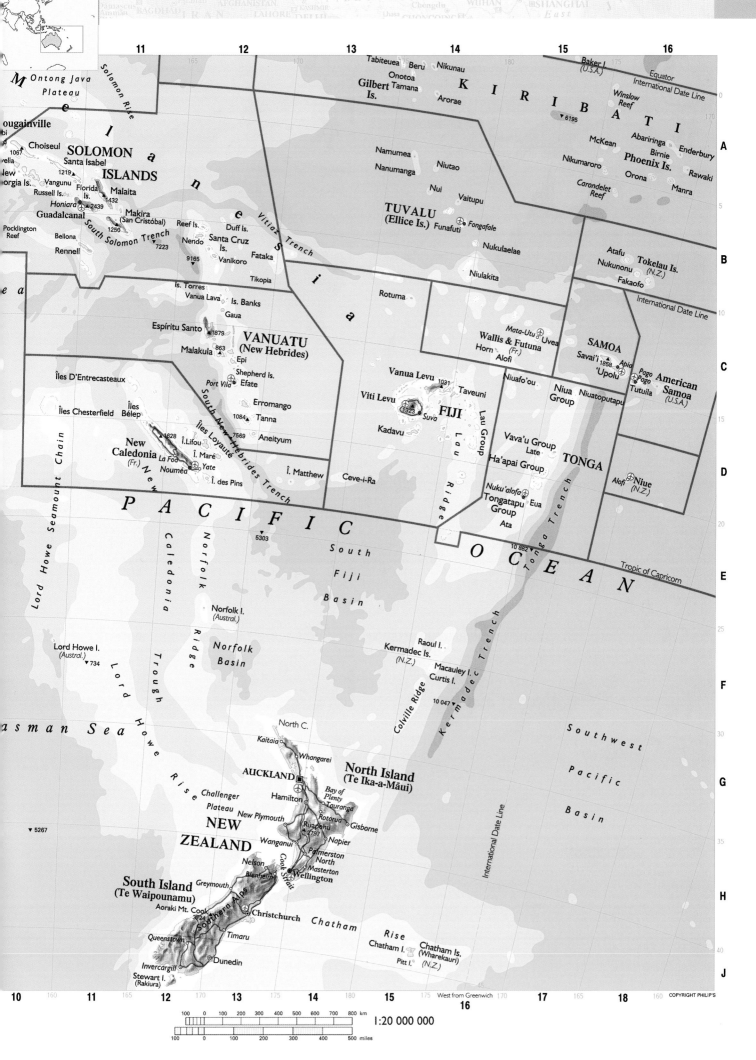

M e l a n e s i a

Ontong Java
Plateau

Solomon Rise

Tabiteuea Beru Nikunau
Onotoa Tamana
Gilbert Tamana
Is.
Arorae

K I R I B A T I

Baker I.
(U.S.A.)

Equator
International Date Line

▼6195

Winslow
Reef

ougainville
bi

Choiseul 1067
New Santa Isabel
orgia Is. Vangunu 1219▲
Russell Is. Florida
Is. Malaita 1432
Honiara 2439▲
Guadalcanal 1250

SOLOMON
ISLANDS

McKean Abariringa Enderbury
Nikumaroro Birnie
Phoenix Is. Rawaki
Orona Manra
Carondelet
Reef

A

Namumea Niutao
Nanumanga
Nui Vaitupu

TUVALU
(Ellice Is.) Funafuti Fongafale

Atafu
Nukunonu Tokelau Is.
(N.Z.)
Fakaofo

B

South Solomon Trench

Pocklington
Reef
Bellona
Rennell

Makira
(San Cristóbal)

Reef Is. Duff Is.
Nendo Santa Cruz
7223 Is.
9165 Vanikoro
Fataka
Tikopia

Is. Torres
Vanua Lava Is. Banks
Gaua

Nukulaelae

Niulakita

Vitiaz Trench

Rotuma

Niuafo'ou

International Date Line

ea

Espíritu Santo 1879▲
Malakula 863▲ Epi
Shepherd Is.
Port Vila Efate

VANUATU
(New Hebrides)

Wallis & Futuna
Mata-Utu Uvea
(Fr.)
Horn
Alofi

SAMOA
Savai'i 1858 Apia
'Upolu Pago
Pago
Tutuila American
Samoa
(U.S.A.)

C

Îles D'Entrecasteaux

Îles Chesterfield

Îles
Bélep

Erromango
1084▲ Tanna

Vanua Levu
1031▲
Viti Levu Taveuni
1323▲ FIJI
Suva
Kadavu

Niua
Group Niuatoputapu

New
Caledonia 1628▲
(Fr.) Î.Lifou
La Foa Î. Maré
Nouméa Yate
Î. des Pins

7569
Aneityum

Î. Matthew Ceve-i-Ra

Lau Group

Vava'u Group
Late
Ha'apai Group

TONGA

Alofi Niue
(N.Z.)

D

Îles Loyauté

Nuku'alofa
Tongatapu Eua
Group
Ata

Lord Howe Seamount Chain

New Hebrides Trench

P A C I F I C

South
Fiji
Basin

O C E A N

Lau Ridge

10 882

Tonga Trench

Tropic of Capricorn

E

5303

Caledonia Trough

Norfolk Ridge

Norfolk I.
(Austral.)

Norfolk
Basin

Lord Howe I.
(Austral.) ▼734

Raoul I.
Kermadec Is.
(N.Z.)
Macauley I.
Curtis I.

Southwest

Pacific

F

Lord Howe Rise

Colville Ridge

Kermadec Trench

10 047

Basin

asman Sea

North C.
Kaitaia
Whangarei

AUCKLAND
Hamilton Bay of
Plenty
Challenger New Plymouth Tauranga
Plateau Rotorua Gisborne
Ruapehu
NEW 2797▲ Napier
Wanganui
ZEALAND Palmerston
North

North Island
(Te Ika-a-Māui)

International Date Line

G

▼5267

Nelson Masterton
Blenheim Wellington
Greymouth Cook Strait

South Island
(Te Waipounamu)
Aoraki Mt. Cook
3724▲ Christchurch

Southern Alps

Chatham
Rise
Chatham I. Chatham Is.
(Wharekauri)
Pitt I. (N.Z.)

H

Queenstown
Timaru
Invercargill Dunedin
Stewart I.
(Rakiura)

J

100 0 100 200 300 400 500 600 700 800 km

1:20 000 000

100 0 100 200 300 400 500 miles

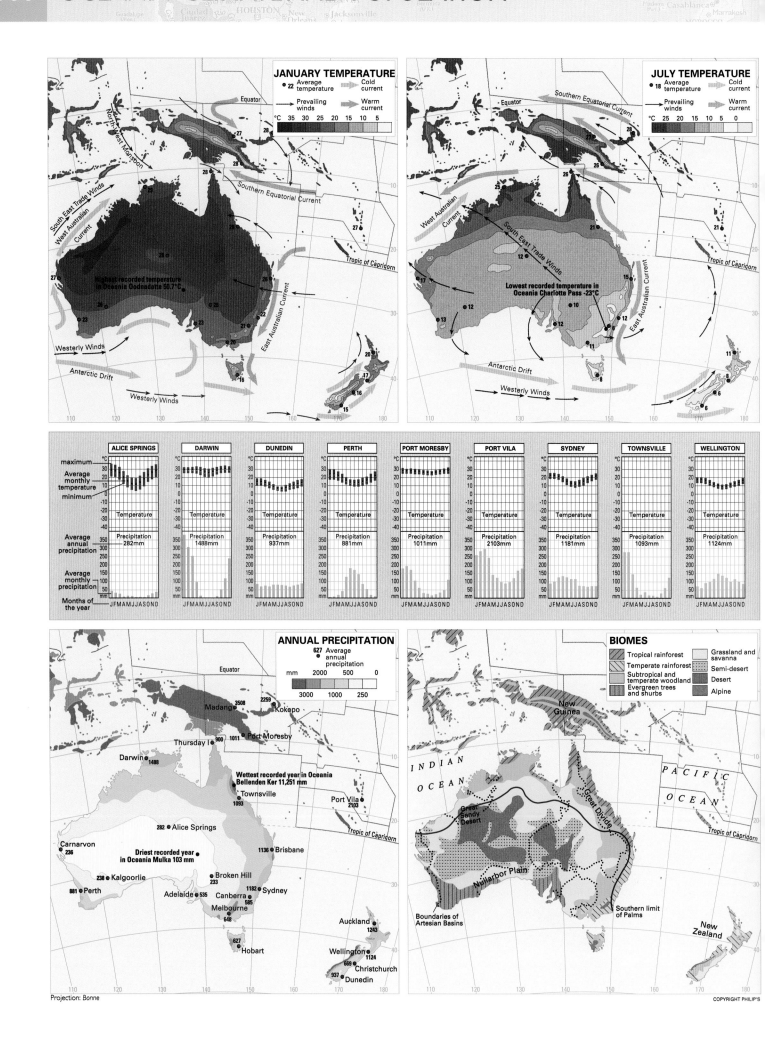

JANUARY TEMPERATURE

- • 22 Average temperature
- ➡ Cold current
- → Prevailing winds
- ➡ Warm current

°C 35 30 25 20 15 10 5

Highest recorded temperature in Oceania Oodnadatta 50.7°C.

JULY TEMPERATURE

- • 18 Average temperature
- ➡ Cold current
- → Prevailing winds
- ➡ Warm current

°C 25 20 15 10 5 0

Lowest recorded temperature in Oceania Charlotte Pass -23°C

Climate graphs (maximum, Average monthly temperature, minimum; Temperature; Average annual precipitation; Average monthly precipitation; Months of the year — J F M A M J J A S O N D):

- ALICE SPRINGS — Precipitation 282mm
- DARWIN — Precipitation 1488mm
- DUNEDIN — Precipitation 937mm
- PERTH — Precipitation 881mm
- PORT MORESBY — Precipitation 1011mm
- PORT VILA — Precipitation 2103mm
- SYDNEY — Precipitation 1181mm
- TOWNSVILLE — Precipitation 1093mm
- WELLINGTON — Precipitation 1124mm

ANNUAL PRECIPITATION

- • 627 Average annual precipitation

mm 2000 500 0 / 3000 1000 250

- Madang 3508
- Kokopo 2259
- Port Moresby 1011
- Thursday I 900
- Darwin 1488
- Wettest recorded year in Oceania Bellenden Ker 11,251 mm
- Townsville 1093
- Port Vila 2103
- Alice Springs 282
- Carnarvon 236
- Driest recorded year in Oceania Mulka 103 mm
- Brisbane 1136
- Kalgoorlie 238
- Broken Hill 233
- Perth 881
- Sydney 1182
- Adelaide 535
- Canberra 585
- Melbourne 648
- Auckland 1243
- Hobart 627
- Wellington 1124
- Christchurch 669
- Dunedin 937

BIOMES

- ▨ Tropical rainforest
- ▨ Temperate rainforest
- Subtropical and temperate woodland
- ▥ Evergreen trees and shurbs
- Grassland and savanna
- Semi-desert
- Desert
- Alpine

New Guinea
Great Sandy Desert
Great Divide
Nullarbor Plain
Boundaries of Artesian Basins
Southern limit of Palms
New Zealand

Projection: Bonne

COPYRIGHT PHILIP'S

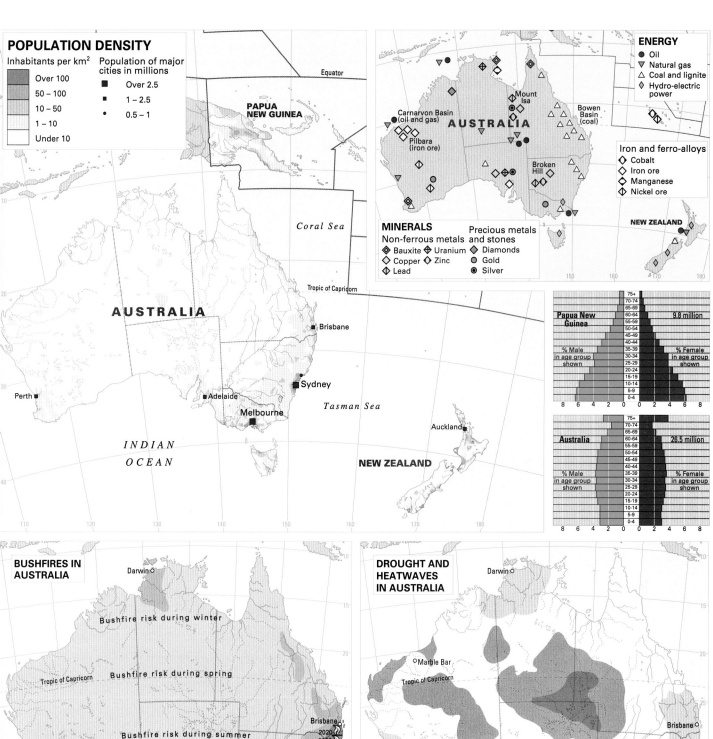

POPULATION DENSITY

Inhabitants per km²

	Over 100
	50 – 100
	10 – 50
	1 – 10
	Under 10

Population of major cities in millions

- ■ Over 2.5
- ▪ 1 – 2.5
- • 0.5 – 1

ENERGY

- ● Oil
- ▽ Natural gas
- △ Coal and lignite
- ◇ Hydro-electric power

Iron and ferro-alloys

- ◇ Cobalt
- ◇ Iron ore
- ◇ Manganese
- ◇ Nickel ore

MINERALS

Non-ferrous metals

- ◈ Bauxite
- ◇ Copper
- ◈ Lead
- ⊕ Uranium
- ◇ Zinc

Precious metals and stones

- ◇ Diamonds
- ● Gold
- ● Silver

Carnarvon Basin (oil and gas)
Pilbara (iron ore)
Mount Isa
Bowen Basin (coal)
Broken Hill

PAPUA NEW GUINEA
AUSTRALIA
NEW ZEALAND

Coral Sea
Tropic of Capricorn
Brisbane
Sydney
Perth ■   Adelaide
Melbourne
Tasman Sea
Auckland
INDIAN OCEAN
NEW ZEALAND

Equator

Papua New Guinea   9.8 million

% Male in age group shown   % Female in age group shown

Australia   26.5 million

% Male in age group shown   % Female in age group shown

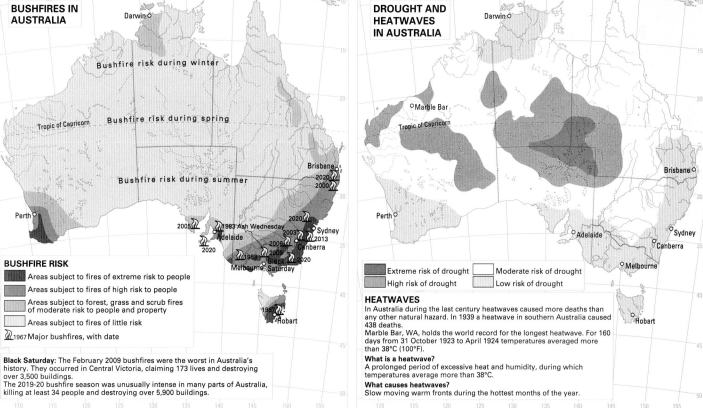

BUSHFIRES IN AUSTRALIA

Darwin

Bushfire risk during winter
Bushfire risk during spring
Tropic of Capricorn
Bushfire risk during summer
Brisbane
2020
2000
2020
2005
1983 Ash Wednesday
Adelaide
2003
Sydney
2006
2013
2020
Canberra
1983
2009
Melbourne   Black   2020
Saturday
Perth
1967
Hobart

BUSHFIRE RISK

	Areas subject to fires of extreme risk to people
	Areas subject to fires of high risk to people
	Areas subject to forest, grass and scrub fires of moderate risk to people and property
	Areas subject to fires of little risk
🔥1967	Major bushfires, with date

Black Saturday: The February 2009 bushfires were the worst in Australia's history. They occurred in Central Victoria, claiming 173 lives and destroying over 3,500 buildings.
The 2019-20 bushfire season was unusually intense in many parts of Australia, killing at least 34 people and destroying over 5,900 buildings.

DROUGHT AND HEATWAVES IN AUSTRALIA

Darwin
Marble Bar
Tropic of Capricorn
Brisbane
Perth
Adelaide
Sydney
Canberra
Melbourne
Hobart

	Extreme risk of drought		Moderate risk of drought
	High risk of drought		Low risk of drought

HEATWAVES

In Australia during the last century heatwaves caused more deaths than any other natural hazard. In 1939 a heatwave in southern Australia caused 438 deaths.
Marble Bar, WA, holds the world record for the longest heatwave. For 160 days from 31 October 1923 to April 1924 temperatures averaged more than 38°C (100°F).

What is a heatwave?
A prolonged period of excessive heat and humidity, during which temperatures average more than 38°C.

What causes heatwaves?
Slow moving warm fronts during the hottest months of the year.

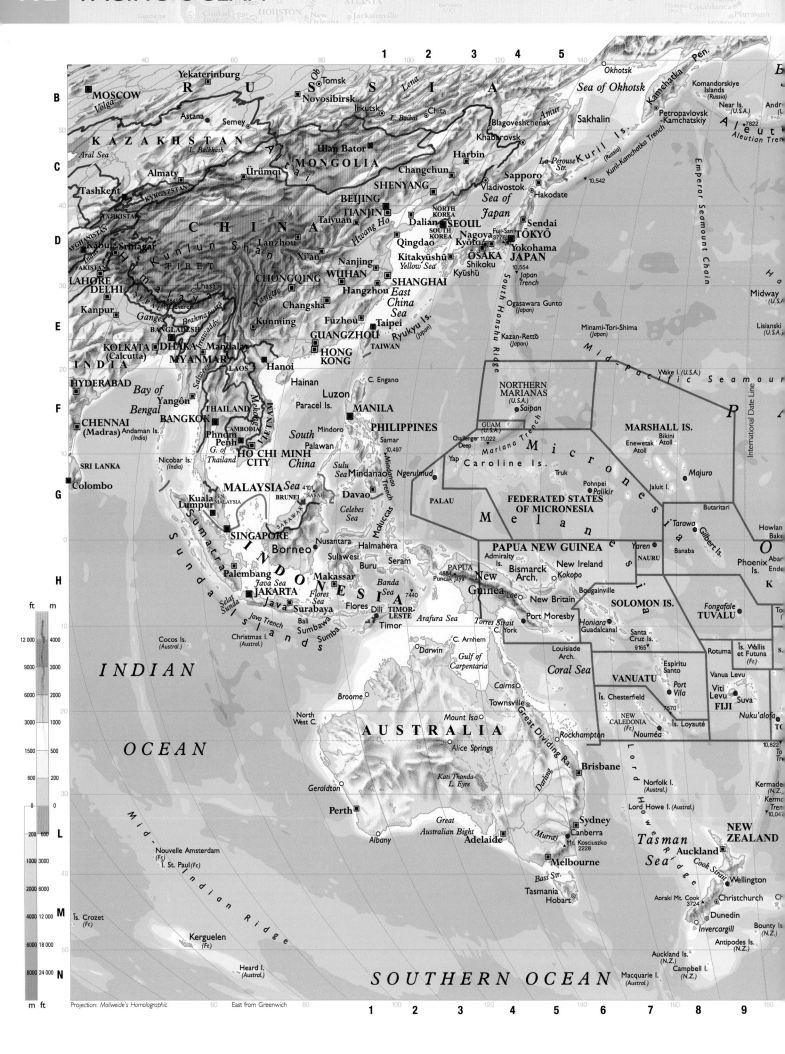

SAN FRANCISCO Lake City Kansas City Cincinnati NEW YORK PHILADELPHIA PORTUGAL MADRID
Las Vegas St. Louis WASHINGTON Baltimore Lisbon SPAIN
STATES Memphis D.C. Azores Tangier Rabat
HOUSTON ATLANTA Madeira Casablanca MOROCCO
New Jacksonville A T L A N T I C Marrakesh
Orleans

1 2 3 4 5

MOSCOW Yekaterinburg Ob Tomsk Okhotsk Komandorskiye B
Volga R U S S I A Lena Sea of Okhotsk Islands (Russia)
B Astana Novosibirsk Kamchatka Near Is. (U.S.A.) Andr
KAZAKHSTAN Irkutsk Chita Petropavlovsk 7822
Semey L. Baikal Blagoveshchensk -Kamchatskiy Aleut Aleutian Tren
50 Almaty Ürümqi Ulan Bator Khabarovsk Kuril Is. (Russia)
Tashkent L. Balkhash MONGOLIA Sapporo La Pérouse Kuril-Kamchatka Trench
C KYRGYZSTAN Changchun Vladivostok Hakodate Str. 10,542
TAJIKISTAN SHENYANG Sea of
Kabul Srinagar BEIJING Dalian SEOUL Japan Emperor Seamount Chain
AFGHANISTAN C H I N A TIANJIN NORTH Nagoya Fuji-San TŌKYŌ
PAKISTAN Taiyuan KOREA Kyōto 3776 Yokohama
LAHORE Lanzhou Qingdao SOUTH OSAKA JAPAN
DELHI Xi'an Hwang Ho KOREA Shikoku 10,554 Midway
Kanpur Nanjing CHONGQING WUHAN Kyūshū Japan (U.S.A.)
Ganges Lhasa Changsha SHANGHAI Trench
E Brahmaputra 8848 Hangzhou East Kazan-Rettō Minami-Tori-Shima Lisianski
INDIA Mt. Everest Kunming Fuzhou China (Japan) (Japan) (U.S.A.)
BANGLADESH GUANGZHOU Sea Ogasawara Gunto Mid-Pacific Seamou
KOLKATA DHAKA Mandalay Taipei (Japan)
(Calcutta) MYANMAR HONG Ryukyu Is. Wake I. (U.S.A.) P
HYDERABAD LAOS Hanoi KONG (Japan) NORTHERN
Yangôn TAIWAN South Honshu Ridge MARIANAS MARSHALL IS.
THAILAND Hainan (U.S.A.)
CHENNAI Andaman Is. Luzon Saipan Enewetak Bikini
(Madras) (India) Paracel Is. GUAM Atoll Atoll
BANGKOK C. Engano (U.S.A.)
Phnom CAMBODIA MANILA Challenger 11,022 Majuro
SRI LANKA Penh Mindoro PHILIPPINES Deep
Colombo HO CHI MINH Palawan Samar Mariana Trench Caroline Is. Jaluit I.
CITY South 10,497 Yap Truk
MALAYSIA China Sulu Mindanao Ngerulmud Pohnpei Butaritari
Kuala Sea Sea Davao Palikir Tarawa
Lumpur PEN. SABAH Celebes PALAU FEDERATED STATES Gilbert Is. Howlan
0 MALAYSIA BRUNEI Sea OF MICRONESIA Bake
SINGAPORE Nusantara Moluccas Yaren Phoenix
Palembang Borneo Sulawesi Halmahera PAPUA NEW GUINEA NAURU Abar
JAKARTA Java Sea Makassar Buru Seram Admiralty New Ireland Banaba Ende
INDONESIA Flores Banda Is. Bismarck Kokopo
Surabaya Sea Sea 7440 PAPUA Arch. SOLOMON IS. Fongafale K
Java Bali Flores Dili TIMOR- Puncak Jaya New New Britain Bougainville TUVALU
Christmas I. Sumbawa LESTE 4884 Guinea Lae Honiara Îs. Wallis
Cocos Is. (Austral.) Sumba Timor Arafura Sea Torres Strait Port Moresby Guadalcanal Rotuma et Futuna (Fr.)
(Austral.) Java Trench C. York Santa Espíritu Vanua Levu
C. Arnhem Cruz Is. Santo Viti
Darwin Louisiade 9165 Levu Nuku'alofa
Gulf of Arch. Coral Sea VANUATU Port Suva 10,822
Carpentaria Îs. Chesterfield Vila FIJI To
Broome Cairns Îs. Loyauté 7570 Tre
North Townsville Great Dividing Ra. NEW Nouméa
West C. Mount Isa CALEDONIA
AUSTRALIA Rockhampton (Fr.) Kermadec
Alice Springs Brisbane Norfolk I. (N.Z.)
Geraldton Kati Thanda Darling (Austral.) Kerma
L. Eyre Lord Howe I. (Austral.) Tren
L Perth 10,04
Great Sydney NEW
Australian Bight Canberra Tasman ZEALAND
Albany Adelaide Mt. Kosciuszko Sea Auckland
Murray 2228 Melbourne Cook Strait
Bass Str. Wellington
M Tasmania Aoraki Mt. Cook Christchurch
Hobart 3724
Dunedin
Invercargill Bounty Is.
SOUTHERN OCEAN Auckland Is. Antipodes Is. (N.Z.)
(N.Z.) (N.Z.)
N Macquarie I. Campbell I.
(Austral.) (N.Z.)

INDIAN

OCEAN

Nouvelle Amsterdam
(Fr.)
I. St. Paul (Fr.)

Mid-Indian Ridge

Îs. Crozet
(Fr.)

Kerguelen
(Fr.)

Heard I.
(Austral.)

ft m
12 000 4000
9000 3000
6000 2000
3000 1000
1500 500
600 200
0 0
200 600
1000 3000
2000 6000
4000 12 000
6000 18 000
8000 24 000
m ft

Projection: Mollweide's Homolographic East from Greenwich

1 2 3 4 5 6 7 8 9

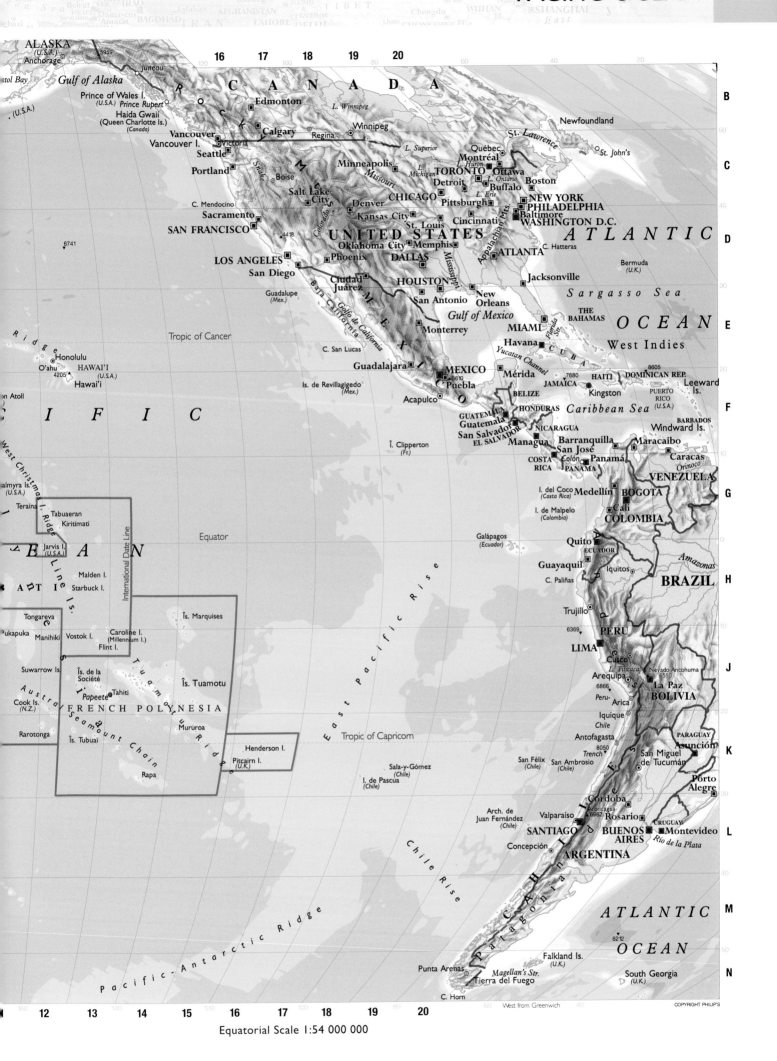

ALASKA
(U.S.A.)
Anchorage
5959
Juneau
stol Bay
Gulf of Alaska
Prince of Wales I.
(U.S.A.) Prince Rupert
Haida Gwaii
(Queen Charlotte Is.)
(Canada)
(U.S.A.)
ROCKY
CANADA
Edmonton
L. Winnipeg
Newfoundland
Vancouver
Vancouver I.
Seattle
Victoria
Calgary
Regina
Winnipeg
St. Lawrence
Québec
Montréal
St. John's
Portland
Boise
Minneapolis
L. Superior
L. Huron
Ottawa
TORONTO
Detroit
L. Michigan
Buffalo
Boston
Salt Lake
City
Denver
CHICAGO
L. Ontario
L. Erie
Pittsburgh
NEW YORK
PHILADELPHIA
C. Mendocino
Sacramento
4418
Kansas City
St. Louis
Cincinnati
Baltimore
WASHINGTON D.C.
SAN FRANCISCO
6741
UNITED STATES
Oklahoma City
Memphis
ATLANTA
C. Hatteras
ATLANTIC
LOS ANGELES
Phoenix
DALLAS
Appalachian Mts.
San Diego
HOUSTON
Jacksonville
Bermuda
(U.K.)
Guadalupe
(Mex.)
Ciudad
Juárez
San Antonio
New
Orleans
Sargasso Sea
Gulf of Mexico
MIAMI
THE
BAHAMAS
OCEAN
Tropic of Cancer
C. San Lucas
Monterrey
Havana
West Indies
Honolulu
O'ahu
4205
HAWAI'I
(U.S.A.)
Hawai'i
Is. de Revillagigedo
(Mex.)
Guadalajara
MEXICO
5610
Puebla
Mérida
Yucatan Channel
CUBA
8605
HAITI
7680
JAMAICA
DOMINICAN REP.
PUERTO
RICO
(U.S.A.)
Leeward
Is.
IFIC
Acapulco
BELIZE
Kingston
Caribbean Sea
BARBADOS
almyra Is.
(U.S.A.)
Palmyra Is.
West Christmas I. Ridge
Teraina
Tabuaeran
Kiritimati
GUATEMALA
Guatemala
San Salvador
EL SALVADOR
HONDURAS
NICARAGUA
Managua
Barranquilla
San José
COSTA
RICA
Colón
PANAMA
Panamá
Windward Is.
Maracaibo
Caracas
VENEZUELA
Jarvis I.
(U.S.A.)
EAN
Tongareva
Malden I.
Starbuck I.
Equator
I. del Coco
(Costa Rica)
I. de Malpelo
(Colombia)
Medellín
Cali
BOGOTA
COLOMBIA
Orinoco
Pukapuka
Manihiki
Vostok I.
Caroline I.
(Millennium I.)
Flint I.
Is. Marquises
Galápagos
(Ecuador)
Quito
ECUADOR
BRAZIL
Suwarrow Is
Î. de la
Société
Papeete Tahiti
Is. Tuamotu
Guayaquil
C. Palinas
Iquitos
Amazonas
Cook Is.
(N.Z.)
FRENCH POLYNESIA
Tuamotu Ridge
Seamount Chain
Mururoa
Trujillo
6369
PERU
LIMA
Iquique
Rarotonga
Is. Tubuaï
Rapa
Henderson I.
Pitcairn I.
(U.K.)
Tropic of Capricorn
East Pacific Rise
Cusco
L. Titicaca
Arequipa
6866
Peru-
Arica
Nevado Ancohuma
6550
La Paz
BOLIVIA
Austral Seamount Chain
Chile
PARAGUAY
Asunción
Antofagasta
San Miguel
de Tucumán
San Félix
(Chile)
8050
Trench
San Ambrosio
(Chile)
Sala-y-Gómez
(Chile)
I. de Pascua
(Chile)
ANDES
Córdoba
Porto
Alegre
Arch. de
Juan Fernández
(Chile)
Valparaíso
Aconcagua
6962
Rosario
URUGUAY
Montevideo
SANTIAGO
Concepción
BUENOS
AIRES
Río de la Plata
ARGENTINA
Chile Rise
ATLANTIC
Patagonia
Pacific-Antarctic Ridge
OCEAN
6212
Falkland Is.
(U.K.)
South Georgia
(U.K.)
Punta Arenas
Magellan's Str.
Tierra del Fuego
C. Horn
West from Greenwich
COPYRIGHT PHILIP'S

Equatorial Scale 1:54 000 000

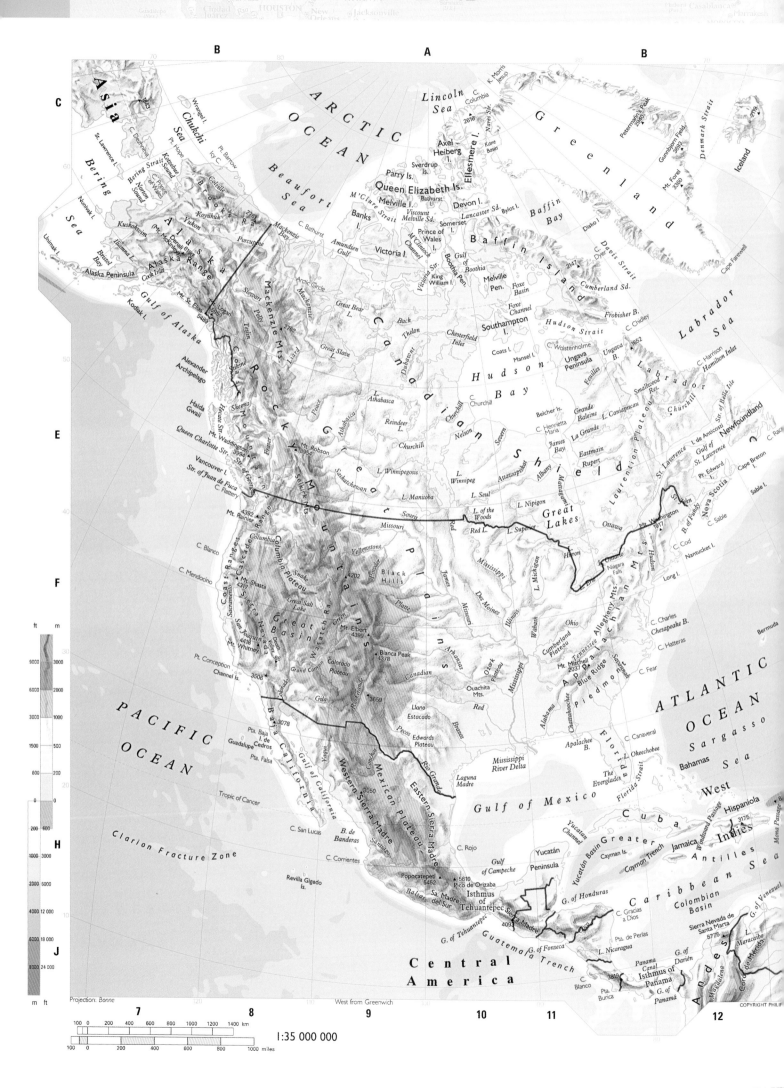

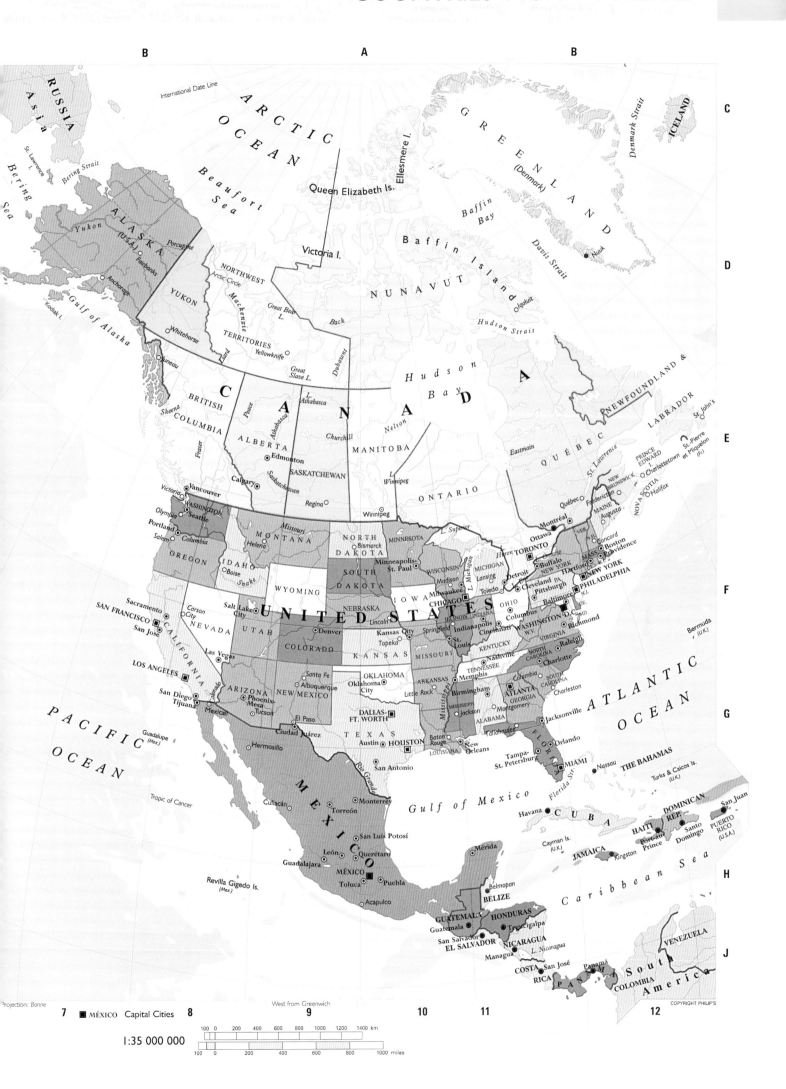

RUSSIA
Asia

ARCTIC OCEAN

Bering Strait

St. Lawrence I.

Bering Sea

ALASKA (USA)

Yukon

Fairbanks

Anchorage

Kodiak I.

Gulf of Alaska

Beaufort Sea

International Date Line

Queen Elizabeth Is.

Ellesmere I.

Victoria I.

Arctic Circle

Porcupine

NORTHWEST

YUKON

Whitehorse

Mackenzie

Great Bear L.

TERRITORIES

Yellowknife

Great Slave L.

Juneau

BRITISH COLUMBIA

Skeena

Fraser

Peace

Athabasca

L. Athabasca

ALBERTA

Edmonton

CANADA

Back

Dubawnt L.

NUNAVUT

Baffin Bay

GREENLAND (Denmark)

Denmark Strait

ICELAND

Nuuk

Davis Strait

Baffin Island

Hudson Strait

Iqaluit

Hudson Bay

Nelson

Churchill

MANITOBA

SASKATCHEWAN

Calgary

Saskatchewan

Regina

Victoria

Vancouver

WASHINGTON

Olympia

Seattle

Portland

Salem

Columbia

OREGON

Winnipeg

L. Winnipeg

ONTARIO

Eastmain

QUÉBEC

St. Lawrence

L. Superior

NEWFOUNDLAND & LABRADOR

St. John's

St-Pierre et Miquelon (Fr.)

PRINCE EDWARD I.

Charlottetown

NOVA SCOTIA

Halifax

NEW BRUNSWICK

Fredericton

Québec

Montréal

Ottawa

MAINE

Augusta

N.H. Concord

VER.

MASS. Boston

Providence

Hartford

L. Huron

L. Michigan

TORONTO

Buffalo

NEW YORK

NEW YORK

N.J.

PHILADELPHIA

DE.

MD.

Baltimore

WASHINGTON D.C.

Richmond

Bermuda (U.K.)

MONTANA

Missouri

Helena

IDAHO

Boise

Snake

NORTH DAKOTA

Bismarck

MINNESOTA

Minneapolis-St. Paul

Madison

WISCONSIN

Lansing

MICHIGAN

Detroit

Cleveland

PA.

Pittsburgh

OHIO

Columbus

W.V.

VIRGINIA

Sacramento

Carson City

Salt Lake City

SOUTH DAKOTA

UNITED STATES

IOWA

Milwaukee

CHICAGO

Toledo

Erie

SAN FRANCISCO

San Jose

CALIFORNIA

NEVADA

UTAH

WYOMING

NEBRASKA

Lincoln

Denver

Kansas City

Topeka

ILLINOIS

Springfield

St. Louis

INDIANA

Indianapolis

Cincinnati

KENTUCKY

Nashville

TENNESSEE

NORTH CAROLINA

Raleigh

Charlotte

Las Vegas

LOS ANGELES

San Diego

Tijuana

Mexicali

Colorado

ARIZONA

Phoenix

Mesa

Tucson

COLORADO

Santa Fe

Albuquerque

NEW MEXICO

KANSAS

MISSOURI

ARKANSAS

Little Rock

Memphis

MISSISSIPPI

Birmingham

Jackson

ALABAMA

Montgomery

Columbia

SOUTH CAROLINA

Charleston

ATLANTA

GEORGIA

ATLANTIC OCEAN

Guadalupe (Mex.)

PACIFIC OCEAN

Hermosillo

El Paso

Ciudad Juárez

Oklahoma City

OKLAHOMA

TEXAS

DALLAS-FT. WORTH

Austin

HOUSTON

San Antonio

Rio Grande

Baton Rouge

LOUISIANA

New Orleans

Jacksonville

Tallahassee

FLORIDA

Orlando

Tampa-St. Petersburg

MIAMI

Nassau

THE BAHAMAS

Turks & Caicos Is. (U.K.)

Tropic of Cancer

MEXICO

Culiacán

Torreón

Monterrey

San Luis Potosí

León

Querétaro

Guadalajara

MÉXICO

Toluca

Puebla

Acapulco

Revilla Gigedo Is. (Mex.)

Mérida

Belmopan

BELIZE

GUATEMALA

Guatemala

San Salvador

EL SALVADOR

HONDURAS

Tegucigalpa

NICARAGUA

Managua

L. Nicaragua

Gulf of Mexico

Florida Str.

Havana

CUBA

Cayman Is. (U.K.)

JAMAICA

Kingston

HAITI

Port-au-Prince

DOMINICAN REP.

Santo Domingo

San Juan

PUERTO RICO (U.S.A.)

Caribbean Sea

COSTA RICA

San José

PANAMA

Panamá

COLOMBIA

VENEZUELA

South America

Projection: Bonne

■ MÉXICO Capital Cities

West from Greenwich

COPYRIGHT PHILIP'S

1:35 000 000

100 0 200 400 600 800 1000 1200 1400 km

100 0 200 400 600 800 1000 miles

7 8 9 10 11 12

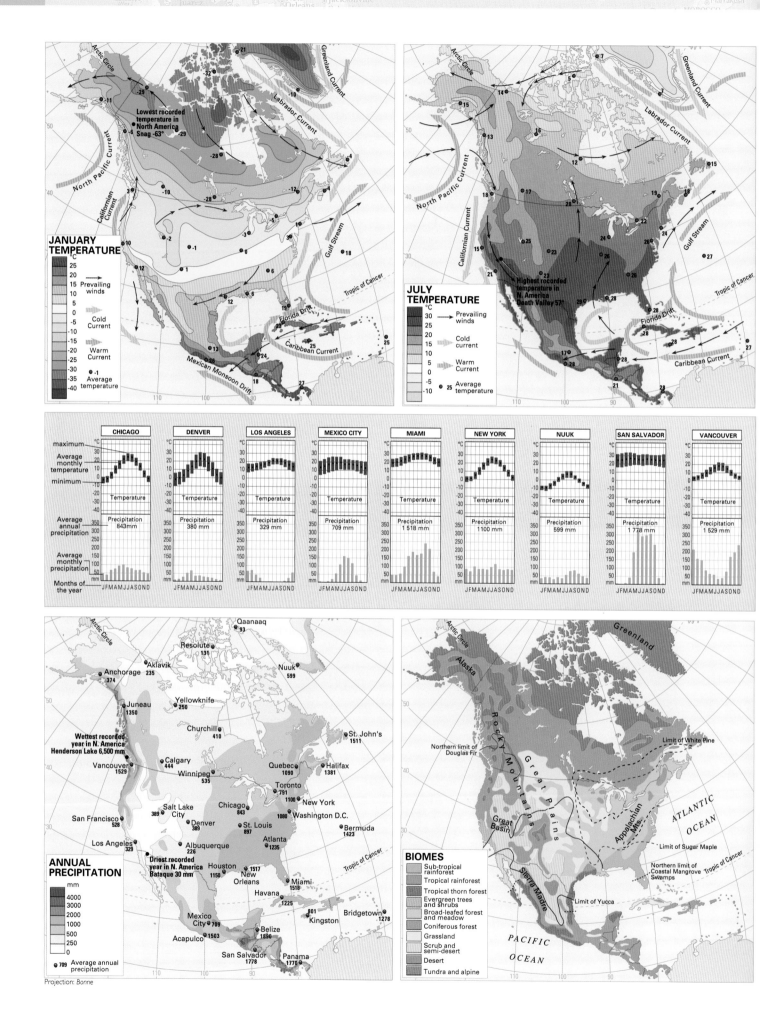

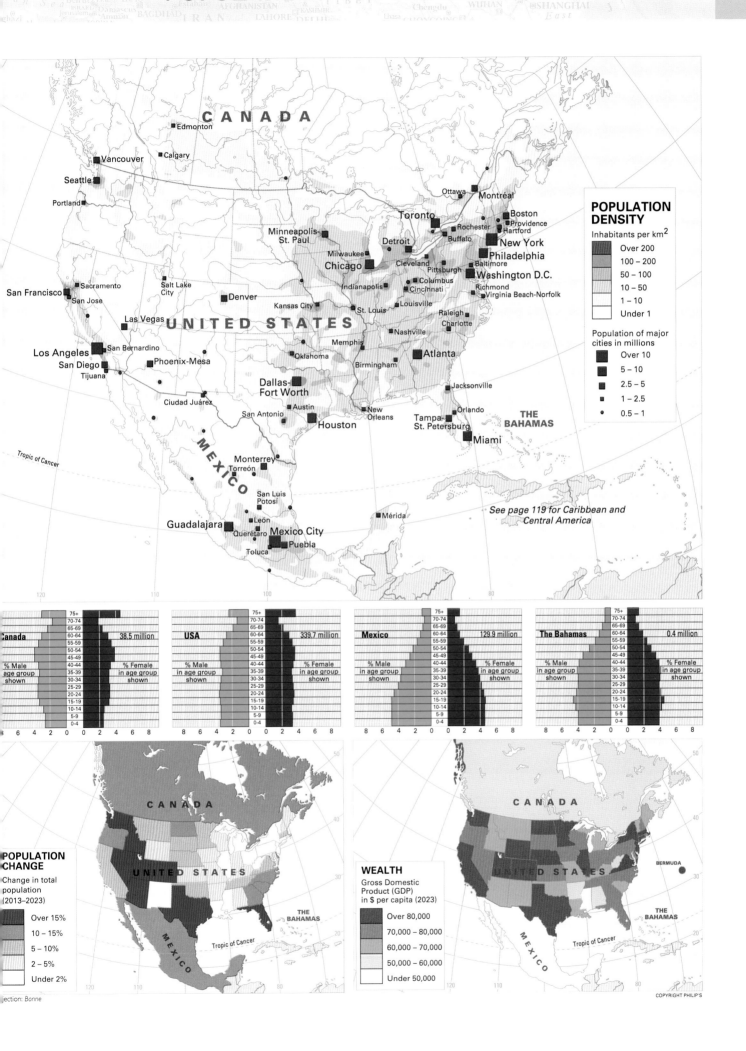

POPULATION DENSITY

Inhabitants per km²

- Over 200
- 100 – 200
- 50 – 100
- 10 – 50
- 1 – 10
- Under 1

Population of major cities in millions

- Over 10
- 5 – 10
- 2.5 – 5
- 1 – 2.5
- 0.5 – 1

See page 119 for Caribbean and Central America

CANADA — 38.5 million
% Male in age group shown / % Female in age group shown

USA — 339.7 million
% Male in age group shown / % Female in age group shown

Mexico — 129.9 million
% Male in age group shown / % Female in age group shown

The Bahamas — 0.4 million
% Male in age group shown / % Female in age group shown

POPULATION CHANGE

Change in total population (2013–2023)

- Over 15%
- 10 – 15%
- 5 – 10%
- 2 – 5%
- Under 2%

WEALTH

Gross Domestic Product (GDP) in $ per capita (2023)

- Over 80,000
- 70,000 – 80,000
- 60,000 – 70,000
- 50,000 – 60,000
- Under 50,000

Projection: Bonne

COPYRIGHT PHILIP'S

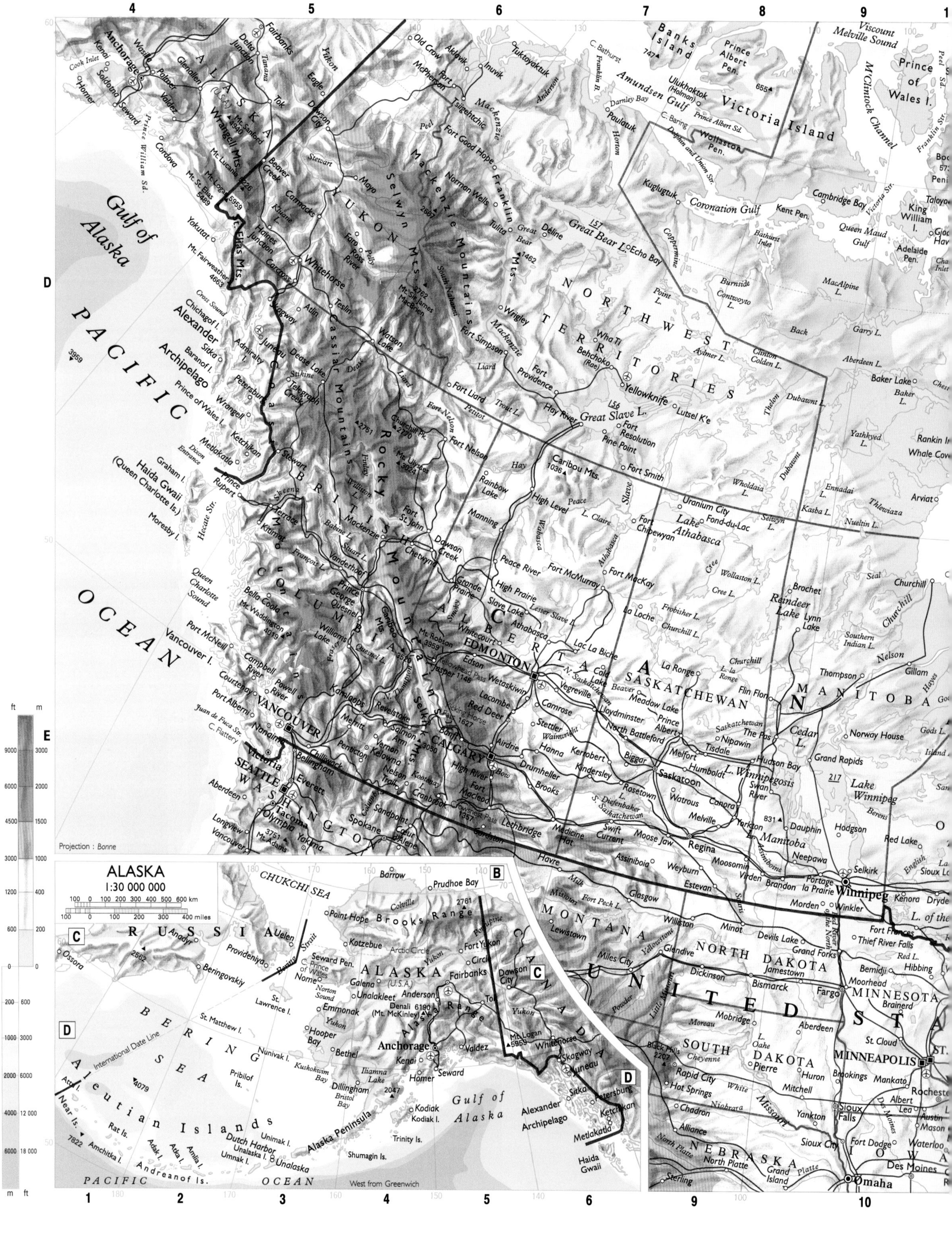

PACIFIC OCEAN

Gulf of Alaska

ALASKA

YUKON

Mackenzie Mountains

Selwyn Mts.

NORTHWEST TERRITORIES

Victoria Island

Banks Island

Prince Albert Pen.

Prince of Wales I.

M'Clintock Channel

Amundsen Gulf

Coronation Gulf

Great Bear L.

Great Slave L.

Yellowknife

BRITISH COLUMBIA

ALBERTA

SASKATCHEWAN

MANITOBA

Rocky Mountains

Columbia Mts.

Vancouver Island

Haida Gwaii (Queen Charlotte Is.)

Queen Charlotte Sound

Alexander Archipelago

EDMONTON

CALGARY

VANCOUVER

Victoria

SEATTLE WASHINGTON

Lake Athabasca

Reindeer Lake

Lake Winnipeg

Lake Winnipegosis

Winnipeg

Regina

Saskatoon

MONTANA

NORTH DAKOTA

SOUTH DAKOTA

NEBRASKA

MINNESOTA

MINNEAPOLIS

UNITED STATES

Lake of the Woods

Baker Lake

Queen Maud Gulf

Projection : Bonne

ALASKA
1:30 000 000

CHUKCHI SEA

RUSSIA

BERING SEA

Aleutian Islands

ALASKA (U.S.A.)

Brooks Range

Fairbanks

Anchorage

Denali 6190 (Mt. McKinley)

Prudhoe Bay

Barrow

Point Hope

Kotzebue

Nome

Bethel

Gulf of Alaska

Kodiak I.

Alaska Peninsula

Alexander Archipelago

Haida Gwaii

International Date Line

PACIFIC OCEAN

West from Greenwich

ft m

E

9000 3000

6000 2000

4500 1500

3000 1000

1200 400

600 200

0 0

200 600

1000 3000

2000 6000

4000 12 000

6000 18 000

m ft

NORTHERN CANADA
Continuation northwards on same
scale as main map

West from Greenwich   COPYRIGHT PHILIP'S

1:15 000 000

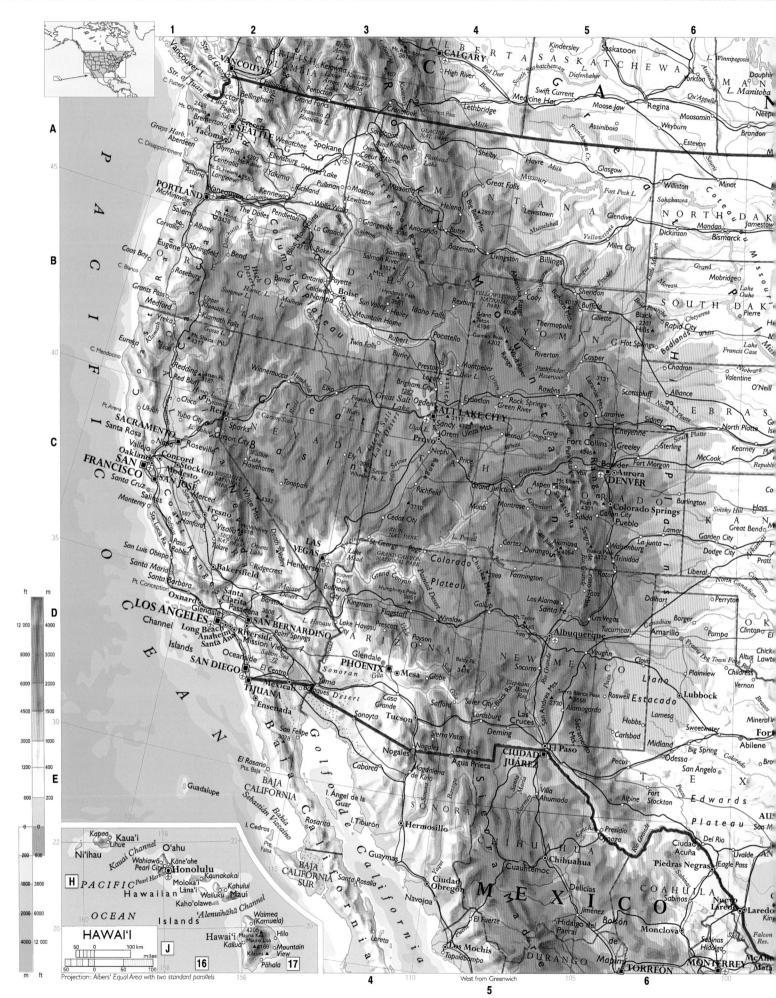

See page 108 for map of Alaska

Projection: Albers' Equal Area with two standard parallels

West from Greenwich

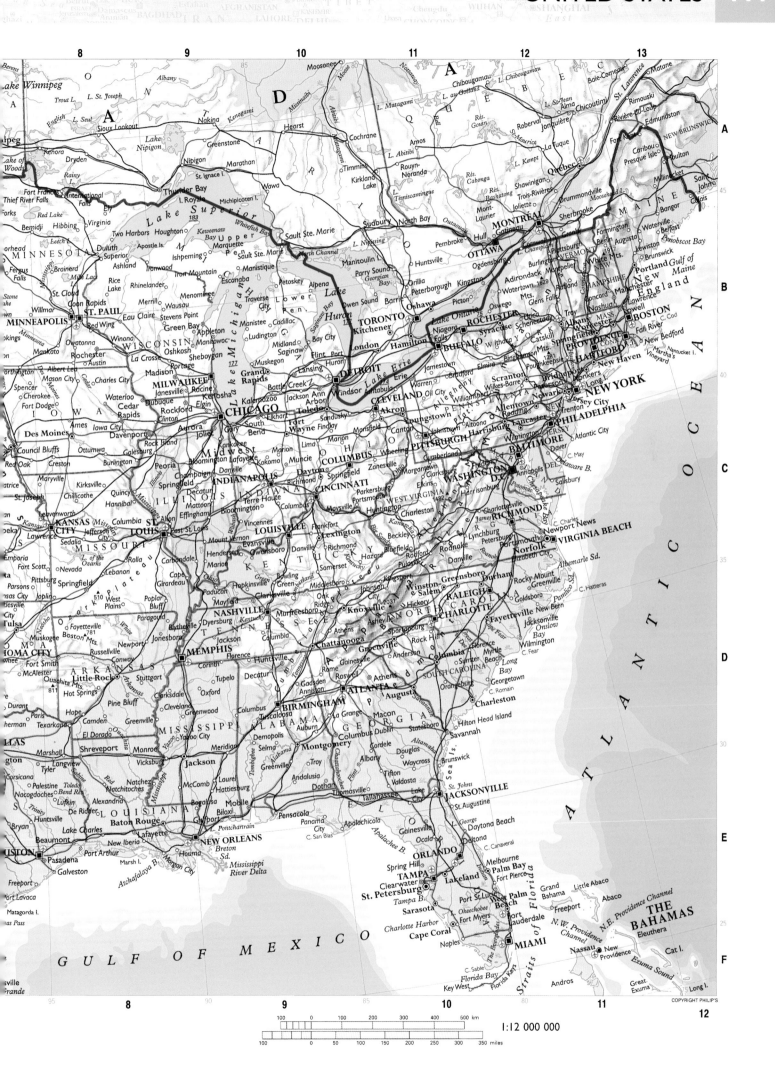

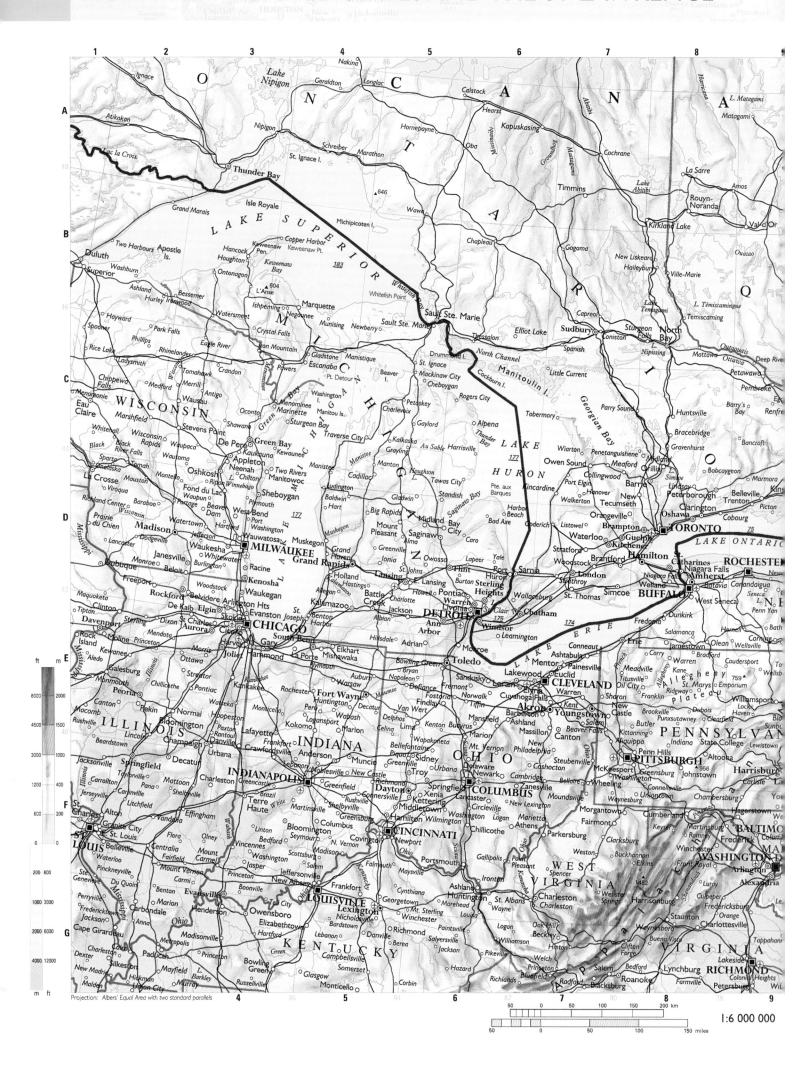

Projection: Albers' Equal Area with two standard parallels

1:6 000 000

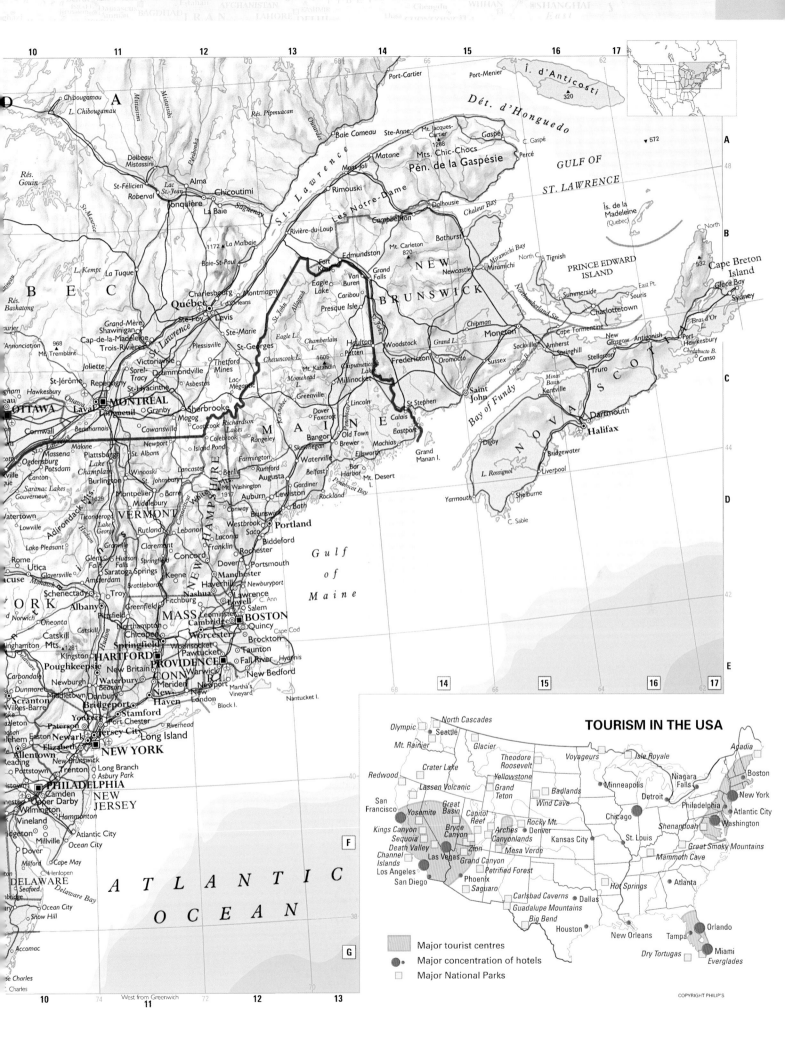

TOURISM IN THE USA

Major tourist centres

Major concentration of hotels

Major National Parks

COPYRIGHT PHILIP'S

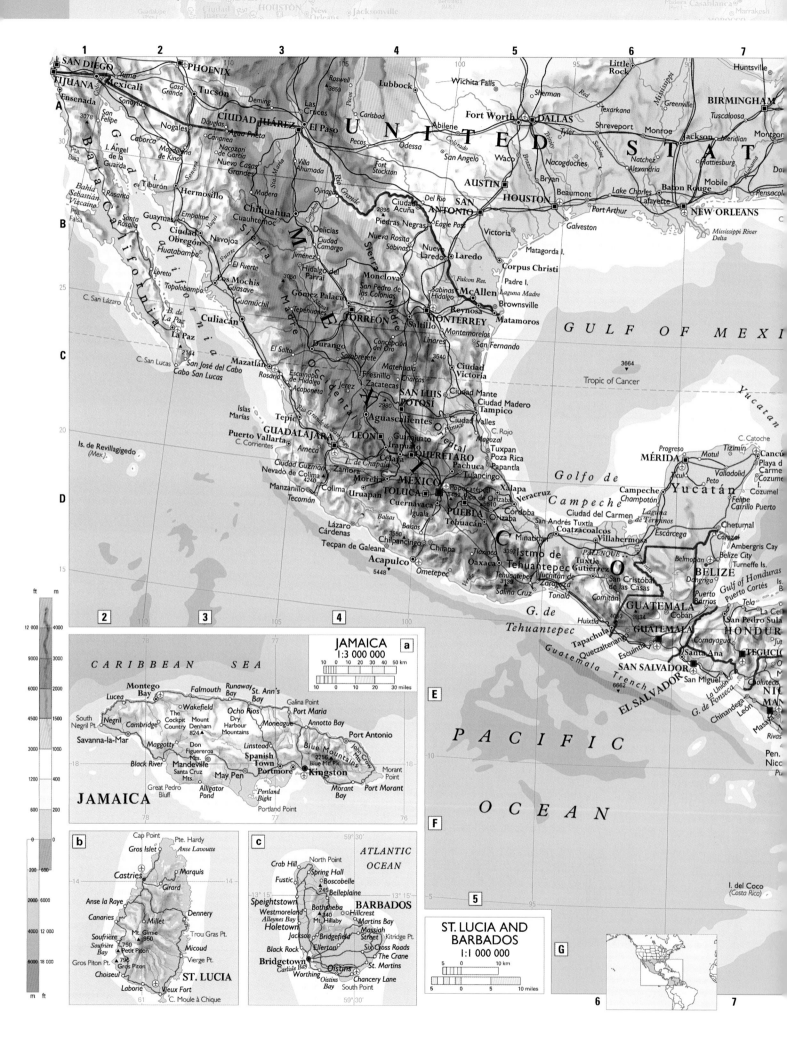

MEXICO, CENTRAL AMERICA AND THE CARIBBEAN

1   2   3   4   5   6   7

SAN FRANCISCO
Lake City   Kansas City   Cincinnati   PHILADELPHIA   PORTUGAL   MADRID
Las Vegas   St. Louis   WASHINGTON   Baltimore   Lisbon   SPAIN
STATES   Memphis   NEW YORK   Azores (Port.)   Rabat   Casablanca   Tangier
Los Angeles   Kansas City   Cincinnati   Marrakech   MOROCCO

SAN DIEGO   PHOENIX   Roswell   Wichita Falls   Little Rock   Huntsville
TIJUANA   Mexicali   Yuma   Casa Grande   Tucson   Lubbock   Memphis
Ensenada   Sonoyta   CIUDAD JUÁREZ   El Paso   UNITED   STAT
Nogales   Douglas   Agua Prieta   Cananea   Las Cruces   Carlsbad   Fort Worth   DALLAS   Texarkana   Tuscaloosa   BIRMINGHAM
I. Ángel de la Guarda   Caborca   Nacozari de García   Abilene   Tyler   Shreveport   Monroe   Jackson   Meridian   Montg
Pta. Baja   Magdalena de Kino   Nuevo Casas Grandes   Odessa   San Angelo   Waco   Nacogdoches   Alexandria   Natchez   Hattiesburg   Mobile   Pensacol
Bahía Sebastián Vizcaíno   Hermosillo   Chihuahua   Villa Ahumada   Ojinaga   Fort Stockton   Del Rio   SAN   HOUSTON   Beaumont   Lake Charles   Baton Rouge
Pta. Falsa   Guaymas   Empalme   Cuauhtémoc   Delicias   Ciudad Acuña   ANTONIO   Port Arthur   Lafayette   NEW ORLEANS
Ciudad Obregón   Navojoa   Ciudad Camargo   Jiménez   Piedras Negras   Eagle Pass   AUSTIN   Bryan   Galveston   Mississippi River Delta
Huatabampo   Los Mochis   El Fuerte   Hidalgo del Parral   Monclova   Nueva Rosita   Sabinas   Nuevo Laredo   Victoria   Matagorda I.
Topolobampo   Guasave   Guamúchil   Gómez Palacio   San Pedro de las Colonias   Sabinas Hidalgo   Laredo   Corpus Christi
C. San Lázaro   Culiacán   TORREÓN   Saltillo   MONTERREY   McAllen   Reynosa   Brownsville   Padre I.   Laguna Madre
La Paz   Durango   Concepción del Oro   Montemorelos   Matamoros   GULF OF MEXI
C. San Lucas   Mazatlán   El Salto   Sombrerete   Linares   San Fernando
San José del Cabo   Rosario   Fresnillo   Zacatecas   Matehuala   Ciudad Victoria   Tropic of Cancer
Cabo San Lucas   Escuinapa de Hidalgo   Charcas   Ciudad Mante
Islas Marías   Acaponeta   Ciudad Madero   Tampico
Is. de Revillagigedo (Mex.)   Tepic   Aguascalientes   SAN LUIS POTOSÍ   Ciudad Valles   C. Rojo   Yucatan
GUADALAJARA   Puerto Vallarta   LEÓN   Guanajuato   Tuxpan   Poza Rica   C. Catoche
C. Corrientes   Ameca   Irapuato   Celaya   QUERÉTARO   Papantla   Progreso   Tizimín   Cancú
L. de Chapala   Zamora   Morelia   Pachuca   Tulancingo   MÉRIDA   Motul   Valladolid   Playa d
Ciudad Guzmán   Uruapan   MEXICO   Xalapa   Golfo de   Ticul   Peto   Cozume
Nevado de Colima   TOLUCA   Popocatépetl   Veracruz   Campeche   Champotón   Yucatán   Cozumel
Manzanillo   Colima   Cuernavaca   Córdoba   Campeche   Ciudad del Carmen   Felipe Carrillo Puerto
Tecomán   PUEBLA   Orizaba   Laguna de Términos   Chetumal
Lázaro Cárdenas   Iguala   Tehuacán   San Andrés Tuxtla   Villahermosa   Escárcega   Corozal   Ambergris Cay
Tecpan de Galeana   Chilpancingo   Chilapa   Oaxaca   Minatitlán   PALENQUE   Belize City   Turneffe Is.
Acapulco   Ometepec   Istmo de Tehuantepec   Coatzacoalcos   Belmopan   Dangriga   Gulf of Honduras
Tuxtla Gutiérrez   San Cristóbal de las Casas   BELIZE   Puerto Barrios   Puerto Cortés
Juchitán de Zaragoza   Comitán   GUATEMALA   San Pedro Sula   Tela   La Cei
G. de Tehuantepec   Salina Cruz   Tonalá   Huixtla   Cobán   HONDUR
Tapachula   GUATEMALA   Santa Ana   TEGUCIG
Quetzaltenango   Escuintla   San Salvador   San Miguel   NIC
Guatemala Trench   SAN SALVADOR   EL SALVADOR   León   MAN
PACIFIC   G. de Fonseca   Chinandega   Masas
Chalchuapa   La Unión   Choluteca   Rivas
OCEAN   Pen. Nico
I. del Coco (Costa Rica)

JAMAICA 1:3 000 000
10   0   10   20   30   40   50 km
10   0   10   20   30 miles

JAMAICA

CARIBBEAN SEA

Montego Bay   Falmouth   Runaway Bay   St. Ann's Bay   Galina Point
Lucea   Wakefield   Ocho Rios   Port Maria
Negril   The Cockpit Country   Mount Denham 824▲   Dry Harbour Mountains   Moneague   Annotto Bay
South Negril Pt.   Cambridge   Maggotty   Don Figuereroa Mts.   Linstead   Blue Mountains   Port Antonio
Savanna-la-Mar   Mandeville   Santa Cruz Mts.   Spanish Town   Blue Mt. Pk. 2256   John Crow Mts.
Black River   May Pen   Portmore   Kingston   Morant Point
Great Pedro Bluff   Alligator Pond   Portland Bight   Morant Bay   Port Morant
Portland Point

---

b
Cap Point   Pte. Hardy
Gros Islet   Anse Lavoutte
Castries   Marquis
Girard
ATLANTIC
Anse la Raye   Dennery   OCEAN
Canaries   Millet   c
Soufrière   Mt. Gimie   Crab Hill   North Point
Soufrière   750 ▲   950   Trou Gras Pt.   Fustic   Spring Hall
Bay   Petit Piton   Micoud   Boscobelle
Gros Piton Pt.   796   Vierge Pt.   Speightstown   Bathsheba   245 Belleplaine
▲ Gros Piton   Westmoreland   BARBADOS
Choiseul   Alleynes Bay   Martins Bay
Laborie   ST. LUCIA   Holetown   Mt. Hillaby   Hillcrest
Vieux Fort   Jackson   ▲340   Massiah
C. Moule à Chique   Black Rock   Bridgefield   Street   Kitridge Pt.
Bridgetown   Ellerton   Six Cross Roads   The Crane
Carlisle Bay   Oistins   St. Martins
Worthing   Oistins Bay   Chancery Lane
South Point

ST. LUCIA AND BARBADOS 1:1 000 000
5   0   5   10 km
5   0   5   10 miles

ft   m
12 000   4000
9000   3000
6000   2000
4500   1500
3000   1000
1200   400
600   200
0   0
200   600
2000   6000
4000   12 000
6000   18 000
m   ft

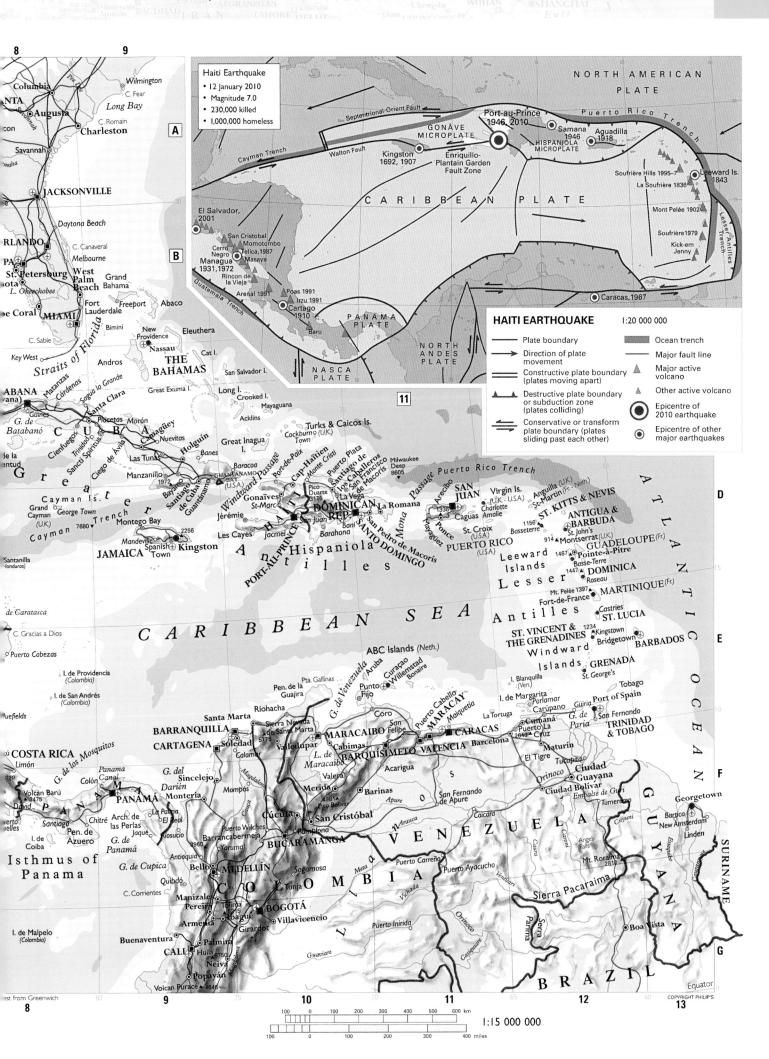

8 **9**

Columbia
Wilmington
C. Fear
Long Bay
Augusta
Charleston
C. Romain
Savannah

A

JACKSONVILLE

Daytona Beach
ORLANDO
C. Canaveral
Melbourne
West Palm Beach
St. Petersburg
Grand Bahama
L. Okeechobee
Coral
MIAMI
C. Sable
Fort Lauderdale
Freeport
Abaco

B

Key West
New Providence
Eleuthera
Nassau
THE BAHAMAS
Andros
San Salvador I.
Cat I.
Straits of Florida
ABANA
Matanzas
Cárdenas
Sagua la Grande
Great Exuma I.
Long I.
Santa Clara
Crooked I.
G. de Batabanó
Güines
Placetas
Morón
Camagüey
Mayaguana
Acklins
CUBA
Cienfuegos
Trinidad
Sancti Spíritus
Ciego de Ávila
Nuevitas
Turks & Caicos Is.
Cockburn
Town (U.K.)
entud
Manzanillo
Las Tunas
Holguín
Banes
Great Inagua I.
Bayamo
Baracoa
Santiago de Cuba
GUANTÁNAMO BAY (U.S.A.)
Cayman Is.
Grand Cayman (U.K.)
George Town
7680
Cayman Trench
Montego Bay
2256
Mandeville
Spanish Town
Kingston
Santanilla (Honduras)
JAMAICA

HAITI EARTHQUAKE Inset

Haiti Earthquake
• 12 January 2010
• Magnitude 7.0
• 230,000 killed
• 1,000,000 homeless

NORTH AMERICAN PLATE

Septentrional-Orient Fault
Puerto Rico Trench
Port-au-Prince 1946, 2010
Samana 1946
Aguadilla 1918
GONÂVE MICROPLATE
HISPANIOLA MICROPLATE
Cayman Trench
Walton Fault
Kingston 1692, 1907
Enriquillo-Plantain Garden Fault Zone
Soufrière Hills 1995-7
Leeward Is. 1843
La Soufrière 1836
CARIBBEAN PLATE
Mont Pelée 1902
El Salvador, 2001
San Cristobal
Momotombo
Telica, 1987
Soufrière 1979
Cerro Negro
Masaya
Kick-em Jenny
Managua 1931,1972
Rincon de la Vieja
Guatemala Trench
Arenal 1991
Poas 1991
Irzu 1991
Caracas,1967
Cartago 1910
PANAMA PLATE
Baru
NORTH ANDES PLATE
NASCA PLATE

HAITI EARTHQUAKE 1:20 000 000

— Plate boundary
→ Direction of plate movement
═ Constructive plate boundary (plates moving apart)
▲ Destructive plate boundary or subduction zone (plates colliding)
⇄ Conservative or transform plate boundary (plates sliding past each other)
▨ Ocean trench
— Major fault line
▲ Major active volcano
▲ Other active volcano
◉ Epicentre of 2010 earthquake
◉ Epicentre of other major earthquakes

11

Port-de-Paix
Cap-Haïtien
Monte Cristi
Puerto Plata
Santiago de los Caballeros
San Francisco de Macorís
Milwaukee Deep 8605
Puerto Rico Trench
Gonaïves
St-Marc
Pico Duarte 3175
La Vega
Mona Passage
Arecibo
SAN JUAN
Virgin Is. (U.K. - U.S.A.)
Anguilla (U.K.)
St-Martin (Fr.- Neth.)
HAITI
DOMINICAN REP.
La Romana
1338
Charlotte Amalie
ST. KITTS & NEVIS
Jérémie
PORT-AU-PRINCE
San Juan
Caguas
914
Montserrat (U.K.)
ANTIGUA & BARBUDA
St. John's
Les Cayes
Jacmel
Bani
SANTO DOMINGO
San Pedro de Macorís
Mayagüez
Ponce
St. Croix (U.S.A.)
1156
Basseterre
Barahona
PUERTO RICO (U.S.A.)
GUADELOUPE (Fr.)
Hispaniola
Antilles
Leeward Islands
1467
Pointe-à-Pitre
Basse-Terre
1447
DOMINICA
Roseau
Lesser
Mt. Pelée 1397
MARTINIQUE (Fr.)
Fort-de-France
Castries
ST. LUCIA
Antilles
ST. VINCENT & THE GRENADINES
1234
Kingstown
Windward
Bridgetown
BARBADOS
Islands
GRENADA
St. George's
ATLANTIC OCEAN

CARIBBEAN SEA

de Caratasca
C. Gracias a Dios
Puerto Cabezas
I. de Providencia (Colombia)
I. de San Andrés (Colombia)
uefields
ABC Islands (Neth.)
Aruba
Curaçao
Willemstad
Bonaire
Pta. Gallinas
Pen. de la Guajira
Punto Fijo
I. Blanquilla (Ven.)
Tobago
I. de Margarita
Porlamar
St. George's
Ríohacha
Santa Marta
Sierra Nevada de Santa Marta
Coro
San Felipe
Puerto Cabello
MARACAY
Maiquetía
La Tortuga
Carúpano
Güiria Port of Spain
TRINIDAD & TOBAGO
COSTA RICA
Limón
BARRANQUILLA
Soledad
Calamar
Valledupar
MARACAIBO
CARACAS
Cumaná
Puerto La Cruz
2640
San Fernando
G. de Paria
CARTAGENA
Cabimas
BARQUISIMETO
VALENCIA
Barcelona
Maturín
G. de los Mosquitos
Panama Canal
G. del Sincelejo
Darién
Montería
Mompós
L. de Maracaibo
Valera
Acarigua
El Tigre
Tucupita
Ciudad Guayana
Volcán Barú 3475
PANAMÁ
Colón
4981
Mérida
Pico Bolívar
Barinas
Apure
San Fernando de Apure
Orinoco
Ciudad Bolívar
Embalse de Guri
David
Santiago
Chitré
Arch. de las Perlas
La Palma
El Real
Ríosucio
Cúcuta
Pamplona
Caicara
Angel Falls
Tumeremo
Georgetown
Bartica
New Amsterdam
I. de Coiba
Pen. de Azuero
G. de Panamá
Jaqué
3960
Barrancabermeja
Yarumal
Puerto Wilches
BUCARAMANGA
San Cristóbal
Arauca
Cuyuni
Mt. Roraima 2810
Linden
Isthmus of Panama
Antioquia
Bello
MEDELLÍN
Sogamoso
VENEZUELA
Puerto Carreño
Puerto Ayacucho
SURINAME
Quibdó
Sierra Pacaraima
Boa Vista
C. Corrientes
COLOMBIA
Tunja
Meta
Vichada
GUYANA
Manizales
Pereira
Tolima
5215
Ibagué
BOGOTÁ
Villavicencio
Puerto Inírida
Orinoco
I. de Malpelo (Colombia)
Armenia
Girardot
Sierra Parima
Buenaventura
Palmira
Guaviare
CALI
Huila 5750
Casiquiare
BRAZIL
Neiva
Popayán
Volcán Puracé 4646
Equator
COPYRIGHT PHILIP'S

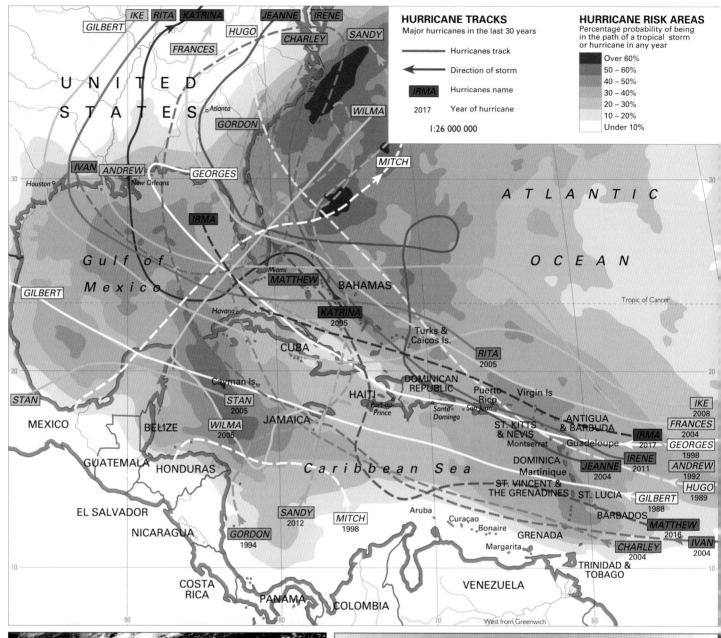

HURRICANE TRACKS
Major hurricanes in the last 30 years

— Hurricanes track

← Direction of storm

IRMA Hurricanes name

2017 Year of hurricane

1:26 000 000

HURRICANE RISK AREAS
Percentage probability of being in the path of a tropical storm or hurricane in any year

- Over 60%
- 50 – 60%
- 40 – 50%
- 30 – 40%
- 20 – 30%
- 10 – 20%
- Under 10%

Hurricane Irma, with winds of 295km per hour, was the most powerful in over ten years when it made landfall on Barbuda in September 2017. It caused catastrophic damage in St. Barthélemy, St. Martin, Anguilla and the Virgin Islands.

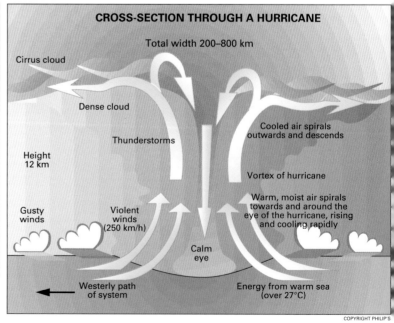

CROSS-SECTION THROUGH A HURRICANE

Total width 200–800 km

Cirrus cloud

Dense cloud

Thunderstorms

Cooled air spirals outwards and descends

Vortex of hurricane

Height 12 km

Warm, moist air spirals towards and around the eye of the hurricane, rising and cooling rapidly

Gusty winds

Violent winds (250 km/h)

Calm eye

Westerly path of system

Energy from warm sea (over 27°C)

COPYRIGHT PHILIP'S

Projection: Lambert's Azimuthal Equal Area

1:35 000 000

West from Greenwich

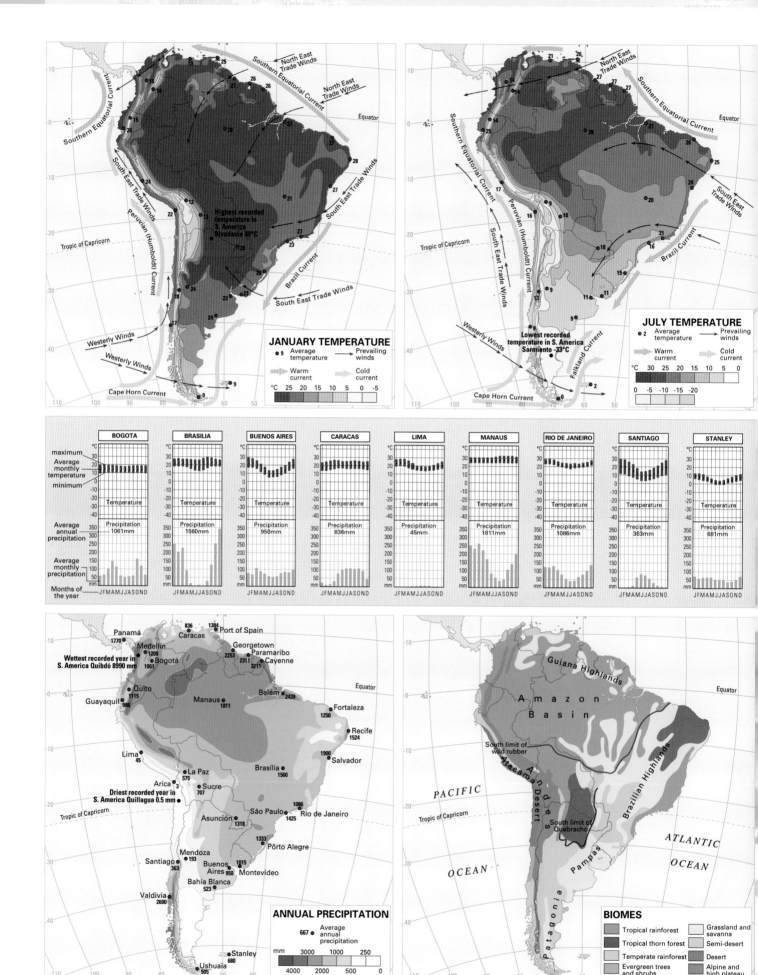

JANUARY TEMPERATURE
- 9 Average temperature
- → Prevailing winds
- Warm current
- Cold current
- °C 25 20 15 10 5 0 -5

Highest recorded temperature in S. America Rivadavia 49°C

North East Trade Winds
Southern Equatorial Current
North East Trade Winds
Southern Equatorial Current
Equator
South East Trade Winds
Peruvian (Humboldt) Current
Southern Equatorial Current
Tropic of Capricorn
Brazil Current
South East Trade Winds
Westerly Winds
Westerly Winds
Cape Horn Current

JULY TEMPERATURE
- 2 Average temperature
- → Prevailing winds
- Warm current
- Cold current
- °C 30 25 20 15 10 5 0
- 0 -5 -10 -15 -20

North East Trade Winds
Southern Equatorial Current
Equator
Southern Equatorial Current
Peruvian (Humboldt) Current
South East Trade Winds
Tropic of Capricorn
South East Trade Winds
Brazil Current
Westerly Winds
Lowest recorded temperature in S. America Sarmiento -33°C
Falkland Current
Cape Horn Current

Climate graphs: BOGOTA, BRASILIA, BUENOS AIRES, CARACAS, LIMA, MANAUS, RIO DE JANEIRO, SANTIAGO, STANLEY

- maximum
- Average monthly temperature
- minimum
- Average annual precipitation
- Average monthly precipitation
- Months of the year

Temperature / Precipitation values:
- BOGOTA — 1061mm
- BRASILIA — 1560mm
- BUENOS AIRES — 950mm
- CARACAS — 836mm
- LIMA — 45mm
- MANAUS — 1811mm
- RIO DE JANEIRO — 1086mm
- SANTIAGO — 363mm
- STANLEY — 681mm

ANNUAL PRECIPITATION
- 667 Average annual precipitation
- mm 3000 1000 250
- 4000 2000 500 0

Panamá 1770
Caracas 836
Port of Spain 1384
Medellín 1200
Bogotá 1061
Georgetown 2253
Paramaribo 2311
Cayenne 3211
Wettest recorded year in S. America Quibdó 8990 mm
Quito 1115
Guayaquil 986
Manaus 1811
Belém 2439
Fortaleza 1250
Recife 1524
Lima 45
La Paz 575
Arica 3
Sucre 707
Driest recorded year in S. America Quillagua 0.5 mm
Salvador 1900
Brasília 1560
São Paulo 1425
Rio de Janeiro 1086
Asunción 1318
Pôrto Alegre 1333
Mendoza 193
Santiago 363
Buenos Aires 950
Bahía Blanca 523
Montevideo 1015
Valdivia 2600
Stanley 680
Ushuaia 505

BIOMES
- Tropical rainforest
- Tropical thorn forest
- Temperate rainforest
- Evergreen trees and shrubs
- Grassland and savanna
- Semi-desert
- Desert
- Alpine and high plateau

Guiana Highlands
Amazon Basin
South limit of wild rubber
Andes
Atacama Desert
South limit of Quebracho
Brazilian Highlands
PACIFIC OCEAN
Pampas
ATLANTIC OCEAN
Patagonia
Tropic of Capricorn
Equator

Projection: Lambert's Equivalent Azimuthal

COPYRIGHT PHILIP'S

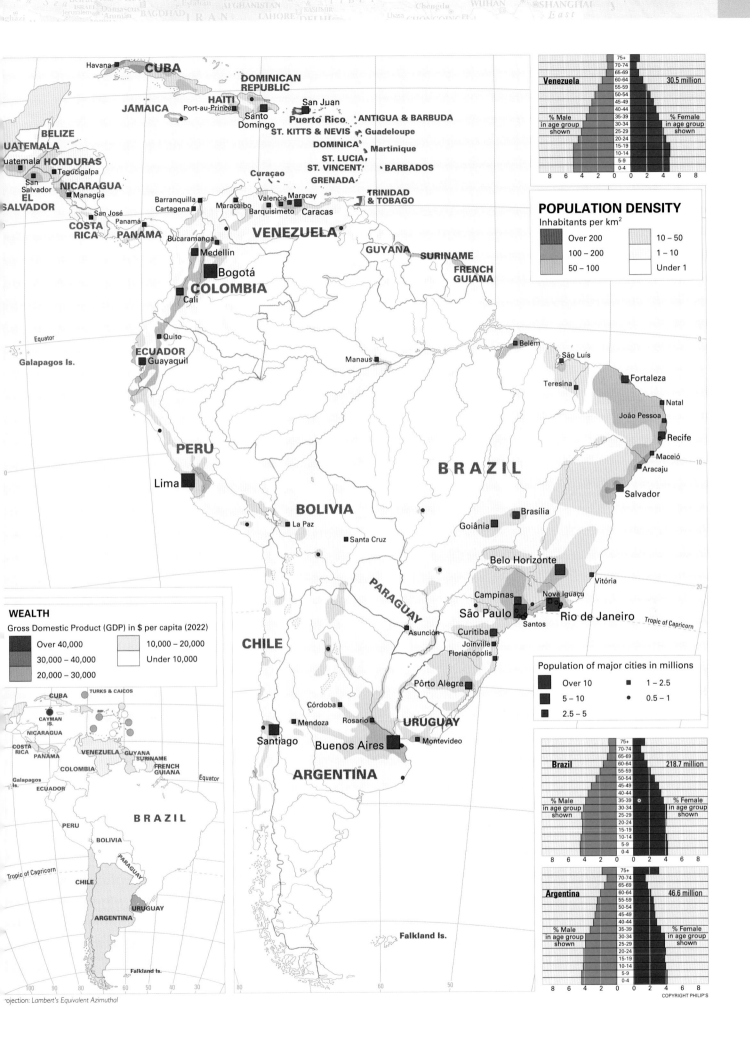

Venezuela   30.5 million

% Male in age group shown   % Female in age group shown

75+
70-74
65-69
60-64
55-59
50-54
45-49
40-44
35-39
30-34
25-29
20-24
15-19
10-14
5-9
0-4

8 6 4 2 0 0 2 4 6 8

POPULATION DENSITY

Inhabitants per km²

Over 200
100 – 200
50 – 100
10 – 50
1 – 10
Under 1

WEALTH

Gross Domestic Product (GDP) in $ per capita (2022)

Over 40,000
30,000 – 40,000
20,000 – 30,000
10,000 – 20,000
Under 10,000

Population of major cities in millions

Over 10
5 – 10
2.5 – 5
1 – 2.5
0.5 – 1

Brazil   218.7 million

% Male in age group shown   % Female in age group shown

75+
70-74
65-69
60-64
55-59
50-54
45-49
40-44
35-39
30-34
25-29
20-24
15-19
10-14
5-9
0-4

8 6 4 2 0 0 2 4 6 8

Argentina   46.6 million

% Male in age group shown   % Female in age group shown

75+
70-74
65-69
60-64
55-59
50-54
45-49
40-44
35-39
30-34
25-29
20-24
15-19
10-14
5-9
0-4

8 6 4 2 0 0 2 4 6 8

Projection: Lambert's Equivalent Azimuthal

COPYRIGHT PHILIP'S

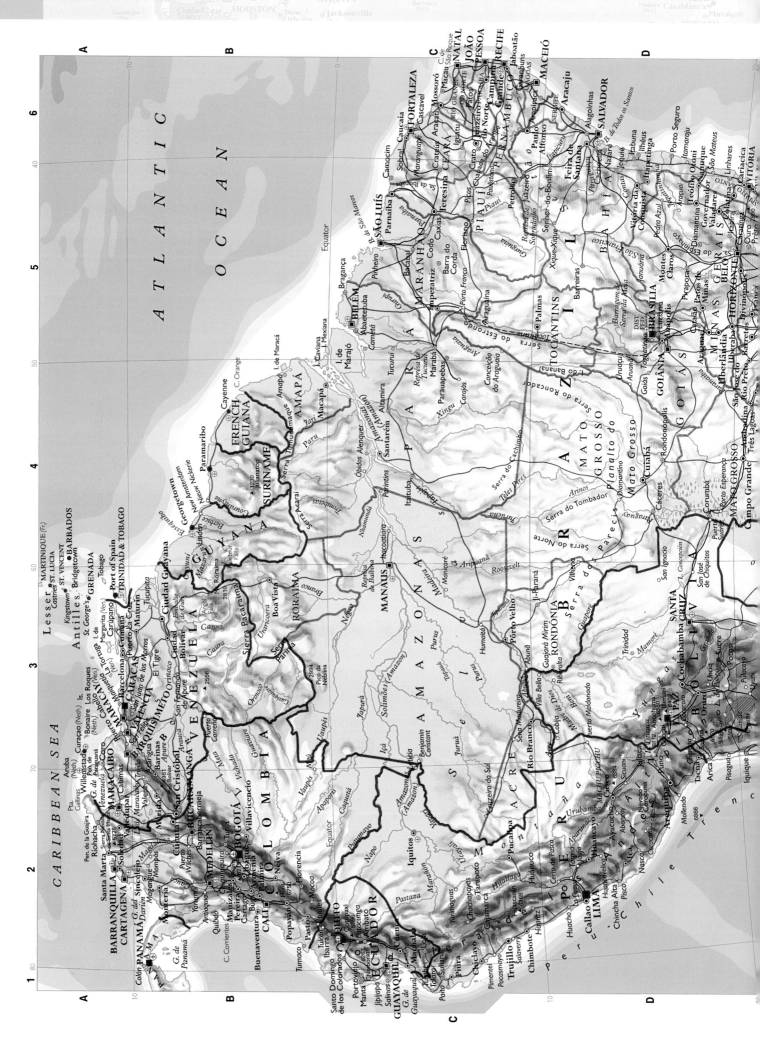

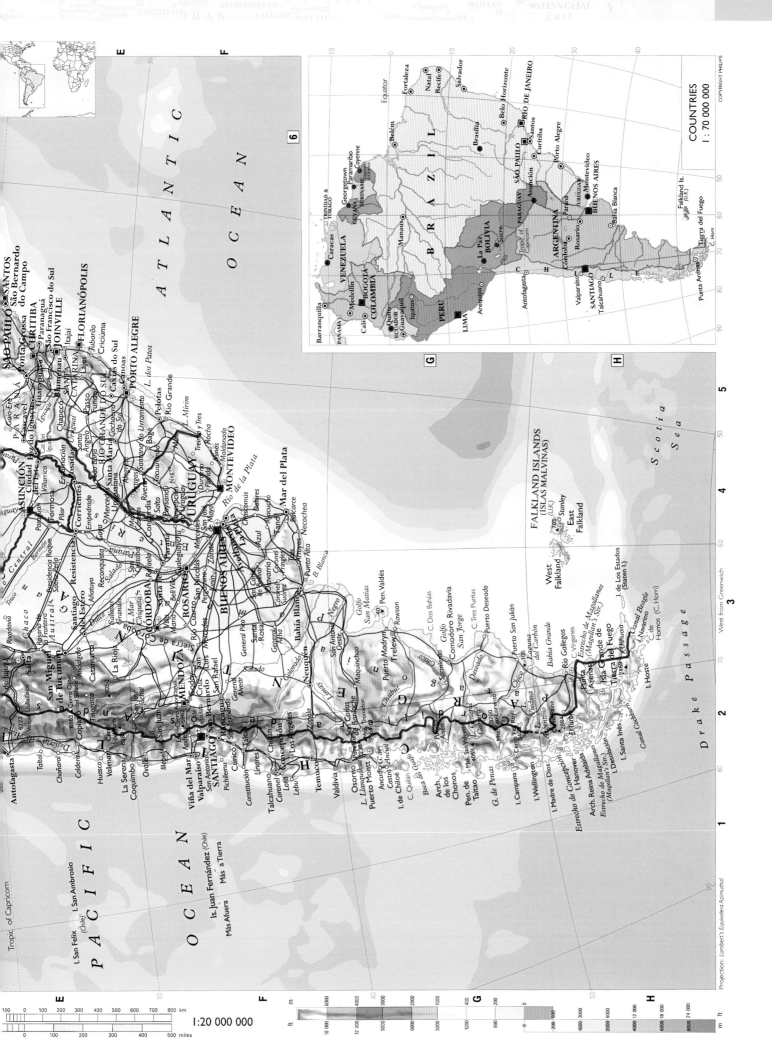

ATLANTIC

ATLANTIC OCEAN

Projection : Lambert's Equivalent Azimuthal

West from Greenwich

1:8 000 000

50   0   50   100   150   200   250   300 km

50   0   50   100   150   200 miles

WORLD THEMES

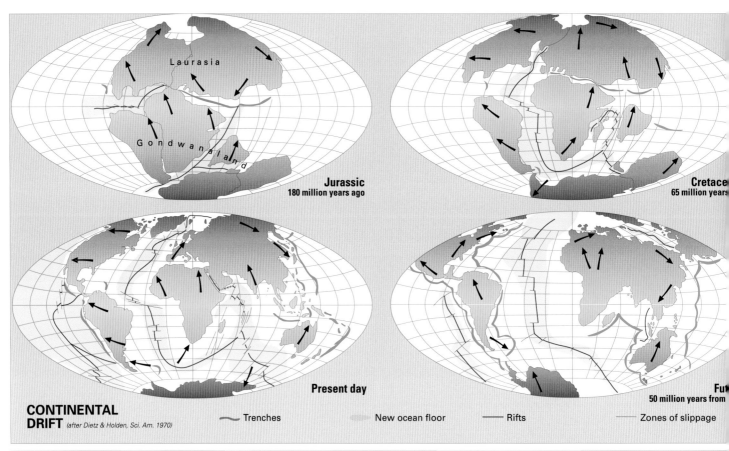

Jurassic
180 million years ago

Cretaceous
65 million years

Present day

Future
50 million years from

CONTINENTAL DRIFT *(after Dietz & Holden, Sci. Am. 1970)*

〜 Trenches   ▨ New ocean floor   — Rifts   — Zones of slippage

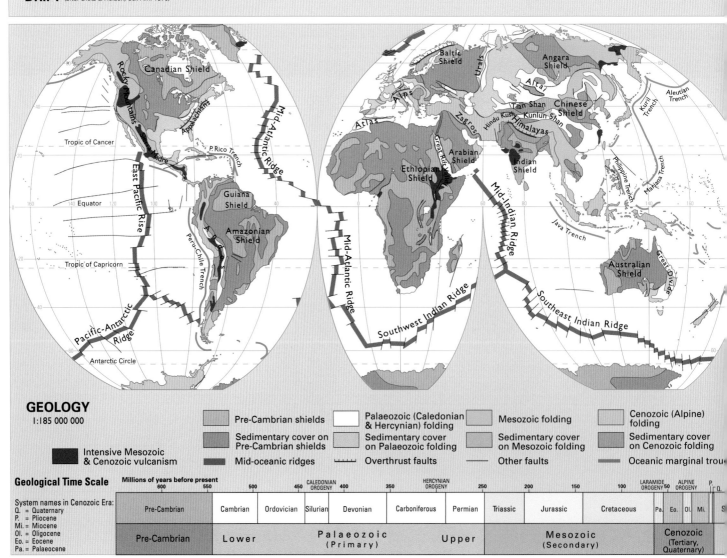

GEOLOGY
1:185 000 000

■ Intensive Mesozoic & Cenozoic vulcanism

Pre-Cambrian shields	Palaeozoic (Caledonian & Hercynian) folding
Sedimentary cover on Pre-Cambrian shields	Sedimentary cover on Palaeozoic folding
Mid-oceanic ridges	Overthrust faults
Mesozoic folding	Cenozoic (Alpine) folding
Sedimentary cover on Mesozoic folding	Sedimentary cover on Cenozoic folding
Other faults	Oceanic marginal trough

Geological Time Scale

System names in Cenozoic Era:
Q. = Quaternary
P. = Pliocene
Mi. = Miocene
Ol. = Oligocene
Eo. = Eocene
Pa. = Palaeocene

Millions of years before present														
600	550	500	450	400	350	250	200	150	100	50				
			CALEDONIAN OROGENY			HERCYNIAN OROGENY				LARAMIDE OROGENY	ALPINE OROGENY			
Pre-Cambrian		Cambrian	Ordovician	Silurian	Devonian	Carboniferous	Permian	Triassic	Jurassic	Cretaceous	Pa.	Eo.	Ol.	Mi.
Pre-Cambrian		Lower			Palaeozoic (Primary)		Upper	Mesozoic (Secondary)			Cenozoic (Tertiary, Quaternary)			

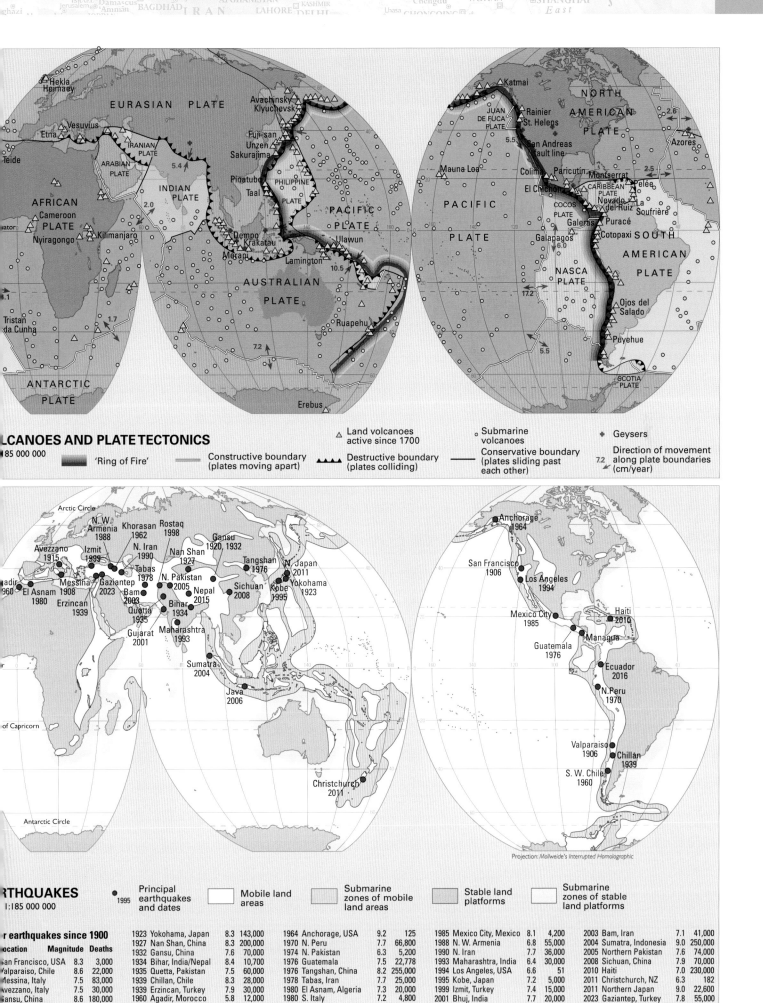

VOLCANOES AND PLATE TECTONICS

1:85 000 000

███ 'Ring of Fire'	
══════ Constructive boundary (plates moving apart)	△ Land volcanoes active since 1700
▲▲▲ Destructive boundary (plates colliding)	○ Submarine volcanoes
	────── Conservative boundary (plates sliding past each other)
	✦ Geysers
	7.2 ⬌ Direction of movement along plate boundaries (cm/year)

EARTHQUAKES

1:185 000 000

● 1995 Principal earthquakes and dates	▢ Mobile land areas
▢ Submarine zones of mobile land areas	▢ Stable land platforms
▢ Submarine zones of stable land platforms	

Major earthquakes since 1900

Location	Magnitude	Deaths								
San Francisco, USA	8.3	3,000	1923 Yokohama, Japan	8.3	143,000	1964 Anchorage, USA	9.2	125	1985 Mexico City, Mexico	8.1	4,200	2003 Bam, Iran	7.1	41,000
Valparaiso, Chile	8.6	22,000	1927 Nan Shan, China	8.3	200,000	1970 N. Peru	7.7	66,800	1988 N. W. Armenia	6.8	55,000	2004 Sumatra, Indonesia	9.0	250,000
Messina, Italy	7.5	83,000	1932 Gansu, China	7.6	70,000	1974 N. Pakistan	6.3	5,200	1990 N. Iran	7.7	36,000	2005 Northern Pakistan	7.6	74,000
Avezzano, Italy	7.5	30,000	1934 Bihar, India/Nepal	8.4	10,700	1976 Guatemala	7.5	22,778	1993 Maharashtra, India	6.4	30,000	2008 Sichuan, China	7.9	70,000
Gansu, China	8.6	180,000	1935 Quetta, Pakistan	7.5	60,000	1976 Tangshan, China	8.2	255,000	1994 Los Angeles, USA	6.6	51	2010 Haiti	7.0	230,000
			1939 Chillan, Chile	8.3	28,000	1978 Tabas, Iran	7.7	25,000	1995 Kobe, Japan	7.2	5,000	2011 Christchurch, NZ	6.3	182
			1939 Erzincan, Turkey	7.9	30,000	1980 El Asnam, Algeria	7.3	20,000	1999 Izmit, Turkey	7.4	15,000	2011 Northern Japan	9.0	22,600
			1960 Agadir, Morocco	5.8	12,000	1980 S. Italy	7.2	4,800	2001 Bhuj, India	7.7	20,000	2023 Gaziantep, Turkey	7.8	55,000

Projection: Mollweide's Interrupted Homolographic

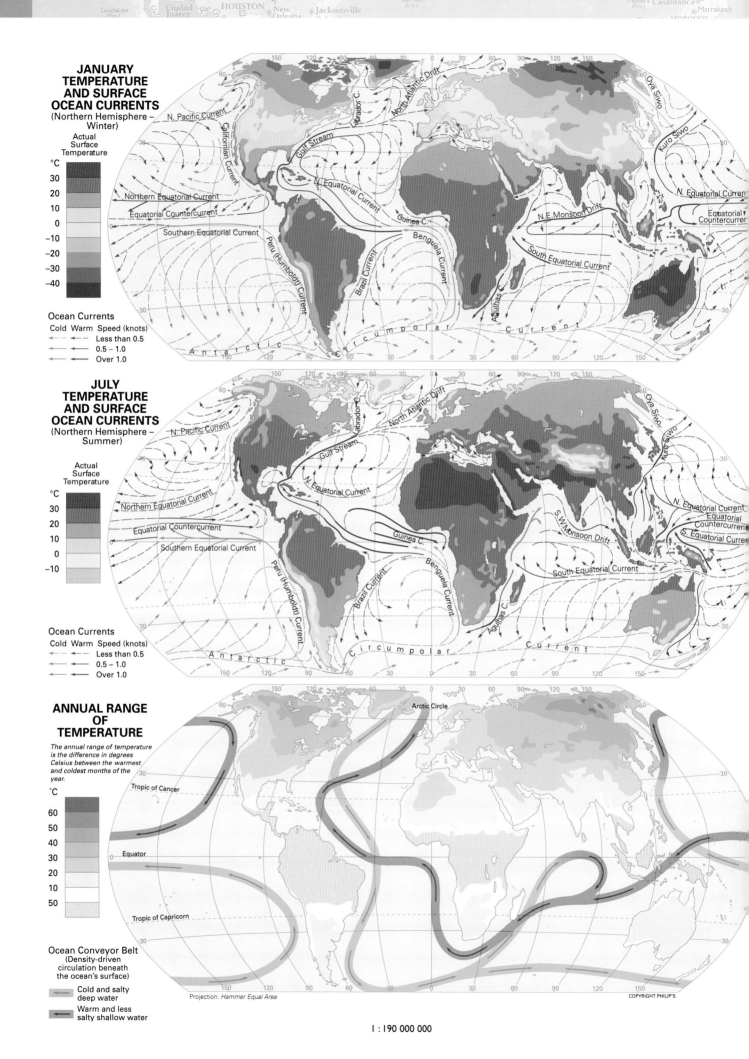

JANUARY TEMPERATURE AND SURFACE OCEAN CURRENTS
(Northern Hemisphere – Winter)

Actual Surface Temperature

°C
30
20
10
0
-10
-20
-30
-40

Ocean Currents

Cold	Warm	Speed (knots)
		Less than 0.5
		0.5 – 1.0
		Over 1.0

JULY TEMPERATURE AND SURFACE OCEAN CURRENTS
(Northern Hemisphere – Summer)

Actual Surface Temperature

°C
30
20
10
0
-10

Ocean Currents

Cold	Warm	Speed (knots)
		Less than 0.5
		0.5 – 1.0
		Over 1.0

ANNUAL RANGE OF TEMPERATURE

The annual range of temperature is the difference in degrees Celsius between the warmest and coldest months of the year.

°C
60
50
40
30
20
10
50

Ocean Conveyor Belt
(Density-driven circulation beneath the ocean's surface)

Cold and salty deep water

Warm and less salty shallow water

Projection: Hammer Equal Area

COPYRIGHT PHILIP'S

1 : 190 000 000

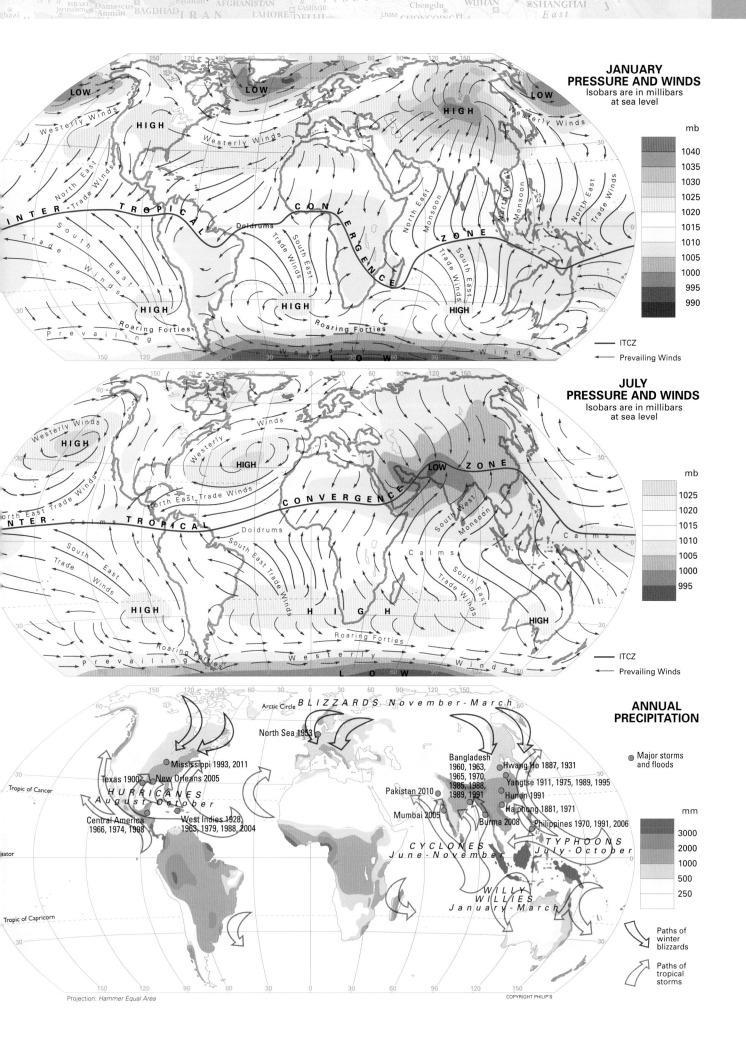

JANUARY
PRESSURE AND WINDS
Isobars are in millibars
at sea level

mb
1040
1035
1030
1025
1020
1015
1010
1005
1000
995
990

ITCZ
Prevailing Winds

JULY
PRESSURE AND WINDS
Isobars are in millibars
at sea level

mb
1025
1020
1015
1010
1005
1000
995

ITCZ
Prevailing Winds

ANNUAL
PRECIPITATION

Major storms
and floods

mm
3000
2000
1000
500
250

Paths of
winter
blizzards

Paths of
tropical
storms

Projection: Hammer Equal Area

COPYRIGHT PHILIP'S

KEY TO CLIMATE REGIONS MAP

Climate group	Climate	Temperature	Rainfall
A TROPICAL RAINY CLIMATES	**Af** RAIN FOREST CLIMATE / **Am** MONSOON CLIMATE / **Aw** SAVANNA CLIMATE	All mean monthly temperatures above 18°C	*Rainfall during the driest month (mm)* chart: Af, Aw, Am vs Annual rainfall (mm) 0–3000
B DRY CLIMATES	**BS** STEPPE CLIMATE / **BW** DESERT CLIMATE	Mean annual temperature. **h** = above 18°C, **k** = below 18°C	BW/BS boundary, BS/Wet Climates Boundary chart; Mean annual temperature (°C) vs Annual rainfall (mm); Wet Climates A,C,D. --- summer rainfall, — winter rainfall, -·- rainfall evenly distributed
C WARM TEMPERATE RAINY CLIMATES	**Cw** DRY WINTER CLIMATE / **Cs** DRY SUMMER CLIMATE (Mediterranean) / **Cf** CLIMATE WITH NO DRY SEASON	Mean temperature of the coldest month between −3°C to 18°C	**a** Mean temperature of hottest month above 22°C, and with more than 4 months of over 10°C. **b** Mean temperature of hottest month below 22°C and with more than 4 months of over 10°C.	**w** dry winter — Rainfall of the driest month of the cold season is one-tenth or less of the rainfall of the wettest month of the hot season. **s** dry summer — Rainfall of the driest month of the hot season is less than one-third of the rainfall of the wettest month of the cold season and less than 40mm.
D COLD TEMPERATE RAINY CLIMATES	**Dw** DRY WINTER CLIMATE / **Df** CLIMATE WITH NO DRY SEASON	Mean temperature of the coldest month below −3°C	**c** Mean temperature of hottest month below 22°C, but with less than 4 months of over 10°C. **d** Mean temperature of hottest month below 22°C, and of the coldest month below −38°C.	**f** with no dry season — Rainfall does not correspond to **w** or **s** climates
E POLAR CLIMATES	**ET** TUNDRA CLIMATE / **EF** PERPETUAL FROST	Mean temperature of the hottest month below 10°C. Mean temperature of the hottest month between 0°C and 10°C. Mean temperature of the hottest month below 0°C	**H** More than 1500m above sea level

CLIMATE RECORDS

Highest recorded temperature: Death Valley, California, USA, 56.7°C, 10 July 1913.

Lowest recorded temperature (outside poles): Verkhoyansk, Siberia, −68°C, 7 February 1892. Verkhoyansk also registered the greatest annual range of temperature: −68°C to 37°C.

Highest barometric pressure: Agata, Siberia, 1,083.8 mb at altitude 262 m, 31 December 1968.

Lowest barometric pressure: Typhoon Tip, 480 km west of Guam, Pacific Ocean, 870 mb, 12 October 1979.

Driest place: Quillagua, N. Chile, 0.5 mm, 1964–2001.

Wettest place (12 months): Cherrapunji, Meghalaya, N.E. India: 26,461 mm, August 1860 to August 1861. Cherrapunji also holds the record for rainfall in one month: 2930 mm, July 1861.

Highest recorded wind speed: Mt Washington, New Hampshire, USA, 371 km/h, 12 April 1934. This is three times as strong as hurricane force on the Beaufort Scale.

Windiest place: Commonwealth Bay, George V Coast, Antarctica, where gales frequently reach over 320 km/h.

Projection: Interrupted Mollweide's Homolographic

WINDCHILL FACTOR

In sub-zero weather, even moderate winds significantly reduce effective temperatures. The chart below shows the windchill effect across a range of speeds.

	Wind speed in kilometres per hour				
	16	32	48	64	80
0°C	−8	−14	−17	−19	−20
−5°C	−14	−21	−25	−27	−28
−10°C	−20	−28	−33	−35	−36
−15°C	−26	−36	−40	−43	−44
−20°C	−32	−42	−48	−51	−52
−25°C	−38	−49	−56	−59	−60
−30°C	−44	−57	−63	−66	−68
−35°C	−51	−64	−72	−74	−76
−40°C	−57	−71	−78	−82	−84
−45°C	−63	−78	−86	−90	−92
−50°C	−69	−85	−94	−98	−100

ITCZ AND ATMOSPHERIC CIRCULATION

The Trade Winds converge on the Earth's surface at the Inter-Tropical Convergence Zone (ITCZ), where the hot and moist air rises rapidly to the upper limit of the Earth's troposphere to be carried by the Hadley Cell towards the mid-latitudes where it descends as dry air. Two lesser circulation cells – the Ferrel Cell and the Polar Cell carry the air further towards the Poles. The pattern of this circulation may vary from year to year and may affect the huge Pacific Cell, resulting in El Niño or La Niña events – see diagrams opposite.

High pressure
Low pressure
Warm air
Cold air
Surface winds
Clouds

Polar Jet
Subtropical Jet
Ferrel Cell
Polar Cell
Hadley Cell
North Pole
EASTERLY WINDS
SOUTHWESTERLY WINDS
NORTHEASTERLY TRADES
ITCZ Inter-Tropical Convergence Zone
Equator
DOLDRU
SOUTHEASTERLY TRADES

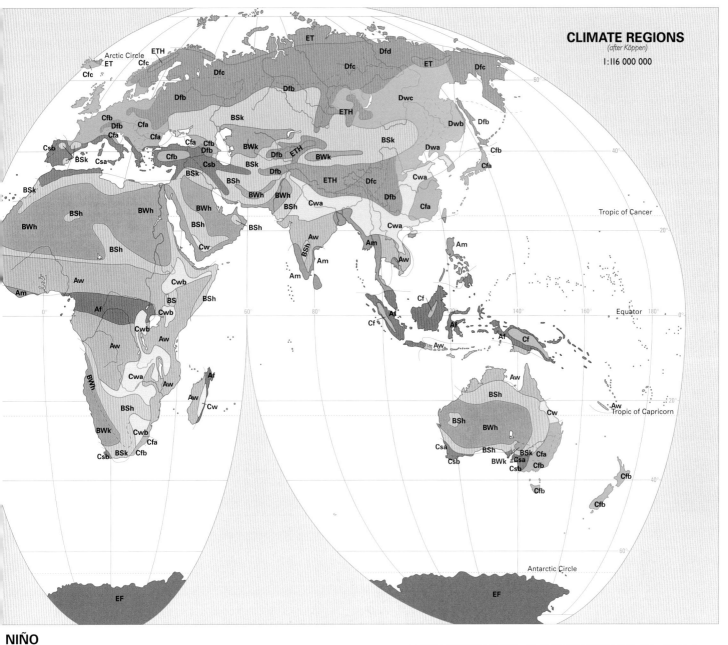

CLIMATE REGIONS
(after Köppen)
1:116 000 000

NIÑO

iño, 'The Little Boy' in Spanish, was the name given by local fishermen to the warm
ent that can appear off the Pacific coast of South America. In a normal year,
h-easterly trade winds drive surface waters westwards off the coast of South America,
ving cold, nutrient-rich water up from below. In an El Niño year, warm water from the
t Pacific suppresses upwelling in the east, depriving the region of nutrients and driving
fish away. The water is warmed by as much as 7°C, disturbing the circulation of the Pacific
. During an intense El Niño, the south-east trade winds change direction and become
atorial westerlies, resulting in climatic extremes in many regions of the world, such as
ught in parts of Australia and India, and heavy rainfall in the SE USA.

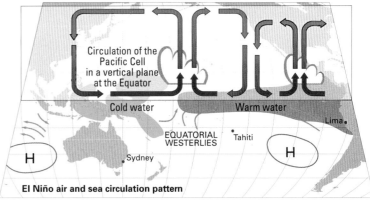

El Niño air and sea circulation pattern

El Niño events occur about every 4 to 7 years and typically last for around 12 to 18
months. El Niño usually results in reduced rainfall across northern and eastern Australia.
This can lead to widespread and severe drought, as well as increased temperatures and
bushfire risk. However, each El Niño event is unique in terms of its strength as well as its
impact. It is measured by the Southern Oscillation Index (SOI) and the changes in ocean
temperatures.
La Niña, or 'The Little Girl', is associated with cooler waters in the central and eastern
Pacific. A La Niña year can result in cooler land temperatures across the tropics and
subtropics and more storms in the North Atlantic.

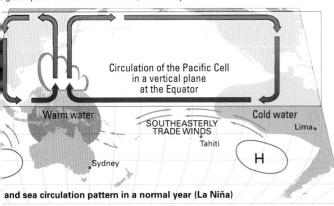

and sea circulation pattern in a normal year (La Niña)

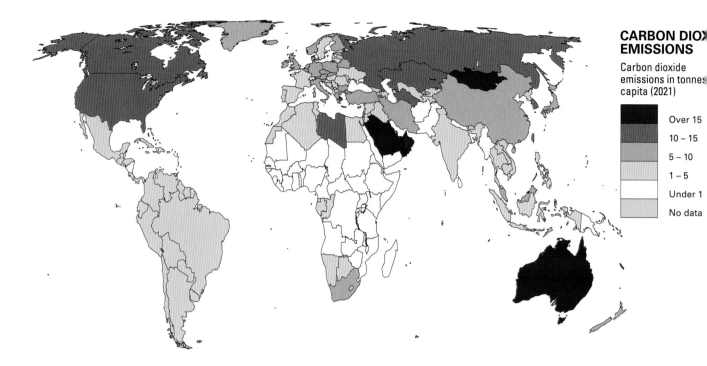

CARBON DIOX[IDE] EMISSIONS

Carbon dioxide emissions in tonnes [per] capita (2021)

- Over 15
- 10 – 15
- 5 – 10
- 1 – 5
- Under 1
- No data

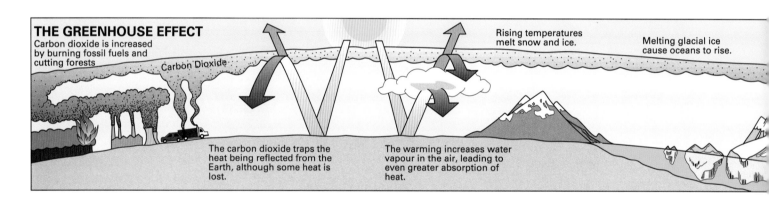

THE GREENHOUSE EFFECT

Carbon dioxide is increased by burning fossil fuels and cutting forests

Carbon Dioxide

Rising temperatures melt snow and ice.

Melting glacial ice cause oceans to rise.

The carbon dioxide traps the heat being reflected from the Earth, although some heat is lost.

The warming increases water vapour in the air, leading to even greater absorption of heat.

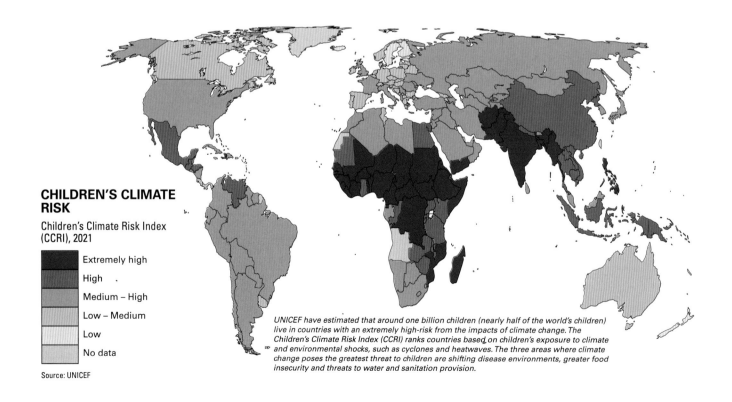

CHILDREN'S CLIMATE RISK

Children's Climate Risk Index (CCRI), 2021

- Extremely high
- High
- Medium – High
- Low – Medium
- Low
- No data

Source: UNICEF

UNICEF have estimated that around one billion children (nearly half of the world's children) live in countries with an extremely high-risk from the impacts of climate change. The Children's Climate Risk Index (CCRI) ranks countries based on children's exposure to climate and environmental shocks, such as cyclones and heatwaves. The three areas where climate change poses the greatest threat to children are shifting disease environments, greater food insecurity and threats to water and sanitation provision.

PREDICTED CHANGE IN TEMPERATURE

The difference between actual annual average surface air temperature, 1960–90, and predicted annual average surface air temperature, 2070–2100. This map shows the predicted increase, assuming a 'medium growth' of the global economy and assuming that no measures to combat the emission of greenhouse gases are taken.

- 5 – 10°C warmer
- 3 – 5°C warmer
- 2 – 3°C warmer
- 1 – 2°C warmer
- 0 – 1°C warmer

Source: The Hadley Centre of Climate Prediction and Research, The Met. Office.

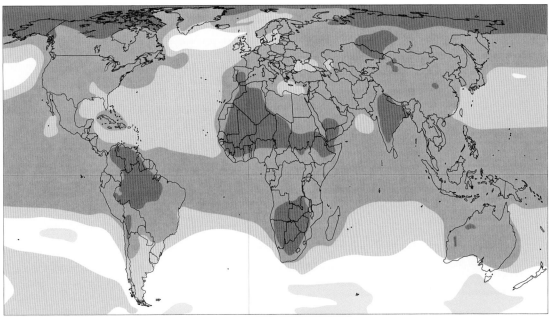

PREDICTED CHANGE IN PRECIPITATION

The difference between actual annual average precipitation, 1960–90, and predicted annual average precipitation, 2070–2100. It should be noted that these predicted annual mean changes mask quite significant seasonal detail.

- Over 2 mm more rain per day
- 1 – 2 mm more rain per day
- 0.5 – 1 mm more rain per day
- 0.2 – 0.5 mm more rain per day
- No change
- 0.2 – 0.5 mm less rain per day
- 0.5 – 1 mm less rain per day
- 1 – 2 mm less rain per day
- Over 2 mm less rain per day

DESERTIFICATION AND DEFORESTATION

- Existing deserts and dry areas
- Areas with a high risk of desertification
- Areas with a moderate risk of desertification
- Former extent of rainforest
- Existing rainforest

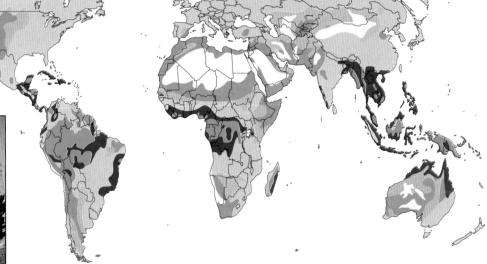

COPYRIGHT PHILIP'S

Global warming and climate change have affected agricultural through increased desertification.

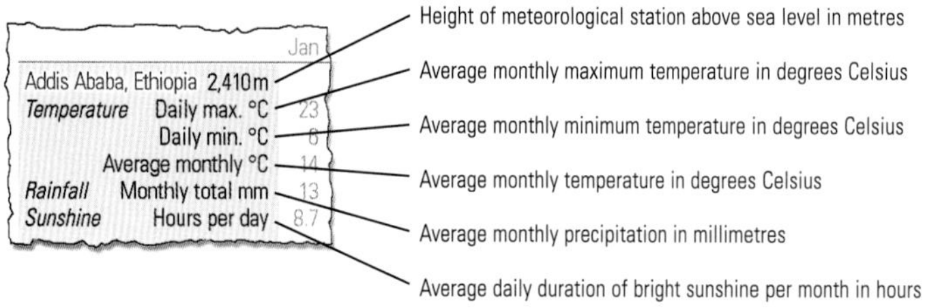
Jan
Addis Ababa, Ethiopia 2,410m
Temperature Daily max. °C 23
Daily min. °C 6
Average monthly °C 14
Rainfall Monthly total mm 13
Sunshine Hours per day 8.7
Height of meteorological station above sea level in metres
Average monthly maximum temperature in degrees Celsius
Average monthly minimum temperature in degrees Celsius
Average monthly temperature in degrees Celsius
Average monthly precipitation in millimetres
Average daily duration of bright sunshine per month in hours

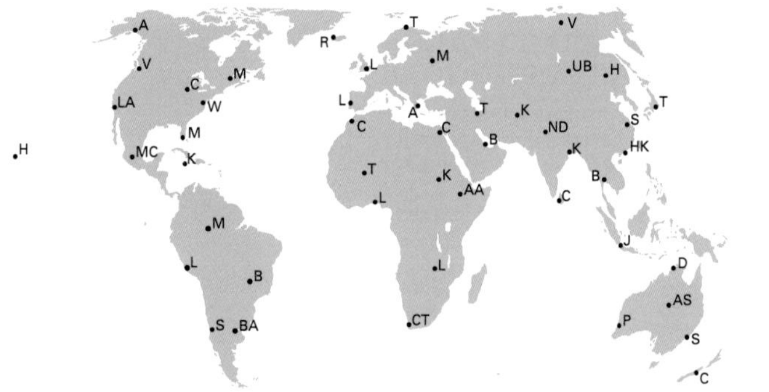

	Jan	Feb	Mar	Apr	May	June	July	Aug	Sept	Oct	Nov	Dec	Year
Addis Ababa, Ethiopia 2,410m													
Temperature Daily max. °C	23	24	25	24	25	23	20	20	21	22	23	22	23
Daily min. °C	6	7	9	10	9	10	11	11	10	7	5	5	8
Average monthly °C	14	15	17	17	17	16	16	15	15	15	14	14	15
Rainfall Monthly total mm	13	35	67	91	81	117	247	255	167	29	8	5	1,115
Sunshine Hours per day	8.7	8.2	7.6	8.1	6.5	4.8	2.8	3.2	5.2	7.6	6.7	7	6.4
Alice Springs, Australia 580m													
Temperature Daily max. °C	35	35	32	27	23	19	19	23	27	31	33	35	28
Daily min. °C	21	20	17	12	8	5	4	6	10	15	18	20	13
Average monthly °C	28	27	25	20	15	12	12	14	18	23	25	27	21
Rainfall Monthly total mm	44	33	27	10	15	13	7	8	7	18	29	38	249
Sunshine Hours per day	10.3	10.4	9.3	9.2	8	8	8.9	9.8	10	9.7	10.1	10	9.5
Anchorage, USA 183m													
Temperature Daily max. °C	−7	−3	0	7	13	18	19	17	13	6	−2	−6	−6
Daily min. °C	−15	−12	−9	−2	4	8	10	9	5	−2	−9	−14	−2
Average monthly °C	−11	−7	−4	3	9	13	15	13	9	2	−5	−10	−4
Rainfall Monthly total mm	20	18	13	11	13	25	47	64	64	47	28	24	374
Sunshine Hours per day	2.4	4.1	6.6	8.3	8.3	9.2	8.5	6	4.4	3.1	2.6	1.6	5.4
Athens, Greece 107m													
Temperature Daily max. °C	13	14	16	20	25	30	33	33	29	24	19	15	23
Daily min. °C	6	7	8	11	16	20	23	23	19	15	12	8	14
Average monthly °C	10	10	12	16	20	25	28	28	24	20	15	11	18
Rainfall Monthly total mm	62	37	37	23	23	14	6	7	15	51	56	71	402
Sunshine Hours per day	3.9	5.2	5.8	7.7	8.9	10.7	11.9	11.5	9.4	6.8	4.8	3.8	7.3
Bahrain City, Bahrain 2m													
Temperature Daily max. °C	20	21	25	29	33	36	37	38	36	32	27	22	30
Daily min. °C	14	15	18	22	25	29	31	32	29	25	22	16	23
Average monthly °C	17	18	21	25	29	32	34	35	32	29	25	19	26
Rainfall Monthly total mm	18	12	10	9	2	0	0	0	0	0.4	3	16	70
Sunshine Hours per day	5.9	6.9	7.9	8.8	10.6	13.2	12.1	12	12	10.3	7.7	6.4	9.5
Bangkok, Thailand 10m													
Temperature Daily max. °C	32	33	34	35	34	33	32	32	32	31	31	31	33
Daily min. °C	20	23	24	26	25	25	25	24	24	24	23	20	24
Average monthly °C	26	28	29	30	30	29	28	28	28	28	27	26	28
Rainfall Monthly total mm	9	30	36	82	165	153	168	183	310	239	55	8	1,438
Sunshine Hours per day	8.2	8	8	10	7.5	6.1	4.7	5.2	5.2	6.1	7.3	7.8	7
Brasilia, Brazil 910m													
Temperature Daily max. °C	28	28	28	28	27	27	27	29	30	29	28	27	28
Daily min. °C	18	18	18	17	15	13	13	14	16	18	18	18	16
Average monthly °C	23	23	23	22	21	20	20	21	23	24	23	22	22
Rainfall Monthly total mm	252	204	227	93	17	3	6	3	30	127	255	343	1,560
Sunshine Hours per day	5.8	5.7	6	7.4	8.7	9.3	9.6	9.8	7.9	6.5	4.8	4.4	7.2
Buenos Aires, Argentina 25m													
Temperature Daily max. °C	30	29	26	22	18	14	14	16	18	21	25	28	22
Daily min. °C	17	17	16	12	9	5	6	6	8	10	14	16	11
Average monthly °C	23	23	21	17	13	10	10	11	13	15	19	22	16
Rainfall Monthly total mm	79	71	109	89	76	61	56	61	79	86	84	99	950
Sunshine Hours per day	9.2	8.5	7.5	6.8	4.9	3.5	3.8	5.2	6	6.8	8.1	8.5	6.6
Cairo, Egypt 75m													
Temperature Daily max. °C	19	21	24	28	32	35	35	35	33	30	26	21	28
Daily min. °C	9	9	12	14	18	20	22	22	20	18	14	10	16
Average monthly °C	14	15	18	21	25	28	29	28	26	24	20	16	22
Rainfall Monthly total mm	4	4	3	1	2	1	0	0	1	1	3	7	27
Sunshine Hours per day	6.9	8.4	8.7	9.7	10.5	11.9	11.7	11.3	10.4	9.4	8.3	6.4	9.5
Cape Town, South Africa 44m													
Temperature Daily max. °C	26	26	25	23	20	18	17	18	19	21	24	25	22
Daily min. °C	15	15	14	11	9	7	7	7	8	10	13	15	11
Average monthly °C	21	20	20	17	14	13	12	12	14	16	18	20	16
Rainfall Monthly total mm	12	19	17	42	67	98	68	76	36	45	12	13	505
Sunshine Hours per day	11.4	10.2	9.4	7.7	6.1	5.7	6.4	6.6	7.6	8.6	10.2	10.9	8.4
Casablanca, Morocco 59m													
Temperature Daily max. °C	17	18	20	21	22	24	26	26	26	24	21	18	22
Daily min. °C	8	9	11	12	15	18	19	20	18	15	12	10	14
Average monthly °C	13	13	15	16	18	21	23	23	22	20	17	14	18
Rainfall Monthly total mm	78	61	54	37	20	3	0	1	6	28	58	94	440
Sunshine Hours per day	5.2	6.3	7.3	9	9.4	9.7	10.2	9.7	9.1	7.4	5.9	5.3	7.9

	Jan	Feb	Mar	Apr	May	June	July	Aug	Sept	Oct	Nov	Dec	Year
Chicago, USA 186m													
Temperature Daily max. °C	1	2	6	14	21	26	29	28	24	17	8	2	
Daily min. °C	−7	−6	−2	5	11	16	20	19	14	8	0	−5	
Average monthly °C	−3	−2	2	9	16	21	24	23	19	13	4	−2	
Rainfall Monthly total mm	47	41	70	77	96	103	86	80	69	71	56	48	8
Sunshine Hours per day	4	5	6.6	6.9	8.9	10.2	10	9.2	8.2	6.9	4.5	3.7	
Christchurch, New Zealand 5m													
Temperature Daily max. °C	21	21	19	17	13	11	10	11	14	17	19	21	
Daily min. °C	12	12	10	7	4	2	1	3	5	7	8	11	
Average monthly °C	16	16	15	12	9	6	6	7	9	12	13	16	
Rainfall Monthly total mm	56	46	43	46	76	69	61	58	51	51	51	61	6
Sunshine Hours per day	7	6.5	5.6	4.7	4.3	3.9	4.1	4.7	5.6	6.1	6.9	6.3	5
Colombo, Sri Lanka 10m													
Temperature Daily max. °C	30	31	31	31	30	30	29	29	30	29	29	30	
Daily min. °C	22	22	23	24	25	25	25	25	25	24	23	22	
Average monthly °C	26	26	27	28	28	27	27	27	27	27	26	26	
Rainfall Monthly total mm	101	66	118	230	394	220	140	102	174	348	333	142	2,3
Sunshine Hours per day	7.9	9	8.1	7.2	6.4	5.4	6.1	6.3	6.2	6.5	6.4	7.8	[illegible]
Darwin, Australia 30m													
Temperature Daily max. °C	32	32	33	33	33	31	31	32	33	34	34	33	
Daily min. °C	25	25	25	24	23	21	19	21	23	25	26	26	
Average monthly °C	29	29	29	29	28	26	25	26	28	29	30	29	
Rainfall Monthly total mm	405	309	279	77	8	2	0	1	15	48	108	214	1,4
Sunshine Hours per day	5.8	5.8	6.6	9.8	9.3	10	9.9	10.4	10.1	9.4	9.6	6.8	[illegible]
Harbin, China 175m													
Temperature Daily max. °C	−14	−9	0	12	21	26	29	27	20	12	−1	−11	
Daily min. °C	−26	−23	−12	−1	7	14	18	16	8	0	−12	−22	
Average monthly °C	−20	−16	−6	6	14	20	23	22	14	6	−7	−17	
Rainfall Monthly total mm	4	6	17	23	44	92	167	119	52	36	12	5	5
Sunshine Hours per day	6.4	7.8	8	7.8	8.3	8.6	8.6	8.2	7.2	6.9	6.1	5.7	7
Hong Kong, China 35m													
Temperature Daily max. °C	18	18	20	24	28	30	31	31	30	27	24	20	
Daily min. °C	13	13	16	19	23	26	26	26	25	23	19	15	
Average monthly °C	16	15	18	22	25	28	28	28	27	25	21	17	
Rainfall Monthly total mm	30	60	70	133	332	479	286	415	364	33	46	17	2,2
Sunshine Hours per day	4.7	3.5	3.1	3.8	5	5.4	6.8	6.5	6.6	7	6.2	5.5	5
Honolulu, Hawaii 5m													
Temperature Daily max. °C	26	26	26	27	28	29	29	29	30	29	28	26	
Daily min. °C	19	19	19	20	21	22	23	23	23	22	21	20	
Average monthly °C	23	22	23	23	24	26	26	26	26	26	24	23	
Rainfall Monthly total mm	96	84	73	33	25	8	11	23	25	47	55	76	5
Sunshine Hours per day	7.3	7.7	8.3	8.6	8.8	9.1	9.4	9.3	9.2	8.3	7.5	6.2	[illegible]
Jakarta, Indonesia 10m													
Temperature Daily max. °C	29	29	30	31	31	31	31	31	31	31	30	29	
Daily min. °C	23	23	23	24	24	23	23	23	23	23	23	23	
Average monthly °C	26	26	27	27	27	27	27	27	27	27	27	26	
Rainfall Monthly total mm	300	300	211	147	114	97	64	43	66	112	142	203	1,7
Sunshine Hours per day	6.1	6.5	7.7	8.5	8.4	8.5	9.1	9.5	9.6	9	7.7	7.1	[illegible]
Kabul, Afghanistan 1,791m													
Temperature Daily max. °C	2	4	12	19	26	31	33	33	30	22	17	8	
Daily min. °C	−8	−6	1	6	11	13	16	15	11	6	1	−3	
Average monthly °C	−3	−1	6	13	18	22	25	24	20	14	9	3	
Rainfall Monthly total mm	28	61	72	117	33	1	7	1	0	1	37	14	3
Sunshine Hours per day	5.9	6	5.7	6.8	10.1	11.5	11.4	11.2	9.8	9.4	7.8	6.1	8
Khartoum, Sudan 380m													
Temperature Daily max. °C	32	33	37	40	42	41	38	36	38	39	35	32	
Daily min. °C	16	17	20	23	26	27	26	25	25	25	21	17	
Average monthly °C	24	25	28	32	34	34	32	30	32	32	28	25	
Rainfall Monthly total mm	0	0	0	1	7	5	56	80	28	2	0	0	1
Sunshine Hours per day	10.6	11.2	10.4	10.8	10.4	10.1	8.6	8.6	9.6	10.3	10.8	10.6	10
Kingston, Jamaica 35m													
Temperature Daily max. °C	30	30	30	31	31	32	32	32	32	31	31	31	
Daily min. °C	20	20	20	21	22	24	23	23	23	23	22	21	
Average monthly °C	25	25	25	26	26	28	28	28	27	27	26	26	
Rainfall Monthly total mm	23	15	23	31	102	89	38	91	99	180	74	36	8
Sunshine Hours per day	8.3	8.8	8.7	8.7	8.3	7.8	8.5	8.5	7.6	7.3	8.3	7.7	8

olkata (Calcutta), India 5m		Jan	Feb	Mar	Apr	May	June	July	Aug	Sept	Oct	Nov	Dec	Year
emperature	Daily max. °C	27	29	34	36	35	34	32	32	32	32	29	26	31
	Daily min. °C	13	15	21	24	25	26	26	26	26	23	18	13	21
	Average monthly °C	20	22	27	30	30	30	29	29	29	28	23	20	26
ainfall	Monthly total mm	10	30	34	44	140	297	325	332	253	114	20	5	1,604
unshine	Hours per day	8.6	8.7	8.9	9	8.7	5.4	4.1	4.1	5.1	6.5	8.3	8.4	7.1

agos, Nigeria 40m		Jan	Feb	Mar	Apr	May	June	July	Aug	Sept	Oct	Nov	Dec	Year
emperature	Daily max. °C	32	33	33	32	31	29	28	28	29	30	31	32	31
	Daily min. °C	22	23	23	23	23	22	22	21	22	22	23	22	22
	Average monthly °C	27	28	28	28	27	26	25	24	25	26	27	27	26
ainfall	Monthly total mm	28	41	99	99	203	300	180	56	180	190	63	25	1,464
unshine	Hours per day	5.9	6.8	6.3	6.1	5.6	3.8	2.8	3.3	3	5.1	6.6	6.5	5.2

ma, Peru 120m		Jan	Feb	Mar	Apr	May	June	July	Aug	Sept	Oct	Nov	Dec	Year
emperature	Daily max. °C	28	29	29	27	24	20	20	19	20	22	24	26	24
	Daily min. °C	19	20	19	17	16	15	14	14	14	15	16	17	16
	Average monthly °C	24	24	24	22	20	17	17	16	17	18	20	21	20
ainfall	Monthly total mm	1	1	1	1	5	5	8	8	8	3	3	1	45
unshine	Hours per day	6.3	6.8	6.9	6.7	4	1.4	1.1	1	1.1	2.5	4.1	5	3.9

sbon, Portugal 77m		Jan	Feb	Mar	Apr	May	June	July	Aug	Sept	Oct	Nov	Dec	Year
emperature	Daily max. °C	14	15	17	20	21	25	27	28	26	22	17	15	21
	Daily min. °C	8	8	10	12	13	15	17	17	17	14	11	9	13
	Average monthly °C	11	12	14	16	17	20	22	23	21	18	14	12	17
ainfall	Monthly total mm	111	76	109	54	44	16	3	4	33	62	93	103	708
unshine	Hours per day	4.7	5.9	6	8.3	9.1	10.6	11.4	10.7	8.4	6.7	5.2	4.6	7.7

ondon (Kew), UK 5m		Jan	Feb	Mar	Apr	May	June	July	Aug	Sept	Oct	Nov	Dec	Year
emperature	Daily max. °C	6	7	10	13	17	20	22	21	19	14	10	7	14
	Daily min. °C	2	2	3	6	8	12	14	13	11	8	5	4	7
	Average monthly °C	4	5	7	9	12	16	18	17	15	11	8	5	11
ainfall	Monthly total mm	54	40	37	37	46	45	57	59	49	57	64	48	593
unshine	Hours per day	1.7	2.3	3.5	5.7	6.7	7	6.6	6	5	3.3	1.9	1.4	4.3

os Angeles, USA 30m		Jan	Feb	Mar	Apr	May	June	July	Aug	Sept	Oct	Nov	Dec	Year
emperature	Daily max. °C	18	18	18	19	20	22	24	24	24	23	22	19	21
	Daily min. °C	7	8	9	11	13	15	17	17	16	14	11	9	12
	Average monthly °C	12	13	14	15	17	18	21	21	20	18	16	14	17
ainfall	Monthly total mm	69	74	46	28	3	3	0	0	5	10	28	61	327
unshine	Hours per day	6.9	8.2	8.9	8.8	9.5	10.3	11.7	11	10.1	8.6	8.2	7.6	9.2

usaka, Zambia 1,154m		Jan	Feb	Mar	Apr	May	June	July	Aug	Sept	Oct	Nov	Dec	Year
emperature	Daily max. °C	26	26	26	27	25	23	23	26	29	31	29	27	27
	Daily min. °C	17	17	16	15	12	10	9	11	15	18	18	17	15
	Average monthly °C	22	22	21	21	18	17	16	19	22	25	23	22	21
ainfall	Monthly total mm	224	173	90	19	3	1	0	1	1	17	85	196	810
unshine	Hours per day	5.1	5.4	6.9	8.9	9	9	9.1	9.6	9.5	9	7	5.5	7.8

lanaus, Brazil 45m		Jan	Feb	Mar	Apr	May	June	July	Aug	Sept	Oct	Nov	Dec	Year
emperature	Daily max. °C	31	31	31	31	31	31	32	33	34	34	33	32	32
	Daily min. °C	24	24	24	24	24	24	24	24	24	25	25	24	24
	Average monthly °C	28	28	28	27	28	28	28	29	29	29	29	28	28
ainfall	Monthly total mm	278	278	300	287	193	99	61	41	62	112	165	220	2,096
unshine	Hours per day	3.9	4	3.6	3.9	5.4	6.9	7.9	8.2	7.5	6.6	5.9	4.9	5.7

lexico City, Mexico 2,309m		Jan	Feb	Mar	Apr	May	June	July	Aug	Sept	Oct	Nov	Dec	Year
emperature	Daily max. °C	21	23	26	27	26	25	23	24	23	22	21	21	24
	Daily min. °C	5	6	7	9	10	11	11	11	11	9	6	5	8
	Average monthly °C	13	15	16	18	18	18	17	17	17	16	14	13	16
ainfall	Monthly total mm	8	4	9	23	57	111	160	149	119	46	16	7	709
unshine	Hours per day	7.3	8.1	8.5	8.1	7.8	7	6.2	6.4	5.6	6.3	7	7.3	7.1

liami, USA 2m		Jan	Feb	Mar	Apr	May	June	July	Aug	Sept	Oct	Nov	Dec	Year
emperature	Daily max. °C	24	25	27	28	30	31	32	32	31	29	27	25	28
	Daily min. °C	14	15	16	19	21	23	24	24	24	22	18	15	20
	Average monthly °C	19	20	21	23	25	27	28	28	27	25	22	20	24
ainfall	Monthly total mm	51	48	58	99	163	188	170	178	241	208	71	43	1,518
unshine	Hours per day	7.7	8.3	8.7	9.4	8.9	8.5	8.7	8.4	7.1	6.5	7.5	7.1	8.1

lontreal, Canada 57m		Jan	Feb	Mar	Apr	May	June	July	Aug	Sept	Oct	Nov	Dec	Year
emperature	Daily max. °C	−6	−4	2	11	18	23	26	25	20	14	5	−3	11
	Daily min. °C	−13	−11	−5	2	9	14	17	16	11	6	0	−9	3
	Average monthly °C	−9	−8	−2	6	13	19	22	20	16	10	3	−6	7
ainfall	Monthly total mm	87	76	86	83	81	91	98	87	96	84	89	89	1,047
unshine	Hours per day	2.8	3.4	4.5	5.2	6.7	7.7	8.2	7.7	5.6	4.3	2.4	2.2	5.1

oscow, Russia 156m		Jan	Feb	Mar	Apr	May	June	July	Aug	Sept	Oct	Nov	Dec	Year
emperature	Daily max. °C	−6	−4	1	9	18	22	24	22	17	10	1	−5	9
	Daily min. °C	−14	−16	−11	−1	5	9	12	9	4	−2	−6	−12	−2
	Average monthly °C	−10	−10	−5	4	12	15	18	16	10	4	−2	−8	4
ainfall	Monthly total mm	31	28	33	35	52	67	74	74	58	51	36	36	575
unshine	Hours per day	1	1.9	3.7	5.2	7.8	8.3	8.4	7.1	4.4	2.4	1	0.6	4.4

ew Delhi, India 220m		Jan	Feb	Mar	Apr	May	June	July	Aug	Sept	Oct	Nov	Dec	Year
emperature	Daily max. °C	21	24	29	36	41	39	35	34	34	34	28	23	32
	Daily min. °C	6	10	14	20	26	28	27	26	24	17	11	7	18
	Average monthly °C	14	17	22	28	33	34	31	30	29	26	20	15	25
ainfall	Monthly total mm	25	21	13	8	13	77	178	184	123	10	2	11	665
unshine	Hours per day	7.7	8.2	8.2	8.7	9.2	7.9	6	6.3	6.9	9.4	8.7	8.3	8

Perth, Australia 60m		Jan	Feb	Mar	Apr	May	June	July	Aug	Sept	Oct	Nov	Dec	Year
Temperature	Daily max. °C	29	30	27	25	21	18	17	18	19	21	25	27	23
	Daily min. °C	17	18	16	14	12	10	9	9	10	11	14	16	13
	Average monthly °C	23	24	22	19	16	14	13	13	15	16	19	22	18
Rainfall	Monthly total mm	8	13	22	44	128	189	177	145	84	58	19	13	900
Sunshine	Hours per day	10.4	9.8	8.8	7.5	5.7	4.8	5.4	6	7.2	8.1	9.6	10.4	7.8

Reykjavik, Iceland 18m		Jan	Feb	Mar	Apr	May	June	July	Aug	Sept	Oct	Nov	Dec	Year
Temperature	Daily max. °C	2	3	5	6	10	13	15	14	12	8	5	4	8
	Daily min. °C	−3	−3	−1	1	4	7	9	8	6	3	0	−2	3
	Average monthly °C	0	0	2	4	7	10	12	11	9	5	3	1	5
Rainfall	Monthly total mm	89	64	62	56	42	42	50	56	67	94	78	79	779
Sunshine	Hours per day	0.8	2	3.6	4.5	5.9	6.1	5.8	5.4	3.5	2.3	1.1	0.3	3.7

Santiago, Chile 520m		Jan	Feb	Mar	Apr	May	June	July	Aug	Sept	Oct	Nov	Dec	Year
Temperature	Daily max. °C	30	29	27	24	19	15	15	17	19	22	26	29	23
	Daily min. °C	12	11	10	7	5	3	3	4	6	7	9	11	7
	Average monthly °C	21	20	18	15	12	9	9	10	12	15	17	20	15
Rainfall	Monthly total mm	3	3	5	13	64	84	76	56	31	15	8	5	363
Sunshine	Hours per day	10.8	8.9	8.5	5.5	3.6	3.3	3.3	3.6	4.8	6.1	8.7	10.1	6.4

Shanghai, China 5m		Jan	Feb	Mar	Apr	May	June	July	Aug	Sept	Oct	Nov	Dec	Year
Temperature	Daily max. °C	8	8	13	19	24	28	32	32	27	23	17	10	20
	Daily min. °C	−1	0	4	9	14	19	23	23	19	13	7	2	11
	Average monthly °C	3	4	8	14	19	23	27	27	23	18	12	6	15
Rainfall	Monthly total mm	48	59	84	94	94	180	147	142	130	71	51	36	1,136
Sunshine	Hours per day	4	3.7	4.4	4.8	5.4	4.7	6.9	7.5	5.3	5.6	4.7	4.5	5.1

Sydney, Australia 40m		Jan	Feb	Mar	Apr	May	June	July	Aug	Sept	Oct	Nov	Dec	Year
Temperature	Daily max. °C	26	26	25	22	19	17	17	18	20	22	24	25	22
	Daily min. °C	18	19	17	14	11	9	8	9	11	13	16	17	14
	Average monthly °C	22	22	21	18	15	13	12	13	16	18	20	21	18
Rainfall	Monthly total mm	89	101	127	135	127	117	117	76	74	71	74	74	1,182
Sunshine	Hours per day	7.5	7	6.4	6.1	5.7	5.3	6.1	7	7.3	7.5	7.5	7.5	6.8

Tehran, Iran 1,191m		Jan	Feb	Mar	Apr	May	June	July	Aug	Sept	Oct	Nov	Dec	Year
Temperature	Daily max. °C	9	11	16	21	29	30	37	36	29	24	16	11	22
	Daily min. °C	−1	1	4	10	16	20	23	23	18	12	6	1	11
	Average monthly °C	4	6	10	15	22	25	30	29	23	18	11	6	17
Rainfall	Monthly total mm	37	23	36	31	14	2	1	1	1	5	29	27	207
Sunshine	Hours per day	5.9	6.7	7.5	7.4	8.6	11.6	11.2	11	10.1	7.6	6.9	6.3	8.4

Timbuktu, Mali 269m		Jan	Feb	Mar	Apr	May	June	July	Aug	Sept	Oct	Nov	Dec	Year
Temperature	Daily max. °C	31	35	38	41	43	42	38	35	38	40	37	31	37
	Daily min. °C	13	16	18	22	26	27	25	24	24	23	18	14	21
	Average monthly °C	22	25	28	31	34	34	32	30	31	31	28	23	29
Rainfall	Monthly total mm	0	0	0	1	4	20	54	93	31	3	0	0	206
Sunshine	Hours per day	9.1	9.6	9.6	9.7	9.8	9.4	9.6	9	9.3	9.5	9.5	8.9	9.4

Tokyo, Japan 5m		Jan	Feb	Mar	Apr	May	June	July	Aug	Sept	Oct	Nov	Dec	Year
Temperature	Daily max. °C	9	9	12	18	22	25	29	30	27	20	16	11	19
	Daily min. °C	−1	−1	3	4	13	17	22	23	19	13	7	1	10
	Average monthly °C	4	4	8	11	18	21	25	26	23	17	11	6	14
Rainfall	Monthly total mm	48	73	101	135	131	182	146	147	217	220	101	61	1,562
Sunshine	Hours per day	6	5.9	5.7	6	6.2	5	5.8	6.6	4.5	4.4	4.8	5.4	5.5

Tromsø, Norway 100m		Jan	Feb	Mar	Apr	May	June	July	Aug	Sept	Oct	Nov	Dec	Year
Temperature	Daily max. °C	−2	−2	0	3	7	12	16	14	10	5	2	0	5
	Daily min. °C	−6	−6	−5	−2	1	6	9	8	5	1	−2	−4	0
	Average monthly °C	−4	−4	−3	0	4	9	13	11	7	3	0	−2	3
Rainfall	Monthly total mm	96	79	91	65	61	59	56	80	109	115	88	95	994
Sunshine	Hours per day	0.1	1.6	2.9	6.1	5.7	6.9	7.9	4.8	3.5	1.7	0.3	0	3.5

Ulan Bator, Mongolia 1,305m		Jan	Feb	Mar	Apr	May	June	July	Aug	Sept	Oct	Nov	Dec	Year
Temperature	Daily max. °C	−19	−13	−4	7	13	21	22	21	14	6	−6	−16	4
	Daily min. °C	−32	−29	−22	−8	−2	7	11	8	2	−8	−20	−28	−11
	Average monthly °C	−26	−21	−13	−1	6	14	16	14	8	−1	−13	−22	−4
Rainfall	Monthly total mm	1	1	2	5	10	28	76	51	23	5	5	2	209
Sunshine	Hours per day	6.4	7.8	8	7.8	8.3	8.6	8.6	8.2	7.2	6.9	6.1	5.7	7.5

Vancouver, Canada 5m		Jan	Feb	Mar	Apr	May	June	July	Aug	Sept	Oct	Nov	Dec	Year
Temperature	Daily max. °C	6	7	10	14	17	20	23	22	19	14	9	7	14
	Daily min. °C	0	1	3	5	8	11	13	12	10	7	3	2	6
	Average monthly °C	3	4	6	9	13	16	18	17	14	10	6	4	10
Rainfall	Monthly total mm	214	161	151	90	69	65	39	44	83	172	198	243	1,529
Sunshine	Hours per day	1.6	3	3.8	5.9	7.5	7.4	9.5	8.2	6	3.7	2	1.4	5

Verkhoyansk, Russia 137m		Jan	Feb	Mar	Apr	May	June	July	Aug	Sept	Oct	Nov	Dec	Year
Temperature	Daily max. °C	−47	−40	−20	−1	11	21	24	21	12	−8	−33	−42	−8
	Daily min. °C	−51	−48	−40	−25	−7	4	6	1	−6	−20	−39	−50	−23
	Average monthly °C	−49	−44	−30	−13	2	12	15	11	3	−14	−36	−46	−16
Rainfall	Monthly total mm	7	5	5	4	5	25	33	30	13	11	10	7	155
Sunshine	Hours per day	0	2.6	6.9	9.6	9.7	10	9.7	7.5	4.1	2.4	0.6	0	5.4

Washington, D.C., USA 22m		Jan	Feb	Mar	Apr	May	June	July	Aug	Sept	Oct	Nov	Dec	Year
Temperature	Daily max. °C	7	8	12	19	25	29	31	30	26	20	14	8	19
	Daily min. °C	−1	−1	2	8	13	18	21	20	16	10	4	−1	9
	Average monthly °C	3	3	7	13	19	24	26	25	21	15	9	4	14
Rainfall	Monthly total mm	84	68	96	85	103	88	108	120	100	78	75	75	1,080
Sunshine	Hours per day	4.4	5.7	6.7	7.4	8.2	8.8	8.6	8.2	7.5	6.5	5.3	4.5	6.8

Tropical Rain Forest
Tall broadleaved evergreen forest, trees 30–50m high with climbers and epiphytes forming continuous canopies. Associated with wet climate, 2–3000mm precipitation per year and high temperatures 24–28°C. High diversity of species, typically 100 per ha, including lianas, bamboo, palms, rubber, mahogany. Mangrove swamps form in coastal areas.

This diagram shows the highly stratified nature of the tropical rain forest. Crowns of trees form numerous layers at different heights and the dense shade limits undergrowth.

Subtropical and Temperate Rain Forest
Precipitation, which is less than in the Tropical Rain Forest, falls in the long wet season interspersed with a season of reduced rainfall and lower temperatures. As a result there are fewer species, thinner canopies, fewer lianas and denser ground level foliage. Vegetation consists of evergreen oak, laurel, bamboo, magnolia and tree ferns.

Monsoon Woodland and Open Jungle
Mostly deciduous trees, because of the long dry season and lower tempe Trees can reach 30m but are sparser than in the rain forests. There competition for light and thick jungle vegetation grows at lower level species diversity includes lianas, bamboo, teak, sandalwood, sal and b

Temperate Deciduous and Coniferous Forest
A transition zone between broadleaves and conifers. Broadleaves are better suited to the warmer, damper and flatter locations.

Coniferous Forest (Taiga or Boreal)
Forming a large continuous belt across Northern America and Eurasia with a uniformity in tree species. Characteristically trees are tall, conical with short branches and wax-covered needle-shaped leaves to retain moisture. Cold climate with prolonged harsh winters and cool summers where average temperatures are under 0°C for more than six months of the year Undergrowth is sparse with mosses and lichens. Tree species include pine, fir, spruce, larch, tamarisk.

Mountainous Forest, mainly Coniferous
Mild winters, high humidity and high levels of rainfall throughout the year provide habitat for dense needle-leaf evergreen forests and the largest trees in the world, up to 100m, including the Douglas fir, redwood and giant sequoia.

High Plateau Steppe and Tundra
Similar to arctic tundra with frozen ground for the majority of the year. Very sparse ground coverage of low, shallow-rooted herbs, small shrubs, mosses, lichens and heather interspersed with bare soil.

Arctic Tundra
Average temperatures are 0°C, precipitation is mainly snowfall and the ground remains frozen for 10 months of the year. Vegetation flourishes when the shallow surface layer melts in the long summer days. Underlying permafrost remains frozen and surface water cannot drain away, making conditions marshy. Consists of sedges, snow lichen, arctic meadow grass, cotton grasses and dwarf willow.

Polar and Mountainous Ice Desert
Areas of bare rock and ice with patches of rock-strewn lithosols, low in organic matter and low water content. In sheltered patches only a few mosses, lichens and low shrubs can grow, including woolly moss and purple saxifrage.

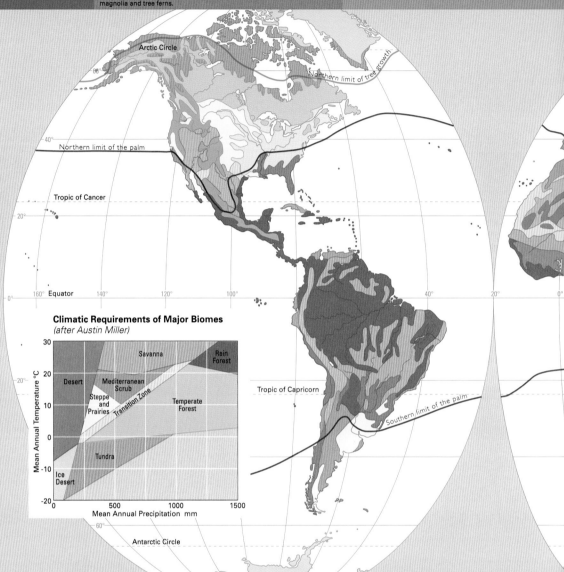

Climatic Requirements of Major Biomes
(after Austin Miller)

SOIL REGIONS
1:220 000 000

- Tundra soil
- Podzols
- Brown forest soil
- Lightly leached dry forest soil
- Red and yellow subtropical forest soil
- Reddish savanna soil and tropical red earths
- Laterites
- Chernozem
- Degraded chernozem
- Black savanna soil
- Chestnut steppe soil
- Desertic (arid) soil
- Alluvium
- Mountain and high plateau soils
- Oases soil
- Tropical and mangrove swamp

(after Glinka, Stremme, Marbut, and others)

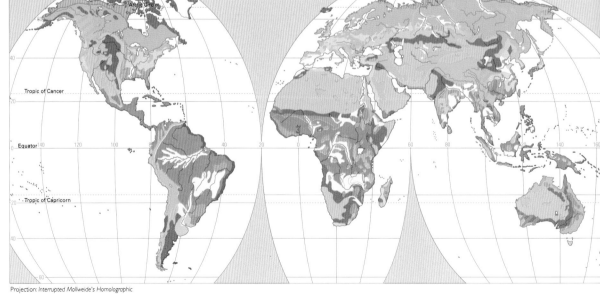

Projection: Interrupted Mollweide's Homolographic

Tropical and Temperate Woodland, Scrub and Bush
Clearings with woody shrubs and tall grasses. Trees are fire-resistant and deciduous or xerophytic because of long dry periods. Species include eucalyptus, acacia, mimosa and euphorbia.

Tropical Savanna with Low Trees and Bush
Tall, coarse grass with enough precipitation to support a scattering of short deciduous trees and thorn scrub. Vegetation consists of elephant grass, acacia, palms and baobob and is limited by aridity, grazing animals and periodic fires; trees have developed thick, woody bark, small leaves or thorns.

Tropical Savanna and Grassland
Areas with a hot climate and long dry season. Extensive areas of tall grasses often reach 3.5m with scattered fire and drought resistant bushes, low trees and thickets of elephant grass. Shrubs include acacia, baobab and palms.

BIOMES
Classified by Climax Vegetation
1:116 000 000

Dry Semi-desert with Shrub and Grass
Xerophytic shrubs with thin grass cover and few trees, limited by a long dry season and short, hot, rainy period. Sagebrush, bunch grass and acacia shrubs are common.

Desert Shrub
Scattered xerophytic plants able to withstand daytime extremes in temperature and long periods of drought. There is a large diversity of desert flora such as cacti, yucca, tamarisk, hard grass and artemisia.

Desert
Precipitation less than 250mm per year. Vegetation is very sparse, mainly bare rock, sand dunes and salt flats. Vegetation comprises a few xerophytic shrubs and ephemeral flowers.

Dry Steppe and Shrub
Semi-arid with cold, dry winters and hot summers. Bare soil with sparsely distributed short grasses and scattered shrubs and short trees. Species include acacia, artemisia, saksaul and tamarisk.

Temperate Grasslands, Prairie and Steppe
Continuous, tall, dense and deep-rooted swards of ancient grasslands, considered to be natural climax vegetation as determined by soil and climate. Average precipitation 250–750mm, with a long dry season, limits growth of trees and shrubs. Includes Stipa grass, buffalo grass, blue stems and loco weed.

Mediterranean Hardwood Forest and Scrub
Areas with hot and arid summers. Sparse evergreen trees are short and twisted with thick bark, interspersed with areas of scrub land. Trees have waxy leaves or thorns and deep root systems to resist drought. Many of the hardwood forests have been cleared by man, resulting in extensive scrub formation – maquis and chaparral. Species found are evergreen oak, stone pine, cork, olive and myrtle.

Temperate Deciduous Forest and Meadow
Areas of relatively high, well-distributed rainfall and temperature favourable for forest growth. The Tall broadleaved trees form a canopy in the summer, but shed their leaves in the winter. The undergrowth is sparse and poorly developed, but in the spring, herbs and flowers develop quickly. Diverse species, with up to 20 per ha, including oak, beech, birch, maple, ash, elm, chestnut and hornbeam. Many of these forests have been cleared for urbanization and farming.

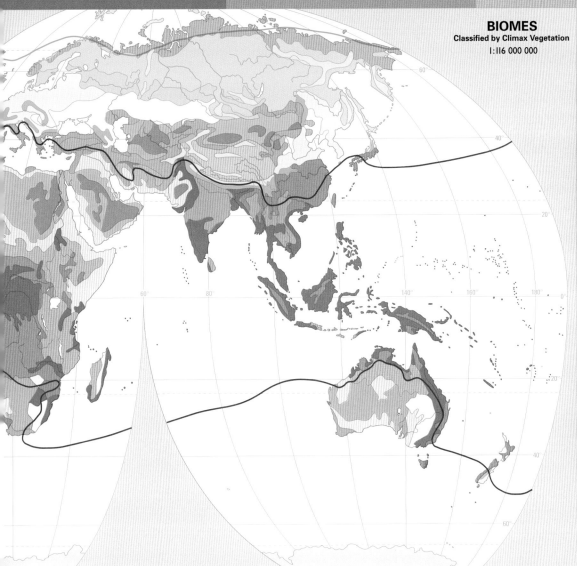

SOIL DEGRADATION
1:220 000 000

Areas of Concern
- Areas of serious concern
- Areas of some concern
- Stable terrain
- Non-vegetated land

Causes of soil degradation (by region)
- Grazing practices
- Other agricultural practices
- Industrialization
- Deforestation
- Fuelwood collection

(after Wageningen)

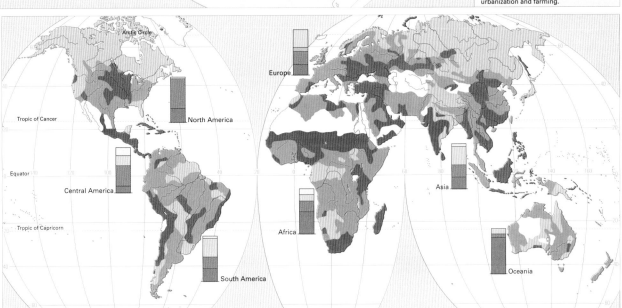

COPYRIGHT PHILIP'S

AGRICULTURAL PRODUCTION

Crops

Wheat

China 17.0%
India 13.3%
Russia 12.9%
USA 5.6%
Australia 4.5%
France 4.3%
Canada 4.2%

World total (2022): 808,441,568 tonnes

Rice

China 26.9%
India 25.3%
Bangladesh 7.4%
Indonesia 7.1%
Vietnam 7.1%
Thailand 4.4%
Myanmar 3.2%

World total (2022): 776,461,457 tonnes

Cassava

Nigeria 18.4%
Congo (D.R.) 14.8%
Thailand 10.3%
Ghana 7.7%
Cambodia 5.4%
Brazil 5.3%

World total (2022): 330,408,754 tonnes

Barley

Russia 15.1%
Australia 9.3%
France 7.3%
Germany 7.2%
Canada 6.4%
Turkey 5.5%

World total (2022): 154,877,140 tonnes

Maize

USA 30.0%
China 23.8%
Brazil 9.4%

World total (2022): 1,163,497,383 tonnes

Potatoes

China 25.5%
India 15.0%
Ukraine 5.6%
Russia 5.0%
USA 4.7%

World total (2022): 374,777,763 tonnes

Soybeans

Brazil 34.6%
USA 33.4%
Argentina 12.6%
China 5.9%
India 3.7%

World total (2022): 348,856,427 tonnes

Millet

India 38.4%
Niger 11.9%
China 8.7%
Nigeria 6.3%
Mali 6.0%
Sudan 5.4%

World total (2022): 30,859,664 tonnes

Sugar Cane

Brazil 37.7%
India 22.9%
China 5.4%
Thailand 4.8%
Pakistan 4.6%
Mexico 2.9%

World total (2022): 1,922,059,851 tonnes

Sugar Beet

Russia 18.7%
France 12.1%
USA 11.3%
Germany 10.8%
Turkey 7.3%
Poland 5.4%
Egypt 5.2%
Ukraine 3.8%

World total (2022): 260,998,614 tonnes

Animal Products

Milk

India 23.0%
USA 11.0%
Pakistan 6.1%
China 4.3%
Brazil 3.9%
Russia 3.5%
Germany 3.5%

World total (2022): 930,271,530 tonnes

Eggs

China 36.6%
India 7.1%
USA 7.0%
Indonesia 6.8%

World total (2022): 92,933,319 tonnes

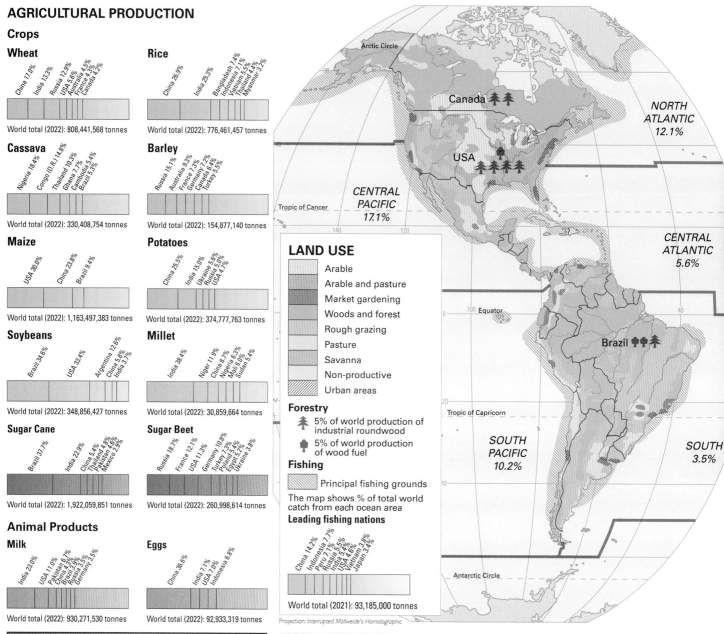

LAND USE

- Arable
- Arable and pasture
- Market gardening
- Woods and forest
- Rough grazing
- Pasture
- Savanna
- Non-productive
- Urban areas

Forestry

🌲 5% of world production of industrial roundwood

🌳 5% of world production of wood fuel

Fishing

Principal fishing grounds

The map shows % of total world catch from each ocean area

Leading fishing nations

China 14.2%
Indonesia 7.7%
Peru 7.1%
Russia 5.5%
India 5.4%
USA 4.6%
Vietnam 3.8%
Japan 3.4%

World total (2021): 93,185,000 tonnes

Projection: Interrupted Mollweide's Homolographic

NORTH ATLANTIC 12.1%
CENTRAL PACIFIC 17.1%
CENTRAL ATLANTIC 5.6%
SOUTH PACIFIC 10.2%
SOUTH 3.5%

This aerial photo shows shrimp farms, near Mahajanga, in north-western Madagascar. Shrimp farming is being used to stimulate the country's economy.

WILL THE WORLD RUN OUT OF FOOD?

At present-day rates, the world's population is predicted to reach at least 9 billion people by 2050. To sustain this population there will have to be a 70% increase in food production.

Currently, many people struggle to achieve the minimum food intake to sustain life. Globally, about 1 billion people are malnourished compared with 1 billion who are overweight.

Over 30% of the world's grain is fed to livestock because more and more people like to eat meat. But animals (and humans) are very inefficient in their utilization of nutrients; generally less than 20% of the nitrogen in their food is used; the rest is excreted, causing air and water pollution.

Meat is also very expensive in terms of water consumption: 0.5 kg of beef requires 8,442 litres of water to produce it. By 2030 there will be a 30% increase in water demand. Over 71% of the Earth's surface is covered in water but less than 3% of this is fresh water, of which over two-thirds is frozen in ice-caps and glaciers. Its over-exploitation in developed areas and availability in regions where it is scarce are major problems. For example, China currently has 20% of the world's population, but only 11% of its water.

How can we feed 9 billion people adequately and sustainably? The Royal Society has said that we need 'Sustainable Intensification', that is, to produce more using less and with less of an impact on the environment through good soil management, maintaining or enhancing crop genetic diversity, and introducing pest and disease resistance, as well as better fertiliser use.

Some, however, reject technological approach and advocate extensive systems described as 'organic', 'bio-dynamic' or 'ecological', objecting the reliance on chemical fertilisers and pesticide.

We need to reduce the 30% of the world's crop yield lost to pests, diseases and weeds; protect the fertile soil that irregularly covers only 11% of the global land surface and is a non-renewab asset; and cut back on food waste. In the UK it is estimated that 8.3 million tonnes of food worth £20 billion is sent to landfill each year. Some people now live on the food thrown away by shops – called 'skipping'.

If we adopt appropriate techniques and modif our behaviour, we stand a good chance of feedi the future, predominantly urban, population.

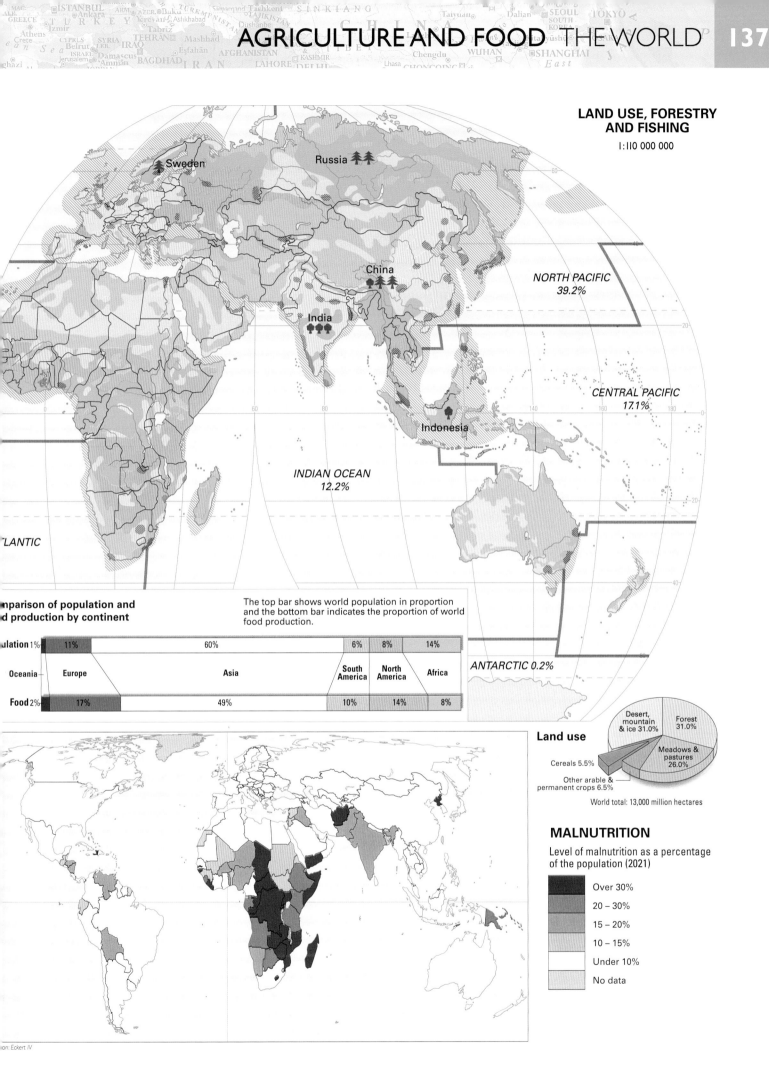

LAND USE, FORESTRY AND FISHING
1:110 000 000

Sweden

Russia

China

India

NORTH PACIFIC
39.2%

CENTRAL PACIFIC
17.1%

Indonesia

INDIAN OCEAN
12.2%

ATLANTIC

ANTARCTIC 0.2%

Comparison of population and food production by continent

The top bar shows world population in proportion and the bottom bar indicates the proportion of world food production.

Population	Oceania 1%	Europe 11%	Asia 60%	South America 6%	North America 8%	Africa 14%
Food	2%	17%	49%	10%	14%	8%

Land use

- Desert, mountain & ice 31.0%
- Forest 31.0%
- Meadows & pastures 26.0%
- Cereals 5.5%
- Other arable & permanent crops 6.5%

World total: 13,000 million hectares

MALNUTRITION

Level of malnutrition as a percentage of the population (2021)

- Over 30%
- 20 – 30%
- 15 – 20%
- 10 – 15%
- Under 10%
- No data

Projection: Eckert IV

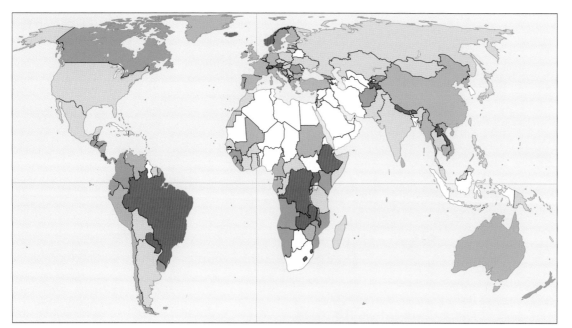

RENEWABLE ENERGY

Electricity gereration from renewable sources as a percentage of total electricity generation per country (20

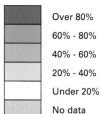

- Over 80%
- 60% - 80%
- 40% - 60%
- 20% - 40%
- Under 20%
- No data

WORLD ENERGY CONSUMPTION BY SOURCE (2021)

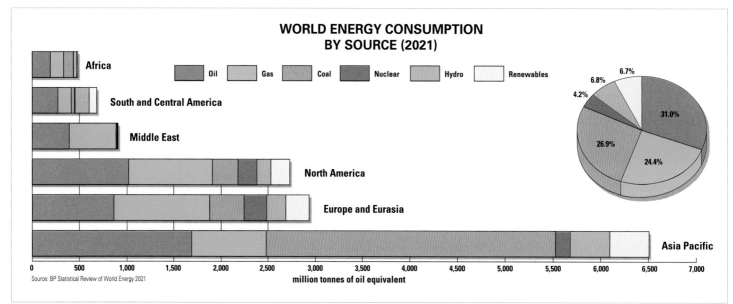

Oil | Gas | Coal | Nuclear | Hydro | Renewables

Africa
South and Central America
Middle East
North America
Europe and Eurasia
Asia Pacific

million tonnes of oil equivalent

Source: BP Statistical Review of World Energy 2021

Pie chart: 31.0%, 24.4%, 26.9%, 4.2%, 6.8%, 6.7%

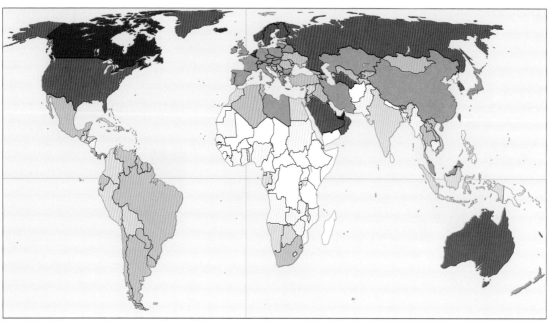

ENERGY CONSUMPTION

Consumption per capita kwh (2020)

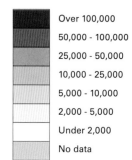

- Over 100,000
- 50,000 - 100,000
- 25,000 - 50,000
- 10,000 - 25,000
- 5,000 - 10,000
- 2,000 - 5,000
- Under 2,000
- No data

Projection: Eckert IV

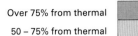

ELECTRICITY GENERATION

Percentage of electricity generated by source (latest available data)

- Over 75% from thermal
- 50 – 75% from thermal
- Over 75% from hydro
- 50 – 75% from hydro
- Over 50% from nuclear
- 50% from other renewables
- No dominant source
- No data
- Selected geothermal plants ●
- Selected hydroelectric plants ◇

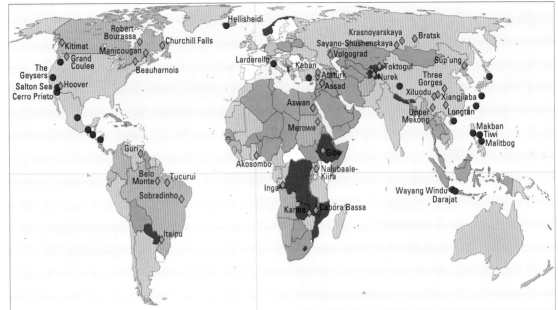

An aerial view of a thermal power station.

The power of water to generate electricity is harnessed by hydro-electric power stations.

MINERAL PRODUCTION

Diamonds

Russia 40.0%	Congo (DR) 17.8%	Botswana 15.6%	S. Africa 13.3%	Zimbabwe 8.9%

World total (2023): 45,000,000 carats

Gold

China 12.3%	Australia 10.3%	Russia 10.3%	Canada 6.7%	USA 5.7%

World total (2023): 3,000,000 kg

Silver

Mexico 24.6%	China 13.1%	Peru 11.9%	Chile 5.4%	Poland 5.0%

World total (2023): 26,000 tonnes

Phosphate fertilizer

China 40.9%	Morocco 15.9%	USA 9.1%	Russia 6.4%	Jordan 5.5%

World total (2023): 220,000,000 tonnes

Iron ore

Australia 38.4%	Brazil 17.6%	China 11.2%	India 10.8%

World total (2023): 2,500,000 tonnes

Copper

Chile 27.1%	Peru 14.1%	Congo (DR) 13.6%	China 9.2%	USA 6.0%

World total (2023): 18,450,000 tonnes

Lead

China 42.2%	Australia 9.8%	Mexico 6.0%	USA 6.0%	Peru 5.6%

World total (2023): 4,500,000 tonnes

Zinc

China 33.3%	Peru 11.7%	Australia 9.2%	India 6.3%	Mexico 5.8%

World total (2023): 12,000,000 tonnes

Bauxite

Australia 24.5%	Guinea 24.3%	China 23.3%	Brazil 7.8%	Indonesia 5.0%

World total (2023): 400,000,000 tonnes

Nickel ore

Indonesia 50.0%	Philippines 11.1%	New Caledonia 6.4%	Russia 5.6%	Canada 5.0%

World total (2023): 3,600,000 tonnes

Chromium

South Africa 43.9%	Kazakhstan 14.6%	Turkey 14.6%	India 10.2%

World total (2023): 41,000,000 tonnes

Precious metals
- ◇ Diamonds
- ◇ Gold
- ● Silver

Iron and ferro-alloys
- ◇ Iron ore
- ◆ Nickel ore
- ◇ Chromium

Non-ferrous metals
- ◈ Bauxite
- ◇ Copper
- ◆ Lead
- ◇ Zinc
- △ Phosphates

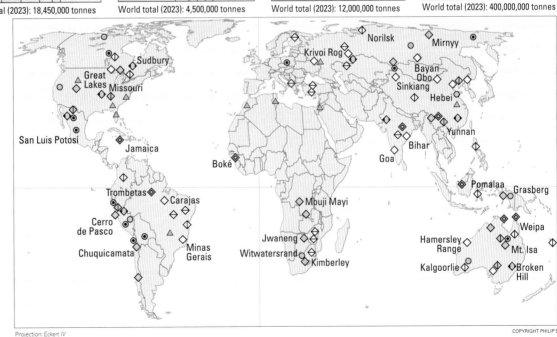

Projection: Eckert IV

COPYRIGHT PHILIP'S

SHARE OF WORLD TRADE

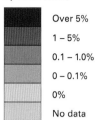

Percentage share of total world export by value (2022)

■	Over 5%
■	1 – 5%
■	0.1 – 1.0%
■	0 – 0.1%
■	0%
■	No data

Countries with the largest share of world trade (2022)

USA	11.4%	Netherlands	3.4%
China	10.5%	France	3.4%
Germany	6.4%	Singapore	2.8%
UK	3.7%	Ireland	2.4%
Japan	3.5%	South Korea	2.4%

EMPLOYMENT BY INDUSTRY

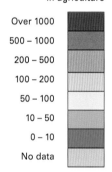

Workers employed in industry for every 100 workers engaged in agriculture

Over 1000	■
500 – 1000	■
200 – 500	■
100 – 200	■
50 – 100	■
10 – 50	■
0 – 10	■
No data	■

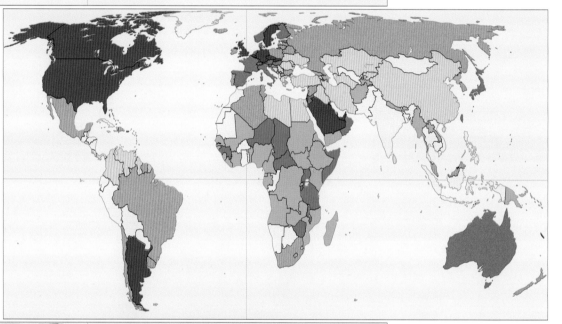

GLOBALIZATION INDEX

2021 KOF Index

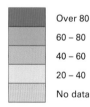

■	Over 80
■	60 – 80
■	40 – 60
■	20 – 40
■	No data

The index is a measure of economic, political and social globalization. The higher values show a greater level of globalization.

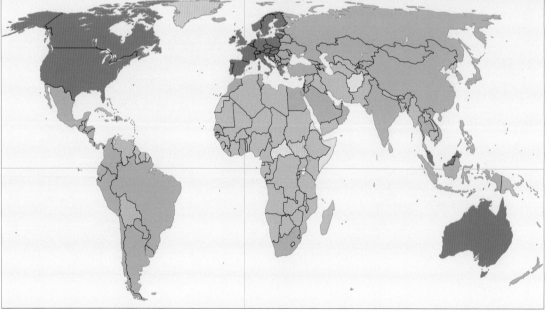

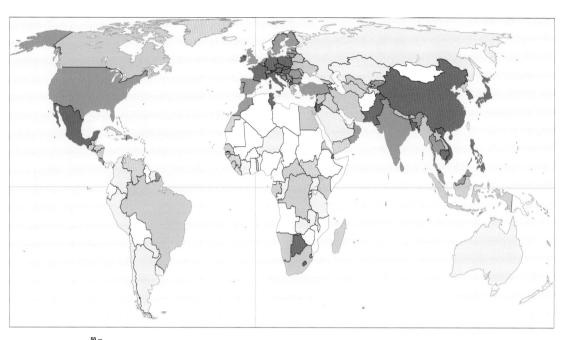

INDUSTRY AND TRADE

Manufactured exports as a percentage of total exports (2023)

- Over 75%
- 50 – 75%
- 25 – 50%
- 10 – 25%
- 0 – 10%
- No data

Countries most dependent on the export of manufactured goods (2023)

Andorra	96%
Bangladesh	96%
China	93%
Botswana	92%
Djibouti	92%
Cambodia	91%

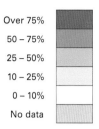

f Shanghai in Hangzhou Bay lies the container port shan.

Top Ten Container Ports

Total container traffic, in million TEU (2023) ('TEU' stands for Twenty-foot Equivalent Unit, the equivalent of a standard container)

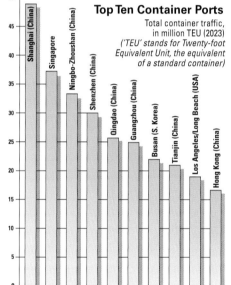

- Shanghai (China)
- Singapore
- Ningbo-Zhoushan (China)
- Shenzhen (China)
- Qingdao (China)
- Guangzhou (China)
- Busan (S. Korea)
- Tianjin (China)
- Los Angeles/Long Beach (USA)
- Hong Kong (China)

Types of Vessels

World fleet by type of vessel

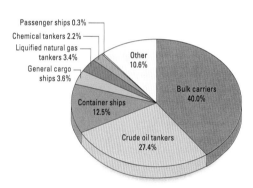

- Passenger ships 0.3%
- Chemical tankers 2.2%
- Liquified natural gas tankers 3.4%
- General cargo ships 3.6%
- Other 10.6%
- Container ships 12.5%
- Bulk carriers 40.0%
- Crude oil tankers 27.4%

SERVICE SECTOR

Percentage of GDP from services (2022)

- Over 70%
- 60 – 70%
- 50 – 60%
- 40 – 50%
- Under 40%
- No data

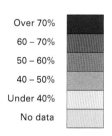

ountries with the highest and lowest rcentage of GDP from services (2022)

hest		Lowest	
anon	94%	Sudan	6%
naco	88%	Guyana	19%
embourg	80%	Libya	26%
Bahamas	79%	Chad	26%
Tomé & Príncipe	79%	Sierra Leone	29%

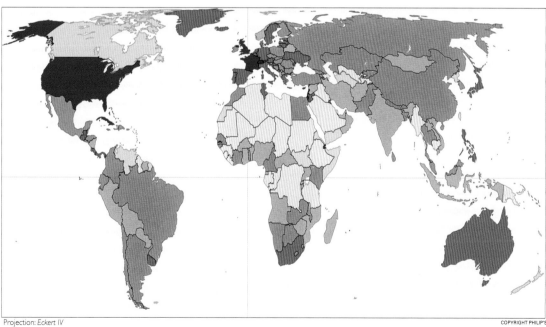

Projection: Eckert IV

COPYRIGHT PHILIP'S

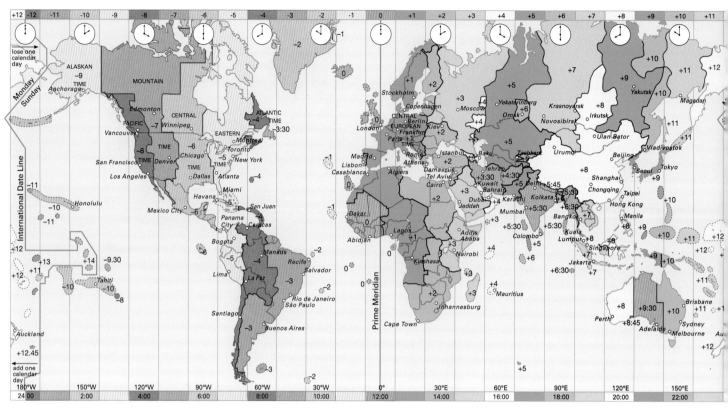

TIME ZONES

Zones using UT (Universal Time)	
Zones behind UT (Universal Time)	
Zones ahead of UT (Universal Time)	
Half-hour zones	
10 Hours behind or ahead of UT (Universal Time)	

- - - - - International boundaries
――――― Time zone boundaries

Actual solar time, when it is noon at Greenwich, is shown at the top of the map.

――――― International Date Line and Prime Meridian

Note: Certain time zones are affected by the incidence daylight saving time in countries where it is adopted. UT (Universal Time) has replaced GMT (Greenwich Mea

AIR TRAVEL

Major airports
Number of passengers (international and domestic, 2023)

- ◯ Over 100 million
- ◦ 75 – 100 million
- ∘ 50 – 75 million

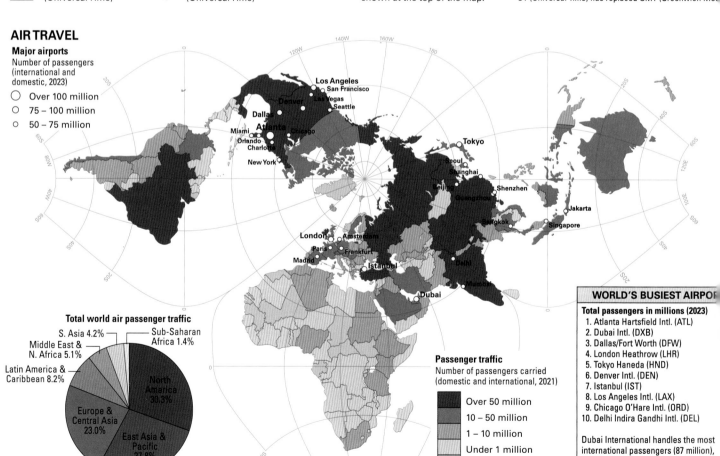

Total world air passenger traffic

- S. Asia 4.2%
- Sub-Saharan Africa 1.4%
- Middle East & N. Africa 5.1%
- Latin America & Caribbean 8.2%
- North America 30.3%
- Europe & Central Asia 23.0%
- East Asia & Pacific 27.8%

Total air passenger traffic (2021)
2,280,000,000

Passenger traffic
Number of passengers carried (domestic and international, 2021)

	Over 50 million
	10 – 50 million
	1 – 10 million
	Under 1 million
	No data available

WORLD'S BUSIEST AIRPOR

Total passengers in millions (2023)
1. Atlanta Hartsfield Intl. (ATL)
2. Dubai Intl. (DXB)
3. Dallas/Fort Worth (DFW)
4. London Heathrow (LHR)
5. Tokyo Haneda (HND)
6. Denver Intl. (DEN)
7. Istanbul (IST)
8. Los Angeles Intl. (LAX)
9. Chicago O'Hare Intl. (ORD)
10. Delhi Indira Gandhi Intl. (DEL)

Dubai International handles the most international passengers (87 million), followed by London's Heathrow (75 million).

Projection: Peirce

SCO WORLD HERITAGE SITES 2023
tes = 1,199 (933 cultural, 227 natural and 39 mixed)

	Cultural sites	Natural sites	Mixed sites
	56	42	5
ates	84	6	3
Pacific	205	72	12
& North	485	69	11
nerica & an	103	38	8

sites are trans-boundary, therefore the total figures may not add up

Europe at larger scale

Fjords, Saimaa, St.-Petersburg, Edinburgh, Dublin, Öland, London, Copenhagen, Amsterdam, Disneyland, Brittany, Paris, Prague, Tatra, Vienna, Budapest, Lourdes, Alps, Costa Brava, Venice, Black Sea Coast, Pyrenees, Florence, Lisbon, Barcelona, Côte d'Azur, Rome, Istanbul, Algarve, Balearic Islands, Pompeii, Aegean Is., Costa del Sol, Costa Blanca, Ionian Islands, Athens, Crete, Rhodes

Destinations
- ■ Cultural & historical centres
- □ Coastal resorts
- □ Ski resorts
- ■ Centres of entertainment
- ■ Places of pilgrimage
- ■ Places of great natural beauty

Other tourist destinations

TOURIST EARNINGS
Countries receiving the most from overseas tourism, US$ billion (2022)

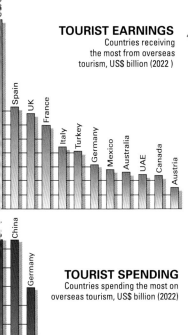

Spain, UK, France, Italy, Turkey, Germany, Mexico, Australia, UAE, Canada, Austria

Movement of tourists
- More than 10 million
- 5 – 10 million
- 3 – 5 million
- Less than 3 million

TOURIST SPENDING
Countries spending the most on overseas tourism, US$ billion (2022)

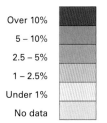

China, Germany, France, UK, Italy, India, Canada, Spain, South Korea, UAE, Belgium

TOURIST DESTINATIONS
Projection: Peirce

South Island, Fiji, Gold Coast, Sydney, Great Barrier Reef, Uluru National Park, Bali, Hawaii, Manila, Singapore, Kuala Lumpur, Tokyo, Osaka, Hong Kong, Kyoto, Shanghai, Macau, Penang, Sapporo, Everland Yong-in, Guilin, Phuket, Beijing, Xi'an, Bangkok, Great Wall of China, Chiang Mai, Sri Lanka, Himalayas, Benares, Kashmir, Agra (Taj Mahal), Mumbai, Goa, Maldives, Alaska, Moscow, Dubai, San Francisco, Disneyland, Yosemite, Crimea, Baja California, Banff, Turkey, Jerusalem, Las Vegas, Grand Canyon, Yellowstone Park, Aspen, Iceland, Cyprus, Red Sea, Mecca, Mexico City, New Orleans, Great Smoky Mts, Cairo (Pyramids), Acapulco, Niagara Falls, Quebec, Seychelles, Palenque, Belize, Walt Disney World, New York, Cape Cod, Djerba, Costa Rica, Miami, Bahamas, Bermuda, Serengeti National Park, Jamaica, Dominican Rep., Canary Islands, Marrakesh, Mombasa, Tahiti, ABC Islands, Virgin Islands, Margarita, Barbados, Mauritius, Gambia, Victoria Falls, Machu Picchu, Kruger National Park, Amazon Rainforest, Durban, Iguaçu National Park, Rio de Janeiro, Cape Town, Buenos Aires

See inset of Europe

PORTANCE OF TOURISM
Tourism receipts as a percentage of Gross National Income (2022)

- Over 10%
- 5 – 10%
- 2.5 – 5%
- 1 – 2.5%
- Under 1%
- No data

Countries with highest percentage of GNI from tourism receipts (2022)

St Lucia	63.1
Kosovo	40.6
Maldives	39.8
Liberia	35.7
St Kitts & Nevis	34.0
Antigua & Barbuda	29.8

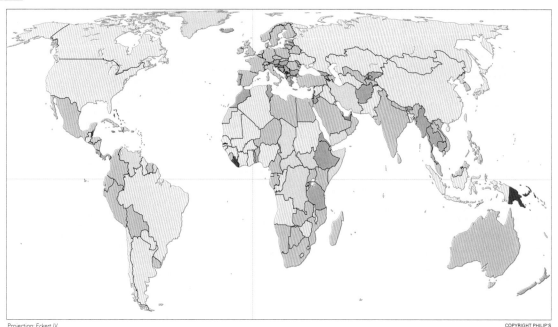

Projection: Eckert IV

WEALTH

The value of total production divided by the population (the Gross National Income per capita in 2022)

Over 400% of world average

200 – 400% of world average

100 – 200% of world average

World average US$11,566

50 – 100% of world average

25 – 50% of world average

10 – 25% of world average

Under 10% of world average

No data

Wealthiest countries		Poorest countries	
Norway	$95,520	Burundi	$24
Switzerland	$95,490	Afghanistan	$38
Luxembourg	$89,200	Mozambique	$44
		UK $49,240	

WATER SUPPLY

Mortality rate attributed to unsafe water, unsafe sanitation and lack of hygiene per 100,000 population

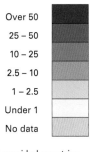

Over 50

25 – 50

10 – 25

2.5 – 10

1 – 2.5

Under 1

No data

Least well-provided countries

Chad	101.0
Somalia	86.6
Central African Rep.	82.1
Sierra Leone	81.3

One person in eight in the world has no access to a safe water supply.

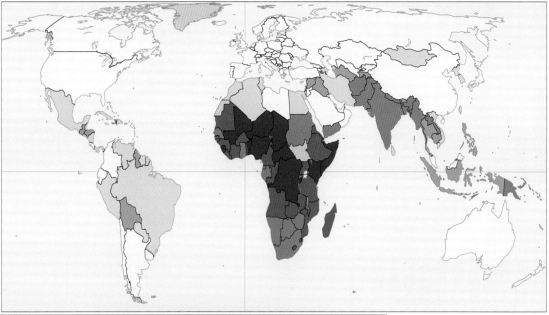

HUMAN DEVELOPMENT INDEX

The Human Development Index (HDI), calculated by the UN Development Programme (UNDP), gives a value to countries using indicators of life expectancy, education and standards of living in 2021 . Higher values show more developed countries.

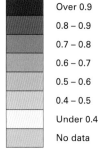

Over 0.9

0.8 – 0.9

0.7 – 0.8

0.6 – 0.7

0.5 – 0.6

0.4 – 0.5

Under 0.4

No data

Highest values		Lowest values	
Switzerland	0.962	Niger	0.400
Norway	0.961	Chad	0.394
Iceland	0.959	South Sudan	0.385
		UK 0.929	

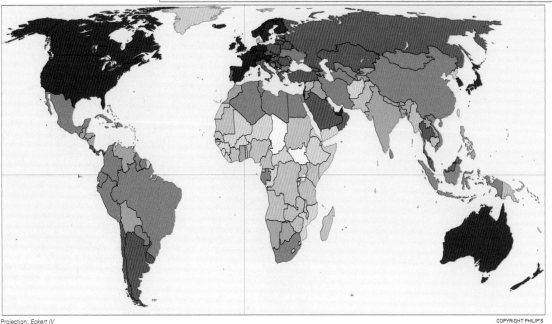

Projection: *Eckert IV*

COPYRIGHT PHILIP'S

HEALTH CARE

Health expenditure
US$ per capita 2023

- Over 2,500
- 1,000 – 2,500
- 500 – 1,000
- 100 – 500
- Under 100
- No data

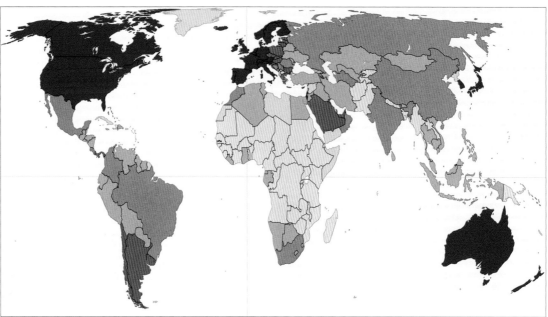

Countries spending the most and least on health care (US$)

Most		Least	
USA	12,012.2	Madagascar	17.6
Switzerland	10,897.5	Sudan	21.6
Norway	90,20.6	DRC	22.3
Monaco	8,634.3	The Gambia	24.3
Luxembourg	7,635.7	Eritrea	25.4

UK 5738.5

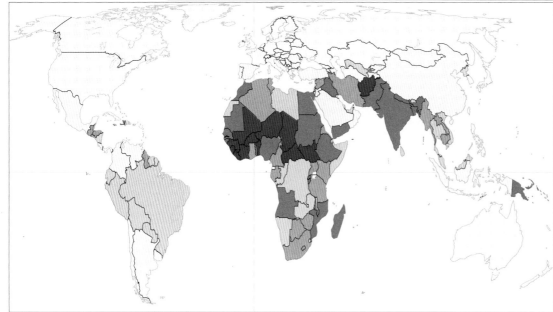

ILLITERACY

Percentage of adult total
population unable to read or
write (2021)

- Over 50%
- 25 – 50%
- 10 – 25%
- 5 – 10%
- 1 – 5%
- Under 1%
- No data

Countries with the highest illiteracy rates (%)

Niger	80.9	CAR	62.6
Chad	77.7	Burkina Faso	58.8
Guinea	69.6	Benin	57.6
South Sudan	65.5	Afghanistan	57.0
Mali	64.5	Sierra Leone	56.8

GENDER INEQUALITY INDEX

The Gender Inequality Index (GII) is a
composite measure reflecting inequality in
achievements between women and men in
three categories: reproductive health,
empowerment and the labour market.
It varies between 0, when women and men
fare equally, and 1, when women or men
fare poorly compared to the other in all
categories (2021).

- Over 0.65
- 0.5 – 0.65
- 0.25 – 0.5
- Under 0.25
- No data

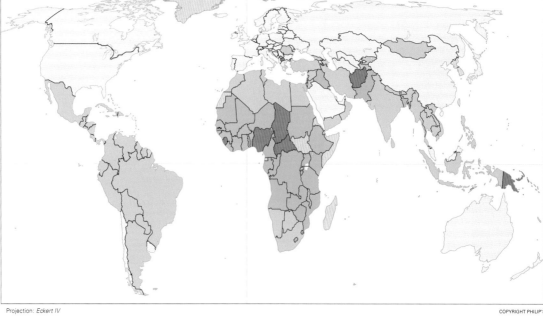

Most equal		Least equal	
Denmark	0.013	PNG	0.725
Norway	0.016	N. Macedonia	0.720
Switzerland	0.018	Nigeria	0.680

UK 0.098

Projection: Eckert IV

AGE DISTRIBUTION PYRAMIDS

The bars represent the percentage of the total population (males plus females) in each age group. More Economically Developed Countries (MEDCs), such as New Zealand, have populations spread evenly across age groups and usually a growing percentage of elderly people. Less Economically Developed Countries (LEDCs), such as Kenya, have the great majority of their people in the younger age groups, about to enter their most fertile years.

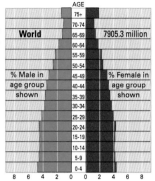

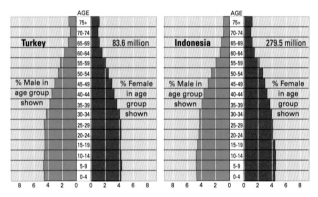

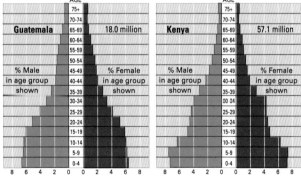

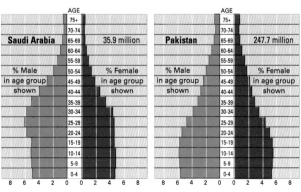

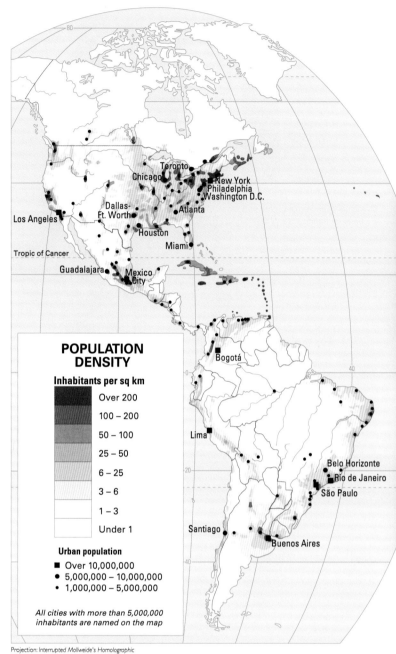

POPULATION DENSITY

Inhabitants per sq km

- Over 200
- 100 – 200
- 50 – 100
- 25 – 50
- 6 – 25
- 3 – 6
- 1 – 3
- Under 1

Urban population
- ■ Over 10,000,000
- ● 5,000,000 – 10,000,000
- • 1,000,000 – 5,000,000

All cities with more than 5,000,000 inhabitants are named on the map

Projection: Interrupted Mollweide's Homolographic

POPULATION CHANGE 1930–2020   Population totals are in millions

Figures in italics represent the percentage average annual increase for the period shown

	1930	1930–1960	1960	1960–1990	1990	1990–2020	2020
World	2,013	1.4%	3,019	1.9%	5,292	1.2%	7,631
Africa	155	2.0%	281	2.9%	648	2.5%	1,286
North America	135	1.3%	199	1.1%	276	1.0%	370
Latin America*	129	1.8%	218	2.4%	448	1.3%	647
Asia	1,073	1.5%	1,669	2.1%	3,108	1.3%	4,542
Europe	355	0.6%	425	0.6%	508	0.3%	549
Oceania	10	1.4%	16	1.8%	27	1.3%	39
CIS†	176	0.7%	214	1.0%	281	0.1%	285

* South America plus Central America, Mexico and the West Indies
† Commonwealth of Independent States, formerly the USSR

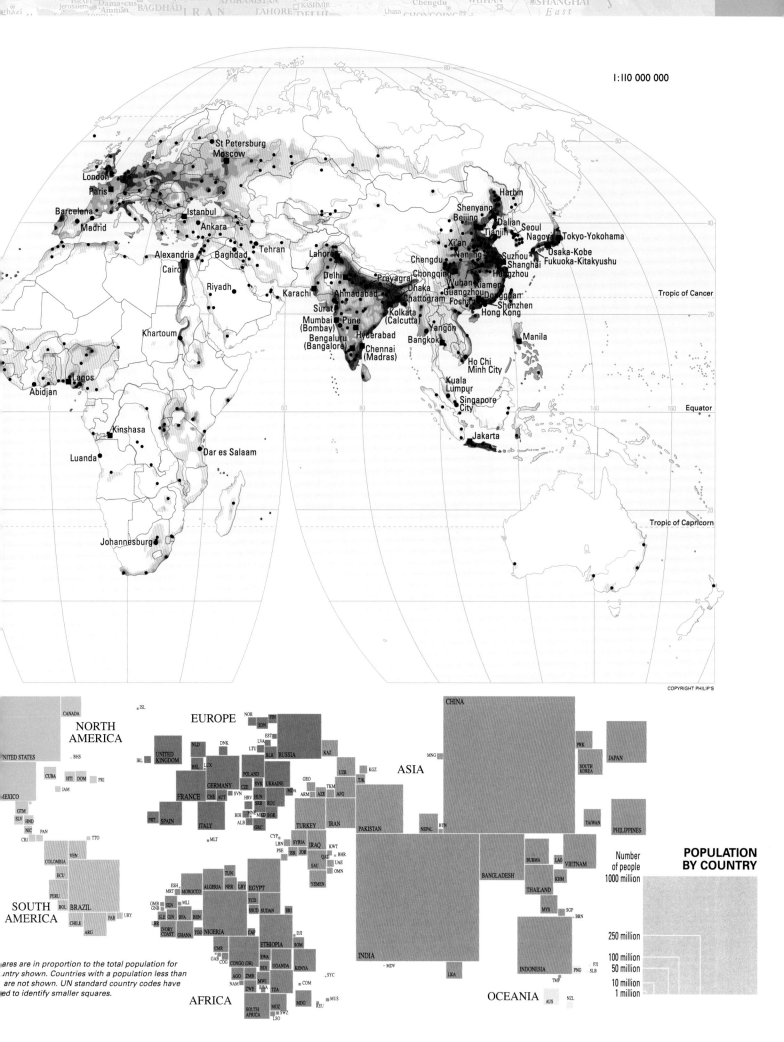

1:110 000 000

St Petersburg
Moscow
London
Paris
Barcelona
Madrid
Istanbul
Ankara
Harbin
Shenyang
Beijing
Dalian
Tianjin
Seoul
Nagoya
Tokyo-Yokohama
Xi'an
Nanjing
Suzhou
Osaka-Kobe
Fukuoka-Kitakyushu
Alexandria
Baghdad
Tehran
Lahore
Chengdu
Chongqing
Shanghai
Hangzhou
Cairo
Delhi
Prayagraj
Wuhan
Xiamen
Dhaka
Guangzhou
Dongguan
Riyadh
Karachi
Ahmadabad
Chattogram
Foshan
Shenzhen
Surat
Kolkata
(Calcutta)
Hong Kong
Khartoum
Mumbai
(Bombay)
Pune
Hyderabad
Yangon
Bangkok
Manila
Bengaluru
(Bangalore)
Chennai
(Madras)
Ho Chi
Minh City
Lagos
Abidjan
Kuala
Lumpur
Singapore
City
Kinshasa
Dar es Salaam
Jakarta
Luanda
Johannesburg

Tropic of Cancer
Equator
Tropic of Capricorn

COPYRIGHT PHILIP'S

POPULATION BY COUNTRY

Number
of people
1000 million

250 million

100 million
50 million
10 million
1 million

ares are in proportion to the total population for
untry shown. Countries with a population less than
are not shown. UN standard country codes have
ed to identify smaller squares.

NORTH
AMERICA
EUROPE
ASIA
CHINA

SOUTH
AMERICA
AFRICA
OCEANIA

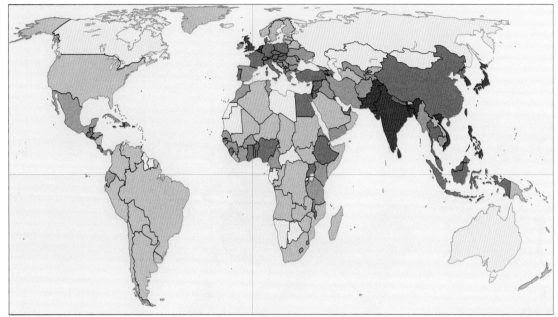
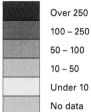

POPULATION DENSITY BY COUNTRY

Density of people per square kilometre (2023)

- Over 250
- 100 – 250
- 50 – 100
- 10 – 50
- Under 10
- No data

Most and least densely populated countries

Most per km²		Least per km²
Singapore	8,787	Mongolia
Bahrain	2,252	Australia
Malta	1,460	Namibia
Maldives	1,299	Iceland
Bangladesh	1,161	Guyana

UK 282 per km²

POPULATION CHANGE

The projected population change for the years 2004–2050

- Over 125% gain
- 100 – 125% gain
- 50 – 100% gain
- 25 – 50% gain
- 0 – 25% gain
- No change or loss

Based on estimates for the year 2050, the ten most populous nations in the world will be, in millions:

India	1,657	Pakistan	291
China	1,304	Bangladesh	250
USA	400	Brazil	232
Indonesia	300	Ethiopia	228
Nigeria	391	Philippines	172

UK (2050) 71 million

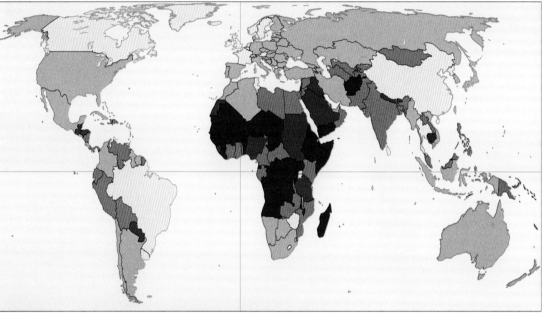

URBAN POPULATION

Percentage of total population living in towns and cities (2023)

- Over 80%
- 60 – 80%
- 40 – 60%
- 20 – 40%
- Under 20%
- No data

Countries that are the most and least urbanized (%)

Most urbanized		Least urbanized	
Kuwait	100	Papua N. Guinea	14
Monaco	100	Liechtenstein	15
Singapore	100	Burundi	15

UK 85% urban

In 2008, for the first time in history, more than half the world's population lived in urban areas.

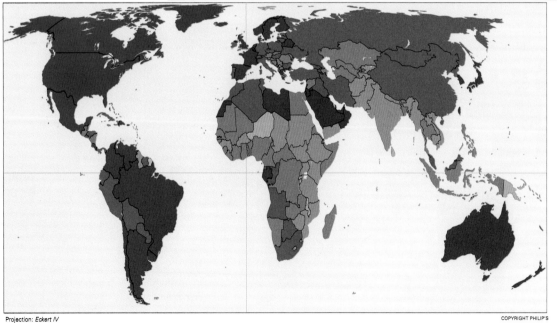

Projection: *Eckert IV*

COPYRIGHT PHILIP'S

INFANT MORTALITY

Number of babies who died under the age of one, per 1,000 live births (2022)

- Over 70
- 50 – 70
- 25 – 50
- 10 – 25
- Under 10
- No data

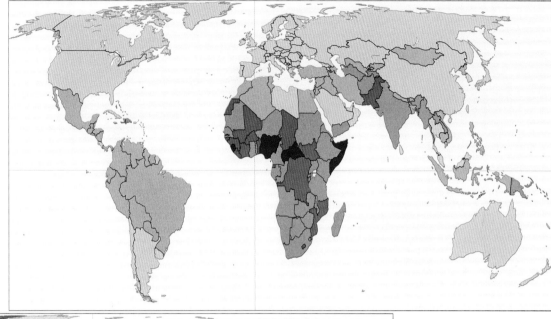

Countries with the highest and lowest child mortality

Highest		Lowest	
Sierra Leone	80.1	Iceland	1.5
CAR	77.5	San Marino	1.6
Somalia	72.7	Estonia	1.7

UK 3.6 babies

LIFE EXPECTANCY

The average expected lifespan of babies born in 2023

- Over 80
- 75 – 80
- 70 – 75
- 65 – 70
- Under 65
- No data

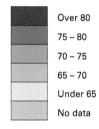

Countries with the highest and lowest life expectancy at birth in years

Highest		Lowest	
Singapore	87	Afghanistan	54
Japan	85	CAR	56
Canada	84	Somalia	56
Iceland	84	Mozambique	58
Switzerland	84	Sierra Leone	59

UK 82 years

FAMILY SIZE

Children born per woman (2021)

- More than 5
- 4 – 5
- 3 – 4
- 2 – 3
- Less than 2
- No data

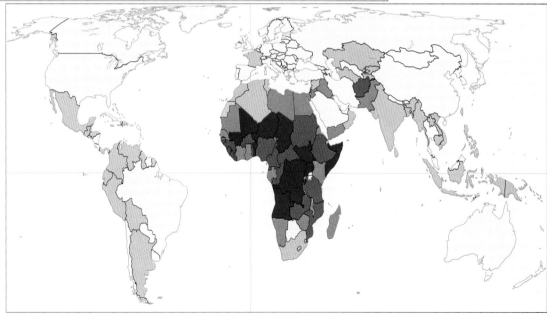

Countries with the largest and smallest family size

Largest		Smallest	
Niger	6.9	South Korea	1.1
Angola	5.9	Singapore	1.2
DRC	5.7	Puerto Rico	1.2
Mali	5.6	Montserrat	1.3
Chad	5.6	Bosnia-Herz.	1.4

UK 1.9 children

Projection: Eckert IV

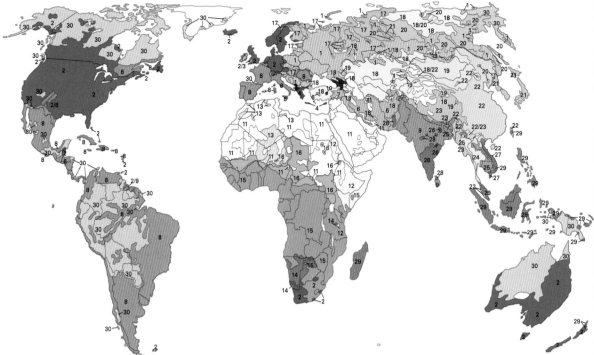

Languages of the W

Language can be classifi
by ancestry and structur
For example, the Roman
and Germanic groups ar
both derived from an Ind
European language
believed to have been
spoken 5,000 years ago.

**First-language speakers
millions**
Mandarin Chinese 850,
Spanish 430, English 340,
Hindi 260, Arabic 240,
Portuguese 215, Bengali 1
Russian 160, Japanese 13
Javanese 84, French 80,
German 78, Wu Chinese 7
Korean 77, Telugu 74, Mar
Tamil 69, Vietnamese 68,
Italian 64, Punjabi 63.

**Distribution of living
languages**
The figures refer to the n
of languages currently in
in the regions shown
Asia 2,303
Africa 2,146
Pacific 1,312
The Americas 1,060
Europe 285

LANGUAGES

INDO-EUROPEAN FAMILY
1	Balto-Slavic group (incl. Russian, Ukrainian)
2	Germanic group (incl. English, German)
3	Celtic group
4	Greek
5	Albanian
6	Iranian group
7	Armenian
8	Romance group (incl. Spanish, Portuguese, French, Italian)
9	Indo-Aryan group (incl. Hindi, Bengali, Urdu, Punjabi, Marathi)
10	CAUCASIAN FAMILY

AFRO-ASIATIC FAMILY
111	Semitic group (incl. Arabic)
21	Kushitic group
3	Berber group
14	KHOISAN FAMILY
15	NIGER-CONGO FAMILY
16	NILO-SAHARAN FAMILY
17	URALIC FAMILY

ALTAIC FAMILY
181	Turkic group (incl. Turkish)
92	Mongolian group
02	Tungus-Manchu group
1	Japanese and Korean

SINO-TIBETAN FAMILY
22	Sinitic (Chinese) languages (incl. Mandarin, Wu, Yue)
23	Tibetic-Burmic languages
24	TAI FAMILY

AUSTRO-ASIATIC FAM
25	Mon-Khmer group
26	Munda group
27	Vietnamese
28	DRAVIDIAN FAMILY (incl. Telugu, Tamil)
29	AUSTRONESIAN FAM (incl. Malay-Indonesia Javanese)
30	OTHER LANGUAGES

RELIGIONS

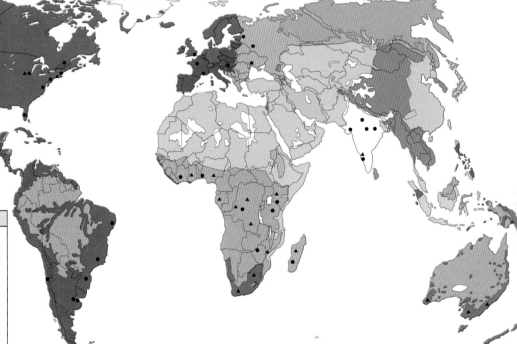

Roman Catholicism	
Orthodox and other Eastern Churches	
Protestantism	
Sunni Islam	
Shiite Islam	
Buddhism	
Hinduism	
Confucianism	
Judaism	
Shintoism	
Tribal Religions	

Religious Adherents

Religious adherents in millions

Christianity	2,000	Hinduism	900
Roman Catholic	1,500	Chinese folk	394
Orthodox	225	Buddhism	360
Anglican	70	Sikhism	23
Lutheran	66	Taoism	20
Methodist	8	Judaism	14
Others	131	Mormonism	12
Islam	1,300	Spiritualism	11
Sunni	940	Baha'i	6
Shi'ite	120	Confucianism	5
Others	240	Jainism	4
Non-religious/ Agnostic/Atheist	1,100	Shintoism	4

United Nations

Created in 1945 to promote peace and co-operation, and based in New York, the United Nations is the world's largest international organization, with 193 members and a budget for 2024 of US $3.59 billion. Each member of the General Assembly has one vote, while the five permanent members of the 15-nation Security Council – China, France, Russia, the UK and the USA – hold a veto. The Secretariat is the UN's principal administrative arm. The 54 members of the Economic and Social Council are responsible for economic, social, cultural, educational, health and related matters. The UN has 16 specialized agencies – based in Canada, France, Switzerland and Italy, as well as the USA – which help members in fields such as education (UNESCO), agriculture (FAO), medicine (WHO) and finance (IFC). By the end of 1994, all the original 11 Trust territories of the Trusteeship Council had become independent.

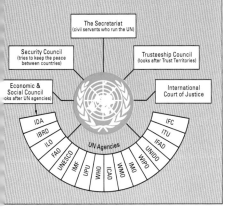

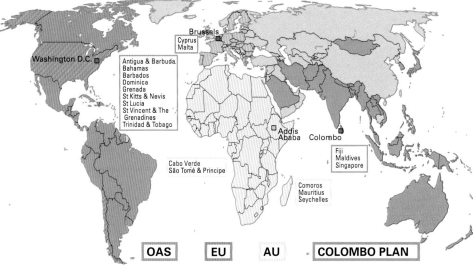

OAS   **EU**   **AU**   **COLOMBO PLAN**

AU The African Union was set up in 2002, taking over from the Organization of African Unity (1963). It has 55 members. Working languages are Arabic, English, French and Portuguese.

COLOMBO PLAN (formed in 1951) Its 27 members aim to promote economic and social development in Asia and the Pacific. Chile joined in 2021.

OAS Organization of American States (formed in 1948). It aims to promote social and economic co-operation between countries in the developed North America and developing Latin America.

EU European Union (evolved from the European Community in 1993). Cyprus, Czechia, Estonia, Hungary, Latvia, Lithuania, Malta, Poland, Slovakia and Slovenia joined the EU in May 2004, Bulgaria and Romania joined in 2007, Croatia joined in 2013. The other 15 members of the EU are Austria, Belgium, Denmark, Finland, France, Germany, Greece, Ireland, Italy, Luxembourg, Netherlands, Portugal, Spain and Sweden. The UK left the EU in 2020. Together, the 27 members aim to integrate economies, co-ordinate social developments and bring about political union. Its member states have set up common institutions to which they delegate some of their sovereignty so that decisions on specific matters of joint interest can be made democratically at European level.

APEC Asia-Pacific Economic Co-operation (formed in 1989). It aims to support sustainable economic growth and prosperity for the region and to strengthen the Asia-Pacific community. APEC is the only intergovernmental grouping in the world operating on the basis of non-binding commitments, open dialogue, and equal respect for the views of all participants. There are 21 member economies.

G7 Group of seven leading industrialized nations, comprising Canada, France, Germany, Italy, Japan, the UK and the USA. Periodic meetings are held to discuss major world issues, such as world recessions.

OACPS The **Organisation of African, Caribbean and Pacific States** (formerly APC) was formed in 1975. Members enjoy economic ties with the EU.

OECD Organization for Economic Co-operation and Development (formed in 1961). It comprises 37 major free-market economies. The 'G7' is its 'inner group' of leading industrial nations.

OPEC Organization of Petroleum Exporting Countries (formed in 1960). It controls about three-quarters of the world's oil supply. Angola left in 2024.

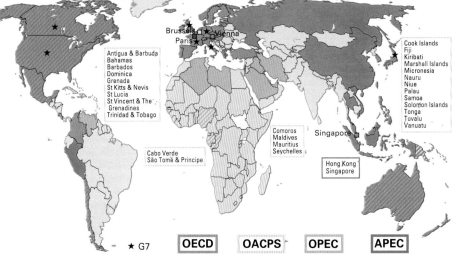

★ G7   **OECD**   **OACPS**   **OPEC**   **APEC**

ARAB LEAGUE (1945) Aims to promote economic, social, political and military co-operation. There are 22 member nations.

ASEAN Association of South-east Asian Nations (formed in 1967).

BRICS Originally formed of the emerging market countries of Brazil, Russia, India, China, and South Africa. Egypt, Ethiopia, Iran, Saudi Arabia and UAE joined in 2024.

COMMONWEALTH The Commonwealth of Nations evolved from the British Empire. Pakistan was suspended in 1999, but reinstated in 2004. Zimbabwe was suspended in 2002 and, in response to its continued suspension, left the Commonwealth in 2003. Fiji was suspended in 2006 following a military coup. Rwanda joined the Commonwealth in 2009, with Gabon and Togo in 2022, adding to the number of countries that were not formerly a British colony to be admitted to the group. The Gambia left between 2013 and 2018. There are currently 56 Commonwealth members.

LAIA The Latin American Integration Association (formed in 1980) superceded the Latin American Free Trade Association formed in 1961. Its aim is to promote freer regional trade.

NATO North Atlantic Treaty Organization (formed in 1949). It continues despite the winding-up of the Warsaw Pact in 1991. Bulgaria, Estonia, Latvia, Lithuania, Romania, Slovakia and Slovenia became members in 2004 and Albania and Croatia in 2009. Montenegro joined in 2017, North Macedonia in 2020, Finland in 2023 and Sweden in 2024.

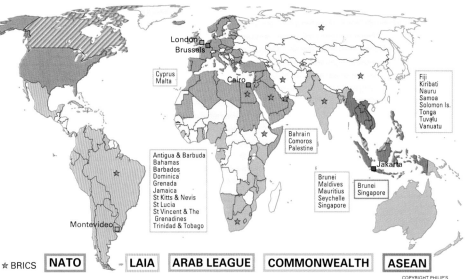

★ BRICS   **NATO**   **LAIA**   **ARAB LEAGUE**   **COMMONWEALTH**   **ASEAN**

GLOBAL PEACE INDEX

The Global Peace Index (GPI) is calculated [by the]
Institute for Economics and Peace. The GPI [measures]
158 nations using 23 qualitative and quantat[ive]
indicators which gauge three broad themes [the]
level of security in society; the extent of dom[estic]
or international conflict; and the degree of
militarization.

Global Peace Index (2023)

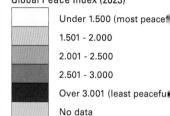

	Under 1.500 (most peaceful)
	1.501 - 2.000
	2.001 - 2.500
	2.501 - 3.000
	Over 3.001 (least peaceful)
	No data

Most peaceful		Least peaceful	
Cyprus	1.093	Afghanistan	3.448
Iceland	1.124	Yemen	3.350
The Gambia	1.189	Syria	3.294
Denmark	1.310	South Sudan	3.221
Ireland	1.312	DRC	3.214
	UK 1.693		

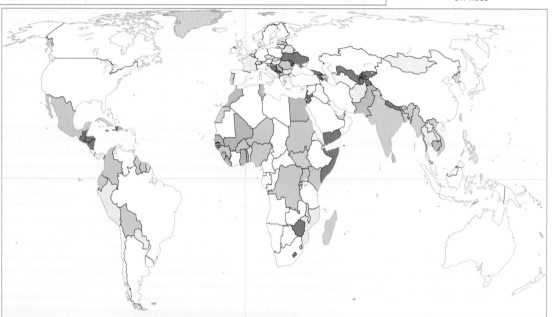

MONEY SENT HOME BY MIGRANTS

Remittances as a percentage
share of GDP (2022)

	Over 10%
	5% - 10%
	2.5% - 5%
	1% - 2.5%
	Under 1%
	No data

Most money sent home

Tajikistan	50.9%	Lebanon	27.5%
Tonga	46.2%	Honduras	26.8%
Samoa	33.6%	Lesotho	25.7%
The Gambia	28.1%	El Salvador	23.7%
Kyrgyzstan	27.9%	Nepal	22.8%

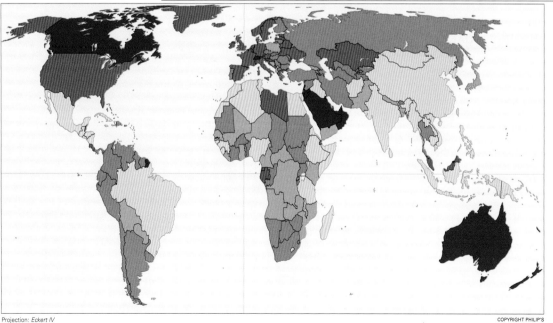

INTERNATIONAL MIGRA[TION]

Migrant Stock as percentage of
total population

	Over 20%
	10% - 20%
	2.5% - 10%
	1% - 2.5%
	Under 1%
	No data

UAE	88.1%
Qatar	77.7%
Kuwait	72.8%
Liechtenstein	67.9%
Monaco	67.8%
Andorra	59.0%
Bahrain	55.0%
Luxembourg	47.6%
Oman	46.5%
Singapore	43.1%

Projection: *Eckert IV*

GLOBAL TERRORISM

Calculation of the Global Terrorism ndex (GTI) takes into account deaths, ncidents, hostages and injuries from terrorism (2022)

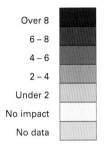

- Over 8
- 6 – 8
- 4 – 6
- 2 – 4
- Under 2
- No impact
- No data

untries with highest impact from terrorism

ghanistan	8.8	Pakistan	8.2
rkina Faso	8.6	Iraq	8.1
malia	8.5	Nigeria	8.1
ali	8.4	Niger	7.6
ria	8.2	Cameroon	7.3

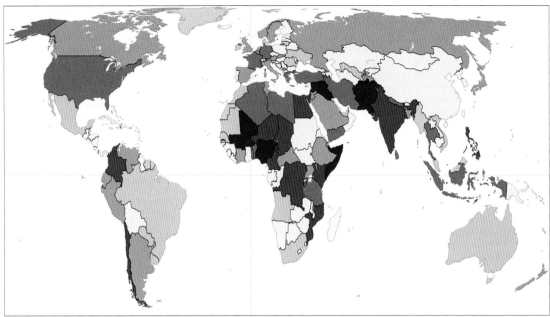

COVID-19 CASES

Cumulative total number of cases per 100,000 people (April 2023)

- Over 40,000
- 20,000 – 40,000
- 10,000 – 20,000
- 1,000 – 10,000
- Under 1,000
- No data

Countries with highest number of cases per 100,000 people

Cyprus	73,800
San Marino	70,300
Austria	68,000
Brunei	65,000
Slovenia	64,000

TRAFFIC IN DRUGS

Countries producing illegal drugs

- Cannabis
- Opium poppy
- Coca leaves
- Cocaine
- Amphetamines ■

Major routes of drug trafficking

- Opium
- Coca leaves
- Cocaine
- Heroin
- Cannabis
- Amphetamines (usually used within producing countries)
- Conflicts relating to drug trafficking

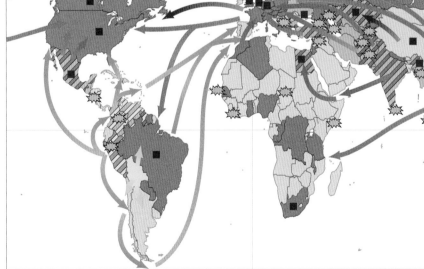

Projection: Eckert IV

	POPULATION						WEALTH						TRADE	
	Total population (millions 2023)	Population density (persons per km² 2023)	Population change (average annual % 2023)	Birth rate (births per thousand people 2023)	Death rate (deaths per thousand people 2023)	Urban population (% of total 2023)	Gross National Income (million US$ 2022)	Gross National Income per capita (PPP US$ 2022)	GDP growth rate (percentage 2022)	GDP from agriculture (% of GDP)	GDP from industry (% of GDP)	GDP from services (% of GDP 2022)	Imports (% of GDP 2022)	Exports (% of GDP 2022)
Afghanistan	39.2	60	2.3	35	12	27	15,387	380	-6.2	23.0	21.1	47.2	37	14
Albania	3.1	108	2.3	13	7	65	18,815	6,770	4.8	21.7	21.7	47.4	48	37
Algeria	44.7	19	1.6	21	4	74	176,171	3,920	3.6	12.4	39.3	38.6	24	35
Angola	35.9	29	3.4	41	8	69	66,998	1,880	3.0	10.2	62.4	42.6	25	43
Argentina	46.6	17	0.8	15	7	93	535,914	11,590	5.0	10.8	28.1	53.1	15	16
Armenia	3.0	100	-0.4	11	10	64	16,574	5,960	12.6	16.7	28.2	55.5	51	50
Australia	26.5	3	1.3	12	7	93	1,582,213	60,840	3.8	3.6	25.3	63.3	20	25
Austria	8.9	107	0.3	9	10	60	503,844	55,720	4.8	1.3	28.4	62.1	62	62
Azerbaijan	10.4	120	0.4	12	7	58	57,394	5,660	4.6	6.1	53.5	32.2	27	60
Bahamas, The	0.4	26	1.6	13	6	84	12,923	31,520	14.4	2.3	7.7	79.4	43	38
Bahrain	1.5	2252	0.9	12	3	90	40,804	27,720	4.9	0.3	39.3	47.9	70	90
Bangladesh	167.1	1161	1.0	18	6	41	483,359	2,820	7.1	14.2	29.3	51.0	21	13
Barbados	0.3	706	0.2	11	8	41	5,489	19,490	13.8	1.5	9.8	73.0	43	35
Belarus	9.3	45	-0.4	9	13	81	66,549	7,210	-4.7	8.1	40.8	48.8	58	64
Belgium	11.9	391	0.6	11	10	98	629,745	53,890	3.0	0.6	19.1	48.3	97	96
Belize	0.4	18	1.5	18	5	47	2,687	6,630	8.7	10.3	21.6	61.4	56	52
Benin	14.2	126	3.3	41	8	50	18,644	1,400	6.3	26.1	22.8	46.9	29	22
Bhutan	0.9	19	1.0	16	6	44	2,559	3,290	4.8	16.2	41.8	50.2	48	50
Bolivia	12.2	11	1.1	18	7	71	42,675	3,490	3.6	13.8	37.8	49.6	35	32
Bosnia-Herzegovina	3.8	74	-0.2	8	10	50	24,785	7,660	4.2	6.8	28.9	54.4	62	48
Botswana	2.4	4	1.4	20	9	73	19,556	7,430	5.8	1.8	27.5	55.9	42	43
Brazil	218.7	26	0.6	13	7	88	1,753,188	8,140	3.0	6.6	20.7	58.9	19	20
Brunei	0.5	84	1.4	16	4	79	14,102	31,410	-1.6	1.2	56.6	32.5	61	86
Bulgaria	6.8	62	-0.7	8	14	77	86,291	13,350	3.9	4.3	28.0	59.6	69	69
Burkina Faso	22.4	82	2.5	33	8	33	19,374	850	1.8	31.0	23.9	42.7	33	32
Burundi	13.1	86	3.7	35	6	15	3,118	240	1.8	39.5	16.4	45.4	23	5
Cabo Verde	0.6	151	1.2	18	6	68	2,344	3,950	17.1	8.9	17.5	66.2	57	41
Cambodia	17.0	93	1.0	19	6	26	28,373	1,690	5.1	25.3	32.8	33.9	55	68
Cameroon	30.1	63	2.7	35	8	59	45,911	1,640	3.6	16.7	26.5	50.0	22	19
Canada	38.5	4	0.7	10	8	82	2,075,403	53,310	3.8	1.6	28.2	70.2	34	34
Central African Rep.	5.5	9	1.8	32	12	44	2,666	480	0.5	43.2	16	42.4	33	19
Chad	18.5	14	3.1	40	9	24	12,183	690	3.1	52.3	14.7	26.2	40	51
Chile	18.5	24	0.6	13	7	88	301,194	15,360	2.1	4.2	32.8	54.3	39	36
China	1413.1	147	0.2	10	8	65	18,151,669	12,850	3.0	7.9	40.5	52.8	17	21
Colombia	49.3	43	0.5	15	8	82	336,943	6,500	7.3	7.2	30.8	54.6	28	21
Comoros	0.9	403	1.3	22	7	31	1,346	1,610	2.6	47.7	11.8	50.2	35	13
Congo	5.6	17	2.4	29	5	70	13,697	2,290	8.8	9.3	51.0	37.3	34	64
Congo (Dem. Rep.)	111.8	48	3.1	40	8	48	60,646	610	1.7	19.7	43.6	32.1	49	46
Costa Rica	5.2	103	0.7	11	6	83	66,934	12,920	4.6	5.5	20.6	67.3	39	41
Côte d'Ivoire	29.3	87	2.1	28	8	53	73,645	2,620	6.9	20.1	26.6	53.7	27	25
Croatia	4.2	74	-0.5	9	13	59	75,567	19,600	6.3	3.7	26.2	60.9	65	59
Cuba	10.9	99	-0.2	10	9	78	100,934	8,920	1.7	4.0	22.7	70.0	49	40
Cyprus	1.3	141	1.0	10	7	67	28,769	31,520	5.1	2.0	12.6	74.3	95	95
Czechia	10.7	136	0.1	10	12	75	278,546	26,100	2.3	2.3	36.7	59.2	75	76
Denmark	5.9	138	0.4	11	10	89	434,002	73,520	2.7	1.3	22.9	76.8	59	70
Djibouti	0.9	42	2.0	22	7	79	3,708	3,310	3.9	2.4	17.3	76.8	171	169
Dominican Republic	10.8	223	0.7	17	7	84	101,620	8,430	4.9	5.6	33.0	54.4	32	22
Ecuador	17.4	61	1.0	18	7	65	113,428	6,300	6.2	6.7	32.9	53.7	29	29
Egypt	109.5	109	1.6	21	4	43	455,137	4,100	6.7	11.7	34.3	51.4	22	15
El Salvador	6.6	314	0.5	18	6	75	29,899	4,720	2.8	12.0	27.7	59.6	56	31
Equatorial Guinea	1.7	62	3.4	30	9	74	8,775	5,240	3.2	2.5	54.6	45.1	36	52
Eritrea	6.3	53	1.1	27	7	43	1,941	610	5.0	11.7	29.6	58.7	–	–
Estonia	1.2	27	-0.7	9	13	70	36,576	27,120	-0.5	2.6	29.2	61.5	86	86
Eswatini	1.1	64	0.7	22	10	25	4,509	3,750	0.5	6.5	45.0	53.0	48	44
Ethiopia	116.5	106	2.4	30	6	23	126,126	1,020	6.4	34.5	21.6	36.6	18	8
Fiji	0.9	52	0.4	16	6	59	5,014	5,390	20.0	13.6	17.4	54.8	69	48
Finland	5.6	17	0.2	10	10	89	304,992	54,890	1.3	2.7	28.2	59.1	48	45
France	68.5	124	0.2	11	10	82	3,078,220	45,290	2.5	1.7	19.5	70.7	39	35
Gabon	2.4	9	2.4	26	6	91	17,994	7,530	3.0	5.0	44.7	33.2	17	61
Gambia, The	2.5	219	2.2	28	6	65	2,158	800	4.9	20.2	14.2	52.3	31	5
Gaza Strip (OPT)*	2.0	5660	2.1	28	3	77	–	4,610	3.9	3.0	21.1	75.0	–	–
Georgia	4.9	71	-0.9	12	14	61	20,158	5,600	11	8.2	23.7	59.6	63	53
Germany	84.2	236	-0.1	9	12	78	4,527,641	54,030	1.8	0.7	30.7	62.7	49	51
Ghana	33.8	1425	2.2	28	6	59	79,641	2,380	3.1	18.3	24.5	42.0	36	35
Greece	10.5	80	-0.4	8	12	81	227,407	21,810	5.6	4.1	16.9	67.4	59	49

	ENERGY			LAND & AGRICULTURE				SOCIAL INDICATORS							
	Energy consumed (% of world total 2022)	Renewable energy consumption (% of world total 2022)	CO₂ emissions (tonnes per capita 2022)	Land area (thousand km²)	Arable and Permanent crops (% of land area)	Permanent pasture (% of land area)	Forest (% of land area)	Human Development Index (HDI value 2022)	Life expectancy (years 2023)	Infant Mortality (deaths per 1,000 live births before age 1 2022)	Malnutrition undernourished (% of population)	Health expenditure (US$ per capita 2023)	Gender Inequality Index (GII value 2022)	Global Peace Index (GPI 2023)	Children's Climate Risk Index (CCRI 2021)
anistan	0.60	0.03	0.14	652	21	79	2	0.478	54	102.1	30	81.3	0.678	3.448	7.6
nia	0.02	0.08	1.52	28.7	59	40	28	0.796	80	10.5	4	465	0.144	1.754	4.8
ria	0.42	0.01	3.97	2,382	20	79	1	0.745	78	18.8	3	204.5	0.499	2.094	4.6
la	0.06	0.09	0.58	1,247	9	79	47	0.586	63	57.3	22	64.2	0.537	2.200	–
ntina	0.60	0.50	3.97	2,780	17	39	11	0.842	79	9.1	3	1,044.7	0.287	1.837	4.1
enia	0.02	0.04	2.15	29.8	18	42	9	0.759	76	11.9	3	612.8	0.216	1.929	3.7
ralia	1.00	1.50	15.12	7,741	12	88	16	0.951	83	3.0	3	7,055.3	0.073	1.525	3.6
ria	0.24	0.40	6.94	83.9	17	21	47	0.916	83	3.2	3	6,504.0	0.053	1.316	2.1
baijan	0.10	0.02	3.62	86.6	25	32	11	0.745	75	11.9	3	248.0	0.294	2.090	3.8
mas, The	0.01	0.00	3.49	13.9	1	0	51	0.812	76	9.6	–	1,961.7	0.329	–	–
ain	0.12	0.00	21.31	0.69	6	5	1	0.875	80	10.0	–	1,146.5	0.181	2.145	3.1
adesh	0.30	0.03	0.63	144	65	5	11	0.661	75	29.6	11	57.9	0.530	2.051	7.6
ados	0.00	0.00	2.34	0.43	28	5	19	0.790	79	9.8	3	1,400.4	0.268	–	–
us	0.20	0.01	6.12	208	28	16	43	0.808	75	2.1	3	457.5	0.104	2.248	3.2
um	0.45	0.60	7.72	30.5	28	16	22	0.937	82	3.2	3	5,680.2	0.048	1.523	2.5
e	0.00	0.00	0.65	23	5	2	61	0.683	74	11.3	7	310.2	0.364	–	3.8
n	0.02	0.00	0.75	113	26	5	40	0.525	63	54.3	10	35.1	0.602	2.177	7.6
an	0.01	0.05	2.01	47	4	11	85	0.666	73	25.6	–	120.4	0.415	1.496	3.8
ia	0.05	0.03	1.85	1,099	4	30	52	0.692	73	22.3	19	273.0	0.418	2.001	5.0
ia-Herzegovina	0.04	0.03	6.26	51.2	21	20	43	0.780	78	5.1	3	619.5	0.136	1.892	3.0
wana	0.02	0.00	3.29	582	0	45	20	0.693	66	24.4	23	457.5	0.468	1.762	4.8
l	2.20	5.60	2.15	8,514	9	23	62	0.754	76	13.1	5	761.3	0.390	2.462	5.3
ei	0.03	0.20	20.65	5.8	2	1	72	0.829	79	10.3	–	693.4	0.259	–	2.4
aria	0.13	0.25	7.32	111	31	16	38	0.795	76	13.8	3	1,040.0	0.210	1.643	3.6
na Faso	0.01	0.00	0.26	274	21	22	21	0.449	64	48.2	16	57.0	0.621	2.686	7.6
ndi	0.00	0.00	0.07	27.8	55	19	7	0.462	68	36.8	–	24.3	0.505	2.393	6.1
Verde	0.00	0.00	1.74	4	12	6	21	0.654	74	23.0	18	247.9	0.349	–	–
bodia	0.03	0.05	1.03	181	24	9	51	0.593	71	28.8	5	122.4	0.461	1.947	6.5
eroon	0.03	0.05	0.37	475	15	4	41	0.576	64	47.7	6	63.8	0.565	2.660	7.9
da	2.30	1.30	15.22	9,971	5	2	34	0.936	84	4.3	3	6,470.1	0.069	1.350	3.7
ral African Rep.	0.00	0.00	0.05	623	3	5	36	0.404	56	81.7	49	42.9	0.672	2.934	8.7
	0.00	0.00	0.12	1,284	4	36	9	0.394	60	64.0	31	35.6	0.652	2.699	8.5
	0.30	0.70	4.96	757	2	19	22	0.855	80	6.4	3	1,518.0	0.187	1.874	4.0
a	26.40	29.40	8.85	9,597	13	42	22	0.768	78	6.5	3	670.5	0.192	2.009	6.7
mbia	0.40	0.20	1.74	1,139	3	35	55	0.752	75	11.7	7	557.5	0.424	2.693	6.4
oros	0.00	0.00	0.38	2.2	77	8	1	0.558	68	56.0	14	99.4	–	–	–
go	0.01	0.01	1.24	342	2	29	66	0.479	72	31.4	33	80.5	0.564	2.210	6.4
go (Dem. Rep.)	0.02	0.11	0.03	2,345	3	8	68	0.571	62	59.1	35	22.3	0.601	3.214	8.0
a Rica	0.04	0.11	1.68	51.1	12	25	1	0.809	80	7.0	3	948.9	0.265	1.731	2.9
e d'Ivoire	0.03	0.03	0.53	322	23	42	33	0.550	63	54.0	8	81.9	0.613	2.053	7.5
tia	0.07	0.1	4.23	56.5	17	6	34	0.858	78	8.6	3	1,384.1	0.093	1.450	3.2
a	0.06	0.01	2.15	111	38	23	27	0.764	80	4.1	3	–	0.303	2.103	4.7
us	0.02	0.00	6.10	9.3	13	0	19	0.896	80	8.2	3	2,989.7	0.123	1.093	2.5
hia	0.30	0.2	9.55	78.9	42	13	34	0.889	78	2.6	3	2,598.5	0.120	1.379	2.4
mark	0.12	0.6	4.99	43.1	59	4	13	0.948	82	3.0	3	7,382.2	0.013	1.310	2.4
uti	0.00	0.00	0.74	23.2	0	73	0	0.509	66	46.0	17	87.8	–	2.196	5.8
inican Republic	0.06	0.03	2.07	48.5	27	25	41	0.767	72	22.7	7	416.9	0.429	2.019	6.2
dor	0.12	0.21	2.59	284	10	20	39	0.740	75	11.7	14	494.3	0.362	2.095	5.4
t	0.70	0.20	2.50	1,001	3	0	0	0.731	75	17.3	7	179.7	0.442	2.267	5.6
vador	0.02	0.04	1.22	21	44	31	14	0.657	76	11.7	8	442.2	0.376	2.279	5.1
torial Guinea	0.01	0.01	3.37	28.1	6	4	57	0.596	64	77.9	–	255.4	–	2.103	7.5
ea	0.00	0.00	0.14	118	7	68	15	0.492	67	40.6	–	25.4	–	2.505	7.1
nia	0.02	0.10	8.39	45.1	14	7	52	0.890	78	3.4	3	2,094.5	0.100	1.563	1.7
tini	0.00	0.01	0.91	17.4	11	58	32	0.597	60	38.1	12	279.9	0.540	2.166	5.2
pia	0.10	0.13	0.18	1,104	16	20	12	0.498	67	33.0	22	26.5	0.520	2.872	7.6
	0.01	0.01	1.81	18.3	14	10	55	0.730	75	9.9	7	250.0	0.318	–	–
nd	0.20	0.70	6.64	338	7	0	73	0.940	82	2.1	3	5,487.9	0.033	1.399	1.7
ce	1.40	1.80	4.76	552	35	18	29	0.903	83	3.1	3	5,380.9	0.083	1.939	4.1
on	0.01	0.01	2.46	268	2	17	81	0.706	70	27.7	23	233.8	0.541	2.068	5.1
bia, The	0.00	0.00	0.26	11.3	40	26	48	0.500	68	36.4	20	24.6	0.611	1.189	6.8
Strip (OPT)*	0.01	0.02	–	0.4	–	–	–	0.690	75	–	–	–	–	–	–
gia	0.04	0.11	3.10	69.7	8	28	40	0.802	72	22.6	3	417.1	0.280	2.071	2.6
nany	2.01	5.40	8.16	357	35	14	32	0.942	82	3.1	3	6,626.0	0.073	1.456	2.6
a	0.05	0.06	0.76	239	33	37	21	0.632	70	31.9	5	100.08	0.529	1.799	6.9
ce	0.20	0.40	5.14	132	29	35	30	0.887	82	3.5	3	1,845.8	0.119	1.890	3.3

	POPULATION						WEALTH						TRADE		
	Total population (millions 2023)	Population density (persons per km² 2023)	Population change (average annual % 2023)	Birth rate (births per thousand people 2023)	Death rate (deaths per thousand people 2023)	Urban Population (% of total 2023)	Gross National Income (million US$ 2022)	Gross National Income per capita (PPP US$ 2022)	GDP growth rate (percentage 2022)	GDP from agriculture (% of GDP)	GDP from industry (% of GDP)	GDP from services (% of GDP)	Imports (% of GDP 2022)	Exports (% of GDP 2022)	Tourism receipts (% OF GNI 2022)
Guatemala	18.0	165	1.5	22	5	53	92,836	5,350	4.1	13.3	23.4	62.0	36	19	
Guinea	13.6	55	2.8	36	8	38	16,502	1,190	4.0	18.8	32.1	35.5	64	44	
Guinea-Bissau	2.0	58	2.8	36	7	46	1,717	820	4.2	50.0	13.1	36.9	–	–	
Guyana	0.8	4	0.3	17	7	27	12,067	14,920	62.3	15.4	16.3	19.3	–	–	
Haiti	11.4	413	1.2	22	8	60	18,624	1,610	-1.7	22.1	20.3	48.2	29	7	
Honduras	9.6	86	1.3	20	6	60	28,670	2,750	4.0	14.2	28.8	56.	69	42	
Hungary	9.7	104	-0.3	9	15	73	183,348	19,010	4.6	3.9	31.3	57.2	96	91	
Iceland	0.4	4	0.9	13	7	94	26,229	68.660	8.9	5.8	19.7	64.5	47	47	
India	1339.1	426	0.7	17	10	36	3,384,775	2,390	7.0	15.4	23.0	48.8	26	23	
Indonesia	279.5	147	0.8	15	7	59	1,260,906	4,580	5.3	13.7	41.0	41.8	21	24	
Iran	87.6	53	0.9	15	5	77	352,591	3,980	3.8	9.6	35.8	45.0	25	27	
Iraq	41.3	95	1.9	24	4	72	234,694	5,370	7.0	3.3	51.0	34.8	24	38	
Ireland	5.3	76	1.1	11	7	65	408,767	79,730	9.4	1.2	38.6	52.6	97	137	
Israel	9.0	439	1.6	19	5	93	527,023	55,140	6.5	2.4	26.5	72.4	29	32	
Italy	61.0	203	-0.1	7	11	72	2,251,550	38,200	4.0	2.1	23.9	64.3	38	37	
Jamaica	2.8	257	0.1	16	7	57	16,273	5,760	4.2	7.0	21.1	5.3	–	–	
Japan	123.7	327	-0.4	7	12	92	5,324,575	42,550	1.0	1.2	30.1	69.9	25	22	
Jordan	11.1	124	0.8	22	4	92	49,137	4,350	2.4	4.5	28.8	60.4	–	–	
Kazakhstan	19.5	7	0.9	18	8	58	188,688	9,620	3.3	4.7	34.1	52.4	26	42	
Kenya	57.0	94	2.1	26	5	30	117,313	2,170	4.8	34.5	17.8	55.1	22	12	
Korea, North	26.0	216	0.4	13	10	63	–	–	-1.1	22.5	47.6	29.9	–	–	
Korea, South	51.9	523	0.2	7	7	82	1,868,326	36,190	2.6	2.2	39.3	58.0	48	48	
Kosovo	1.9	180	0.6	15	8	–	9,979	5,660	4.3	11.9	17.7	45.5	71	38	
Kuwait	3.1	174	1.1	18	2	100	173,298	40,600	6.1	0.4	58.7	69.1	–	–	
Kyrgyzstan	6.1	31	0.8	19	6	38	10,063	1,440	6.3	14.6	31.2	52.4	–	–	
Laos	7.8	33	1.3	20	6	38	17,367	2,310	2.3	20.9	33.2	40.3	–	–	
Latvia	1.8	28	-1.1	9	15	69	41,058	21,850	3.0	3.9	22.4	61.7	77	72	
Lebanon	5.3	512	0.6	13	6	89	27,768	4,970	-7.0	3.9	13.1	94.1	53	26	
Lesotho	2.2	71	0.8	23	11	30	2,827	1,230	1.6	5.8	39.2	56.6	101	48	
Liberia	5.5	50	2.4	33	9	54	3,591	1,320	4.8	34.0	13.8	37.3	–	–	
Libya	7.3	4	1.5	21	4	82	49,473	7,260	-8.3	1.3	52.3	25.5	–	–	
Lithuania	2.7	41	-1.0	9	15	68	67,585	23,870	2.4	3.5	29.5	61.2	89	86	
Luxembourg	0.6	254	1.6	12	7	92	58,2581	89,200	1.4	0.3	12.8	80.4	177	211	
Macedonia, North	2.1	83	0.1	10	10	60	13,707	6,660	2.1	10.9	23.5	55.2	96		
Madagascar	28.8	47	2.2	29	6	40	15,158	510	4.0	24.0	19.5	47.1	39	30	
Malawi	21.2	172	2.3	27	5	18	13,133	640	0.8	28.6	15.4	54.9	–	–	
Malaysia	34.2	102	1.0	14	6	79	401,460	11,830	8.7	8.8	37.6	50.9	70	77	
Maldives	0.4	1302	-0.2	15	4	42	5,697	10,880	13.9	3.0	16.0	73.3	–	–	
Mali	21.4	16	2.9	41	8	46	19,126	850	3.5	41.8	18.9	35.6	40	29	
Malta	0.5	1440	0.6	10	9	95	17,455	32,860	8.1	41.8	18.1	78.9	152	165	
Mauritania	4.2	4	2.0	28	7	58	9,843	2,080	6.4	27.8	29.3	33.7	55	49	
Mauritius	1.3	655	0.1	10	9	41	13,082	10,360	8.9	4.0	21.8	65.8	63	59	
Mexico	129.9	67	0.6	14	7	82	1,397,146	10,820	3.9	3.6	31.9	57.6	45	39	
Moldova	3.3	96	-0.6	9	14	43	13,965	5,500	-5.0	17.7	20.3	58.1	69	41	
Mongolia	3.2	2	0.8	15	6	69	14,468	4,260	5.0	12.5	38.2	49.7	71	65	
Montenegro	0.6	43	-0.4	11	10	69	6,466	10,480	6.4	7.5	15.9	61.5	74	52	
Morocco	37.0	83	0.9	17	7	65	139,595	3,670	1.3	14.0	29.5	54.5	56	45	
Mozambique	32.5	41	2.6	37	10	39	14,395	440	4.4	23.9	19.3	40.6	–	–	
Myanmar	57.9	86	0.7	16	7	32	68,904	1,270	-4.0	24.1	35.6	39.4	–	–	
Namibia	2.8	3	1.7	25	8	55	12,861	5,010	4.6	6.7	26.3	54.2	55	37	
Nepal	30.8	210	0.7	17	6	22	40,940	1,340	5.6	27.0	13.6	52.6	43	7	
Netherlands	17.5	421	0.5	11	10	93	1,066,103	60,230	4.3	1.6	17.9	68.7	83	94	
New Zealand	5.1	19	1.1	13	7	87	251,517	49,090	2.4	5.7	21.5	72.8	30	24	
Nicaragua	6.3	48	1.0	17	5	60	14,505	2,090	3.8	15.5	24.4	46.5	65	50	
Niger	25.4	20	3.7	47	10	17	15,143	580	11.9	41.6	19.5	34.7	27	9	
Nigeria	230.8	250	2.5	34	9	54	471,252	2,160	3.3	21.1	22.5	44.0	–	–	
Norway	5.6	17	0.6	10	8	84	515,900	94,540	3.0	2.3	33.7	43.2	27	55	
Oman	3.8	12	1.8	22	3	88	91,616	20,020	4.3	1.8	46.4	44.5	41	53	
Pakistan	247.6	311	1.9	26	6	38	369,926	1,560	6.2	24.4	19.1	52.2	23	11	
Panama	4.4	58	1.5	18	6	70	74,752	16,960	10.8	2.4	15.7	68.1	–	–	
Papua New Guinea	9.8	21	2.3	29	6	14	27,408	2,700	5.2	22.1	42.9	30.0	–	–	
Paraguay	7.4	18	1.1	16	5	63	40,130	5,920	0.2	17.9	27.7	68.1	39	35	
Peru	32.3	25	0.5	17	11	80	229,498	6,740	2.7	7.6	32.7	49.5	29	30	
Philippines	116.4	388	1.6	22	6	48	457,021	3,950	7.6	9.6	30.6	61.5	44	28	
Poland	37.9	118	-1.0	9	13	60	695,816	18,900	5.3	2.4	40.2	58.2	61	63	

	ENERGY			LAND & AGRICULTURE				SOCIAL INDICATORS							
	Energy consumed (% of world total 2022)	Renewable energy consumption (% of world total 2022)	CO₂ emissions (tonnes per capita 2018)	Land area (thousand km²)	Arable and permanent crops (% of land area)	Permanent pasture (% of land area)	Forest (% of land area)	Human Development Index (HDI) value 2022	Life expectancy (years 2023)	Infant Mortality (deaths per 1,000 live births before age 1 2022)	Malnutrition undernourished 2022 (% of population)	Health expenditure (US$ per capita 2023)	Gender Inequality Index (GII value 2022)	Global Peace Index (GPI 2023)	Children's Climate Risk Index (CCRI 2021)
emala	0.05	0.08	1.08	109	23	18	34	0.627	73	25.6	13	289.1	0.481	2.130	5.9
ea	0.01	0.01	0.26	246	15	44	27	0.465	64	48.3	13	44.9	0.621	2.359	8.4
ea-Bissau	0.00	0.00	0.17	36.1	15	30	55	–	64	47.7	3.4	68.9	0.627	2.045	8.4
na	0.01	0.00	4.76	215	2	6	77	0.714	72	21.6	3	470.6	0.454	2.134	4.8
	0.01	0.00	0.30	27.8	48	18	4	0.535	65	38.8	45	57.9	0.635	2.395	7.3
uras	0.03	0.07	1.05	112	13	16	45	0.621	72	14.4	19	253.9	0.431	2.695	5.5
ary	0.20	0.20	4.95	93	50	8	22	0.846	75	4.8	3	1,381.6	0.221	1.508	3.2
d	0.04	0.10	10.23	103	1	17	0	0.959	84	1.6	3	6,716.4	0.043	1.124	1.0
	6.00	4.80	1.91	3,287	57	3	23	0.945	68	30.4	17	740.0	0.490	2.314	7.4
esia	1.50	1.60	2.5	1,905	25	6	52	0.705	73	19.3	6	160.6	0.444	1.829	6.5
	2.10	0.23	8.08	1,648	12	18	7	0.775	75	14.6	6	392.5	0.459	2.800	5.3
	0.44	0.10	4.43	438	9	9	2	0.686	74	19.2	16	248.9	0.558	3.006	5.4
d	0.11	0.30	7.61	70.3	16	50	11	0.945	82	3.2	3	6,764.3	0.074	1.312	2.1
	0.20	0.20	4.24	20.6	18	6	7	0.919	82	3.0	3	4,338.9	0.083	2.706	3.7
	1.01	1.70	5.58	301	31	16	31	0.895	83	3.1	3	3,349.6	0.056	1.662	4.1
ca	0.02	0.01	2.08	11	20	21	31	0.709	76	10.9	8	372.5	0.335	1.986	–
n	3.00	3.40	8.61	378	12	0	68	0.925	85	1.9	3	4,347.3	0.083	1.336	4.5
	0.17	0.02	2.27	89.3	3	8	1	0.720	76	13.6	–	299.1	0.471	1.895	4.5
khstan	0.52	0.10	12.85	2,725	9	69	1	0.811	72	8.1	3	403.0	0.161	1.980	4.1
a	0.06	0.10	0.38	580	10	37	6	0.575	70	26.9	28	94.7	0.506	2.254	6.3
a, North	0.10	0.13	0.97	121	22	0	46	–	73	16.2	46	–	–	2.848	6.9
a, South	2.17	1.100	12.26	99.3	17	1	64	0.926	83	2.8	3	3,260.5	–	1.760	5.2
vo	0.01	0.00	4.30	10.9	29	23	42	–	72	24.9	–	–	–	1.946	–
it	0.30	0.00	24.90	17.8	1	8	0	0.831	79	7.3	3	1,898.0	0.305	1.669	3.3
zstan	0.01	0.14	1.60	200	7	48	5	0.692	73	25.1	5	72.9	0.370	2.110	4.5
	0.17	0.12	2.74	237	7	4	68	0.607	69	36.6	5	68.9	0.478	1.779	6.7
	0.03	0.04	3.61	64.6	19	10	54	0.863	76	4.8	3	1,898.0	0.151	1.582	2.6
on	0.10	0.00	4.05	10.4	24	39	13	0.706	79	6.9	–	307.1	0.432	2.581	3.6
tho	0.00	0.01	0.33	30.4	10	66	1	0.514	60	47	46	114.7	0.557	2.191	5.4
a	0.00	0.00	0.30	111	7	21	45	0.481	61	56.1	38	112.3	0.648	1.946	7.5
	0.10	0.00	9.20	1,760	1	8	0	0.718	77	11.0	8	–	0.259	2.605	4.4
ania	0.10	0.10	4.69	65.2	35	9	35	0.875	76	3.6	3	1,858.6	0.105	1.671	2.4
nbourg	0.03	0.03	12.26	2.6	25	26	33	0.930	83	3.2	3	7,635.7	0.044	–	1.5
donia, North	0.01	0.03	3.16	25.7	19	26	40	–	77	4.5	–	–	0.720	1.713	3.4
gascar	0.01	0.01	0.11	587	7	64	22	0.501	69	38.6	51	17.6	–	1.846	7.9
vi	0.00	0.01	0.26	118	39	20	34	0.512	73	32.7	18	46.6	0.554	1.970	6.7
sia	0.80	0.20	8.23	330	22	1	62	0.803	76	6.5	3	487.0	0.228	1.513	5.4
ves	0.00	0.00	4.26	0.3	20	3	3	0.747	77	25.0	–	1,038.7	0.348	–	–
	0.01	0.01	0.31	1,240	4	28	10	0.428	63	59.0	13	40.1	0.613	2.963	7.3
	0.02	0.00	3.93	0.3	32	0	1	0.918	83	4.5	5	3,641.6	0.167	–	2.1
tania	0.01	0.00	0.92	1,026	0	38	0	0.556	66	50.0	9	89.3	0.634	2.228	6.7
tius	0.02	0.01	3.35	2	40	3	17	0.802	75	11.8	7	564.9	0.347	1.546	–
co	1.40	1.00	3.56	1,958	13	42	33	0.758	74	12.0	3	610.7	0.309	2.599	5.9
ova	0.02	0.01	2.17	33.9	64	11	12	0.767	70	14.1	3	410.0	0.205	1.873	4.1
olia	0.04	0.01	6.71	1,567	1	73	7	0.735	72	19.8	8	315.6	0.313	1.765	4.2
enegro	0.01	0.02	4.02	14	14	24	40	0.832	78	3.2	3	985.0	0.119	1.772	2.7
cco	0.20	0.1	1.92	447	24	47	11	0.676	74	1.8	6	985.1	0.425	2.020	5.4
mbique	0.04	0.14	0.29	802	6	50	44	0.446	58	59.8	31	44.5	0.537	2.259	7.9
mar	0.10	0.13	0.67	677	19	0	48	0.585	70	33.4	4	65.1	0.489	2.741	7.1
bia	0.01	0.02	1.53	824	1	46	9	0.615	64	14.7	17	456.4	0.445	1.895	5.1
	0.03	0.06	0.51	147	16	12	25	0.602	73	24.6	5	65.3	0.452	2.006	6.1
erlands	0.64	1.1	7.79	41.5	31	24	11	0.941	82	3.7	3	6,539.2	0.025	1.490	2.7
Zealand	0.15	0.3	6.59	271	2	41	31	0.937	83	3.7	3	4,906.1	0.088	1.313	1.6
agua	0.02	0.03	0.86	130	15	27	25	0.667	75	14.7	18	198.1	0.424	2.264	4.6
	0.01	0.00	0.10	1,267	12	23	1	0.400	62	65.5	16	34.3	0.611	2.625	8.2
ia	0.30	0.06	0.57	924	45	33	10	0.535	62	55.2	16	83.8	0.680	2.713	8.5
ay	0.32	0.4	7.62	324	2	1	28	0.961	83	1.8	3	9,020.6	0.016	1.550	2.1
	0.23	0.00	17.09	310	0	5	0	0.816	77	14.2	3	852.6	0.300	1.794	4.4
an	0.61	0.10	0.92	796	29	7	2	0.544	70	52.7	19	43.1	0.534	2.746	7.7
na	0.10	0.09	2.58	75.5	10	21	44	0.795	78	15.3	5	1,415.2	0.329	1.942	3.6
New Guinea	0.02	0.01	0.52	463	2	0	64	0.558	70	32.8	23	61.4	0.725	2.096	7.0
uay	0.10	0.44	1.37	407	11	43	44	0.717	79	22.6	4	478.7	0.445	1.942	3.9
	0.20	0.10	1.81	1,285	4	15	53	0.762	69	10.8	7	412.2	0.390	2.130	5.0
pines	0.32	0.40	1.38	300	36	5	26	0.669	71	22.1	5	203.2	0.419	2.229	7.1
d	0.73	0.90	8.53	323	37	11	31	0.876	76	5.1	3	1,159.3	0.109	1.634	3.5

	POPULATION						WEALTH						TRADE		
	Total population (millions 2023)	Population density (persons per km² 2023)	Population change (average annual % 2023)	Birth rate (births per thousand people 2023)	Death rate (deaths per thousand people 2023)	Urban population (% of total 2023)	Gross National income (million US$ 2022)	Gross National income per capita (PPP US$ 2022)	GDP growth rate (percentage 2022)	GDP from agriculture (% of GDP)	GDP from industry (% of GDP)	GDP from services (% of GDP)	Imports (% of GDP 2022)	Exports (% of GDP 2022)	Tourism received (% OF GNI 2022)
Portugal	10.2	115	-0.2	8	11	68	270,087	25,950	6.8	2.4	40.2	66.1	52	50	
Qatar	2.5	230	1.0	9	1	99	188,980	79,120	4.2	0.2	50.3	38.5	32	68	
Romania	18.3	77	-1.1	9	15	57	296,591	15,570	4.6	4.2	33.2	57.6	50	43	
Russia	141.6	8	-0.5	9	14	75	1,870,592	12,750	-2.0	4.7	32.4	54.0	16	28	
Rwanda	13.4	5	1.7	26	6	18	12,768	930	8.2	30.9	17.6	46.5	39	22	
Saudi Arabia	36.0	16	1.7	14	4	85	1,007,790	27,680	8.8	2.6	44.2	39.8	23	40	
Senegal	18.3	93	2.5	4	5	50	28,070	1,620	4.1	16.9	24.3	50.0	53	27	
Serbia	7.0	86	-0.6	9	15	57	61,938	9,290	2.6	9.8	41.1	52.0	75	64	
Sierra Leone	6.7	124	2.4	32	9	44	5,204	600	3.5	60.7	6.6	28.9	56	32	
Singapore	5.9	8787	1.0	9	4	100	378,814	64,010	3.7	0.0	24.8	70.9	150	187	
Slovakia	5.4	111	-0.1	10	12	54	119,855	35,260	1.8	3.8	35.0	58.5	105	99	
Slovenia	2.1	104	-0.1	8	11	56	62,487	29,590	2.5	1.8	32.2	58.0	92	94	
Solomon Is.	0.7	24	1.7	22	4	26	1,603	2,750	4.0	34.3	7.6	48.6	–	–	
Somalia	12.1	19	2.5	38	11	48	10,491	600	2.4	60.2	7.4	58.1	79	17	
South Africa	58.0	48	1.1	18	7	69	406,039	6,780	1.9	2.8	29.7	62.3	32	34	
Spain	47.2	95	-0.1	7	10	82	1,533,031	32,090	5.8	2.6	23.2	67.9	32	41	
Sri Lanka	23.3	355	0.6	16	7	19	80,075	3,610	-7.8	7.8	30.5	56.1	25	21	
Sudan	49.1	26	2.6	33	6	36	35,819	760	-1.0	39.6	2.6	6.4	1	2	
Sudan, South	12.1	18	4.8	37	9	21	11,669	1,080	-5.2	10.4	33.1	–	29	37	
Suriname	0.6	4	1.1	15	7	66	3,073	4,970	2.4	11.6	31.1	44.7	61	69	
Sweden	10.5	23	0.5	11	10	89	665,875	65,940	2.8	1.6	33.0	63.6	50	53	
Switzerland	8.5	207	0.8	10	8	74	837,996	96,490	2.6	0.7	25.6	71.8	63	77	
Syria	22.9	124	6.4	22	4	57	12,091	560	1.3	20.0	19.6	43.3	–	–	
Taiwan	23.6	655	0.0	7	8	80	–	–	2.7	1.8	36.0	61..2	–	–	
Tajikistan	9.2	64	1.9	26	5	28	12,041	1,210	8.0	28.6	25.5	33.4	41	16	
Tanzania	65.6	70	2.8	33	5	37	75,938	1,200	4.6	23.4	28.6	30.7	20	15	
Thailand	69.7	136	0.2	10	8	54	518,438	7,230	2.6	8.2	36.2	56.2	68	66	
Timor-Leste	1.4	95	2.1	30	6	33	2,652	1,980	-20.5	9.1	56.7	37.2	42	56	
Togo	8.7	153	2.5	31	5	46	8,949	1,010	5.8	28.8	21.8	59.7	34	24	
Trinidad & Tobago	1.4	276	0.1	11	9	53	24,788	16,190	1.48	0.4	47.8	47.8	–	–	
Tunisia	11.9	73	0.6	14	6	70	47,353	3,830	2.4	10.1	26.2	60.3	61	49	
Turkey	83.5	108	0.6	14	6	77	904,190	1.064	5.5	6.8	32.3	51.7	43	39	
Turkmenistan	5.7	12	1.0	17	6	54	53,547	6,970	1.7	7.5	44.9	47.7	12	23	
Uganda	47.7	198	3.2	40	5	27	43,9439	930	4.6	28.2	21.1	41.7	22	12	
Ukraine	43.3	72	2.3	6	20	70	150,812	4,260	-29.1	12.2	28.6	60.8	52	35	
United Arab Emirates	9.9	119	0.6	11	2	89	464,105	49,160	7.8	0.9	49.8	47.7	68	92	
United Kingdom	68.1	282	0.5	11	9	85	3,297,975	49,240	4.4	0.7	20.2	72.2	36	33	
USA	339.6	35	0.7	12	9	83	25,586,010	76,770	1.9	0.9	19.1	77.6	16	12	
Uruguay	3.4	19	0.3	13	9	96	61,597	18,000	4.9	6.2	24.1	63.2	26	26	
Uzbekistan	31.6	90	1.6	22	5	50	78,149	2,190	5.7	17.9	33.7	35.5	44	27	
Vanuatu	0.3	26	1.7	21	4	26	1,191	3,650	1.8	27.3	11.8	60.8	54	15	
Venezuela	30.5	34	2.4	17	7	88	393,924	–	-19.7	4.7	40.4	54.9	31	17	
Vietnam	104.8	316	1.0	15	6	39	393943	4,010	8.0	15.3	33.3	41.6	92	94	
West Bank (OPT)*	3.1	517	1.7	28	4	77	23,250	–	3.9	2.9	19.5	77.6	67	19	
Yemen	31.5	60	1.8	24	6	40	–	–	0.8	20.3	11.8	67.9	–	–	
Zambia	20.2	27	2.9	35	6	46	24,883	1,240	5.3	7.5	35.3	55.2	29	40	
Zimbabwe	15.4	39	2.0	29	7	32	27,910	1,710	6.5	12.0	22.2	40.7	37	28	

NOTES

The tables list information for the main states and territories of the world using the latest available data in each category.

OPT*
Occupied Palestinian Territory.

POPULATION TOTAL
These are estimates of the mid-year total in 2023.

POPULATION DENSITY
The total population divided by the land area (both are recorded in the table above).

BIRTH/DEATH RATES
These are 2023 estimates from the CIA World Factbook.

URBAN POPULATION
The urban population shows the percentage of the total population living in towns and cities (each country will differ with regard to the size or type of town that is defined as an urban area).

GNI
Gross National Income is a good indication of a country's wealth. It is the income in US dollars from goods and services in a country for one year, including income from overseas.

GNI PER CAPITA
The GNI (see note) divided by the total population by using the PPP method (see note).

PER CAPITA
An amount divided by the total population of a country or the amount per person.

PPP
Purchasing Power Parity (PPP) is a method used to enable real comparisons to be made between countries when measuring wealth. The UN International Comparison Programme gives estimates of the PPP for each country, so it can be used as an indicator of real price levels for goods and services rather than using currency exchange rates (see GNI and GNI per capita).

AGRICULTURE, INDUSTRY AND SERVICES
The percentage contributions that each of these three sectors makes a country's Gross Domestic Produ (GDP).

IMPORTS AND EXPORTS
The value of goods and services imported into a country and expor to other countries, given as a perce of a country's Gross Domestic Pro (GDP).

TOURISM RECEIPTS
The amount of income generated f tourism as a percentage of GNI

ENERGY CONSUMED
The total amount of commercial e consumed in a country given as a percentage of the world total.

ENERGY — LAND & AGRICULTURE — SOCIAL INDICATORS

	Energy consumed (% of world total 2022)	Renewable energy consumption (% of world total 2022)	CO₂ emissions (tonnes per capita 2022)	Land area (thousand km²)	Arable and permanent crops (% of land area)	Permanent pasture (% of land area)	Forest (% of land area)	Human Development Index (HDI value 2022)	Life expectancy (years 2023)	Infant Mortality (deaths per 1,000 live births before age 1 2022)	Malnutrition undernourished (% of population 2022)	Health expenditure (US$ per capita 2023)	Gender Inequality Index (GII value 2022)	Global Peace Index (GPI 2023)	Children's Climate Risk Index (CCRI 2021)
gal	0.20	0.50	4.07	88.8	20	20	38	0.866	82	2.5	3	2,746.7	0.067	1.333	3.0
r	0.33	0.00	35.52	11	1	4	0	0.855	80	6.5	–	1,934.1	0.220	1.524	3.1
nia	0.24	0.20	4.03	238	41	19	28	0.821	76	5.7	3	962.0	0.282	1.649	4.1
a	4.80	0.20	13.31	17,075	7	6	49	0.829	72	6.6	3	935.7	0.203	3.142	4.6
da	0.00	0.00	0.12	26.3	57	17	18	0.534	66	25.6	32	60.2	0.388	2.051	5.7
Arabia	1.90	0.00	16.89	2,150	2	79	0	0.875	77	12.0	4	1442.0	0.247	2.260	4.7
gal	0.02	0.01	0.67	197	17	29	44	0.511	70	31.8	6	71.2	0.530	1.827	7.5
a	0.12	0.13	6.13	77.5	41	16	32	0.802	75	4.6	3	919.2	0.131	1.921	3.9
Leone	0.00	0.00	0.13	71.7	26	30	38	0.477	59	72.3	28	43.2	0.663	1.792	7.4
pore	0.50	0.02	8.85	0.7	1	0	3	0.939	87	1.5	–	3,969.9	0.040	1.332	–
kia	0.12	0.10	6.46	49	29	11	40	0.848	77	5.3	3	1,684.5	0.180	1.589	2.9
nia	0.10	0.11	6.70	20.3	10	13	62	0.918	82	1.5	3	2,775.0	0.071	1.334	2.3
on Is.	0.00	0.00	0.47	28.9	3	0	79	0.564	77	19.5	19	106.4	–	–	5.2
lia	0.00	0.00	0.06	638	2	69	11	–	56	85.1	49	–	–	3.036	8.4
Africa	0.84	0.30	6.75	1,221	13	69	8	0.713	71	24.4	8	583.7	0.406	2.405	5.2
	1.00	2.30	5.48	498	35	21	36	0.905	82	2.4	3	3,234.3	0.059	1.649	3.7
nka	0.10	0.07	0.87	65.6	37	7	29	0.782	77	6.8	5	166.2	0.383	2.136	5.4
	0.10	0.10	0.44	1,886	16	84	0	0.508	68	41.4	12	21.6	0.553	3.023	7.6
, South	0.00	0.00	0.13	620	–	–	–	0.385	60	61.4	–	32.7	–	3.221	8.2
ame	0.01	0.01	5.60	163	0	0	95	0.730	73	15.8	9	289.9	0.429	–	5.0
en	0.40	1.20	3.69	450	6	1	69	0.847	83	2.3	3	6,900.8	0.023	1.625	1.8
erland	0.20	0.20	4.11	41.3	11	28	31	0.962	84	3.0	3	10,897.5	0.018	1.339	2.4
	0.10	0.01	1.38	185	31	45	3	0.577	75	15.5	–	–	0.477	3.294	4.8
n	0.80	0.30	11.52	36	23	–	58	–	81	3.9	–	–	–	1.649	–
stan	0.04	0.17	1.07	143	7	28	3	0.685	71	23.1	9	72.4	0.285	2.114	5.4
nia	0.03	0.02	0.25	945	17	27	37	0.549	71	30.4	24	32.2	0.560	2.058	6.7
nd	0.80	0.70	4.06	513	40	2	37	0.800	78	6.4	5	364.4	0.333	2.061	6.2
-Leste	0.00	0.00	0.40	14.9	15	10	49	–	70	32.9	22	135.0	0.378	1.796	–
	0.01	0.00	0.28	56.8	48	18	6	0.745	72	30.4	17	54.2	0.580	2.130	7.6
ad & Tobago	0.15	0.00	21.17	5.1	9	1	44	0.810	76	15.4	12	1,125.4	0.344	1.946	–
a	0.07	0.01	2.96	164	3	31	7	0.731	77	11.6	3	265.5	0.259	2.010	3.6
y	1.20	1.50	5.66	775	31	19	14	0.838	77	18.9	3	441.1	0.272	2.800	4.4
nenistan	0.30	-0.01	11.27	488	4	68	9	0.745	72	36.7	6	565.3	0.177	2.107	4.6
da	0.02	0.04	0.15	241	45	26	15	0.525	69	29.4	32	43.55	0.530	2.300	6.8
ne	0.40	0.20	3.07	604	57	14	17	0.773	70	9.0	5	367.9	0.200	3.043	3.8
d Arab Emirates	0.77	0.10	21.75	83.6	1	4	4	0.911	80	5.1	3	2,353.8	0.049	1.979	4.3
d Kingdom	1.20	3.00	5.00	242	25	46	12	0.929	82	3.8	3	5,738.5	0.098	1.693	3.8
	15.90	18.7	14.44	9,629	17	27	33	0.921	81	5.1	3	12,012.2	0.179	2.448	5.0
ay	0.04	0.14	2.43	175	10	77	10	0.809	76	8.1	3	1,620.3	0.235	1.798	3.0
kistan	0.30	0.06	3.89	447	11	52	8	0.727	75	18.9	3	157.2	0.227	2.033	5.4
tu	0.00	0.00	0.71	12.2	12	3	36	0.607	75	14.0	10	133.2	–	–	–
uela	0.44	0.57	2.86	912	4	20	53	0.691	74	14.1	18	160.1	0.429	2.693	5.5
am	0.80	0.70	3.27	332	32	2	45	0.703	76	14.4	5	172.6	0.296	1.745	6.8
Bank (OPT)*	0.01	0.02	–	5.9	18	25	2	–	76	–	–	–	–	–	–
n	0.02	0.00	0.39	528	3	42	1	0.455	68	45.5	35	–	0.492	3.350	7.4
ia	0.04	0.13	0.47	753	5	27	66	0.565	66	36.3	30	75.3	0.540	1.898	6.6
abwe	0.03	0.05	0.55	391	11	31	40	0.590	63	34.0	38	62.7	0.532	2.300	6.1

...WABLE ENERGY
...mption of energy generated from ...in renewable sources given as a ...tage of the world total.

...ON DIOXIDE EMISSIONS
...nount of carbon dioxide that each ...y produces per capita.

...AREA
...the total land area of a country, ...e area of major lakes and rivers, ...re kilometres.

...E AND PERMANENT CROPS
...figures give a percentage of the ...nd area that is used for crops and ...ncluding temporary fallow land or ...ws).

...ANENT PASTURE
...the percentage of land area that

has permanent forage crops for cattle or horses, cultivated or wild. Some land may be classified both as permanent pasture or as forest.

FOREST
Natural/planted trees including cleared land that will be reforested in the near future as a percentage of the land area.

HUMAN DEVELOPMENT INDEX (HDI)
Produced by the UN Development Programme using indicators of life expectancy, knowledge and standards of living to give a value between 0 and 1 for each country. A high value shows a higher human development.

LIFE EXPECTANCY
The average age that a child born today is expected to live to, if mortality levels

of today last throughout its lifetime. It is a measure of the overall quality of life.

INFANT MORTALITY
This is the number of deaths of infants under one year old in a year per 1,000 live births. This is often used as an indicator of the level of health in a country.

MALNUTRITION
Percentage of the total population whose food intake is insufficient to meet dietary energy requirements, referred to as the prevalence of undernourishment.

HEALTH EXPENDITURE
The amount of money that a country's government spends on health care per capita in one year.

GENDER INEQUALITY INDEX
Like the HDI (see note), the GII uses the same UNDP indicators but gives a value between 0 and 1 to measure the social and economic differences between men and women. The higher the value, the more equality exists between men and women.

GLOBAL PEACE INDEX
This index is an attempt to measure the relative position of nations' peacefulness. It quantifies: levels of security and safety; domestic and international conflict; and degree of militarization.

CHILDREN'S CLIMATE RISK INDEX
This index, ranks countries based on children's exposure to climate and environmental shocks, such as cyclones and heatwaves.

Each topic list is divided into continents and within a continent the items are listed in order of size. The bottom part of many of the lists is selective in order to give examples from as many different countries as possible. The figures are rounded as appropriate.

WORLD, CONTINENTS, OCEANS

	km²	miles²	%
The World	509,450,000	196,672,000	–
Land	149,450,000	57,688,000	29.3
Water	360,000,000	138,984,000	70.7
Asia	44,500,000	17,177,000	29.8
Africa	30,302,000	11,697,000	20.3
North America	24,241,000	9,357,000	16.2
South America	17,793,000	6,868,000	11.9
Antarctica	14,100,000	5,443,000	9.4
Europe	9,957,000	3,843,000	6.7
Australia & Oceania	8,557,000	3,303,000	5.7
Pacific Ocean	155,557,000	60,061,000	46.4
Atlantic Ocean	76,762,000	29,638,000	22.9
Indian Ocean	68,556,000	26,470,000	20.4
Southern Ocean	20,327,000	7,848,000	6.1
Arctic Ocean	14,056,000	5,427,000	4.2

OCEAN DEPTHS

Atlantic Ocean	m	ft
Puerto Rico (Milwaukee) Deep	8,605	28,232
Cayman Trench	7,680	25,197
Gulf of Mexico	5,203	17,070
Mediterranean Sea	5,121	16,801
Black Sea	2,211	7,254
North Sea	660	2,165

Indian Ocean	m	ft
Java Trench	7,450	24,442
Red Sea	2,635	8,454

Pacific Ocean	m	ft
Mariana Trench	11,022	36,161
Tonga Trench	10,882	35,702
Japan Trench	10,554	34,626
Kuril Trench	10,542	34,587

Arctic Ocean	m	ft
Molloy Deep	5,608	18,399

Southern Ocean	m	ft
South Sandwich Trench	7,235	23,737

MOUNTAINS

Europe		m	ft
Elbrus	Russia	5,642	18,510
Dykh-Tau	Russia	5,205	17,076
Shkhara	Russia/Georgia	5,201	17,064
Koshtan-Tau	Russia	5,152	16,903
Kazbek	Russia/Georgia	5,047	16,558
Pushkin	Russia/Georgia	5,033	16,512
Katyn-Tau	Russia/Georgia	4,979	16,335
Shota Rustaveli	Russia/Georgia	4,860	15,945
Mont Blanc	France/Italy	4,808	15,774
Monte Rosa	Italy/Switzerland	4,634	15,203
Dom	Switzerland	4,545	14,911
Liskamm	Switzerland	4,527	14,852
Weisshorn	Switzerland	4,505	14,780
Taschorn	Switzerland	4,490	14,730
Matterhorn/Cervino	Italy/Switzerland	4,478	14,691
Grossglockner	Austria	3,797	12,457
Mulhacén	Spain	3,478	11,411
Zugspitze	Germany	2,962	9,718
Olympus	Greece	2,917	9,570
Galdhøpiggen	Norway	2,469	8,100
Kebnekaise	Sweden	2,117	6,946
Ben Nevis	UK	1,345	4,413

Asia		m	ft
Everest	China/Nepal	8,849	29,032
K2 (Godwin Austen)	China/Kashmir	8,611	28,251
Kanchenjunga	India/Nepal	8,598	28,208
Lhotse	China/Nepal	8,516	27,939
Makalu	China/Nepal	8,481	27,824
Cho Oyu	China/Nepal	8,201	26,906
Dhaulagiri	Nepal	8,167	26,795
Manaslu	Nepal	8,156	26,758
Nanga Parbat	Kashmir	8,126	26,660
Annapurna	Nepal	8,078	26,502
Gasherbrum	China/Kashmir	8,068	26,469
Broad Peak	China/Kashmir	8,051	26,414
Xixabangma	China	8,012	26,286
Kangbachen	Nepal	7,858	25,781
Trivor	Pakistan	7,720	25,328
Pik Imeni Ismail Samani	Tajikistan	7,495	24,590
Demavend	Iran	5,604	18,386
Ararat	Turkey	5,165	16,945
Gunong Kinabalu	Malaysia (Borneo)	4,101	13,455
Fuji-San	Japan	3,776	12,388

Africa		m	ft
Kilimanjaro	Tanzania	5,895	19,340
Mt Kenya	Kenya	5,199	17,057
Ruwenzori	Uganda/Congo (D.R.)	5,109	16,762
Meru	Tanzania	4,565	14,977
Ras Dashen	Ethiopia	4,553	14,937
Karisimbi	Rwanda/Congo (D.R.)	4,507	14,787
Mt Elgon	Kenya/Uganda	4,321	14,176
Batu	Ethiopia	4,307	14,130
Toubkal	Morocco	4,165	13,665
Mt Cameroun	Cameroon	4,070	13,353

Oceania		m	ft
Puncak Jaya	Indonesia	4,884	16,024
Puncak Trikora	Indonesia	4,730	15,518
Puncak Mandala	Indonesia	4,702	15,427
Mt Wilhelm	Papua New Guinea	4,508	14,790
Mauna Kea	USA (Hawaii)	4,205	13,796
Mauna Loa	USA (Hawaii)	4,169	13,678
Aoraki Mt Cook	New Zealand	3,724	12,218
Mt Kosciuszko	Australia	2,228	7,310

North America		m	ft
Denali (Mt McKinley)	USA (Alaska)	6,190	20,310
Mt Logan	Canada	5,959	19,551
Pico de Orizaba	Mexico	5,610	18,405
Mt St Elias	USA/Canada	5,489	18,008
Popocatépetl	Mexico	5,452	17,887
Mt Foraker	USA (Alaska)	5,304	17,401
Iztaccihuatl	Mexico	5,286	17,342
Lucania	Canada	5,226	17,146
Mt Steele	Canada	5,073	16,644
Mt Bona	USA (Alaska)	5,005	16,420
Mt Whitney	USA	4,418	14,495
Tajumulco	Guatemala	4,220	13,845
Chirripó Grande	Costa Rica	3,837	12,589
Pico Duarte	Dominican Rep.	3,175	10,417

South America		m	ft
Aconcagua	Argentina	6,962	22,841
Ojos del Salado	Argentina/Chile	6,863	22,516
Pissis	Argentina	6,793	22,288
Mercedario	Argentina/Chile	6,770	22,211
Huascarán	Peru	6,768	22,204
Bonete	Argentina	6,759	22,176
Llullaillaco	Argentina/Chile	6,723	22,057
Nevado de Cachi	Argentina	6,720	22,047
Yerupaja	Peru	6,632	21,758
Sajama	Bolivia	6,520	21,391
Chimborazo	Ecuador	6,267	20,561
Pico Cristóbal Colón	Colombia	5,775	18,948
Pico Bolivar	Venezuela	4,981	16,343

Antarctica		m	ft
Vinson Massif		4,897	16,066
Mt Kirkpatrick		4,528	14,855

RIVERS

Europe		km	miles
Volga	Caspian Sea	3,700	2,300
Danube	Black Sea	2,850	1,770
Ural	Caspian Sea	2,535	1,575
Dnieper	Black Sea	2,285	1,420
Kama	Volga	2,030	1,260
Don	Black Sea	1,990	1,240
Petchora	Arctic Ocean	1,790	1,110
Oka	Volga	1,480	920
Dniester	Black Sea	1,400	870
Vyatka	Kama	1,370	850
Rhine	North Sea	1,320	820
North Dvina	Arctic Ocean	1,290	800
Elbe	North Sea	1,145	710

Asia		km	miles
Yangtse	Pacific Ocean	6,380	3,960
Yenisey–Angara	Arctic Ocean	5,550	3,445
Huang He	Pacific Ocean	5,464	3,395
Ob–Irtysh	Arctic Ocean	5,410	3,360
Mekong	Pacific Ocean	4,500	2,795
Amur	Pacific Ocean	4,442	2,760
Lena	Arctic Ocean	4,402	2,735
Irtysh	Ob	4,250	2,640
Yenisey	Arctic Ocean	4,090	2,540
Ob	Arctic Ocean	3,680	2,285
Indus	Indian Ocean	3,100	1,925
Brahmaputra	Indian Ocean	2,900	1,800
Syrdarya	Aralkum Desert	2,860	1,775
Salween	Indian Ocean	2,800	1,740
Euphrates	Indian Ocean	2,700	1,675
Amudarya	Aralkum Desert	2,540	1,575

Africa		km	miles
Nile	Mediterranean	6,695	4,160
Congo	Atlantic Ocean	4,670	2,900
Niger	Atlantic Ocean	4,180	2,595
Zambezi	Indian Ocean	3,540	2,200
Oubangi/Uele	Congo (Dem. Rep.)	2,250	1,400
Kasai	Congo (Dem. Rep.)	1,950	1,210
Shaballe	Indian Ocean	1,930	1,200
Orange	Atlantic Ocean	1,860	1,155
Cubango	Okavango Delta	1,800	1,120
Limpopo	Indian Ocean	1,770	1,100
Senegal	Atlantic Ocean	1,640	1,020

Australia		km	miles
Murray–Darling	Southern Ocean	3,750	2,330
Darling	Murray	3,070	1,905
Murray	Southern Ocean	2,575	1,600
Murrumbidgee	Murray	1,690	1,050

North America		km	miles
Mississippi–Missouri	Gulf of Mexico	5,971	3,710
Mackenzie	Arctic Ocean	4,240	2,630
Missouri	Mississippi	4,088	2,540
Mississippi	Gulf of Mexico	3,782	2,350
Yukon	Pacific Ocean	3,185	1,980
Rio Grande	Gulf of Mexico	3,030	1,880

		km	miles
Arkansas	Mississippi	2,340	1,450
Colorado	Pacific Ocean	2,330	1,445
Red	Mississippi	2,040	1,270
Columbia	Pacific Ocean	1,950	1,210
Saskatchewan	Lake Winnipeg	1,940	1,205

South America		km	miles
Amazon	Atlantic Ocean	6,450	4,010
Paraná–Plate	Atlantic Ocean	4,500	2,800
Purus	Amazon	3,350	2,080
Madeira	Amazon	3,200	1,990
São Francisco	Atlantic Ocean	2,900	1,800
Paraná	Plate	2,800	1,740
Tocantins	Atlantic Ocean	2,750	1,710
Orinoco	Atlantic Ocean	2,740	1,700
Paraguay	Paraná	2,550	1,580
Pilcomayo	Paraná	2,500	1,550
Araguaia	Tocantins	2,250	1,400

LAKES

Europe		km²	miles²
Lake Ladoga	Russia	17,700	6,800
Lake Onega	Russia	9,700	3,700
Saimaa system	Finland	8,000	3,100
Vänern	Sweden	5,500	2,100

Asia		km²	miles²
Caspian Sea	Asia	371,000	143,000
Lake Baikal	Russia	30,500	11,780
Tonlé Sap	Cambodia	20,000	7,700
Lake Balqash	Kazakhstan	18,500	7,100
Aral Sea	Kazakhstan/Uzbekistan	17,160	6,625

Africa		km²	miles²
Lake Victoria	East Africa	68,000	26,000
Lake Tanganyika	Central Africa	33,000	13,000
Lake Malawi/Nyasa	East Africa	29,600	11,430
Lake Chad	Central Africa	25,000	9,700
Lake Turkana	Ethiopia/Kenya	8,500	3,290
Lake Volta	Ghana	8,480	3,270

Australia		km²	miles²
Kati- Thanda-Lake Eyre	Australia	8,900	3,400
Lake Torrens	Australia	5,800	2,200
Lake Gairdner	Australia	4,800	1,900

North America		km²	miles²
Lake Superior	Canada/USA	82,350	31,800
Lake Huron	Canada/USA	59,600	23,010
Lake Michigan	USA	58,000	22,400
Great Bear Lake	Canada	31,800	12,280
Great Slave Lake	Canada	28,500	11,000
Lake Erie	Canada/USA	25,700	9,900
Lake Winnipeg	Canada	24,400	9,400
Lake Ontario	Canada/USA	19,500	7,500
Lake Nicaragua	Nicaragua	8,200	3,200

South America		km²	miles²
Lake Titicaca	Bolivia/Peru	8,300	3,200
Lake Poopo	Bolivia	2,800	1,100

ISLANDS

Europe		km²	miles²
Great Britain	UK	229,880	88,700
Iceland	Atlantic Ocean	103,000	39,800
Ireland	Ireland/UK	84,400	32,600
Novaya Zemlya (N.)	Russia	48,200	18,600
Sicily	Italy	25,500	9,800

Asia		km²	miles²
Borneo	South-east Asia	744,360	287,400
Sumatra	Indonesia	473,600	182,860
Honshu	Japan	230,500	88,980
Celebes	Indonesia	189,000	73,000
Java	Indonesia	126,700	48,900
Luzon	Philippines	104,700	40,400
Hokkaido	Japan	78,400	30,300

Africa		km²	miles²
Madagascar	Indian Ocean	587,040	226,660
Socotra	Indian Ocean	3,600	1,400
Réunion	Indian Ocean	2,500	965

Oceania		km²	miles²
New Guinea	Indonesia/Papua NG	821,030	317,000
New Zealand (S.)	Pacific Ocean	150,500	58,100
New Zealand (N.)	Pacific Ocean	114,700	44,300
Tasmania	Australia	67,800	26,200
New Caledonia	Pacific Ocean	16,650	6,470

North America		km²	miles²
Greenland	Atlantic Ocean	2,175,600	839,800
Baffin I.	Canada	508,000	196,100
Victoria I.	Canada	212,200	81,900
Ellesmere I.	Canada	212,000	81,800
Cuba	Caribbean Sea	110,860	42,800
Hispaniola	Dominican Rep./Haiti	76,200	29,400
Jamaica	Caribbean Sea	11,400	4,400
Puerto Rico	Atlantic Ocean	8,900	3,400

South America		km²	miles²
Tierra del Fuego	Argentina/Chile	47,000	18,100
Chiloé	Chile	8,480	3,275
Falkland I. (E.)	Atlantic Ocean	6,800	2,600

How to use the Index

The index contains the names of all the principal places and features shown on the maps. Each name is followed by an additional entry in italics giving the country or region within which it is located. The alphabetical order of names composed of two or more words is governed primarily by the first word and then by the second. This is an example of the rule:

Albert, L. *Africa* 1°30N 31°0E **96** D6
Albert Lea *U.S.A.* 43°39N 93°22W **111** B8
Albert Nile → *Uganda* 3°36N 32°2E **96** D6
Alberta □ *Canada* 54°40N 115°0W **108** D8
Albertville *France* 45°40N 6°22E **66** D7

Physical features composed of a proper name (Erie) and a description (Lake) are positioned alphabetically by the proper name. The description is positioned after the proper name and is usually abbreviated:

Erie, L. *N. Amer.* 42°15N 81°0W **112** D7

Where a description forms part of a settlement or administrative name, however, it is always written in full and put in its true alphabetical position:

Mount Isa *Australia* 20°42S 139°26E **98** E6

Names beginning with M' and Mc are indexed as if they were spelled Mac. Names beginning St. are alphabetized under Saint, but Santa and San are spelled in full and are alphabetized accordingly. If the same place name occurs two or more times in the index and all are in the same country, each is followed by the name of the administrative subdivision in which it is located.

The geographical co-ordinates that follow each name in the index give the latitude and longitude of each place. The first co-ordinate indicates latitude – the distance north or south of the Equator. The second co-ordinate indicates longitude – the distance east or west of the Greenwich Meridian. Both latitude and longitude are measured in degrees and minutes (there are 60 minutes in a degree).

The latitude is followed by N(orth) or S(outh) and the longitude by E(ast) or W(est).

The number in bold type that follows the geographical co-ordinates refers to the number of the map page where that feature or place will be found. This is usually the largest scale at which the place or feature appears.

The letter and figure that are immediately after the page number give the grid square on the map page, within which the feature is situated. The letter represents the latitude and the figure the longitude. A lower-case letter immediately after the page number refers to an inset map on that page.

In some cases the feature itself may fall within the specified square, while the name is outside. This is usually the case only with features that are larger than a grid square.

Rivers are indexed to their mouths or confluences, and carry the symbol → after their names. The following symbols are also used in the index: ■ country, ⧄ overseas territory or dependency, □ first-order administrative area, △ national park, ✈ (LHR) principal airport (and location identifier).

Abbreviations used in the Index

Afghan. – Afghanistan
Ala. – Alabama
Alta. – Alberta
Amer. – America(n)
Arch. – Archipelago
Ariz. – Arizona
Ark. – Arkansas
Atl. Oc. – Atlantic Ocean
B. – Baie, Bahía, Bay, Bucht, Bugt
B.C. – British Columbia
Bangla. – Bangladesh
C. – Cabo, Cap, Cape, Coast
C.A.R. – Central African Republic
Calif. – California
Cent. – Central
Chan. – Channel
Colo. – Colorado
Conn. – Connecticut
Cord. – Cordillera
Cr. – Creek
D.C. – District of Columbia
Del. – Delaware
Dom. Rep. – Dominican Republic
E. – East
El Salv. – El Salvador
Eq. Guin. – Equatorial Guinea
Fla. – Florida
Falk. Is. – Falkland Is.
G. – Golfe, Golfo, Gulf
Ga. – Georgia
Hd. – Head
Hts. – Heights
I.(s). – Île, Ilha, Insel, Isla, Island, Isle(s)
Ill. – Illinois
Ind. – Indiana
Ind. Oc. – Indian Ocean
Kans. – Kansas
Ky. – Kentucky
L. – Lac, Lacul, Lago, Lagoa, Lake, Limni, Loch, Lough
La. – Louisiana
Lux. – Luxembourg
Madag. – Madagascar
Man. – Manitoba
Mass. – Massachusetts
Md. – Maryland
Me. – Maine
Mich. – Michigan
Minn. – Minnesota
Miss. – Mississippi
Mo. – Missouri
Mont. – Montana
Mozam. – Mozambique
Mt.(s) – Mont, Monte, Monti, Montaña, Mountain
N. – Nord, Norte, North, Northern,
N.B. – New Brunswick
N.C. – North Carolina
N. Cal. – New Caledonia
N. Dak. – North Dakota
N.H. – New Hampshire
N.J. – New Jersey
N. Mex. – New Mexico
N.S. – Nova Scotia
N.S.W. – New South Wales
N.W.T. – North West Territory
N.Y. – New York
N.Z. – New Zealand
Nat. Park – National Park
Nebr. – Nebraska
Neths. – Netherlands
Nev. – Nevada
Nfld. – Newfoundland and Labrador
Nic. – Nicaragua
Okla. – Oklahoma
Ont. – Ontario
Oreg. – Oregon
P.E.I. – Prince Edward Island
Pa. – Pennsylvania
Pac. Oc. – Pacific Ocean
Papua N.G. – Papua New Guinea
Pen. – Peninsula, Péninsule
Phil. – Philippines
Pk. – Peak
Plat. – Plateau
Prov. – Province, Provincial
Pt. – Point
Pta. – Ponta, Punta
Pte. – Pointe
Qué. – Québec
Queens. – Queensland
R. – Rio, River
R.I. – Rhode Island
Ra.(s) – Range(s)
Reg. – Region
Rep. – Republic
Res. – Reserve, Reservoir
S. – San, South
Si. Arabia – Saudi Arabia
S.C. – South Carolina
S. Dak. – South Dakota
Sa. – Serra, Sierra
Sask. – Saskatchewan
Scot. – Scotland
Sd. – Sound
Sib. – Siberia
St. – Saint, Sankt, Sint
Str. – Strait, Stretto
Switz. – Switzerland
Tas. – Tasmania
Tenn. – Tennessee
Tex. – Texas
Trin. & Tob. – Trinidad & Tobago
U.A.E. – United Arab Emirates
U.K. – United Kingdom
U.S.A. – United States of America
Va. – Virginia
Vic. – Victoria
Vol. – Volcano
Vt. – Vermont
W. – West
W. Va. – West Virginia
Wash. – Washington
Wis. – Wisconsin

A

Aachen *Germany* 50°45N 6°6E **64** C4
Aalborg *Denmark* 57°2N 9°54E **63** F5
Aarau *Switz.* 47°23N 8°4E **64** E5
Aare → *Switz.* 47°33N 8°14E **64** E5
Aarhus *Denmark* 56°8N 10°11E **63** F6
Aba *Nigeria* 5°10N 7°19E **94** G7
Abaco *The Bahamas* 26°25N 77°10W **115** B9
Ābādān *Iran* 30°22N 48°20E **86** D7
Abaetetuba *Brazil* 1°40S 48°50W **120** C5
Abakan *Russia* 53°40N 91°10E **77** D10
Abancay *Peru* 13°35S 72°55W **120** D2
Abariringa *Kiribati* 2°50S 171°40W **99** A16
Abaya, L. *Ethiopia* 6°30N 37°50E **89** F2
Abbé, L. *Ethiopia* 11°8N 41°47E **89** E3
Abbeville *France* 50°6N 1°49E **66** A4
Abbey Town *U.K.* 54°51N 3°17W **26** C2
Abbot Ice Shelf *Antarctica* 73°0S 92°0W **55** D16
Abbots Bromley *U.K.* 52°50N 1°52W **27** G5
Abbotsbury *U.K.* 50°40N 2°37W **30** E3
ABC Islands *W. Indies* 12°15N 69°0W **115** E11
Abéché *Chad* 13°50N 20°35E **95** F10
Abeokuta *Nigeria* 7°3N 3°19E **94** G6
Aberaeron *U.K.* 52°15N 4°15W **28** C5
Aberchirder *U.K.* 57°34N 2°37W **23** G12
Aberdare *U.K.* 51°43N 3°27W **28** D7
Aberdaugleddau = Milford Haven *U.K.* 51°42N 5°7W **28** D3
Aberdeen *China* 22°14N 114°8E **79** a
Aberdeen *U.K.* 57°9N 2°5W **23** H13
Aberdeen *S. Dak., U.S.A.* 45°28N 98°29W **110** A7
Aberdeen *Wash., U.S.A.* 46°59N 123°50W **110** A2
Aberdeenshire □ *U.K.* 57°17N 2°36W **23** H12
Aberdovey = Aberdyfi *U.K.* 52°33N 4°3W **28** B5
Aberdyfi *U.K.* 52°33N 4°3W **28** B5
Aberfeldy *U.K.* 56°37N 3°51W **25** A8
Aberfoyle *U.K.* 56°11N 4°23W **24** B7
Abergavenny *U.K.* 51°49N 3°1W **28** D7
Abergele *U.K.* 53°17N 3°35W **28** A6
Abergwaun = Fishguard *U.K.* 52°0N 4°58W **28** D4
Aberhonddu = Brecon *U.K.* 51°57N 3°23W **28** D7
Abermaw = Barmouth *U.K.* 52°44N 4°4W **28** B5
Aberpennar = Mountain Ash *U.K.* 51°40N 3°23W **28** D7
Aberporth *U.K.* 52°8N 4°33W **28** C4
Abersoch *U.K.* 52°49N 4°30W **28** B5
Abersychan *U.K.* 51°44N 3°3W **28** D7
Abert, L. *U.S.A.* 42°38N 120°14W **110** B2
Abertawe = Swansea *U.K.* 51°37N 3°57W **29** D6
Aberteifi = Cardigan *U.K.* 52°5N 4°40W **28** C4
Abertillery *U.K.* 51°44N 3°8W **28** D7
Aberystwyth *U.K.* 52°25N 4°5W **28** C5
Abhā *Si. Arabia* 18°0N 42°34E **89** D3
Abidjan *Côte d'Ivoire* 5°26N 3°58W **94** G5
Abilene *U.S.A.* 32°28N 99°43W **110** D7
Abingdon-on-Thames *U.K.* 51°40N 1°17W **30** C6
Abitibi, L. *Canada* 48°40N 79°40W **109** E12
Abkhazia □ *Georgia* 43°12N 41°5E **71** F7
Abomey *Benin* 7°10N 2°5E **94** G6
Aboyne *U.K.* 57°4N 2°47W **23** H12
Abrolhos, Banco dos *Brazil* 18°0S 38°0W **122** C3
Absaroka Range *U.S.A.* 44°45N 109°50W **110** B5
Abu Dhabi *U.A.E.* 24°28N 54°22E **87** E8
Abu Hamed *Sudan* 19°32N 33°13E **95** E12
Abuja *Nigeria* 9°5N 7°32E **94** G7
Abunã *Brazil* 9°40S 65°20W **120** C3
Abunã → *Brazil* 9°41S 65°20W **120** C3
Abyei ⧄ *Sudan* 9°30N 28°30E **95** G11
Acaponeta *Mexico* 22°30N 105°22W **114** C3
Acapulco *Mexico* 16°51N 99°55W **114** D5
Acarai Mts. *Brazil* 1°50N 57°50W **120** B4
Acarigua *Venezuela* 9°33N 69°12W **120** B3
Accomac *U.S.A.* 37°43N 75°40W **113** G10
Accra *Ghana* 5°35N 0°6W **94** G5
Accrington *U.K.* 53°45N 2°22W **27** E4
Aceh □ *Indonesia* 4°15N 97°30E **82** D1
Acharnes *Greece* 38°5N 23°44E **69** E10
Acheloos → *Greece* 38°19N 21°7E **69** E9
Achill Hd. *Ireland* 53°58N 10°15W **18** D1
Achill I. *Ireland* 53°58N 10°1W **18** D1
Acklins *The Bahamas* 22°30N 74°0W **115** C10
Acle *U.K.* 52°39N 1°33E **31** A12
Aconcagua, Cerro *Argentina* 32°39S 70°0W **121** F3
Acre □ *Brazil* 9°1S 71°0W **120** C2
Acre → *Brazil* 8°45S 67°22W **120** C3
Acton Burnell *U.K.* 52°37N 2°41W **27** G3
Ad Dammām *Si. Arabia* 26°20N 50°5E **86** E7
Ad Dīwānīyah *Iraq* 32°0N 45°0E **86** D6
Adair, C. *Canada* 71°30N 71°34W **109** B12
Adak I. *U.S.A.* 51°45N 176°45W **108** D2
Adamaoua, Massif de l' *Cameroon* 7°20N 12°20E **95** G8
Adam's Bridge *Sri Lanka* 9°15N 79°40E **84** Q11
Adana *Turkey* 37°0N 35°16E **71** G6
Adare, C. *Antarctica* 71°0S 171°0E **55** D11
Addis Ababa *Ethiopia* 9°2N 38°42E **89** F2
Adelaide *Australia* 34°52S 138°30E **98** G6
Adelaide I. *Antarctica* 67°15S 68°30W **55** C17
Adelaide Pen. *Canada* 68°15N 97°30W **108** C10
Adélie, Terre *Antarctica* 68°0S 140°0E **55** C10
Aden *Yemen* 12°45N 45°0E **89** E4
Aden, G. of *Ind. Oc.* 12°30N 47°30E **89** E4
Adige → *Italy* 45°9N 12°20E **68** B5
Adigrat *Ethiopia* 14°20N 39°26E **89** E2
Adirondack Mts. *U.S.A.* 44°0N 74°0W **113** D10
Admiralty Is. *Papua N. G.* 2°0S 147°0E **102** H6
Adour → *France* 43°32N 1°32W **66** E3
Adrar *Mauritania* 20°30N 7°30W **94** D3
Adrian *U.S.A.* 41°54N 84°2W **112** E5
Adriatic Sea *Medit. S.* 43°0N 16°0E **68** C6
Adwa *Ethiopia* 14°15N 38°52E **89** E2
Adwick le Street *U.K.* 53°34N 1°10W **27** E6
Adygea □ *Russia* 45°0N 40°0E **71** F7
Ægean Sea *Medit. S.* 38°30N 25°0E **69** E11
Afghanistan ■ *Asia* 33°0N 65°0E **87** C11
Africa 10°0N 20°0E **90** E6
Afyon *Turkey* 38°45N 30°33E **71** G5
Agadez *Niger* 16°58N 7°59E **94** E7
Agadir *Morocco* 30°28N 9°55W **94** B4
Agartala *India* 23°50N 91°23E **85** H17
Agen *France* 44°12N 0°38E **66** D4
Agra *India* 27°17N 77°58E **84** F10
Ağri *Turkey* 39°44N 43°3E **71** G7
Agrigento *Italy* 37°19N 13°34E **68** F5
Agua Prieta *Mexico* 31°18N 109°34W **114** A3
Aguascalientes *Mexico* 21°53N 102°18W **114** C4
Aguja, C. de la *Colombia* 11°18N 74°12W **117** B3
Agulhas, C. *S. Africa* 34°52S 20°0E **97** L4
Ahaggar *Algeria* 23°0N 6°30E **94** D7
Ahmadabad *India* 23°0N 72°40E **84** H8
Ahmadnagar *India* 19°7N 74°46E **84** K9
Ahmadpur East *Pakistan* 29°12N 71°10E **84** E7
Ahvāz *Iran* 31°20N 48°40E **86** D7
Ahvenanmaa *Finland* 60°15N 20°0E **63** E8
Aḩwar *Yemen* 13°30N 46°40E **89** E4
Ailsa Craig *U.K.* 55°15N 5°6W **24** D5
Aimorés *Brazil* 19°30S 41°4W **122** C2
Aïn Témouchent *Algeria* 35°16N 1°8W **94** A5
Ainsdale *U.K.* 53°37N 3°2W **27** E2
Aïr *Niger* 18°30N 8°0E **94** E7
Air Force I. *Canada* 67°58N 74°5W **109** C12
Aird, The *U.K.* 57°25N 4°33W **23** H8
Airdrie *Canada* 51°18N 114°2W **108** D8
Airdrie *U.K.* 55°52N 3°57W **25** C8
Aire → *U.K.* 53°43N 0°55W **27** E7
Aisgill *U.K.* 54°23N 2°21W **26** D4
Aisne → *France* 49°26N 2°50E **66** B5
Aix-en-Provence *France* 43°32N 5°27E **66** E6
Aix-les-Bains *France* 45°41N 5°53E **66** D6
Aizawl *India* 23°40N 92°44E **85** H18
Aizuwakamatsu *Japan* 37°30N 139°56E **81** E6
Ajaccio *France* 41°55N 8°40E **66** F8
Ajanta Ra. *India* 20°28N 75°50E **84** J9
Ajaria □ *Georgia* 41°30N 42°0E **71** F7
Ajdābiyā *Libya* 30°54N 20°4E **95** B10
'Ajmān *U.A.E.* 25°25N 55°30E **87** E8
Ajmer *India* 26°28N 74°37E **84** F9
Aketi *Dem. Rep. of the Congo* 2°38N 23°47E **96** D4
Akhisar *Turkey* 38°56N 27°48E **71** G4
Akimiski I. *Canada* 52°50N 81°30W **109** D11
Akita *Japan* 39°45N 140°7E **81** D7
'Akko *Israel* 32°55N 35°4E **86** C3
Aklavik *Canada* 68°12N 135°0W **108** C6
Akola *India* 20°42N 77°2E **84** J10
Akpatok I. *Canada* 60°25N 68°8W **109** C13
Akranes *Iceland* 64°19N 22°5W **63** B1
Akron *U.S.A.* 41°5N 81°31W **112** E7
Aksai Chin *China* 35°15N 79°55E **84** B11
Aksaray *Turkey* 38°25N 34°2E **71** G5
Akşehir Gölü *Turkey* 38°30N 31°25E **71** G5
Aksu *China* 41°5N 80°10E **78** C5
Aksum *Ethiopia* 14°5N 38°40E **89** E2
Akure *Nigeria* 7°15N 5°5E **94** G7
Akureyri *Iceland* 65°40N 18°6W **63** A2
Al 'Amārah *Iraq* 31°55N 47°15E **86** D6
Al 'Aqabah *Jordan* 29°31N 35°0E **86** D3
Al 'Aramah *Si. Arabia* 25°30N 46°0E **86** E6
Al 'Ayn *U.A.E.* 24°15N 55°45E **87** E8
Al 'Azīzīyah *Libya* 32°30N 13°1E **95** B8
Al Bayḑā *Libya* 32°50N 21°44E **95** B10
Al Fallūjah *Iraq* 33°20N 43°55E **86** C5
Al Fāw *Iraq* 30°0N 48°30E **86** D7
Al Ḩadīthah *Iraq* 34°0N 41°13E **86** C5
Al Ḩasakah *Syria* 36°35N 40°45E **86** B5
Al Ḩillah *Iraq* 32°30N 44°25E **86** C6
Al Hoceïma *Morocco* 35°8N 3°58W **94** A5
Al Ḩudaydah *Yemen* 14°50N 43°0E **89** E3
Al Hufūf *Si. Arabia* 25°25N 49°45E **86** E7
Al Jahrah *Kuwait* 29°25N 47°40E **86** D6
Al Jawf *Libya* 24°10N 23°24E **95** D10
Al Jubayl *Si. Arabia* 27°0N 49°50E **86** E7
Al Khalīl *West Bank* 31°32N 35°6E **86** D3
Al Khums *Libya* 32°40N 14°17E **95** B8
Al Kufrah *Libya* 24°17N 23°15E **95** D10
Al Kūt *Iraq* 32°30N 46°0E **86** C6
Al Manāmah *Bahrain* 26°10N 50°30E **87** E7
Al Mubarraz *Si. Arabia* 25°30N 49°40E **86** E7
Al Mukallā *Yemen* 14°33N 49°2E **89** E4
Al Musayyib *Iraq* 32°49N 44°20E **86** C6
Al Qāmishlī *Syria* 37°2N 41°14E **86** B5
Al Qaţīf *Si. Arabia* 26°35N 50°0E **86** E7
Al Qunfudhah *Si. Arabia* 19°3N 41°4E **89** D3
Al Qurayyāt *Si. Arabia* 31°20N 37°20E **86** D4
Ala Tau *Asia* 45°30N 80°40E **78** B5
Alabama □ *U.S.A.* 33°0N 87°0W **111** D9
Alabama → *U.S.A.* 31°8N 87°57W **111** D9
Alagoas □ *Brazil* 9°0S 36°0W **122** A3
Alagoinhas *Brazil* 12°7S 38°20W **122** B3
Alai Range *Asia* 39°45N 72°0E **87** B13
Alamogordo *U.S.A.* 32°54N 105°57W **110** D5
Alamosa *U.S.A.* 37°28N 105°52W **110** C5
Åland = Ahvenanmaa *Finland* 60°15N 20°0E **63** E8
Alanya *Turkey* 36°38N 32°0E **71** G5
Alappuzha *India* 9°30N 76°28E **84** Q10
Alaşehir *Turkey* 38°23N 28°30E **71** G4
Alaska □ *U.S.A.* 64°0N 154°0W **108** C5
Alaska, G. of *Pac. Oc.* 58°0N 145°0W **108** D5
Alaska Peninsula *U.S.A.* 56°0N 159°0W **108** D4
Alaska Range *U.S.A.* 62°50N 151°0W **108** C4
Alba-Iulia *Romania* 46°8N 23°39E **65** E12
Albacete *Spain* 39°0N 1°50W **67** C5
Albanel, L. *Canada* 50°55N 73°12W **109** D12
Albania ■ *Europe* 41°0N 20°0E **69** D9
Albany *Australia* 35°1S 117°58E **98** H2
Albany *Ga., U.S.A.* 31°35N 84°10W **111** D10
Albany *N.Y., U.S.A.* 42°39N 73°45W **113** D11
Albany *Oreg., U.S.A.* 44°38N 123°6W **110** B2
Albany → *Canada* 52°17N 81°31W **109** D11
Albemarle Sd. *U.S.A.* 36°5N 76°0W **111** C11
Albert, L. *Africa* 1°30N 31°0E **96** D6
Albert Lea *U.S.A.* 43°39N 93°22W **111** B8
Albert Nile → *Uganda* 3°36N 32°2E **96** D6
Alberta □ *Canada* 54°40N 115°0W **108** D8
Albertville *France* 45°40N 6°22E **66** D7
Albi *France* 43°56N 2°9E **66** E5
Albion *U.S.A.* 42°15N 84°45W **112** D5
Alboran Sea *Medit. S.* 36°0N 3°30W **67** E3
Albrighton *U.K.* 52°38N 2°16W **27** G4

Albuquerque U.S.A. 35°5N 106°39W 110 C5
Albury Australia 36°3S 146°56E 98 H8
Alcalá de Henares Spain 40°28N 3°22W 67 B4
Alcester U.K. 52°14N 1°52W 30 B5
Alcoy Spain 38°43N 0°30W 67 C5
Aldabra Is. Seychelles 9°22S 46°28E 91 G8
Aldan Russia 58°40N 125°30E 77 D13
Aldan → Russia 63°28N 129°35E 77 C13
Aldborough U.K. 54°5N 1°22W 26 D6
Aldbourne U.K. 51°29N 1°37W 30 D5
Aldbrough U.K. 53°49N 0°6W 27 E8
Aldeburgh U.K. 52°10N 1°37E 31 B12
Alderbury U.K. 51°3N 1°44W 30 D5
Alderley Edge U.K. 53°18N 2°13W 27 F4
Alderney U.K. 49°42N 2°11W 29 H9
Aldershot U.K. 51°15N 0°44W 31 D7
Aledo U.S.A. 41°12N 90°45W 112 E2
Alegrete Brazil 29°40S 56°0W 121 E4
Além Paraíba Brazil 21°52S 42°41W 122 D2
Alençon France 48°27N 0°4E 66 B4
Alenquer Brazil 1°56S 54°46W 120 C4
'Alenuihāhā Channel
U.S.A. 20°30N 156°0W 110 H17
Aleppo Syria 36°10N 37°15E 86 B4
Alert Canada 83°2N 60°0W 109 A13
Alès France 44°9N 4°5E 66 D6
Alessándria Italy 44°54N 8°37E 68 B3
Ålesund Norway 62°28N 6°12E 63 E5
Aleutian Is. Pac. Oc. 52°0N 175°0W 102 B10
Aleutian Trench Pac. Oc. 48°0N 180°0E 102 C10
Alexander Arch. U.S.A. 56°0N 136°0W 108 D6
Alexander I. Antarctica 69°0S 70°0W 55 C17
Alexandria Egypt 31°13N 29°58E 95 B11
Alexandria U.K. 55°59N 4°35W 24 C6
Alexandria La., U.S.A. 31°18N 92°27W 111 D8
Alexandria Va., U.S.A. 38°49N 77°5W 112 F9
Alford Aberds., U.K. 57°14N 2°41W 23 H12
Alford Lincs., U.K. 53°15N 0°10E 27 F9
Alfreton U.K. 53°6N 1°24W 27 F6
Alfriston U.K. 50°48N 0°10E 31 E9
Algarve Portugal 36°58N 8°20W 67 D1
Algeciras Spain 36°9N 5°28W 67 D3
Algeria ■ Africa 28°30N 2°0E 94 C6
Algiers Algeria 36°42N 3°8E 94 A6
Algoa B. S. Africa 33°50S 25°45E 90 K6
Alicante Spain 38°23N 0°30W 67 C5
Alice Springs Australia 23°40S 133°50E 98 E5
Aligarh India 27°55N 78°10E 84 F11
Alipur Duar India 26°30N 89°35E 85 F16
Aliquippa U.S.A. 40°37N 80°15W 112 E7
Aliwal North S. Africa 30°45S 26°45E 97 L5
Alkmaar Neths. 52°37N 4°45E 64 B3
Allahabad = Prayagraj India 25°25N 81°58E 85 G12
Allegan U.S.A. 42°32N 85°51W 112 D5
Allegheny → U.S.A. 40°27N 80°1W 112 E8
Allegheny Mts. U.S.A. 38°15N 80°10W 111 C11
Allen → U.S.A. 54°58N 2°18W 26 C4
Allen, Bog of Ireland 53°15N 7°0W 21 B9
Allen, L. Ireland 54°8N 8°4W 18 C5
Allendale Town U.K. 54°53N 2°14W 26 C4
Allenheads U.K. 54°49N 2°12W 26 C4
Allentown U.S.A. 40°37N 75°29W 113 E10
Alleynes B. Barbados 13°13N 59°39W 114 c
Alliance U.S.A. 42°6N 102°52W 110 B6
Allier → France 46°57N 3°4E 66 C5
Alligator Pond Jamaica 17°52N 77°34W 114 a
Alloa U.K. 56°7N 3°47W 25 B8
Allonby U.K. 54°46N 3°26W 26 C2
Alma U.S.A. 43°23N 84°39W 112 D5
Alma Ata = Almaty
Kazakhstan 43°15N 76°57E 76 E8
Almada Portugal 38°41N 9°8W 67 C1
Almaty Kazakhstan 43°15N 76°57E 76 E8
Almelo Neths. 52°22N 6°42E 64 B4
Almería Spain 36°52N 2°27W 67 D4
Almondsbury U.K. 51°32N 2°34W 30 C3
Aln → U.K. 55°24N 1°37W 26 B5
Alness U.K. 57°41N 4°16W 23 G9
Alnmouth U.K. 55°24N 1°37W 26 B5
Alnwick U.K. 55°24N 1°42W 26 B5
Alor Indonesia 8°15S 124°30E 83 F6
Alor Setar Malaysia 6°7N 100°22E 82 C2
Alpena U.S.A. 45°4N 83°27W 112 C6
Alpes Maritimes Europe 44°10N 7°10E 66 D7
Alphington U.K. 50°42N 3°31W 29 F7
Alpine U.S.A. 30°22N 103°40W 110 D6
Alps Europe 46°30N 9°30E 64 E5
Alrewas U.K. 52°44N 1°44W 27 G5
Alsace France 48°15N 7°25E 66 B7
Alsager U.K. 53°6N 2°18W 27 F4
Alston U.K. 54°49N 2°25W 26 C4
Altai Mongolia 46°40N 92°45E 78 B7
Altamira Brazil 3°12S 52°10W 120 C4
Altamura Italy 40°49N 16°33E 68 D7
Altarnun U.K. 50°35N 4°32W 29 F4
Altay China 47°48N 88°10E 78 B6
Altay Mongolia 46°22N 96°15E 78 B8
Altiplano Bolivia 17°0S 68°0W 120 D3
Alton U.K. 51°9N 0°59W 31 D7
Alton U.S.A. 38°53N 90°11W 112 F2
Alton Towers U.K. 52°59N 1°52W 27 G5
Altoona U.S.A. 40°31N 78°24W 112 E8
Altrincham U.K. 53°24N 2°21W 27 F4
Altun Shan China 38°30N 88°0E 78 D6
Altus U.S.A. 34°38N 99°20W 110 D7
Alucra Turkey 40°22N 38°47E 71 F6
Alvechurch U.K. 52°21N 1°57W 30 B5
Alwar India 27°38N 76°34E 84 F10
Alwinton U.K. 55°21N 2°7W 26 B4
Alxa Zuoqi China 38°50N 105°40E 78 D10
Alyth U.K. 56°38N 3°13W 23 J11
Amadjuak L. Canada 65°0N 71°8W 109 C12
Amagasaki Japan 34°42N 135°23E 81 F4
Amapá Brazil 2°5N 50°50W 120 B4
Amapá □ Brazil 1°40N 52°0W 120 B4
Amarillo U.S.A. 35°13N 101°50W 110 C6
Amasya Turkey 40°40N 35°50E 71 F6
Amazon = Amazonas →
S. Amer. 0°5S 50°0W 120 C4
Amazonas □ Brazil 5°0S 65°0W 120 C3

Amazonas → S. Amer. 0°5S 50°0W 120 C4
Ambala India 30°23N 76°56E 84 D10
Ambato Ecuador 1°5S 78°42W 120 C2
Ambergris Cay Belize 18°0N 87°55W 114 D7
Ambikapur India 23°15N 83°15E 85 H13
Ambilobé Madag. 13°10S 49°3E 97 G9
Amble U.K. 55°20N 1°36W 26 B5
Ambleside U.K. 54°26N 2°58W 26 D3
Ambon Indonesia 3°43S 128°12E 83 E7
Amchitka I. U.S.A. 51°32N 179°0E 108 D1
Amderma Russia 69°45N 61°30E 76 C7
Amdo China 32°20N 91°40E 78 E7
Ameca Mexico 20°33N 104°2W 114 C4
Ameland Neths. 53°27N 5°45E 64 B3
American Highland Antarctica 73°0S 75°0E 55 D6
American Samoa ☑ Pac. Oc. 14°20S 170°0W 99 C16
Americana Brazil 22°45S 47°20W 122 D1
Amersham U.K. 51°40N 0°36W 31 C7
Ames U.S.A. 42°2N 93°37W 111 B8
Amesbury U.K. 51°10N 1°46W 30 D5
Amherst Canada 45°48N 64°8W 109 E13
Amiens France 49°54N 2°16E 66 B5
Amirante Is. Seychelles 6°0S 53°0E 72 J7
Amlia I. U.S.A. 52°4N 173°30W 108 D2
Amlwch U.K. 53°24N 4°20W 28 A5
'Ammān Jordan 31°57N 35°52E 86 D3
Ammanford U.K. 51°48N 3°59W 28 D6
Amos Canada 48°35N 78°5W 109 E12
Ampleforth U.K. 54°13N 1°6W 26 D6
Ampthill U.K. 52°2N 0°30W 31 B8
Amravati India 20°55N 77°45E 84 J10
Amreli India 21°35N 71°17E 84 J7
Amritsar India 31°35N 74°57E 84 D9
Amroha India 28°53N 78°30E 84 E11
Amsterdam Neths. 52°23N 4°54E 64 B3
Amsterdam U.S.A. 42°56N 74°11W 113 D10
Amsterdam I. Ind. Oc. 38°30S 77°30E 53 F13
Amudarya → Uzbekistan 43°58N 59°34E 87 A9
Amund Ringnes I. Canada 78°20N 96°25W 109 B10
Amundsen Gulf Canada 71°0N 124°0W 108 B7
Amundsen Sea Antarctica 72°0S 115°0W 55 D15
Amuntai Indonesia 2°28S 115°25E 82 E5
Amur → Russia 52°56N 141°10E 77 D15
An Najaf Iraq 32°3N 44°15E 86 C6
Anaconda U.S.A. 46°8N 112°57W 110 A4
Anadyr Russia 64°35N 177°20E 77 C18
Anadyr, G. of Russia 64°0N 180°0E 77 C19
Anaheim U.S.A. 33°50N 117°55W 110 D3
Anambas, Kepulauan
Indonesia 3°20N 106°30E 82 D3
Anamur Turkey 36°8N 32°58E 71 G5
Anantapur India 14°39N 77°42E 84 M10
Anápolis Brazil 16°15S 48°50W 122 C1
Anār Iran 30°55N 55°13E 87 D8
Anatolia Turkey 39°0N 30°0E 71 G5
Añatuya Argentina 28°20S 62°50W 121 E3
Ancaster U.K. 52°59N 0°32W 27 F7
Ancholme → U.K. 53°40N 0°32W 27 E7
Anchorage U.S.A. 61°13N 149°54W 108 C5
Anci China 39°20N 116°40E 79 D12
Ancohuma Bolivia 16°0S 68°50W 120 D3
Ancona Italy 43°38N 13°30E 68 C5
Ancrum U.K. 55°31N 2°35W 25 C10
Ancud Chile 42°0S 73°50W 121 G2
Ancud, G. de Chile 42°0S 73°0W 121 G2
Anda China 46°24N 125°19E 79 B14
Andalgalá Argentina 27°40S 66°30W 121 E3
Andalucía □ Spain 37°35N 5°0W 67 D3
Andalusia U.S.A. 31°18N 86°29W 111 D9
Andaman Is. Ind. Oc. 12°30N 92°45E 53 D14
Anderson Alaska, U.S.A. 64°25N 149°15W 108 C5
Anderson Ind., U.S.A. 40°10N 85°41W 112 E5
Anderson S.C., U.S.A. 34°31N 82°39W 111 D10
Anderson → Canada 69°42N 129°0W 108 C7
Andes, Cord. de los S. Amer. 20°0S 68°0W 121 E3
Andhra Pradesh □ India 18°0N 79°0E 84 L11
Andijon Uzbekistan 41°10N 72°15E 87 A13
Andorra ■ Europe 42°30N 1°30E 66 E4
Andorra La Vella Andorra 42°31N 1°32E 66 E4
Andover U.K. 51°12N 1°29W 30 D6
Andradina Brazil 20°54S 51°23W 120 E4
Andreanof Is. U.S.A. 51°30N 176°0W 108 D2
Ándria Italy 41°13N 16°17E 68 D7
Andros Greece 37°50N 24°57E 69 F11
Andros The Bahamas 24°30N 78°0W 115 C9
Aneityum Vanuatu 20°12S 169°45E 99 E12
Angara → Russia 58°5N 94°20E 77 D10
Angarsk Russia 52°30N 104°0E 77 D11
Ange Sweden 62°31N 15°35E 63 E7
Angel Falls Venezuela 5°57N 62°30W 120 B3
Angeles Phil. 15°9N 120°33E 83 A6
Ångermanälven → Sweden 63°0N 17°20E 63 E7
Angers France 47°30N 0°35W 66 C3
Anglesey □ U.K. 53°16N 4°18W 28 A5
Angoche Mozam. 16°8S 39°55E 97 H7
Angola ■ Africa 12°0S 18°0E 97 G3
Angoulême France 45°39N 0°10E 66 D4
Angoumois France 45°50N 0°25E 66 D3
Angra dos Reis Brazil 23°0S 44°10W 122 D2
Angren Uzbekistan 41°1N 70°12E 87 A12
Anguilla ☑ W. Indies 18°14N 63°5W 115 D12
Angus □ U.K. 56°46N 2°56S 23 J11
Angus, Braes of U.K. 56°51N 3°10W 23 J11
Anhui □ China 32°0N 117°0E 79 E12
Anjou France 47°20N 0°15W 66 C3
Ankang China 32°40N 109°1E 79 E10
Ankara Turkey 39°57N 32°54E 71 G5
Ann, C. U.S.A. 42°38N 70°35W 113 D12
Ann Arbor U.S.A. 42°17N 83°45W 112 D6
Annaba Algeria 36°50N 7°46E 94 A7
Annalee → Ireland 54°2N 7°24W 18 C7
Annan U.K. 54°59N 3°16W 25 E9
Annan → U.K. 54°58N 3°16W 25 E9
Annandale U.K. 55°10N 3°25W 25 D9
Annapolis U.S.A. 38°59N 76°30W 112 F9
Annapurna Nepal 28°34N 83°50E 85 E14
Annecy France 45°55N 6°8E 66 D7
Annfield Plain U.K. 54°52N 1°44W 26 C5
Anniston U.S.A. 33°39N 85°50W 111 D9
Annobón Atl. Oc. 1°25S 5°36E 90 G4
Annotto B. Jamaica 18°17N 76°45W 114 a

Anqing China 30°30N 117°3E 79 E12
Anse la Raye St. Lucia 13°55N 61°3W 114 b
Anshan China 41°5N 122°58E 79 C13
Anshun China 26°18N 105°57E 78 F10
Anstey U.K. 52°41N 1°12W 27 G6
Anstruther U.K. 56°14N 2°41W 25 B10
Antalaha Madag. 14°57S 50°20E 97 G10
Antalya Turkey 36°52N 30°45E 71 G5
Antalya Körfezi Turkey 36°15N 31°30E 71 G5
Antananarivo Madag. 18°55S 47°31E 97 H9
Antarctic Pen. Antarctica 67°0S 60°0W 55 C18
Antarctica 90°0S 0°0 55 E3
Anti Atlas Morocco 30°0N 8°30W 94 C4
Antibes France 43°34N 7°6E 66 E7
Anticosti, Î. d' Canada 49°30N 63°0W 109 E13
Antigo U.S.A. 45°9N 89°9W 112 C3
Antigonish Canada 45°38N 61°58W 109 E13
Antigua & Barbuda ■
W. Indies 17°20N 61°48W 115 D12
Antilles Cent. Amer. 15°0N 65°0W 115 E12
Antioch = Hatay Turkey 36°14N 36°10E 71 G6
Antioquia Colombia 6°40N 75°55W 120 B2
Antipodes Is. Pac. Oc. 49°45S 178°40E 102 M9
Antofagasta Chile 23°50S 70°30W 121 E2
Antrim U.K. 54°43N 6°14W 19 B9
Antrim, Mts. of U.K. 55°3N 6°14W 19 A9
Antrim & Newtownabbey □
U.K. 54°40N 6°11W 19 B9
Antsirabe Madag. 19°55S 47°2E 97 H9
Antsiranana Madag. 12°25S 49°20E 97 G9
Antwerp Belgium 51°13N 4°25E 64 C3
Anuradhapura Sri Lanka 8°22N 80°28E 84 Q12
Anxi China 40°30N 95°43E 78 C8
Anxious Colombia 6°40N 75°55W 120 B2
Anyang China 36°5N 114°21E 79 D11
Anzhero-Sudzhensk Russia 56°10N 86°0E 76 D9
Ánzio Italy 41°27N 12°37E 68 D5
Aomori Japan 40°45N 140°45E 81 C7
Aoraki Mount Cook N.Z. 43°36S 170°9E 99 J13
Aosta Italy 45°45N 7°20E 68 B2
Aozou Strip Chad 22°0N 19°0E 95 D9
Apalachee B. U.S.A. 30°0N 84°0W 111 E10
Apaporis → Colombia 1°23S 69°25W 120 C3
Aparecida de Goiânia Brazil 16°49S 49°14W 122 C1
Apatity Russia 67°34N 33°22E 70 A5
Apeldoorn Neths. 52°13N 5°57E 64 B3
Apia Samoa 13°50S 171°50W 99 C16
Apostle Is. U.S.A. 47°0N 90°40W 112 B2
Appalachian Mts. U.S.A. 38°0N 80°0W 112 G7
Appennini Italy 44°30N 10°0E 68 B4
Appleby-in-Westmorland
U.K. 54°35N 2°29W 26 C4
Applecross Forest U.K. 57°27N 5°40W 22 H6
Appledore Devon, U.K. 51°3N 4°13W 29 E5
Appledore Kent, U.K. 51°1N 0°47E 31 D10
Appleton U.S.A. 44°16N 88°25W 112 C3
Apure → Venezuela 7°37N 66°25W 120 B3
Apurímac → Peru 12°17S 73°56W 120 D2
Aqaba, G. of Red Sea 29°0N 34°40E 86 D3
Aqtaū Kazakhstan 43°39N 51°12E 71 F9
Aqtöbe Kazakhstan 50°17N 57°10E 71 D10
Aquitain, Bassin France 44°0N 0°30W 66 D3
Ar Ramādī Iraq 33°25N 43°20E 86 C5
Ar Raqqah Syria 35°59N 39°8E 86 B4
Ara India 25°35N 84°32E 85 G14
'Arab, Bahr el → South Sudan 9°0N 29°30E 95 G11
Arab, Shatt al → Asia 29°57N 48°34E 86 D7
Arabia Asia 25°0N 45°0E 72 F6
Arabian Sea Ind. Oc. 16°0N 65°0E 72 G8
Aracaju Brazil 10°55S 37°4W 122 B3
Aracati Brazil 4°30S 37°44W 120 C6
Araçatuba Brazil 21°10S 50°30W 120 E4
Araçuaí Brazil 16°52S 42°4W 122 C2
Arad Romania 46°10N 21°20E 65 E11
Arafura Sea E. Indies 9°0S 135°0E 98 B5
Aragón □ Spain 41°25N 0°40W 67 B5
Araguacema Brazil 8°50S 49°20W 120 C5
Araguaia → Brazil 5°21S 48°41W 120 C5
Araguari Brazil 18°38S 48°11W 122 C1
Arāk Iran 34°0N 49°40E 86 C7
Arakan Coast Myanmar 19°0N 94°0E 85 K19
Arakan Yoma Myanmar 20°0N 94°40E 85 K19
Aral Kazakhstan 46°41N 61°45E 76 E7
Aral Sea Asia 45°0N 58°20E 76 E7
Aran I. = Arranmore Ireland 55°0N 8°30W 18 B4
Aran Is. Ireland 53°6N 9°38W 20 B3
Aransas Pass U.S.A. 27°55N 97°9W 111 E7
Arapiraca Brazil 9°45S 36°39W 122 A3
Ar'ar Si. Arabia 30°59N 41°2E 86 D5
Araraquara Brazil 21°50S 48°0W 122 D1
Araras Brazil 22°22S 47°23W 122 D1
Ararat Turkey 39°50N 44°15E 71 G7
Araripe, Chapada do Brazil 7°20S 40°0W 120 C5
Aras, Rūd-e → Asia 40°5N 48°29E 86 A7
Arauca → Venezuela 7°24N 66°35W 120 B3
Araxá Brazil 19°35S 46°55W 122 C1
Arbroath U.K. 56°34N 2°35W 25 A10
Arcachon France 44°40N 1°10W 66 D3
Arctic Bay Canada 73°1N 85°7W 109 B11
Arctic Ocean Arctic 78°0N 160°0W 54 B18
Ardabīl Iran 38°15N 48°18E 86 B7
Ardee Ireland 53°52N 6°33W 19 C8
Ardennes Belgium 49°50N 5°5E 64 D3
Arderin Ireland 53°2N 7°39W 21 B7
Ardgour U.K. 56°45N 5°25W 22 J7
Ardingly U.K. 51°3N 0°4W 31 D8
Ardivachar Pt. U.K. 57°23N 7°26W 22 H3
Ardmore U.S.A. 34°10N 97°8W 111 D7
Ardnamurchan U.K. 56°43N 6°0W 22 J5
Ardnamurchan, Pt. of U.K. 56°43N 6°14W 22 J5
Ardnave Pt. U.K. 55°53N 6°20E 24 C6
Ardrossan U.K. 55°39N 4°49W 24 C6
Ards & North Down □ U.K. 54°33N 5°34W 19 B10
Ards Pen. U.K. 54°33N 5°34W 19 B10
Arecibo Puerto Rico 18°29N 66°43W 115 D11
Arena, Pt. U.S.A. 38°57N 123°44W 110 C2
Arendal Norway 58°28N 8°46E 63 F5
Arequipa Peru 16°20S 71°30W 120 D2
Arezzo Italy 43°25N 11°53E 68 C4
Argentan France 48°45N 0°1W 66 B3
Argentina ■ S. Amer. 35°0S 66°0W 121 F3
Argentino, L. Argentina 50°10S 73°0W 121 H2

Argostoli Greece 38°11N 20°29E 69 E9
Argun → Russia 53°20N 121°28E 79 A13
Argyle, L. Australia 16°20S 128°40E 98 D4
Argyll U.K. 56°10N 5°20W 24 B5
Argyll & Bute □ U.K. 56°13N 5°28W 24 B4
Ariana, L' Tunisia 36°52N 10°12E 95 A8
Arica Chile 18°32S 70°20W 120 D2
Arinos → Brazil 10°25S 58°20W 120 D4
Aripuanã → Brazil 5°7S 60°25W 120 C3
Arisaig U.K. 56°55N 5°51W 22 J6
Arizona □ U.S.A. 34°0N 112°0W 110 D4
Arkaig, L. U.K. 56°59N 5°10W 22 J7
Arkansas □ U.S.A. 35°0N 92°30W 111 D8
Arkansas → U.S.A. 33°47N 91°4W 111 D8
Arkansas City U.S.A. 37°4N 97°2W 111 C7
Arkhangelsk Russia 64°38N 40°36E 70 B7
Arkle → U.K. 54°24N 1°56W 26 D5
Arklow Ireland 52°48N 6°10W 21 C10
Arles France 43°41N 4°40E 66 E6
Arlington U.S.A. 38°53N 77°7W 112 F9
Arlon Belgium 49°42N 5°49E 64 D3
Armagh U.K. 54°21N 6°39W 19 C8
Armagh, Bansbridge & Craigavon □
U.K. 54°20N 6°39W 19 C8
Armavir Russia 45°2N 41°7E 71 E7
Armenia Colombia 4°35N 75°45W 120 B2
Armenia ■ Asia 40°20N 45°0E 71 F7
Arnaud → Canada 59°59N 69°46W 109 D13
Arnhem Neths. 51°58N 5°55E 64 C3
Arnhem, C. Australia 12°20S 137°30E 98 C6
Arnhem Land Australia 13°10S 134°30E 98 C5
Arno → Italy 43°41N 10°17E 68 C4
Arnold U.K. 53°1N 1°7W 27 F6
Arnprior Canada 45°26N 76°21W 112 C9
Arnside U.K. 54°12N 2°49W 26 D3
Arra Mts. Ireland 52°50N 8°22W 20 C6
Arran U.K. 55°34N 5°12W 24 C5
Arranmore Ireland 55°0N 8°30W 18 B4
Arras France 50°17N 2°46E 66 A5
Arrecife Canary Is. 28°57N 13°37W 94 C3
Arrow, L. Ireland 54°3N 8°19W 18 C5
Artigas Uruguay 30°20S 56°30W 121 F4
Artois France 50°20N 2°30E 66 A5
Artux China 39°40N 76°10E 78 D4
Artvin Turkey 41°14N 41°44E 71 F7
Aru, Kepulauan Indonesia 6°0S 134°30E 83 F8
Arua Uganda 3°1N 30°58E 96 D6
Aruanã Brazil 14°54S 51°10W 120 D4
Aruba ☑ W. Indies 12°30N 70°0W 115 E11
Arun → U.K. 50°49N 0°33W 31 E7
Arunachal Pradesh □ India 28°0N 95°0E 85 F19
Arundel U.K. 50°51N 0°33W 31 E7
Arusha Tanzania 3°20S 36°40E 96 E7
Aruwimi →
Dem. Rep. of the Congo 1°13N 23°36E 96 D4
Arvayheer Mongolia 46°15N 102°48E 78 B9
Arviat Canada 61°6N 93°59W 108 C10
Arxan China 47°11N 119°57E 79 B12
Arzamas Russia 55°27N 43°55E 70 C7
As Sulaymānīyah Iraq 35°35N 45°29E 86 C6
As Sulaymānīyah Si. Arabia 24°9N 47°18E 86 E6
As Suwayq Oman 23°51N 57°26E 89 C6
Aş Şuwayrah Iraq 32°55N 45°0E 86 C6
Asahikawa Japan 43°46N 142°22E 81 B8
Asama-Yama Japan 36°24N 138°31E 81 E6
Asamankese Ghana 5°50N 0°40W 94 G5
Asansol India 23°40N 87°1E 85 H15
Asbestos Canada 45°47N 71°58W 113 C12
Asbury Park U.S.A. 40°13N 74°1W 113 E10
Ascension I. Atl. Oc. 7°57S 14°23W 52 E9
Áscoli Piceno Italy 42°51N 13°34E 68 C5
Ascot U.K. 51°25N 0°41W 31 D7
Aseb Eritrea 13°0N 42°40E 89 E3
Asenovgrad Bulgaria 42°1N 24°51E 69 C11
Asfordby U.K. 52°47N 0°57W 27 G7
Ash Kent, U.K. 51°16N 1°17E 31 D11
Ash Surrey, U.K. 51°15N 0°43W 31 D7
Ashbourne U.K. 53°2N 1°43W 27 F5
Ashburton N.Z. 43°53S 171°48E 99 J13
Ashby-de-la-Zouch U.K. 52°46N 1°29W 27 G6
Ashchurch U.K. 52°0N 2°5W 30 C4
Ashdown Forest U.K. 51°3N 0°5E 31 D9
Asheville U.S.A. 35°36N 82°33W 111 C10
Ashford Derby., U.K. 53°14N 1°42W 27 F5
Ashford Kent, U.K. 51°8N 0°53E 31 D10
Ashgabat Turkmenistan 37°58N 58°24E 87 B9
Ashington U.K. 55°11N 1°33W 26 B5
Ashkhabad = Ashgabat
Turkmenistan 37°58N 58°24E 87 B9
Ashland Ky., U.S.A. 38°28N 82°38W 112 F6
Ashland Ohio, U.S.A. 40°52N 82°19W 112 E6
Ashland Wis., U.S.A. 46°35N 90°53W 111 A8
Ashqelon Israel 31°42N 34°35E 86 D3
Ashtabula U.S.A. 41°52N 80°47W 112 E7
Ashton-in-Makerfield U.K. 53°30N 2°40W 27 F3
Ashton-under-Lyne U.K. 53°29N 2°6W 27 F4
Ashuanipi, L. Canada 52°45N 66°15W 109 D13
Ashwater U.K. 50°43N 4°19W 29 F5
Ashwick U.K. 51°13N 2°31W 30 D3
Axios → Greece 40°57N 22°35E 69 D10
Asia 45°0N 75°0E 72 E9
Asinara Italy 41°4N 8°16E 68 D3
'Asīr Si. Arabia 18°40N 42°30E 89 D3
Asir, Ras Somalia 11°55N 51°10E 89 E5
Askrigg U.K. 54°19N 2°6W 26 D5
Aslackby U.K. 52°53N 0°24W 27 G8
Asmera Eritrea 15°19N 38°55E 89 D2
Aspatria U.K. 54°47N 3°19W 26 C2
Aspen U.S.A. 39°11N 106°49W 110 C5
Assal, L. Djibouti 11°40N 42°26E 89 E3
Assam □ India 26°0N 93°0E 85 G18
Assen Neths. 53°0N 6°35E 64 B4
Assiniboia Canada 49°40N 105°59W 108 E9
Assiniboine → Canada 49°53N 97°8W 108 E10
Assisi Italy 43°4N 12°37E 68 C5
Assynt U.K. 58°12N 5°12W 22 F7
Assynt, L. U.K. 58°10N 5°3W 22 F7
Astana Kazakhstan 51°10N 71°30E 76 D8
Asti Italy 44°54N 8°12E 68 B3
Astipálaia Greece 36°32N 26°22E 69 F12
Astoria U.S.A. 46°11N 123°50W 110 A2
Astrakhan Russia 46°25N 48°5E 71 E8

Asturias □ Spain 43°15N 6°0W 67 A3
Astwood Bank U.K. 52°15N 1°56W 30 B5
Asunción Paraguay 25°10S 57°30W 121 E4
Aswân Egypt 24°4N 32°57E 95 D12
Aswan High Dam Egypt 23°54N 32°54E 95 D12
Asyût Egypt 27°11N 31°4E 95 C12
Aţ Ţā'if Si. Arabia 21°5N 40°27E 89 C3
Atacama, Desierto de Chile 24°0S 69°20W 121 E3
Atatürk Barajı Turkey 37°28N 38°30E 71 G6
Atbara Sudan 17°42N 33°59E 95 E12
Atbara → Sudan 17°40N 33°56E 95 E12
Atchafalaya B. U.S.A. 29°25N 91°25W 111 E8
Athabasca Canada 54°45N 113°20W 108 D8
Athabasca → Canada 58°40N 110°50W 108 D8
Athabasca, L. Canada 59°15N 109°15W 108 D9
Athboy Ireland 53°36N 6°56W 19 C8
Athenry Ireland 53°18N 8°44W 20 B5
Athens Greece 37°58N 23°43E 69 F10
Athens Ga., U.S.A. 33°57N 83°23W 111 D10
Athens Ohio, U.S.A. 39°20N 82°6W 112 F6
Atherstone U.K. 52°35N 1°33W 27 G5
Atherton U.K. 53°32N 2°30W 27 F4
Athlone Ireland 53°25N 7°56W 20 B7
Atholl, Forest of U.K. 56°51N 3°50W 23 J10
Athos Greece 40°9N 24°22E 69 D11
Athy Ireland 53°0N 7°0W 21 B8
Atikokan Canada 48°45N 91°37W 112 A2
Atka I. U.S.A. 52°7N 174°30W 108 D2
Atlanta U.S.A. 33°45N 84°23W 111 D10
Atlantic City U.S.A. 39°21N 74°27W 113 F10
Atlantic Ocean 0°0 20°0W 50 D8
Atlas Saharien Algeria 33°30N 1°0E 94 B6
Atlin Canada 59°31N 133°41W 108 D6
Attawapiskat Canada 52°56N 82°24W 109 D11
Attawapiskat → Canada 52°57N 82°18W 109 D11
Attleborough U.K. 52°32N 1°1E 31 A11
Attu I. U.S.A. 52°55N 172°55E 108 D1
Atyraū Kazakhstan 47°5N 52°0E 71 E9
Au Sable → U.S.A. 44°25N 83°20W 112 C6
Aube → France 48°34N 3°43E 66 B5
Auburn Ind., U.S.A. 41°22N 85°4W 112 E5
Auburn N.Y., U.S.A. 42°56N 76°34W 112 D9
Aubusson France 45°57N 2°11E 66 D5
Auch France 43°39N 0°36E 66 E4
Auchterarder U.K. 56°18N 3°41W 25 B8
Auchtermuchty U.K. 56°18N 3°13W 25 B9
Auckland N.Z. 36°52S 174°46E 99 H13
Auckland Is. Pac. Oc. 50°40S 166°5E 102 N8
Aude → France 43°13N 3°14E 66 E5
Audlem U.K. 52°59N 2°30W 27 G4
Aughnacloy U.K. 54°25N 6°59W 19 C8
Augsburg Germany 48°25N 10°52E 64 D6
Augusta Australia 34°19S 115°9E 98 G2
Augusta U.S.A. 33°28N 81°58W 111 D10
Aunis France 46°5N 0°50W 66 C3
Aurangabad Bihar, India 24°45N 84°18E 85 G14
Aurangabad Maharashtra,
India 19°50N 75°23E 84 K9
Aurillac France 44°55N 2°26E 66 D5
Aurora Colo., U.S.A. 39°43N 104°49W 110 C6
Aurora Ill., U.S.A. 41°45N 88°19W 112 E3
Austin U.S.A. 30°17N 97°45W 110 D7
Australia ■ Oceania 23°0S 135°0E 98 E3
Australian Capital Territory □
Australia 35°30S 149°0E 98 H8
Austria ■ Europe 47°0N 14°0E 64 E8
Autun France 46°58N 4°17E 66 C6
Auvergne France 45°20N 3°15E 66 D5
Auvergne, Mts. d' France 45°20N 2°55E 66 D5
Auxerre France 47°48N 3°32E 66 C5
Avallon France 47°30N 3°53E 66 C5
Avaré Brazil 23°4S 48°58W 122 D1
Avebury U.K. 51°26N 1°50W 30 D5
Avellaneda Argentina 34°40S 58°22W 121 F4
Avellino Italy 40°54N 14°47E 68 D6
Aversa Italy 40°58N 14°12E 68 D6
Aveton Gifford U.K. 50°18N 3°50W 29 G6
Aveyron → France 44°5N 1°16E 66 D4
Aviemore U.K. 57°12N 3°50W 23 H10
Avignon France 43°57N 4°50E 66 E6
Ávila Spain 40°39N 4°43W 67 B3
Avilés Spain 43°35N 5°57W 67 A3
Avoca → Ireland 52°48N 6°10W 21 C10
Avon → Bristol, U.K. 51°29N 2°41W 30 D3
Avon → Dorset, U.K. 50°44N 1°46W 30 E5
Avon → Warks., U.K. 52°0N 2°8W 30 B4
Avonmouth U.K. 51°30N 2°42W 30 D3
Avranches France 48°40N 1°20W 66 B3
Awasa Ethiopia 7°2N 38°28E 89 F2
Awash Ethiopia 9°1N 40°10E 89 F3
Awbārī, Idehan Libya 27°10N 11°30E 95 C8
Awe, L. U.K. 56°17N 5°16W 24 B5
Axbridge U.K. 51°17N 2°49W 30 D3
Axe → U.K. 50°42N 3°4W 29 F7
Axe Edge U.K. 53°14N 1°57W 27 F5
Axel Heiberg I. Canada 80°0N 90°0W 109 B11
Axholme, Isle of U.K. 53°32N 0°50W 27 E7
Axminster U.K. 50°46N 3°0W 29 F7
Axmouth U.K. 50°42N 3°3W 29 F7
Ayacucho Argentina 37°5S 58°20W 121 F4
Ayacucho Peru 13°0S 74°0W 120 D2
Ayaköz Kazakhstan 38°30N 43°45E 71 G7
Ayakkum Hu China 37°30N 89°20E 78 D6
Aydın Turkey 37°51N 27°51E 71 G4
Aydingkol Hu China 42°40N 89°15E 78 C6
Ayers Rock = Uluru Australia 25°23S 131°5E 98 F5
Ayeyawadi → Myanmar 15°50N 95°6E 85 M19
Aylesbury U.K. 51°49N 0°49W 31 C7
Aylesford U.K. 51°18N 0°30E 31 D10
Aylmer, L. Canada 64°5N 108°30W 108 C8
Aylsham U.K. 52°48N 1°15E 31 A11
Aynho U.K. 52°0N 1°15W 30 B6
Ayr U.S.A. 55°28N 4°38W 24 D6
Ayr → U.K. 55°28N 4°38W 24 D6
Aysgarth U.K. 54°18N 2°1W 26 D5
Ayton Borders., U.K. 55°51N 2°6W 25 C11
Ayton N. Yorks., U.K. 54°15N 0°28W 26 D7
Ayutthaya Thailand 14°25N 100°30E 82 B2
Az Zarqā Jordan 32°5N 36°4E 86 C4
Az Zāwiyah Libya 32°52N 12°56E 95 B8

Azad Kashmir □ *Pakistan* 33°50N 73°50E **84** B8
Azamgarh *India* 26°5N 83°13E **85** F13
Āzarbāyjān □ *Iran* 37°0N 44°30E **86** B6
Azare *Nigeria* 11°55N 10°10E **94** F8
Azerbaijan ■ *Asia* 40°20N 48°0E **71** F8
Azov *Russia* 38°0N 27°0W **91** C1
Azov, Sea of *Europe* 47°3N 39°25E **71** E6
Azores *Atl. Oc.* 46°0N 36°30E **71** E6
Azuero, Pen. de *Panama* 7°30N 80°30W **115** F8
Azul *Argentina* 36°42S 59°43W **121** F4

B

Bab el Mandeb *Red Sea* 12°35N 43°25E **89** E3
Bābā, Koh-i- *Afghan.* 34°30N 67°0E **84** B5
Babine L. *Canada* 54°48N 126°0W **108** D7
Bābol *Iran* 36°40N 52°50E **87** B8
Babruysk *Belarus* 53°10N 29°15E **65** B15
Babuyan Chan. *Phil.* 18°40N 121°30E **83** A6
Babylon *Iraq* 32°34N 44°22E **86** C6
Bac Lieu *Vietnam* 9°17N 105°43E **82** C3
Bacabal *Brazil* 4°15S 44°45W **120** C5
Bacău *Romania* 46°35N 26°55E **65** E14
Back → *Canada* 65°10N 104°0W **108** C9
Bacolod *Phil.* 10°40N 122°57E **83** B6
Bacton *U.K.* 52°52N 1°27E **31** A11
Bacup *U.K.* 53°42N 2°11W **27** E4
Bad Axe *U.S.A.* 43°48N 83°0W **112** D6
Badain Jaran Desert *China* 40°23N 102°0E **78** C9
Badajoz *Spain* 38°50N 6°59W **67** C2
Badakhshān □ *Afghan.* 36°30N 71°0E **87** B12
Badalona *Spain* 41°26N 2°15E **67** B7
Baden-Württemberg □
Germany 48°20N 8°40E **64** D5
Badenoch *U.K.* 56°59N 4°15W **23** J9
Badlands *U.S.A.* 43°55N 102°30W **110** B6
Baffin B. *N. Amer.* 72°0N 64°0W **109** B13
Baffin I. *Canada* 68°0N 75°0W **109** C12
Bafoulabé *Mali* 13°50N 10°55W **94** F3
Bafoussam *Cameroon* 5°28N 10°25E **96** C2
Bafra *Turkey* 41°34N 35°54E **71** F6
Bagamoyo *Tanzania* 6°28S 38°55E **96** F7
Bagé *Brazil* 31°20S 54°15W **121** F4
Bagenalstown *Ireland* 52°42N 6°58W **21** D9
Baggy Pt. *U.K.* 51°8N 4°16W **29** E5
Baghdād *Iraq* 33°20N 44°23E **86** C6
Baghlān *Afghan.* 32°12N 68°46E **87** B12
Bagshot *U.K.* 51°22N 0°41W **31** D7
Baguio *Phil.* 16°26N 120°34E **83** A6
Bahamas, The ■ *N. Amer.* 24°0N 75°0W **115** C10
Baharampur *India* 24°2N 88°27E **85** G16
Bahawalpur *Pakistan* 29°24N 71°40E **84** E7
Bahía = Salvador *Brazil* 13°0S 38°30W **122** B3
Bahía □ *Brazil* 12°0S 42°0W **122** B2
Bahía Blanca *Argentina* 38°35S 62°13W **121** F3
Bahir Dar *Ethiopia* 11°37N 37°10E **89** E2
Bahr el Ghazal □ *South Sudan* 7°30N 25°30E **95** G11
Bahraich *India* 27°38N 81°37E **85** F12
Bahrain ■ *Asia* 26°0N 50°35E **87** E7
Baia Mare *Romania* 47°40N 23°35E **65** E12
Baicheng *China* 45°38N 122°42E **79** B13
Baie-Comeau *Canada* 49°12N 68°10W **109** D13
Baie-St-Paul *Canada* 47°28N 70°32W **113** B12
Baie Verte *Canada* 49°55N 56°12W **109** E14
Ba'iji *Iraq* 35°0N 43°30E **86** C5
Baikal, L. *Russia* 53°0N 108°0E **77** D11
Baildon *U.K.* 53°51N 1°46W **27** E5
Baile Sear = Baleshare *U.K.* 57°31N 7°22W **22** G3
Bain → *U.K.* 53°6N 0°12W **27** F8
Bainbridge *U.K.* 54°18N 2°6W **26** D4
Baja, Pta. *Mexico* 29°58N 115°49W **114** B1
Baja California *Mexico* 31°10N 115°12W **114** A1
Baker, L. *Canada* 64°0N 96°0W **108** C10
Baker City *U.S.A.* 44°47N 117°50W **110** B3
Baker I. *Pac. Oc.* 0°10N 176°35W **99** A15
Baker Lake *Canada* 64°20N 96°3W **108** C10
Bakers Dozen Is. *Canada* 56°45N 78°45W **109** D12
Bakersfield *U.S.A.* 35°23N 119°1W **110** C3
Bakewell *U.K.* 53°13N 1°40W **27** F5
Bakhmut *Ukraine* 48°35N 38°0E **71** E6
Baku *Azerbaijan* 40°29N 49°56E **71** F8
Bala *U.K.* 52°54N 3°36W **28** B6
Bala, L. *U.K.* 52°53N 3°37W **28** B6
Balabac Str. *E. Indies* 7°53N 117°5E **82** C5
Balaghat Ra. *India* 18°50N 76°30E **84** K10
Balaklava *Ukraine* 44°30N 33°30E **71** F5
Balakovo *Russia* 52°4N 47°55E **70** D8
Balashov *Russia* 51°30N 43°10E **71** D7
Balaton *Hungary* 46°50N 17°40E **65** E9
Balbi, Mt. *Papua N. G.* 5°55S 154°58E **99** B10
Balbina, Represa de *Brazil* 2°0S 59°30W **120** C4
Balbriggan *Ireland* 53°37N 6°11W **19** D9
Balcarce *Argentina* 38°0S 58°10W **121** F4
Balderton *U.K.* 53°3N 0°47W **27** F7
Baldock *U.K.* 52°0N 0°11W **31** C8
Baldoyle *Ireland* 53°24N 6°8W **21** B10
Baldwin *U.S.A.* 43°54N 85°51W **112** D5
Baldy Peak *U.S.A.* 33°54N 109°34W **110** D5
Balearic Is. *Spain* 39°30N 3°0E **67** C7
Baleine → *Canada* 58°15N 67°40W **109** D13
Baleshare *U.K.* 57°31N 7°22W **22** G3
Baleshwar *India* 21°35N 87°3E **85** J15
Bali □ *Indonesia* 8°20S 115°0E **82** F4
Balıkeşir *Turkey* 39°39N 27°53E **71** G4
Balıkpapan *Indonesia* 1°10S 116°55E **82** E5
Balkan Mts. *Bulgaria* 43°15N 23°0E **69** C10
Balkanabat *Turkmenistan* 39°30N 54°22E **87** B8
Balkhash, L. *Kazakhstan* 46°0N 74°50E **76** E8
Ballachulish *U.K.* 56°41N 5°8W **22** J7
Ballaghadereen *Ireland* 53°55N 8°34W **18** D4
Ballantrae *U.K.* 55°6N 4°59W **24** D6
Ballarat *Australia* 37°33S 143°50E **98** H7
Ballari *India* 15°10N 76°56E **84** M10
Ballater *U.K.* 57°3N 3°3W **23** H11
Ballenas, B. de *Mexico* 26°45N 113°26W **114** B2
Balleny Is. *Antarctica* 66°30S 163°0E **55** C11
Ballina *Ireland* 54°7N 9°9W **18** C3
Ballinasloe *Ireland* 53°20N 8°13W **20** B6
Ballincollig *Ireland* 51°53N 8°35W **20** E5
Ballinrobe *Ireland* 53°38N 9°13W **18** D3
Ballinskelligs B. *Ireland* 51°48N 10°13W **20** E2

Ballybunion *Ireland* 52°31N 9°40W **20** C3
Ballycastle *U.K.* 55°12N 6°15W **19** A9
Ballyclare *U.K.* 54°46N 6°0W **19** B10
Ballycroy △ *Ireland* 54°5N 9°50W **18** C2
Ballycummin *Ireland* 52°38N 8°38W **20** C5
Ballyhaunis *Ireland* 53°46N 8°46W **18** D4
Ballyhoura Mts. *Ireland* 52°18N 8°33W **20** D5
Ballymena *U.K.* 54°52N 6°17W **19** B9
Ballymoney *U.K.* 55°5N 6°31W **19** A8
Ballymote *Ireland* 54°5N 8°31W **18** C4
Ballynahinch *U.K.* 54°24N 5°54W **19** C10
Ballyquintin Pt. *U.K.* 54°20N 5°30W **19** C11
Ballyshannon *Ireland* 54°30N 8°11W **18** B5
Balmoral Forest *U.K.* 57°0N 3°15W **23** J11
Balrampur *India* 27°30N 82°20E **85** F13
Balsas → *Mexico* 17°55N 102°10W **114** D4
Baltic Sea *Europe* 57°0N 19°0E **63** F7
Baltimore *Ireland* 51°29N 9°22W **20** E4
Baltimore *U.S.A.* 39°17N 76°36W **112** F9
Baluchistan □ *Pakistan* 27°30N 65°0E **84** F4
Bam *Iran* 29°7N 58°14E **87** D9
Bamako *Mali* 12°34N 7°55W **94** F4
Bambari *C.A.R.* 5°40N 20°35E **96** C4
Bamberg *Germany* 49°54N 10°54E **64** D6
Bamburgh *U.K.* 55°37N 1°43W **26** A5
Bamenda *Cameroon* 5°57N 10°11E **96** C2
Bamford *U.K.* 53°22N 1°41W **27** F5
Bampton *Devon, U.K.* 50°59N 3°29W **29** F7
Bampton *Oxon., U.K.* 51°44N 1°32W **30** C5
Banaba *Kiribati* 0°45S 169°50E **102** H8
Bananal, I. do *Brazil* 11°30S 50°30W **120** D4
Banbridge *U.K.* 54°22N 6°16W **19** C9
Banbury *U.K.* 52°4N 1°20W **30** B6
Banchory *U.K.* 57°3N 2°29W **23** H13
Bancroft *Canada* 45°3N 77°51W **112** C9
Banda *India* 25°30N 80°26E **84** G12
Banda, Kepulauan *Indonesia* 4°37S 129°50E **83** E7
Banda Aceh *Indonesia* 5°35N 95°20E **82** C1
Banda Sea *Indonesia* 6°0S 130°0E **83** F7
Bandar-e Abbās *Iran* 27°15N 56°15E **87** E9
Bandar-e Anzalī *Iran* 37°30N 49°30E **86** B7
Bandar-e Ma'shur *Iran* 30°35N 49°10E **86** D7
Bandar-e Torkeman *Iran* 37°0N 54°10E **87** B8
Bandar Lampung *Indonesia* 5°20S 105°10E **82** F3
Bandar Seri Begawan *Brunei* 4°52N 115°0E **82** C4
Bandeira, Pico da *Brazil* 20°26S 41°47W **122** D2
Bandırma *Turkey* 40°20N 28°0E **71** F4
Bandon *Ireland* 51°44N 8°44W **20** E5
Bandon → *Ireland* 51°43N 8°37W **20** E5
Bandundu
Dem. Rep. of the Congo 3°15S 17°22E **96** E3
Bandung *Indonesia* 6°54S 107°36E **82** F3
Banes *Cuba* 21°0N 75°42W **115** C9
Banff *Canada* 51°10N 115°34W **108** D8
Banff *U.K.* 57°40N 2°33W **23** G12
Bangalore = Bengaluru
India 12°59N 77°40E **84** N10
Bangassou *C.A.R.* 4°55N 23°7E **96** D4
Banggai, Kepulauan *Indonesia* 1°40S 123°30E **83** E6
Bangka *Indonesia* 2°0S 105°50E **82** E3
Bangkok *Thailand* 13°45N 100°35E **82** B2
Bangladesh ■ *Asia* 24°0N 90°0E **85** H17
Bangor *Gwynedd, U.K.* 53°14N 4°8W **28** A5
Bangor *Newry M. & D., U.K.* 54°40N 5°40W **19** B10
Bangui *C.A.R.* 4°23N 18°35E **96** D3
Bangweulu, L. *Zambia* 11°0S 30°0E **96** G6
Banham *U.K.* 52°27N 1°2E **31** B11
Bani *Dom. Rep.* 18°16N 70°22W **115** D10
Banja Luka *Bos.-H.* 44°49N 17°11E **68** B7
Banjarmasin *Indonesia* 3°20S 114°35E **82** E4
Banjul *Gambia* 13°28N 16°40W **94** F2
Bankend *U.K.* 55°1N 3°33W **25** D8
Banks I. *Canada* 73°15N 121°30W **108** B7
Banks Is. *Vanuatu* 13°50S 167°30E **99** C12
Bann → *U.K.* 55°8N 6°41W **19** A8
Bannockburn *U.K.* 56°5N 3°55W **24** B8
Bannu *Pakistan* 33°0N 70°18E **84** C7
Banská Bystrica *Slovakia* 48°46N 19°14E **65** D10
Bantry *Ireland* 51°41N 9°27W **20** E4
Bantry B. *Ireland* 51°37N 9°44W **20** E3
Banwell *U.K.* 51°19N 2°52W **30** D3
Banyak, Kepulauan *Indonesia* 2°10N 97°10E **82** D1
Banyuwangi *Indonesia* 8°13S 114°21E **82** F4
Bao'an *China* 22°34N 113°52E **79** a
Baoding *China* 38°50N 115°28E **79** D12
Baoji *China* 34°20N 107°5E **78** E10
Baoshan *China* 25°10N 99°5E **78** F8
Baotou *China* 40°32N 110°2E **79** C11
Ba'qūbah *Iraq* 33°45N 44°50E **86** C6
Bar Harbor *U.S.A.* 44°23N 68°13W **113** C13
Bar-le-Duc *France* 48°47N 5°10E **66** B6
Baraboo *U.S.A.* 43°28N 89°45W **112** D3
Baracoa *Cuba* 20°20N 74°30W **115** C10
Barahona *Dom. Rep.* 18°13N 71°7W **115** D10
Barail Range *India* 25°15N 93°20E **85** G18
Barakaldo *Spain* 43°18N 2°59W **67** A4
Baranavichy *Belarus* 53°10N 26°0E **65** B14
Baranof I. *U.S.A.* 57°0N 135°0W **108** D6
Barbacena *Brazil* 21°15S 43°56W **122** D2
Barbados ■ *W. Indies* 13°10N 59°30W **114** c
Barberton *U.S.A.* 41°1N 81°39W **112** E7
Barcelona *Spain* 41°22N 2°10E **67** B7
Barcelona *Venezuela* 10°10N 64°40W **120** A3
Barddhaman *India* 23°14N 87°39E **85** H15
Bardīyah *Libya* 31°45N 25°5E **95** B10
Bardney *U.K.* 53°13N 0°19W **27** F8
Bardsey I. *U.K.* 52°45N 4°47W **28** B4
Bardstown *U.S.A.* 37°49N 85°28W **112** G5
Bareilly *India* 28°22N 79°27E **84** E11
Barents Sea *Arctic* 73°0N 39°0E **54** B9
Barford *U.K.* 52°16N 1°35W **30** B5
Bargoed *U.K.* 51°42N 3°15W **28** D7
Barham *U.K.* 51°12N 1°11E **31** D11
Barhi *India* 24°15N 85°25E **85** G14
Bari *Italy* 41°8N 16°51E **68** D7
Bari Doab *Pakistan* 30°20N 73°0E **84** D8
Barīm *Yemen* 12°39N 43°25E **90** E8
Barinas *Venezuela* 8°36N 70°15W **120** B2
Baring, C. *Canada* 70°0N 117°30W **108** C8
Barisal *Bangla.* 22°45N 90°20E **85** H17
Barking and Dagenham □
U.K. 51°32N 0°10E **31** C9

Barkly Tableland *Australia* 17°50S 136°40E **98** D6
Barlborough *U.K.* 53°17N 1°17W **27** F6
Barlby *U.K.* 53°48N 1°2W **27** E6
Barlee, L. *Australia* 29°15S 119°30E **98** F2
Barletta *Italy* 41°19N 16°17E **68** D7
Barmby Moor *U.K.* 53°56N 0°49W **27** E7
Barmer *India* 25°45N 71°20E **84** G7
Barmoor Castle *U.K.* 55°39N 1°59W **26** A5
Barmouth *U.K.* 52°44N 4°4W **28** B5
Barnard Castle *U.K.* 54°33N 1°55W **26** C5
Barnaul *Russia* 53°20N 83°40E **76** D9
Barnet □ *U.K.* 51°38N 0°9W **31** C8
Barnetby le Wold *U.K.* 53°34N 0°24W **27** E8
Barnoldswick *U.K.* 53°55N 2°11W **27** E4
Barnsley *U.K.* 53°34N 1°27W **27** E6
Barnstaple *U.K.* 51°5N 4°4W **29** E5
Barnstaple Bay = Bideford Bay
U.K. 51°5N 4°20W **29** E5
Barotseland *Zambia* 15°0S 24°0E **97** H4
Barques, Pt. Aux *U.S.A.* 44°4N 82°58W **112** C6
Barquísimeto *Venezuela* 10°4N 69°19W **120** A3
Barra *Brazil* 11°5S 43°10W **122** B2
Barra *U.K.* 57°0N 7°29W **22** J2
Barra, Sd. of *U.K.* 57°4N 7°25W **22** H3
Barra do Corda *Brazil* 5°30S 45°10W **120** C5
Barra do Piraí *Brazil* 22°30S 43°50W **122** D2
Barra Hd. *U.K.* 56°47N 7°40W **22** J2
Barra Mansa *Brazil* 22°35S 44°12W **122** D2
Barrancabermeja *Colombia* 7°0N 73°50W **120** B2
Barranquilla *Colombia* 11°0N 74°50W **120** A2
Barre *U.S.A.* 44°12N 72°30W **113** C11
Barreiras *Brazil* 12°8S 45°0W **122** B2
Barreiro *Portugal* 38°39N 9°5W **67** C1
Barreiros *Brazil* 8°49S 35°12W **122** A3
Barretos *Brazil* 20°30S 48°35W **122** D1
Barrhead *U.K.* 55°48N 4°23W **24** C7
Barrie *Canada* 44°24N 79°40W **109** E12
Barrow *U.S.A.* 71°18N 156°47W **108** B4
Barrow → *Ireland* 52°25N 6°58W **21** D9
Barrow-in-Furness *U.K.* 54°7N 3°14W **26** D2
Barrow upon Humber *U.K.* 53°41N 0°23W **27** E8
Barrowford *U.K.* 53°51N 2°14W **27** E4
Barry *U.K.* 51°24N 3°16W **29** D7
Barry I. *U.K.* 51°23N 3°16W **29** E7
Barry's Bay *Canada* 45°29N 77°41W **112** C9
Barstow *U.S.A.* 34°54N 117°1W **110** D3
Bartlesville *U.S.A.* 36°45N 95°59W **111** C7
Barton *U.K.* 54°29N 1°38W **26** D5
Barton-upon-Humber *U.K.* 53°41N 0°25W **27** E8
Barú, Volcan *Panama* 8°55N 82°35W **115** F8
Baruun-Urt *Mongolia* 46°46N 113°15E **79** B11
Barwell *U.K.* 52°35N 1°21W **27** G6
Barysaw *Belarus* 54°17N 28°28E **65** A15
Bashkortostan □ *Russia* 54°0N 57°0E **70** D10
Basilan I. *Phil.* 6°35N 122°0E **83** C6
Basildon *U.K.* 51°34N 0°28E **31** C9
Basingstoke *U.K.* 51°15N 1°5W **30** D6
Baskatong, Rés. *Canada* 46°46N 75°50W **113** B10
Basle *Switz.* 47°35N 7°35E **64** E4
Basque Provinces = País Vasco □
Spain 42°50N 2°45W **67** A4
Basra *Iraq* 30°30N 47°50E **86** D6
Bass Rock *U.K.* 56°5N 2°38W **25** B10
Bass Str. *Australia* 39°15S 146°30E **98** H8
Bassas da India *Ind. Oc.* 22°0S 39°0E **97** J7
Basse-Terre *Guadeloupe* 16°0N 61°44W **115** D12
Bassenthwaite L. *U.K.* 54°40N 3°14W **26** C2
Basseterre *St. Kitts & Nevis* 17°17N 62°43W **115** D12
Basti *India* 26°52N 82°55E **85** F13
Bastia *France* 42°40N 9°30E **66** E8
Baston *U.K.* 52°43N 0°21W **27** G8
Bata *Eq. Guin.* 1°57N 9°50E **96** D1
Batabanó, G. de *Cuba* 22°30N 82°30W **115** C8
Batangas *Phil.* 13°35N 121°10E **83** B6
Batatais *Brazil* 20°54S 47°37W **122** D1
Batavia *U.S.A.* 43°0N 78°11W **112** D8
Bataysk *Russia* 47°3N 39°45E **71** E6
Batdambang *Cambodia* 13°7N 103°12E **82** B2
Bath *Maine, U.S.A.* 43°55N 69°49W **113** D13
Bath *N.Y., U.S.A.* 42°20N 77°19W **112** D9
Bathford *U.K.* 51°24N 2°18W **30** D4
Bathgate *U.K.* 55°54N 3°39W **25** C8
Bathsheba *Barbados* 13°13N 59°32W **114** c
Bathurst *Australia* 33°25S 149°31E **98** G8
Bathurst *Canada* 47°37N 65°43W **109** E13
Bathurst, C. *Canada* 70°34N 128°0W **108** B7
Bathurst Inlet *Canada* 66°50N 108°1W **108** C9
Batley *U.K.* 53°43N 1°38W **27** E5
Batman *Turkey* 37°55N 41°5E **71** G7
Batna *Algeria* 35°34N 6°15E **94** A7
Baton Rouge *U.S.A.* 30°27N 91°11W **111** D8
Batticaloa *Sri Lanka* 7°43N 81°45E **84** R12
Battle *U.K.* 50°55N 0°30E **31** E9
Battle Creek *U.S.A.* 42°19N 85°11W **112** D5
Batu, Kepulauan *Indonesia* 0°30S 98°25E **82** E1
Batu Pahat *Malaysia* 1°50N 102°56E **82** D2
Batumi *Georgia* 41°39N 41°44E **71** F7
Bauld, C. *Canada* 51°38N 55°26W **109** D14
Bauru *Brazil* 22°10S 49°0W **122** D1
Bavaria = Bayern □ *Germany* 48°50N 12°0E **64** D6
Bawdsey *U.K.* 52°1N 1°27E **31** B11
Bawtry *U.K.* 53°26N 1°2W **27** F6
Bay City *U.S.A.* 43°36N 83°54W **112** D6
Bay Is. *Honduras* 16°45N 86°15W **114** D7
Bayamo *Cuba* 20°20N 76°40W **115** C9
Bayan Har Shan *China* 34°0N 98°0E **78** E8
Bayan Obo *China* 41°52N 109°59E **79** C10
Baydhabo *Somalia* 3°8N 43°30E **89** G3
Bayern □ *Germany* 48°50N 12°0E **64** D6
Bayeux *France* 49°17N 0°42W **66** B3
Bayonne *France* 43°30N 1°28E **66** E3
Beachley *U.K.* 51°37N 2°39W **30** C3
Beachy Hd. *U.K.* 50°44N 0°15E **31** E9
Beacon *U.S.A.* 41°30N 73°58W **113** E11
Beaconsfield *U.K.* 51°36N 0°38W **31** C7
Beadnell *U.K.* 55°33N 1°38W **26** A5
Beagle, Canal *S. Amer.* 55°0S 68°30W **121** H3
Beaminster *U.K.* 50°48N 2°44W **30** E3
Bear → *U.S.A.* 41°30N 112°8W **110** B4
Bear I. *Arctic* 74°30N 19°0E **54** B8

Bear I. *Ireland* 51°38N 9°50W **20** E3
Bear L. *U.S.A.* 41°59N 111°21W **110** B4
Beardmore Glacier *Antarctica* 84°30S 170°0E **55** E11
Beardstown *U.S.A.* 40°1N 90°26W **112** E2
Béarn *France* 43°20N 0°30W **66** E3
Bearsden *U.K.* 55°55N 4°21W **24** C7
Bearsted *U.K.* 51°16N 0°35E **31** D10
Beatrice *U.S.A.* 40°16N 96°45W **111** B7
Beattock *U.K.* 55°20N 3°28W **25** D9
Beattock Summit *U.K.* 55°25N 3°32W **25** D8
Beattock Summit *U.K.* 55°20N 3°28W **25** D9
Beauce, Plaine de la *France* 48°10N 1°45E **66** B4
Beaufort Sea *Arctic* 72°0N 140°0W **54** B1
Beaufort West *S. Africa* 32°18S 22°36E **97** L4
Beauharnois *Canada* 45°20N 73°52W **113** C11
Beauly *U.K.* 57°30N 4°28W **23** H9
Beauly → *U.K.* 57°29N 4°27W **23** H9
Beauly Firth *U.K.* 57°30N 4°20W **23** H9
Beaumaris *U.K.* 53°16N 4°6W **28** A5
Beaumont *U.S.A.* 30°5N 94°6W **111** D8
Beaune *France* 47°2N 4°50E **66** C6
Beauvais *France* 49°25N 2°8E **66** B5
Beaver → *Canada* 55°26N 107°45W **108** D9
Beaver Creek *Canada* 63°0N 141°0W **108** C5
Beaver Dam *U.S.A.* 43°28N 88°50W **112** D3
Beaver Falls *U.S.A.* 40°46N 80°20W **112** E7
Beaver I. *U.S.A.* 45°40N 85°33W **112** C5
Beawar *India* 26°3N 74°18E **84** F9
Bebedouro *Brazil* 21°0S 48°25W **122** D1
Bebington *U.K.* 53°22N 3°0W **27** F3
Beccles *U.K.* 52°27N 1°35E **31** B12
Béchar *Algeria* 31°38N 2°18W **94** B5
Beckermet *U.K.* 54°27N 3°30W **26** D1
Beckfoot *U.K.* 54°50N 3°24W **26** C2
Beckingham *U.K.* 53°24N 0°50W **27** F7
Beckley *U.S.A.* 37°47N 81°11W **112** G7
Bedale *U.K.* 54°18N 1°36W **26** D5
Beddgelert *U.K.* 53°1N 4°6W **28** A5
Bedford *U.K.* 52°8N 0°28W **31** B8
Bedford *Ind., U.S.A.* 38°52N 86°29W **112** F4
Bedford *Va., U.S.A.* 37°20N 79°31W **112** G8
Bedford □ *U.K.* 52°4N 0°28W **31** B8
Bedford Level *U.K.* 52°32N 0°7W **31** A8
Bedlington *U.K.* 55°8N 1°35W **26** B5
Bedworth *U.K.* 52°29N 1°28W **30** B6
Beeford *U.K.* 53°58N 0°17W **27** E8
Beer *U.K.* 50°41N 3°6W **29** F7
Be'er Sheva *Israel* 31°15N 34°48E **86** D3
Beeston *U.K.* 52°56N 1°14W **27** G6
Behchokǫ̀ *Canada* 62°50N 116°3W **108** C8
Bei Jiang → *China* 23°2N 112°58E **79** G11
Bei Shan *China* 41°30N 96°0E **78** C8
Bei'an *China* 48°10N 126°20E **79** B14
Beighton *U.K.* 53°21N 1°20W **27** F6
Beihai *China* 21°28N 109°6E **79** G10
Beijing *China* 39°53N 116°21E **79** D12
Beinn na Faoghla = Benbecula
U.K. 57°26N 7°21W **22** H3
Beira *Mozam.* 19°50S 34°52E **97** H6
Beirut *Lebanon* 33°53N 35°31E **86** C3
Beitbridge *Zimbabwe* 22°12S 30°0E **97** J6
Beith *U.K.* 55°45N 4°38W **24** C6
Béja *Tunisia* 36°43N 9°12E **95** A7
Bejaïa *Algeria* 36°42N 5°2E **94** A7
Békéscsaba *Hungary* 46°40N 21°5E **65** E11
Bela *Pakistan* 26°12N 66°20E **84** F5
Belagavi *India* 15°55N 74°35E **84** M9
Belarus ■ *Europe* 53°30N 27°0E **70** D4
Belau = Palau ■ *Palau* 7°30N 134°30E **102** G5
Belbroughton *U.K.* 52°24N 2°7W **30** B4
Belcher Chan. *Canada* 77°15N 95°0W **109** B10
Belcher Is. *Canada* 56°15N 78°45W **109** D12
Beledweyne *Somalia* 4°30N 45°5E **89** G4
Belém *Brazil* 1°20S 48°30W **120** C5
Belep, Îs. *N. Cal.* 19°45S 163°40E **99** D11
Belfast *U.K.* 54°37N 5°56W **19** B10
Belfast L. *U.K.* 54°40N 5°50W **19** B10
Belford *U.K.* 55°36N 1°49W **26** A5
Belfort *France* 47°38N 6°50E **66** C7
Belgium ■ *Europe* 50°30N 5°0E **64** C3
Belgorod *Russia* 50°35N 36°35E **71** D6
Belgrade *Serbia* 44°50N 20°37E **69** B9
Belitung *Indonesia* 3°10S 107°50E **82** E3
Belize ■ *Cent. Amer.* 17°0N 88°30W **114** D7
Belize City *Belize* 17°25N 88°10W **114** D7
Bell Peninsula *Canada* 63°50N 82°0W **109** C11
Bell Ville *Argentina* 32°40S 62°40W **121** F3
Bella Coola *Canada* 52°25N 126°40W **108** D7
Bellaire *U.S.A.* 40°1N 80°45W **112** E7
Belle Fourche → *U.S.A.* 44°26N 102°18W **110** B6
Belle-Île *France* 47°20N 3°10W **66** C2
Belle Isle *Canada* 51°57N 55°25W **109** D14
Belle Isle, Str. of *Canada* 51°30N 56°30W **109** D14
Bellefontaine *U.S.A.* 40°22N 83°46W **112** E6
Belleplaine *Barbados* 13°15N 59°34W **114** c
Belleville *Canada* 44°10N 77°23W **109** E12
Belleville *U.S.A.* 38°31N 89°59W **112** F3
Bellingham *U.K.* 55°9N 2°16W **26** B4
Bellingham *U.S.A.* 48°46N 122°29W **110** A2
Bellingshausen Sea *Antarctica* 66°0S 80°0W **55** C17
Bellinzona *Switz.* 46°11N 9°1E **64** E5
Belmonte *Brazil* 16°0S 39°0W **122** C3
Belmopan *Belize* 17°18N 88°30W **114** D7
Belmullet *Ireland* 54°14N 9°58W **18** C2
Belo Horizonte *Brazil* 19°55S 43°56W **122** C2
Belo Jardim *Brazil* 8°20S 36°26W **122** A3
Belogorsk *Russia* 51°0N 128°20E **77** D13
Beloit *U.S.A.* 42°31N 89°2W **112** D3
Belomorsk *Russia* 64°35N 34°54E **70** B5
Beloretsk *Russia* 53°58N 58°24E **70** D10
Beloye, L. *Russia* 60°10N 37°35E **70** B6
Belper *U.K.* 53°2N 1°29W **27** F6
Belsay *U.K.* 55°6N 1°51W **26** B5
Belton *N. Lincs., U.K.* 53°33N 0°48W **27** E7
Belton *Norfolk, U.K.* 52°35N 1°39E **31** B12
Beltsy *Moldova* 47°48N 27°58E **65** E14
Belturbet *Ireland* 54°6N 7°26W **18** C7
Belukha *Russia* 49°50N 86°50E **76** E9
Belvidere *U.S.A.* 42°15N 88°50E **112** D3
Bembridge *U.K.* 50°41N 1°5W **30** E6
Bemidji *U.S.A.* 47°28N 94°53W **111** A8

Ben Cruachan *U.K.* 56°26N 5°8W **24** B5
Ben Dearg *U.K.* 57°47N 4°56W **23** G8
Ben Hope *U.K.* 58°25N 4°36W **23** F8
Ben Lawers *U.K.* 56°32N 4°14W **24** A7
Ben Lomond *U.K.* 56°11N 4°38W **24** B6
Ben Macdhui *U.K.* 57°4N 3°40W **23** H10
Ben Mhor *U.K.* 57°15N 7°18W **22** H3
Ben More *Argyll & Bute, U.K.* 56°26N 6°1W **24** B3
Ben More *Stirling, U.K.* 56°23N 4°32W **24** B6
Ben More Assynt *U.K.* 58°8N 4°52W **23** F8
Ben Nevis *U.K.* 56°48N 5°1W **22** J7
Ben Vorlich *U.K.* 56°21N 4°14W **24** B7
Ben Wyvis *U.K.* 57°40N 4°35W **23** G8
Benares = Varanasi *India* 25°22N 83°0E **85** G13
Benbecula *U.K.* 57°26N 7°21W **22** H3
Bend *U.S.A.* 44°4N 121°19W **110** B2
Benderloch *U.K.* 56°30N 5°22W **24** A5
Bendery *Moldova* 46°50N 29°30E **65** E15
Bendigo *Australia* 36°40S 144°15E **98** H7
Benevento *Italy* 41°8N 14°45E **68** D6
Bengal, Bay of *Ind. Oc.* 15°0N 90°0E **85** M17
Bengaluru *India* 12°59N 77°40E **84** N10
Bengbu *China* 32°58N 117°20E **79** E12
Benghazi *Libya* 32°11N 20°3E **95** B10
Bengkulu *Indonesia* 3°50S 102°12E **82** E2
Benguela *Angola* 12°37S 13°25E **97** G2
Beni → *Bolivia* 10°23S 65°24W **120** D3
Beni Mellal *Morocco* 32°21N 6°21W **94** B4
Beni Suef *Egypt* 29°5N 31°6E **95** C12
Benidorm *Spain* 38°33N 0°9W **67** C5
Benin ■ *Africa* 10°0N 2°0E **94** G6
Benin, Bight of *W. Afr.* 5°0N 3°0E **94** H6
Benin City *Nigeria* 6°20N 5°31E **94** G7
Benington *U.K.* 53°0N 0°5E **27** F9
Benjamin Constant *Brazil* 4°40S 70°15W **120** C2
Benoni *S. Africa* 26°11S 28°18E **97** K5
Benson *U.K.* 51°37N 1°6W **30** C6
Bentley *Hants., U.K.* 51°12N 0°52W **31** D7
Bentley *S. Yorks., U.K.* 53°33N 1°8W **27** E6
Bentley Subglacial Trench
Antarctica 80°0S 115°0W **55** E14
Benton *U.S.A.* 38°0N 88°55W **112** G3
Benton Harbor *U.S.A.* 42°6N 86°27W **112** D4
Benue → *Nigeria* 7°48N 6°46E **94** G7
Benxi *China* 41°20N 123°48E **79** C13
Beppu *Japan* 33°15N 131°30E **81** G2
Berber *Sudan* 18°0N 34°0E **95** E12
Berbera *Somalia* 10°30N 45°2E **89** E4
Berbérati *C.A.R.* 4°15N 15°40E **96** D3
Berbice → *Guyana* 6°20N 57°32W **120** B4
Berdyansk *Ukraine* 46°45N 36°50E **71** E6
Berdychiv *Ukraine* 49°57N 28°30E **71** E4
Bere Alston *U.K.* 50°29N 4°13W **29** G5
Bere Regis *U.K.* 50°45N 2°14W **30** E4
Berea *U.S.A.* 37°34N 84°17W **112** G5
Berens → *Canada* 52°25N 97°2W **108** D10
Berezník *Russia* 62°51N 42°40E **70** B7
Berezniki *Russia* 59°24N 56°46E **70** C10
Bérgamo *Italy* 45°41N 9°43E **68** B3
Bergen *Norway* 60°20N 5°20E **63** E5
Bergerac *France* 44°51N 0°30E **66** D4
Bering Sea *Pac. Oc.* 58°0N 171°0W **102** B10
Bering Strait *Pac. Oc.* 65°30N 169°0W **108** C3
Berkeley *U.K.* 51°41N 2°27W **30** C4
Berkhamsted *U.K.* 51°45N 0°33W **31** C7
Berkner I. *Antarctica* 79°30S 50°0W **55** D18
Berkshire Downs *U.K.* 51°33N 1°29W **30** C6
Berlin *Germany* 52°31N 13°23E **64** B7
Berlin *U.S.A.* 44°28N 71°11W **113** C12
Bermejo → *Argentina* 26°51S 58°23W **121** E4
Bermuda ⊠ *Atl. Oc.* 32°18N 64°45W **52** C6
Bern *Switz.* 46°57N 7°28E **64** E4
Berneray *U.K.* 57°43N 7°11W **22** G3
Berry *France* 46°50N 2°0E **66** C5
Berry Hd. *U.K.* 50°24N 3°29W **29** G7
Bertraghboy B. *Ireland* 53°22N 9°54W **20** B3
Berwick *U.S.A.* 41°3N 76°14W **112** E9
Berwick-upon-Tweed *U.K.* 55°46N 2°0W **26** A5
Berwyn Mts. *U.K.* 52°54N 3°26W **28** B7
Besançon *France* 47°15N 6°2E **66** C7
Bessarabiya *Moldova* 47°0N 28°10E **65** E15
Bessemer *U.S.A.* 46°29N 90°3W **112** B2
Bethel *U.S.A.* 60°48N 161°45W **108** C3
Bethesda *U.K.* 53°10N 4°3W **28** A5
Bethlehem *S. Africa* 28°14S 28°18E **97** K5
Bethlehem *U.S.A.* 40°37N 75°23W **113** E10
Béthune *France* 50°30N 2°38E **66** A5
Betim *Brazil* 19°58S 44°7W **122** C2
Bettiah *India* 26°48N 84°33E **85** F14
Betul *India* 21°58N 77°59E **84** J10
Betws-y-Coed *U.K.* 53°5N 3°48W **28** A6
Beverley *U.K.* 53°51N 0°26W **27** E8
Bewdley *U.K.* 52°23N 2°19W **30** B4
Bexhill *U.K.* 50°51N 0°29E **31** E9
Bexley □ *U.K.* 51°27N 0°9E **31** D9
Beyneu *Kazakhstan* 45°18N 55°9E **71** E10
Beypazarı *Turkey* 40°10N 31°56E **71** F5
Beyşehir Gölü *Turkey* 37°41N 31°33E **71** G5
Béziers *France* 43°20N 3°12E **66** E5
Bhagalpur *India* 25°10N 87°0E **85** G15
Bhaktapur *Nepal* 27°38N 85°24E **85** F14
Bhanrer Ra. *India* 23°40N 79°45E **84** H11
Bharatpur *India* 27°15N 77°30E **84** F10
Bharraig = Barra *U.K.* 57°0N 7°29W **22** J2
Bharuch *India* 21°47N 73°0E **84** J8
Bhatarsaigh = Vatersay *U.K.* 56°55N 7°32W **22** J2
Bhatpara *India* 22°50N 88°25E **85** H16
Bhavnagar *India* 21°45N 72°10E **84** J8
Bhearnaraigh = Berneray
U.K. 57°43N 7°11W **22** G3
Bhilainagar-Durg *India* 21°13N 81°26E **85** J12
Bhilwara *India* 25°25N 74°38E **84** G9
Bhima → *India* 16°25N 77°17E **84** L10
Bhiwandi *India* 19°20N 73°0E **84** K8
Bhiwani *India* 28°50N 76°9E **84** E10
Bhopal *India* 23°20N 77°30E **84** H10
Bhubaneshwar *India* 20°15N 85°50E **85** J14
Bhuj *India* 23°15N 69°49E **84** H6
Bhusawal *India* 21°3N 75°46E **84** J9
Bhutan ■ *Asia* 27°25N 90°30E **85** F17
Biała Podlaska *Poland* 52°4N 23°6E **65** B12

Białystok   Burnmouth

Białystok *Poland* 53°10N 23°10E **65** B12
Biarritz *France* 43°29N 1°33W **66** E3
Bibury *U.K.* 51°45N 1°49W **30** C5
Bicester *U.K.* 51°54N 1°9W **30** C6
Bicton *U.K.* 52°44N 2°48W **27** G3
Bida *Nigeria* 9°3N 5°58E **94** G7
Biddeford *U.S.A.* 43°30N 70°28W **113** D12
Biddenden *U.K.* 51°7N 0°40E **31** D10
Biddulph *U.K.* 53°7N 2°10W **27** F4
Bideford *U.K.* 51°1N 4°13W **29** E5
Bideford Bay *U.K.* 51°5N 4°20W **29** E5
Bidford-on-Avon *U.K.* 52°11N 1°50W **30** B5
Bié Plateau *Angola* 12°0S 16°0E **97** G3
Biel *Switz.* 47°8N 7°14E **64** E4
Bielefeld *Germany* 52°1N 8°33E **64** B5
Biella *Italy* 45°34N 8°3E **68** B3
Bielsko-Biała *Poland* 49°50N 19°2E **65** D10
Bien Hoa *Vietnam* 10°57N 106°49E **82** B3
Bienville, L. *Canada* 55°5N 72°40W **109** D12
Big Belt Mts. *U.S.A.* 46°30N 111°25W **110** A4
Big Rapids *U.S.A.* 43°42N 85°29W **112** D5
Big Sioux → *U.S.A.* 42°29N 96°27W **111** B7
Big Spring *U.S.A.* 32°15N 101°28W **110** D6
Big Trout L. *Canada* 53°40N 90°0W **109** D11
Bigbury *U.K.* 50°18N 3°53W **29** G6
Bigbury B. *U.K.* 50°16N 3°54W **29** G6
Biggar *Canada* 52°4N 108°0W **108** D9
Biggar *U.K.* 55°38N 3°32W **25** C8
Biggleswade *U.K.* 52°5N 0°14W **31** B8
Bighorn → *U.S.A.* 46°10N 107°28W **110** A5
Bighorn Mts. *U.S.A.* 44°25N 107°0W **110** B5
Bihar *India* 25°5N 85°40E **85** G14
Bihar □ *India* 25°0N 86°0E **85** G15
Bijagós, Arquipélago dos
  Guinea-Biss. 11°15N 16°10W **94** F2
Bikaner *India* 28°2N 73°18E **84** E8
Bikini Atoll *Marshall Is.* 12°0N 167°30E **102** F8
Bila Tserkva *Ukraine* 49°45N 30°10E **65** D16
Bilaspur *India* 22°2N 82°15E **85** H13
Bilbao *Spain* 43°16N 2°56W **67** A4
Bilecik *Turkey* 40°5N 30°5E **71** F5
Bilhorod-Dnistrovskyi
  Ukraine 46°11N 30°23E **71** E5
Billericay *U.K.* 51°38N 0°26E **31** C9
Billesdon *U.K.* 52°38N 0°54W **27** G7
Billingham *U.K.* 54°36N 1°17W **26** C6
Billinghay *U.K.* 53°5N 0°15W **27** F8
Billings *U.S.A.* 45°47N 108°30W **110** A5
Billingshurst *U.K.* 51°2N 0°27W **31** D8
Bingley *U.K.* 53°51N 1°50W **27** E5
Bioko *Eq. Guin.* 3°30N 8°40E **96** D1
Biratnagar *Nepal* 26°27N 87°17E **85** F15
Birchington *U.K.* 51°22N 1°19E **31** D11
Birdlip *U.K.* 51°50N 2°5W **30** C4
Birkdale *U.K.* 53°38N 3°1W **27** E2
Birkenhead *U.K.* 53°23N 3°2W **27** F2
Birmingham *U.K.* 52°29N 1°52W **27** H5
Birmingham *U.S.A.* 33°31N 86°48W **111** D9
Birmingham Int. ✈ (BHX)
  U.K. 52°26N 1°45W **27** H5
Birnin Kebbi *Nigeria* 12°32N 4°12E **94** F6
Birobidzhan *Russia* 48°50N 132°50E **77** E14
Birr *Ireland* 53°6N 7°54W **20** B7
Birtley *Northumberland, U.K.* 55°6N 2°12W **26** B4
Birtley *Tyne & W., U.K.* 54°54N 1°34W **26** C5
Biscay, B. of *Atl. Oc.* 45°0N 2°0W **66** C1
Bishkek *Kyrgyzstan* 42°54N 74°46E **76** E8
Bishop Auckland *U.K.* 54°39N 1°40W **26** C5
Bishop's Castle *U.K.* 52°30N 2°59W **27** H3
Bishop's Cleeve *U.K.* 51°57N 2°3W **30** C4
Bishop's Frome *U.K.* 52°8N 2°29W **30** B4
Bishop's Nympton *U.K.* 51°0N 3°47W **29** F6
Bishop's Stortford *U.K.* 51°52N 0°10E **31** C9
Bishop's Waltham *U.K.* 50°57N 1°11W **30** E6
Bishopsteignton *U.K.* 50°33N 3°33W **29** F6
Bishopstoke *U.K.* 50°58N 1°19W **30** E6
Biskra *Algeria* 34°50N 5°44E **94** B7
Bismarck *U.S.A.* 46°48N 100°47W **110** A6
Bismarck Arch. *Papua N. G.* 2°30S 150°0E **98** A9
Bissau *Guinea-Biss.* 11°45N 15°45W **94** F2
Bitola *N. Macedonia* 41°1N 21°20E **69** D9
Bitterfontein *S. Africa* 31°1S 18°32E **97** L3
Bitterroot Range *U.S.A.* 46°0N 114°20W **110** A4
Bitton *U.K.* 51°25N 2°27W **30** D4
Biu *Nigeria* 10°40N 12°3E **95** F8
Biwa-Ko *Japan* 35°15N 136°10E **81** F5
Biysk *Russia* 52°40N 85°0E **76** D9
Bizerte *Tunisia* 37°15N 9°50E **95** A7
Blaby *U.K.* 52°35N 1°10W **27** G6
Black Combe *U.K.* 54°16N 3°20W **26** D2
Black Esk → *U.K.* 55°12N 3°11W **25** D9
Black Forest = Schwarzwald
  Germany 48°30N 8°20E **64** D5
Black Hd. *Ireland* 53°9N 9°16W **20** B4
Black Hd. *U.K.* 50°0N 5°7W **29** H3
Black Hills *U.S.A.* 44°0N 103°45W **110** B6
Black Isle *U.K.* 57°35N 4°16W **23** G9
Black Mt. = Mynydd Du *U.K.* 51°52N 3°50W **28** D7
Black Mts. *U.K.* 51°55N 3°7W **28** D7
Black Range *U.S.A.* 33°15N 107°50W **110** D5
Black River *Jamaica* 18°0N 77°50W **114** a
Black River Falls *U.S.A.* 44°18N 90°51W **112** C2
Black Rock *Barbados* 13°7N 59°37W **114** c
Black Sea *Eurasia* 43°30N 35°0E **71** F6
Blackburn *U.K.* 53°45N 2°29W **27** E4
Blackdown Hills *U.K.* 50°57N 3°15W **30** E2
Blackmoor Vale *U.K.* 50°54N 2°28W **30** E4
Blackpool *U.K.* 53°49N 3°3W **27** E2
Blackrock *Ireland* 53°18N 6°11W **21** B10
Blacksburg *U.S.A.* 37°14N 80°25W **112** G7
Blacksod B. *Ireland* 54°6N 10°0W **18** C1
Blackwater → *Meath, Ireland* 53°39N 6°41W **19** D7
Blackwater → *Waterford,
  Ireland* 52°4N 7°52W **20** D7

Blackwater → *Armagh B. & C.,
  U.K.* 54°31N 6°35W **19** B8
Blackwater → *Essex, U.K.* 51°44N 0°53E **31** C10
Blaenau Ffestiniog *U.K.* 53°0N 3°56W **28** B6
Blaenavon *U.K.* 51°46N 3°5W **28** D7
Blagdon *U.K.* 51°20N 2°43W **30** D3
Blagoevgrad *Bulgaria* 42°2N 23°5E **69** C10
Blagoveshchensk *Russia* 50°20N 127°30E **77** D13
Blair Atholl *U.K.* 56°46N 3°50W **23** J10
Blairgowrie *U.K.* 56°35N 3°21W **25** A9
Blakeney *Gloucs., U.K.* 51°46N 2°28W **30** C4
Blakeney *Norfolk, U.K.* 52°58N 1°1E **31** A11
Blanc, Mont *Europe* 45°48N 6°50E **66** D7
Blanca, B. *Argentina* 39°10S 61°30W **121** F3
Blanca, Costa *Spain* 38°25N 0°10W **67** C5
Blanca Peak *U.S.A.* 37°35N 105°29W **110** C5
Blanchardstown *Ireland* 53°23N 6°23W **21** B10
Blanco, C. *U.S.A.* 42°51N 124°34W **110** B2
Blandford Forum *U.K.* 50°51N 2°9W **30** E4
Blanquilla, I. *Venezuela* 11°51N 64°37W **115** E12
Blantyre *Malawi* 15°45S 35°0E **97** H7
Blarney *Ireland* 51°56N 8°33W **20** E5
Blaydon *U.K.* 54°58N 1°42W **26** C5
Blean *U.K.* 51°18N 1°3E **31** D11
Bleasdale Moors *U.K.* 53°55N 2°35W **27** E3
Blenheim *N.Z.* 41°38S 173°57E **99** J13
Bletchingdon *U.K.* 51°51N 1°15W **30** C6
Bletchley *U.K.* 51°59N 0°44W **31** C7
Blida *Algeria* 36°30N 2°49E **94** A6
Blisworth *U.K.* 52°10N 0°56W **31** B7
Blitar *Indonesia* 8°5S 112°11E **82** F4
Blockley *U.K.* 52°1N 1°44W **30** B5
Bloemfontein *S. Africa* 29°6S 26°7E **97** K5
Blofield *U.K.* 52°38N 1°26E **31** A11
Blois *France* 47°35N 1°20E **66** C4
Bloody Foreland *Ireland* 55°10N 8°17W **18** A5
Bloomington *Ill., U.S.A.* 40°28N 89°0W **112** E3
Bloomington *Ind., U.S.A.* 39°10N 86°32W **112** F4
Bloomsburg *U.S.A.* 41°0N 76°27W **112** E9
Bloxham *U.K.* 52°1N 1°21W **30** B6
Blue Mountain Pk. *Jamaica* 18°3N 76°36W **114** a
Blue Mt. *U.S.A.* 40°30N 76°30W **112** E9
Blue Mts. *Jamaica* 18°3N 76°36W **114** a
Blue Mts. *U.S.A.* 45°0N 118°20W **110** A3
Blue Nile → *Sudan* 15°38N 32°31E **95** E12
Blue Ridge *U.S.A.* 36°40N 80°50W **111** C10
Blue Stack Mts. *Ireland* 54°42N 8°12W **18** B5
Bluefield *U.S.A.* 37°15N 81°17W **112** G7
Bluefields *Nic.* 12°20N 83°50W **115** E8
Blumenau *Brazil* 27°0S 49°0W **121** E5
Blundeston *U.K.* 52°31N 1°42E **31** A12
Blyth *Northumberland, U.K.* 55°8N 1°31W **26** B5
Blyth *Notts., U.K.* 53°22N 1°3W **27** F6
Blyth → *U.K.* 55°8N 1°33W **26** B5
Blyth Bridge *U.K.* 55°42N 3°22W **25** C9
Blyton *U.K.* 53°27N 0°42W **27** F7
Bo *S. Leone* 7°55N 11°50W **94** G3
Bo Hai *China* 39°0N 119°0E **79** D12
Boa Vista *Brazil* 2°48N 60°30W **120** B3
Bobcaygeon *Canada* 44°33N 78°33W **112** C8
Bobo-Dioulasso *Burkina Faso* 11°8N 4°13W **94** F5
Bóbr → *Poland* 52°4N 15°4E **64** B8
Bochum *Germany* 51°28N 7°13E **64** C4
Boddam *U.K.* 59°56N 1°17W **22** C15
Boden *Sweden* 65°50N 21°42E **63** D8
Bodiam *U.K.* 51°0N 0°34E **31** D10
Bodinnick *U.K.* 50°20N 4°38W **29** G4
Bodmin *U.K.* 50°28N 4°43W **29** G4
Bodmin Moor *U.K.* 50°33N 4°36W **29** F4
Bodø *Norway* 67°17N 14°24E **63** D6
Bodrog → *Hungary* 48°11N 21°22E **65** D11
Bodrum *Turkey* 37°3N 27°30E **71** G4
Bogalusa *U.S.A.* 30°47N 89°52W **111** D9
Bogda Shan *China* 43°35N 89°40E **78** C6
Boggeragh Mts. *Ireland* 52°2N 8°55W **20** D5
Bognor Regis *U.K.* 50°47N 0°40W **31** E7
Bogor *Indonesia* 6°36S 106°48E **82** F3
Bogotá *Colombia* 4°34N 74°0W **120** B2
Bogura *Bangla.* 24°51N 89°22E **85** G16
Böhmerwald *Germany* 49°8N 13°14E **64** D7
Bohol Sea *Phil.* 9°0N 124°0E **83** C6
Boise *U.S.A.* 43°37N 116°13W **110** B3
Bole *China* 44°55N 81°37E **78** C5
Bolívar, Pico *Venezuela* 8°32N 71°2W **115** F10
Bolivia ■ *S. Amer.* 17°6S 64°0W **120** D3
Bollington *U.K.* 53°18N 2°6W **27** F4
Bolney *U.K.* 50°59N 0°12W **31** E8
Bologna *Italy* 44°29N 11°20E **68** B4
Bologoye *Russia* 57°55N 34°5E **70** C5
Bolsena, L. di *Italy* 42°36N 11°56E **68** C4
Bolsover *U.K.* 53°14N 1°16W **27** F6
Bolt Head *U.K.* 50°12N 3°48W **29** G6
Bolt Tail *U.K.* 50°14N 3°52W **29** G6
Bolton *U.K.* 53°35N 2°26W **27** E4
Bolton Abbey *U.K.* 53°59N 1°53W **27** E5
Bolton by Bowland *U.K.* 53°56N 2°20W **27** E4
Bolton-le-Sands *U.K.* 54°6N 2°48W **26** D3
Bolu *Turkey* 40°45N 31°35E **71** F5
Bolvadin *Turkey* 38°45N 31°4E **71** G5
Bolzano *Italy* 46°31N 11°22E **68** A4
Bom Despacho *Brazil* 19°43S 45°15W **122** C1
Bom Jesus da Lapa *Brazil* 13°15S 43°25W **122** B2
Boma *Dem. Rep. of the Congo* 5°50S 13°4E **96** F2
Bombala *Australia* 36°56S 149°15E **98** H8
Bombay = Mumbai *India* 18°56N 72°50E **84** K8
Bomi *China* 29°50N 95°45E **78** F8
Bomu → *C.A.R.* 4°40N 22°30E **96** D4
Bon, C. *Tunisia* 37°1N 11°2E **90** C5
Bonaire *W. Indies* 12°10N 68°15W **115** E11
Bonar Bridge *U.K.* 57°54N 4°20W **23** G9
Bonavista *Canada* 48°40N 53°5W **109** E14
Bonchester Bridge *U.K.* 55°24N 2°39W **25** D10
Bonchurch *U.K.* 50°37N 1°11W **30** E6
Bo'ness *U.K.* 56°1N 3°37W **25** B9
Bongor *Chad* 10°35N 15°20E **95** F9
Bongos, Massif des *C.A.R.* 8°40N 22°25E **96** C4
Bonifacio *France* 41°24N 9°10E **66** F8
Bonn *Germany* 50°46N 7°6E **64** C4
Bonnyrigg *U.K.* 55°53N 3°6W **25** C9
Böön Tsagaan Nuur *Mongolia* 45°35N 99°9E **78** B8

Boonville *U.S.A.* 38°3N 87°16W **112** F4
Boosaaso *Somalia* 11°12N 49°18E **89** E4
Boot *U.K.* 54°24N 3°13W **26** D2
Boothia, Gulf of *Canada* 71°0N 90°0W **109** B11
Boothia Pen. *Canada* 71°0N 94°0W **108** B10
Bootle *Cumb., U.K.* 54°18N 3°22W **26** D2
Bootle *Mersey., U.K.* 53°28N 3°1W **27** F2
Borås *Sweden* 57°43N 12°56E **63** F6
Borborema, Planalto da *Brazil* 7°0S 37°0W **117** D7
Bordeaux *France* 44°50N 0°36W **66** D3
Borden I. *Canada* 78°30N 111°30W **109** B8
Borden Pen. *Canada* 73°0N 83°0W **109** B11
Borders = Scottish Borders □
  U.K. 55°35N 2°50W **25** C10
Bordon *U.K.* 51°8N 0°52W **31** D7
Borehamwood *U.K.* 51°40N 0°15W **31** C8
Boreland *U.K.* 55°12N 3°16W **25** D9
Borger *U.S.A.* 35°39N 101°24W **110** C6
Borhoyn Tal *Mongolia* 43°50N 111°58E **79** C11
Borisoglebsk *Russia* 51°27N 42°5E **71** D7
Borkou *Chad* 18°15N 18°50E **95** E9
Borneo *E. Indies* 1°0N 115°0E **82** D5
Bornholm *Denmark* 55°10N 15°0E **63** F7
Borohoro Shan *China* 44°6N 83°10E **78** C5
Boroughbridge *U.K.* 54°6N 1°24W **26** D6
Borovichi *Russia* 58°25N 33°55E **70** C5
Borrowdale *U.K.* 54°31N 3°10W **26** D2
Borth *U.K.* 52°29N 4°2W **28** C5
Borüjerd *Iran* 33°55N 48°50E **86** C7
Bosbury *U.K.* 52°5N 2°26W **30** B4
Boscastle *U.K.* 50°41N 4°42W **29** F4
Boscobelle *Barbados* 13°17N 59°35W **114** c
Bose *China* 23°53N 106°35E **78** G10
Bosham *U.K.* 50°49N 0°51W **31** E7
Bosnia-Herzegovina ■ *Europe* 44°0N 18°0E **69** B7
Bosporus *Turkey* 41°5N 29°3E **71** F4
Bossangoa *C.A.R.* 6°35N 17°30E **96** C3
Bosten Hu *China* 41°55N 87°40E **78** C6
Boston *U.K.* 52°59N 0°2W **27** G8
Boston *U.S.A.* 42°22N 71°3W **113** D12
Bothel *U.K.* 54°45N 3°15W **26** C2
Bothnia, G. of *Europe* 62°0N 20°0E **63** E8
Botletle → *Botswana* 20°10S 23°15E **97** J4
Botoşani *Romania* 47°42N 26°41E **65** E14
Botswana ■ *Africa* 22°0S 24°0E **97** J4
Bottesford *U.K.* 52°57N 0°47W **27** G7
Botucatu *Brazil* 22°55S 48°30W **122** D1
Bou Saâda *Algeria* 35°11N 4°9E **94** A6
Bouaké *Côte d'Ivoire* 7°40N 5°2W **94** G4
Bouar *C.A.R.* 6°0N 15°40E **96** C3
Bouârfa *Morocco* 32°32N 1°58W **94** B5
Bougainville I. *Papua N. G.* 6°0S 155°0E **99** B10
Boulder *U.S.A.* 40°1N 105°17W **110** B5
Boulogne-sur-Mer *France* 50°42N 1°36E **66** A4
Bounty Is. *Pac. Oc.* 48°0S 178°30E **102** M9
Bourbonnais *France* 46°28N 3°0E **66** C5
Bourg-en-Bresse *France* 46°13N 5°12E **66** C6
Bourges *France* 47°9N 2°25E **66** C5
Bourgogne *France* 47°0N 4°50E **66** C6
Bourke *Australia* 30°8S 145°55E **98** G8
Bourne *U.K.* 52°47N 0°22W **27** G8
Bournemouth *U.K.* 50°43N 1°52W **30** E5
Bourton-on-the-Water *U.K.* 51°52N 1°45W **30** C5
Bouvet I. *Antarctica* 54°26S 3°24E **52** G10
Bovey Tracey *U.K.* 50°36N 3°41W **29** F6
Bow → *Canada* 49°57N 111°41W **108** D8
Bowes *U.K.* 54°32N 1°59W **26** C5
Bowland, Forest of *U.K.* 54°0N 2°30W **27** E3
Bowling Green *Ky., U.S.A.* 36°59N 86°27W **112** G4
Bowling Green *Ohio, U.S.A.* 41°23N 83°39W **112** E6
Bowmore *U.K.* 55°45N 6°17W **24** C3
Bowness-on-Solway *U.K.* 54°57N 3°12W **26** C2
Bowness-on-Windermere
  U.K. 54°22N 2°55W **26** D3
Box *U.K.* 51°25N 2°14W **30** D4
Box Hill *U.K.* 51°15N 0°16W **31** D8
Boxworth *U.K.* 52°17N 0°1W **31** B9
Boyle *Ireland* 53°59N 8°18W **18** D5
Boyne → *Ireland* 53°43N 6°15W **19** D9
Boyoma, Chutes
  Dem. Rep. of the Congo 0°35N 25°23E **90** F6
Bozeat *U.K.* 52°14N 0°40W **31** B7
Bozeman *U.S.A.* 45°41N 111°2W **110** A4
Bozoum *C.A.R.* 6°25N 16°35E **96** C3
Brač *Croatia* 43°20N 16°40E **68** C7
Bracadale, L. *U.K.* 57°20N 6°30W **22** H4
Bracebridge *Canada* 45°2N 79°19W **112** C8
Bracebridge Heath *U.K.* 53°12N 0°32W **27** F7
Bräcke *Sweden* 62°45N 15°26E **63** E7
Brackley *U.K.* 52°2N 1°8W **30** B6
Bracknell *U.K.* 51°25N 0°43W **31** D7
Bradford *U.K.* 53°47N 1°45W **27** E5
Bradford *U.S.A.* 41°58N 78°38W **112** E8
Brading *U.K.* 50°41N 1°8W **30** E6
Bradwell-on-Sea *U.K.* 51°43N 0°56E **31** C10
Bradworthy *U.K.* 50°53N 4°24W **29** F5
Braemar *U.K.* 57°2N 3°26W **23** H11
Braga *Portugal* 41°35N 8°25W **67** B1
Bragança *Brazil* 1°0S 47°2W **120** C5
Bragança *Portugal* 41°48N 6°50W **67** B2
Bragança Paulista *Brazil* 22°55S 46°32W **122** D1
Brahmanbaria *Bangla.* 23°58N 91°15E **85** H17
Brahmani → *India* 20°39N 86°46E **85** J15
Brahmapur *India* 19°15N 84°54E **85** K14
Brahmaputra → *Asia* 23°40N 90°35E **85** H16
Braich-y-pwll *U.K.* 52°47N 4°46W **28** B4
Brăila *Romania* 45°19N 27°59E **65** F14
Brailsford *U.K.* 52°58N 1°35W **27** G5
Brainerd *U.S.A.* 46°22N 94°12W **111** A8
Braintree *U.K.* 51°53N 0°34E **31** C10
Bramford *U.K.* 52°4N 1°7E **31** B11
Brampton *Canada* 43°45N 79°45W **112** D8
Brampton *Cambs., U.K.* 52°19N 0°14W **31** B8
Brampton *Cumb., U.K.* 54°57N 2°44W **26** C3
Brancaster *U.K.* 52°58N 0°38E **31** A10
Branco → *Brazil* 1°20S 61°50W **120** C3
Brandenburg *Germany* 52°25N 12°33E **64** B7
Brandenburg □ *Germany* 52°50N 13°0E **64** B7
Brandon *Canada* 49°50N 99°57W **108** E10
Brandon *Durham, U.K.* 54°46N 1°37W **26** C5
Brandon *Suffolk, U.K.* 52°27N 0°38E **31** B10

Brandon B. *Ireland* 52°17N 10°8W **20** D2
Brandon Mt. *Ireland* 52°15N 10°15W **20** D2
Branston *U.K.* 53°12N 0°27W **27** F8
Brantford *Canada* 43°10N 80°15W **112** D7
Bras d'Or L. *Canada* 45°50N 60°50W **113** C17
Brasília *Brazil* 15°47S 47°55W **122** C1
Braşov *Romania* 45°38N 25°35E **65** F13
Bratislava *Slovakia* 48°10N 17°7E **65** D9
Bratsk *Russia* 56°10N 101°30E **77** D11
Bratsk Res. *Russia* 56°15N 101°45E **77** D11
Brattleboro *U.S.A.* 42°51N 72°34W **113** D11
Braunschweig *Germany* 52°15N 10°31E **64** B6
Braunton *U.K.* 51°7N 4°10W **29** E5
Brava, Costa *Spain* 41°30N 3°0E **67** B7
Bray *Ireland* 53°13N 6°7W **21** B10
Bray *U.K.* 51°30N 0°41W **31** D7
Brazil *U.S.A.* 39°32N 87°8W **112** F4
Brazil ■ *S. Amer.* 12°0S 50°0W **120** D4
Brazilian Highlands *Brazil* 18°0S 46°30W **117** E6
Brazos → *U.S.A.* 28°53N 95°23W **111** E7
Brazzaville *Congo* 4°9S 15°12E **96** E3
Breadalbane *U.K.* 56°30N 4°15W **24** A7
Breage *U.K.* 50°6N 5°20W **29** G3
Breamish → *U.K.* 55°35N 2°2W **26** A4
Brechin *U.K.* 56°44N 2°39W **23** J12
Breckland *U.K.* 52°30N 0°40E **31** B10
Brecon *U.K.* 51°57N 3°23W **28** D7
Brecon Beacons △ *U.K.* 51°50N 3°30W **28** D6
Breda *Neths.* 51°35N 4°45E **64** C3
Brede *U.K.* 50°56N 0°36E **31** E10
Bredon Hill *U.K.* 52°3N 2°2W **30** B4
Bregenz *Austria* 47°30N 9°45E **64** E5
Breiðafjörður *Iceland* 65°15N 23°15W **63** A1
Bremen *Germany* 53°4N 8°47E **64** B5
Bremerhaven *Germany* 53°33N 8°36E **64** B5
Bremerton *U.S.A.* 47°34N 122°37W **110** A2
Brendon Hills *U.K.* 51°6N 3°25W **30** D2
Brennerpass *Austria* 47°2N 11°30E **64** E6
Brent □ *U.K.* 51°33N 0°16W **31** C8
Brentwood *U.K.* 51°37N 0°19E **31** C9
Bréscia *Italy* 45°33N 10°15E **68** B4
Bressay *U.K.* 60°9N 1°6W **22** B15
Brest *Belarus* 52°10N 23°40E **65** B12
Brest *France* 48°24N 4°31W **66** B1
Bretagne □ *France* 48°10N 3°0W **66** B2
Breton Sd. *U.S.A.* 29°35N 89°15W **111** E9
Brewer *U.S.A.* 44°48N 68°46W **113** C13
Brewood *U.K.* 52°41N 2°9W **27** G4
Briançon *France* 44°54N 6°39E **66** D7
Bridestowe *U.K.* 50°41N 4°7W **29** F5
Bridge *U.K.* 51°15N 1°8E **31** D11
Bridgefield *Barbados* 13°9N 59°36W **114** c
Bridgend *U.K.* 51°30N 3°34W **29** D6
Bridgeport *U.S.A.* 41°11N 73°12W **113** E11
Bridgeton *U.S.A.* 39°26N 75°14W **113** F10
Bridgetown *Barbados* 13°6N 59°37W **114** c
Bridgewater *Canada* 44°25N 64°31W **109** E13
Bridgnorth *U.K.* 52°32N 2°25W **27** G4
Bridgwater *U.K.* 51°8N 2°59W **30** D3
Bridgwater B. *U.K.* 51°15N 3°15W **30** D2
Bridlington *U.K.* 54°5N 0°12W **26** D8
Bridlington B. *U.K.* 54°4N 0°10W **27** D8
Bridport *U.K.* 50°44N 2°45W **30** E3
Brierfield *U.K.* 53°49N 2°14W **27** E4
Brierley Hill *U.K.* 52°29N 2°6W **27** H4
Brigg *U.K.* 53°34N 0°28W **27** E8
Brigham City *U.S.A.* 41°31N 112°1W **110** B4
Brighouse *U.K.* 53°42N 1°46W **27** E5
Brighstone *U.K.* 50°38N 1°23W **30** E6
Brightlingsea *U.K.* 51°49N 1°2E **31** C11
Brighton *U.K.* 50°49N 0°7W **31** E8
Brigstock *U.K.* 52°27N 0°36W **31** B7
Brill *U.K.* 51°49N 1°1W **30** C6
Brimfield *U.K.* 52°18N 2°42W **30** B3
Bríndisi *Italy* 40°39N 17°55E **69** D7
Brinklow *U.K.* 51°15N 10°1W **31** D8   (Brinklow 52°25N 1°22W **30** B6)
Brinkworth *U.K.* 51°33N 1°59W **30** C5
Brisbane *Australia* 27°25S 153°2E **98** F9
Bristol *U.K.* 51°26N 2°35W **30** D3
Bristol *U.S.A.* 58°0N 160°0W **108** C4
Bristol B. *U.S.A.* 51°18N 4°30W **29** F7
Bristol Channel *U.K.* 51°18N 4°30W **29** F7
Briston *U.K.* 52°51N 1°4E **31** A11
British Columbia □ *Canada* 55°0N 125°15W **108** D7
British Isles *Europe* 54°0N 4°0W **62** D5
British Virgin Is. ☑
  W. Indies 18°30N 64°30W **115** D12
Brittany = Bretagne □ *France* 48°10N 3°0W **66** B2
Brive-la-Gaillarde *France* 45°10N 1°32E **66** D4
Brixham *U.K.* 50°23N 3°31W **29** G6
Brixworth *U.K.* 52°20N 0°54W **31** B7
Brize Norton *U.K.* 51°46N 1°34W **30** C5
Brno *Czechia* 49°10N 16°35E **65** D9
Broad B. *U.K.* 58°14N 6°18E **22** F2
Broad Chalke *U.K.* 51°2N 1°56W **30** D5
Broad Haven *Ireland* 54°20N 9°55W **18** C2
Broad Law *U.K.* 55°30N 3°21W **25** C9
Broad Sd. *U.K.* 49°55N 6°21W **29** H1
Broadclyst *U.K.* 50°46N 3°27W **29** F7
Broadhembury *U.K.* 50°49N 3°18W **30** E2
Broadstairs *U.K.* 51°21N 1°27E **31** D11
Broadway *U.K.* 52°2N 1°50W **30** B5
Broadwindsor *U.K.* 50°48N 2°47W **30** E3
Brochet *Canada* 57°53N 101°40W **108** D9
Brock I. *Canada* 77°52N 114°19W **109** B8
Brocken *Germany* 51°47N 10°37E **64** C6
Brockenhurst *U.K.* 50°49N 1°34W **30** E5
Brockville *Canada* 44°35N 75°41W **113** C10
Brodeur Pen. *Canada* 72°30N 88°10W **109** B11
Brodick *U.K.* 55°35N 5°9W **24** C4
Broken Hill *Australia* 31°58S 141°29E **98** G7
Bromfield *U.K.* 52°23N 2°45W **27** H3
Bromham *U.K.* 51°23N 2°1W **30** D4
Brompton *U.K.* 54°21N 1°25W **26** D6
Bromsgrove *U.K.* 52°21N 2°2W **30** B4
Bromyard *U.K.* 52°11N 2°30W **30** B4
Brookings *U.S.A.* 44°19N 96°48W **111** B7
Brooks *Canada* 50°35N 111°55W **108** D8
Brooks Range *U.S.A.* 68°0N 152°0W **108** C5
Broom, L. *U.K.* 57°55N 5°15W **22** G7

Broome *Australia* 18°0S 122°15E **98** D3
Broomhill *U.K.* 55°18N 1°36W **26** B5
Brora *U.K.* 58°0N 3°52W **23** F10
Brora → *U.K.* 58°0N 3°51W **23** F10
Broseley *U.K.* 52°37N 2°29W **27** G4
Brosna → *Ireland* 53°14N 7°58W **20** B7
Brothertoft *U.K.* 53°0N 0°7W **27** F8
Brotton *U.K.* 54°35N 0°56W **26** C7
Brough *Cumb., U.K.* 54°32N 2°18W **26** C4
Brough *E. Riding, U.K.* 53°44N 0°36W **27** E7
Brough Hd. *U.K.* 59°8N 3°20W **23** D11
Broughton *Borders, U.K.* 55°37N 3°24W **25** C9
Broughton *N. Lincs., U.K.* 53°34N 0°34W **27** E7
Broughton *N. Northants., U.K.* 52°22N 0°46W **31** B7
Broughton-in-Furness *U.K.* 54°17N 3°13W **26** D2
Broughty Ferry *U.K.* 56°29N 2°51W **25** B10
Brown Willy *U.K.* 50°35N 4°37W **29** F4
Brownhills *U.K.* 52°39N 1°54W **27** G5
Brownsville *U.S.A.* 25°54N 97°30W **111** E7
Brownwood *U.S.A.* 31°43N 98°59W **110** D7
Broxburn *U.K.* 55°56N 3°28W **25** C9
Bruay-la-Buissière *France* 50°29N 2°33E **66** A5
Bruce, Mt. *Australia* 22°37S 118°8E **98** E2
Brue → *U.K.* 51°13N 2°59W **30** D3
Brugge *Belgium* 51°13N 3°13E **64** C2
Brumado *Brazil* 14°14S 41°40W **122** B2
Brunei ■ *Asia* 4°50N 115°0E **82** D4
Brunswick *Ga., U.S.A.* 31°10N 81°30W **111** D10
Brunswick *Maine, U.S.A.* 43°55N 69°58W **113** D13
Brunton *U.K.* 55°2N 2°6W **26** B4
Brussels *Belgium* 50°51N 4°21E **64** C3
Bruton *U.K.* 51°7N 2°27W **30** D4
Bryan *Ohio, U.S.A.* 41°28N 84°33W **112** E5
Bryan *Tex., U.S.A.* 30°40N 96°22W **111** D7
Bryansk *Russia* 53°13N 34°25E **70** D5
Bryher *U.K.* 49°57N 6°22W **29** H1
Brynamman *U.K.* 51°49N 3°51W **28** D6
Brynmawr *U.K.* 51°48N 3°10W **28** D7
Bucaramanga *Colombia* 7°0N 73°0W **120** B2
Buchan *U.K.* 57°32N 2°21W **23** G13
Buchan Ness *U.K.* 57°29N 1°46W **23** H14
Buchanan *Liberia* 5°57N 10°2W **94** G3
Bucharest *Romania* 44°27N 26°10E **65** F14
Buckden *U.K.* 52°18N 0°14W **31** B8
Buckfastleigh *U.K.* 50°28N 3°48W **29** G6
Buckhannon *U.S.A.* 39°0N 80°8W **112** F7
Buckhaven *U.K.* 56°11N 3°3W **25** B9
Buckie *U.K.* 57°41N 2°58W **23** G12
Buckingham *Canada* 45°37N 75°24W **113** C10
Buckingham *U.K.* 51°59N 0°57W **31** C7
Buckinghamshire □ *U.K.* 51°53N 0°55W **31** C7
Buckland Brewer *U.K.* 50°58N 4°15W **29** F5
Buckland Newton *U.K.* 50°50N 2°26W **30** E4
Buckley *U.K.* 53°10N 3°5W **28** A7
Budapest *Hungary* 47°29N 19°3E **65** E10
Bude *U.K.* 50°49N 4°34W **29** F4
Bude B. *U.K.* 50°49N 4°35W **29** F4
Budle B. *U.K.* 55°37N 1°45W **26** A5
Budleigh Salterton *U.K.* 50°37N 3°19W **29** F7
Buena Vista *U.S.A.* 37°44N 79°21W **112** G8
Buenaventura *Colombia* 3°53N 77°4W **120** B2
Buenos Aires *Argentina* 34°36S 58°22W **121** F4
Buffalo *N.Y., U.S.A.* 42°53N 78°53W **112** D8
Buffalo *Wyo., U.S.A.* 44°21N 106°42W **110** B5
Bug → *Poland* 52°31N 21°5E **65** B11
Bug → *Ukraine* 46°59N 31°58E **71** E5
Bugle *U.K.* 50°24N 4°47W **29** G4
Bugulma *Russia* 54°33N 52°48E **70** D9
Buguruslan *Russia* 53°39N 52°26E **70** D9
Buir Nur *Mongolia* 47°50N 117°42E **79** B12
Buji *China* 22°37N 114°5E **79** a
Bujumbura *Burundi* 3°16S 29°18E **96** E5
Bukavu *Dem. Rep. of the Congo* 2°20S 28°52E **96** E5
Bukhara *Uzbekistan* 39°48N 64°25E **87** B11
Bukittinggi *Indonesia* 0°20S 100°20E **82** E2
Bulawayo *Zimbabwe* 20°7S 28°32E **97** J5
Bulford *U.K.* 51°11N 1°45W **30** D5
Bulgaria ■ *Europe* 42°35N 25°30E **69** C11
Bullhead City *U.S.A.* 35°8N 114°32W **110** C4
Bunbury *Australia* 33°20S 115°35E **98** G2
Bunclody *Ireland* 52°39N 6°40W **21** C9
Buncrana *Ireland* 55°8N 7°27W **18** A7
Bundaberg *Australia* 24°54S 152°22E **98** E9
Bundi *India* 25°30N 75°35E **84** G9
Bundoran *Ireland* 54°28N 8°18W **18** C5
Bungay *U.K.* 52°27N 1°28E **31** B11
Buntingford *U.K.* 51°56N 0°1W **31** C8
Bunwell *U.K.* 52°30N 1°9E **31** A11
Buon Ma Thuot *Vietnam* 12°40N 108°3E **82** B3
Buôr Sagaa *Egypt* 26°43N 33°57E **95** C12
Buraydah *Si. Arabia* 26°20N 43°59E **86** E5
Burbage *Derby, U.K.* 53°15N 1°55W **27** F5
Burbage *Leics., U.K.* 52°32N 1°21W **27** G6
Burbage *Wilts., U.K.* 51°21N 1°39W **30** D5
Burco *Somalia* 9°32N 45°32E **89** F4
Burdur *Turkey* 37°45N 30°17E **71** G5
Bure → *U.K.* 52°38N 1°43E **31** A12
Burford *U.K.* 51°49N 1°38W **30** C5
Burgas *Bulgaria* 42°33N 27°29E **69** C12
Burgess Hill *U.K.* 50°58N 0°6W **31** E8
Burgh le Marsh *U.K.* 53°9N 0°15E **27** F9
Burghead *U.K.* 57°43N 3°30W **23** G11
Burgos *Spain* 42°21N 3°41W **67** A4
Burgundy = Bourgogne *France* 47°0N 4°50E **66** C6
Burhanpur *India* 21°18N 76°14E **84** J10
Burkina Faso ■ *Africa* 12°0N 1°0W **94** F5
Burley *U.S.A.* 42°32N 113°48W **110** B4
Burley in Wharfedale *U.K.* 53°55N 1°45W **27** E5
Burlington *Colo., U.S.A.* 39°18N 102°16W **110** C6
Burlington *Iowa, U.S.A.* 40°49N 91°14W **112** E2
Burlington *Vt., U.S.A.* 44°29N 73°12W **113** C11
Burma = Myanmar ■ *Asia* 21°0N 96°30E **85** J20
Burnham Market *U.K.* 52°57N 0°44E **31** A10
Burnham-on-Crouch *U.K.* 51°38N 0°49E **31** C10
Burnham-on-Sea *U.K.* 51°14N 3°0W **30** D2
Burnie *Australia* 41°4S 145°56E **98** J8
Burnley *U.K.* 53°47N 2°14W **27** E4
Burnmouth *U.K.* 55°50N 2°4W **25** C11

Burns U.S.A. 43°35N 119°3W 110 B3
Burnside → Canada 66°51N 108°4W 108 C9
Burntisland U.K. 56°4N 3°13W 25 B9
Burqin China 47°43N 87°0E 78 B6
Burray U.K. 58°51N 2°54W 23 E12
Burren △ Ireland 53°9N 9°5W 20 B4
Burrow Hd. U.K. 54°41N 4°24W 24 E7
Burry Port U.K. 51°41N 4°15W 28 D5
Bursa Turkey 40°15N 29°5E 71 F4
Burstwick U.K. 53°44N 0°8W 27 E8
Burton U.K. 54°11N 2°43W 26 D3
Burton Agnes U.K. 54°4N 0°18W 26 D8
Burton Bradstock U.K. 50°42N 2°43W 30 E3
Burton Fleming U.K. 54°8N 0°20W 26 D8
Burton Latimer U.K. 52°22N 0°41W 31 B7
Burton upon Stather U.K. 53°39N 0°41W 27 E7
Burton upon Trent U.K. 52°48N 1°38W 27 G5
Buru Indonesia 3°30S 126°30E 83 E7
Burundi ■ Africa 3°15S 30°0E 96 E5
Burwash U.K. 50°59N 0°23E 31 E9
Burwell U.K. 52°17N 0°20E 31 B9
Burwick U.K. 58°45N 2°58W 23 E12
Bury U.K. 53°35N 2°17W 27 E4
Bury St. Edmunds U.K. 52°15N 0°43E 31 B10
Buryatia □ Russia 53°0N 110°0E 77 D11
Busan S. Korea 35°5N 129°0E 79 D14
Büshehr Iran 28°55N 50°55E 87 D7
Bushey U.K. 51°38N 0°22W 31 C8
Busto Arsizio Italy 45°37N 8°51E 68 B3
Buta Dem. Rep. of the Congo 2°50N 24°53E 96 D4
Butare Rwanda 2°31S 29°52E 96 E5
Butaritari Kiribati 3°30N 174°0E 102 G9
Bute U.K. 55°48N 5°2W 24 C5
Bute, Kyles of U.K. 55°55N 5°10W 24 C5
Butembo Dem. Rep. of the Congo 0°9N 29°18E 96 D5
Butler U.S.A. 40°52N 79°54W 112 E8
Buton Indonesia 5°0S 122°45E 83 E6
Butte U.S.A. 46°0N 112°32W 110 A4
Buttermere U.K. 54°32N 3°16W 26 C2
Butterworth Malaysia 5°24N 100°23E 82 C2
Buttevant Ireland 52°14N 8°40W 20 D5
Butuan Phil. 8°57N 125°33E 83 C7
Buurhakaba Somalia 3°12N 44°20E 89 G3
Buxton U.K. 53°16N 1°54W 27 F5
Buyant-Uhaa Mongolia 44°55N 110°11E 79 C11
Buzău Romania 45°10N 26°50E 65 F14
Buzuluk Russia 52°48N 52°12E 70 D9
Byarezina → Belarus 52°33N 30°14E 70 D5
Bydgoszcz Poland 53°10N 18°0E 65 B9
Byfield U.K. 52°10N 1°14W 30 B6
Bylot I. Canada 73°13N 78°34W 109 B12
Byrranga Ra. Russia 75°0N 100°0E 77 B11
Bytom Poland 50°25N 18°54E 65 C10

C
Ca Mau Vietnam 9°7N 105°8E 82 C3
Cabanatuan Phil. 15°30N 120°58E 83 A6
Cabedelo Brazil 7°0S 34°50W 120 C6
Cabimas Venezuela 10°23N 71°25W 120 A2
Cabinda Angola 5°33S 12°11E 96 F2
Cabinda □ Angola 5°0S 12°30E 96 F2
Cabo Frio Brazil 22°51S 42°3W 122 D2
Cabo San Lucas Mexico 22°53N 109°54W 114 C3
Cabonga, Réservoir Canada 47°20N 76°40W 109 E12
Cabora Bassa Dam Mozam. 15°20S 32°50E 97 H6
Cabot Str. Canada 47°15N 59°40W 109 E14
Čačak Serbia 43°54N 20°20E 69 C9
Cáceres Brazil 16°5S 57°40W 120 D4
Cáceres Spain 39°26N 6°23W 67 C2
Cachimbo, Serra do Brazil 9°30S 55°30W 120 C4
Cachoeira Brazil 12°30S 39°0W 122 B3
Cachoeira do Sul Brazil 30°3S 52°53W 121 F4
Cachoeiro de Itapemirim Brazil 20°51S 41°7W 122 D2
Cader Idris U.K. 52°42N 3°53W 28 B6
Cadillac U.S.A. 44°15N 85°24W 112 C5
Cádiz Spain 36°30N 6°20W 67 D2
Cádiz, G. de Spain 36°40N 7°0W 67 D2
Caen France 49°10N 0°22W 66 B3
Caenby Corner U.K. 53°24N 0°33W 27 F7
Caerdydd = Cardiff U.K. 51°29N 3°10W 29 E7
Caerfyrddin = Carmarthen U.K. 51°52N 4°19W 28 D5
Caergybi = Holyhead U.K. 53°18N 4°38W 28 A4
Caernarfon U.K. 53°8N 4°16W 28 A5
Caernarfon B. U.K. 53°4N 4°40W 28 A4
Caerphilly U.K. 51°35N 3°13W 29 D7
Caersws U.K. 52°31N 3°26W 28 B7
Caetê Brazil 19°55S 43°40W 122 D2
Caetité Brazil 13°50S 42°32W 122 B2
Cagayan de Oro Phil. 8°30N 124°40E 83 C6
Cágliari Italy 39°13N 9°7E 68 E3
Caguas Puerto Rico 18°14N 66°2W 115 D11
Caha Mts. Ireland 51°45N 9°40W 20 E3
Caherciveen Ireland 51°56N 10°14W 20 E2
Cahir Ireland 52°22N 7°56W 20 D7
Cahore Pt. Ireland 52°33N 6°12W 21 D10
Cahors France 44°27N 1°27E 66 D4
Cairn Gorm U.K. 57°7N 3°39W 23 H10
Cairngorm Mts. U.K. 57°6N 3°42W 23 H10
Cairngorms △ U.K. 57°10N 3°50W 23 H10
Cairnryan U.K. 54°59N 5°1W 24 E5
Cairns Australia 16°57S 145°45E 98 D8
Cairnsmore of Fleet U.K. 54°59N 4°20W 24 E7
Cairo Egypt 30°2N 31°13E 95 B12
Cairo U.S.A. 37°0N 89°11W 112 G3
Caister-on-Sea U.K. 52°40N 1°43E 31 A12
Caistor U.K. 53°30N 0°18W 27 E7
Caithness U.K. 58°25N 3°35W 23 F10
Caithness, Ord of U.K. 58°8N 3°36W 23 F10
Cajamarca Peru 7°5S 78°28W 120 C2
Calabar Nigeria 4°57N 8°20E 94 H7
Calábria □ Italy 39°0N 16°30E 68 E7
Calais France 50°57N 1°56E 66 A4
Calais U.S.A. 45°11N 67°17W 113 C14
Calama Chile 22°30S 68°55W 121 E3
Calamian Group Phil. 11°50N 119°55E 83 B5
Calanscio, Sarir Libya 27°30N 22°30E 95 C10
Calapan Phil. 13°25N 121°7E 83 B6

Calbayog Phil. 12°4N 124°38E 83 B6
Calcutta = Kolkata India 22°34N 88°21E 85 H16
Caldbeck U.K. 54°45N 3°3W 26 C2
Calder → U.K. 53°44N 1°22W 27 E6
Calder Bridge U.K. 54°27N 3°29W 26 D2
Caldera Chile 27°5S 70°55W 121 E2
Caldew → U.K. 54°54N 2°56W 26 C3
Caldwell U.S.A. 43°40N 116°41W 110 B3
Caledonian Canal U.K. 57°29N 4°15W 23 H9
Calgary Canada 51°0N 114°10W 108 D8
Cali Colombia 3°25N 76°35W 120 B2
Cálida, Costa Spain 37°30N 1°30W 67 D5
California □ U.S.A. 37°30N 119°30W 110 C2
California, G. de Mexico 27°0N 111°0W 114 B2
Callan Ireland 52°32N 7°24W 21 C8
Callander U.K. 56°15N 4°13W 24 B7
Callao Peru 12°3S 77°8W 120 D2
Calne U.K. 51°26N 2°0W 30 D5
Calshot U.K. 50°48N 1°19W 30 E6
Calstock U.K. 50°30N 4°13W 29 F5
Caltanissetta Italy 37°29N 14°4E 68 F6
Calvi France 42°34N 8°45E 66 E8
Calvinia S. Africa 31°28S 19°45E 97 L3
Cam → U.K. 52°21N 0°16E 31 B9
Cam Ranh Vietnam 11°54N 109°12E 82 B3
Camagüey Cuba 21°20N 77°55W 115 C9
Camargue France 43°34N 4°34E 66 E6
Camberley U.K. 51°20N 0°44W 31 D7
Cambodia ■ Asia 12°15N 105°0E 82 B3
Camborne U.K. 50°12N 5°19W 29 G3
Cambrai France 50°11N 3°14E 66 A5
Cambrian Mts. U.K. 52°3N 3°57W 28 C6
Cambridge Jamaica 18°18N 77°54W 114 a
Cambridge U.K. 52°12N 0°8E 31 B9
Cambridge Mass., U.S.A. 42°23N 71°7W 113 D12
Cambridge Md., U.S.A. 38°34N 76°5W 113 F9
Cambridge Ohio, U.S.A. 40°2N 81°35W 112 E7
Cambridge Bay Canada 69°10N 105°0W 108 C9
Cambridgeshire □ U.K. 52°25N 0°7W 31 B8
Camden Ark., U.S.A. 33°35N 92°50W 111 D8
Camden N.J., U.S.A. 39°55N 75°7W 113 F10
Camden U.K. 51°32N 0°8W 31 C8
Camel → U.K. 50°31N 4°51W 29 F4
Cameroon ■ Africa 6°0N 12°30E 96 C2
Cameroun, Mt. Cameroon 4°13N 9°10E 96 D1
Camocim Brazil 2°55S 40°50W 120 C5
Campana, I. Chile 48°20S 75°20W 121 G2
Campánia □ Italy 41°0N 14°30E 68 D6
Campbell I. Pac. Oc. 52°30S 169°0E 102 N8
Campbell River Canada 50°5N 125°20W 108 D7
Campbellsville U.S.A. 37°21N 85°20W 112 G5
Campbellton Canada 47°57N 66°43W 109 E13
Campbeltown U.K. 55°26N 5°36W 24 D4
Campeche Mexico 19°51N 90°32W 114 D6
Campeche, Golfo de Mexico 19°30N 93°0W 114 D6
Campina Grande Brazil 7°20S 35°47W 120 C6
Campinas Brazil 22°50S 47°0W 122 D1
Campo Belo Brazil 20°52S 45°16W 122 D1
Campo Grande Brazil 20°25S 54°40W 120 E4
Campobasso Italy 41°34N 14°39E 68 D6
Campos Brazil 21°50S 41°20W 122 D2
Campos Belos Brazil 13°10S 47°3W 122 B1
Can Tho Vietnam 10°2N 105°46E 82 B3
Canada ■ N. Amer. 60°0N 100°0W 108 D10
Canadian → U.S.A. 35°28N 95°3W 111 C7
Canadian Shield Canada 53°0N 75°0W 104 C9
Çanakkale Turkey 40°8N 26°24E 71 F4
Cananaigua U.S.A. 42°54N 77°17W 112 D9
Cananea Mexico 31°0N 110°18W 114 A2
Canaries St. Lucia 13°55N 61°4W 114 b
Canary Is. Atl. Oc. 28°30N 16°0W 94 C2
Canaveral, C. U.S.A. 28°27N 80°32W 111 E10
Canavieiras Brazil 15°39S 39°0W 122 C3
Canberra Australia 35°15S 149°8E 98 H8
Cancún Mexico 21°8N 86°44W 114 C7
Cangzhou China 38°19N 116°52E 79 D12
Caniapiscau → Canada 56°40N 69°30W 109 D13
Caniapiscau, L. Canada 54°10N 69°55W 109 D13
Çankırı Turkey 40°40N 33°37E 71 F5
Canna U.K. 57°3N 6°33W 22 H4
Canna, Sd. of U.K. 57°1N 6°30W 22 H5
Cannes France 43°32N 7°1E 66 E7
Cannington U.K. 51°9N 3°4W 30 D2
Cannock U.K. 52°41N 2°1W 27 G4
Cannock Chase U.K. 52°44N 2°4W 27 G4
Canoas Brazil 29°56S 51°11W 121 E4
Cañon City U.S.A. 38°27N 105°14W 110 C5
Canonbie U.K. 55°5N 2°58W 25 D10
Canora Canada 51°40N 102°30W 108 D9
Canso Canada 45°20N 61°0W 113 C17
Cantabria □ Spain 43°10N 4°0W 67 A4
Cantábrica, Cordillera Spain 43°0N 5°10W 67 A3
Canterbury U.K. 51°16N 1°6E 31 D11
Canton = Guangzhou China 23°6N 113°13E 79 G11
Canton Ill., U.S.A. 40°33N 90°2W 112 E2
Canton N.Y., U.S.A. 44°36N 75°10W 113 C10
Canton Ohio, U.S.A. 40°48N 81°23W 112 E7
Canvey Island U.K. 51°31N 0°37E 31 C10
Cap-de-la-Madeleine Canada 46°22N 72°31W 113 B11
Cap-Haïtien Haiti 19°40N 72°20W 115 D10
Cap Pt. St. Lucia 14°7N 60°57W 114 b
Cape Breton I. Canada 46°0N 60°30W 113 C17
Cape Charles U.S.A. 37°16N 76°1W 113 G10
Cape Coast Ghana 5°5N 1°15W 94 G5
Cape Coral U.S.A. 26°33N 81°57W 111 E10
Cape Fear → U.S.A. 33°53N 78°1W 111 D11
Cape Girardeau U.S.A. 37°19N 89°32W 112 G3
Cape May U.S.A. 38°56N 74°56W 113 F10
Cape Town S. Africa 33°55S 18°22E 97 L3
Cape York Peninsula Australia 12°0S 142°30E 98 C7
Capela Brazil 10°30S 37°0W 122 B3
Capreol Canada 46°43N 80°56W 112 B7
Capri Italy 40°33N 14°14E 68 D6
Caprivi Strip Namibia 18°0S 23°0E 97 H4
Caquetá → Colombia 1°15S 69°15W 120 C3

Caracas Venezuela 10°30N 66°55W 120 A3
Caracol Brazil 9°15S 43°22W 122 A2
Carangola Brazil 20°44S 42°5W 122 D2
Caratasca, L. de Honduras 15°20N 83°40W 115 D8
Caratinga Brazil 19°50S 42°10W 122 C2
Caravelas Brazil 17°45S 39°15W 122 C3
Carbón, L. del Argentina 49°35S 68°21W 121 G3
Carbondale Ill., U.S.A. 37°44N 89°13W 112 G3
Carbondale Pa., U.S.A. 41°35N 75°30W 113 E10
Carbonear Canada 47°42N 53°13W 109 E14
Carcassonne France 43°13N 2°20E 66 E5
Carcross Canada 60°13N 134°45W 108 C6
Cardamon Hills India 9°30N 77°15E 84 Q10
Cárdenas Cuba 23°0N 81°30W 115 C8
Cardiff U.K. 51°29N 3°10W 29 E7
Cardigan U.K. 52°5N 4°40W 28 C4
Cardigan B. U.K. 52°30N 4°30W 28 B4
Cardington U.K. 52°6N 0°25W 31 B8
Cardston Canada 49°15N 113°20W 108 E8
Cariacica Brazil 20°16S 40°25W 122 D2
Caribbean Sea W. Indies 15°0N 75°0W 115 E10
Cariboo Mts. Canada 53°0N 121°0W 108 D7
Caribou U.S.A. 46°52N 68°1W 113 B13
Caribou Mts. Canada 59°12N 115°40W 108 D8
Carinhanha Brazil 14°15S 44°46W 122 B2
Carinhanha → Brazil 14°20S 43°47W 122 B2
Carinthia = Kärnten □ Austria 46°52N 13°30E 64 E8
Carisbrooke U.K. 50°41N 1°19W 30 E6
Cark U.K. 54°11N 2°58W 26 D3
Carleton Place Canada 45°8N 76°9W 113 C9
Carleton Rode U.K. 52°30N 1°7E 31 A11
Carlingford L. U.K. 54°3N 6°9W 19 C9
Carlinville U.S.A. 39°17N 89°53W 112 F3
Carlisle U.K. 54°54N 2°56W 26 C3
Carlisle U.S.A. 40°12N 77°12W 112 E9
Carlisle B. Barbados 13°5N 59°37W 114 c
Carlops U.K. 55°47N 3°20W 25 C9
Carlow Ireland 52°50N 6°56W 21 C9
Carlow □ Ireland 52°43N 6°50W 21 C9
Carlsbad U.S.A. 32°25N 104°14W 110 D6
Carlton U.K. 52°59N 1°5W 27 G6
Carlton Colville U.K. 52°27N 1°43E 31 B12
Carlton Miniott U.K. 54°12N 1°22W 26 D6
Carluke U.K. 55°45N 3°50W 25 C8
Carmacks Canada 62°5N 136°16W 108 C6
Carman Canada 49°30N 98°0W 108 E10
Carmarthen U.K. 51°52N 4°19W 28 D5
Carmarthen B. U.K. 51°40N 4°30W 28 D5
Carmarthenshire □ U.K. 51°55N 4°13W 28 D5
Carmaux France 44°3N 2°10E 66 D5
Carmi U.S.A. 38°5N 88°10W 112 F3
Carn Ban U.K. 57°7N 4°15W 23 H9
Carn Eige U.K. 57°17N 5°8W 22 H7
Carnarvon Australia 24°51S 113°42E 98 E1
Carnarvon S. Africa 30°56S 22°8E 97 L4
Carndonagh Ireland 55°16N 7°15W 19 A7
Carnegie, L. Australia 26°5S 122°30E 98 F3
Carnforth U.K. 54°7N 2°45W 26 D3
Carno U.K. 52°34N 3°30W 28 B6
Carnoustie U.K. 56°30N 2°42W 25 A10
Carnsore Pt. Ireland 52°10N 6°22W 21 D10
Caro U.S.A. 43°29N 83°24W 112 D6
Caroline I. Kiribati 9°58S 150°13W 103 H12
Caroline Is. Micronesia 8°0N 150°0E 102 G6
Carondelet Reef Kiribati 5°33S 173°50E 99 B16
Caroní → Venezuela 8°21N 62°43W 120 B3
Carpathians Europe 49°30N 21°0E 65 D11
Carpentaria, G. of Australia 14°0S 139°0E 98 C6
Carpentras France 44°3N 5°2E 66 D6
Carpi Italy 44°47N 10°53E 68 B4
Carrara Italy 44°5N 10°6E 68 B4
Carrauntoohill Ireland 52°0N 9°45W 20 D3
Carrick-on-Shannon Ireland 53°57N 8°7W 18 D5
Carrick-on-Suir Ireland 52°21N 7°24W 21 D8
Carrickfergus U.K. 54°43N 5°49W 19 B10
Carrickmacross Ireland 53°59N 6°43W 19 D8
Carrigaline Ireland 51°48N 8°23W 20 E6
Carrollton U.S.A. 39°18N 90°24W 112 F2
Carron → U.K. 57°53N 4°22W 23 G9
Carron, L. U.K. 57°22N 5°35W 22 H6
Carson City U.S.A. 39°10N 119°46W 110 C3
Carson Sink U.S.A. 39°50N 118°25W 110 C3
Cartagena Colombia 10°25N 75°33W 120 A2
Cartagena Spain 37°38N 0°59W 67 D5
Cartago Colombia 4°45N 75°55W 120 B2
Carter Bar U.K. 55°21N 2°29W 25 D10
Carthage Tunisia 36°52N 10°20E 95 A8
Cartmel U.K. 54°12N 2°57W 26 D3
Cartwright Canada 53°41N 56°58W 109 D14
Caruaru Brazil 8°15S 35°55W 122 A3
Carúpano Venezuela 10°39N 63°15W 120 A3
Cas-gwent = Chepstow U.K. 51°38N 2°40W 30 C3
Casa Grande U.S.A. 32°53N 111°45W 110 D4
Casa Nova Brazil 9°25S 41°5W 122 A2
Casablanca Morocco 33°36N 7°36W 94 B4
Cascade Ra. U.S.A. 47°0N 121°30W 110 A2
Cascavel Ceará, Brazil 4°7S 38°14W 120 C6
Cascavel Paraná, Brazil 24°57S 53°28W 121 E4
Caserta Italy 41°4N 14°20E 68 D6
Cashel Ireland 52°30N 7°53W 20 D7
Casiquiare → Venezuela 2°1N 67°7W 120 B3
Casnewydd = Newport U.K. 51°35N 3°0W 29 D8
Casper U.S.A. 42°51N 106°19W 110 B5
Caspian Depression Eurasia 47°0N 48°0E 71 E8
Caspian Sea Eurasia 43°0N 50°0E 71 F8
Cassiar Mts. Canada 59°30N 130°30W 108 D6
Castell-Nedd = Neath U.K. 51°39N 3°48W 29 D7
Castellammare di Stábia Italy 40°42N 14°29E 68 D6
Castelló de la Plana Spain 39°58N 0°3W 67 C5
Castelsarrasin France 44°2N 1°7E 66 E4
Castilla-La Mancha □ Spain 39°30N 3°30W 67 C4
Castilla y Leon □ Spain 42°0N 5°0W 67 B3
Castle Acre U.K. 52°42N 0°42E 31 A10
Castle Cary U.K. 51°6N 2°31W 30 D5
Castle Donington U.K. 52°51N 1°20W 27 G6
Castle Douglas U.K. 54°56N 3°56W 25 E8
Castlebar Ireland 53°52N 9°18W 18 D3
Castlebay U.K. 56°57N 7°31W 22 J2
Castleblayney Ireland 54°7N 6°44W 19 C8
Castlederg U.K. 54°42N 7°36W 18 B6
Castleford U.K. 53°43N 1°21W 27 E6

Castlemaine Harbour Ireland 52°8N 9°50W 20 D3
Castlepollard Ireland 53°41N 7°19W 18 D7
Castlerea Ireland 53°46N 8°29W 18 D5
Castleside U.K. 54°50N 1°52W 26 C5
Castleton Derby, U.K. 53°22N 1°46W 27 F5
Castleton N. Yorks., U.K. 54°28N 0°57W 26 D7
Castletown I. of Man 54°5N 4°38W 19 C12
Castletown Bearhaven Ireland 51°39N 9°55W 20 E3
Castres France 43°37N 2°13E 66 E5
Castries St. Lucia 14°2N 60°58W 114 b
Castro Chile 42°30S 73°50W 121 G2
Castro Alves Brazil 12°46S 39°33W 122 B3
Cat I. The Bahamas 24°30N 75°30W 115 C9
Cataguases Brazil 21°23S 42°39W 122 D2
Catalão Brazil 18°10S 47°57W 122 C1
Cataluña □ Spain 41°40N 1°15E 67 B6
Catamarca Argentina 28°30S 65°50W 121 E3
Catanduanes Phil. 13°50N 124°20E 83 B6
Catanduva Brazil 21°5S 48°58W 122 D1
Catánia Italy 37°30N 15°6E 68 F6
Catanzaro Italy 38°54N 16°35E 68 E7
Catcleugh U.K. 55°20N 2°24W 26 B4
Caterham U.K. 51°15N 0°4W 31 D8
Catoche, C. Mexico 21°35N 87°5W 114 C7
Caton U.K. 54°5N 2°42W 26 D3
Catsfield U.K. 50°54N 0°28E 31 E9
Catskill U.S.A. 42°14N 73°52W 113 D11
Catskill Mts. U.S.A. 42°10N 74°25W 113 D10
Catterick U.K. 54°23N 1°37W 26 D5
Catterick Garrison U.K. 54°22N 1°42W 26 D5
Catton U.K. 54°55N 2°15W 26 C4
Cauca → Colombia 8°54N 74°28W 120 B2
Caucaia Brazil 3°40S 38°35W 120 C6
Caucasus Mountains Eurasia 42°50N 44°0E 71 F7
Caulkerbush U.K. 54°54N 3°41W 25 E9
Caura → Venezuela 7°38N 64°53W 120 B3
Causeway Coast & Glens □ U.K. 55°5N 6°33W 19 A8
Cauvery → India 11°9N 78°52E 84 P11
Cavan Ireland 54°0N 7°22W 18 D7
Cavan □ Ireland 54°1N 7°16W 19 C7
Caviana, I. Brazil 0°10N 50°10W 120 B4
Cawood U.K. 53°50N 1°8W 27 E6
Cawston U.K. 52°47N 1°9E 31 A11
Caxias Brazil 4°55S 43°20W 120 C5
Caxias do Sul Brazil 29°10S 51°10W 121 E4
Cayenne Fr. Guiana 5°5N 52°18W 120 B4
Cayman Is. ☑ W. Indies 19°40N 80°30W 115 D8
Cayman Trench Caribbean 17°0N 83°0W 115 D8
Cayuga L. U.S.A. 42°41N 76°41W 112 D9
Ceará □ Brazil 5°0S 40°0W 120 C6
Cebu Phil. 10°18N 123°54E 83 B6
Cedar City U.S.A. 37°41N 113°4W 110 C4
Cedar L. Canada 53°10N 100°0W 108 D10
Cedar Rapids U.S.A. 41°59N 91°40W 111 E8
Cefalù Italy 38°2N 14°1E 68 E6
Cegléd Hungary 47°11N 19°47E 65 E10
Celaya Mexico 20°31N 100°37W 114 C4
Celebes Sea Indonesia 3°0N 123°0E 83 D6
Celina U.S.A. 40°33N 84°35W 112 E5
Cellar Hd. U.K. 58°25N 6°11W 22 F5
Celtic Sea Atl. Oc. 50°9N 9°34W 62 F2
Cemaes U.K. 53°24N 4°27W 28 A5
Central, Cordillera Colombia 5°0N 75°0W 117 C3
Central African Rep. ■ Africa 7°0N 20°0E 96 C4
Central Bedfordshire □ U.K. 52°5N 0°20W 31 B8
Central Makran Range Pakistan 26°30N 64°15E 84 F4
Central Russian Uplands Europe 54°0N 36°0E 56 E13
Central Siberian Plateau Russia 65°0N 105°0E 72 B12
Centralia Ill., U.S.A. 38°32N 89°8W 112 F3
Centralia Wash., U.S.A. 46°43N 122°58W 110 A2
Cephalonia = Kefalonia Greece 38°15N 20°30E 69 E9
Ceredigion □ U.K. 52°16N 4°15W 28 C5
Cerignola Italy 41°17N 15°53E 68 D6
Cerne Abbas U.K. 50°49N 2°29W 30 E4
Cerrigydrudion U.K. 53°1N 3°35W 28 A6
Cerro de Pasco Peru 10°45S 76°10W 120 D2
Cesena Italy 44°8N 12°15E 68 B5
České Budějovice Czechia 48°55N 14°25E 64 D8
Çeşme Turkey 38°20N 26°23E 71 G4
Ceuta N. Afr. 35°52N 5°18W 67 E3
Ceve-i-Ra Fiji 21°46S 174°31E 99 E13
Cévennes France 44°10N 3°50E 66 D5
Chacewater U.K. 50°15N 5°11W 29 G3
Chachapoyas Peru 6°15S 77°50W 120 C2
Chaco Austral S. Amer. 27°0S 61°30W 121 E3
Chaco Boreal S. Amer. 22°0S 60°0W 121 E4
Chaco Central S. Amer. 24°0S 61°0W 121 E3
Chad ■ Africa 15°0N 17°15E 95 F8
Chad, L. Chad 13°30N 14°30E 95 F8
Chadron U.S.A. 42°50N 103°0W 110 B6
Chagford U.K. 50°40N 3°50W 29 F6
Chaghcharān Afghan. 34°31N 65°15E 87 C11
Chagos Arch. ☑ Ind. Oc. 6°0S 72°0E 53 E13
Chāh Gay Hills Afghan. 29°30N 64°0E 87 D10
Chakradharpur India 22°45N 85°40E 85 H14
Chaleur B. Canada 47°55N 65°30W 113 B15
Chalisgaon India 20°30N 75°10E 84 J9
Challenger Deep Pac. Oc. 11°30N 142°0E 102 F6
Chalon-sur-Saône France 46°48N 4°50E 66 C6
Châlons-en-Champagne France 48°58N 4°20E 66 B6
Chambal → India 26°29N 79°15E 84 F11
Chambersburg U.S.A. 39°56N 77°40W 112 F9
Chambéry France 45°34N 5°55E 66 D6
Chamonix-Mont Blanc France 45°55N 6°51E 66 D7
Champagne France 48°40N 4°20E 66 B6
Champaign U.S.A. 40°7N 88°15W 112 E3
Champlain, L. U.S.A. 44°40N 73°20W 113 C11
Chañaral Chile 26°23S 70°40W 121 E2
Chancery Lane Barbados 13°3N 59°30W 114 c
Chandigarh India 30°43N 76°47E 84 D10
Chandler's Ford U.K. 50°59N 1°22W 30 E6
Chandpur Bangla. 23°8N 90°45E 85 H17
Chandrapur India 19°57N 79°25E 84 K11
Changbai Shan China 42°20N 129°0E 79 C14
Changchun China 43°57N 125°17E 79 C14

Changde China 29°4N 111°35E 79 F11
Changhua Taiwan 24°2N 120°30E 79 G13
Changji China 44°1N 87°19E 78 C6
Changsha China 28°12N 113°0E 79 F11
Changzhi China 36°10N 113°6E 79 D11
Changzhou China 31°47N 119°58E 79 E12
Chania Greece 35°30N 24°4E 69 G11
Channel Is. U.K. 49°19N 2°24W 29 J9
Channel Is. U.S.A. 33°40N 119°15W 110 D2
Channel-Port aux Basques Canada 47°30N 59°9W 109 E14
Chantrey Inlet Canada 67°48N 96°20W 108 C10
Chaoyang China 41°35N 120°22E 79 C13
Chaozhou China 23°42N 116°32E 79 G12
Chapala, L. de Mexico 20°15N 103°0W 114 C4
Chapayevsk Russia 53°0N 49°40E 70 D8
Chapel-en-le-Frith U.K. 53°20N 1°54W 27 F5
Chapel St. Leonards U.K. 53°13N 0°20E 27 F9
Chapleau Canada 47°50N 83°24W 112 B6
Charaña Bolivia 17°30S 69°25W 120 D3
Chard U.K. 50°52N 2°58W 30 E3
Chari → Chad 12°58N 14°31E 95 F8
Chārīkār Afghan. 35°0N 69°10E 87 C12
Charing U.K. 51°12N 0°49E 31 D10
Charlbury U.K. 51°53N 1°28W 30 C6
Charleroi Belgium 50°24N 4°27E 64 C3
Charles, C. U.S.A. 37°7N 75°58W 113 G10
Charles City U.S.A. 43°4N 92°41W 111 B8
Charleston Ill., U.S.A. 39°30N 88°10W 112 F3
Charleston Mo., U.S.A. 36°55N 89°21W 112 G3
Charleston S.C., U.S.A. 32°46N 79°56W 111 D11
Charleston W. Va., U.S.A. 38°21N 81°38W 112 F7
Charlestown Ireland 53°58N 8°48W 18 D4
Charlestown of Aberlour U.K. 57°28N 3°14W 23 H11
Charleville Australia 26°24S 146°15E 98 F8
Charleville Ireland 52°21N 8°40W 20 D5
Charleville-Mézières France 49°44N 4°40E 66 B6
Charlevoix U.S.A. 45°19N 85°16W 112 C5
Charlotte Mich., U.S.A. 42°34N 84°50W 112 D5
Charlotte N.C., U.S.A. 35°13N 80°50W 111 C10
Charlotte Amalie U.S. Virgin Is. 18°21N 64°56W 115 D12
Charlotte Harbor U.S.A. 26°57N 82°4W 111 E10
Charlottesville U.S.A. 38°2N 78°30W 112 F8
Charlottetown Canada 46°14N 63°8W 113 B16
Charlton I. Canada 52°0N 79°20W 109 D12
Charlton Kings U.K. 51°53N 2°3W 30 C4
Charlwood U.K. 51°9N 0°13W 31 D8
Charminster U.K. 50°44N 2°28W 30 E4
Charmouth U.K. 50°44N 2°54W 30 E3
Charnwood Forest U.K. 52°44N 1°17W 27 G6
Charolles France 46°27N 4°16E 66 C6
Charters Towers Australia 20°5S 146°13E 98 E8
Chartham U.K. 51°14N 1°1E 31 D11
Chartres France 48°29N 1°30E 66 B4
Chascomús Argentina 35°30S 58°0W 121 F4
Châteaubriant France 47°43N 1°23W 66 C3
Châteaulin France 48°11N 4°8W 66 B1
Châteauroux France 46°50N 1°40E 66 C4
Châtellerault France 46°50N 0°30E 66 C4
Chatham = Miramichi Canada 47°2N 65°28W 109 E13
Chatham Canada 42°24N 82°11W 112 D6
Chatham U.K. 51°22N 0°32E 31 D10
Chatham Is. Pac. Oc. 44°0S 176°40W 99 J15
Chatsworth U.K. 53°13N 1°36W 27 F6
Chattanooga U.S.A. 35°3N 85°19W 111 C9
Chatteris U.K. 52°28N 0°2E 31 B9
Chattogram Bangla. 22°19N 91°48E 85 H17
Chatton U.K. 55°35N 2°0W 26 A5
Chaumont France 48°7N 5°8E 66 B6
Chaykovskiy Russia 56°47N 54°9E 70 C9
Cheadle Gt. Man., U.K. 53°23N 2°12W 27 F4
Cheadle Staffs., U.K. 52°59N 1°58W 27 G5
Cheb Czechia 50°9N 12°28E 64 C7
Cheboksary Russia 56°8N 47°12E 70 C8
Cheboygan U.S.A. 45°39N 84°29W 112 C5
Chech, Erg Africa 25°0N 2°15W 94 D5
Chechnia □ Russia 43°30N 45°29E 71 F8
Chedabucto B. Canada 45°25N 61°8W 113 C17
Cheddar U.K. 51°17N 2°46W 30 D3
Cheddleton U.K. 53°4N 2°2W 27 F4
Cheduba I. Myanmar 18°45N 93°40E 85 K18
Chegutu Zimbabwe 18°10S 30°14E 97 H6
Chek Lap Kok China 22°18N 113°56E 79 a
Chelm Poland 51°8N 23°30E 65 C12
Chelmer → U.K. 51°44N 0°30E 31 C10
Chelmsford U.K. 51°44N 0°29E 31 C9
Cheltenham U.K. 51°54N 2°4W 30 C4
Chelyabinsk Russia 55°10N 61°24E 76 D7
Chelyuskin, C. Russia 77°30N 103°0E 72 B11
Chemnitz Germany 50°51N 12°54E 64 C7
Chenab → Pakistan 30°23N 71°2E 84 D7
Chengde China 40°59N 117°58E 79 C12
Chengdu China 30°38N 104°2E 78 E9
Chennai India 13°8N 80°19E 84 N12
Cheò, Eilean a' = Skye U.K. 57°15N 6°10W 22 H5
Chepstow U.K. 51°38N 2°41W 30 C3
Cher → France 47°21N 0°29E 66 C4
Cherbourg-Octeville France 49°39N 1°40W 66 B3
Cheremkhovo Russia 53°8N 103°1E 78 A9
Cherepovets Russia 59°5N 37°55E 70 C6
Chergui, Chott ech Algeria 34°21N 0°25E 94 B6
Cheriton U.K. 51°3N 1°9W 30 D6
Cheriton Fitzpaine U.K. 50°51N 3°35W 29 F6
Cherkasy Ukraine 49°27N 32°4E 71 E5
Cherkessk Russia 44°15N 42°5E 71 F7
Chernihiv Ukraine 51°28N 31°20E 70 D5
Chernivtsi Ukraine 48°15N 25°52E 65 D13
Cherokee U.S.A. 42°45N 95°33W 111 B7
Cherrapunji India 25°17N 91°47E 85 G17
Cherski Ra. Russia 65°0N 143°0E 77 C15
Chertsey U.K. 51°23N 0°30W 31 D8
Chervonohrad Ukraine 50°25N 24°10E 71 D3
Cherwell → U.K. 51°44N 1°14W 30 C6
Chesapeake B. U.S.A. 38°0N 76°10W 112 F9
Chesha B. Russia 67°20N 47°0E 70 A8
Cheshire East □ U.K. 53°15N 2°15W 27 F4
Cheshire West and Chester □ U.K. 53°15N 2°40W 27 F3

Cheshunt

Culm

Cheshunt U.K. 51°43N 0°1W **31** C8
Chesil Beach U.K. 50°37N 2°33W **30** E3
Chester U.K. 53°12N 2°53W **27** F3
Chester U.S.A. 39°51N 75°22W **113** F10
Chester-le-Street U.K. 54°51N 1°34W **26** C5
Chesterfield U.K. 53°15N 1°25W **27** F6
Chesterfield, Îs. N. Cal. 19°52S 158°15E **99** D10
Chesterfield Inlet Canada 63°30N 90°45W **108** C10
Chesuncook L. U.S.A. 46°0N 69°21W **113** B13
Chetumal Mexico 18°30N 88°20W **114** D7
Chetwynd Canada 55°45N 121°36W **108** D7
Cheviot, The U.K. 55°29N 2°9W **26** B4
Cheviot Hills U.K. 55°20N 2°30W **26** B3
Chew Bahir Ethiopia 4°40N 36°50E **89** G2
Chew Magna U.K. 51°22N 2°37W **30** D3
Cheyenne U.S.A. 41°8N 104°49W **110** B6
Cheyenne → U.S.A. 44°41N 101°18W **110** B6
Chhapra India 25°48N 84°44E **85** G14
Chhattisgarh □ India 22°0N 82°0E **85** J12
Chi → Thailand 15°11N 104°43E **82** A3
Chiai Taiwan 23°29N 120°25E **79** G13
Chiávari Italy 44°19N 9°19E **68** B3
Chiba Japan 35°30N 140°7E **81** F7
Chibougamau Canada 49°56N 74°24W **109** E12
Chibougamau, L. Canada 49°50N 74°20W **113** A10
Chic-Chocs, Mts. Canada 48°55N 66°0W **113** A14
Chicago U.S.A. 41°52N 87°38W **112** E4
Chichagof I. U.S.A. 57°30N 135°30W **108** D6
Chichester U.K. 50°50N 0°47W **31** E7
Chickasha U.S.A. 35°3N 97°58W **110** C7
Chiclayo Peru 6°42S 79°50W **120** C2
Chico U.S.A. 39°44N 121°50W **110** C2
Chico → Chubut, Argentina 44°0S 67°0W **121** G3
Chico → Santa Cruz, Argentina 50°0S 68°30W **121** G3
Chicopee U.S.A. 42°9N 72°37W **113** D11
Chicoutimi Canada 48°28N 71°5W **113** A12
Chiddingfold U.K. 51°7N 0°37W **31** D7
Chidley, C. Canada 60°23N 64°26W **109** C13
Chieti Italy 42°21N 14°10E **68** C6
Chifeng China 42°18N 118°58E **79** C12
Chihuahua Mexico 28°38N 106°5W **114** B3
Chilapa Mexico 17°36N 99°10W **114** D5
Chilaw Sri Lanka 7°30N 79°50E **84** R11
Childress U.S.A. 34°25N 100°13W **110** D6
Chile ■ S. Amer. 35°0S 72°0W **121** F2
Chilham U.K. 51°15N 0°59E **31** D10
Chililabombwe Zambia 12°18S 27°43E **97** G5
Chilka L. India 19°40N 85°25E **85** K14
Chillán Chile 36°40S 72°10W **121** F2
Chillicothe Ill., U.S.A. 40°55N 89°29W **112** E3
Chillicothe Ohio, U.S.A. 39°20N 82°59W **112** F6
Chilliwack Canada 49°10N 121°54W **108** E7
Chiloé, I. de Chile 42°30S 73°50W **121** G2
Chilpancingo Mexico 17°33N 99°30W **114** D5
Chiltern Hills U.K. 51°40N 0°53W **31** C7
Chilton U.S.A. 44°2N 88°10W **112** C3
Chilung Taiwan 25°3N 121°45E **79** F13
Chilwa, L. Malawi 15°15S 35°40E **97** H7
Chimborazo Ecuador 1°29S 78°55W **120** C2
Chimbote Peru 9°0S 78°35W **120** C2
Chimoio Mozam. 19°4S 33°30E **97** H6
Chin □ Myanmar 22°0N 93°0E **85** J18
Chin Hills Myanmar 22°30N 93°30E **85** H18
China ■ Asia 30°0N 110°0E **79** E11
China, Great Plain of Asia 35°0N 115°0E **72** E13
Chinandega Nic. 12°35N 87°12W **114** E7
Chincha Alta Peru 13°25S 76°7W **120** D2
Chindwin → Myanmar 21°26N 95°15E **85** J19
Chingola Zambia 12°31S 27°53E **97** G5
Chinhoyi Zimbabwe 17°20S 30°8E **97** H6
Chiniot Pakistan 31°45N 73°0E **84** D8
Chinmen Tao Taiwan 24°26N 118°22E **79** G12
Chinon France 47°10N 0°15E **66** C4
Chióggia Italy 45°13N 12°17E **68** B5
Chipata Zambia 13°38S 32°28E **97** G6
Chipman Canada 46°6N 65°53W **113** B15
Chippenham U.K. 51°27N 2°6W **30** D4
Chippewa Falls U.S.A. 44°56N 91°24W **112** C2
Chipping Campden U.K. 52°3N 1°45W **30** B5
Chipping Norton U.K. 51°56N 1°32W **30** C5
Chipping Ongar U.K. 51°42N 0°15E **31** C9
Chipping Sodbury U.K. 51°33N 2°23W **30** C4
Chiquinquira Colombia 5°37N 73°50W **120** B2
Chirbury U.K. 52°35N 3°4W **27** G2
Chirchiq Uzbekistan 41°29N 69°35E **87** A12
Chiredzi Zimbabwe 21°0S 31°38E **97** J6
Chirnside U.K. 55°48N 2°12W **25** C11
Chisasibi Canada 53°50N 79°0W **109** D12
Chiseldon U.K. 51°31N 1°44W **30** C5
Chișinău Moldova 47°2N 28°50E **65** E15
Chistopol Russia 55°25N 50°38E **70** C9
Chita Russia 52°0N 113°35E **77** D12
Chitral Pakistan 35°50N 71°56E **84** B7
Chittagong = Chattogram Bangla. 22°19N 91°48E **85** H17
Chitungwiza Zimbabwe 18°0S 31°6E **97** H6
Choiseul St. Lucia 13°47N 61°3W **114** b
Choiseul Solomon Is. 7°0S 156°40E **99** B10
Chōkai-San Japan 39°6N 140°3E **81** D7
Cholet France 47°4N 0°52W **66** C3
Chollerton U.K. 55°4N 2°7W **26** B4
Cholsey U.K. 51°35N 1°8W **30** C6
Choluteca Honduras 13°20N 87°14W **114** E7
Chon Buri Thailand 13°21N 101°1E **82** B2
Ch'ŏngjin N. Korea 41°47N 129°50E **79** C14
Chongqing China 29°35N 106°25E **78** F10
Chongqing Shi □ China 30°0N 108°0E **78** F10
Chonos, Arch. de los Chile 45°0S 75°0W **121** G2
Chorley U.K. 53°39N 2°38W **27** E3
Chornobyl Ukraine 51°20N 30°15E **65** C16
Chorzów Poland 50°18N 18°57E **65** C10
Choybalsan Mongolia 48°4N 114°30E **79** B11
Choyr Mongolia 46°24N 108°30E **79** B10
Christchurch N.Z. 43°33S 172°47E **99** J13
Christchurch U.K. 50°44N 1°47W **30** E5
Christmas I. Ind. Oc. 10°30S 105°40E **102** J2
Chubut → Argentina 43°20S 65°5W **121** G3
Chudleigh U.K. 50°36N 3°36W **29** F6
Chudskoye, L. Russia 58°13N 27°30E **70** C4
Chukchi Sea Russia 68°0N 175°0W **77** C19
Chukot Ra. Russia 68°0N 175°0E **77** C18

Chulmleigh U.K. 50°54N 3°51W **29** F6
Chuncheon S. Korea 37°58N 127°44E **79** D14
Chuquicamata Chile 22°15S 69°0W **121** E3
Chur Switz. 46°52N 9°32E **64** E5
Church Stretton U.K. 52°32N 2°48W **27** G3
Churchdown U.K. 51°52N 2°10W **30** C4
Churchill Canada 58°47N 94°11W **108** D10
Churchill → Man., Canada 58°47N 94°12W **108** D10
Churchill → Nfld. & L., Canada 53°19N 60°10W **109** D13
Churchill, C. Canada 58°46N 93°12W **108** D10
Churchill Falls Canada 53°36N 64°19W **109** D13
Churchill L. Canada 55°55N 108°20W **108** D9
Churchill Pk. Canada 58°10N 125°10W **108** D7
Churu India 28°20N 74°50E **84** E9
Chuska Mts. U.S.A. 36°15N 108°50W **110** C5
Chusovoy Russia 58°22N 57°50E **70** C10
Chuvashia □ Russia 55°30N 47°0E **70** C8
Chuxiong China 25°2N 101°28E **78** F9
Cícero U.S.A. 41°51N 87°44W **112** E4
Ciechanów Poland 52°52N 20°38E **65** B11
Ciego de Ávila Cuba 21°50N 78°50W **115** C9
Cienfuegos Cuba 22°10N 80°30W **115** C8
Cilo Dağı Turkey 37°28N 43°55E **71** G7
Cimarron → U.S.A. 36°10N 96°16W **111** C7
Cincinnati U.S.A. 39°9N 84°27W **112** F5
Cinderford U.K. 51°49N 2°30W **30** C3
Cinto, Mte. France 42°24N 8°54E **66** E8
Circle U.S.A. 65°50N 144°4W **108** C5
Circleville U.S.A. 39°36N 82°57W **112** F6
Cirebon Indonesia 6°45S 108°32E **82** F3
Cirencester U.K. 51°43N 1°57W **30** C5
Ciudad Acuña Mexico 29°18N 100°55W **114** B4
Ciudad Bolívar Venezuela 8°5N 63°36W **120** B3
Ciudad del Carmen Mexico 18°38N 91°50W **114** D6
Ciudad del Este Paraguay 25°30S 54°50W **121** E4
Ciudad Guayana Venezuela 8°0N 62°30W **120** B3
Ciudad Guzmán Mexico 19°41N 103°29W **114** D4
Ciudad Juárez Mexico 31°44N 106°29W **114** A3
Ciudad Madero Mexico 22°19N 97°50W **114** C5
Ciudad Mante Mexico 22°44N 98°59W **114** C5
Ciudad Obregón Mexico 27°29N 109°56W **114** B3
Ciudad Real Spain 38°59N 3°55W **67** C4
Ciudad Valles Mexico 21°59N 99°1W **114** C5
Ciudad Victoria Mexico 23°44N 99°8W **114** C5
Civitavécchia Italy 42°6N 11°48E **68** C4
Cizre Turkey 37°19N 42°10E **71** G7
Clackmannan U.K. 56°7N 3°45W **25** B8
Clacton-on-Sea U.K. 51°47N 1°11E **31** C11
Claire, L. Canada 58°35N 112°5W **108** D8
Clara Ireland 53°21N 7°37W **18** E6
Clare U.K. 52°4N 0°34E **31** B9
Clare □ Ireland 52°45N 9°0W **20** C4
Clare → Ireland 53°20N 9°2W **18** E3
Clare I. Ireland 53°47N 10°0W **18** D1
Claremont U.S.A. 43°23N 72°20W **113** D11
Clark Fork → U.S.A. 48°9N 116°15W **110** A3
Clarksburg U.S.A. 39°17N 80°30W **112** F7
Clarksdale U.S.A. 34°12N 90°35W **111** D8
Clarksville U.S.A. 36°32N 87°21W **111** C9
Claverley U.K. 52°32N 2°18W **27** G4
Clay Cross U.K. 53°10N 1°25W **27** F6
Claydon U.K. 52°7N 1°8E **31** B11
Clear, C. Ireland 51°25N 9°32W **20** F3
Clear I. Ireland 51°26N 9°30W **20** F3
Clearfield U.S.A. 41°2N 78°27W **112** E8
Clearwater U.S.A. 27°59N 82°48W **111** E10
Cleator Moor U.K. 54°33N 3°30W **26** C2
Clee Hills U.K. 52°26N 2°35W **27** H3
Cleethorpes U.K. 53°33N 0°3W **27** E8
Cleeve Cloud U.K. 51°56N 2°0W **30** C5
Clent Hills U.K. 52°25N 2°4W **30** B4
Cleobury Mortimer U.K. 52°22N 2°28W **27** H4
Clermont-Ferrand France 45°46N 3°4E **66** D5
Clevedon U.K. 51°26N 2°52W **30** D3
Cleveland Miss., U.S.A. 33°45N 90°43W **111** D8
Cleveland Ohio, U.S.A. 41°29N 81°41W **112** E7
Cleveland Hills U.K. 54°25N 1°11W **26** D6
Clew B. Ireland 53°50N 9°49W **18** D2
Cley U.K. 52°57N 1°2E **31** A11
Clifden Ireland 53°29N 10°1W **18** E1
Cliffe U.K. 51°28N 0°31E **31** D10
Clifford U.K. 52°7N 3°6W **30** B2
Clinton Iowa, U.S.A. 41°51N 90°12W **112** E2
Clinton Okla., U.S.A. 35°31N 98°58W **110** C7
Clinton Colden L. Canada 63°58N 107°27W **108** C9
Clipperton, Î. Pac. Oc. 10°18N 109°13W **103** F17
Clipston U.K. 52°37N 0°58W **31** B7
Clitheroe U.K. 53°53N 2°22W **27** E4
Cloghaneely Ireland 55°8N 8°5W **18** A3
Clogher Hd. Ireland 53°48N 6°14W **19** D9
Clonakilty Ireland 51°37N 8°53W **20** E5
Clonakilty B. Ireland 51°35N 8°51W **20** E5
Cloncurry → Australia 18°37S 140°40E **98** E7
Clondalkin Ireland 53°19N 6°25W **21** B10
Clones Ireland 54°11N 7°15W **19** C7
Clonmel Ireland 52°21N 7°42W **21** D7
Clontarf Ireland 53°22N 6°11W **21** B10
Cloughton U.K. 54°20N 0°26W **26** D8
Clovelly U.K. 51°0N 4°25W **29** F5
Clovis U.S.A. 34°24N 103°12W **110** D6
Clowne U.K. 53°16N 1°17W **27** F6
Cluj-Napoca Romania 46°47N 23°38E **65** E12
Clun Forest U.K. 52°27N 3°7W **27** H2
Clunbury U.K. 52°25N 2°55W **27** H3
Clwyd → U.K. 53°19N 3°31W **28** A6
Clwyd → U.K. 53°19N 3°30W **28** A6
Clyde River Canada 70°30N 68°30W **109** B13
Clyde → U.K. 55°55N 4°30W **24** C6
Clyde, Firth of U.K. 55°22N 5°1W **24** D5
Clydebank U.K. 55°54N 4°23W **24** C7
Clydesdale U.K. 55°43N 3°51W **25** C8
Coalbrookdale U.K. 52°39N 2°30W **27** G3
Coalisland U.K. 54°33N 6°42W **19** B8
Coalville U.K. 52°44N 1°23W **27** G6
Coast Mts. Canada 55°0N 129°20W **108** D7
Coast Ranges U.S.A. 39°0N 123°0W **110** B2
Coatbridge U.K. 55°52N 4°6W **24** C7
Coaticook Canada 45°10N 71°46W **113** C12
Coats I. Canada 62°30N 83°0W **109** C11
Coats Land Antarctica 77°0S 25°0W **55** D1

Coatzacoalcos Mexico 18°7N 94°25W **114** D6
Cobán Guatemala 15°30N 90°21W **114** D6
Cobar Australia 31°27S 145°48E **98** G8
Cobh Ireland 51°51N 8°17W **20** E6
Cobija Bolivia 11°0S 68°50W **120** D3
Cobourg Canada 43°58N 78°10W **112** D8
Cochabamba Bolivia 17°26S 66°10W **120** D3
Cochrane Canada 49°0N 81°0W **109** E11
Cockburn, Canal Chile 54°30S 72°0W **121** H2
Cockburn I. Canada 45°55N 83°22W **112** C6
Cockburn Town The Bahamas 24°2N 74°31W **115** C10
Cockerham U.K. 53°58N 2°49W **27** E3
Cockermouth U.K. 54°40N 3°22W **26** C2
Cockfield U.K. 52°10N 0°48E **31** B10
Cockpit Country, The Jamaica 18°15N 77°45W **114** a
Coco → Cent. Amer. 15°0N 83°8W **115** E8
Cocos I. Ind. Oc. 12°10S 96°55E **102** J1
Cod, C. U.S.A. 42°5N 70°10W **113** D12
Coddenham U.K. 52°9N 1°8E **31** B11
Codó Brazil 4°30S 43°55W **120** C5
Cody U.S.A. 44°32N 109°3W **110** B5
Coeur d'Alene U.S.A. 47°41N 116°46W **110** A3
Coggeshall U.K. 51°52N 0°42E **31** C10
Cognac France 45°41N 0°20W **66** D3
Coigach U.K. 57°59N 5°14W **22** G7
Coigeach, Rubha U.K. 58°6N 5°26W **22** F7
Coimbatore India 11°2N 76°59E **84** P10
Coimbra Portugal 40°15N 8°27W **67** B1
Colatina Brazil 19°32S 40°37W **122** C2
Colchester U.K. 51°54N 0°55E **31** C10
Cold Fell U.K. 54°53N 2°36W **26** C3
Coldstream U.K. 55°39N 2°15W **25** C11
Colebrook U.S.A. 44°54N 71°30W **113** C12
Colebrooke U.K. 50°47N 3°44W **29** F6
Coleford U.K. 51°47N 2°36W **30** C3
Coleraine U.K. 55°8N 6°41W **19** A8
Coleshill U.K. 52°30N 1°41W **27** G5
Colgrave Sd. U.K. 60°36N 0°58W **22** A16
Colima Mexico 19°14N 103°43W **114** D4
Colima, Nevado de Mexico 19°33N 103°38W **114** D4
Coll U.K. 56°39N 6°34W **24** J4
Collier Law U.K. 54°47N 1°59W **26** C5
Collin U.K. 55°4N 3°31W **25** D9
Collingbourne Kingston U.K. 51°18N 1°40W **30** D5
Collingham U.K. 53°8N 0°46W **27** F7
Collingwood Canada 44°29N 80°13W **112** C7
Collooney Ireland 54°11N 8°29W **18** C5
Colmar France 48°5N 7°20E **66** B7
Colne U.K. 53°51N 2°9W **27** E4
Colne → Bucks., U.K. 51°27N 0°32W **31** D7
Colne → Essex, U.K. 51°51N 0°58E **31** C10
Cologne Germany 50°56N 6°57E **64** C4
Colombia ■ S. Amer. 3°45N 73°0W **120** B2
Colombo Sri Lanka 6°56N 79°58E **84** R11
Colonsay U.K. 56°5N 6°12W **24** B3
Colorado □ U.S.A. 39°30N 105°30W **110** C5
Colorado → Argentina 39°50S 62°8W **121** F3
Colorado → N. Amer. 31°45N 114°40W **110** D4
Colorado → U.S.A. 28°36N 95°59W **111** E7
Colorado Plateau U.S.A. 37°0N 111°0W **110** C4
Colorado Springs U.S.A. 38°50N 104°49W **110** C6
Colsterworth U.K. 52°49N 0°37W **27** G7
Coltishall U.K. 52°44N 1°21E **31** A11
Columbia Mo., U.S.A. 38°57N 92°20W **111** C8
Columbia S.C., U.S.A. 34°0N 81°2W **111** D10
Columbia Tenn., U.S.A. 35°37N 87°2W **111** C9
Columbia → N. Amer. 46°15N 124°5W **110** A2
Columbia, District of □ U.S.A. 38°55N 77°0W **112** F9
Columbia Plateau U.S.A. 44°0N 117°30W **110** B4
Columbus Ga., U.S.A. 32°28N 84°59W **111** D10
Columbus Ind., U.S.A. 39°13N 85°55W **112** F5
Columbus Miss., U.S.A. 33°30N 88°25W **111** D9
Columbus Nebr., U.S.A. 41°26N 97°22W **111** E7
Columbus Ohio, U.S.A. 39°58N 83°0W **112** F6
Colville → U.S.A. 70°25N 150°30W **108** B4
Colwell U.K. 55°5N 2°4W **26** B4
Colwich U.K. 52°48N 1°58W **27** G5
Colwyn Bay U.K. 53°18N 3°44W **28** A6
Colyton U.K. 50°44N 3°5W **29** F7
Comayagua Honduras 14°25N 87°37W **114** E7
Combe Martin U.K. 51°12N 4°3W **29** E5
Comber U.K. 54°33N 5°45W **19** B6
Comeragh Mts. Ireland 52°18N 7°34W **21** D7
Comitán Mexico 16°15N 92°8W **114** D6
Committee B. Canada 68°30N 86°30W **109** C11
Como Italy 45°47N 9°5E **68** B3
Como, L. di Italy 46°0N 9°11E **68** B3
Comodoro Rivadavia Argentina 45°50S 67°40W **121** G3
Comoros ■ Ind. Oc. 12°10S 44°15E **91** H8
Compass Mt. S. Africa 31°45S 24°32E **90** K6
Compiègne France 49°24N 2°50E **66** B5
Conakry Guinea 9°29N 13°49W **94** G3
Conceição da Barra Brazil 18°35S 39°45W **122** C3
Concepción Chile 36°50S 73°0W **121** F2
Concepción Paraguay 23°22S 57°26W **121** E4
Concepción, Est. de Chile 50°30S 74°55W **121** H2
Concepción del Oro Mexico 24°38N 101°25W **114** C4
Concepción del Uruguay Argentina 32°35S 58°20W **121** F4
Conception, Pt. U.S.A. 34°27N 120°28W **110** D2
Conchos → Mexico 29°35N 104°25W **114** B4
Concord Calif., U.S.A. 37°59N 122°2W **110** C2
Concord N.H., U.S.A. 43°12N 71°32W **113** D12
Concordia Argentina 31°20S 58°2W **121** F4
Concordia U.S.A. 39°34N 97°40W **110** C7
Condeúba Brazil 14°52S 42°0W **122** B2
Condover U.K. 52°39N 2°44W **27** G3
Congleton U.K. 53°10N 2°13W **27** F4
Congo ■ Africa 1°0S 16°0E **96** E3
Congo → Africa 6°4S 12°24E **96** F2
Congo, Dem. Rep. of the ■ Africa 3°0S 23°0E **96** E4
Congo Basin Africa 0°10S 24°30E **96** E4
Congresbury U.K. 51°22N 2°48W **30** D3
Coningsby U.K. 53°7N 0°10W **27** F8
Conisbrough U.K. 53°29N 1°14W **27** F6
Coniston Canada 46°29N 80°51W **112** B7
Coniston U.K. 54°22N 3°5W **26** D2

Coniston Water U.K. 54°20N 3°5W **26** D2
Conn, L. Ireland 54°3N 9°15W **18** C3
Connah's Quay U.K. 53°13N 3°4W **28** A7
Connaught □ Ireland 53°43N 9°12W **18** D3
Conneaut U.S.A. 41°57N 80°34W **112** E7
Connecticut □ U.S.A. 41°30N 72°45W **113** E11
Connecticut → U.S.A. 41°16N 72°20W **113** E11
Connellsville U.S.A. 40°1N 79°35W **112** E8
Connemara Ireland 53°29N 9°45W **18** E2
Connemara △ Ireland 53°32N 9°52W **18** E2
Connersville U.S.A. 39°39N 85°8W **112** F5
Conselheiro Lafaiete Brazil 20°40S 43°48W **122** D2
Consett U.K. 54°51N 1°50W **26** C5
Constance, L. Europe 47°35N 9°25E **64** E5
Constanța Romania 44°14N 28°38E **65** F15
Constantine Algeria 36°25N 6°42E **94** A7
Constitución Chile 35°20S 72°30W **121** F2
Contagem Brazil 19°56S 44°3W **122** C2
Contas → Brazil 14°17S 39°1W **122** B3
Contwoyto L. Canada 65°42N 110°50W **108** C8
Conway Ark., U.S.A. 35°5N 92°26W **111** C8
Conway N.H., U.S.A. 43°59N 71°7W **113** D12
Conwy U.K. 53°17N 3°50W **28** A6
Conwy □ U.K. 53°10N 3°44W **28** A6
Conwy → U.K. 53°17N 3°50W **28** A6
Coober Pedy Australia 29°1S 134°43E **98** F6
Cook Inlet U.S.A. 60°0N 152°0W **108** D4
Cook Is. ☑ Pac. Oc. 17°0S 160°0W **103** J12
Cook Strait N.Z. 41°15S 174°29E **99** J13
Cookstown U.K. 54°38N 6°45W **19** B8
Cooktown Australia 15°30S 145°16E **98** D8
Coondapoor India 13°42N 74°40E **84** N9
Coos Bay U.S.A. 43°22N 124°13W **110** B2
Cootehill Ireland 54°4N 7°5W **19** C7
Copenhagen Denmark 55°40N 12°26E **63** F6
Copiapó Chile 27°30S 70°20W **121** E2
Copper Harbor U.S.A. 47°28N 87°53W **112** B4
Coppermine → Canada 67°49N 116°4W **108** C8
Coquet → U.K. 55°20N 1°32W **26** B5
Coquet I. U.K. 55°20N 1°36W **26** B5
Coquimbo Chile 30°0S 71°20W **121** E2
Coracora Peru 15°5S 73°45W **120** D2
Coral Harbour Canada 64°8N 83°10W **109** C11
Coral Sea Pac. Oc. 15°0S 150°0E **98** C9
Corbin U.S.A. 36°57N 84°6W **112** G5
Corbridge U.K. 54°58N 2°0W **26** C5
Corby U.K. 52°30N 0°41W **31** A7
Corby Glen U.K. 52°49N 0°30W **27** G7
Cordele U.S.A. 31°58N 83°47W **111** D10
Córdoba Argentina 31°20S 64°10W **121** F3
Córdoba Mexico 18°53N 96°56W **114** D5
Córdoba Spain 37°50N 4°50W **67** D3
Córdoba, Sierra de Argentina 31°10S 64°25W **121** F3
Cordova U.S.A. 60°33N 145°45W **108** C5
Corfe Castle U.K. 50°38N 2°3W **30** E4
Corfe Mullen U.K. 50°46N 2°1W **30** E4
Corfu Greece 39°38N 19°50E **69** E8
Corinth Greece 37°56N 22°55E **69** F10
Corinth U.S.A. 34°56N 88°31W **111** D9
Corinto Brazil 18°20S 44°30W **122** C2
Cork Ireland 51°54N 8°29W **20** E6
Cork □ Ireland 51°57N 8°40W **20** E5
Cork Harbour Ireland 51°47N 8°16W **20** E6
Corner Brook Canada 48°57N 57°58W **109** E14
Corning U.S.A. 42°9N 77°3W **112** D9
Cornwall Canada 45°2N 74°44W **113** C10
Cornwall □ U.K. 50°26N 4°40W **29** G4
Cornwall, C. U.K. 50°8N 5°43W **29** G2
Cornwall I. Canada 77°37N 94°38W **109** B10
Cornwallis I. Canada 75°8N 95°0W **109** B10
Coro Venezuela 11°25N 69°41W **120** A3
Corocoro Bolivia 17°15S 68°28W **120** D3
Coromandel Coast India 12°30N 81°0E **84** N12
Coronation Gulf Canada 68°25N 110°0W **108** C8
Coronel Chile 37°0S 73°10W **121** F2
Coronel Fabriciano Brazil 19°31S 42°38W **122** C2
Coronel Pringles Argentina 38°0S 61°30W **121** F3
Coronel Suárez Argentina 37°30S 61°52W **121** F3
Coropuna, Nevado Peru 15°30S 72°41W **120** D2
Corpus Christi U.S.A. 27°47N 97°24W **110** E7
Corrain Pen. Ireland 53°54N 9°54W **18** D2
Corrib, L. Ireland 53°27N 9°16W **20** B4
Corrientes Argentina 27°30S 58°45W **121** E4
Corrientes, C. Colombia 5°30N 77°34W **120** B2
Corrientes, C. Mexico 20°25N 105°42W **114** C3
Corringham U.K. 53°25N 0°41W **27** F7
Corry U.S.A. 41°55N 79°39W **112** E8
Corse, C. France 43°1N 9°25E **66** E8
Corsham U.K. 51°27N 2°10W **30** D4
Corsica □ France 42°0N 9°0E **66** F8
Corsicana U.S.A. 32°6N 96°28W **111** D7
Corsley U.K. 51°13N 2°14W **30** D4
Corte France 42°19N 9°11E **66** E8
Cortez U.S.A. 37°21N 108°35W **110** C5
Cortland U.S.A. 42°36N 76°11W **113** D9
Corton U.K. 52°31N 1°45E **31** A12
Çorum Turkey 40°30N 34°57E **71** F5
Corumbá Brazil 19°0S 57°30W **120** D4
Corunna = La Coruña Spain 43°20N 8°25W **67** A1
Corvallis U.S.A. 44°34N 123°16W **110** B2
Corve → U.K. 52°22N 2°43W **27** H3
Coseley U.K. 52°33N 2°5W **27** G4
Cosenza Italy 39°18N 16°15E **68** E7
Cosham U.K. 50°51N 1°2W **30** E6
Coshocton U.S.A. 40°16N 81°51W **112** E7
Costa Blanca Spain 38°25N 0°10W **67** C5
Costa Brava Spain 41°30N 3°0E **67** B7
Costa del Sol Spain 36°30N 4°30W **67** D3
Costa Dorada Spain 41°12N 1°15E **67** B6
Costa Rica ■ Cent. Amer. 10°0N 84°0W **115** F8
Costessey U.K. 52°40N 1°11E **31** A11
Cotabato Phil. 7°14N 124°15E **83** C6
Côte d'Azur France 43°25N 7°10E **66** E7
Côte-d'Ivoire ■ Africa 7°30N 5°0W **94** G4
Coteau du Missouri U.S.A. 47°0N 100°0W **110** A6
Cotentin France 49°15N 1°30W **66** B3
Cotherstone U.K. 54°35N 1°59W **26** C5
Cotonou Benin 6°20N 2°25E **94** G6
Cotopaxi Ecuador 0°40S 78°30W **120** C2
Cotswold Hills U.K. 51°42N 2°10W **30** C4
Cottbus Germany 51°45N 14°20E **64** C8
Cottenham U.K. 52°18N 0°9E **31** B9

Coudersport U.S.A. 41°46N 78°1W **112** E8
Council Bluffs U.S.A. 41°16N 95°52W **111** B7
Courantyne → S. Amer. 5°50N 57°8W **120** B4
Courtenay Canada 49°45N 125°0W **108** E7
Cove U.K. 56°0N 4°51W **24** B6
Coventry U.K. 52°25N 1°28W **30** B6
Cover → U.K. 54°17N 1°47W **26** D5
Coverack U.K. 50°1N 5°7W **29** G3
Covington U.S.A. 39°5N 84°30W **112** F5
Cowal U.K. 56°5N 5°8W **24** B5
Cowbridge U.K. 51°27N 3°27W **29** F7
Cowdenbeath U.K. 56°7N 3°21W **25** B9
Cowes U.K. 50°45N 1°18W **30** E6
Cowfold U.K. 50°59N 0°16W **31** E8
Cowpen U.K. 55°8N 1°32W **26** B5
Cox's Bazar Bangla. 21°26N 91°59E **85** J17
Cozumel, Isla Mexico 20°30N 86°40W **114** C7
Crab Hill Barbados 13°19N 59°38W **114** c
Cradock S. Africa 32°8S 25°36E **97** L5
Craig U.S.A. 40°31N 107°33W **110** B5
Craigavon U.K. 54°27N 6°23W **19** C9
Crail U.K. 56°16N 2°37W **25** B10
Craiova Romania 44°21N 23°48E **65** F12
Cramlington U.K. 55°6N 1°34W **26** B5
Cranborne U.K. 50°55N 1°54W **30** E5
Cranborne Chase U.K. 50°56N 2°6W **30** E4
Cranbrook Canada 49°30N 115°46W **108** E8
Cranbrook U.K. 51°6N 0°34E **31** D10
Crandon U.S.A. 45°34N 88°54W **112** C3
Crane, The Barbados 13°6N 59°27W **114** c
Cranleigh U.K. 51°8N 0°28W **31** D8
Cranwell U.K. 53°3N 0°27W **27** F8
Crateús Brazil 5°10S 40°39W **120** C5
Crato Brazil 7°10S 39°25W **120** C6
Craven Arms U.K. 52°26N 2°50W **27** H3
Crawfordsville U.S.A. 40°2N 86°54W **112** E4
Crawley U.K. 51°7N 0°11W **31** D8
Credenhill U.K. 52°5N 2°48W **30** B3
Crediton U.K. 50°47N 3°40W **29** F6
Cree → Canada 58°57N 105°47W **108** D9
Cree → U.K. 54°55N 4°25W **24** E7
Cree L. Canada 57°30N 106°30W **108** D9
Cremona Italy 45°7N 10°2E **68** B4
Cres Croatia 44°58N 14°25E **68** B6
Crete Greece 35°15N 25°0E **69** G11
Créteil France 48°47N 2°27E **66** B5
Creuse → France 47°0N 0°34E **66** C4
Crewe U.K. 53°6N 2°26W **27** F4
Crewkerne U.K. 50°53N 2°48W **30** E3
Crianlarich U.K. 56°24N 4°37W **24** B6
Criccieth U.K. 52°55N 4°13W **28** B5
Crick U.K. 52°22N 1°8W **30** B6
Crickhowell U.K. 51°52N 3°8W **28** D7
Cricklade U.K. 51°38N 1°50W **30** C5
Crieff U.K. 56°22N 3°50W **25** B8
Criffell U.K. 54°56N 3°39W **25** E9
Crimea □ Ukraine 45°30N 33°10E **71** E5
Crimean Pen. Ukraine 45°0N 34°0E **71** F5
Crișul Alb → Romania 46°42N 21°17E **65** E11
Crișul Negru → Romania 46°42N 21°16E **65** E11
Croagh Patrick Ireland 53°46N 9°40W **18** D2
Croaghan Ireland 53°59N 10°10W **18** D1
Croatia ■ Europe 45°20N 16°0E **68** B7
Croglin U.K. 54°50N 2°39W **26** C3
Crohy Hd. Ireland 54°55N 8°26W **18** B4
Croker, C. Australia 10°58S 132°35E **98** C5
Cromarty U.K. 57°40N 4°2W **23** G9
Cromarty Firth U.K. 57°40N 4°15W **23** G9
Cromdale, Hills of U.K. 57°20N 3°28W **23** H11
Cromer U.K. 52°56N 1°17E **31** A11
Crondall U.K. 51°14N 0°51W **31** D7
Crook U.K. 54°43N 1°45W **26** C6
Crooked I. The Bahamas 22°50N 74°10W **115** C10
Crooklands U.K. 54°16N 2°42W **26** D3
Crosby Cumb., U.K. 54°45N 3°25W **26** C2
Crosby Mersey., U.K. 53°30N 3°3W **27** F2
Crosby Ravensworth U.K. 54°33N 2°35W **26** C3
Cross Fell U.K. 54°43N 2°28W **26** C4
Cross Sound U.S.A. 58°0N 135°0W **108** D6
Crosshaven Ireland 51°47N 8°17W **20** E6
Crossmaglen U.K. 54°5N 6°36W **19** C8
Crotone Italy 39°5N 17°8E **68** E7
Crouch → U.K. 51°37N 0°53E **31** C10
Crow Hd. Ireland 51°35N 10°9W **20** E2
Crow Sound U.K. 49°56N 6°16W **29** H1
Crowborough U.K. 51°3N 0°11E **31** D9
Crowland U.K. 52°41N 0°10W **27** G8
Crowle U.K. 53°36N 0°49W **27** E7
Crowsnest Pass Canada 49°40N 114°40W **108** E8
Croyde U.K. 51°7N 4°14W **29** E5
Croydon □ U.K. 51°22N 0°5W **31** D8
Crozet, Îs. Ind. Oc. 46°27S 52°0E **53** G12
Cruden Bay U.K. 57°25N 1°52W **23** H14
Crudgington U.K. 52°46N 2°32W **27** G3
Crummock Water U.K. 54°33N 3°18W **26** C2
Cruz das Almas Brazil 12°0S 39°6W **122** B3
Cruzeiro Brazil 22°33S 45°0W **122** D1
Cruzeiro do Sul Brazil 7°35S 72°35W **120** C2
Crystal Falls U.S.A. 46°5N 88°20W **112** B3
Cuando → Angola 17°30S 23°15E **97** H4
Cuango → Dem. Rep. of the Congo 3°14S 17°22E **96** E3
Cuanza → Angola 9°21S 13°9E **96** F2
Cuauhtémoc Mexico 28°25N 106°52W **114** B3
Cuba ■ W. Indies 22°0N 79°0W **115** C9
Cubango → Africa 18°50S 22°25E **97** H4
Cuckfield U.K. 51°1N 0°8W **31** D8
Cúcuta Colombia 7°54N 72°31W **120** B2
Cuddalore India 11°46N 79°45E **84** P11
Cuenca Ecuador 2°50S 79°9W **120** C2
Cuenca Spain 40°5N 2°10W **67** B4
Cuernavaca Mexico 18°55N 99°15W **114** D5
Cuiabá Brazil 15°30S 56°0W **120** D4
Cuihangcun China 22°27N 113°32E **79** a
Cuillin Hills U.K. 57°13N 6°15W **22** H5
Cuillin Sd. U.K. 57°4N 6°20W **22** H5
Cuito → Angola 18°1S 20°48E **97** H4
Culiacán Mexico 24°50N 107°23W **114** C3
Cullen U.K. 57°42N 2°49W **23** G12
Cullompton U.K. 50°51N 3°24W **29** F7
Culm → U.K. 50°46N 3°31W **29** F7

Culpeper

East Timor

Culpeper U.S.A. 38°30N 78°0W 112 F9
Cumaná Venezuela 10°30N 64°5W 120 A3
Cumberland U.K. 54°40N 3°30W 26 C2
Cumberland U.S.A. 39°39N 78°46W 112 F8
Cumberland → U.S.A. 37°9N 88°25W 111 C9
Cumberland Pen. Canada 67°0N 64°0W 109 C13
Cumberland Plateau U.S.A. 36°0N 85°0W 111 C10
Cumberland Sd. Canada 65°30N 66°0W 109 C13
Cumbernauld U.K. 55°57N 3°58W 25 C8
Cumbrae Is. U.K. 55°46N 4°54W 24 C6
Cumbrian Mts. U.K. 54°30N 3°0W 26 D2
Cumilla Bangla. 23°28N 91°10E 85 H17
Cummertrees U.K. 54°59N 3°20W 25 E9
Cumnock U.K. 55°28N 4°17W 24 D7
Cumnor U.K. 51°44N 1°19W 30 C6
Cumwhinton U.K. 54°52N 2°50W 26 C3
Cunene → Angola 17°20S 11°50E 97 H2
Cúneo Italy 44°23N 7°32E 68 B2
Cunnamulla Australia 28°2S 145°38E 98 F8
Cunninghame U.K. 55°38N 4°35W 24 C6
Cupar U.K. 56°19N 3°1W 25 B9
Curaçao W. Indies 12°10N 69°0W 115 E11
Curicó Chile 34°55S 71°20W 121 F2
Curitiba Brazil 25°20S 49°10W 122 E1
Curlew Mts. Ireland 54°0N 8°20W 18 D5
Curry Rivel U.K. 51°1N 2°52W 30 D3
Curvelo Brazil 18°45S 44°27W 122 C2
Cusco Peru 13°32S 72°0W 120 D3
Cuttack India 20°25N 85°57E 85 J14
Cuxhaven Germany 53°51N 8°41E 64 B5
Cuyahoga Falls U.S.A. 41°8N 81°29W 112 E7
Cuyuni → Guyana 6°23N 58°41W 120 B4
Cwmbran U.K. 51°39N 3°2W 28 D7
Cyclades Greece 37°0N 24°30E 69 F11
Cynthiana U.S.A. 38°23N 84°18W 112 F5
Cyprus ■ Asia 35°0N 33°0E 86 C3
Cyrenaica Libya 27°0N 23°0E 95 C10
Czech Rep. = Czechia ■ Europe 50°0N 15°0E 64 D8
Czechia ■ Europe 50°0N 15°0E 64 D8
Częstochowa Poland 50°49N 19°7E 65 C10

D
Da Lat Vietnam 11°56N 108°25E 82 B3
Da Nang Vietnam 16°4N 108°13E 82 A3
Da Yunhe → Hopei, China 39°10N 117°10E 79 D12
Da Yunhe → Jiangsu, China 34°25N 120°5E 79 E13
Daba Shan China 32°0N 109°0E 79 E10
Dabie Shan China 31°20N 115°20E 79 E12
Dadra & Nagar Haveli □ India 20°5N 73°0E 84 J8
Dadu Pakistan 26°45N 67°45E 84 F5
Daegu S. Korea 35°50N 128°37E 79 D14
Daejeon S. Korea 36°20N 127°28E 79 D14
Dagana Phil. 16°3N 120°20E 83 A6
Dagestan □ Russia 42°30N 47°0E 71 F8
Dagupan Phil. 16°3N 120°20E 83 A6
Dahod India 22°50N 74°15E 84 H9
Dahongliutan China 35°45N 79°20E 78 D4
Daingean Ireland 53°18N 7°17W 21 B8
Dajarra Australia 21°42S 139°30E 98 E6
Dakar Senegal 14°34N 17°29W 94 F2
Dakhla W. Sahara 23°50N 15°53W 94 D2
Dakhla, El Wâhât el Egypt 25°30N 28°50E 95 C11
Dalandzadgad Mongolia 43°27N 104°30E 78 C9
Dalbeattie U.K. 54°56N 3°50W 25 E8
Dalhart U.S.A. 36°4N 102°31W 110 C6
Dalhousie Canada 48°5N 66°26W 113 A14
Dali China 25°40N 100°10E 78 F9
Dalian China 38°50N 121°40E 79 D13
Daliang Shan China 28°0N 102°45E 78 F9
Dalkeith U.K. 55°54N 3°4W 25 C9
Dalkey Ireland 53°16N 6°6W 21 B10
Dallas U.S.A. 32°47N 96°48W 111 D7
Dalles, The U.S.A. 45°36N 121°10W 110 A2
Dalmatia Croatia 43°20N 17°0E 68 C7
Dalmellington U.K. 55°19N 4°23W 24 D7
Daloa Côte d'Ivoire 7°0N 6°30W 94 G4
Dalry U.K. 55°42N 4°43W 24 C6
Dalrymple, L. Australia 20°40S 147°0E 98 E8
Dalton Dumf. & Gall., U.K. 55°4N 3°24W 25 D9
Dalton N. Yorks., U.K. 54°28N 1°32W 26 D5
Dalton-in-Furness U.K. 54°10N 3°11W 26 D2
Daly Waters Australia 16°15S 133°24E 98 D5
Daman India 20°25N 72°57E 84 J8
Damanhûr Egypt 31°0N 30°30E 95 B12
Damaraland Namibia 20°0S 15°0E 97 H2
Damascus Syria 33°30N 36°18E 86 C4
Damavand Iran 35°57N 52°7E 87 C8
Damerham U.K. 50°56N 1°51W 30 E5
Dampier Australia 20°41S 116°42E 98 E2
Danakil Desert Ethiopia 12°45N 41°0E 89 E3
Danbury U.S.A. 41°24N 73°28W 113 E11
Dandong China 40°10N 124°20E 79 C13
Danube → Europe 45°20N 29°40E 65 F15
Danville Ill., U.S.A. 40°8N 87°37W 112 E4
Danville Ky., U.S.A. 37°39N 84°46W 112 G5
Danville Va., U.S.A. 36°36N 79°23W 111 C11
Daqing China 46°35N 125°0E 79 B13
Dar Banda Africa 8°0N 23°0E 90 F6
Dar es Salaam Tanzania 6°50S 39°12E 96 F7
Darbhanga India 26°15N 85°55E 85 F14
Dardanelles Turkey 40°17N 26°32E 69 D12
Darent → U.K. 51°28N 0°14E 31 D9
Dârfûr Sudan 13°40N 24°0E 95 F10
Darhan Mongolia 49°37N 106°21E 78 B10
Darién, G. del Caribbean 9°0N 77°0W 120 B2
Darjiling India 27°3N 88°18E 85 F16
Darling → Australia 34°4S 141°54E 98 G7
Darling Ra. Australia 32°30S 116°20E 98 G2
Darlington U.K. 54°32N 1°33W 26 C5
Darmstadt Germany 49°51N 8°39E 64 D5
Darnah Libya 32°45N 22°45E 95 B10
Darnley, C. Antarctica 68°0S 69°0E 55 C6
Darnley B. Canada 69°30N 123°30W 108 C7
Dart → U.K. 50°24N 3°39W 29 G6
Dartford U.K. 51°26N 0°13E 31 D9
Dartington U.K. 50°27N 3°43W 29 G6
Dartmoor △ U.K. 50°38N 3°57W 29 F6
Dartmouth Canada 44°40N 63°30W 113 C16
Dartmouth U.K. 50°21N 3°36W 29 G6
Darton U.K. 53°35N 1°31W 27 E5
Darwen U.K. 53°42N 2°29W 27 E4

Darwin Australia 12°25S 130°51E 98 C5
Dashen, Ras Ethiopia 13°8N 38°26E 89 E2
Dasht → Pakistan 25°10N 61°40E 84 G2
Daşoguz Turkmenistan 41°49N 59°58E 87 A9
Datong China 40°6N 113°18E 79 C11
Daugava → Latvia 57°4N 24°3E 63 F9
Daugavpils Latvia 55°53N 26°32E 63 F9
Dauphin Canada 51°9N 100°5W 108 D9
Dauphiné France 45°15N 5°25E 66 D6
Daurada, Costa Spain 41°12N 1°15E 67 B6
Davangere India 14°25N 75°55E 84 M9
Davao Phil. 7°0N 125°40E 83 C7
Davenport U.S.A. 41°32N 90°35W 112 E2
Daventry U.K. 52°16N 1°10W 30 B6
David Panama 8°30N 82°30W 115 F8
Davis Str. N. Amer. 65°0N 58°0W 104 C14
Dawlish U.K. 50°35N 3°28W 29 F7
Dawmat al Jandal Si. Arabia 29°55N 39°40E 86 D4
Dawna Ra. Myanmar 16°30N 98°30E 85 L21
Dawros Hd. Ireland 54°50N 8°33W 18 B4
Dawson City Canada 64°10N 139°30W 108 C6
Dawson Creek Canada 55°45N 120°15W 108 D7
Dax France 43°44N 1°3W 66 E3
Daxian China 31°15N 107°23E 78 E10
Daxue Shan China 30°30N 101°30E 78 E9
Dayr az Zawr Syria 35°20N 40°5E 86 C5
Dayton U.S.A. 39°45N 84°12W 112 F5
Daytona Beach U.S.A. 29°13N 81°1W 111 E10
De Aar S. Africa 30°39S 24°0E 97 L4
De Pere U.S.A. 44°27N 88°4W 112 D3
Dead Sea Asia 31°30N 35°30E 86 D3
Deal U.K. 51°13N 1°25E 31 D11
Dean, Forest of U.K. 51°45N 2°33W 30 C3
Dearham U.K. 54°44N 3°25W 26 C2
Dease → Canada 59°56N 128°32W 108 D7
Dease Lake Canada 58°25N 130°6W 108 D6
Death Valley U.S.A. 36°15N 116°50W 110 C3
Deben → U.K. 52°0N 1°25E 31 B11
Debenham U.K. 52°14N 1°12E 31 B11
Debre Markos Ethiopia 10°20N 37°40E 89 E2
Debre Tabor Ethiopia 11°50N 38°26E 89 E2
Debrecen Hungary 47°33N 21°42E 65 E11
Decatur Ala., U.S.A. 34°36N 86°59W 111 D9
Decatur Ill., U.S.A. 39°51N 88°57W 112 F3
Decatur Ind., U.S.A. 40°50N 84°56W 112 E5
Deccan India 18°0N 79°0E 84 L11
Deddington U.K. 51°59N 1°18W 30 C6
Dee → Aberds., U.K. 57°9N 2°5W 23 H13
Dee → Dumf. & Gall., U.K. 54°51N 4°3W 24 E7
Dee → Wales, U.K. 53°22N 3°17W 28 A7
Deeping Fen U.K. 52°45N 0°15W 27 G8
Deeping St. Nicholas U.K. 52°44N 0°12W 27 G8
Deer Lake Canada 49°11N 57°27W 109 E14
Defiance U.S.A. 41°17N 84°22W 112 E5
Dehra Dun India 30°20N 78°4E 84 D11
DeKalb U.S.A. 41°56N 88°46W 112 E3
Del Rio U.S.A. 29°22N 100°54W 110 E6
Delabole U.K. 50°37N 4°46W 29 F4
Delaware U.S.A. 40°18N 83°4W 112 E6
Delaware □ U.S.A. 39°0N 75°20W 113 F10
Delaware → U.S.A. 39°15N 75°20W 113 F10
Delaware B. U.S.A. 39°0N 75°10W 111 C12
Delgado, C. Mozam. 10°45S 40°40E 96 G8
Delhi India 28°39N 77°13E 84 E10
Delice Turkey 39°54N 34°2E 71 G5
Delicias Mexico 28°13N 105°28W 114 B3
Déline Canada 65°11N 123°25W 108 C7
Delphos U.S.A. 40°51N 84°21W 112 E5
Delta Junction U.S.A. 64°2N 145°44W 108 C5
Demanda, Sierra de la Spain 42°15N 3°0W 67 A4
Deming U.S.A. 32°16N 107°46W 110 D5
Demopolis U.S.A. 32°31N 87°50W 111 D9
Den Helder Neths. 52°57N 4°45E 64 B3
Denali U.S.A. 63°4N 151°0W 108 C4
Denbigh U.K. 53°12N 3°25W 28 A7
Denbighshire □ U.K. 53°8N 3°22W 28 A7
Denby Dale U.K. 53°34N 1°40W 27 E5
Denham, Mt. Jamaica 18°13N 77°32W 114 a
Denia Spain 38°49N 0°8E 67 C6
Denizli Turkey 37°42N 29°2E 71 G4
Denmark ■ Europe 55°45N 10°0E 63 F6
Denmark Str. Atl. Oc. 66°0N 30°0W 54 C6
Dennery St. Lucia 13°55N 60°54W 114 b
Denny U.K. 56°1N 3°55W 25 B8
Denpasar Indonesia 8°39S 115°13E 82 F5
Dent U.K. 54°17N 2°27W 26 D4
Denton Gt. Man., U.K. 53°27N 2°9W 27 F4
Denton Lincs., U.K. 52°53N 0°43W 27 G7
Denton U.S.A. 33°13N 97°8W 111 D7
D'Entrecasteaux Is. Papua N. G. 9°0S 151°0E 98 B9
Denver U.S.A. 39°42N 104°59W 110 C5
Deoghar India 24°30N 86°42E 85 G15
Deolali India 19°58N 73°50E 84 K8
Deosai Mts. Pakistan 35°40N 75°0E 84 B9
Dera Ghazi Khan Pakistan 30°5N 70°43E 84 D7
Dera Ismail Khan Pakistan 31°50N 70°50E 84 D7
Derbent Russia 42°5N 48°15E 71 F8
Derby Australia 17°18S 123°38E 98 D3
Derby U.K. 52°56N 1°28W 27 G6
Derbyshire □ U.K. 53°11N 1°38W 27 F5
Dereham U.K. 52°41N 0°57E 31 A10
Derg → U.K. 54°44N 7°26W 18 B7
Derg, L. Ireland 53°0N 8°20W 20 C6
Deridder U.S.A. 30°51N 93°17W 111 D8
Derry = Londonderry U.K. 55°0N 7°20W 18 A7
Derry & Strabane □ U.K. 54°47N 7°22W 18 B6
Derrynasaggart Mts. Ireland 51°58N 9°15W 20 E4
Derryveagh Mts. Ireland 54°56N 8°11W 18 B5
Derwent → Derby, U.K. 52°57N 1°28W 27 G6
Derwent → N. Yorks., U.K. 53°45N 0°58W 27 E7
Derwent → Tyne & W., U.K. 54°58N 1°41W 26 C5
Derwent Water U.K. 54°35N 3°9W 26 D2
Des Moines U.S.A. 41°35N 93°37W 111 B8
Des Moines → U.S.A. 40°23N 91°25W 111 B8
Desborough U.K. 52°27N 0°49W 31 B7
Deschutes → U.S.A. 45°38N 120°55W 110 A2
Dese Ethiopia 11°5N 39°40E 89 E2
Deseado → Argentina 47°45S 65°54W 121 G3
Desolación, I. Chile 53°0S 74°0W 121 H2
Dessau Germany 51°51N 12°14E 64 C7

Detour, Pt. U.S.A. 45°40N 86°40W 112 C4
Detroit U.S.A. 42°19N 83°12W 112 D6
Deutsche Bucht Germany 54°15N 8°0E 64 A5
Deventer Neths. 52°15N 6°10E 64 B4
Deveron → U.K. 57°41N 2°32W 23 G12
Devils Lake U.S.A. 48°7N 98°52W 110 A7
Devizes U.K. 51°22N 1°58W 30 D5
Devon □ U.K. 50°50N 3°40W 29 F6
Devon I. Canada 75°10N 85°0W 109 B11
Devonport U.K. 50°22N 4°11W 29 G5
Dewsbury U.K. 53°42N 1°37W 27 E5
Dexter U.S.A. 36°48N 89°57W 112 G3
Deyang China 31°3N 104°27E 78 E9
Dezfûl Iran 32°20N 48°30E 86 C7
Dezhneva, C. Russia 66°5N 169°40W 77 C20
Dezhou China 37°26N 116°18E 79 D12
Dhahran Si. Arabia 26°10N 50°7E 86 E7
Dhaka Bangla. 23°43N 90°26E 85 H17
Dhaka □ Bangla. 23°30N 90°0E 85 G17
Dhamār Yemen 14°30N 44°20E 89 E3
Dhamtari India 20°42N 81°35E 85 J12
Dhanbad India 23°50N 86°30E 85 H15
Dharwad India 15°30N 75°4E 84 M9
Dhaulagiri Nepal 28°39N 83°28E 85 E13
Dhenkanal India 20°45N 85°35E 85 J14
Dhuburi India 26°2N 89°59E 85 F16
Dhule India 20°58N 74°50E 84 J9
Diamantina Brazil 18°17S 43°40W 122 C2
Diamantina → Australia 26°45S 139°10E 98 F6
Diamantino Brazil 14°30S 56°30W 120 D4
Dibrugarh India 27°29N 94°55E 85 F19
Dickinson U.S.A. 46°53N 102°47W 110 A6
Didcot U.K. 51°36N 1°14W 30 C6
Diefenbaker, L. Canada 51°0N 106°55W 108 D9
Dieppe France 49°54N 1°4E 66 B4
Digby Canada 44°38N 65°50W 109 E13
Digne-les-Bains France 44°5N 6°12E 66 D7
Dijon France 47°20N 5°3E 66 C6
Dikson Russia 73°40N 80°5E 76 B9
Dili Timor-Leste 8°39S 125°34E 83 F7
Dillingham U.S.A. 59°3N 158°28W 108 D4
Dimitrovgrad Bulgaria 42°5N 25°35E 69 C11
Dimitrovgrad Russia 54°14N 49°39E 70 D8
Dinajpur Bangla. 25°33N 88°43E 85 G16
Dinan France 48°28N 2°2W 66 B2
Dinant Belgium 50°16N 4°55E 64 C3
Dinaric Alps Croatia 44°0N 16°30E 68 C7
Dinbych-y-Pysgod = Tenby U.K. 51°40N 4°42W 28 D4
Dingle Ireland 52°9N 10°17W 20 D2
Dingle B. Ireland 52°3N 10°20W 20 D2
Dingle Pen. Ireland 52°12N 10°5W 20 D2
Dingwall U.K. 57°36N 4°26W 23 G9
Dipolog Phil. 8°36N 123°20E 83 C6
Dire Dawa Ethiopia 9°35N 41°45E 89 F3
Dirranbandi Australia 28°33S 148°17E 98 F8
Disappointment, C. U.S.A. 46°18N 124°5W 110 A2
Disappointment, L. Australia 23°20S 122°40E 98 E3
Diss U.K. 52°23N 1°7E 31 B11
Distington U.K. 54°36N 3°32W 26 C1
Distrito Federal □ Brazil 15°45S 47°45W 122 C1
Ditchingham U.K. 52°28N 1°28E 31 B11
Ditchling Beacon U.K. 50°54N 0°6W 31 E8
Ditton Priors U.K. 52°30N 2°34W 27 H3
Diu India 20°45N 70°58E 84 J7
Divinópolis Brazil 20°10S 44°54W 122 D2
Dixon U.S.A. 41°50N 89°29W 112 E3
Dixon Entrance U.S.A. 54°30N 132°0W 108 D6
Diyarbakır Turkey 37°55N 40°18E 71 G7
Dizzard Pt. U.K. 50°44N 4°40W 29 F4
Djerba, Î. de Tunisia 33°50N 10°48E 95 B8
Djerid, Chott Tunisia 33°42N 8°30E 94 B7
Djibouti Djibouti 11°30N 43°5E 89 E3
Djibouti ■ Africa 12°0N 43°0E 89 E3
Djourab, Erg du Chad 16°40N 18°50E 95 E9
Dmitri Laptev Str. Russia 73°0N 140°0E 77 B15
Dnepropetrovsk = Dnipro Ukraine 48°30N 35°0E 71 E6
Dnieper → Ukraine 46°30N 32°18E 71 E5
Dniester → Europe 46°18N 30°17E 65 E16
Dnipro Ukraine 48°30N 35°0E 71 E6
Doba Chad 8°40N 16°50E 95 G9
Doberai, Jazirah Indonesia 1°25S 133°0E 83 E8
Dobrich Bulgaria 43°37N 27°49E 69 C12
Dobruja Europe 44°30N 28°15E 65 F15
Docking U.K. 52°54N 0°38E 31 A10
Doddington Cambs., U.K. 52°30N 0°3E 31 B9
Doddington Northumberland, U.K. 55°33N 1°54W 26 A5
Dodecanese Greece 36°35N 27°0E 69 F12
Dodge City U.S.A. 37°45N 100°1W 110 C6
Dodman Pt. U.K. 50°13N 4°48W 29 G4
Dodoma Tanzania 6°8S 35°45E 96 F7
Doha Qatar 25°15N 51°35E 87 E7
Dokdo = Liancourt Rocks Asia 37°15N 131°52E 81 E2
Dolbeau-Mistassini Canada 48°53N 72°14W 109 E12
Dole France 47°7N 5°31E 66 C6
Dolgarrog U.K. 53°11N 3°50W 28 A6
Dolgellau U.K. 52°45N 3°53W 28 B6
Dolo Ethiopia 4°11N 42°3E 89 G3
Dolomites Italy 46°23N 11°51E 68 A4
Dolores Argentina 36°20S 57°40W 121 F4
Dolphin and Union Str. Canada 69°5N 114°45W 108 C8
Dolphinton U.K. 55°42N 3°28W 25 C9
Dolton U.K. 50°53N 4°2W 29 F5
Dominica ■ W. Indies 15°20N 61°20W 115 D12
Dominican Rep. ■ W. Indies 19°0N 70°30W 115 D10
Don → Russia 47°4N 39°18E 71 E6
Don → Aberds., U.K. 57°11N 2°5W 23 H13
Don → S. Yorks., U.K. 53°41N 0°52W 27 E7
Don Figueroroa Mts. Jamaica 18°5N 77°36W 114 a
Donaghadee U.K. 54°39N 5°33W 19 B10
Doncaster U.K. 53°32N 1°6W 27 E6
Dondra Head Sri Lanka 5°55N 80°40E 84 S12
Donegal Ireland 54°39N 8°5W 18 B5
Donegal □ Ireland 54°53N 8°0W 18 B5
Donegal B. Ireland 54°31N 8°49W 18 B4
Donets → Russia 47°33N 40°55E 71 E7

Donetsk Ukraine 48°0N 37°45E 71 E6
Dong Hoi Vietnam 17°29N 106°36E 82 A3
Dongchuan China 26°8N 103°1E 78 F9
Dongguan China 22°58N 113°44E 79 G11
Dongola Sudan 19°9N 30°22E 95 E12
Dongsha Dao S. China Sea 20°45N 116°43E 79 G12
Dongting Hu China 29°18N 112°45E 79 F11
Donhead U.K. 51°1N 2°7W 30 D4
Donington U.K. 52°54N 0°12W 27 G8
Donna Nook U.K. 53°29N 0°8E 27 F9
Donostia-San Sebastián Spain 43°17N 1°58W 67 A5
Doon → U.K. 55°27N 4°39W 24 D6
Dorchester Dorset, U.K. 50°42N 2°27W 30 E4
Dorchester Oxon., U.K. 51°39N 1°10W 30 C6
Dorchester, C. Canada 65°27N 77°27W 109 C12
Dordogne → France 45°2N 0°36W 66 D3
Dordrecht Neths. 51°48N 4°39E 64 C3
Dores do Indaiá Brazil 19°27S 45°36W 122 C1
Dorking U.K. 51°14N 0°19W 31 D8
Dornie U.K. 57°17N 5°31W 22 H6
Dornoch U.K. 57°53N 4°2W 23 G9
Dornoch Firth U.K. 57°51N 4°4W 23 G9
Dörgön Nuur Mongolia 48°0N 93°0E 78 B7
Dorset □ U.K. 50°45N 2°26W 30 E4
Dorstone U.K. 52°3N 2°59W 30 B3
Dortmund Germany 51°30N 7°28E 64 C4
Dos Bahías, C. Argentina 44°58S 65°32W 121 G3
Dos Hermanas Spain 37°16N 5°55W 67 D3
Dothan U.S.A. 31°13N 85°24W 111 D9
Douai France 50°21N 3°4E 66 A5
Douala Cameroon 4°0N 9°45E 96 D1
Douglas Ireland 51°52N 8°25W 20 E6
Douglas I. of Man 54°10N 4°28W 19 C13
Douglas U.S.A. 31°21N 109°33W 110 D5
Dounreay U.K. 58°35N 3°44W 23 E10
Dourados Brazil 22°9S 54°50W 120 E4
Douro → Europe 41°8N 8°40W 67 B1
Dove → Derby, U.K. 52°51N 1°36W 27 G5
Dove → N. Yorks., U.K. 54°15N 0°55W 26 D7
Dove Dale U.K. 53°7N 1°46W 27 F5
Dover U.K. 51°7N 1°19E 31 D11
Dover Del., U.S.A. 39°10N 75°32W 113 F10
Dover N.H., U.S.A. 43°12N 70°56W 113 D12
Dover, Str. of Europe 51°0N 1°30E 62 F7
Dover-Foxcroft U.S.A. 45°11N 69°13W 113 C13
Doveridge U.K. 52°54N 1°49W 27 G5
Dovey = Dyfi → U.K. 52°32N 4°3W 28 B5
Dovrefjell Norway 62°15N 9°33E 63 E5
Downham U.K. 52°26N 0°14E 31 B9
Downham Market U.K. 52°37N 0°23E 31 A9
Downpatrick U.K. 54°20N 5°43W 19 C10
Downpatrick Hd. Ireland 54°20N 9°21W 18 C3
Downton U.K. 50°59N 1°44W 30 E5
Drâa, Oued → Morocco 28°40N 11°10W 94 C3
Draguignan France 43°32N 6°27E 66 E7
Drake Passage S. Ocean 58°0S 68°0W 55 B17
Drakensberg S. Africa 31°0S 28°0E 97 L5
Drammen Norway 59°42N 10°12E 63 F6
Drava → Croatia 45°33N 18°55E 69 B8
Dresden Germany 51°3N 13°44E 64 C7
Dreux France 48°44N 1°23E 66 B4
Driffield U.K. 54°0N 0°26W 27 D8
Drina → Bos.-H. 44°53N 19°21E 69 B8
Drobeta-Turnu Severin Romania 44°39N 22°41E 65 F12
Drogheda Ireland 53°43N 6°22W 19 D9
Drohobych Ukraine 49°20N 23°30E 71 E3
Droitwich U.K. 52°16N 2°8W 30 B4
Dromore U.K. 54°31N 7°28W 18 B7
Dromore West Ireland 54°15N 8°52W 18 C4
Dronfield U.K. 53°19N 1°27W 27 F6
Dronning Maud Land Antarctica 72°30S 12°0E 55 D3
Drum Hills Ireland 52°1N 7°45W 20 D7
Drumheller Canada 51°25N 112°40W 108 D8
Drummond I. U.S.A. 46°1N 83°39W 112 B5
Drummondville Canada 45°55N 72°25W 113 C11
Drumochter, Pass of U.K. 56°50N 4°15W 23 J9
Druridge B. U.K. 55°17N 1°32W 26 B5
Dry Harbour Mts. Jamaica 18°19N 77°24W 114 a
Dryden Canada 49°47N 92°50W 108 E10
Drygalski I. Antarctica 66°0S 92°0E 55 C7
Du Quoin U.S.A. 38°1N 89°14W 112 F3
Duarte, Pico Dom. Rep. 19°2N 70°59W 115 D10
Dubai U.A.E. 25°18N 55°20E 87 E8
Dubawnt → Canada 64°33N 100°6W 108 C9
Dubawnt L. Canada 63°8N 101°28W 108 C9
Dubbo Australia 32°11S 148°35E 98 G8
Dublin Ireland 53°21N 6°15W 21 B10
Dublin U.S.A. 32°32N 82°54W 111 D10
Dublin □ Ireland 53°24N 6°20W 21 B10
Dublin ✈ (DUB) Ireland 53°26N 6°15W 21 B10
DuBois U.S.A. 41°7N 78°46W 112 E8
Dubrovnik Croatia 42°39N 18°6E 69 C8
Dubuque U.S.A. 42°30N 90°41W 112 D2
Duddington U.K. 52°36N 0°32W 31 A7
Duddon → U.K. 54°12N 3°15W 26 D2
Dudinka Russia 69°30N 86°13E 77 C9
Dudley U.K. 52°31N 2°5W 27 G4
Duffield U.K. 52°59N 1°29W 27 G6
Dufftown U.K. 57°27N 3°8W 23 H11
Dugi Otok Croatia 44°0N 15°3E 68 C6
Duisburg Germany 51°26N 6°45E 64 C4
Dukinfield U.K. 53°28N 2°4W 27 F4
Dulce → Argentina 30°32S 62°33W 121 F3
Duluth U.S.A. 46°47N 92°6W 112 B1
Dulverton U.K. 51°2N 3°33W 29 E6
Dumaguete Phil. 9°17N 123°15E 83 C6
Dumbarton U.K. 55°57N 4°33W 24 C6
Dumfries U.K. 55°4N 3°37W 25 D8
Dumfries & Galloway □ U.K. 55°9N 3°58W 25 D8
Dumyât Egypt 31°24N 31°48E 95 B12
Dún Laoghaire Ireland 53°17N 6°8W 21 B10
Dunbar U.K. 56°0N 2°31W 25 B10
Dunblane U.K. 56°11N 3°58W 25 B8
Duncan U.S.A. 34°30N 97°57W 110 D7
Duncansby Head U.K. 58°38N 3°1W 23 E11
Dunchurch U.K. 52°21N 1°17W 30 B6
Dundalk Ireland 54°1N 6°24W 19 C9

Dundalk Bay Ireland 53°55N 6°15W 19 D9
Dundee U.K. 56°28N 2°59W 25 B10
Dundrum Ireland 53°18N 6°14W 21 B10
Dundrum U.K. 54°16N 5°52W 19 C10
Dundrum B. U.K. 54°13N 5°47W 19 C10
Dunedin N.Z. 45°50S 170°33E 99 K13
Dunfermline U.K. 56°5N 3°27W 25 B9
Dungannon U.K. 54°31N 6°46W 19 B8
Dungarvan Ireland 52°5N 7°37W 21 D7
Dungarvan Harbour Ireland 52°4N 7°35W 21 D7
Dungeness U.K. 50°54N 0°59E 31 E10
Dunhua China 43°20N 128°14E 79 C14
Dunhuang China 40°8N 94°36E 78 C7
Dunkeld U.K. 56°34N 3°35W 25 A8
Dunkerque France 51°2N 2°20E 66 A5
Dunkery Beacon U.K. 51°9N 3°36W 29 E6
Dunkirk U.S.A. 42°29N 79°20W 112 D8
Dunleer Ireland 53°50N 6°24W 19 D9
Dunmanway Ireland 51°43N 9°6W 20 E4
Dunmore U.S.A. 41°25N 75°38W 113 E10
Dunnet Hd. U.K. 58°40N 3°21W 23 E11
Dunoon U.K. 55°57N 4°56W 24 C6
Duns U.K. 55°47N 2°20W 25 C11
Dunsford U.K. 50°41N 3°42W 29 F6
Dunstable U.K. 51°53N 0°32W 31 C7
Dunster U.K. 51°11N 3°27W 30 D2
Dunston U.K. 52°46N 2°7W 27 G4
Dunvegan U.K. 57°27N 6°35W 22 H4
Duolun China 42°12N 116°28E 79 C12
Duque de Caxias Brazil 22°46S 43°18W 122 D2
Durance → France 43°55N 4°45E 66 E6
Durango Mexico 24°3N 104°39W 114 C4
Durango U.S.A. 37°16N 107°53W 110 C5
Durant U.S.A. 33°59N 96°25W 111 D7
Durazno Uruguay 33°25S 56°31W 121 F4
Durban S. Africa 29°49S 31°1E 97 K6
Düren Germany 50°48N 6°29E 64 C4
Durgapur India 23°30N 87°20E 85 H15
Durham U.K. 54°47N 1°34W 26 C5
Durham U.S.A. 35°59N 78°54W 111 C11
Durham □ U.K. 54°42N 1°45W 26 C5
Durlston Hd. U.K. 50°36N 1°57W 30 E5
Durness U.K. 58°34N 4°45W 23 E8
Durrës Albania 41°19N 19°28E 69 D8
Durrington U.K. 51°12N 1°47W 30 D5
Durrow Ireland 52°51N 7°24W 21 C8
Dursey I. Ireland 51°36N 10°12W 20 E2
Dursley U.K. 51°40N 2°21W 30 C4
Dushanbe Tajikistan 38°33N 68°48E 87 B12
Düsseldorf Germany 51°14N 6°47E 64 C4
Dutch Harbor U.S.A. 53°53N 166°32W 108 D3
Duyun China 26°18N 107°29E 78 F10
Dvina, N. → Russia 64°32N 40°30E 70 B7
Dvina B. Russia 65°0N 39°0E 70 B6
Dwarka India 22°18N 69°8E 84 H6
Dyce U.K. 57°13N 2°12W 23 H13
Dyer, C. Canada 66°37N 61°16W 109 C13
Dyersburg U.S.A. 36°3N 89°23W 111 C9
Dyfi → U.K. 52°32N 4°3W 28 B5
Dymchurch U.K. 51°1N 1°0E 31 D11
Dymock U.K. 51°59N 2°26W 30 C4
Dzavhan Gol → Mongolia 48°54N 93°23E 78 B7
Dzerzhinsk Russia 56°14N 43°30E 70 C7
Dzhankoy Ukraine 45°40N 34°20E 71 E5
Dzhugdzhur Ra. Russia 57°30N 138°0E 77 D14
Dzungarian Basin China 44°30N 86°0E 78 B6
Dzungarian Gate Asia 45°10N 82°0E 78 B5
Dzüünmod Mongolia 47°45N 106°58E 78 B10

E
Eagle U.S.A. 64°47N 141°12W 108 C5
Eagle L. U.S.A. 46°20N 69°22W 113 B13
Eagle Pass U.S.A. 28°43N 100°30W 110 E6
Eagle River U.S.A. 47°25N 88°18W 112 B3
Eaglesfield U.K. 55°4N 3°12W 25 D9
Eakring U.K. 53°9N 0°58W 27 F7
Ealing □ U.K. 51°31N 0°20W 31 C8
Earby U.K. 53°55N 2°7W 27 E4
Eardisley U.K. 52°8N 3°1W 30 B2
Earith U.K. 52°22N 0°2E 31 B9
Earl Shilton U.K. 52°35N 1°18W 27 G6
Earl Soham U.K. 52°14N 1°18E 31 B11
Earls Barton U.K. 52°16N 0°45W 31 B7
Earl's Colne U.K. 51°56N 0°43E 31 C10
Earlston U.K. 55°39N 2°40W 25 C10
Earn → U.K. 56°21N 3°18W 25 B9
Earn, L. U.K. 56°23N 4°13W 24 B7
Earsdon U.K. 55°3N 1°29W 26 B6
Easebourne U.K. 51°0N 0°43W 31 E7
Easington Durham, U.K. 54°47N 1°21W 26 C6
Easington E. Riding, U.K. 53°39N 0°6E 27 E9
Easington Colliery U.K. 54°48N 1°19W 26 C6
Easingwold U.K. 54°8N 1°11W 26 D6
East Ayrshire □ U.K. 55°26N 4°11W 24 C7
East Bengal Bangla. 24°0N 90°0E 85 H17
East Bergholt U.K. 51°59N 1°3E 31 C11
East Beskids Europe 49°20N 22°0E 65 D11
East Brent U.K. 51°15N 2°56W 30 D3
East C. = Dezhneva, C. Russia 66°5N 169°40W 77 C20
East China Sea Asia 30°0N 126°0E 79 F14
East Cowes U.K. 50°45N 1°16W 30 E6
East Falkland Falk. Is. 51°30S 58°30W 121 H4
East Fen U.K. 53°4N 0°5E 27 F9
East Grinstead U.K. 51°7N 0°0 31 D9
East Harling U.K. 52°26N 0°56E 31 B10
East Ilsley U.K. 51°33N 1°16W 30 C6
East Indies Asia 0°0 120°0E 72 J14
East Kilbride U.K. 55°47N 4°11W 24 C7
East Lansing U.S.A. 42°44N 84°29W 112 D5
East London S. Africa 33°0S 27°55E 97 L5
East Lothian □ U.K. 55°58N 2°44W 25 C10
East Markham U.K. 53°15N 0°53W 27 F7
East Moor U.K. 53°16N 1°34W 27 F5
East Pt. Canada 46°27N 61°58W 113 B17
East St. Louis U.S.A. 38°37N 90°9W 112 F3
East Sea = Japan, Sea of Asia 40°0N 135°0E 81 D4
East Siberian Sea Russia 73°0N 160°0E 77 B17
East Sussex □ U.K. 50°56N 0°19E 31 E9
East Timor = Timor-Leste ■ Asia 8°50S 126°0E 83 F7

East Wittering U.K. 50°46N 0°52W **31 E7**
East Woodhay U.K. 51°21N 1°25W **30 D6**
Eastbourne U.K. 50°46N 0°18E **31 E9**
Eastchurch U.K. 51°24N 0°53E **31 D10**
Eastern Desert Egypt 27°30N 32°30E **95 C12**
Eastern Ghats India 14°0N 78°50E **84 N11**
Eastern Group Fiji 17°0S 178°30W **99 D15**
Eastleigh U.K. 50°58N 1°21W **30 E6**
Eastmain Canada 52°10N 78°30W **109 D12**
Eastmain → Canada 52°27N 78°26W **109 D12**
Eastnor U.K. 52°2N 2°23W **30 B4**
Easton Dorset, U.K. 50°33N 2°26W **30 E4**
Easton N. Northants., U.K. 52°37N 0°31W **31 A7**
Easton Md., U.S.A. 38°47N 76°5W **113 F9**
Easton Pa., U.S.A. 40°41N 75°13W **113 E10**
Easton-in-Gordano U.K. 51°28N 2°42W **30 D3**
Eastport U.S.A. 44°56N 67°0W **113 C14**
Eastry U.K. 51°14N 1°19E **31 D11**
Eastwood U.K. 53°1N 1°18W **27 F6**
Eaton U.K. 52°51N 0°49W **27 G7**
Eaton Socon U.K. 52°14N 0°17W **31 B8**
Eau Claire U.S.A. 44°49N 91°30W **112 C2**
Eau Claire, L. à l' Canada 56°10N 74°25W **109 D12**
Ebberston U.K. 54°14N 0°37W **26 D7**
Ebbw Vale U.K. 51°46N 3°12W **28 D7**
Eberswalde-Finow Germany 52°50N 13°49E **64 B7**
Ebetsu Japan 43°7N 141°34E **81 B7**
Ebinur Hu China 44°55N 82°55E **78 C5**
Ebolowa Cameroon 2°55N 11°10E **96 D2**
Ebro → Spain 40°43N 0°54E **67 B6**
Ecclefechan U.K. 55°4N 3°16W **25 D9**
Eccleshall U.K. 52°52N 2°15W **27 G4**
Ech Chélif Algeria 36°10N 1°20E **94 A6**
Echo Bay Canada 66°5N 117°55W **108 C8**
Eckington U.K. 53°18N 1°22W **27 F6**
Eclipse Sd. Canada 72°38N 79°0W **109 B12**
Ecuador ■ S. Amer. 2°0S 78°0W **120 C2**
Ed Damazin Sudan 11°46N 34°21E **95 F12**
Eday U.K. 59°11N 2°47W **23 D12**
Eddrachillis B. U.K. 58°17N 5°14W **22 F7**
Eddystone U.K. 50°11N 4°16W **29 G5**
Eden → U.K. 54°57N 3°1W **26 C2**
Edenbridge U.K. 51°12N 0°5E **31 D9**
Edenderry Ireland 53°21N 7°4W **21 B8**
Edfu Egypt 24°55N 32°49E **95 D12**
Edge Hill U.K. 52°8N 1°26W **30 B6**
Edinburgh U.K. 55°57N 3°13W **25 C9**
Edinburgh ✈ (EDI) U.K. 55°54N 3°22W **25 C9**
Edington U.K. 51°17N 2°5W **30 D4**
Edirne Turkey 41°40N 26°34E **71 F4**
Edmonton Canada 53°30N 113°30W **108 D8**
Edmundbyers U.K. 54°50N 1°58W **26 C5**
Edmundston Canada 47°23N 68°20W **109 E13**
Edremit Turkey 39°34N 27°0E **86 B1**
Edson Canada 53°35N 116°28W **108 D8**
Edward, L. Africa 0°25S 29°40E **96 E5**
Edward VII Land Antarctica 80°0S 150°0W **55 E13**
Edwards Plateau U.S.A. 30°45N 101°20W **110 D6**
Effingham U.S.A. 39°7N 88°33W **112 F3**
Égadi, Ísole Italy 37°55N 12°16E **68 F5**
Eganville Canada 45°32N 77°5W **112 C9**
Eger Hungary 47°53N 20°27E **65 E11**
Egham U.K. 51°25N 0°32W **31 D7**
Eglinton I. Canada 75°48N 118°30W **109 B8**
Egremont U.K. 54°29N 3°32W **26 D1**
Eğridir Turkey 37°52N 30°51E **71 G5**
Eğridir Gölü Turkey 37°53N 30°50E **71 G5**
Egton U.K. 54°28N 0°44W **26 D7**
Egypt ■ Africa 28°0N 31°0E **95 C12**
Eifel Germany 50°15N 6°50E **64 C4**
Eigg U.K. 56°54N 6°10W **22 J5**
Eil, L. U.K. 56°51N 5°16W **22 J7**
Eilat Israel 29°30N 34°56E **86 D3**
Eilean Siar □ U.K. 57°30N 7°10W **22 G3**
Eindhoven Neths. 51°26N 5°28E **64 C3**
Eire = Ireland ■ Europe 53°50N 7°52W **62 E2**
Eiriosgaigh = Eriskay U.K. 57°4N 7°18W **22 H3**
Eivissa Spain 38°54N 1°26E **67 C6**
Ekaterinburg Russia 56°50N 60°30E **76 D7**
Ekibastuz Kazakhstan 51°50N 75°10E **76 D8**
El Aaiún W. Sahara 27°9N 13°12W **94 C3**
El Alamein Egypt 30°48N 28°58E **95 B11**
El Centro U.S.A. 32°48N 115°34W **110 D3**
El Djouf Mauritania 21°25N 6°40W **94 D4**
El Dorado U.S.A. 33°12N 92°40W **111 D8**
El Faiyûm Egypt 29°19N 30°50E **95 C12**
El Fâsher Sudan 13°33N 25°26E **95 F11**
El Fuerte Mexico 26°25N 108°39W **114 B3**
El Geneina Sudan 13°27N 22°45E **95 F10**
El Gezira □ Sudan 15°0N 33°0E **95 F12**
El Giza Egypt 30°0N 31°12E **95 C12**
El Istiwa'iya Sudan 5°0N 28°0E **95 G11**
El Jadida Morocco 33°11N 8°17W **94 B4**
El Khârga Egypt 25°30N 30°33E **95 C12**
El Mahalla el Kubra Egypt 31°0N 31°0E **95 B12**
El Mansûra Egypt 31°0N 31°19E **95 B12**
El Minyâ Egypt 28°7N 30°33E **95 C12**
El Obeid Sudan 13°8N 30°10E **95 F12**
El Oued Algeria 33°20N 6°58E **94 B7**
El Paso U.S.A. 31°45N 106°29W **110 D5**
El Puerto de Santa María Spain 36°36N 6°13W **67 D2**
El Reno U.S.A. 35°32N 97°57W **110 C7**
El Salvador ■ Cent. Amer. 13°50N 89°0W **114 E7**
El Tigre Venezuela 8°44N 64°15W **120 B3**
El Uqsur Egypt 25°41N 32°38E **95 C12**
Elâzığ Turkey 38°37N 39°14E **71 G6**
Elba Italy 42°46N 10°17E **68 C4**
Elbasan Albania 41°9N 20°9E **69 D9**
Elbe → Europe 53°50N 9°0E **64 B5**
Elbert, Mt. U.S.A. 39°7N 106°27W **110 C5**
Elbeuf France 49°17N 1°2E **66 B4**
Elblag Poland 54°10N 19°25E **65 A10**
Elbrus Russia 43°21N 42°30E **71 F7**
Elburz Mts. Iran 36°0N 52°0E **87 B8**
Elche Spain 38°15N 0°42W **67 C5**
Elda Spain 38°29N 0°47W **67 C5**
Eldoret Kenya 0°30N 35°17E **96 D7**
Elektrostal Russia 55°41N 38°32E **70 C6**
Elephant Butte Res. U.S.A. 33°9N 107°11W **110 D5**
Elephant I. Antarctica 61°0S 55°0W **55 C18**

Eleuthera The Bahamas 25°0N 76°20W **115 C9**
Elgin U.K. 57°39N 3°19W **23 G11**
Elgin U.S.A. 42°2N 88°17W **112 D3**
Elgon, Mt. Africa 1°10N 34°30E **96 D6**
Elham U.K. 51°9N 1°8E **31 D11**
Elishaw U.K. 55°15N 2°14W **26 B4**
Elizabeth U.S.A. 40°39N 74°12W **113 E10**
Elizabeth City U.S.A. 36°18N 76°14W **111 C11**
Elizabethtown U.S.A. 37°42N 85°52W **112 G5**
Elkhart U.S.A. 41°41N 85°58W **112 E5**
Elkins U.S.A. 38°55N 79°51W **112 F8**
Elko U.S.A. 40°50N 115°46W **110 B3**
Elland U.K. 53°41N 1°50W **27 E5**
Ellef Ringnes I. Canada 78°30N 102°2W **109 B9**
Ellen → U.K. 54°44N 3°30W **26 C2**
Ellensburg U.S.A. 46°59N 120°34W **110 A2**
Ellerton Barbados 13°7N 59°33W **114 c**
Ellesmere U.K. 52°55N 2°53W **27 G3**
Ellesmere I. Canada 79°30N 80°0W **109 B12**
Ellesmere Port U.K. 53°17N 2°54W **27 F3**
Ellington U.K. 55°14N 1°33W **26 B5**
Elliot Lake Canada 46°25N 82°35W **109 E11**
Ellon U.K. 57°22N 2°4W **23 H13**
Ellsworth Land Antarctica 76°0S 89°0W **55 D16**
Elmalı Turkey 36°44N 29°56E **71 G4**
Elmira U.S.A. 42°6N 76°48W **112 D9**
Elmswell U.K. 52°15N 0°55E **31 B10**
Eluru India 16°48N 81°8E **85 L12**
Ely U.K. 52°24N 0°16E **31 B9**
Ely U.S.A. 39°15N 114°54W **110 C4**
Elyria U.S.A. 41°22N 82°7W **112 E6**
eMalahleni S. Africa 25°51S 29°14E **97 K5**
Emämrüd Iran 36°30N 55°0E **87 B8**
Embarcación Argentina 23°10S 64°0W **121 E3**
Embleton U.K. 55°29N 1°38W **26 B5**
Emden Germany 53°21N 7°12E **64 B4**
Emerald Australia 37°56S 145°29E **98 E8**
Emmen Neths. 52°48N 6°57E **64 B4**
Emmonak U.S.A. 62°47N 164°31W **108 C3**
Empalme Mexico 27°58N 110°51W **114 B2**
Empangeni S. Africa 28°50S 31°52E **97 K6**
Empedrado Argentina 28°0S 58°46W **121 E4**
Emporia U.S.A. 38°25N 96°11W **111 C7**
Emporium U.S.A. 41°31N 78°14W **112 E8**
Empty Quarter = Rub' al Khālī Si. Arabia 19°0N 48°0E **89 D4**
Ems → Germany 53°20N 7°12E **64 B4**
En Nahud Sudan 12°45N 28°25E **95 F11**
Enard B. U.K. 58°5N 5°20W **22 F7**
Encarnación Paraguay 27°15S 55°50W **121 E4**
Encounter B. Australia 35°45S 138°45E **98 H6**
Ende Indonesia 8°45S 121°40E **83 F6**
Enderbury Kiribati 3°8S 171°5W **102 H10**
Enderby U.K. 52°36N 1°13W **27 G6**
Enderby Land Antarctica 66°0S 53°0E **55 C5**
Endicott U.S.A. 42°6N 76°4W **113 D9**
Enewetak Atoll Marshall Is. 11°30N 162°15E **102 F8**
Enez Turkey 40°45N 26°5E **71 F4**
Enfield □ U.K. 51°38N 0°5W **31 C8**
Engadin Switz. 46°45N 10°10E **64 E6**
Engels Russia 51°28N 46°6E **71 D8**
Enggano Indonesia 5°20S 102°40E **82 F2**
England □ U.K. 53°0N 2°0W **62 E6**
English → Canada 49°12N 91°5W **108 D10**
English Channel Europe 50°0N 2°0W **62 F6**
Enid U.S.A. 36°24N 97°53W **110 C7**
Ennadai L. Canada 60°58N 101°20W **108 C9**
Ennedi Chad 17°15N 22°0E **95 E10**
Ennerdale Water U.K. 54°32N 3°24W **26 C2**
Ennis Ireland 52°51N 8°59W **20 C5**
Enniscorthy Ireland 52°30N 6°34W **21 D9**
Enniskillen U.K. 54°21N 7°39W **18 C6**
Ennistymon Ireland 52°57N 9°17W **20 C4**
Enns → Austria 48°14N 14°32E **64 D8**
Enschede Neths. 52°13N 6°53E **64 B4**
Ensenada Mexico 31°52N 116°37W **114 A1**
Enshi China 30°18N 109°29E **79 E10**
Enstone U.K. 51°55N 1°27W **30 C6**
Entebbe Uganda 0°4N 32°28E **96 D6**
Entre Ríos □ Argentina 30°30S 58°30W **121 F4**
Enugu Nigeria 6°30N 7°30E **94 G7**
Eólie, Ís. Italy 38°30N 14°57E **68 E6**
Épernay France 49°3N 3°56E **66 B5**
Épinal France 48°10N 6°27E **66 B7**
Epping U.K. 51°41N 0°7E **31 C9**
Epping Forest U.K. 51°40N 0°5E **31 C9**
Epsom U.K. 51°19N 0°16W **31 D8**
Epworth U.K. 53°32N 0°48W **27 E7**
Equatorial Guinea ■ Africa 2°0N 8°0E **96 D1**
Er Rachidia Morocco 31°58N 4°20W **94 B5**
Ercıyaş Dağı Turkey 38°30N 35°30E **86 B3**
Erebus, Mt. Antarctica 77°35S 167°0E **55 D11**
Ereğli Konya, Turkey 37°31N 34°4E **71 G5**
Ereğli Zonguldak, Turkey 41°15N 31°24E **71 F5**
Erenhot China 43°48N 112°2E **79 C11**
Erfurt Germany 50°58N 11°2E **64 C6**
Ergeni Lowlands Russia 47°0N 44°0E **71 E7**
Eriboll, L. U.K. 58°30N 4°42W **23 E8**
Erie U.S.A. 42°8N 80°5W **112 D7**
Erie, L. N. Amer. 42°15N 81°0W **112 D7**
Eriskay U.K. 57°4N 7°18W **22 H3**
Eritrea ■ Africa 14°0N 38°30E **89 D2**
Erlangen Germany 49°36N 11°0E **64 D6**
Ermoupoli Greece 37°28N 24°57E **69 F11**
Ernakulam India 9°59N 76°22E **84 Q10**
Erne → Ireland 54°30N 8°16W **18 C5**
Erne, Lower L. U.K. 54°28N 7°47W **18 C6**
Erne, Upper L. U.K. 54°14N 7°32W **18 C6**
Erode India 11°24N 77°45E **84 P10**
Erramala Hills India 15°30N 78°15E **84 M11**
Errigal Ireland 55°2N 8°6W **18 A5**
Erris Hd. Ireland 54°17N 10°0W **18 C1**
Erromango Vanuatu 18°45S 169°5E **99 D12**
Erzgebirge Germany 50°27N 12°55E **64 C7**
Erzincan Turkey 39°46N 39°30E **71 G6**
Erzurum Turkey 39°57N 41°15E **71 G7**
Esbjerg Denmark 55°29N 8°29E **63 F5**
Escanaba U.S.A. 45°45N 87°4W **112 C4**
Esch-sur-Alzette Lux. 49°32N 6°0E **64 D3**

Escrick U.K. 53°53N 1°2W **27 E6**
Escuinapa de Hidalgo Mexico 22°50N 105°50W **114 C3**
Escuintla Guatemala 14°20N 90°48W **114 E6**
Eşfahān Iran 32°39N 51°43E **87 C7**
Esha Ness U.K. 60°29N 1°38W **22 B14**
Esk → Cumb., U.K. 54°20N 3°24W **26 D2**
Esk → Dumf. & Gall., U.K. 54°58N 3°2W **25 E9**
Esk → N. Yorks., U.K. 54°30N 0°37W **26 D7**
Eskdale U.K. 55°12N 3°4W **25 D9**
Esker Siding Canada 53°53N 66°25W **109 D13**
Eskilstuna Sweden 59°22N 16°32E **63 F7**
Eskişehir Turkey 39°50N 30°30E **71 G5**
Eslāmābād-e Gharb Iran 34°10N 46°30E **86 C6**
Esna Egypt 25°17N 32°30E **95 C12**
Esperance Australia 33°45S 121°55E **98 G3**
Espinhaço, Serra do Brazil 17°30S 43°30W **122 C2**
Espírito Santo □ Brazil 20°0S 40°45W **122 C2**
Espíritu Santo Vanuatu 15°15S 166°50E **99 D12**
Espoo Finland 60°12N 24°40E **63 E8**
Essaouira Morocco 31°32N 9°42W **94 B4**
Essen Germany 51°28N 7°2E **64 C4**
Essequibo → Guyana 6°50N 58°30W **120 B4**
Essex □ U.K. 51°54N 0°27E **31 C9**
Esslingen Germany 48°44N 9°18E **64 D5**
Estância, I. de Los Argentina 54°40S 64°30W **121 H3**
Estância Brazil 11°16S 37°26W **122 B3**
Estevan Canada 49°10N 102°59W **108 E9**
Eston U.K. 54°34N 1°8W **26 C6**
Estonia ■ Europe 58°30N 25°30E **63 F8**
Estrela, Serra da Portugal 40°10N 7°45W **67 B2**
Estrondo, Serra do Brazil 7°20S 48°0W **120 C5**
Eswatini ■ Africa 26°30S 31°30E **97 K6**
Etawah India 26°48N 79°6E **84 F11**
Etchingham U.K. 51°0N 0°26E **31 D9**
Ethiopia ■ Africa 8°0N 40°0E **89 F3**
Ethiopian Highlands Ethiopia 10°0N 37°0E **89 F2**
Etive, L. U.K. 56°29N 5°10W **24 B5**
Etna Italy 37°50N 14°55E **68 F6**
Eton U.K. 51°30N 0°36W **31 C7**
Etosha Pan Namibia 18°40S 16°30E **97 H3**
Ettington U.K. 52°8N 1°35W **30 B5**
Ettrick Forest U.K. 55°30N 3°0W **25 C9**
Ettrick Water → U.K. 55°31N 2°55W **25 C10**
Euclid U.S.A. 41°34N 81°32W **112 E7**
Eugene U.S.A. 44°5N 123°4W **110 B2**
Euphrates → Asia 31°0N 47°25E **86 D6**
Eureka Canada 80°0N 85°56W **109 B11**
Eureka U.S.A. 40°47N 124°9W **110 B2**
Europa, Île Ind. Oc. 22°20S 40°22E **97 J8**
Europa, Picos de Spain 43°10N 4°49W **67 A3**
Europe 50°0N 20°0E **56 E10**
Eurotunnel Terminal U.K. 51°6N 1°10E **31 D11**
Euxton U.K. 53°41N 2°41W **27 E3**
Evanston Ill., U.S.A. 42°3N 87°40W **112 D4**
Evanston Wyo., U.S.A. 41°16N 110°58W **110 B4**
Evansville U.S.A. 37°58N 87°35W **112 G4**
Evercreech U.K. 51°9N 2°30W **30 D4**
Everest, Mt. Nepal 28°5N 86°58E **85 E15**
Everett U.S.A. 47°59N 122°12W **110 A2**
Everglades, The U.S.A. 25°50N 81°0W **111 E10**
Evesham U.K. 52°6N 1°56W **30 B5**
Evia Greece 38°30N 24°0E **69 E11**
Évora Portugal 38°33N 7°57W **67 C2**
Évreux France 49°3N 1°8E **66 B4**
Evros → Greece 41°40N 26°34E **69 D12**
Ewe, L. U.K. 57°49N 5°38W **22 G6**
Ewell U.K. 51°20N 0°14W **31 D8**
Ewhurst U.K. 51°9N 0°25W **31 D8**
Exe → U.K. 50°41N 3°29W **29 F7**
Exeter U.K. 50°43N 3°31W **29 F6**
Exminster U.K. 50°40N 3°29W **29 F7**
Exmoor △ U.K. 51°8N 3°42W **29 E6**
Exmouth U.K. 50°37N 3°25W **29 F7**
Exton U.K. 52°42N 0°38W **27 G7**
Extremadura □ Spain 39°30N 6°5W **67 C2**
Eyam U.K. 53°17N 1°40W **27 F5**
Eyasi, L. Tanzania 3°30S 35°0E **96 E6**
Eye Cambs., U.K. 52°37N 0°11W **31 A8**
Eye Suffolk, U.K. 52°19N 1°9E **31 B11**
Eyemouth U.K. 55°52N 2°5W **25 C11**
Eyjafjallajökull Iceland 63°38N 19°36W **63 B2**
Eynsham U.K. 51°47N 1°22W **30 C6**
Eyre Pen. Australia 33°30S 136°17E **98 G6**

F

Faenza Italy 44°17N 11°53E **68 B4**
Fair Hd. U.K. 55°14N 6°9W **19 A9**
Fair Isle U.K. 59°32N 1°38W **22 C14**
Fairbanks U.S.A. 64°51N 147°43W **108 C5**
Fairfield U.S.A. 38°23N 88°22W **112 F3**
Fairford U.K. 51°43N 1°46W **30 C5**
Fairlight U.K. 50°52N 0°40E **31 E10**
Fairmont U.S.A. 39°29N 80°9W **112 F7**
Fairweather, Mt. U.S.A. 58°55N 137°32W **108 D6**
Faisalabad Pakistan 31°30N 73°5E **84 D8**
Faizabad India 26°45N 82°10E **85 F13**
Fakenham U.K. 52°51N 0°51E **31 A10**
Falcon Res. U.S.A. 26°34N 99°10W **110 E7**
Faldingworth U.K. 53°21N 0°24W **27 F8**
Falkirk U.K. 56°0N 3°47W **25 C8**
Falkland U.K. 56°16N 3°12W **25 B9**
Falkland Is. ☒ Atl. Oc. 51°30S 59°0W **121 H4**
Fall River U.S.A. 41°43N 71°10W **113 E12**
Falmouth Jamaica 18°30N 77°40W **114 a**
Falmouth U.K. 50°9N 5°5W **29 G3**
Falmouth B. U.K. 50°6N 5°5W **29 G3**
Falstone U.K. 55°11N 2°26W **26 B4**
Falun Sweden 60°37N 15°37E **63 E7**
Famagusta Cyprus 35°8N 33°55E **86 C3**
Fanad Ireland 55°7N 7°38W **18 A6**
Fanad Hd. Ireland 55°17N 7°38W **18 A6**
Fannich, L. U.K. 57°38N 4°59W **23 G8**
Fano Italy 43°50N 13°1E **68 C5**
Far East Asia 40°0N 130°0E **72 E14**
Farāh Afghan. 32°20N 62°7E **87 C10**
Farasān Si. Arabia 16°45N 41°55E **89 D3**
Fareham U.K. 50°51N 1°11W **30 E6**
Farewell, C. Greenland 59°48N 43°55W **54 D5**

Fargo U.S.A. 46°53N 96°48W **111 A7**
Farg'ona Uzbekistan 40°23N 71°19E **76 E7**
Faridabad India 28°26N 77°19E **84 E10**
Faringdon U.K. 51°39N 1°34W **30 C5**
Farmington U.S.A. 36°44N 108°12W **110 C5**
Farmville U.S.A. 37°18N 78°24W **112 G8**
Farnborough U.K. 51°16N 0°45W **31 D7**
Farne Is. U.K. 55°38N 1°37W **26 A5**
Farnham U.K. 51°13N 0°47W **31 D7**
Farnworth U.K. 53°34N 2°25W **27 E4**
Faro Canada 62°11N 133°22W **108 C6**
Faro Portugal 37°2N 7°55W **67 D2**
Faroe Is. ☒ Atl. Oc. 62°0N 7°0W **57 C4**
Färs □ Iran 29°30N 55°0E **87 D8**
Faslane U.K. 56°5N 4°49W **24 B6**
Fataka Solomon Is. 11°55S 170°12E **99 C12**
Fatehgarh India 27°25N 79°35E **84 F11**
Fatehpur Raj., India 28°0N 74°40E **84 F9**
Fatehpur U. P., India 25°56N 81°13E **85 G12**
Fauldhouse U.K. 55°50N 3°43W **25 C8**
Faversham U.K. 51°19N 0°56E **31 D10**
Fawley U.K. 50°50N 1°20W **30 E6**
Fayetteville Ark., U.S.A. 36°4N 94°10W **111 C8**
Fayetteville N.C., U.S.A. 35°3N 78°53W **111 D11**
Fazeley U.K. 52°37N 1°40W **27 G5**
Fazilka India 30°27N 74°2E **84 D9**
Fdérik Mauritania 22°40N 12°45W **94 D3**
Feale → Ireland 52°27N 9°37W **20 D3**
Fear, C., U.S.A. 33°50N 77°58W **111 D11**
Fécamp France 49°45N 0°22E **66 B4**
Fehmarn Germany 54°27N 11°7E **64 A6**
Feira de Santana Brazil 12°15S 38°57W **122 B3**
Felipe Carrillo Puerto Mexico 19°38N 88°3W **114 D7**
Felixstowe U.K. 51°58N 1°23E **31 C11**
Felton U.K. 55°18N 1°42W **26 B5**
Feltwell U.K. 52°30N 0°32E **31 B10**
Fenny Bentley U.K. 53°3N 1°45W **27 F5**
Fenny Compton U.K. 52°10N 1°23W **30 B6**
Fenny Stratford U.K. 52°0N 0°44W **31 C7**
Fens, The U.K. 52°38N 0°2W **31 B8**
Fenyang China 37°18N 111°48E **79 D11**
Feodosiya Ukraine 45°2N 35°16E **71 E6**
Fergus Falls U.S.A. 46°17N 96°4W **111 A7**
Ferkéssédougou Côte d'Ivoire 9°35N 5°6W **94 G4**
Fermanagh & Omagh □ U.K. 54°34N 7°24W **18 C6**
Fermont Canada 52°47N 67°5W **109 D13**
Fermoy Ireland 52°9N 8°16W **20 D6**
Fernhurst U.K. 51°3N 0°43W **31 D7**
Ferrara Italy 44°50N 11°35E **68 B4**
Ferret, C. France 44°38N 1°15W **66 D3**
Ferrol Spain 43°29N 8°15W **67 A1**
Ferryhill U.K. 54°41N 1°33W **26 C5**
Fès Morocco 34°0N 5°0W **94 B5**
Fethiye Turkey 36°36N 29°6E **71 G4**
Fetlar U.K. 60°36N 0°52W **22 A16**
Feuilles → Canada 58°47N 70°4W **109 D12**
Feyzābād Afghan. 37°7N 70°33E **87 B12**
Fezzan Libya 27°0N 13°0E **95 C8**
Ffestiniog U.K. 52°57N 3°55W **28 B6**
Fianarantsoa Madag. 21°26S 47°5E **97 J9**
Fife □ U.K. 56°16N 3°1W **25 B9**
Fife Ness U.K. 56°17N 2°35W **25 B10**
Figeac France 44°37N 2°2E **66 D5**
Figueres Spain 42°18N 2°58E **67 A7**
Fiji ■ Pac. Oc. 17°20S 179°0E **99 D14**
Filby U.K. 52°40N 1°39E **31 A12**
Filey U.K. 54°12N 0°18W **26 D8**
Filey B. U.K. 54°12N 0°15W **26 D8**
Filton U.K. 51°30N 2°34W **30 C3**
Fincham U.K. 52°38N 0°30E **31 A9**
Findhorn → U.K. 57°38N 3°38W **23 G10**
Findlay U.S.A. 41°2N 83°39W **112 E6**
Finedon U.K. 52°21N 0°39W **31 B7**
Fingal's Cave U.K. 56°27N 6°21W **24 B3**
Finglas Ireland 53°23N 6°19W **21 B10**
Finike Turkey 36°21N 30°10E **86 B2**
Finland ■ Europe 63°0N 27°0E **63 E9**
Finland, G. of Europe 60°0N 26°0E **63 F9**
Finlay → Canada 57°0N 125°10W **108 D7**
Finn → Ireland 54°51N 7°28W **18 B7**
Firozabad India 27°10N 78°25E **84 F11**
Firozpur India 30°55N 74°40E **84 D9**
Fish → Namibia 28°7S 17°10E **97 K3**
Fishguard U.K. 52°0N 4°58W **28 D4**
Fishtoft U.K. 52°58N 0°1E **27 G9**
Fisterra, C. Spain 42°50N 9°19W **67 A1**
Fitchburg U.S.A. 42°35N 71°48W **113 D12**
Flagstaff U.S.A. 35°12N 111°39W **110 C4**
Flamborough U.K. 54°7N 0°7W **26 D8**
Flamborough Hd. U.K. 54°10N 0°5W **26 D8**
Flandre Europe 50°50N 2°30E **64 C2**
Flathead L. U.S.A. 47°51N 114°8W **110 A4**
Flattery, C., U.S.A. 48°23N 124°29W **110 A2**
Fleet U.K. 51°17N 0°50W **31 D7**
Fleetwood U.K. 53°55N 3°1W **27 E2**
Flensburg Germany 54°47N 9°27E **64 A5**
Flers France 48°47N 0°33W **66 B3**
Flimby U.K. 54°42N 3°30W **26 C2**
Flin Flon Canada 54°46N 101°53W **108 D9**
Flinders → Australia 17°36S 140°36E **98 D7**
Flinders I. Australia 40°0S 148°0E **98 H8**
Flinders Ranges Australia 31°30S 138°30E **98 G6**
Flint U.K. 53°15N 3°8W **28 A7**
Flint U.S.A. 43°1N 83°41W **112 D6**
Flint → U.S.A. 30°57N 84°34W **111 D10**
Flint I. Kiribati 11°26S 151°48W **103 J12**
Flintshire □ U.K. 53°17N 3°17W **28 A7**
Flitwick U.K. 52°0N 0°30W **31 C8**
Flodden U.K. 55°37N 2°8W **26 A4**
Flora U.S.A. 38°40N 88°29W **112 F3**
Florence Italy 43°46N 11°15E **68 C4**
Florence U.S.A. 34°12N 79°46W **111 D11**
Florencia Colombia 1°36N 75°36W **120 B2**
Flores Indonesia 8°35S 121°0E **83 F6**
Flores Sea Indonesia 6°30S 120°0E **83 F6**
Florianópolis Brazil 27°30S 48°30W **121 E5**
Florida Uruguay 34°7S 56°10W **121 F4**
Florida □ U.S.A. 28°0N 82°0W **111 E10**
Florida, Straits of U.S.A. 25°0N 80°0W **115 C9**
Florida Keys U.S.A. 24°40N 81°0W **111 F10**
Florø Norway 61°35N 5°1E **63 E5**

Fly → Papua N. G. 8°25S 143°0E **98 B7**
Fochabers U.K. 57°37N 3°6W **23 G11**
Focşani Romania 45°41N 27°15E **65 F14**
Fóggia Italy 41°27N 15°34E **68 D6**
Foix France 42°58N 1°38E **66 E4**
Foligno Italy 42°57N 12°42E **68 C5**
Folkestone U.K. 51°5N 1°12E **31 D11**
Fond-du-Lac Canada 59°19N 107°12W **108 D9**
Fond du Lac U.S.A. 43°47N 88°27W **112 D3**
Fongafale Tuvalu 8°31S 179°13E **99 B14**
Fontainebleau France 48°24N 2°40E **66 B5**
Fontenay-le-Comte France 46°28N 0°48W **66 C3**
Fordham U.K. 52°19N 0°23E **31 B9**
Fordingbridge U.K. 50°56N 1°47W **30 E5**
Forel, Mt. Greenland 66°52N 36°55W **54 C6**
Forest Row U.K. 51°5N 0°3E **31 D9**
Forfar U.K. 56°39N 2°53W **23 J12**
Forli Italy 44°13N 12°3E **68 B5**
Formartine U.K. 57°20N 2°15W **23 H13**
Formby U.K. 53°34N 3°4W **27 E2**
Formby Pt. U.K. 53°33N 3°6W **27 E2**
Formentera Spain 38°43N 1°27E **67 C6**
Formiga Brazil 20°27S 45°25W **122 D1**
Formosa Argentina 26°15S 58°10W **121 E4**
Formosa Brazil 15°32S 47°20W **122 C1**
Forres U.K. 57°37N 3°37W **23 G10**
Forsayth Australia 18°33S 143°34E **98 D7**
Fort Albany Canada 52°15N 81°35W **109 D11**
Fort Augustus U.K. 57°9N 4°42W **23 H8**
Fort Chipewyan Canada 58°42N 111°8W **108 D8**
Fort Collins U.S.A. 40°35N 105°5W **110 B5**
Fort-Coulonge Canada 45°50N 76°45W **112 C9**
Fort-de-France Martinique 14°36N 61°5W **115 E12**
Fort Dodge U.S.A. 42°30N 94°11W **111 B8**
Fort Good Hope Canada 66°14N 128°40W **108 C7**
Fort Kent U.S.A. 47°15N 68°36W **113 B13**
Fort Lauderdale U.S.A. 26°7N 80°8W **111 E10**
Fort Liard Canada 60°14N 123°30W **108 C7**
Fort MacKay Canada 57°12N 111°41W **108 D8**
Fort Macleod Canada 49°45N 113°30W **108 E8**
Fort McMurray Canada 56°44N 111°7W **108 D8**
Fort McPherson Canada 67°30N 134°55W **108 C6**
Fort Morgan U.S.A. 40°15N 103°48W **110 B6**
Fort Myers U.S.A. 26°39N 81°52W **111 E10**
Fort Nelson Canada 58°50N 122°44W **108 D7**
Fort Nelson → Canada 59°32N 124°0W **108 D7**
Fort Peck L. U.S.A. 48°0N 106°26W **110 A5**
Fort Providence Canada 61°3N 117°40W **108 C8**
Fort Resolution Canada 61°10N 113°40W **108 C8**
Fort St. John Canada 56°15N 120°50W **108 D7**
Fort Scott U.S.A. 37°50N 94°42W **111 C8**
Fort Shevchenko Kazakhstan 44°35N 50°23E **71 F9**
Fort Simpson Canada 61°45N 121°15W **108 C7**
Fort Smith Canada 60°0N 111°51W **108 C8**
Fort Smith U.S.A. 35°23N 94°25W **111 C8**
Fort Stockton U.S.A. 30°53N 102°53W **110 D6**
Fort Wayne U.S.A. 41°4N 85°9W **112 E5**
Fort William U.K. 56°49N 5°7W **22 J7**
Fort Worth U.S.A. 32°43N 97°19W **111 D7**
Fort Yukon U.S.A. 66°34N 145°16W **108 C5**
Fortaleza Brazil 3°45S 38°35W **120 C6**
Forth → U.K. 56°9N 3°50W **25 B8**
Forth, Firth of U.K. 56°5N 2°55W **25 B10**
Fortrose U.K. 57°35N 4°9W **23 G9**
Foshan China 23°3N 113°9E **79 G11**
Fostoria U.S.A. 41°10N 83°25W **112 E6**
Fothergill U.K. 54°43N 3°29W **26 C2**
Fotheringhay U.K. 52°32N 0°27W **31 A8**
Fougères France 48°21N 1°14W **66 B3**
Foula U.K. 60°10N 2°5W **22 B13**
Foulness I. U.K. 51°36N 0°55E **31 C10**
Foulness Pt. U.K. 51°37N 0°58E **31 C10**
Foulsham U.K. 52°48N 0°59E **31 A10**
Fountainhall U.K. 55°44N 2°53W **25 C10**
Fouta Djallon Guinea 11°20N 12°10W **94 F3**
Fovant U.K. 51°4N 2°0W **30 D5**
Fowey U.K. 50°20N 4°39W **29 G4**
Fownhope U.K. 52°0N 2°36W **30 B3**
Foxe Basin Canada 66°0N 77°0W **109 C12**
Foxe Chan. Canada 65°0N 80°0W **109 C11**
Foxe Pen. Canada 65°0N 76°0W **109 C12**
Foyle → U.K. 55°3N 7°15W **19 A7**
Foyle, Lough U.K. 55°7N 7°4W **19 A7**
Foynes Ireland 52°37N 9°7W **20 C4**
Foz do Iguaçu Brazil 25°30S 54°30W **121 E4**
Framlingham U.K. 52°11N 1°21E **31 B11**
Franca Brazil 20°33S 47°30W **122 D1**
France ■ Europe 47°0N 3°0E **66 C5**
Franceville Gabon 1°40S 13°32E **96 E2**
Franche-Comté France 46°50N 5°55E **66 C6**
Francis Case, L. U.S.A. 43°4N 98°34W **110 B7**
Francistown Botswana 21°7S 27°33E **97 J5**
François L. Canada 54°0N 125°30W **108 D7**
Frankfort Ind., U.S.A. 40°17N 86°31W **112 E4**
Frankfort Ky., U.S.A. 38°12N 84°52W **112 F5**
Frankfurt Brandenburg, Germany 52°20N 14°32E **64 B8**
Frankfurt Hessen, Germany 50°7N 8°41E **64 C5**
Fränkische Alb Germany 49°10N 11°23E **64 D6**
Franklin N.H., U.S.A. 43°27N 71°39W **113 D12**
Franklin Pa., U.S.A. 41°24N 79°50W **112 E8**
Franklin B. Canada 69°45N 126°0W **108 C7**
Franklin D. Roosevelt L. U.S.A. 48°18N 118°9W **110 A3**
Franklin L. U.S.A. 40°25N 115°22W **110 B3**
Franklin Mts. Canada 65°0N 125°0W **108 C7**
Franklin Str. Canada 72°0N 96°0W **108 B10**
Franz Josef Land Arctic 82°0N 55°0E **54 A10**
Fraser → Canada 49°7N 123°11W **108 E7**
Fraserburgh U.K. 57°42N 2°1W **23 G13**
Frederick U.S.A. 39°25N 77°25W **112 F9**
Fredericksburg U.S.A. 38°18N 77°28W **112 F9**
Fredericktown U.S.A. 37°34N 90°18W **112 G2**
Fredericton Canada 45°57N 66°40W **113 C14**
Frederikshavn Denmark 57°28N 10°31E **63 F6**
Fredonia U.S.A. 42°26N 79°20W **112 D8**
Fredrikstad Norway 59°13N 10°57E **63 F6**
Free State □ S. Africa 28°30S 27°0E **97 K5**
Freeport The Bahamas 26°30N 78°47W **115 B9**
Freeport Ill., U.S.A. 42°17N 89°36W **112 D3**

Freeport

Guantánamo

Freeport *Tex., U.S.A.* 28°57N 95°21W **111** E7
Freetown *S. Leone* 8°30N 13°17W **94** G3
Freiburg *Germany* 47°59N 7°51E **64** E4
Fréjus *France* 43°25N 6°44E **66** E7
Fremont *U.S.A.* 41°21N 83°7W **112** E6
French Creek → *U.S.A.* 41°24N 79°50W **112** E8
French Guiana ☑ *S. Amer.* 4°0N 53°0W **120** B4
French Polynesia ☑ *Pac. Oc.* 20°0S 145°0W **103** J13
Frenchman Cr. →
  N. Amer. 48°31N 107°10W **110** A5
Freshwater *U.K.* 50°41N 1°31W **30** E5
Fresnillo *Mexico* 23°10N 102°53W **114** C4
Fresno *U.S.A.* 36°44N 119°47W **110** C3
Fria, C. *Namibia* 18°0S 12°0E **90** H5
Fridaythorpe *U.K.* 54°2N 0°39W **27** D7
Friedrichshafen *Germany* 47°39N 9°30E **64** E5
Frimley *U.K.* 51°19N 0°44W **31** D7
Frinton-on-Sea *U.K.* 51°49N 1°15E **31** C11
Frio, C. *Brazil* 22°50S 41°50W **117** F6
Frizington *U.K.* 54°33N 3°28W **26** C2
Frobisher B. *Canada* 62°30N 66°0W **109** C13
Frobisher L. *Canada* 56°20N 108°15W **108** D9
Frodsham *U.K.* 53°18N 2°43W **27** F3
Frome *U.K.* 51°14N 2°19W **30** D4
Frome → *U.K.* 50°41N 2°6W **30** E4
Front Range *U.S.A.* 40°25N 105°45W **110** B5
Front Royal *U.S.A.* 38°55N 78°12W **112** F8
Frutal *Brazil* 20°0S 49°0W **122** C1
Frýdek-Místek *Czechia* 49°40N 18°20E **65** D10
Fuchū *Japan* 34°34N 133°14E **81** F3
Friedrichshafen *Germany* 36°32N 4°41W **67** D3
Fuerte → *Mexico* 25°54N 109°22W **114** B3
Fuerteventura *Canary Is.* 28°30N 14°0W **94** C3
Fuidhaigh = Wiay *U.K.* 57°24N 7°13W **22** F3
Fuji *Japan* 35°9N 138°39E **81** F6
Fuji-San *Japan* 35°22N 138°44E **81** F6
Fujian ☑ *China* 26°0N 118°0E **79** F12
Fujin *China* 47°16N 132°1E **79** B15
Fukui *Japan* 36°5N 136°10E **81** E5
Fukuoka *Japan* 33°39N 130°21E **81** G2
Fukushima *Japan* 37°44N 140°28E **81** E7
Fukuyama *Japan* 34°35N 133°20E **81** F3
Fulda *Germany* 50°32N 9°40E **64** C5
Fulda → *Germany* 51°25N 9°39E **64** C5
Fulton *U.S.A.* 43°19N 76°25W **112** D9
Fulwood *U.K.* 53°47N 2°40W **27** E3
Funabashi *Japan* 35°45N 140°0E **81** F7
Funchal *Madeira* 32°38N 16°54W **94** B2
Fundy, B. of *Canada* 45°0N 66°0W **113** C15
Furnas, Represa de *Brazil* 20°50S 45°30W **122** D1
Furneaux Group *Australia* 40°10S 147°50E **98** J8
Fürth *Germany* 49°28N 10°59E **64** D6
Fury and Hecla Str. *Canada* 69°56N 84°0W **109** C11
Fushun *China* 41°50N 123°56E **79** C13
Fustic *Barbados* 13°16N 59°38W **114** c
Fuxin *China* 42°5N 121°48E **79** C13
Fuyang *China* 33°0N 115°48E **79** E12
Fuyang *China* 22°40N 113°49E **79** a
Fuyu *Heilongjiang, China* 47°49N 124°27E **79** B13
Fuyu *Jilin, China* 45°12N 124°43E **79** B13
Fuyun *China* 47°0N 89°28E **78** B6
Fuzhou *China* 26°5N 119°16E **79** F12
Fylingdales Moor *U.K.* 54°25N 0°41W **26** D7
Fyn *Denmark* 55°20N 10°30E **63** F6
Fyne, L. *U.K.* 55°59N 5°23W **24** C5

G

Gaalkacyo *Somalia* 6°30N 47°30E **89** F4
Gabès *Tunisia* 33°53N 10°2E **95** B8
Gabès, G. de *Tunisia* 34°0N 10°30E **95** B8
Gabon ■ *Africa* 0°10S 10°0E **96** E2
Gaborone *Botswana* 24°45S 25°57E **97** J5
Gabrovo *Bulgaria* 42°52N 25°19E **69** C11
Gachsārān *Iran* 30°15N 50°45E **87** D7
Gadarwara *India* 22°50N 78°50E **84** H11
Gadsden *U.S.A.* 34°1N 86°1W **111** D9
Gafsa *Tunisia* 34°24N 8°43E **95** B7
Găgăuzia ☑ *Moldova* 46°10N 28°40E **65** E15
Gagnoa *Côte d'Ivoire* 6°56N 6°16W **94** G4
Gagnon *Canada* 51°50N 68°5W **109** D13
Gainesville *Fla., U.S.A.* 29°40N 82°20W **111** E10
Gainesville *Ga., U.S.A.* 34°18N 83°50W **111** D10
Gainford *U.K.* 54°34N 1°43W **26** C5
Gairdner, L. *Australia* 31°30S 136°0E **98** G6
Gairloch *U.K.* 57°43N 5°41W **22** G6
Gairloch, L. *U.K.* 57°43N 5°45W **22** G6
Galapagos *Ecuador* 0°0 91°0W **117** D1
Galashiels *U.K.* 55°37N 2°49W **25** C10
Galați *Romania* 45°27N 28°2E **65** F15
Galdhøpiggen *Norway* 61°38N 8°18E **63** E5
Galena *U.S.A.* 64°44N 156°56W **108** C4
Galesburg *U.S.A.* 40°57N 90°22W **112** E2
Galgate *U.K.* 53°59N 2°46W **27** E3
Galicia ☑ *Spain* 42°43N 7°45W **67** A2
Galilee, Sea of *Israel* 32°45N 35°35E **86** C3
Galina Pt. *Jamaica* 18°24N 76°58W **114** a
Gallan Hd. *U.K.* 58°15N 7°2W **22** F3
Galle *Sri Lanka* 6°5N 80°10E **84** R12
Galley Hd. *Ireland* 51°32N 8°55W **20** E5
Gallinas, Pta. *Colombia* 12°28N 71°40W **120** A2
Gallipolis *U.S.A.* 38°49N 82°12W **112** F6
Gallivare *Sweden* 67°9N 20°40E **63** D8
Galloway *U.K.* 55°1N 4°29W **24** D7
Galloway, Mull of *U.K.* 54°39N 4°52W **24** E7
Gallup *U.S.A.* 35°32N 108°45W **110** C5
Galmudug *Somalia* 5°0N 47°0E **89** F4
Galston *U.K.* 55°36N 4°24W **24** D7
Galty Mts. *Ireland* 52°22N 8°10W **20** D6
Galtymore *Ireland* 52°21N 8°11W **20** D6
Galveston *U.S.A.* 29°18N 94°48W **111** E8
Galway *Ireland* 53°17N 9°3W **20** B4
Galway ☑ *Ireland* 53°22N 9°1W **20** B4
Galway B. *Ireland* 53°13N 9°10W **20** B4
Gambia ■ *W. Afr.* 13°25N 16°0W **94** F2
Gambia → *W. Afr.* 13°28N 16°34W **94** F2
Gamlingay *U.K.* 52°10N 0°11W **31** B8
Gan Jiang → *China* 29°15N 116°0E **79** F12
Gananoque *Canada* 44°20N 76°10W **113** C9

Gäncä *Azerbaijan* 40°45N 46°20E **71** F8
Gand = Gent *Belgium* 51°2N 3°42E **64** C2
Gandak → *India* 25°39N 85°13E **85** G14
Gander *Canada* 48°58N 54°35W **109** E14
Gandhi Sagar *India* 24°40N 75°40E **84** G9
Gandia *Spain* 38°58N 0°9W **67** C5
Gangdisê Shan *China* 31°20N 81°0E **78** E5
Ganges → *India* 23°20N 90°30E **85** H17
Gangneung *S. Korea* 37°45N 128°54E **79** D14
Gangtok *India* 27°20N 88°37E **85** F16
Gannett Peak *U.S.A.* 43°11N 109°39W **110** B5
Gansu ☑ *China* 36°0N 104°0E **78** D9
Ganzhou *China* 25°51N 114°56E **79** F11
Gao *Mali* 16°15N 0°5W **94** E5
Gap *France* 44°33N 6°5E **66** D7
Gar *China* 32°10N 79°58E **78** E4
Garanhuns *Brazil* 8°50S 36°30W **122** A3
Garboldisham *U.K.* 52°23N 0°57E **31** B10
Garda, L. di *Italy* 45°40N 10°41E **68** B4
Garden City *U.S.A.* 37°58N 100°53W **110** C6
Gardēz *Afghan.* 33°37N 69°9E **87** C12
Gare L. *U.K.* 56°1N 4°50W **24** B6
Garforth *U.K.* 53°47N 1°24W **27** E6
Gargrave *U.K.* 53°59N 2°7W **27** E4
Garioch *U.K.* 57°18N 2°40W **23** H12
Garissa *Kenya* 0°25S 39°40E **96** E7
Garonne → *France* 45°2N 0°36W **66** D3
Garoowe *Somalia* 8°25N 48°33E **89** F4
Garoua *Cameroon* 9°19N 13°21E **95** G8
Garron Pt. *U.K.* 55°3N 5°59W **19** A10
Garry → *U.K.* 56°44N 3°47W **23** J10
Garry, L. *Canada* 65°58N 100°18W **108** C9
Garsdale Head *U.K.* 54°20N 2°20W **26** D4
Garstang *U.K.* 53°55N 2°46W **27** E3
Gary *U.S.A.* 41°36N 87°20W **112** E4
Garzê *China* 31°38N 100°1E **78** E9
Gascogne *France* 43°45N 0°20E **66** E4
Gascogne, G. de *Europe* 44°0N 2°0W **66** D2
Gashua *Nigeria* 12°54N 11°0E **95** F8
Gaspé *Canada* 48°52N 64°30W **109** E13
Gaspé, C. de *Canada* 48°48N 64°7W **113** A15
Gaspésie, Pén. de la *Canada* 48°45N 65°40W **113** A15
Gata, Sierra de *Spain* 40°20N 6°45W **67** B2
Gatehouse of Fleet *U.K.* 54°53N 4°12W **24** E7
Gateshead *U.K.* 54°57N 1°35W **26** C6
Gatineau *Canada* 45°29N 75°39W **113** C10
Gatineau → *Canada* 45°27N 75°42W **113** C10
Gatley *U.K.* 53°24N 2°15W **27** F4
Gävle *Sweden* 60°40N 17°9E **63** E7
Gawilgarh Hills *India* 21°15N 76°45E **84** J10
Gawthwaite *U.K.* 54°16N 3°8W **26** D2
Gaxun Nur *China* 42°22N 100°30E **78** C9
Gaya *India* 24°47N 85°4E **85** G14
Gaylord *U.S.A.* 45°2N 84°41W **112** C5
Gayton *U.K.* 52°45N 0°36E **31** A10
Gaywood *U.K.* 52°46N 0°26E **31** A9
Gaza *Gaza Strip* 31°30N 34°28E **86** D3
Gaza Strip ☑ *Asia* 31°29N 34°25E **86** D3
Gaziantep *Turkey* 37°6N 37°23E **71** G6
Gdańsk *Poland* 54°22N 18°40E **65** A10
Gdynia *Poland* 54°35N 18°33E **65** A10
Gebze *Turkey* 40°47N 29°25E **71** F4
Gedaref *Sudan* 14°2N 35°28E **95** F13
Gedney *U.K.* 52°48N 0°4E **27** G9
Gedser *Denmark* 54°35N 11°55E **63** G6
Geelong *Australia* 38°10S 144°22E **98** H7
Gejiu *China* 23°20N 103°10E **78** G9
Gela *Italy* 37°4N 14°15E **68** F6
Gelibolu *Turkey* 40°28N 26°43E **71** F4
Gelsenkirchen *Germany* 51°32N 7°6E **64** C4
General Acha *Argentina* 37°20S 64°38W **121** F3
General Alvear *Argentina* 35°0S 67°40W **121** F3
General Santos *Phil.* 6°5N 125°14E **83** C7
Geneva *Switz.* 46°12N 6°9E **64** E4
Geneva *U.S.A.* 42°52N 76°59W **112** D9
Geneva, L. = Léman, L. *Europe* 46°26N 6°30E **64** E4
Gennargentu, Mti. del *Italy* 40°1N 9°19E **68** D3
Genoa *Italy* 44°25N 8°57E **68** B3
Génova, G. di *Italy* 44°0N 9°0E **68** C3
Gent *Belgium* 51°2N 3°42E **64** C2
George *S. Africa* 33°58S 22°29E **97** L4
George → *Canada* 58°49N 66°10W **109** D13
George, L. *U.S.A.* 29°17N 81°36W **111** E10
George Town *Cayman Is.* 5°25N 100°20E **82** C2
George Town *Malaysia* 5°25N 100°20E **82** C2
George V Land *Antarctica* 69°0S 148°0E **55** C10
Georgetown *Guyana* 6°50N 58°12W **120** B4
Georgetown *Ky., U.S.A.* 38°13N 84°33W **112** F5
Georgetown *S.C., U.S.A.* 33°23N 79°17W **111** D11
Georgia ☑ *Asia* 42°0N 43°0E **71** F7
Georgia ■ *U.S.A.* 32°50N 83°15W **111** D10
Georgian B. *Canada* 45°15N 81°0W **112** C7
Georgiyevsk *Russia* 44°12N 43°28E **71** F7
Gera *Germany* 50°53N 12°4E **64** C7
Geraldton *Australia* 28°48S 114°32E **98** F1
Germany ■ *Europe* 51°0N 10°0E **64** C6
Germiston *S. Africa* 26°13S 28°10E **97** K5
Gerrans B. *U.K.* 50°12N 4°57W **29** G4
Gerrards Cross *U.K.* 51°35N 0°33W **31** C7
Getafe *Spain* 40°18N 3°43W **67** B4
Ghadāmis *Libya* 30°11N 9°29E **95** B7
Ghaghara → *India* 25°45N 84°40E **85** G14
Ghana ■ *W. Afr.* 8°0N 1°0W **94** G5
Ghardaïa *Algeria* 32°20N 3°37E **94** B6
Gharyān *Libya* 32°10N 13°0E **95** B8
Ghats, Eastern *India* 14°0N 78°50E **84** N11
Ghats, Western *India* 14°0N 75°0E **84** N9
Ghazal, Bahr el → *Chad* 13°0N 15°47E **95** F9
Ghazal, Bahr el → *South Sudan* 9°31N 30°25E **95** G12
Ghaziabad *India* 28°42N 77°26E **84** E10
Ghazipur *India* 25°38N 83°35E **85** G13
Ghaznī *Afghan.* 33°30N 68°28E **87** C12
Ghent = Gent *Belgium* 51°2N 3°42E **64** C2
Giant's Causeway *U.K.* 55°16N 6°29W **19** A9
Gibraltar ☑ *Europe* 36°7N 5°22W **67** D3
Gibraltar, Str. of *Medit.* 35°55N 5°40W **67** E3
Gibraltar Pt. *U.K.* 53°6N 0°19E **27** F9

Gibson Desert *Australia* 24°0S 126°0E **98** E4
Gifu *Japan* 35°30N 136°45E **81** F5
Giggleswick *U.K.* 54°5N 2°17W **26** D4
Goole *U.K.* 53°42N 0°53W **27** E7
Gigha *U.K.* 55°42N 5°44W **24** C4
Gigha L. *U.S.A.* 41°56N 120°26W **110** B2
Gijón *Spain* 43°32N 5°42W **67** A3
Gila → *U.S.A.* 32°43N 114°33W **110** D4
Gilān ☑ *Iran* 37°0N 50°0E **86** B7
Gilbert Is. *Kiribati* 1°0N 172°0E **102** G9
Gilgit *India* 35°50N 74°15E **84** B9
Gilgit-Baltistan ☑ *Pakistan* 36°30N 73°0E **84** B9
Gillam *Canada* 56°20N 94°40W **108** D10
Gillette *U.S.A.* 44°18N 105°30W **110** B5
Gillingham *Dorset, U.K.* 51°2N 2°18W **30** D4
Gillingham *Medway, U.K.* 51°23N 0°33E **31** D10
Gilsland *U.K.* 55°0N 2°34W **26** C3
Gimie, Mt. *St. Lucia* 13°54N 61°0W **114** b
Girdle Ness *U.K.* 57°9N 2°3W **23** H13
Giresun *Turkey* 40°55N 38°30E **71** F6
Girga *Egypt* 26°17N 31°55E **95** C12
Girona *Spain* 41°58N 2°46E **67** B7
Gironde → *France* 45°32N 1°7W **66** D3
Girvan *U.K.* 55°14N 4°51W **24** D6
Gisborne *N.Z.* 38°39S 178°5E **99** H14
Gisburn *U.K.* 53°56N 2°16W **27** E4
Gitega *Burundi* 3°26S 29°56E **96** E5
Gizhiga *Russia* 62°3N 160°30E **77** C17
Gjoa Haven *Canada* 68°38N 95°53W **108** C10
Glace Bay *Canada* 46°11N 59°58W **113** B18
Glacier Nat. Park △ *U.S.A.* 48°42N 113°48W **110** A4
Gladstone *Australia* 23°52S 151°16E **98** E9
Gladstone *U.S.A.* 45°51N 87°1W **112** C4
Gladwin *U.S.A.* 43°59N 84°29W **112** D5
Glamorgan, Vale of ☑ *U.K.* 51°28N 3°25W **29** E7
Glanaruddery Mts. *Ireland* 52°20N 9°27W **20** D4
Glanton *U.K.* 55°26N 1°54W **26** B5
Glasgow *U.K.* 55°51N 4°15W **24** C7
Glasgow *Ky., U.S.A.* 37°0N 85°55W **112** G5
Glasgow *Mont., U.S.A.* 48°12N 106°38W **110** A5
Glasgow Int. ✈ (GLA) *U.K.* 55°51N 4°21W **29** D5
Glasnevin *Ireland* 53°22N 6°15W **21** B10
Glastonbury *U.K.* 51°9N 2°43W **30** D4
Glazov *Russia* 58°9N 52°40E **70** C9
Glemsford *U.K.* 52°6N 0°40E **31** B10
Glen → *U.K.* 52°51N 0°7W **27** G8
Glen Affric *U.K.* 57°17N 5°1W **22** H7
Glen Almond *U.K.* 56°28N 3°50W **25** B8
Glen Coe *U.K.* 56°40N 5°0W **22** J7
Glen Etive *U.K.* 56°37N 5°0W **24** A5
Glen Garry *Highl., U.K.* 57°3N 5°7W **22** H6
Glen Garry *Perth & Kinr., U.K.* 56°47N 4°5W **23** J9
Glen Mor *U.K.* 57°9N 4°37W **23** H8
Glen Moriston *U.K.* 57°11N 4°52W **23** H8
Glen Orchy *U.K.* 56°27N 4°52W **24** B6
Glen Orrin *U.K.* 57°31N 4°45W **23** G8
Glen Oykel *U.K.* 58°5N 4°50W **23** F8
Glen Roy *U.K.* 56°56N 4°50W **23** J8
Glen Shee *U.K.* 56°50N 3°28W **23** J11
Glen Shiel *U.K.* 57°9N 5°18W **22** H7
Glen Spean *U.K.* 56°53N 4°40W **23** J8
Glenamaddy *Ireland* 53°37N 8°33W **18** D4
Glendale *Ariz., U.S.A.* 33°32N 112°11W **110** D4
Glendale *Calif., U.S.A.* 34°9N 118°15W **110** D3
Glenelg → *U.K.* 57°15N 5°37W **22** H6
Gleneagles *U.K.* 56°17N 3°43W **25** B8
Glenfinnan *U.K.* 56°53N 5°27W **22** J7
Glengarriff *Ireland* 51°45N 9°34W **20** E3
Glenkens, The *U.K.* 55°11N 4°12W **24** D7
Glenluce *U.K.* 54°52N 4°48W **24** E6
Glennallen *U.S.A.* 62°7N 145°33W **108** C5
Glenrothes *U.K.* 56°12N 3°10W **25** B9
Glens Falls *U.S.A.* 43°19N 73°39W **113** D11
Glenties *Ireland* 54°48N 8°17W **18** B5
Glenveagh △ *Ireland* 55°3N 8°1W **18** A5
Gliwice *Poland* 50°22N 18°41E **65** C10
Globe *U.S.A.* 33°24N 110°47W **110** D4
Glogów *Poland* 51°37N 16°5E **64** C9
Glomma → *Norway* 59°12N 10°57E **63** F6
Glossop *U.K.* 53°27N 1°56W **27** F5
Gloucester *U.K.* 51°53N 2°15W **30** C4
Gloucestershire ☑ *U.K.* 51°46N 2°15W **30** C4
Gloversville *U.S.A.* 43°3N 74°21W **113** D10
Glyn Ebwy = Ebbw Vale *U.K.* 51°46N 3°12W **28** D7
Gnosall *U.K.* 52°48N 2°14W **27** G4
Goa *India* 15°33N 73°59E **84** M8
Goa ☑ *India* 15°33N 73°59E **84** M8
Goat Fell *U.K.* 55°38N 5°11W **24** C5
Gobi *Asia* 44°0N 110°0E **79** C10
Godalming *U.K.* 51°11N 0°36W **31** D7
Godavari → *India* 16°25N 82°18E **85** L13
Goderich *Canada* 43°45N 81°41W **112** D7
Godhra *India* 22°49N 73°40E **84** H8
Godmanchester *U.K.* 52°20N 0°11W **31** B8
Godoy Cruz *Argentina* 32°56S 68°52W **121** F3
Gods → *Canada* 56°22N 92°51W **108** D10
Gods L. *Canada* 54°40N 94°15W **108** D10
Godshill *U.K.* 50°38N 1°15W **30** E6
Godstone *U.K.* 51°14N 0°3W **31** D8
Gogama *Canada* 47°35N 81°43W **112** C7
Goiânia *Brazil* 16°43S 49°20W **122** C1
Goiás *Brazil* 15°55S 50°10W **120** D5
Goiás ☑ *Brazil* 12°10S 48°0W **120** D5
Goio-Erê *Brazil* 24°12S 53°1W **121** A5
Gold Coast *Australia* 28°0S 153°25E **98** F9
Gold Coast *W. Afr.* 4°0N 1°40W **94** H5
Golden Vale *Ireland* 52°33N 8°17W **20** D6
Goldsboro *U.S.A.* 35°23N 77°59W **111** C11
Goléstān ☑ *Iran* 37°20N 55°25E **87** B8
Golmud *China* 36°25N 94°53E **78** D7
Golspie *U.K.* 57°58N 3°59W **23** H9
Goma *Dem. Rep. of the Congo* 1°37S 29°10E **96** E5
Gomera *Canary Is.* 28°7N 17°14W **94** C2
Gómez Palacio *Mexico* 25°34N 103°30W **114** B4
Gonābād *Iran* 34°15N 58°45E **87** C9
Gonaïves *Haiti* 19°20N 72°42W **115** D10
Gonbad-e Kāvūs *Iran* 37°20N 55°25E **87** B8
Gonda *India* 27°9N 81°58E **85** F12
Gonder *Ethiopia* 12°39N 37°30E **89** E2
Gongbei *China* 22°12N 113°32E **79** a
Gongga Shan *China* 29°40N 101°55E **78** F9
Good Hope, C. of *S. Africa* 34°24S 18°30E **97** L3

Goodrich *U.K.* 51°52N 2°37W **30** C3
Goodwood *U.K.* 50°53N 0°44W **31** E7
Goole *U.K.* 53°42N 0°53W **27** E7
Goose L. *U.S.A.* 41°56N 120°26W **110** B2
Gorakhpur *India* 26°47N 83°23E **85** F13
Gordon *U.K.* 55°41N 2°34W **25** C10
Gore *Ethiopia* 8°12N 35°32E **89** F2
Gorebridge *U.K.* 55°50N 3°2W **25** C9
Gorey *Ireland* 52°41N 6°18W **21** C10
Gorgān *Iran* 36°55N 54°30E **87** B8
Goring *U.K.* 51°31N 1°7W **30** C6
Goring-by-Sea *U.K.* 50°49N 0°24W **31** E8
Gorleston-on-Sea *U.K.* 52°35N 1°44E **31** A12
Görlitz *Germany* 51°9N 14°58E **64** C8
Gorno-Altay ☑ *Russia* 51°0N 86°0E **76** D9
Gorontalo *Indonesia* 0°35N 123°5E **83** D6
Gort *Ireland* 53°3N 8°49W **20** B5
Gorzów Wielkopolski *Poland* 52°43N 15°15E **64** B8
Gosberton *U.K.* 52°53N 0°9W **27** G8
Gosforth *U.K.* 54°26N 3°27W **26** D2
Gosport *U.K.* 50°48N 1°9W **30** E6
Göta kanal *Sweden* 58°30N 15°58E **63** F7
Götaland *Sweden* 57°30N 14°30E **63** F6
Göteborg *Sweden* 57°43N 11°59E **63** F6
Gotha *Germany* 50°56N 10°42E **64** C6
Gothenburg = Göteborg *Sweden* 57°43N 11°59E **63** F6
Gotland *Sweden* 57°30N 18°33E **63** F7
Gotō-Rettō *Japan* 32°55N 129°5E **81** G1
Göttingen *Germany* 51°31N 9°55E **64** C5
Gouda *Neths.* 52°1N 4°42E **64** B3
Goudhurst *U.K.* 51°6N 0°29E **31** D9
Gouin, Rés. *Canada* 48°35N 74°40W **113** A10
Goulburn *Australia* 34°44S 149°44E **98** G8
Goundam *Mali* 16°27N 3°40W **94** E5
Gourock *U.K.* 55°57N 4°49W **24** C6
Governador Valadares *Brazil* 18°15S 41°57W **122** C2
Gower *U.K.* 51°35N 4°10W **29** D5
Gowna, L. *Ireland* 53°51N 7°34W **18** D6
Goya *Argentina* 29°10S 59°10W **121** E4
Gozo *Malta* 36°3N 14°15E **68** a
Gqeberha *S. Africa* 33°58S 25°40E **97** L5
Graaff-Reinet *S. Africa* 32°13S 24°32E **97** L4
Gracias a Dios, C. *Honduras* 15°0N 83°10W **115** E8
Grafham Water *U.K.* 52°19N 0°18W **31** B8
Grafton *Australia* 29°38S 152°58E **98** F9
Grafton *U.S.A.* 48°25N 97°25W **111** A7
Graham Land *Antarctica* 65°0S 64°0W **55** C17
Grain *Canada* 4°20N 10°0W **94** H3
Grainthorpe *U.K.* 53°27N 0°5E **27** F9
Grampian Mts. *U.K.* 56°50N 4°0W **23** J9
Gran Canaria *Canary Is.* 27°55N 15°35W **94** C2
Gran Chaco *S. Amer.* 25°0S 61°0W **121** E3
Gran Sasso d'Itália *Italy* 42°27N 13°42E **68** C5
Granada *Nic.* 11°58N 86°0W **114** E7
Granada *Spain* 37°10N 3°35W **67** D4
Granard *Ireland* 53°47N 7°30W **18** D6
Granby *Canada* 45°25N 72°45W **109** E12
Grand → *U.S.A.* 45°40N 100°45W **110** A6
Grand Bahama *The Bahamas* 26°40N 78°30W **115** B9
Grand Canyon *U.S.A.* 36°3N 112°9W **110** C4
Grand Canyon Nat. Park △ *U.S.A.* 36°15N 112°30W **110** C4
Grand Cayman *Cayman Is.* 19°20N 81°20W **115** D8
Grand Falls *Canada* 47°3N 67°44W **113** B14
Grand Falls-Windsor *Canada* 48°56N 55°40W **109** E14
Grand Forks *U.S.A.* 47°55N 97°3W **111** A7
Grand Haven *U.S.A.* 43°4N 86°13W **112** D4
Grand Island *U.S.A.* 40°55N 98°21W **110** B7
Grand Junction *U.S.A.* 39°4N 108°33W **110** C5
Grand L. *Canada* 45°57N 66°7W **113** C14
Grand Manan I. *Canada* 44°45N 66°52W **113** C14
Grand-Mère *Canada* 46°36N 72°40W **113** B11
Grand Rapids *Canada* 53°12N 99°19W **108** D10
Grand Rapids *U.S.A.* 42°58N 85°40W **112** D4
Grand St-Bernard, Col du *Europe* 45°50N 7°10E **64** F4
Grand Teton *U.S.A.* 43°54N 110°50W **110** B4
Grande → *Bolivia* 15°51S 64°39W **120** D3
Grande → *Brazil* 11°30S 44°30W **122** B2
Grande, B. *Argentina* 50°30S 68°20W **121** H3
Grande, Rio → *N. Amer.* 25°58N 97°9W **111** E7
Grande Baleine → *Canada* 55°16N 77°47W **109** D12
Grande Prairie *Canada* 55°10N 118°50W **108** D8
Grange-over-Sands *U.K.* 54°12N 2°54W **26** D3
Grangemouth *U.K.* 56°1N 3°42W **25** B8
Grangeville *U.S.A.* 45°56N 116°7W **110** A3
Grantham *U.K.* 52°55N 0°38W **27** G7
Grantown-on-Spey *U.K.* 57°20N 3°36W **23** H10
Grants Pass *U.S.A.* 42°26N 123°19W **110** B2
Granville *U.S.A.* 43°24N 73°16W **113** D11
Grasmere *U.K.* 54°28N 3°1W **26** D2
Grasse *France* 43°38N 6°56E **66** E7
Grassington *U.K.* 54°5N 1°59W **26** D5
Gravelbourg *Canada* 49°50N 106°35W **108** E9
Gravesend *U.K.* 51°26N 0°22E **31** D9
Grayling *U.S.A.* 44°40N 84°43W **112** C5
Grayrigg *U.K.* 54°23N 2°39W **26** D3
Grays *U.K.* 51°28N 0°21E **31** D9
Graz *Austria* 47°4N 15°27E **64** E8
Great Australian Bight *Australia* 33°30S 130°0E **98** G5
Great Ayton *U.K.* 54°30N 1°8W **26** D6
Great Baddow *U.K.* 51°43N 0°31E **31** C10
Great Barrier Reef *Australia* 18°0S 146°50E **98** D8
Great Basin *U.S.A.* 40°0N 117°0W **110** B3
Great Bear → *Canada* 65°0N 126°0W **108** C7
Great Bear L. *Canada* 65°30N 120°0W **108** C7
Great Bend *U.S.A.* 38°22N 98°46W **110** C7
Great Bentley *U.K.* 51°51N 1°4E **31** C11
Great Bernera *U.K.* 58°14N 6°50W **22** F4
Great Blasket I. *Ireland* 52°6N 10°32W **20** D1
Great Britain *Europe* 54°0N 2°15W **62** D5
Great Broughton *U.K.* 54°26N 1°9W **26** D6
Great Chesterford *U.K.* 52°4N 0°13E **31** B9
Great Clifton *U.K.* 54°39N 3°29W **26** C2
Great Dividing Ra. *Australia* 23°0S 146°0E **98** E8
Great Dunmow *U.K.* 51°52N 0°23E **31** C9
Great Exuma *The Bahamas* 23°30N 75°50W **115** C9

Great Falls *U.S.A.* 47°30N 111°17W **110** A4
Great Glen = Glen Mor *U.K.* 57°9N 4°37W **23** H8
Great Harwood *U.K.* 53°47N 2°24W **27** E4
Great Inagua *The Bahamas* 21°0N 73°20W **115** C10
Great Karoo *S. Africa* 31°55S 21°0E **97** L4
Great Khingan Mts. *China* 48°0N 121°0E **79** B13
Great Malvern *U.K.* 52°7N 2°18W **30** B4
Great Massingham *U.K.* 52°47N 0°40E **31** A10
Great Missenden *U.K.* 51°42N 0°41W **31** C7
Great Ormes Head *U.K.* 53°20N 3°52W **28** A6
Great Ouse → *U.K.* 52°48N 0°21E **31** A9
Great Pedro Bluff *Jamaica* 17°51N 77°44W **114** a
Great Plains *N. Amer.* 47°0N 105°0W **110** A6
Great Salt Desert *Iran* 34°30N 55°0E **87** C8
Great Salt L. *U.S.A.* 41°15N 112°40W **110** B4
Great Salt Lake Desert *U.S.A.* 40°50N 113°30W **110** B4
Great Sandy Desert *Australia* 21°0S 124°0E **98** E3
Great Sandy Desert *U.S.A.* 43°35N 120°15W **110** B2
Great Shefford *U.K.* 51°28N 1°28W **30** C6
Great Shelford *U.K.* 52°9N 0°8E **31** B9
Great Shunner Fell *U.K.* 54°22N 2°14W **26** D4
Great Skellig *Ireland* 51°47N 10°33W **20** E1
Great Slave L. *Canada* 61°23N 115°38W **108** C8
Great Snow Mt. *Canada* 57°26N 124°0W **108** D7
Great Torrington *U.K.* 50°57N 4°9W **29** F5
Great Victoria Desert *Australia* 29°30S 126°30E **98** F4
Great Wall of China *China* 38°30N 109°30E **79** D10
Great Waltham *U.K.* 51°47N 0°28E **31** C9
Great Whernside *U.K.* 54°10N 1°58W **26** D5
Great Yarmouth *U.K.* 52°37N 1°44E **31** A12
Greater Antilles *W. Indies* 17°40N 74°0W **115** D10
Greater London ☑ *U.K.* 51°31N 0°6W **31** C8
Greater Manchester ☑ *U.K.* 53°30N 2°15W **27** E4
Greater Sudbury *Canada* 46°30N 81°0W **112** B7
Greater Sunda Is. *Indonesia* 7°0S 112°0E **82** F4
Greatham *U.K.* 54°39N 1°14W **26** C6
Greece ■ *Europe* 40°0N 23°0E **69** E9
Greeley *U.S.A.* 40°25N 104°42W **110** B6
Greely Fd. *Canada* 80°30N 85°0W **109** A11
Green → *Ky., U.S.A.* 37°54N 87°30W **112** G4
Green → *Utah, U.S.A.* 38°11N 109°53W **110** C5
Green B. *U.S.A.* 45°0N 87°30W **112** C4
Green Bay *U.S.A.* 44°31N 88°0W **112** C4
Green Hammerton *U.K.* 54°1N 1°18W **27** D6
Green River *U.S.A.* 41°32N 109°28W **110** B5
Greencastle *U.S.A.* 39°38N 86°52W **112** F4
Greenfield *Ind., U.S.A.* 39°47N 85°46W **112** F5
Greenfield *Mass., U.S.A.* 42°35N 72°36W **113** D11
Greenhead *U.K.* 54°59N 2°30W **26** C3
Greenland ☑ *N. Amer.* 66°0N 45°0W **54** C5
Greenland Sea *Arctic* 73°0N 10°0W **54** B7
Greenlaw *U.K.* 55°43N 2°27W **25** C11
Greenock *U.K.* 55°57N 4°46W **24** C6
Greenodd *U.K.* 54°14N 3°4W **26** D2
Greenore *Ireland* 54°1N 6°9W **19** C9
Greenore Pt. *Ireland* 52°14N 6°19W **21** D10
Greensboro *U.S.A.* 36°4N 79°48W **111** C11
Greensburg *Ind., U.S.A.* 39°20N 85°29W **112** F5
Greensburg *Pa., U.S.A.* 40°18N 79°33W **112** E8
Greenstone Pt. *U.K.* 57°55N 5°37W **22** G6
Greenville *Ala., U.S.A.* 31°50N 86°38W **111** D9
Greenville *Maine, U.S.A.* 45°28N 69°35W **113** C13
Greenville *Mich., U.S.A.* 43°11N 85°15W **112** D5
Greenville *Miss., U.S.A.* 33°24N 91°4W **111** D8
Greenville *Ohio, U.S.A.* 40°6N 84°38W **112** E5
Greenville *S.C., U.S.A.* 34°51N 82°24W **111** D10
Greenwich ☑ *U.K.* 51°29N 0°1E **31** D9
Greenwood *U.S.A.* 33°31N 90°11W **111** D8
Gremikha *Russia* 67°59N 39°47E **70** A6
Grenada ■ *W. Indies* 12°10N 61°40W **115** E12
Grenoble *France* 45°12N 5°42E **66** D6
Greta → *U.K.* 54°9N 2°37W **26** D3
Gretna *U.K.* 55°0N 3°3W **25** E9
Gretna Green *U.K.* 55°1N 3°3W **25** D9
Grey Ra. *Australia* 27°0S 143°30E **98** F7
Greymouth *N.Z.* 42°29S 171°13E **99** J13
Greystoke *U.K.* 54°41N 2°51W **26** C3
Greystones *Ireland* 53°9N 6°5W **21** B10
Griffith *Australia* 34°18S 146°2E **98** G8
Grimsay *U.K.* 57°29N 7°14W **22** H3
Grimsby *U.K.* 53°34N 0°5W **27** E8
Griomasaigh = Grimsay *U.K.* 57°29N 7°14W **22** H3
Gris-Nez, C. *France* 50°52N 1°35E **66** A4
Grise Fiord *Canada* 76°25N 82°57W **109** B11
Grizebeck *U.K.* 54°16N 3°10W **26** D2
Groningen *Neths.* 53°15N 6°35E **64** B4
Groote Eylandt *Australia* 14°0S 136°40E **98** C6
Gros Islet *St. Lucia* 14°5N 60°58W **114** b
Gros Piton *St. Lucia* 13°49N 61°5W **114** b
Gros Piton Pt. *St. Lucia* 13°49N 61°5W **114** b
Grosseto *Italy* 42°46N 11°8E **68** C4
Grossglockner *Austria* 47°5N 12°40E **64** E7
Groundhog → *Canada* 48°45N 82°58W **112** A6
Groznyy *Russia* 43°20N 45°45E **71** F8
Grudziadz *Poland* 53°30N 18°47E **65** B10
Gruinard B. *U.K.* 57°56N 5°35W **22** G6
Guadalajara *Mexico* 20°40N 103°20W **114** C4
Guadalajara *Spain* 40°37N 3°12W **67** B4
Guadalcanal *Solomon Is.* 9°32S 160°12E **99** B11
Guadalete → *Spain* 36°35N 6°13W **67** D2
Guadalquivir → *Spain* 36°47N 6°22W **67** D2
Guadarrama, Sierra de *Spain* 41°0N 4°0W **67** B4
Guadeloupe ☑ *W. Indies* 16°15N 61°40W **114** b
Guadiana → *Portugal* 37°14N 7°22W **67** D2
Guadix *Spain* 37°18N 3°11W **67** D4
Guafo, Boca del *Chile* 43°35S 74°0W **121** G2
Guajará-Mirim *Brazil* 10°50S 65°20W **120** D3
Guajira, Pen. de la *Colombia* 12°0N 72°0W **120** A2
Gualeguaychú *Argentina* 33°3S 59°31W **121** F4
Guam ☑ *Pac. Oc.* 13°27N 144°45E **102** F6
Guamúchil *Mexico* 25°28N 108°6W **114** B3
Guanajuato *Mexico* 21°1N 101°15W **114** C4
Guane *Cuba* 22°10N 84°7W **115** C8
Guangdong ☑ *China* 23°0N 113°0E **79** F10
Guangxi Zhuang ☑ *China* 24°0N 109°0E **79** G10
Guangyuan *China* 32°26N 105°51E **78** E10
Guangzhou *China* 23°6N 113°13E **79** G11
Guantánamo *Cuba* 20°10N 75°14W **115** C9

Guantánamo B.   Húnaflói

Guantánamo B. *Cuba* 19°59N 75°10W **115** D9
Guaporé → *Brazil* 11°55S 65°4W **120** D3
Guaqui *Bolivia* 16°41S 68°54W **120** D3
Guarapuava *Brazil* 25°20S 51°30W **121** E4
Guaratinguetá *Brazil* 22°49S 45°9W **122** D1
Guarulhos *Brazil* 23°29S 46°33W **122** D1
Guatemala *Guatemala* 14°40N 90°22W **114** E6
Guatemala ■ *Cent. Amer.* 15°40N 90°30W **114** D6
Guaviare → *Colombia* 4°3N 67°44W **120** B3
Guaxupé *Brazil* 21°10S 47°5W **122** D1
Guayaquil *Ecuador* 2°15S 79°52W **120** C2
Guayaquil, G. de *Ecuador* 3°10S 81°0W **120** C1
Guaymas *Mexico* 27°56N 110°54W **114** B2
Gubkin *Russia* 51°17N 37°32E **71** D6
Guelmim *Morocco* 28°56N 10°0W **94** C3
Guelph *Canada* 43°35N 80°20W **112** D7
Guéret *France* 46°11N 1°51E **66** C4
Guernsey *U.K.* 49°26N 2°35W **29** J8
Guestling Green *U.K.* 50°53N 0°39E **31** E10
Guiana Highlands *S. Amer.* 5°10N 60°40W **117** C4
Guidónia-Montecélio *Italy* 42°1N 12°45E **68** C5
Guildford *U.K.* 51°14N 0°34W **31** D7
Guilin *China* 25°18N 110°15E **79** F11
Guinea ■ *W. Afr.* 10°20N 11°30W **94** F3
Guinea, Gulf of *Atl. Oc.* 3°0N 2°30E **90** F4
Guinea-Bissau ■ *Africa* 12°0N 15°0W **94** F3
Güines *Cuba* 22°50N 82°0W **115** C8
Guingamp *France* 48°34N 3°10W **66** B2
Guisborough *U.K.* 54°33N 1°4W **26** C6
Guiyang *China* 26°32N 106°40E **78** F10
Guizhou □ *China* 27°0N 107°0E **78** F10
Gujarat □ *India* 23°20N 71°0E **84** H7
Gujranwala *Pakistan* 32°10N 74°12E **84** C9
Gujrat *Pakistan* 32°40N 74°2E **84** C9
Gulf, The = Persian Gulf *Asia* 27°0N 50°0E **87** E7
Gulfport *U.S.A.* 30°22N 89°6W **111** D9
Gulian *China* 52°56N 122°21E **79** A13
Gulu *Uganda* 2°48N 32°17E **96** D6
Guna *India* 24°40N 77°19E **84** G10
Gunnison → *U.S.A.* 39°4N 108°35W **110** C5
Gunsan *S. Korea* 35°59N 126°45E **79** D14
Guntur *India* 16°23N 80°30E **85** L12
Gurbantünggüt Desert *China* 45°8N 87°20E **78** B6
Gurgueia → *Brazil* 6°50S 43°24W **120** C5
Guri, Embalse de *Venezuela* 7°50N 62°52W **120** B3
Gurkha *Nepal* 28°5N 84°40E **85** E14
Gurnard's Hd. *U.K.* 50°11N 5°37W **29** G2
Gürün *Turkey* 38°43N 37°15E **71** G6
Gurupi *Brazil* 11°43S 49°4W **122** B1
Gurupi → *Brazil* 1°13S 46°6W **120** C5
Gurvan Sayhan Uul *Mongolia* 43°50N 104°0E **78** C9
Gusau *Nigeria* 12°12N 6°40E **94** F7
Guwahati *India* 26°10N 91°45E **85** F17
Guyana ■ *S. Amer.* 5°0N 59°0W **120** B4
Guyenne *France* 44°30N 0°40E **66** D4
Gwādar *Pakistan* 25°10N 62°18E **84** G3
Gwalchmai *U.K.* 53°16N 4°25W **28** A5
Gwalior *India* 26°12N 78°10E **84** F11
Gwanda *Zimbabwe* 20°55S 29°0E **97** J5
Gwangju *S. Korea* 35°9N 126°54E **79** D14
Gweebarra B. *Ireland* 54°51N 8°23W **18** B5
Gweedore *Ireland* 55°3N 8°14W **18** A5
Gweek *U.K.* 50°5N 5°13W **29** G3
Gwennap *U.K.* 50°12N 5°11W **29** G3
Gweru *Zimbabwe* 19°28S 29°45E **97** H5
Gwynedd □ *U.K.* 52°52N 4°10W **28** B6
Gyaring Hu *China* 34°50N 97°40E **78** E8
Gydan Peninsula *Russia* 70°0N 78°0E **76** B8
Gympie *Australia* 26°11S 152°38E **98** F9
Győr *Hungary* 47°41N 17°40E **65** E9
Gyumri *Armenia* 40°47N 43°50E **71** F7

H

Ha'apai Group *Tonga* 19°47S 174°27W **99** D16
Haarlem *Neths.* 52°23N 4°39E **64** B3
Hachinohe *Japan* 40°30N 141°29E **81** C7
Hackney □ *U.K.* 51°33N 0°3W **31** C8
Hackthorpe *U.K.* 54°34N 2°42W **26** C3
Hadd, Ra's al *Oman* 22°35N 59°50E **87** F9
Haddenham *U.K.* 51°46N 0°55W **31** C7
Haddington *U.K.* 55°57N 2°47W **25** C10
Hadejia *Nigeria* 12°30N 10°5E **94** F7
Hadleigh *U.K.* 52°3N 0°58E **31** B10
Hadlow *U.K.* 51°13N 0°22E **31** U9
Haḍramawt □ *Yemen* 15°30N 49°30E **89** D4
Hadrian's Wall *U.K.* 55°0N 2°30W **26** B4
Haeju *N. Korea* 38°3N 125°45E **79** D14
Hafizabad *Pakistan* 32°5N 73°40E **84** C8
Hagen *Germany* 51°21N 7°27E **64** C4
Hagerstown *U.S.A.* 39°39N 77°43W **112** F9
Hags Hd. *Ireland* 52°57N 9°28W **20** C4
Hague, C. de la *France* 49°44N 1°56W **66** B3
Hague, The *Neths.* 52°7N 4°17E **64** B3
Haguenau *France* 48°49N 7°47E **66** B7
Haida Gwaii *Canada* 53°20N 132°10W **108** D6
Haifa *Israel* 32°46N 35°0E **86** C3
Haikou *China* 20°1N 110°16E **79** G11
Ḥā'il *Si. Arabia* 27°28N 41°45E **86** E5
Hailar *China* 49°10N 119°38E **79** B12
Hailey *U.S.A.* 43°31N 114°19W **110** B4
Haileybury *Canada* 47°30N 79°38W **112** B8
Hailsham *U.K.* 50°52N 0°16E **31** E9
Hailun *China* 47°28N 126°50E **79** B14
Hainan □ *China* 19°0N 109°30E **79** H10
Hainan Dao *China* 19°0N 109°30E **79** H10
Hainan Str. *China* 20°10N 110°15E **79** G11
Haines Junction *Canada* 60°45N 137°30W **108** C6
Hainton *U.K.* 53°21N 0°14W **27** F8
Haiphong *Vietnam* 20°47N 106°41E **78** D10
Haiti ■ *W. Indies* 19°0N 72°30W **115** D10
Haji Ibrahim *Iraq* 36°40N 44°30E **86** B6
Ḥajjah *Yemen* 15°42N 43°36E **89** D3
Hakkoda-San *Japan* 40°39N 140°53E **81** C7
Hakodate *Japan* 41°45N 140°44E **81** C7
Haku-San *Japan* 36°9N 136°46E **81** E5
Halaib Triangle *Africa* 22°30N 35°20E **95** D12
Halberstadt *Germany* 51°54N 11°3E **64** C6
Halberton *U.K.* 50°54N 3°25W **29** F7
Halden *Norway* 59°9N 11°23E **63** F6
Haldia *India* 22°5N 88°3E **85** H16

Haldwani *India* 29°31N 79°30E **84** E11
Halesowen *U.K.* 52°27N 2°3W **27** H4
Halesworth *U.K.* 52°20N 1°31E **31** B12
Halifax *Canada* 44°38N 63°35W **113** C16
Halifax *U.K.* 53°43N 1°52W **27** E5
Halkirk *U.K.* 58°30N 3°29W **23** E11
Hall Beach *Canada* 68°46N 81°12W **109** C11
Hall Pen. *Canada* 63°30N 66°0W **109** C13
Halle *Germany* 51°30N 11°56E **64** C6
Hallow *U.K.* 52°14N 2°15W **30** B4
Halls Creek *Australia* 18°16S 127°38E **98** D4
Hallworthy *U.K.* 50°39N 4°35W **29** F4
Halmahera *Indonesia* 0°40N 128°0E **83** D7
Halmstad *Sweden* 56°41N 12°52E **63** F6
Halstead *U.K.* 51°57N 0°40E **31** C10
Haltwhistle *U.K.* 54°58N 2°26W **26** C4
Hamadān *Iran* 34°52N 48°32E **86** C7
Ḥamāh *Syria* 35°5N 36°40E **86** C4
Hamamatsu *Japan* 34°45N 137°45E **81** F5
Hamar *Norway* 60°48N 11°7E **63** E6
Hambantota *Sri Lanka* 6°10N 81°10E **84** R12
Hambledon *U.K.* 50°55N 1°5W **30** E6
Hambleton Hills *U.K.* 54°17N 1°12W **26** D6
Hamburg *Germany* 53°33N 9°59E **64** B5
Hämeenlinna *Finland* 61°0N 24°28E **63** E8
Hameln *Germany* 52°6N 9°21E **64** B5
Hamersley Ra. *Australia* 22°0S 117°45E **98** E2
Hamhŭng *N. Korea* 39°54N 127°30E **79** D14
Hami *China* 42°55N 93°25E **78** C7
Hamilton *Canada* 43°15N 79°50W **111** B11
Hamilton *N.Z.* 37°47S 175°19E **99** H14
Hamilton *U.K.* 55°46N 4°2W **24** C7
Hamilton *U.S.A.* 39°24N 84°34W **112** F5
Hamm *Germany* 51°40N 7°50E **64** C4
Hammerfest *Norway* 70°39N 23°41E **63** C8
Hammersmith and Fulham □ *U.K.* 51°30N 0°14W **31** D8
Hammond *U.S.A.* 41°38N 87°30W **112** E4
Hammonton *U.S.A.* 39°39N 74°48W **113** F10
Hampshire □ *U.K.* 51°7N 1°23W **30** D6
Hampshire Downs *U.K.* 51°15N 1°10W **30** D6
Hampton in Arden *U.K.* 52°26N 1°41W **27** H5
Han Shui → *China* 30°34N 114°17E **79** E11
Hancock *U.S.A.* 47°8N 88°35W **112** B3
Handan *China* 36°35N 114°28E **79** D11
Hanford *U.S.A.* 36°20N 119°39W **110** C3
Hangayn Nuruu *Mongolia* 47°30N 99°0E **78** B8
Hangzhou *China* 30°18N 120°11E **79** E13
Hangzhou Wan *China* 30°15N 120°45E **79** E13
Hankö *Finland* 59°50N 22°57E **63** F8
Hanna *Canada* 51°40N 111°54W **108** D8
Hannibal *U.S.A.* 39°42N 91°22W **111** C8
Hanningfield Res. *U.K.* 51°40N 0°31E **31** C10
Hannover *Germany* 52°22N 9°46E **64** B5
Hanoi *Vietnam* 21°5N 105°55E **78** G10
Hanover *U.S.A.* 39°48N 76°59W **112** F9
Hanover, I. *Chile* 51°0S 74°50W **121** H2
Hans I. *Arctic* 80°49N 66°38W **109** A13
Hanzhong *China* 33°10N 107°1E **78** E10
Haora *India* 22°34N 88°18E **85** H16
Haparanda *Sweden* 65°52N 24°8E **63** D8
Happy Valley-Goose Bay *Canada* 53°15N 60°20W **109** D13
Har Hu *China* 38°20N 97°38E **78** D8
Har Us Nuur *Mongolia* 48°0N 92°0E **78** B7
Ḥaraḍ *Si. Arabia* 24°22N 49°0E **86** E7
Harare *Zimbabwe* 17°43S 31°2E **97** H6
Harbin *China* 45°48N 126°40E **79** B14
Harbor Beach *U.S.A.* 43°51N 82°39W **112** D6
Hardangerfjorden *Norway* 60°5N 6°0E **63** E5
Hardy, Pte. *St. Lucia* 14°6N 60°56W **114** b
Harer *Ethiopia* 9°20N 42°8E **89** F3
Harewood *U.K.* 53°54N 1°30W **27** E6
Hargeisa *Somalia* 9°30N 44°2E **89** F3
Haridwar *India* 29°58N 78°9E **84** E11
Haringey □ *U.K.* 51°34N 0°5W **31** C8
Haringhata → *Bangla.* 22°0N 89°58E **85** J16
Harīrūd → *Asia* 37°24N 60°38E **87** B10
Harlech *U.K.* 52°52N 4°6W **28** B5
Harleston *U.K.* 52°24N 1°18E **31** B11
Harlingen *U.S.A.* 26°12N 97°42W **110** E7
Harlow *U.K.* 51°46N 0°8E **31** C9
Harney L. *U.S.A.* 43°14N 119°8W **110** B3
Härnösand *Sweden* 62°38N 17°55E **63** E7
Haroldswick *U.K.* 60°48N 0°50W **22** A16
Harpenden *U.K.* 51°49N 0°21W **31** C8
Harricana → *Canada* 50°56N 79°32W **109** D12
Harrietsham *U.K.* 51°14N 0°41E **31** D10
Harrington *U.K.* 54°37N 3°33W **26** C1
Harris *U.K.* 57°50N 6°55W **22** G4
Harris, Sd. of *U.K.* 57°44N 7°6W **22** G3
Harrisburg *U.S.A.* 40°16N 76°53W **112** E9
Harrison, C. *Canada* 54°55N 57°55W **109** D14
Harrisonburg *U.S.A.* 38°27N 78°52W **112** F8
Harrisville *U.S.A.* 44°39N 83°17W **112** C6
Harrogate *U.K.* 54°0N 1°33W **27** D5
Harrow □ *U.K.* 51°35N 0°21W **31** C8
Hart *U.S.A.* 43°42N 86°22W **112** D4
Hartest *U.K.* 52°8N 0°40E **31** B10
Hartford *Conn., U.S.A.* 41°46N 72°41W **113** E11
Hartford *Ky., U.S.A.* 37°27N 86°55W **112** G4
Hartford *Wis., U.S.A.* 43°19N 88°22W **112** D3
Hartland *U.K.* 50°59N 4°29W **29** F5
Hartland Pt. *U.K.* 51°1N 4°32W **29** E4
Hartlebury *U.K.* 52°20N 2°14W **30** B4
Hartlepool *U.K.* 54°42N 1°13W **26** C6
Hartley *U.K.* 55°5N 1°28W **26** B6
Hartpury *U.K.* 51°55N 2°17W **30** C4
Harvey *U.S.A.* 41°36N 87°50W **112** E4
Harwell *U.K.* 51°36N 1°17W **30** C5
Harwich *U.K.* 51°56N 1°17E **31** C11
Haryana □ *India* 29°0N 76°10E **84** E10
Harz *Germany* 51°38N 10°44E **64** C6
Hasa *Si. Arabia* 25°50N 49°0E **86** E7
Haskovo *Bulgaria* 41°56N 25°30E **69** D11
Haslemere *U.K.* 51°5N 0°43W **31** D7
Haslingden *U.K.* 53°42N 2°19W **27** E4
Hastings *U.K.* 50°51N 0°35E **31** E10
Hastings *U.S.A.* 40°35N 98°23W **110** B7
Hat Yai *Thailand* 7°1N 100°27E **82** C2
Hatay *Turkey* 36°14N 36°10E **71** G6

Hatfield *U.K.* 51°46N 0°13W **31** C8
Hatgal *Mongolia* 50°26N 100°9E **78** A9
Hatherleigh *U.K.* 50°49N 4°5W **29** F5
Hathersage *U.K.* 53°20N 1°39W **27** F5
Hathras *India* 27°36N 78°6E **84** F11
Hatia *Bangla.* 22°30N 91°5E **85** H17
Hatteras, C. *U.S.A.* 35°14N 75°32W **111** C11
Hattiesburg *U.S.A.* 31°20N 89°17W **111** D9
Haugesund *Norway* 59°23N 5°13E **63** F5
Haughley *U.K.* 52°14N 0°57E **31** B10
Haut Atlas *Morocco* 32°30N 5°0W **94** B4
Hauts Plateaux *Algeria* 35°0N 1°0E **94** B6
Havana = La Habana *Cuba* 23°8N 82°22W **115** C8
Havant *U.K.* 50°51N 0°58W **31** E7
Havasu, L. *U.S.A.* 34°18N 114°28W **110** D4
Havel → *Germany* 52°50N 12°3E **64** B7
Haverfordwest *U.K.* 51°48N 4°58W **28** D4
Haverhill *U.K.* 52°5N 0°28E **31** B9
Haverhill *U.S.A.* 42°47N 71°5W **113** D12
Haverigg *U.K.* 54°13N 3°17W **26** D2
Havering □ *U.K.* 51°34N 0°13E **31** C9
Havre *U.S.A.* 48°33N 109°41W **110** A5
Havre-St.-Pierre *Canada* 50°18N 63°33W **109** D13
Hawai'i □ *U.S.A.* 19°30N 155°30W **110** J17
Hawai'i □ *U.S.A.* 19°30N 156°30W **110** H16
Hawaiian Is. *Pac. Oc.* 20°30N 156°0W **103** E12
Hawes *U.K.* 54°19N 2°12W **26** D4
Haweswater → *U.K.* 54°31N 2°47W **26** C3
Hawick *U.K.* 55°26N 2°47W **25** D10
Hawkchurch *U.K.* 50°48N 2°56W **30** F3
Hawkesbury *Canada* 45°37N 74°37W **113** C10
Hawkesbury Upton *U.K.* 51°35N 2°19W **30** C4
Hawkhurst *U.K.* 51°2N 0°32E **31** D10
Hawkshead *U.K.* 54°23N 2°59W **26** D3
Haworth *U.K.* 53°50N 1°58W **27** E5
Hawsker *U.K.* 54°27N 0°34W **26** D7
Haxby *U.K.* 54°1N 1°4W **27** D6
Hay *Australia* 34°30S 144°51E **98** G8
Hay → *Canada* 60°50N 116°26W **108** C8
Hay-on-Wye *U.K.* 52°5N 3°8W **28** C7
Hay River *Canada* 60°51N 115°44W **108** C8
Haydon Bridge *U.K.* 54°58N 2°14W **26** C4
Hayes → *Canada* 57°3N 92°12W **108** D10
Hayle *U.K.* 50°11N 5°26W **29** G3
Hays *U.S.A.* 38°53N 99°20W **110** C7
Hayton *U.K.* 54°55N 2°45W **26** C3
Hayward *U.S.A.* 46°1N 91°29W **112** B2
Haywards Heath *U.K.* 51°0N 0°5W **31** E8
Hazar *Turkmenistan* 39°34N 53°16E **71** G9
Hazard *U.S.A.* 37°15N 83°12W **112** G6
Hazaribag *India* 23°58N 85°26E **85** H14
Heacham *U.K.* 52°54N 0°29E **31** A9
Headcorn *U.K.* 51°10N 0°38E **31** D10
Heanor *U.K.* 53°1N 1°21W **27** F6
Heard I. *Ind. Oc.* 53°6S 72°36E **53** G13
Hearst *Canada* 49°40N 83°41W **109** E11
Heathfield *U.K.* 50°58N 0°16E **31** E9
Hebburn *U.K.* 54°59N 1°32W **26** C5
Hebden Bridge *U.K.* 53°45N 2°0W **27** E5
Hebei □ *China* 39°0N 116°0E **79** D12
Hebrides *U.K.* 57°30N 7°0W **56** D4
Hebrides, Sea of the *U.K.* 57°5N 7°0W **22** H4
Hebron *Canada* 58°5N 62°30W **109** D13
Hecate Str. *Canada* 53°10N 130°30W **108** D6
Hechi *China* 24°40N 108°2E **78** G10
Hechuan *China* 30°2N 106°12E **78** E10
Heckington *U.K.* 52°59N 0°17W **27** F8
Hednesford *U.K.* 52°43N 1°59W **27** G5
Hedon *U.K.* 53°44N 0°12W **27** E8
Heerlen *Neths.* 50°55N 5°58E **64** C3
Hefei *China* 31°52N 117°18E **79** E12
Hegang *China* 47°20N 130°19E **79** B15
Heidelberg *Germany* 49°24N 8°42E **64** D5
Heihe *China* 50°10N 127°30E **79** A14
Heilbronn *Germany* 49°9N 9°13E **64** D5
Heilongjiang □ *China* 48°0N 126°0E **79** B14
Heimaey *Iceland* 63°26N 20°17W **63** B1
Hekla *Iceland* 63°56N 19°35W **63** B2
Helena *U.S.A.* 46°36N 112°2W **110** A4
Helensburgh *U.K.* 56°1N 4°43W **24** B6
Helgoland *Germany* 54°10N 7°53E **64** A4
Hellifield *U.K.* 54°1N 2°12W **27** D4
Helmand → *Afghan.* 31°12N 61°34E **87** D10
Helmsdale *U.K.* 58°7N 3°39W **23** F10
Helmsley *U.K.* 54°15N 1°3W **26** D6
Helperby *U.K.* 54°8N 1°19W **26** D6
Helsby *U.K.* 53°17N 2°46W **27** F3
Helsingborg *Sweden* 56°3N 12°42E **63** F6
Helston *U.K.* 50°6N 5°17W **29** G3
Helvellyn *U.K.* 54°32N 3°1W **26** C2
Helwân *Egypt* 29°50N 31°20E **95** C12
Hemel Hempstead *U.K.* 51°44N 0°28W **31** C8
Hempton *U.K.* 52°50N 0°50E **31** A10
Hemsworth *U.K.* 53°37N 1°21W **27** E6
Hemyock *U.K.* 50°54N 3°15W **29** F7
Henan □ *China* 34°0N 114°0E **79** E11
Henderson *Ky., U.S.A.* 37°50N 87°35W **112** G4
Henderson *Nev., U.S.A.* 36°2N 114°58W **110** C3
Henfield *U.K.* 50°56N 0°16W **31** E8
Hengduan Shan *China* 28°30N 98°50E **78** F8
Hengyang *China* 26°59N 112°22E **79** F11
Henley-in-Arden *U.K.* 52°18N 1°46W **30** B5
Henley-on-Thames *U.K.* 51°32N 0°54W **31** C7
Henlopen, C. *U.S.A.* 38°48N 75°6W **113** F10
Henlow *U.K.* 52°2N 0°17W **31** B8
Henrietta Maria, C. *Canada* 55°9N 82°20W **109** D11
Henstridge *U.K.* 50°58N 2°24W **30** E4
Hentiyn Nuruu *Mongolia* 48°30N 108°30E **78** B10
Herät *Afghan.* 34°20N 62°7E **87** C10
Hereford *U.K.* 52°4N 2°43W **30** B3
Herefordshire □ *U.K.* 52°8N 2°40W **30** B3
Herford *Germany* 52°7N 8°39E **64** B5
Herlen → *Asia* 48°48N 117°0E **79** B12
Herm *U.K.* 49°30N 2°28W **29** J9
Herma Ness *U.K.* 60°50N 0°54W **22** A16
Hermosillo *Mexico* 29°10N 111°0W **114** B2
Hernád → *Hungary* 47°56N 21°8E **65** D11
Herne Bay *U.K.* 51°21N 1°8E **31** D11
Herstmonceux *U.K.* 50°53N 0°20E **31** E9

Hertford *U.K.* 51°48N 0°4W **31** C8
Hertfordshire □ *U.K.* 51°51N 0°5W **31** C8
's-Hertogenbosch *Neths.* 51°42N 5°17E **64** C3
Hessen □ *Germany* 50°30N 9°0E **64** C5
Hessle *U.K.* 53°44N 0°24W **27** E8
Hethersett *U.K.* 52°36N 1°10E **31** A11
Hetton-le-Hole *U.K.* 54°50N 1°26W **26** C6
Hexham *U.K.* 54°58N 2°4W **26** C4
Heybridge *U.K.* 51°45N 0°42E **31** C10
Heysham *U.K.* 54°3N 2°53W **26** D3
Heytesbury *U.K.* 51°11N 2°6W **30** D4
Heywood *U.K.* 53°35N 2°12W **27** E4
Heze *China* 35°14N 115°20E **79** D12
Hibbing *U.S.A.* 47°25N 92°56W **111** A8
Hickman *U.S.A.* 36°34N 89°11W **112** G3
Hidalgo del Parral *Mexico* 26°56N 105°40W **114** B3
Hierro *Canary Is.* 27°44N 18°0W **94** C2
Higashiōsaka *Japan* 34°39N 135°37E **81** F4
High Bentham *U.K.* 54°7N 2°28W **26** D4
High Ercall *U.K.* 52°45N 2°35W **27** G3
High Hesket *U.K.* 54°48N 2°49W **26** C3
High Level *Canada* 58°31N 117°8W **108** D8
High Pike *U.K.* 54°42N 3°4W **26** C2
High Prairie *Canada* 55°30N 116°30W **108** D8
High River *Canada* 50°30N 113°50W **108** D8
High Veld *Africa* 27°0S 27°0E **90** J6
High Willhays *U.K.* 50°40N 4°0W **29** F5
High Wycombe *U.K.* 51°37N 0°45W **31** C7
Higham Ferrers *U.K.* 52°19N 0°35W **31** B7
Highbridge *U.K.* 51°13N 2°58W **30** D3
Highclere *U.K.* 51°20N 1°21W **30** D6
Highland □ *U.K.* 57°17N 4°21W **22** H7
Highley *U.K.* 52°27N 2°23W **27** H4
Hightae *U.K.* 55°6N 3°26W **25** D9
Highworth *U.K.* 51°37N 1°43W **30** C5
Hiiumaa *Estonia* 58°50N 22°45E **63** F8
Ḥijāz *Si. Arabia* 24°0N 40°0E **86** E4
Hildesheim *Germany* 52°9N 9°56E **64** B5
Hilgay *U.K.* 52°34N 0°24E **31** A9
Hillaby, Mt. *Barbados* 13°12N 59°35W **114** c2
Hillcrest *Barbados* 13°13N 59°31W **114** c
Hillingdon □ *U.K.* 51°32N 0°27W **31** C8
Hillsborough *U.K.* 54°28N 6°5W **19** C9
Hillsdale *U.S.A.* 41°56N 84°38W **112** E5
Hilo *U.S.A.* 19°44N 155°5W **110** J17
Hilpsford Pt. *U.K.* 54°3N 3°12W **26** D2
Hilversum *Neths.* 52°14N 5°10E **64** B3
Himachal Pradesh □ *India* 31°30N 77°0E **84** D10
Himalaya *Asia* 29°0N 84°0E **85** E14
Himeji *Japan* 34°50N 134°40E **81** F4
Hinckley *U.K.* 52°33N 1°22W **27** G6
Hinderwell *U.K.* 54°32N 0°45W **26** D7
Hindhead *U.K.* 51°7N 0°43W **31** D7
Hindley *U.K.* 53°33N 2°35W **27** E3
Hindu Kush *Asia* 36°0N 71°0E **87** C12
Hingham *U.K.* 52°35N 1°0E **31** A10
Hingoli *India* 19°41N 77°15E **84** K10
Hinkley Pt. *U.K.* 51°12N 3°8W **30** D2
Hinstock *U.K.* 52°50N 2°27W **27** G4
Hinton *U.S.A.* 37°40N 80°54W **112** G7
Hirakud Dam *India* 21°32N 83°45E **85** J13
Hirosaki *Japan* 40°34N 140°28E **81** C7
Hiroshima *Japan* 34°24N 132°30E **81** F3
Hisar *India* 29°12N 75°45E **84** E9
Hispaniola *W. Indies* 19°0N 71°0W **115** D10
Histon *U.K.* 52°16N 0°7E **31** B9
Hitachi *Japan* 36°36N 140°39E **81** E7
Hitchin *U.K.* 51°58N 0°16W **31** C8
Hjälmaren *Sweden* 59°18N 15°40E **63** F7
Hkakabo Razi *Myanmar* 28°25N 97°23E **85** E20
Ho Chi Minh City *Vietnam* 10°58N 106°40E **82** B3
Hoare B. *Canada* 65°17N 62°30W **109** C13
Hobart *Australia* 42°50S 147°21E **98** J8
Hobbs *U.S.A.* 32°42N 103°8W **110** D6
Hodder → *U.K.* 53°57N 2°27W **27** E4
Hoddesdon *U.K.* 51°45N 0°1W **31** C8
Hodge → *U.K.* 54°16N 0°56W **26** D7
Hodgson *Canada* 51°13N 97°36W **108** D10
Hódmezővásárhely *Hungary* 46°28N 20°22E **65** E11
Hodna, Chott el *Algeria* 35°26N 4°43E **94** A6
Hoek van Holland *Neths.* 52°0N 4°7E **64** B3
Hoff *U.K.* 54°34N 2°31W **26** C3
Hōfu *Japan* 34°3N 131°34E **81** F2
Hog's Back *U.K.* 51°13N 0°38W **31** D7
Hoh Xil Shan *China* 36°30N 89°0E **78** D6
Höher Rhön *Germany* 50°24N 9°58E **64** C5
Hohhot *China* 40°52N 111°40E **79** C11
Hokkaidō □ *Japan* 43°30N 143°0E **81** B8
Holbeach *U.K.* 52°48N 0°1E **27** G9
Holbeach Marsh *U.K.* 52°52N 0°5E **27** F9
Holderness *U.K.* 53°45N 0°5W **27** E8
Holetown *Barbados* 13°11N 59°38W **114** c
Holguín *Cuba* 20°50N 76°20W **115** C9
Holkham *U.K.* 52°57N 0°48E **31** A10
Holland *U.S.A.* 42°47N 86°7W **112** D4
Holland Fen *U.K.* 53°0N 0°8W **27** G8
Holland on Sea *U.K.* 51°48N 1°13E **31** C11
Holme *U.K.* 53°50N 0°46W **27** E7
Holmes Chapel *U.K.* 53°12N 2°21W **27** F4
Holmfirth *U.K.* 53°35N 1°46W **27** E5
Holstebro *Denmark* 56°22N 8°37E **63** F5
Holsworthy *U.K.* 50°48N 4°22W **29** F5
Holt *U.K.* 52°55N 1°6E **31** A11
Holy I. *Anglesey, U.K.* 53°17N 4°37W **28** A4
Holy I. *Northumberland, U.K.* 55°40N 1°47W **26** A6
Holyhead *U.K.* 53°18N 4°38W **28** A4
Holywell *U.K.* 53°16N 3°14W **28** A7
Home B. *Canada* 68°40N 67°10W **109** C13
Homer *U.S.A.* 59°39N 151°33W **108** D4
Homs *Syria* 34°40N 36°45E **86** C4
Homyel *Belarus* 52°28N 31°0E **65** B16
Honduras ■ *Cent. Amer.* 14°40N 86°30W **114** E7
Honduras, G. of *Caribbean* 16°50N 87°0W **114** D7
Hønefoss *Norway* 60°10N 10°18E **63** E6
Honey L. *U.S.A.* 40°15N 120°19W **110** B2
Hong Kong □ *China* 22°11N 114°14E **79** a
Hong Kong Int. ✈ (HKG) *China* 22°10N 111°0W **114** B2
Hongjiang *China* 27°7N 109°59E **79** F10
Hongshui He → *China* 23°48N 109°30E **79** G10
Hongze Hu *China* 33°15N 118°35E **79** E12

Honiara *Solomon Is.* 9°27S 159°57E **99** B10
Honington *U.K.* 52°59N 0°35W **27** G7
Honiton *U.K.* 50°47N 3°11W **29** F7
Honolulu *U.S.A.* 21°19N 157°52W **103** E12
Honshū *Japan* 36°0N 138°0E **81** F6
Hoo St. Werburgh *U.K.* 51°25N 0°35E **31** D10
Hood, Mt. *U.S.A.* 45°23N 121°42W **110** A2
Hook *U.K.* 51°17N 0°57W **31** D7
Hook Hd. *Ireland* 52°7N 6°56W **21** D9
Hooper Bay *U.S.A.* 61°32N 166°6W **108** C3
Hoopeston *U.S.A.* 40°28N 87°40W **112** E4
Hoorn *Neths.* 52°38N 5°4E **64** B3
Hoover Dam *U.S.A.* 36°1N 114°44W **110** C4
Hope *U.S.A.* 33°40N 93°36W **111** D8
Hopedale *Canada* 55°28N 60°13W **109** D13
Horden *U.K.* 54°46N 1°19W **26** C6
Horley *U.K.* 51°10N 0°10W **31** D8
Horlivka *Ukraine* 48°19N 38°5E **71** E6
Hormuz, Str. of *The Gulf* 26°30N 56°30E **87** E9
Horn, C. = Hornos, C. de *Chile* 55°50S 67°30W **121** H3
Horn, Is. *Wall. & F. Is.* 14°16S 178°6W **99** C15
Horn Head *Ireland* 55°14N 8°0W **18** A6
Hornavan *Sweden* 66°15N 17°30E **63** D7
Horncastle *U.K.* 53°13N 0°7W **27** F8
Horndean *U.K.* 50°55N 1°1W **30** E6
Hornell *U.S.A.* 42°20N 77°40W **112** D9
Hornepayne *Canada* 49°14N 84°48W **112** A5
Horningsham *U.K.* 51°10N 2°15W **30** D4
Hornos, C. de *Chile* 55°50S 67°30W **121** H3
Hornsea *U.K.* 53°55N 0°11W **27** E8
Horqin Youyi Qianqi *China* 46°5N 122°3E **79** B13
Horsforth *U.K.* 53°50N 1°39W **27** E5
Horsham *Australia* 36°44S 142°13E **98** H7
Horsham *U.K.* 51°4N 0°20W **31** D8
Horsham St. Faith *U.K.* 52°43N 1°14E **31** A11
Horsted Keynes *U.K.* 51°2N 0°1W **31** D8
Horton → *Canada* 69°56N 126°52W **108** C7
Horton in Ribblesdale *U.K.* 54°9N 2°17W **26** D4
Horwich *U.K.* 53°36N 2°33W **27** E3
Hoste, I. *Chile* 55°0S 69°0W **121** H3
Hot Springs *Ark., U.S.A.* 34°31N 93°3W **111** D8
Hot Springs *S. Dak., U.S.A.* 43°26N 103°29W **110** B6
Hotan *China* 37°25N 79°55E **78** D4
Hotan He → *China* 40°22N 80°56E **78** C5
Houghton *U.S.A.* 47°7N 88°34W **112** B3
Houghton L. *U.S.A.* 44°21N 84°44W **112** C5
Houghton-le-Spring *U.K.* 54°51N 1°28W **26** C6
Houghton Regis *U.K.* 51°54N 0°32W **31** C7
Houlton *U.S.A.* 46°8N 67°51W **113** B14
Houma *U.S.A.* 29°36N 90°43W **111** E8
Hounslow □ *U.K.* 51°28N 0°21W **31** D8
Hourn, L. *U.K.* 57°7N 5°35W **22** H6
Houston *U.S.A.* 29°45N 95°21W **111** E7
Hove *U.K.* 50°50N 0°10W **31** E8
Hoveton *U.K.* 52°43N 1°25E **31** A11
Hovingham *U.K.* 54°11N 0°58W **26** D7
Hövsgöl Nuur *Mongolia* 51°0N 100°30E **78** A9
Howakil *Eritrea* 15°10N 40°16E **89** D3
Howden *U.K.* 53°45N 0°52W **27** E7
Howe, C. *Australia* 37°30S 150°0E **98** H9
Howell *U.S.A.* 42°36N 83°56W **112** D6
Howland I. *Pac. Oc.* 0°48N 176°38W **102** G10
Howth *Ireland* 53°23N 6°7W **21** B10
Howth Hd. *Ireland* 53°22N 6°4W **21** B10
Hoxne *U.K.* 52°21N 1°12E **31** B11
Hoy *U.K.* 58°50N 3°15W **23** E11
Høyanger *Norway* 61°13N 6°4E **63** E5
Hoylake *U.K.* 53°24N 3°4W **27** F2
Hradec Králové *Czechia* 50°15N 15°50E **64** C8
Hrodna *Belarus* 53°42N 23°52E **65** B12
Hron → *Slovakia* 47°49N 18°45E **65** E10
Hsinchu *Taiwan* 24°48N 120°58E **79** F13
Huacho *Peru* 11°10S 77°35W **120** D2
Huai He → *China* 33°0N 118°30E **79** E12
Huaibei *China* 34°0N 116°48E **79** E12
Huaihua *China* 27°32N 109°57E **79** F10
Huainan *China* 32°38N 116°58E **79** E12
Huallaga → *Peru* 5°15S 75°30W **120** C2
Huambo *Angola* 12°42S 15°54E **97** G3
Huancavelica *Peru* 12°50S 75°5W **120** D2
Huancayo *Peru* 12°5S 75°12W **120** D2
Huang He → *China* 37°55N 118°50E **79** D12
Huangshan *China* 29°42N 118°25E **79** F12
Huangshi *China* 30°10N 115°3E **79** E12
Huánuco *Peru* 9°55S 76°15W **120** C2
Huaraz *Peru* 9°30S 77°32W **120** C2
Huascarán, Nevado *Peru* 9°7S 77°37W **120** C2
Huasco *Chile* 28°30S 71°15W **121** E2
Huatabampo *Mexico* 26°50N 109°38W **114** B3
Hubballi *India* 15°22N 75°15E **84** M9
Hubei □ *China* 31°0N 112°0E **79** E11
Hucknall *U.K.* 53°3N 1°13W **27** F6
Huddersfield *U.K.* 53°39N 1°47W **27** E5
Hudiksvall *Sweden* 61°43N 17°10E **63** E7
Hudson → *U.S.A.* 40°42N 74°2W **113** E10
Hudson Bay *Canada* 60°0N 86°0W **109** D11
Hudson Falls *U.S.A.* 43°18N 73°35W **113** D11
Hudson Str. *Canada* 62°0N 70°0W **109** C13
Hue *Vietnam* 16°30N 107°35E **82** A3
Huelva *Spain* 37°18N 6°57W **67** D2
Huesca *Spain* 42°8N 0°25W **67** A5
Hugh Town *U.K.* 49°55N 6°19W **29** H1
Hughenden *Australia* 20°52S 144°10E **98** E7
Hugli → *India* 21°56N 88°4E **85** J16
Huila, Nevado del *Colombia* 3°0N 76°0W **120** B2
Hull = Kingston upon Hull *U.K.* 53°45N 0°21W **27** E8
Hull *Canada* 45°26N 75°43W **113** C10
Hull → *U.K.* 53°44N 0°20W **27** E8
Hullavington *U.K.* 51°32N 2°9W **30** C4
Hulme End *U.K.* 53°8N 1°50W **27** F5
Hulun Nur *China* 49°0N 117°30E **79** B12
Humaitá *Brazil* 7°35S 63°1W **120** C3
Humber → *U.K.* 53°42N 0°27W **27** E8
Humber, Mouth of the *U.K.* 53°32N 0°8E **27** E9
Humboldt *Canada* 52°15N 105°9W **108** D9
Humboldt → *U.S.A.* 39°59N 118°36W **110** B3
Humen *China* 22°50N 113°40E **79** a
Humphreys Peak *U.S.A.* 35°21N 111°41W **110** C4
Humshaugh *U.K.* 55°3N 2°8W **26** B4
Húnaflói *Iceland* 65°50N 20°50W **63** A1

Hunan

Hunan □ China 27°30N 112°0E 79 F11
Hunchun China 42°52N 130°28E 79 C15
Hungary ■ Europe 47°20N 19°20E 65 E10
Hungary, Plain of Europe 47°0N 20°0E 56 F10
Hungerford U.K. 51°25N 1°31W 30 D5
Hüngnam N. Korea 39°49N 127°45E 79 D14
Hunmanby U.K. 54°10N 0°20W 26 D8
Hunsrück Germany 49°56N 7°27E 64 D4
Hunstanton U.K. 52°56N 0°29E 31 A9
Huntingdon U.K. 52°20N 0°11W 31 B8
Huntington Ind., U.S.A. 40°53N 85°30W 112 E15
Huntington W. Va., U.S.A. 38°25N 82°27W 112 F6
Huntly U.K. 57°27N 2°47W 23 H12
Huntsville Canada 45°20N 79°14W 109 E12
Huntsville Ala., U.S.A. 34°44N 86°35W 111 D9
Huntsville Tex., U.S.A. 30°43N 95°33W 111 E7
Hurghada Egypt 27°15N 33°50E 95 C12
Hurley U.S.A. 46°27N 90°11W 112 B2
Huron U.S.A. 44°22N 98°13W 110 B7
Huron, L. U.S.A. 44°30N 82°40W 112 C6
Hursley U.K. 51°2N 1°23W 30 D6
Hurstbourne Tarrant U.K. 51°17N 1°26W 30 D6
Hurstpierpoint U.K. 50°56N 0°11W 31 E8
Húsavík Iceland 66°3N 17°21W 63 A2
Husband's Bosworth U.K. 52°28N 1°4W 27 H6
Hutchinson U.S.A. 38°5N 97°56W 110 C7
Huyton U.K. 53°25N 2°51W 27 F3
Huzhou China 30°51N 120°8E 79 E13
Hvar Croatia 43°11N 16°28E 68 C7
Hwang Ho = Huang He →
China 37°55N 118°50E 79 D12
Hwange Zimbabwe 18°18S 26°30E 97 H5
Hwlffordd = Haverfordwest
U.K. 51°48N 4°58W 28 D4
Hyargas Nuur Mongolia 49°0N 93°0E 78 B7
Hyde U.K. 53°27N 2°4W 27 F4
Hyderabad India 17°22N 78°29E 84 L11
Hyderabad Pakistan 25°23N 68°24E 84 G6
Hyères France 43°8N 6°9E 66 E7
Hyères, Îs. d' France 43°0N 6°20E 66 E7
Hyndman Peak U.S.A. 43°45N 114°8W 110 B4
Hythe U.K. 51°4N 1°5E 31 D11

I
Ialomiţa → Romania 44°42N 27°51E 65 F14
Iaşi Romania 47°10N 27°40E 65 E14
Ibadan Nigeria 7°22N 3°58E 94 G6
Ibagué Colombia 4°20N 75°20W 120 B2
Ibarra Ecuador 0°21N 78°7W 120 B2
Ibb Yemen 14°2N 44°10E 89 E3
Iberian Peninsula Europe 40°0N 5°0W 56 H5
Ibiá Brazil 19°30S 46°30W 122 C1
Ibiapaba, Sa. da Brazil 4°0S 41°30W 122 C5
Ibicaraí Brazil 14°51S 39°36W 122 B3
Ibiza = Eivissa Spain 38°54N 1°26E 67 C6
Ibotirama Brazil 12°13S 43°12W 122 B2
Ibstock U.K. 52°42N 1°24W 27 G6
Ica Peru 14°0S 75°48W 120 D2
Içá → Brazil 2°55S 67°58W 120 C3
Iceland ■ Europe 64°45N 19°0W 63 B2
Ichihara Japan 35°28N 140°5E 81 F7
Ichinomiya Japan 35°18N 136°48E 81 F5
Idaho □ U.S.A. 45°0N 115°0W 110 B4
Idaho Falls U.S.A. 43°30N 112°2W 110 B4
Idar-Oberstein Germany 49°43N 7°16E 64 D4
Idle → U.K. 53°27N 0°49E 27 F7
Idlib Syria 35°55N 36°36E 86 C4
Idmiston U.K. 51°9N 1°42W 30 D5
Ife Nigeria 7°30N 4°31E 94 G6
Iforas, Adrar des Africa 19°40N 1°40E 94 E6
Igarapava Brazil 20°3S 47°47W 122 D1
Igarka Russia 67°30N 86°33E 76 C9
Iglésias Italy 39°19N 8°32E 68 E3
Iglulik Canada 69°20N 81°49W 109 C11
Ignace Canada 49°30N 91°40W 112 A2
Igoumenitsa Greece 39°32N 20°18E 69 E9
Iguaçu → Brazil 25°36S 54°36W 121 E4
Iguaçu, Cat. del Brazil 25°41S 54°26W 121 E4
Iguala Mexico 18°21N 99°32W 114 D5
Iguatu Brazil 6°20S 39°18W 120 C6
Iguidi, Erg Africa 27°0N 6°0W 94 C4
Iisalmi Finland 63°32N 27°10E 63 E9
Ijebu-Ode Nigeria 6°47N 3°58E 94 G6
IJsselmeer Neths. 52°45N 5°20E 64 B3
Ikare Nigeria 7°32N 5°40E 94 G7
Ikaria Greece 37°35N 26°10E 69 F12
Ikeda Japan 34°1N 133°48E 81 F3
Ilagan Phil. 17°7N 121°53E 83 A6
Ĩlam Iran 33°36N 46°36E 86 C6
Ilchester U.K. 51°0N 2°41W 30 D3
Île-de-France □ France 49°0N 2°20E 66 B5
Ilebo Dem. Rep. of the Congo 4°17S 20°55E 96 E4
Ilemi Triangle Africa 5°0N 35°20E 96 C7
Ilesha Nigeria 7°37N 4°40E 94 G6
Ilfracombe U.K. 51°12N 4°8W 29 E5
Ilhéus Brazil 14°49S 39°2W 122 B3
Ili → Kazakhstan 45°53N 77°10E 76 E8
Iliamna L. U.S.A. 59°30N 155°0W 108 D4
Iligan Phil. 8°12N 124°13E 83 C6
Ilkeston U.K. 52°58N 1°19W 27 G6
Ilkley U.K. 53°56N 1°48W 27 E5
Illapel Chile 32°0S 71°10W 121 F2
Iller → Germany 48°23N 9°58E 64 D6
Illimani Bolivia 16°30S 67°50W 120 D3
Illinois □ U.S.A. 40°15N 89°30W 111 B9
Illinois → U.S.A. 38°58N 90°28W 111 C8
Ilmen, L. Russia 58°15N 31°10E 70 C5
Ilminster U.K. 50°55N 2°55W 30 E3
Iloilo Phil. 10°45N 122°33E 83 B6
Ilorin Nigeria 8°30N 4°35E 94 G6
Imabari Japan 34°4N 133°0E 81 F3
Imandra, L. Russia 67°30N 33°0E 70 A5
Imatra Finland 61°12N 28°48E 63 E9
imeni Ismail Samani, Pik
Tajikistan 39°0N 72°2E 87 B13
Immingham U.K. 53°37N 0°13W 27 E8
Imola Italy 44°20N 11°42E 68 B4
Imperatriz Brazil 5°30S 47°29W 120 C5
Impéria Italy 43°53N 8°3E 68 C3
Imphal India 24°48N 93°56E 85 G18

In Salah Algeria 27°10N 2°32E 94 C6
Inari Finland 68°54N 27°1E 63 D9
Inarijärvi Finland 69°0N 28°0E 63 D9
Ince Burun Turkey 42°7N 34°56E 71 F5
Incheon S. Korea 37°27N 126°40E 79 D14
Incomáti → Mozam. 25°46S 32°43E 97 K6
Indalsälven → Sweden 62°36N 17°30E 63 E7
India ■ Asia 20°0N 78°0E 84 K11
Indian Ocean 5°0S 75°0E 53 E13
Indiana U.S.A. 40°37N 79°9W 112 E8
Indiana □ U.S.A. 40°0N 86°0W 112 E4
Indianapolis U.S.A. 39°46N 86°9W 112 F4
Indigirka → Russia 70°48N 148°54E 77 B15
Indira Gandhi Canal India 28°0N 72°0E 84 F8
Indo-China Asia 15°0N 102°0E 72 G12
Indonesia ■ Asia 5°0S 115°0E 82 F5
Indore India 22°42N 75°53E 84 H9
Indre → France 47°16N 0°11E 66 C4
Indus → Pakistan 24°20N 67°47E 84 G5
Inebolu Turkey 41°55N 33°40E 71 F5
Inga, Barrage d'
Dem. Rep. of the Congo 5°39S 13°39E 96 F2
Ingatestone U.K. 51°40N 0°24E 31 C9
Ingleborough U.K. 54°10N 2°22W 26 D4
Ingleton U.K. 54°10N 2°27W 26 D4
Ingolstadt Germany 48°46N 11°26E 64 D6
Ingraj Bazar India 24°58N 88°10E 85 G16
Ingushetia □ Russia 43°20N 44°50E 71 F8
Inishbofin Ireland 53°37N 10°13W 18 D1
Inisheer Ireland 53°3N 9°32W 20 B3
Inishfree B. Ireland 55°4N 8°23W 18 A5
Inishkea North Ireland 54°9N 10°11W 18 C1
Inishkea South Ireland 54°7N 10°12W 18 C1
Inishmaan Ireland 53°5N 9°35W 20 B3
Inishmore Ireland 53°8N 9°45W 20 B3
Inishowen Pen. Ireland 55°14N 7°15W 19 A7
Inishshark Ireland 53°37N 10°16W 18 D1
Inishtrahull Ireland 55°26N 7°13W 19 A7
Inishturk Ireland 53°42N 10°7W 18 D1
Inishvickillane Ireland 52°3N 10°37W 20 D1
Inkberrow U.K. 52°13N 1°58W 30 B5
Inland Sea Japan 34°20N 133°30E 81 F3
Inn → Austria 48°35N 13°28E 64 D7
Inner Hebrides U.K. 57°0N 6°30W 22 J4
Inner Mongolia = Nei Mongol
Zizhiqu □ China 42°0N 112°0E 79 C11
Inner Sound U.K. 57°30N 5°55W 22 H6
Innerleithen U.K. 55°37N 3°4W 25 C9
Innsbruck Austria 47°16N 11°23E 64 E6
Inowrocław Poland 52°50N 18°12E 65 B10
Insein Myanmar 16°50N 96°5E 85 L20
Inta Russia 66°5N 60°8E 70 A11
Interlaken Switz. 46°41N 7°50E 64 E4
Inukjuak Canada 58°25N 78°15W 109 D12
Inuvik Canada 68°16N 133°40W 108 C6
Inveraray U.K. 56°14N 5°5W 24 B5
Inverbervie U.K. 56°51N 2°17W 23 J13
Invercargill N.Z. 46°24S 168°24E 99 K12
Invergordon U.K. 57°41N 4°10W 23 G9
Inverkeithing U.K. 56°2N 3°24W 25 B9
Inverness U.K. 57°29N 4°13W 23 H9
Inverurie U.K. 57°17N 2°23W 23 H13
Ioannina Greece 39°42N 20°47E 69 E9
Iona U.K. 56°20N 6°25W 24 B3
Ionia U.S.A. 42°59N 85°4W 112 D5
Ionian Is. Greece 38°40N 20°0E 69 E9
Ionian Sea Medit. S. 37°30N 17°30E 69 E7
Ios Greece 36°41N 25°20E 69 F11
Iowa □ U.S.A. 42°18N 93°30W 111 B8
Iowa City U.S.A. 41°40N 91°32W 111 B8
Ipameri Brazil 17°44S 48°9W 122 C1
Ipatinga Brazil 19°32S 42°30W 122 C2
Ipiales Colombia 0°50N 77°37W 120 B2
Ipoh Malaysia 4°35N 101°5E 82 D2
Ipswich Australia 27°35S 152°40E 98 F9
Ipswich U.K. 52°4N 1°10E 31 B11
Iqaluit Canada 63°44N 68°31W 109 C13
Iquique Chile 20°19S 70°5W 120 E2
Iquitos Peru 3°45S 73°10W 120 C2
Iraklio Greece 35°20N 25°12E 69 G11
Iran ■ Asia 33°0N 53°0E 87 C8
Ĩrānshahr Iran 27°15N 60°40E 87 E10
Irapuato Mexico 20°41N 101°28W 114 C4
Iraq ■ Asia 33°0N 44°0E 86 C5
Irazú, Volcán Costa Rica 9°59N 83°51W 115 E8
Irbil Iraq 36°15N 44°5E 86 B6
Irchester U.K. 52°18N 0°39W 31 B7
Ireland ■ Europe 53°50N 7°52W 62 E2
Ireland's Eye Ireland 53°24N 6°4W 21 B10
Iringa Tanzania 7°48S 35°43E 96 F7
Irish Sea Europe 53°38N 4°48W 62 E4
Irkutsk Russia 52°18N 104°20E 77 D11
Irlam U.K. 53°26N 2°26W 27 F4
Iron Gate Europe 44°44N 22°30E 65 F12
Iron Mountain U.S.A. 45°49N 88°4W 112 C3
Ironbridge U.K. 52°38N 2°30W 27 G4
Ironton U.S.A. 38°32N 82°41W 112 F6
Ironwood U.S.A. 46°27N 90°9W 112 B2
Irt → U.K. 54°23N 3°26E 26 D2
Irthlingborough U.K. 52°20N 0°37W 31 B7
Irtysh → Russia 61°4N 68°52E 76 C7
Irún Spain 43°20N 1°52W 67 A5
Irvine U.K. 55°37N 4°41W 24 D6
Irvinestown U.K. 54°28N 7°39W 18 C6
Ísafjörður Iceland 66°5N 23°9W 63 A1
Isar → Germany 48°48N 12°57E 64 D7
Ischia Italy 40°44N 13°57E 68 D5
Isère → France 44°59N 4°51E 66 D6
Ishim → Russia 57°45N 71°10E 76 D8
Ishinomaki Japan 38°32N 141°20E 81 D7
Ishpeming U.S.A. 46°29N 87°40W 112 B4
Isiro Dem. Rep. of the Congo 2°53N 27°40E 96 D5
İskenderun Turkey 36°32N 36°10E 71 G6
Isla → U.K. 56°32N 3°20W 23 J11
Islamabad Pakistan 33°40N 73°10E 84 C8
Island L. Canada 53°47N 94°25W 108 D10
Island Pond U.S.A. 44°49N 71°53W 113 C12
Islay U.K. 55°46N 6°10W 24 D3
Isleham U.K. 52°21N 0°25E 31 B9
Islington □ U.K. 51°33N 0°5W 31 C8
Islip U.K. 51°50N 1°12W 30 C6

Ismâ'ilîya Egypt 30°37N 32°18E 95 B12
Isparta Turkey 37°47N 30°30E 71 G5
Israel ■ Asia 32°0N 34°50E 86 D3
Issoire France 45°32N 3°15E 66 D5
Issyk Kul Kyrgyzstan 42°25N 77°15E 72 D9
İstanbul Turkey 41°0N 28°58E 71 F4
Istres France 43°31N 4°59E 66 E6
Istra Croatia 45°10N 14°0E 68 B5
Itaberaba Brazil 12°32S 40°18W 122 B2
Itabira Brazil 19°37S 43°13W 122 C2
Itabuna Brazil 14°48S 39°16W 122 B3
Itacoatiara Brazil 3°8S 58°25W 120 C4
Itaipú, Represa de Brazil 25°30S 54°30W 117 F5
Itajaí Brazil 27°50S 48°39W 121 E5
Itajubá Brazil 22°24S 45°30W 122 D1
Italy ■ Europe 42°0N 13°0E 68 C5
Itaperuna Brazil 21°10S 41°54W 122 D2
Itapetinga Brazil 15°15S 40°15W 122 C2
Itapetininga Brazil 23°36S 48°7W 122 D1
Itapicuru → Brazil 11°47S 37°32W 122 B3
Itararé Brazil 24°6S 49°23W 122 D1
Itaúna Brazil 20°4S 44°34W 122 D2
Itchen → U.K. 50°55N 1°22W 30 E6
Ithaca U.S.A. 42°27N 76°30W 112 D9
Ittoqqortoormiit Greenland 70°20N 23°0W 54 B6
Itu Brazil 23°17S 47°15W 122 D1
Ivanava Belarus 52°7N 25°29E 65 B13
Ivano-Frankivsk Ukraine 48°40N 24°40E 65 D13
Ivanovo Russia 57°5N 41°0E 70 C7
Iveragh Pen. Ireland 51°52N 10°15W 20 D2
Ivinghoe U.K. 51°50N 0°37W 31 C7
Ivory Coast = Côte d'Ivoire ■
Africa 7°30N 5°0W 94 G4
Ivujivik Canada 62°24N 77°55W 109 C12
Ivybridge U.K. 50°23N 3°56W 29 G6
Iwaki Japan 37°3N 140°55E 81 E7
Iwakuni Japan 34°15N 132°8E 81 F3
Iwo Nigeria 7°39N 4°9E 94 G6
Ixworth U.K. 52°18N 0°51E 31 B10
Izhevsk Russia 56°51N 53°14E 70 C9
Izmayil Ukraine 45°22N 28°46E 71 E4
İzmir Turkey 38°25N 27°8E 71 G4
İznik Gölü Turkey 40°27N 29°30E 71 F4
Izumi-Sano Japan 34°23N 135°18E 81 F4

J
Jabalpur India 23°9N 79°58E 84 H11
Jaboatão Brazil 8°7S 35°1W 120 C6
Jaboticabal Brazil 21°15S 48°17W 122 D1
Jacareí Brazil 23°20S 46°0W 122 D1
Jackson Barbados 13°7N 59°36W 114 c
Jackson Ky., U.S.A. 37°33N 83°23W 112 G6
Jackson Mich., U.S.A. 42°15N 84°24W 112 D5
Jackson Miss., U.S.A. 32°18N 90°12W 111 D8
Jackson Mo., U.S.A. 37°23N 89°40W 112 G3
Jackson Tenn., U.S.A. 35°37N 88°49W 111 D9
Jacksonville Fla., U.S.A. 30°20N 81°39W 111 D10
Jacksonville Ill., U.S.A. 39°44N 90°14W 112 F7
Jacmel Haiti 18°14N 72°32W 115 D10
Jacobabad Pakistan 28°20N 68°29E 84 E6
Jacobina Brazil 11°11S 40°30W 122 B2
Jade Mt. Taiwan 23°25N 120°52E 79 G13
Jaén Spain 37°44N 3°43W 67 D4
Jaffna Sri Lanka 9°45N 80°2E 84 Q12
Jahrom Iran 28°30N 53°31E 87 D8
Jaipur India 27°0N 75°50E 84 F9
Jakarta Indonesia 6°9S 106°52E 82 F3
Jalālābād Afghan. 34°30N 70°29E 87 C12
Jalandhar India 31°20N 75°40E 84 D9
Jalgaon India 21°0N 75°42E 84 J9
Jalna India 19°48N 75°38E 84 K9
Jalpaiguri India 26°32N 88°46E 85 F16
Jaluit I. Marshall Is. 6°0N 169°30E 102 G8
Jamaame Somalia 0°4N 42°44E 89 G3
Jamaica ■ W. Indies 18°10N 77°30W 114 a
Jamalpur Bangla. 24°52N 89°56E 85 G16
Jamalpur India 25°18N 86°28E 85 G15
Jambi Indonesia 1°38S 103°30E 82 E2
James → U.S.A. 42°52N 97°18W 111 B7
James B. Canada 54°0N 80°0W 109 D12
Jamestown N. Dak., U.S.A. 46°54N 98°42W 110 A7
Jamestown N.Y., U.S.A. 42°6N 79°14W 112 D8
Jammu India 32°43N 74°54E 84 C9
Jammu & Kashmir □ India 30°50N 75°0E 84 C9
Jamnagar India 22°30N 70°6E 84 H7
Jamshedpur India 22°44N 86°12E 85 H15
Jan Mayen Arctic 71°0N 9°0W 54 B7
Janaúba Brazil 15°48S 43°19W 122 C2
Janesville U.S.A. 42°41N 89°1W 112 D3
Januária Brazil 15°25S 44°25W 122 C2
Jaora India 23°40N 75°10E 84 H9
Japan ■ Asia 36°0N 136°0E 81 F5
Japan, Sea of Asia 40°0N 135°0E 81 D4
Japan Trench Pac. Oc. 32°0N 142°0E 102 D6
Japurá → Brazil 3°8S 65°46W 120 C3
Jari → Brazil 1°9S 51°54W 120 C4
Jarrow U.K. 54°59N 1°28W 26 C6
Jarvis I. Pac. Oc. 0°15S 160°5W 103 H12
Jashore Bangla. 23°10N 89°10E 85 H16
Jāsk Iran 25°38N 57°45E 87 E9
Jasper Canada 52°55N 118°5W 108 D8
Jaú Brazil 22°10S 48°30W 122 D1
Jauja Peru 11°45S 75°15W 120 D2
Jaunpur India 25°46N 82°44E 85 G13
Java Indonesia 7°0S 110°0E 82 F3
Java Sea Indonesia 4°35S 107°15E 82 E3
Java Trench Ind. Oc. 9°0S 105°0E 82 F3
Jawhar Somalia 2°48N 45°30E 89 G4
Jaya, Puncak Indonesia 3°57S 137°17E 83 E9
Jebel, Bahr el → South Sudan 9°30N 30°25E 95 G12
Jedburgh U.K. 55°29N 2°33W 25 D10
Jedda Si. Arabia 21°29N 39°10E 86 F4
Jeffersonville U.S.A. 38°17N 85°44W 112 F5
Jeju S. Korea 33°31N 126°32E 79 E14
Jeju-do S. Korea 33°29N 126°34E 79 E14
Jelenia Góra Poland 50°50N 15°45E 64 C8
Jelgava Latvia 56°41N 23°49E 63 F8
Jena Germany 50°54N 11°35E 64 C6
Jeonju S. Korea 35°50N 127°4E 79 D14
Jequié Brazil 13°51S 40°5W 122 B2

Jequitinhonha Brazil 16°30S 41°0W 122 C2
Jequitinhonha → Brazil 15°51S 38°53W 122 C3
Jérémie Haiti 18°40N 74°10W 115 D10
Jerez de la Frontera Spain 36°41N 6°7W 67 D2
Jersey U.K. 49°11N 2°7W 29 J9
Jersey City U.S.A. 40°42N 74°4W 113 E10
Jerseyville U.S.A. 39°7N 90°20W 112 F2
Jerusalem Israel/West Bank 31°47N 35°10E 86 D3
Jervaulx U.K. 54°16N 1°43W 26 D5
Jhang Maghiana Pakistan 31°15N 72°22E 84 D8
Jhansi India 25°30N 78°36E 84 G11
Jharkhand □ India 24°0N 85°50E 85 H14
Jhelum Pakistan 33°0N 73°45E 84 C8
Jhelum → Pakistan 31°20N 72°10E 84 D8
Jiamusi China 46°40N 130°26E 79 B15
Ji'an Jiangxi, China 27°6N 114°59E 79 F11
Ji'an Jilin, China 41°5N 126°10E 79 C14
Jiangsu □ China 33°0N 120°0E 79 E12
Jiangxi □ China 27°30N 116°0E 79 F12
Jiaxing China 30°49N 120°45E 79 E13
Jiayuguan China 39°49N 98°18E 78 D8
Jihlava Czechia 49°55N 15°36E 65 D9
Jijiga Ethiopia 9°20N 42°50E 89 F3
Jilib Somalia 0°29N 42°46E 89 G3
Jilin China 43°44N 126°30E 79 C14
Jilin □ China 44°0N 127°0E 79 C14
Jima Ethiopia 7°40N 36°47E 89 F2
Jiménez Mexico 27°8N 104°54W 114 B4
Jinan China 36°38N 117°1E 79 D12
Jinchang China 38°30N 102°10E 78 D9
Jincheng China 35°29N 112°50E 79 D11
Jinding China 22°22N 113°33E 79 a
Jingdezhen China 29°20N 117°11E 79 F12
Jingmen China 31°0N 112°10E 79 E11
Jinhua China 29°8N 119°38E 79 F12
Jining Nei Monggol Zizhiqu,
China 41°5N 113°0E 79 C11
Jining Shandong, China 35°22N 116°34E 79 D12
Jinja Uganda 0°25N 33°12E 96 D6
Jinsha Jiang → China 28°50N 104°36E 78 F9
Jinxi China 40°52N 120°50E 79 C13
Jinzhong China 37°42N 112°46E 79 D11
Jinzhou China 41°5N 121°3E 79 C13
Jipijapa Ecuador 1°0S 80°40W 120 C1
Jishou China 28°21N 109°43E 79 F10
Jiujiang China 29°42N 115°58E 79 F12
Jiwani Pakistan 25°1N 61°44E 87 E10
Jixi China 45°20N 130°50E 79 B15
Jīzān Si. Arabia 17°0N 42°20E 89 D3
Jizzax Uzbekistan 40°6N 67°50E 87 A11
João Pessoa Brazil 7°10S 34°52W 120 C6
Jodhpur India 26°23N 73°8E 84 F8
Joensuu Finland 62°37N 29°49E 63 E9
Jõetsu Japan 37°12N 138°10E 81 E6
Johannesburg S. Africa 26°11S 28°2E 97 K5
John Crow Mts. Jamaica 18°5N 76°25W 114 a
John Day → U.S.A. 45°44N 120°39W 110 A2
John o' Groats U.K. 58°38N 3°4W 23 F11
Johnson City U.S.A. 36°19N 82°21W 111 C10
Johnston Atoll Pac. Oc. 17°10N 169°8W 103 F11
Johnstone U.K. 55°49N 4°31W 24 C6
Johor Bahru Malaysia 1°28N 103°46E 82 D2
Joinville Brazil 26°15S 48°55W 121 E5
Joliet U.S.A. 41°32N 88°5W 112 E3
Joliette Canada 46°3N 73°24W 109 E12
Jolo Phil. 6°0N 121°0E 83 C6
Jones Sound Canada 76°0N 85°0W 109 B11
Jönköping Sweden 57°45N 14°8E 63 F6
Jonquière Canada 48°27N 71°14W 113 A12
Joplin U.S.A. 37°6N 94°31W 111 C8
Jordan ■ Asia 31°0N 36°0E 86 D4
Jordan → Asia 31°48N 35°32E 86 D3
Jos Nigeria 9°53N 8°51E 94 G7
Joseph Bonaparte G.
Australia 14°35S 128°50E 98 C4
Jotunheimen Norway 61°35N 8°25E 63 E5
Juan de Fuca, Str. of
N. Amer. 48°15N 124°0W 110 A2
Juan Fernández, Arch. de
Pac. Oc. 33°50S 80°0W 103 L20
Juàzeiro Brazil 9°30S 40°30W 122 A2
Juàzeiro do Norte Brazil 7°10S 39°18W 120 C6
Juba South Sudan 4°50N 31°35E 95 H12
Juba → Somalia 1°30N 42°35E 89 G3
Juchitán de Zaragoza Mexico 16°26N 95°1W 114 D5
Juiz de Fora Brazil 21°43S 43°19W 122 D2
Juliaca Peru 15°25S 70°10W 120 D2
Julianatop Suriname 3°40N 56°30W 120 B4
Junagadh India 21°30N 70°30E 84 J7
Jundiaí Brazil 24°30S 47°0W 122 D1
Juneau U.S.A. 58°18N 134°25W 108 D6
Junín Argentina 34°33S 60°57W 121 F3
Jur → South Sudan 8°45N 29°15E 95 G11
Jura Europe 46°40N 6°5E 66 C7
Jura U.K. 56°0N 5°50W 24 C4
Jura, Sd. of U.K. 55°57N 5°45W 24 C4
Juruá → Brazil 2°37S 65°44W 120 C3
Juruena → Brazil 7°20S 58°3W 120 C4
Juticalpa Honduras 14°40N 86°12W 114 E7
Jutland Denmark 56°25N 9°30E 63 F5
Juventud, I. de la Cuba 21°40N 82°40W 115 C8
Jyväskylä Finland 62°14N 25°50E 63 E9

K
K2 Pakistan 35°58N 76°32E 84 B10
Kabardino-Balkaria □ Russia 43°30N 43°30E 71 F7
Kābul Afghan. 34°28N 69°11E 87 C12
Kabwe Zambia 14°30S 28°29E 97 G5
Kachchh, Gulf of India 22°50N 69°15E 84 H6
Kachchh, Rann of India 24°0N 70°0E 84 H7
Kachin □ Myanmar 26°0N 97°30E 85 G20
Kaçkar Turkey 40°45N 41°10E 71 F7
Kadavu Fiji 19°0S 178°15E 99 E14
Kade Ghana 6°7N 0°56W 94 G5
Kadoma Zimbabwe 18°20S 29°52E 97 H5
Kaduna Nigeria 10°30N 7°21E 94 F7
Kaesŏng N. Korea 37°58N 126°35E 79 D14
Kafue → Zambia 15°30S 29°0E 97 H5

Kaga Bandoro C.A.R. 7°0N 19°10E 96 C3
Kagera → Uganda 0°57S 31°47E 96 E6
Kagoshima Japan 31°35N 130°33E 81 H2
Kaho'olawe U.S.A. 20°33N 156°37W 110 H16
Kahramanmaraş Turkey 37°37N 36°53E 71 G6
Kai, Kepulauan Indonesia 5°55S 132°45E 83 F8
Kaidu He → China 41°46N 86°31E 78 C6
Kaieteur Falls Guyana 5°1N 59°10W 120 B4
Kaifeng China 34°48N 114°21E 79 E11
Kailua Kona U.S.A. 19°39N 155°59W 110 J17
Kainji Res. Nigeria 10°1N 4°40E 94 F6
Kairouan Tunisia 35°45N 10°5E 95 A8
Kaiserslautern Germany 49°26N 7°45E 64 D4
Kaitaia N.Z. 35°8S 173°17E 99 H13
Kaiyuan China 23°40N 103°12E 78 G9
Kajaani Finland 64°17N 27°46E 63 E9
Kajabbi Australia 20°0S 140°1E 98 E7
Kakamega Kenya 0°20N 34°46E 96 D6
Kakhovka Res. Ukraine 47°5N 34°0E 71 E5
Kakinada India 16°57N 82°11E 85 L13
Kalaallit Nunaat = Greenland ☑
N. Amer. 66°0N 45°0W 54 C5
Kalaburagi India 17°20N 76°50E 84 L10
Kalahari Africa 24°0S 21°30E 97 J4
Kalamata Greece 37°3N 22°10E 69 F10
Kalamazoo U.S.A. 42°17N 85°35W 112 D5
Kalamazoo → U.S.A. 42°40N 86°10W 112 D4
Kalemie Dem. Rep. of the Congo 5°55S 29°9E 96 F5
Kalgoorlie-Boulder Australia 30°40S 121°22E 98 G3
Kalimantan Indonesia 0°0 114°0E 82 E4
Kálimnos Greece 37°0N 27°0E 69 F12
Kaliningrad Russia 54°42N 20°32E 63 E8
Kalispell U.S.A. 48°12N 114°19W 110 A4
Kalisz Poland 51°45N 18°8E 65 C10
Kalkaska U.S.A. 44°44N 85°11W 112 C5
Kallsjön Sweden 63°38N 13°0E 63 E6
Kalmar Sweden 56°40N 16°20E 63 F7
Kalmykia □ Russia 46°5N 46°1E 71 E8
Kaluga Russia 54°35N 36°10E 70 D6
Kalutara Sri Lanka 6°35N 80°0E 84 R12
Kalyan India 19°15N 73°9E 84 K8
Kama → Russia 55°45N 52°0E 70 C9
Kamchatka Pen. Russia 57°0N 160°0E 77 D16
Kamensk Uralskiy Russia 56°25N 62°2E 76 D7
Kamina Dem. Rep. of the Congo 8°45S 25°0E 96 F5
Kamloops Canada 50°40N 120°20W 108 D7
Kampala Uganda 0°20N 32°32E 96 D6
Kampong Cham Cambodia 12°0N 105°30E 82 B3
Kampong Saom Cambodia 10°38N 103°30E 82 B2
Kamyanets-Podilskyi
Ukraine 48°45N 26°40E 65 D14
Kamyanske Ukraine 48°32N 34°37E 71 E5
Kamyshin Russia 50°10N 45°24E 71 D8
Kananga Dem. Rep. of the Congo 5°55S 22°18E 96 F4
Kanash Russia 55°30N 47°32E 70 C8
Kanawha → U.S.A. 38°50N 82°9W 112 F6
Kanazawa Japan 36°30N 136°38E 81 E5
Kanchenjunga Nepal 27°50N 88°10E 85 F16
Kanchipuram India 12°52N 79°45E 84 N11
Kandahār Afghan. 31°32N 65°43E 87 D11
Kandalaksha Russia 67°9N 32°30E 70 A5
Kandalaksha, G. of Russia 66°0N 35°0E 70 A6
Kandi Benin 11°7N 2°55E 94 F6
Kandy Sri Lanka 7°18N 80°43E 84 R12
Kane U.S.A. 41°40N 78°49W 112 E8
Käne'ohe U.S.A. 21°25N 157°48W 110 H16
Kangaroo I. Australia 35°45S 137°0E 98 H6
Kangiqsualujjuaq Canada 58°30N 65°59W 109 D13
Kangiqsujuaq Canada 61°30N 72°0W 109 C12
Kangirsuk Canada 60°0N 70°0W 109 D13
Kanin Pen. Russia 68°0N 45°0E 70 A8
Kankakee U.S.A. 41°7N 87°52W 112 E4
Kankakee → U.S.A. 41°23N 88°15W 112 E3
Kankan Guinea 10°23N 9°15W 94 F4
Kannur India 11°53N 75°27E 84 P9
Kannyakumari India 8°3N 77°40E 84 Q10
Kano Nigeria 12°2N 8°30E 94 F7
Kanpur India 26°28N 80°20E 84 F12
Kansas □ U.S.A. 38°30N 99°0W 110 C7
Kansas → U.S.A. 39°7N 94°37W 111 C8
Kansas City U.S.A. 39°6N 94°35W 111 C8
Kansk Russia 56°20N 95°37E 77 D10
Kanturk Ireland 52°11N 8°54W 20 D5
Kanye Botswana 24°55S 25°28E 97 J5
Kaohsiung Taiwan 22°35N 120°16E 79 G13
Kaolack Senegal 14°5N 16°8W 94 F2
Kapa'a U.S.A. 22°5N 159°19W 110 G15
Kapiri Mposhi Zambia 13°59S 28°43E 97 G5
Kaposvár Hungary 46°25N 17°47E 65 E9
Kaptai L. Bangla. 22°40N 92°20E 85 H18
Kapuas → Indonesia 0°25S 109°20E 82 E3
Kapuskasing Canada 49°25N 82°30W 108 E11
Kara Bogaz Gol Turkmenistan 41°0N 53°30E 87 A8
Kara Kum Turkmenistan 39°30N 60°0E 87 B9
Kara Sea Russia 75°0N 70°0E 76 B7
Karabük Turkey 41°12N 32°37E 71 F5
Karachey-Cherkessia □
Russia 43°40N 41°30E 71 F7
Karachi Pakistan 24°50N 67°0E 84 G5
Karaganda Kazakhstan 49°50N 73°10E 76 E8
Karagiye Depression
Kazakhstan 43°27N 51°45E 71 F9
Karakalpakstan □ Uzbekistan 43°0N 58°0E 87 A9
Karakoram Pakistan 35°30N 77°0E 84 B10
Karaman Turkey 37°14N 33°13E 71 G5
Karamay China 45°30N 84°58E 78 B5
Karatax Shan China 35°57N 81°0E 78 D5
Karayazı Turkey 39°41N 42°9E 71 G7
Karbalā' Iraq 32°36N 44°3E 86 C6
Karelia □ Russia 65°30N 32°30E 70 A5
Kariba, L. Zimbabwe 16°40S 28°25E 97 H5
Kariba Dam Zimbabwe 16°30S 28°35E 97 H5
Kariega S. Africa 33°40S 25°58E 97 L5
Karimata, Str. of Indonesia 2°0S 108°40E 82 E3
Karlovac Croatia 45°31N 15°36E 68 B6
Karlskrona Sweden 56°10N 15°35E 63 F7
Karlsruhe Germany 49°0N 8°23E 64 D5
Karlstad Sweden 59°23N 13°30E 63 F6
Karnak Egypt 25°43N 32°39E 86 E3
Karnal India 29°42N 77°2E 84 E10
Karnataka □ India 13°15N 77°0E 84 N10

Karnataka

172 INDEX

Kärnten Lahore

Kärnten □ Austria 46°52N 13°30E 64 E8
Karpathos Greece 35°37N 27°10E 69 G12
Kars Turkey 40°40N 43°5E 71 F7
Karwar India 14°55N 74°13E 84 M9
Kasai → Dem. Rep. of the Congo 3°30S 16°10E 96 E3
Kasaragod India 12°30N 74°58E 84 N9
Kasba L. Canada 60°20N 102°10W 108 C9
Kāshān Iran 34°5N 51°30E 87 C7
Kashi China 39°30N 76°2E 78 D4
Kasongo Dem. Rep. of the Congo 4°30S 26°33E 96 E5
Kaspiysk Russia 42°52N 47°40E 71 F8
Kassalâ Sudan 15°30N 36°0E 95 E13
Kassel Germany 51°18N 9°26E 64 C5
Kastamonu Turkey 41°25N 33°43E 71 F5
Kasur Pakistan 31°5N 74°25E 84 D9
Katanga Dem. Rep. of the Congo 8°0S 25°0E 96 F4
Kathiawar India 22°20N 71°0E 84 H7
Kathmandu Nepal 27°45N 85°20E 85 F14
Kati Thanda-Lake Eyre Australia 29°30S 137°26E 98 F6
Katihar India 25°34N 87°36E 85 G15
Katima Mulilo Namibia 17°28S 24°13E 97 H4
Katiola Côte d'Ivoire 8°10N 5°10W 94 G4
Katowice Poland 50°17N 19°5E 65 C10
Katrine, L. U.K. 56°15N 4°30W 24 B7
Katsina Nigeria 13°0N 7°32E 94 F7
Kattegat Denmark 56°40N 11°20E 63 F6
Kaua'i U.S.A. 22°3N 159°30W 110 H15
Kauai Channel U.S.A. 21°45N 158°50W 110 H15
Kaukauna U.S.A. 44°17N 88°17W 112 C3
Kaunakakai U.S.A. 21°6N 157°1W 110 H16
Kaunas Lithuania 54°54N 23°54E 63 G8
Kavala Greece 40°57N 24°28E 69 D11
Kavieng Papua N. G. 2°36S 150°51E 98 A9
Kawagoe Japan 35°55N 139°29E 81 F6
Kawaguchi Japan 35°52N 139°45E 81 F6
Kawardha India 22°0N 81°17E 85 J12
Kawasaki Japan 35°31N 139°43E 81 F6
Kawawachikamach Canada 54°48N 66°50W 109 D13
Kayes Mali 14°25N 11°30W 94 F3
Kayseri Turkey 38°45N 35°30E 71 G6
Kazan Russia 55°50N 49°10E 70 C8
Kazan-Rettō Pac. Oc. 25°0N 141°0E 102 E6
Kazanlak Bulgaria 42°38N 25°20E 69 C11
Kea Greece 37°35N 24°22E 69 F11
Kea U.K. 50°14N 5°6W 29 G3
Keady U.K. 54°15N 6°42W 19 C8
Kearney U.S.A. 40°42N 99°5W 110 B7
Keban Turkey 38°50N 38°50E 71 G6
Keban Barajı Turkey 38°41N 38°33E 71 G6
Kebnekaise Sweden 67°53N 18°33E 63 D7
Kebri Dehar Ethiopia 6°45N 44°17E 89 F3
Kebumen Indonesia 7°42S 109°40E 82 F3
Kecskemét Hungary 46°57N 19°42E 65 E10
Kediri Indonesia 7°51S 112°1E 82 F4
Keelby U.K. 53°35N 0°16W 27 E8
Keele U.K. 53°0N 2°17W 27 F4
Keene U.S.A. 42°56N 72°17W 113 D11
Keeper Hill Ireland 52°45N 8°16W 20 C6
Keetmanshoop Namibia 26°35S 18°8E 97 K3
Kefalonia Greece 38°15N 20°30E 69 E9
Keflavík Iceland 64°2N 22°35W 63 B1
Kegworth U.K. 52°50N 1°17W 27 G6
Keighley U.K. 53°52N 1°54W 27 E5
Keith U.K. 57°32N 2°57W 23 G12
Keld U.K. 54°24N 2°10W 26 D4
Kelkit → Turkey 40°45N 36°32E 71 F6
Kellett, C. Canada 72°0N 126°0W 109 B7
Kellogg U.S.A. 47°32N 116°7W 110 A3
Kells Ireland 53°44N 6°53W 19 D8
Kelowna Canada 49°50N 119°25W 108 E8
Kelsale U.K. 52°14N 1°31E 31 B12
Kelsall U.K. 53°13N 2°43W 27 F3
Kelso U.K. 55°36N 2°26W 25 C11
Kelvedon U.K. 51°50N 0°43E 31 C10
Kem Russia 65°0N 34°38E 70 B5
Kemble U.K. 51°40N 1°59W 30 C5
Kemerovo Russia 55°20N 86°5E 76 D9
Kemi Finland 65°44N 24°34E 63 D8
Kemijoki → Finland 65°47N 24°32E 63 D8
Kemp Land Antarctica 69°0S 55°0E 55 C5
Kempsey U.K. 52°8N 2°12W 30 B4
Kempston U.K. 52°7N 0°30W 31 B7
Kempten Germany 47°45N 10°17E 64 E6
Kenai U.S.A. 60°33N 151°16W 108 C4
Kendal U.K. 54°20N 2°44W 26 D3
Kendari Indonesia 3°50S 122°30E 83 E6
Kenema S. Leone 7°50N 11°14W 94 G3
Kenilworth U.K. 52°21N 1°34W 30 B5
Kenitra Morocco 34°15N 6°40W 94 B4
Kenmare Ireland 51°53N 9°36W 20 E3
Kenmare River → Ireland 51°48N 9°51W 20 E3
Kennet → U.K. 51°27N 0°57W 31 D7
Kennewick U.S.A. 46°12N 119°7W 110 A3
Kenninghall U.K. 52°26N 1°0E 31 B11
Kenogami → Canada 51°6N 84°28W 109 D11
Kenora Canada 49°47N 94°29W 108 E10
Kenosha U.S.A. 42°35N 87°49W 112 D4
Kent U.S.A. 41°9N 81°22W 112 E7
Kent □ U.K. 51°12N 0°40E 31 D10
Kent Pen. Canada 68°30N 107°0W 108 C9
Kentisbeare U.K. 50°51N 3°20W 29 F7
Kenton U.S.A. 40°39N 83°37W 112 E6
Kentucky □ U.S.A. 37°0N 84°0W 112 G5
Kentucky → U.S.A. 38°41N 85°11W 112 F5
Kentville Canada 45°6N 64°29W 109 E13
Kenya ■ Africa 1°0N 38°0E 96 D7
Kenya, Mt. Kenya 0°10S 37°18E 96 E7
Kerala □ India 11°0N 76°15E 84 P10
Kerch Ukraine 45°20N 36°20E 71 E6
Kerguelen Ind. Oc. 49°15S 69°10E 53 G13
Kericho Kenya 0°22S 35°15E 96 E7
Kerinci Indonesia 1°40S 101°15E 82 E2
Kermadec Is. Pac. Oc. 30°0S 178°15W 99 G15
Kermadec Trench Pac. Oc. 30°30S 176°0W 99 G15
Kermān Iran 30°15N 57°1E 87 D9
Kermānshāh Iran 34°23N 47°0E 86 C6
Kernow = Cornwall □ U.K. 50°26N 4°40W 29 G4
Kerrera U.K. 56°24N 5°33W 24 B4
Kerrobert Canada 51°56N 109°8W 108 D9
Kerry □ Ireland 52°7N 9°35W 20 D3
Kerry Hd. Ireland 52°25N 9°56W 20 D3
Kessingland U.K. 52°26N 1°43E 31 B12
Keswick U.K. 54°36N 3°8W 26 C2
Ketchikan U.S.A. 55°21N 131°39W 108 D6
Kettering U.K. 52°24N 0°43W 31 B7
Kettle Ness U.K. 54°33N 0°42W 26 C7
Kettlewell U.K. 54°9N 2°3W 26 D4
Kewaunee U.S.A. 44°27N 87°31W 112 C4
Keweenaw B. U.S.A. 47°0N 88°15W 112 B3
Keweenaw Pen. U.S.A. 47°15N 88°15W 112 B3
Keweenaw Pt. U.S.A. 47°25N 87°43W 112 B4
Kexby U.K. 53°22N 0°42W 27 F7
Key West U.S.A. 24°33N 81°48W 111 F10
Keyingham U.K. 53°43N 0°7W 27 E8
Keymer U.K. 50°55N 0°7W 31 E8
Keynsham U.K. 51°24N 2°29W 30 D4
Keyser U.S.A. 39°26N 78°59W 112 F8
Keyworth U.K. 52°52N 1°5W 27 G6
Khabarovsk Russia 48°30N 135°5E 77 E14
Khairpur Pakistan 27°32N 68°49E 84 F6
Khambhat India 22°23N 72°33E 84 H8
Khambhat, G. of India 20°45N 72°30E 84 J8
Khamīs Mushayţ Si. Arabia 18°18N 42°44E 89 D3
Khan Tengri, Pik Asia 42°12N 80°10E 78 C5
Khandyga Russia 62°42N 135°35E 77 C14
Khanewal Pakistan 30°20N 71°55E 84 D7
Khanka, L. Asia 45°0N 132°24E 79 C15
Kharagpur India 22°20N 87°25E 85 H15
Kharg Iran 29°15N 50°28E 86 D7
Khârga, El Wâhât el Egypt 25°10N 30°35E 95 C12
Kharkiv Ukraine 49°58N 36°20E 71 E6
Khartoum Sudan 15°31N 32°35E 95 E12
Khasavyurt Russia 43°16N 46°40E 71 F8
Khatanga Russia 72°0N 102°20E 77 B11
Khemisset Morocco 33°50N 6°1W 94 B4
Khenchela Algeria 35°28N 7°11E 94 A7
Kherson Ukraine 46°35N 32°35E 71 E5
Khmelnytskyi Ukraine 49°23N 27°0E 65 D14
Khojak Pass Afghan. 30°51N 66°34E 87 D11
Kholm Afghan. 36°45N 67°40E 87 B11
Khon Kaen Thailand 16°30N 102°47E 82 A2
Khorāsan Iran 34°0N 58°0E 87 C9
Khorramābād Iran 33°30N 48°25E 86 C7
Khorramshahr Iran 30°29N 48°15E 86 D7
Khouribga Morocco 32°58N 6°57W 94 B4
Khūjand Tajikistan 40°17N 69°37E 87 B12
Khulna Bangla. 22°45N 89°34E 85 H16
Khunjerab Pass Asia 36°40N 75°25E 84 A9
Khushab Pakistan 32°20N 72°20E 84 C8
Khuzdar Pakistan 27°52N 66°30E 84 F5
Khūzestān □ Iran 31°0N 49°0E 86 D7
Khvoy Iran 38°35N 45°0E 86 B6
Khyber Pakhtunkhwa □ Pakistan 34°0N 72°0E 84 B8
Khyber Pass Afghan. 34°10N 71°8E 84 B7
Kibworth Beauchamp U.K. 52°33N 0°59W 27 G7
Kicking Horse Pass Canada 51°28N 116°16W 108 D8
Kidderminster U.K. 52°24N 2°15W 30 B4
Kidlington U.K. 51°50N 1°15W 30 C6
Kidsgrove U.K. 53°5N 2°14W 27 F4
Kidstones U.K. 54°13N 2°2W 26 D4
Kidwelly U.K. 51°44N 4°18W 28 D5
Kiel Germany 54°19N 10°8E 64 A6
Kiel Canal = Nord-Ostsee-Kanal Germany 54°12N 9°32E 64 A5
Kielce Poland 50°52N 20°42E 65 C11
Kielder U.K. 55°14N 2°35W 26 B3
Kieler Bucht Germany 54°35N 10°25E 64 A6
Kiev = Kyiv Ukraine 50°30N 30°28E 65 C16
Kigali Rwanda 1°59S 30°4E 96 E6
Kigoma-Ujiji Tanzania 4°55S 29°36E 96 E5
Kikwit Dem. Rep. of the Congo 5°0S 18°45E 96 E3
Kīlauea U.S.A. 19°25N 155°17W 110 J17
Kilbirnie U.K. 55°46N 4°41W 24 C6
Kilbrannan Sd. U.K. 55°37N 5°26W 24 C5
Kildare Ireland 53°9N 6°55W 21 B9
Kildare □ Ireland 53°10N 6°50W 21 B9
Kilfinnane Ireland 52°21N 8°28W 20 D6
Kilham U.K. 54°4N 0°23W 26 D8
Kilifi Kenya 3°40S 39°48E 96 E7
Kilimanjaro Tanzania 3°7S 37°20E 96 E7
Kilindini Kenya 4°4S 39°40E 96 E7
Kilkee Ireland 52°41N 9°39W 20 C3
Kilkeel U.K. 54°7N 5°55W 19 C10
Kilkenny Ireland 52°39N 7°15W 21 C8
Kilkenny □ Ireland 52°35N 7°15W 21 C8
Kilkhampton U.K. 50°52N 4°31W 29 F4
Kilkieran B. Ireland 53°20N 9°41W 20 B3
Killala Ireland 54°13N 9°13W 18 C3
Killala B. Ireland 54°16N 9°8W 18 C3
Killaloe Ireland 52°48N 8°28W 20 C6
Killarney Ireland 52°4N 9°30W 20 D4
Killarney △ Ireland 52°0N 9°33W 20 E3
Killary Harbour Ireland 53°38N 9°52W 18 D2
Killeen U.S.A. 31°7N 97°44W 110 D7
Killin U.K. 56°28N 4°19W 24 B7
Killiney Ireland 53°15N 6°7W 21 B10
Killinghall U.K. 54°2N 1°33W 26 D5
Killorglin Ireland 52°6N 9°47W 20 D3
Killybegs Ireland 54°38N 8°26W 18 B5
Kilmarnock U.K. 55°37N 4°29W 24 C7
Kilrush Ireland 52°38N 9°29W 20 C4
Kilsby U.K. 52°20N 1°10W 30 B6
Kilsyth U.K. 55°59N 4°3W 24 C7
Kilwa Kivinje Tanzania 8°45S 39°25E 96 F7
Kilwinning U.K. 55°39N 4°43W 24 C6
Kimberley Australia 16°20S 127°0E 98 D4
Kimberley S. Africa 28°43S 24°46E 97 K4
Kimbolton U.K. 52°18N 0°24W 31 B8
Kimch'aek N. Korea 40°40N 129°10E 79 C14
Kimmirut Canada 62°50N 69°50W 109 C13
Kimry Russia 56°55N 37°15E 70 C6
Kinabalu, Gunung Malaysia 6°3N 116°14E 82 C5
Kincardine Canada 44°10N 81°40W 112 C7
Kincardine Aberds., U.K. 56°57N 2°25W 23 J13
Kincardine Fife, U.K. 56°4N 3°43W 25 B8
Kinder Scout U.K. 53°24N 1°52W 27 F5
Kindersley Canada 51°30N 109°10W 108 D9
Kindia Guinea 10°0N 12°52W 94 F3
Kindu Dem. Rep. of the Congo 2°55S 25°50E 96 E5
Kineshma Russia 57°30N 42°5E 70 C7
Kineton U.K. 52°10N 1°31W 30 B5
King George I. Antarctica 60°0S 60°0W 55 C18
King George Is. Canada 57°20N 80°30W 109 D11
King I. Australia 39°50S 144°0E 98 H7
King William I. Canada 69°10N 97°25W 108 C10
Kingman U.S.A. 35°12N 114°4W 110 C4
King's Lynn U.K. 52°45N 0°24E 31 A9
King's Sutton U.K. 52°2N 1°15W 30 B6
King's Worthy U.K. 51°6N 1°17W 30 D6
Kingsbridge U.K. 50°17N 3°47W 29 G6
Kingsbury U.K. 52°34N 1°40W 27 G5
Kingscourt Ireland 53°54N 6°48W 19 D8
Kingskerswell U.K. 50°29N 3°35W 29 G6
Kingsland U.K. 52°15N 2°48W 30 B3
Kingsteignton U.K. 50°33N 3°36W 29 F6
Kingston Canada 44°14N 76°30W 109 E12
Kingston Jamaica 17°55N 76°50W 114 a
Kingston N.Y., U.S.A. 41°56N 73°59W 113 E10
Kingston Pa., U.S.A. 41°16N 75°54W 113 E10
Kingston upon Hull U.K. 53°45N 0°21W 27 E8
Kingston-upon-Thames □ U.K. 51°24N 0°17W 31 D8
Kingstown St. Vincent 13°10N 61°10W 115 E12
Kingsville U.S.A. 27°31N 97°52W 110 E7
Kingswear U.K. 50°21N 3°35W 29 G6
Kingswood U.K. 51°27N 2°31W 30 D3
Kington U.K. 52°13N 3°1W 30 B2
Kingussie U.K. 57°6N 4°2W 23 H9
Kinlochleven U.K. 56°43N 5°0W 22 J7
Kinnairds Hd. U.K. 57°43N 2°1W 23 G13
Kinngait Canada 64°14N 76°32W 109 C12
Kinross U.K. 56°13N 3°25W 25 B9
Kinsale Ireland 51°42N 8°31W 20 E5
Kinsale, Old Hd. of Ireland 51°37N 8°33W 20 E5
Kinshasa Dem. Rep. of the Congo 4°20S 15°15E 96 E3
Kintore U.K. 57°14N 2°20W 23 H13
Kintyre U.K. 55°30N 5°35W 24 D4
Kintyre, Mull of U.K. 55°17N 5°47W 24 D4
Kippure Ireland 53°11N 6°21W 21 B10
Kirensk Russia 57°50N 107°55E 77 D11
Kirgiz Steppe Eurasia 50°0N 55°0E 71 E10
Kiribati ■ Pac. Oc. 3°0S 180°0E 102 H10
Kırıkkale Turkey 39°51N 33°32E 71 G5
Kiritimati Kiribati 1°58N 157°27W 103 G12
Kirkbean U.K. 54°55N 3°36W 25 E9
Kirkbride U.K. 54°54N 3°12W 26 C2
Kirkburton U.K. 53°37N 1°42W 27 E5
Kirkby U.K. 53°30N 2°54W 27 F3
Kirkby-in-Ashfield U.K. 53°6N 1°14W 27 F6
Kirkby Lonsdale U.K. 54°12N 2°36W 26 D3
Kirkby Malzeard U.K. 54°10N 1°37W 26 D5
Kirkby Stephen U.K. 54°29N 2°21W 26 D4
Kirkby Thore U.K. 54°37N 2°32W 26 C3
Kirkbymoorside U.K. 54°17N 0°56W 26 D7
Kirkcaldy U.K. 56°7N 3°9W 25 B9
Kirkcudbright U.K. 54°50N 4°2W 24 E7
Kirkham U.K. 53°47N 2°53W 27 E3
Kirkintilloch U.K. 55°56N 4°8W 24 C7
Kirkland Lake Canada 48°9N 80°2W 109 E11
Kırklareli Turkey 41°44N 27°15E 86 A1
Kirkoswald U.K. 54°46N 2°41W 26 C3
Kirksville U.S.A. 40°12N 92°35W 111 B8
Kirkūk Iraq 35°30N 44°21E 86 C6
Kirkwall U.K. 58°59N 2°58W 23 E12
Kirkwhelpington U.K. 55°9N 1°59W 26 B5
Kirov Russia 58°35N 49°40E 70 C8
Kirriemuir U.K. 56°41N 3°1W 23 J11
Kırşehir Turkey 39°14N 34°5E 71 G5
Kirthar Range Pakistan 27°0N 67°0E 84 F5
Kirtling U.K. 52°12N 0°28E 31 B9
Kirtlington U.K. 51°53N 1°15W 30 C6
Kirton U.K. 52°56N 0°3W 27 G8
Kirton in Lindsey U.K. 53°29N 0°34W 27 F7
Kiruna Sweden 67°52N 20°15E 63 D8
Kiryū Japan 36°24N 139°20E 81 E6
Kisangani Dem. Rep. of the Congo 0°35N 25°15E 96 D5
Kiselevsk Russia 54°5N 86°39E 76 D9
Kishanganj India 26°3N 88°14E 85 F16
Kishinev = Chişinău Moldova 47°2N 28°50E 65 E15
Kisii Kenya 0°40S 34°45E 96 E6
Kislovodsk Russia 43°50N 42°45E 71 F7
Kismaayo Somalia 0°22S 42°32E 89 H3
Kisumu Kenya 0°3S 34°45E 96 E6
Kitakyūshū Japan 33°50N 130°50E 81 G2
Kitale Kenya 1°0N 35°0E 96 D7
Kitami Japan 43°48N 143°54E 81 B8
Kitchener Canada 43°27N 80°29W 112 D7
Kíthnos Greece 37°26N 24°27E 69 F11
Kitimat Canada 54°3N 128°38W 108 D7
Kittanning U.S.A. 40°49N 79°31W 112 E8
Kitwe Zambia 12°54S 28°13E 97 G5
Kivu, L. Dem. Rep. of the Congo 1°48S 29°0E 96 E5
Kızıl Irmak → Turkey 41°44N 35°58E 71 F6
Kizlyar Russia 43°51N 46°40E 71 F8
Kladno Czechia 50°10N 14°7E 64 C8
Klagenfurt Austria 46°38N 14°20E 64 E8
Klaipėda Lithuania 55°43N 21°10E 63 F8
Klamath → U.S.A. 41°33N 124°5W 110 B2
Klamath Falls U.S.A. 42°13N 121°46W 110 B2
Klang Malaysia 3°2N 101°26E 82 D2
Klarälven → Sweden 59°23N 13°32E 63 F6
Klerksdorp S. Africa 26°53S 26°38E 97 K5
Kluane L. Canada 61°15N 138°40W 108 C6
Kluang Malaysia 2°3N 103°18E 82 D2
Klyuchevskaya, Sopka Russia 55°50N 160°30E 77 D17
Knaresborough U.K. 54°1N 1°28W 27 D6
Knebworth U.K. 51°52N 0°11W 31 C8
Knighton U.K. 52°21N 3°3W 28 C7
Knock Ireland 53°48N 8°55W 18 D4
Knockmealdown Mts. Ireland 52°14N 7°56W 20 D7
Knossos Greece 35°16N 25°10E 69 G11
Knottingley U.K. 53°43N 1°16W 27 E6
Knowle U.K. 52°24N 1°44W 27 H5
Knoxville U.S.A. 35°58N 83°55W 111 C10
Knoydart U.K. 57°3N 5°33W 22 H6
Knutsford U.K. 53°18N 2°21W 27 F4
Kōbe Japan 34°41N 135°13E 81 F4
Koblenz Germany 50°21N 7°36E 64 C4
Kocaeli Turkey 40°45N 29°50E 71 F4
Koch Bihar India 26°22N 89°29E 85 F16
Kochi India 9°58N 76°20E 84 Q10
Kōchi Japan 33°30N 133°35E 81 G3
Kodiak U.S.A. 57°47N 152°24W 108 D4
Kodiak I. U.S.A. 57°30N 152°45W 108 D4
Koforidua Ghana 6°3N 0°17W 94 G5
Kōfu Japan 35°40N 138°30E 81 F6
Kogalym Russia 62°16N 74°29E 76 C8
Kohat Pakistan 33°40N 71°29E 84 C7
Kohima India 25°35N 94°10E 85 G19
Kohtla-Järve Estonia 59°20N 27°20E 63 F9
Kokkola Finland 63°50N 23°8E 63 E8
Koko Kyunzu Myanmar 14°7N 93°22E 85 M18
Koko Nur China 36°40N 100°10E 78 D9
Kokomo U.S.A. 40°29N 86°8W 112 E4
Kokopo Papua N. G. 4°22S 152°19E 98 A9
Kökshetaū Kazakhstan 53°20N 69°25E 76 D7
Koksoak → Canada 58°30N 68°10W 109 D13
Kola Pen. Russia 67°30N 38°0E 70 A6
Kolar Gold Fields India 12°58N 78°16E 84 N11
Kolguyev Russia 69°20N 48°30E 70 A8
Kolhapur India 16°43N 74°15E 84 L9
Kolkata India 22°34N 88°21E 85 H16
Kollam India 8°50N 76°38E 84 Q10
Kolomna Russia 55°8N 38°45E 70 C6
Kolomyya Ukraine 48°31N 25°2E 71 E4
Kolpino Russia 59°44N 30°39E 70 C5
Kolwezi Dem. Rep. of the Congo 10°40S 25°25E 96 G5
Kolyma → Russia 69°30N 161°0E 77 C17
Kolyma Ra. Russia 63°0N 157°0E 77 C16
Komatsu Japan 36°25N 136°30E 81 E5
Komi □ Russia 64°0N 55°0E 70 B10
Komsomolsk-na-Amur Russia 50°30N 137°0E 77 D14
Kondoz Afghan. 36°50N 68°50E 87 B12
Kongur Shan China 38°34N 75°18E 78 D4
Konin Poland 52°12N 18°15E 65 B10
Konosha Russia 61°0N 40°5E 70 B7
Konotop Ukraine 51°12N 33°7E 71 D5
Konqi He → China 40°45N 90°10E 78 C6
Konya Turkey 37°52N 32°35E 71 G5
Kootenay L. Canada 49°45N 116°50W 108 E8
Kopet Dagh Asia 38°0N 58°0E 87 B9
Korçë Albania 40°37N 20°50E 69 D9
Korčula Croatia 42°56N 16°57E 68 C7
Kordofân Sudan 13°0N 29°0E 95 F11
Korea Bay Korea 39°0N 124°0E 79 D13
Korea Strait Asia 34°0N 129°30E 79 E14
Korhogo Côte d'Ivoire 9°29N 5°28W 94 G4
Kōriyama Japan 37°24N 140°23E 81 E7
Korla China 41°45N 86°4E 78 C6
Körös → Hungary 46°43N 20°12E 65 E11
Korosten Ukraine 50°54N 28°36E 71 D4
Kortrijk Belgium 50°50N 3°17E 64 C2
Koryak Ra. Russia 61°0N 171°0E 77 C18
Kos Greece 36°50N 27°15E 69 F12
Kosciuszko, Mt. Australia 36°27S 148°16E 98 H8
Košice Slovakia 48°42N 21°15E 65 D11
Kosovo ■ Europe 42°30N 21°0E 69 C9
Kôstî Sudan 13°8N 32°43E 95 F12
Kostroma Russia 57°50N 40°58E 70 C7
Koszalin Poland 54°11N 16°8E 64 A9
Kota India 25°14N 75°49E 84 G9
Kota Bharu Malaysia 6°7N 102°14E 82 C2
Kota Kinabalu Malaysia 6°0N 116°4E 82 C5
Kotabumi Indonesia 4°49S 104°54E 82 E2
Kotelnich Russia 58°22N 48°24E 70 C8
Kotka Finland 60°28N 26°58E 63 E9
Kotlas Russia 61°17N 46°43E 70 B8
Kotor Montenegro 42°25N 18°47E 69 C8
Kotri Pakistan 25°22N 68°22E 84 G6
Kotuy → Russia 71°54N 102°6E 77 B11
Kotzebue U.S.A. 66°53N 162°39W 108 C3
Koudougou Burkina Faso 12°10N 2°20W 94 F5
Koumra Chad 8°50N 17°35E 95 G9
Kovel Ukraine 51°11N 24°38E 70 D3
Kovrov Russia 56°25N 41°25E 70 C7
Kowloon China 22°19N 114°11E 79 G11
Kozhikode India 11°15N 75°43E 84 P9
Kpalimé Togo 6°57N 0°44E 94 G6
Kra, Isthmus of Thailand 10°15N 99°30E 82 B1
Kragujevac Serbia 44°2N 20°56E 69 B9
Krakatoa Indonesia 6°10S 105°20E 82 F3
Kraków Poland 50°4N 19°57E 65 C10
Kraljevo Serbia 43°44N 20°41E 69 C9
Kramatorsk Ukraine 48°50N 37°30E 71 E6
Krasnodar Russia 45°5N 39°0E 71 E6
Krasnokamensk Russia 50°3N 118°0E 77 D12
Krasnokamsk Russia 58°4N 55°48E 70 C10
Krasnoturinsk Russia 59°46N 60°12E 70 C11
Krasnoyarsk Russia 56°8N 93°0E 77 D10
Krasnyy Luch Ukraine 48°13N 39°0E 71 E6
Krefeld Germany 51°20N 6°33E 64 C4
Kremenchuk Ukraine 49°5N 33°25E 71 E5
Kribi Cameroon 2°57N 9°56E 96 D1
Krishna → India 15°57N 80°59E 85 M12
Kristiansand Norway 58°8N 8°1E 63 F5
Kristiansund Norway 63°7N 7°45E 63 E5
Krk Croatia 45°8N 14°40E 68 B6
Kronshtadt Russia 59°57N 29°51E 70 B4
Kroonstad S. Africa 27°43S 27°19E 97 K5
Kropotkin Russia 45°28N 40°28E 71 E7
Kropyvnytskyy Ukraine 48°35N 32°20E 71 E5
Krosno Poland 49°42N 21°46E 65 D11
Krugersdorp S. Africa 26°5S 27°46E 97 K5
Kruševac Serbia 43°35N 21°28E 69 C9
Kryvyi Rih Ukraine 47°51N 33°20E 71 E5
Ksar el Kebir Morocco 35°0N 6°0W 94 B4
Kuala Belait Malaysia 4°35N 114°11E 82 D4
Kuala Lumpur Malaysia 3°9N 101°41E 82 D2
Kuala Terengganu Malaysia 5°20N 103°8E 82 C2
Kuantan Malaysia 3°49N 103°20E 82 D2
Kuching Malaysia 1°33N 110°25E 82 D4
Kudymkar Russia 59°1N 54°39E 70 C9
Kugluktuk Canada 67°50N 115°5W 108 C8
Kuito Angola 12°22S 16°55E 97 G3
Kŭlob Tajikistan 37°55N 69°50E 87 B12
Kuma → Russia 44°55N 47°0E 71 F8
Kumagaya Japan 36°9N 139°22E 81 E6
Kumamoto Japan 32°45N 130°45E 81 G2
Kumanovo N. Macedonia 42°9N 21°42E 69 C9
Kumasi Ghana 6°41N 1°38W 94 G5
Kumba Cameroon 4°36N 9°24E 96 D1
Kumbakonam India 10°58N 79°25E 84 P11
Kumertau Russia 52°45N 55°57E 70 D10
Kumtag Desert China 39°40N 92°0E 78 D7
Kungur Russia 57°25N 56°57E 70 C10
Kunlun Shan Asia 36°0N 86°30E 78 D6
Kunming China 25°1N 102°41E 78 F9
Kuopio Finland 62°53N 27°35E 63 E9
Kupang Indonesia 10°19S 123°39E 83 F6
Kuqa China 41°35N 82°30E 78 C5
Kür → Azerbaijan 39°29N 49°15E 71 G8
Kurdistan Asia 37°20N 43°30E 86 B5
Kure Japan 34°14N 132°32E 81 F3
Kurgan Russia 55°26N 65°18E 76 D7
Kuril Is. Russia 45°0N 150°0E 77 E16
Kuril-Kamchatka Trench Pac. Oc. 44°0N 153°0E 102 C7
Kurnool India 15°45N 78°0E 84 M11
Kursk Russia 51°42N 36°11E 70 D6
Kuruktag China 41°0N 89°0E 78 C6
Kurume Japan 33°15N 130°30E 81 G2
Kushiro Japan 43°0N 144°25E 81 B9
Kushtia Bangla. 23°55N 89°5E 85 H16
Kuskokwim B. U.S.A. 59°45N 162°25W 108 D3
Kütahya Turkey 39°30N 30°2E 71 G5
Kutaisi Georgia 42°19N 42°40E 71 F7
Kuujjuaq Canada 58°6N 68°15W 109 D13
Kuujjuarapik Canada 55°20N 77°35W 109 D12
Kuwait Kuwait 29°30N 48°0E 86 D7
Kuwait ■ Asia 29°30N 47°30E 86 D6
Kuybyshev Res. Russia 55°2N 49°30E 70 C8
Kuznetsk Russia 53°12N 46°40E 70 D8
Kuzomen Russia 66°22N 36°50E 70 A6
KwaMashu S. Africa 29°45S 30°58E 97 K6
KwaZulu Natal □ S. Africa 29°0S 30°0E 97 K6
Kwekwe Zimbabwe 18°58S 29°48E 97 H5
Kwun Tong China 22°19N 114°13E 79 a
Kyiv Ukraine 50°30N 30°28E 65 C16
Kyle of Lochalsh U.K. 57°17N 5°44W 22 H6
Kyoga, L. Uganda 1°35N 33°0E 96 D6
Kyōto Japan 35°0N 135°45E 81 F4
Kyrenia Cyprus 35°20N 33°20E 86 C3
Kyrgyzstan ■ Asia 42°0N 75°0E 76 E8
Kythira Greece 36°8N 23°0E 69 F10
Kyūshū Japan 33°0N 131°0E 81 G2
Kyustendil Bulgaria 42°16N 22°41E 69 C10
Kyzyl Russia 51°50N 94°30E 78 A7
Kyzyl Kum Uzbekistan 42°30N 65°0E 87 A10
Kyzyl-Orda Kazakhstan 44°48N 65°28E 76 E7

L

La Alcarria Spain 40°31N 2°45W 67 B4
La Barra Nic. 12°54N 83°33W 115 E8
La Ceiba Honduras 15°40N 86°50W 114 D7
La Coruña Spain 43°20N 8°25W 67 A1
La Crosse U.S.A. 43°48N 91°15W 112 D2
La Grande U.S.A. 45°20N 118°5W 110 A3
La Grande → Canada 53°50N 79°0W 109 D12
La Grange U.S.A. 33°2N 85°2W 111 D10
La Habana Cuba 23°8N 82°22W 115 C8
La Junta U.S.A. 37°59N 103°33W 110 C6
La Línea de la Concepción Spain 36°15N 5°23W 67 D3
La Loche Canada 56°29N 109°26W 108 D9
La Mancha Spain 39°10N 2°54W 67 C4
La Oroya Peru 11°32S 75°54W 120 D2
La Palma Canary Is. 28°40N 17°50W 94 C2
La Paz Bolivia 16°20S 68°10W 120 D3
La Paz Mexico 24°10N 110°18W 114 C2
La Perouse Str. Asia 45°40N 142°0E 79 B17
La Plata Argentina 35°0S 57°55W 121 F4
La Quiaca Argentina 22°5S 65°35W 121 E3
La Rioja Argentina 29°20S 67°0W 121 E3
La Rioja □ Spain 42°20N 2°20W 67 A4
La Roche-sur-Yon France 46°40N 1°25W 66 C3
La Rochelle France 46°10N 1°9W 66 C3
La Romana Dom. Rep. 18°27N 68°57W 115 D11
La Ronge Canada 55°5N 105°20W 108 D9
La Sarre Canada 48°45N 79°15W 112 A8
La Serena Chile 29°55S 71°10W 121 E2
La Seyne-sur-Mer France 43°7N 5°52E 66 E6
La Spézia Italy 44°7N 9°50E 68 B3
La Tortuga, I. Venezuela 11°0N 65°22W 120 A3
La Tuque Canada 47°30N 72°50W 109 E12
La Vega Dom. Rep. 19°20N 70°30W 115 D10
Labé Guinea 11°24N 12°16W 94 F3
Labinsk Russia 44°40N 40°48E 71 F7
Laborie St. Lucia 13°45N 61°2W 114 b
Labrador Canada 53°20N 61°0W 109 D13
Labrador City Canada 52°57N 66°55W 109 D13
Labrador Sea Atl. Oc. 57°0N 54°0W 109 D14
Labuan Malaysia 5°21N 115°13E 82 C5
Lac La Biche Canada 54°45N 111°58W 108 D8
Lac-Mégantic Canada 45°35N 70°53W 113 C12
Laccadive Is. = Lakshadweep Is. India 10°0N 72°30E 72 G9
Laceby U.K. 53°33N 0°10W 27 E8
Lacock U.K. 51°24N 2°7W 30 D4
Lacombe Canada 52°30N 113°44W 108 D8
Laconia U.S.A. 43°32N 71°28W 113 D12
Ladākh □ India 34°0N 77°35E 84 C10
Ladakh Ra. India 34°0N 78°0E 84 C11
Ladder Hills U.K. 57°13N 3°16W 23 H11
Ladock U.K. 50°19N 4°58W 29 G4
Ladoga, L. Russia 61°15N 30°30E 70 B5
Ladysmith S. Africa 28°32S 29°46E 97 K5
Ladysmith U.S.A. 45°28N 91°12W 112 C2
Lae Papua N. G. 6°40S 147°2E 98 B8
Lafayette Ind., U.S.A. 40°25N 86°54W 112 E4
Lafayette La., U.S.A. 30°14N 92°1W 111 D8
Lafia Nigeria 8°30N 8°34E 94 G7
Lagan → U.K. 54°36N 5°55W 19 B10
Lagarto Brazil 10°54S 37°41W 122 B3
Lagdo, L. de Cameroon 8°40N 14°0E 95 G8
Laghouat Algeria 33°50N 2°59E 94 B6
Lagos Nigeria 6°25N 3°27E 94 G6
Lagos Portugal 37°5N 8°41W 67 D1
Lahn → Germany 50°19N 7°37E 64 C4
Lahore Pakistan 31°32N 74°22E 84 D9

Lahti   **Lyubertsy**

Lahti Finland 60°58N 25°40E 63 E9
Lairg U.K. 58°2N 4°24W 23 F9
Laizhou China 37°8N 119°57E 79 D12
Lake Charles U.S.A. 30°14N 93°13W 111 D8
Lake City U.S.A. 30°11N 82°38W 111 D10
Lake District △ U.K. 54°30N 3°21W 26 C2
Lake Havasu City U.S.A. 34°27N 114°22W 110 D4
Lakeland U.S.A. 28°3N 81°57W 111 E10
Lakenheath U.K. 52°25N 0°32E 31 B10
Lakewood U.S.A. 41°28N 81°47W 112 E7
Lakshadweep Is. India 10°0N 72°30E 72 G9
Lamar U.S.A. 38°5N 102°37W 110 C6
Lambaréné Gabon 0°41S 10°12E 96 E2
Lambay I. Ireland 53°29N 6°1W 21 B10
Lamberhurst U.K. 51°5N 0°24E 31 D9
Lambeth □ U.K. 51°28N 0°6W 31 D8
Lambley U.K. 54°56N 2°30W 26 C5
Lambourn U.K. 51°30N 1°32W 30 C5
Lamesa U.S.A. 32°44N 101°58W 110 D6
Lamma I. China 22°12N 114°7E 79 a
Lammermuir U.K. 55°50N 2°25W 25 C11
Lammermuir Hills U.K. 55°50N 2°40W 25 C10
Lamon B. Phil. 14°30N 122°20E 83 B6
Lampedusa Medit. S. 35°36N 12°40E 68 G5
Lampeter U.K. 52°7N 4°4W 28 C5
Lamu Kenya 2°16S 40°55E 96 E8
Lanark U.K. 55°40N 3°47W 25 C8
Lancang Jiang → China 21°40N 101°10E 78 G8
Lancashire □ U.K. 53°50N 2°48W 27 E3
Lancaster U.K. 54°3N 2°48W 26 D3
Lancaster N.H., U.S.A. 44°29N 71°34W 113 C12
Lancaster Pa., U.S.A. 40°2N 76°19W 112 E9
Lancaster Wis., U.S.A. 42°51N 90°43W 112 D2
Lancaster Sd. Canada 74°13N 84°0W 109 B11
Lanchester U.K. 54°50N 1°44W 26 C5
Lancing U.K. 50°49N 0°19W 31 E8
Landes France 44°0N 1°0W 66 D3
Landkey U.K. 51°3N 4°0W 29 E6
Land's End U.K. 50°4N 5°44W 29 G2
Langholm U.K. 55°9N 3°0W 25 D10
Langport U.K. 51°2N 2°50W 30 D5
Langreo Spain 43°18N 5°40W 67 A3
Langres France 47°52N 5°20E 66 C6
Langres, Plateau de France 47°45N 5°3E 66 C6
Langsa Indonesia 4°30N 97°57E 82 D1
Langstrothdale Chase U.K. 54°14N 2°13W 26 D4
Langtoft U.K. 52°42N 0°20W 27 G8
Langtree U.K. 50°55N 4°13W 29 F5
Languedoc France 43°58N 3°55E 66 E5
Lannion France 48°46N 3°29W 66 B2
L'Annonciation Canada 46°25N 74°55W 113 B10
L'Anse U.S.A. 46°45N 88°27W 112 B3
Lansing U.S.A. 42°44N 84°33W 112 D5
Lantau I. China 22°15N 113°56E 79 a
Lanzarote Canary Is. 29°0N 13°40W 94 C3
Lanzhou China 36°1N 103°52E 78 D9
Laoag Phil. 18°7N 120°34E 83 A6
Laois □ Ireland 52°57N 7°27W 21 D7
Laon France 49°33N 3°35E 66 B5
Laos ■ Asia 17°45N 105°0E 82 A3
Lapeer U.S.A. 43°3N 83°19W 112 D6
Lapford U.K. 50°51N 3°48W 29 F6
Lapland Europe 68°7N 24°0E 63 D8
LaPorte U.S.A. 41°36N 86°43W 112 E4
Laptev Sea Russia 76°0N 125°0E 77 B13
Laramie U.S.A. 41°19N 105°35W 110 B5
Laramie Mts. U.S.A. 42°0N 105°30W 110 B5
Laredo U.S.A. 27°30N 99°30W 110 E7
Largs U.K. 55°47N 4°52W 24 C6
Larisa Greece 39°36N 22°27E 69 E10
Larnaca Cyprus 34°55N 33°38E 86 C3
Larne U.K. 54°51N 5°51W 19 B10
Larne L. U.K. 54°50N 5°48W 19 B10
Larrimah Australia 15°35S 133°12E 98 D5
Larsen Ice Shelf Antarctica 67°0S 62°0W 55 C17
Larvik Norway 59°4N 10°2E 63 F6
Las Cruces U.S.A. 32°19N 106°47W 110 D5
Las Palmas de Gran Canaria
  Canary Is. 28°7N 15°26W 94 C2
Las Tunas Cuba 20°58N 76°59W 115 C9
Las Vegas N. Mex., U.S.A. 35°36N 105°13W 110 C5
Las Vegas Nev., U.S.A. 36°10N 115°8W 110 C4
Lashio Myanmar 22°56N 97°45E 85 H20
Lassen Pk. U.S.A. 40°29N 121°30W 110 B2
Lastoursville Gabon 0°55S 12°38E 96 E2
Latacunga Ecuador 0°50S 78°35W 120 C2
Latakia Syria 35°30N 35°45E 86 C3
Latina Italy 41°28N 12°52E 68 D5
Latvia ■ Europe 56°50N 24°0E 63 F8
Lauder U.K. 55°43N 2°43W 25 C10
Lauderdale U.K. 55°44N 2°41W 25 C10
Launceston Australia 41°24S 147°8E 98 J8
Launceston U.K. 50°38N 4°22W 29 F5
Laune → Ireland 52°7N 9°47W 20 D3
Laurel U.S.A. 31°41N 89°8W 111 D9
Laurencekirk U.K. 56°50N 2°28W 23 J13
Laurentian Plateau Canada 52°0N 70°0W 104 E12
Lausanne Switz. 46°32N 6°38E 64 E4
Lavagh More Ireland 54°46N 8°6W 18 B5
Laval Canada 45°33N 73°42W 113 C11
Laval France 48°4N 0°48W 66 B3
Lavendon U.K. 52°11N 0°39W 31 B7
Lavenham U.K. 52°6N 0°48E 31 B10
Lavras Brazil 21°20S 45°0W 122 D2
Lawrence Kans., U.S.A. 38°58N 95°14W 111 C7
Lawrence Mass., U.S.A. 42°43N 71°10W 113 D12
Lawton U.S.A. 34°37N 98°25W 110 D7
Laxey U.K. 54°14N 4°23W 19 C13
Laxfield U.K. 52°18N 1°22E 31 B11
Laxford, L. U.K. 58°24N 5°6W 22 F7
Lazio □ Italy 42°10N 12°30E 68 C5
Lazonby U.K. 54°46N 2°42W 26 C5
Le Creusot France 46°48N 4°24E 66 C6
Le Havre France 49°30N 0°5E 66 B4
Le Mans France 48°0N 0°10E 66 C4
Le Puy-en-Velay France 45°3N 3°52E 66 D5
Lea → U.K. 53°22N 0°45W 27 F7
Lea → U.K. 51°31N 0°1E 31 C9
Leadenham U.K. 53°3N 0°35W 27 F7
Leamington Canada 42°3N 82°36W 112 D6
Leane, L. Ireland 52°2N 9°32W 20 D3

Leatherhead U.K. 51°18N 0°20W 31 D8
Leavenworth U.S.A. 39°19N 94°55W 111 C8
Lebanon Ind., U.S.A. 40°3N 86°28W 112 E4
Lebanon Ky., U.S.A. 37°34N 85°15W 112 G5
Lebanon Mo., U.S.A. 37°41N 92°40W 111 C8
Lebanon Pa., U.S.A. 40°20N 76°26W 112 E9
Lebanon ■ Asia 34°0N 36°0E 86 C3
Lebu Chile 37°40S 73°47W 121 F2
Lecce Italy 40°23N 18°11E 69 D8
Lechlade U.K. 51°42N 1°41W 30 C5
Ledbury U.K. 52°2N 2°25W 30 B4
Lee → Ireland 51°53N 8°56W 20 E5
Lee-on-the-Solent U.K. 50°48N 1°12W 30 E6
Leech L. U.S.A. 47°10N 94°24W 111 A8
Leeds U.K. 53°48N 1°33W 27 E5
Leek U.K. 53°7N 2°1W 27 F4
Leeuwarden Neths. 53°15N 5°48E 64 B3
Leeuwin, C. Australia 34°20S 115°9E 98 G2
Leeward Is. Atl. Oc. 16°30N 63°30W 115 D12
Lefkada Greece 38°40N 20°43E 69 E9
Leganés Spain 40°19N 3°45W 67 B4
Legazpi Phil. 13°10N 123°45E 83 B6
Legionowo Poland 52°25N 20°50E 65 B11
Legnica Poland 51°12N 16°10E 64 C9
Leicester U.K. 52°38N 1°8W 27 G6
Leicestershire □ U.K. 52°41N 1°17W 27 G6
Leiden Neths. 52°9N 4°30E 64 B3
Leigh Gt. Man., U.K. 53°30N 2°32W 27 E3
Leigh Hereford, U.K. 52°11N 2°20W 30 B4
Leighton Buzzard U.K. 51°54N 0°38W 31 C7
Leine → Germany 52°43N 9°36E 64 B5
Leinster □ Ireland 53°3N 7°8W 21 B8
Leinster, Mt. Ireland 52°37N 6°46W 21 C9
Leintwardine U.K. 52°22N 2°51W 30 B3
Leipzig Germany 51°18N 12°22E 64 C7
Leiston U.K. 52°12N 1°36E 31 B12
Leith U.K. 55°59N 3°11W 25 C9
Leith Hill U.K. 51°11N 0°22W 31 D8
Leitholm U.K. 55°41N 2°20W 25 C11
Leitrim Ireland 54°0N 8°5W 18 C5
Leitrim □ Ireland 54°8N 8°0W 18 C5
Leixlip Ireland 53°22N 6°30W 21 B9
Leizhou Pen. China 21°0N 110°0E 79 G11
Lelant U.K. 50°11N 5°28W 29 G3
Léman, L. Europe 46°26N 6°30E 64 E4
Lena → Russia 72°52N 126°40E 77 B13
Lenham U.K. 51°14N 0°44E 31 D10
Leninsk-Kuznetskiy Russia 54°44N 86°10E 76 D9
Lennox Hills U.K. 56°3N 4°12W 24 B7
Lens France 50°26N 2°50E 66 A5
Leodhais = Lewis U.K. 58°9N 6°40W 22 F4
Leominster U.K. 52°14N 2°43W 30 B3
Leominster U.S.A. 42°32N 71°46W 113 D12
León Mexico 21°6N 101°41W 114 C4
León Nic. 12°27N 86°51W 114 E7
León Spain 42°38N 5°34W 67 A3
Leonora Australia 28°49S 121°19E 98 F3
Leopoldina Brazil 21°28S 42°40W 122 D2
Lerwick U.K. 60°9N 1°9W 22 B15
Les Cayes Haiti 18°15N 73°46W 115 D10
Les Sables-d'Olonne France 46°30N 1°45W 66 C3
Lesbos Greece 39°10N 26°20E 69 E12
Lesbury U.K. 55°25N 1°36W 26 B5
Leshan China 29°33N 103°41E 78 F9
Leskovac Serbia 43°0N 21°58E 69 C9
Lesosibirsk Russia 58°14N 92°29E 77 D10
Lesotho ■ Africa 29°40S 28°0E 97 K5
Lesser Antilles W. Indies 15°0N 61°0W 115 E12
Lesser Slave L. Canada 55°30N 115°25W 108 D8
Lesser Sunda Is. Indonesia 8°0S 120°0E 83 F6
Leszno Poland 51°50N 16°30E 65 C9
Letchworth Garden City U.K. 51°59N 0°13W 31 C8
Lethbridge Canada 49°45N 112°45W 108 E8
Leti, Kepulauan Indonesia 8°10S 128°0E 83 F7
Leticia Colombia 4°9S 70°0W 120 C2
Letterkenny Ireland 54°57N 7°45W 18 B6
Leuchars U.K. 56°24N 2°53W 25 B10
Leuven Belgium 50°52N 4°42E 64 C3
Leven E. Riding, U.K. 53°53N 0°18W 27 E8
Leven Fife, U.K. 56°12N 3°0W 25 B10
Leven → U.K. 54°31N 1°19W 26 C6
Leven, L. Highl., U.K. 56°42N 5°6W 22 J7
Leven, L. Perth & Kinr., U.K. 56°12N 3°22W 25 B9
Lévis Canada 46°48N 71°9W 113 B12
Lewes U.K. 50°52N 0°1E 31 E9
Lewis U.K. 58°9N 6°40W 22 F4
Lewis, Butt of U.K. 58°31N 6°16W 22 E4
Lewisham □ U.K. 51°27N 0°1W 31 D8
Lewisporte Canada 49°15N 55°3W 109 E14
Lewiston Idaho, U.S.A. 46°25N 117°1W 110 A3
Lewiston Maine, U.S.A. 44°6N 70°13W 113 C12
Lewistown Mont., U.S.A. 47°4N 109°26W 110 A5
Lewistown Pa., U.S.A. 40°36N 77°34W 112 E9
Lexington U.S.A. 38°3N 84°30W 112 F5
Lexington Park U.S.A. 38°16N 76°27W 112 F9
Leyburn U.K. 54°19N 1°48W 26 D5
Leyland U.K. 53°42N 2°43W 27 E3
Leysdown on Sea U.K. 51°24N 0°56E 31 D10
Leyte Phil. 11°0N 125°0E 83 B6
Lhasa China 29°25N 90°58E 78 F7
Lhazê China 29°5N 87°38E 78 F6
L'Hospitalet de Llobregat Spain 41°21N 2°6E 67 B7
Liancourt Rocks Asia 37°15N 131°52E 81 E2
Lianyungang China 34°40N 119°11E 79 E12
Liaodong Pen. China 40°0N 122°30E 79 D13
Liaoning □ China 41°40N 122°30E 79 C13
Liaotung, G. of China 40°20N 121°10E 79 C13
Liaoyang China 41°15N 122°58E 79 C13
Liaoyuan China 42°58N 125°2E 79 C14
Liard → Canada 61°51N 121°18W 108 C7
Liberal U.S.A. 37°3N 100°55W 110 C6
Liberec Czechia 50°47N 15°7E 64 C8
Liberia ■ W. Afr. 6°30N 9°30W 94 G4
Libourne France 44°55N 0°14W 66 D3
Libreville Gabon 0°25N 9°26E 96 D1
Libya ■ N. Afr. 27°0N 17°0E 95 C9
Libyan Desert Africa 25°0N 25°0E 95 C10
Libyan Plateau Egypt 30°40N 26°30E 95 B11
Lichfield U.K. 52°41N 1°49W 27 G5
Lichinga Mozam. 13°13S 35°11E 97 G7
Liddesdale U.K. 55°14N 2°50W 25 D10
Liechtenstein ■ Europe 47°8N 9°35E 64 E5

Liège Belgium 50°38N 5°35E 64 C3
Liepāja Latvia 56°30N 21°0E 63 F8
Liffey → Ireland 53°21N 6°13W 21 B10
Lifford Ireland 54°51N 7°29W 18 B7
Liguria □ Italy 44°30N 8°50E 68 B3
Ligurian Sea Medit. S. 43°20N 9°0E 68 C3
Lihu'e U.S.A. 21°59N 159°23W 110 H15
Lijiang China 26°55N 100°20E 78 F9
Likasi Dem. Rep. of the Congo 10°55S 26°48E 96 G5
Lille France 50°38N 3°3E 66 A5
Lillehammer Norway 61°8N 10°30E 63 E6
Lilleshall U.K. 52°44N 2°23W 27 G4
Lilongwe Malawi 14°0S 33°48E 97 G6
Lima Peru 12°3S 77°2W 120 D2
Lima U.S.A. 40°44N 84°6W 112 E5
Limassol Cyprus 34°42N 33°1E 86 C3
Limavady U.K. 55°3N 6°56W 19 A8
Limay → Argentina 39°0S 68°0W 121 F3
Limbe Cameroon 4°1N 9°10E 96 D1
Limeira Brazil 22°35S 47°28W 122 D1
Limerick Ireland 52°40N 8°37W 20 C5
Limerick □ Ireland 52°30N 8°50W 20 C5
Limfjorden Denmark 56°55N 9°0E 63 F5
Limnos Greece 39°50N 25°5E 69 E11
Limoges France 45°50N 1°15E 66 D4
Limón Costa Rica 10°0N 83°2W 115 F8
Limousin France 45°30N 1°30E 66 D4
Limoux France 43°4N 2°12E 66 E5
Limpopo → Africa 25°5S 33°30E 97 K6
Linares Chile 35°50S 71°40W 121 F2
Linares Mexico 24°52N 99°34W 114 C5
Linares Spain 38°10N 3°40W 67 C4
Linchuan China 27°57N 116°15E 79 F12
Lincoln U.K. 53°14N 0°32W 27 F7
Lincoln Ill., U.S.A. 40°9N 89°22W 112 E3
Lincoln Maine, U.S.A. 45°22N 68°30W 113 C13
Lincoln Nebr., U.S.A. 40°49N 96°41W 111 B7
Lincoln Sea Arctic 84°0N 55°0W 54 A5
Lincolnshire □ U.K. 53°14N 0°32W 27 F7
Lincolnshire Wolds U.K. 53°26N 0°13W 27 F8
Lindale U.K. 54°14N 2°53W 26 D3
Lindesnes Norway 57°58N 7°3E 63 F5
Lindsay Canada 44°22N 78°43W 112 C8
Linfen China 36°3N 111°30E 79 D11
Lingfield U.K. 51°11N 0°0 31 D8
Lingga, Kepulauan Indonesia 0°10S 104°30E 82 E2
Linhares Brazil 19°25S 40°4W 122 C2
Linhe China 40°48N 107°20E 78 C10
Linkinhorne U.K. 50°32N 4°24W 29 F5
Linköping Sweden 58°28N 15°36E 63 F7
Linnhe, L. U.K. 56°36N 5°25W 24 A5
Linslade U.K. 51°54N 0°41W 31 C7
Linton U.K. 52°6N 0°17E 31 B9
Linton U.S.A. 39°2N 87°10W 112 F4
Linxi China 43°36N 118°2E 79 C12
Linxia China 35°36N 103°10E 78 D9
Linyi China 35°5N 118°21E 79 D12
Linz Austria 48°18N 14°18E 64 D8
Lion, G. du France 43°10N 4°0E 66 E6
Lipa Phil. 13°57N 121°10E 83 B6
Lipari Italy 38°26N 14°58E 68 E6
Lipetsk Russia 52°37N 39°35E 70 D6
Lippe → Germany 51°39N 6°36E 64 C4
Lisbon Portugal 38°42N 9°8W 67 C1
Lisburn U.K. 54°31N 6°3W 19 B9
Lisburn & Castlereagh □ U.K. 54°30N 6°4W 19 B9
Liscannor B. Ireland 52°55N 9°24W 20 C4
Lisianski I. U.S.A. 26°2N 174°0W 102 E10
Lisieux France 49°10N 0°12E 66 B4
Liskeard U.K. 50°27N 4°29W 29 G5
Liski Russia 51°3N 39°30E 70 D6
Lismore Australia 28°44S 153°21E 98 F9
Lismore Ireland 52°8N 7°55W 20 D7
Liss U.K. 51°3N 0°54W 31 D7
Listowel Canada 43°44N 80°58W 112 D7
Listowel Ireland 52°27N 9°29W 20 D4
Litani → Lebanon 33°20N 35°15E 86 C3
Litcham U.K. 52°44N 0°47E 31 A10
Litchfield U.S.A. 39°11N 89°39W 112 F3
Litherland U.K. 53°29N 2°59W 27 F3
Lithuania ■ Europe 55°30N 24°0E 63 F8
Little Current Canada 45°55N 82°0W 112 C6
Little Khingan Mts. China 49°0N 127°0E 79 B14
Little Minch U.K. 57°35N 6°45W 22 G4
Little Missouri → U.S.A. 47°36N 102°25W 110 A6
Little Ouse → U.K. 52°22N 1°12E 31 B11
Little Rock U.S.A. 34°45N 92°17W 111 D8
Little Walsingham U.K. 52°54N 0°52E 31 A10
Littlehampton U.K. 50°49N 0°32W 31 E7
Littleport U.K. 52°27N 0°19E 31 B9
Littlestone-on-Sea U.K. 50°58N 0°58E 31 E10
Liupanshui China 26°38N 104°48E 78 F9
Liuwa Plain Zambia 14°20S 22°30E 97 G4
Liuzhou China 24°22N 109°22E 79 G10
Liverpool Canada 44°5N 64°41W 109 E13
Liverpool U.K. 53°25N 3°0W 27 F3
Livingston U.K. 55°54N 3°30W 25 C9
Livingston U.S.A. 45°40N 110°34W 110 A4
Livingstone Zambia 17°46S 25°52E 97 H5
Livonia U.S.A. 42°23N 83°23W 112 D6
Livorno Italy 43°33N 10°19E 68 C4
Lizard U.K. 49°58N 5°13W 29 H3
Lizard Pt. U.K. 49°57N 5°13W 29 H3
Ljubljana Slovenia 46°4N 14°33E 64 E8
Llandeilo U.K. 51°53N 3°59W 28 D6
Llandovery U.K. 51°59N 3°48W 28 D6
Llandrindod Wells U.K. 52°14N 3°22W 28 C7
Llandudno U.K. 53°19N 3°50W 28 A7
Llanelli U.K. 51°41N 4°10W 28 D5
Llanerchymedd U.K. 53°20N 4°23W 28 A5
Llanfair Caereinion U.K. 52°39N 3°20W 28 B7
Llanfair-ym-Muallt = Builth Wells
  U.K. 52°9N 3°25W 28 C7
Llanfairfechan U.K. 53°15N 3°58W 28 A6
Llangefni U.K. 53°15N 4°18W 28 A5
Llangollen U.K. 52°58N 3°11W 28 B7
Llanidloes U.K. 52°27N 3°31W 28 C6
Llanllyfni U.K. 53°2N 4°17W 28 A5
Llano Estacado U.S.A. 33°30N 103°0W 110 D6
Llanos S. Amer. 5°0N 71°35W 120 B2

Llanquihue, L. Chile 41°10S 72°50W 121 G2
Llanrhystyd U.K. 52°19N 4°7W 28 C5
Llantrisant U.K. 51°32N 3°22W 29 D7
Llantwit Major U.K. 51°24N 3°29W 29 E7
Llanwrtyd Wells U.K. 52°7N 3°38W 28 C6
Llanyblodwel U.K. 52°48N 3°8W 28 B7
Llanymynech U.K. 52°47N 3°5W 28 B7
Lleida Spain 41°37N 0°39E 67 B6
Lleyn Peninsula U.K. 52°51N 4°36W 28 B4
Llobregat → Spain 41°19N 2°5E 67 B7
Lloret de Mar Spain 41°41N 2°53E 67 B7
Lloydminster Canada 53°17N 110°0W 108 D9
Llullaillaco, Volcán S. Amer. 24°43S 68°30W 121 E3
Lobamba Eswatini 26°28S 31°12E 97 K6
Lobatse Botswana 25°12S 25°40E 97 K5
Lobito Angola 12°18S 13°35E 97 G2
Loch Lomond and the Trossachs △
  U.K. 56°10N 4°40W 24 B6
Lochaber U.K. 56°59N 5°1W 22 J7
Locharbriggs U.K. 55°7N 3°35W 25 D8
Lochboisdale U.K. 57°9N 7°20W 22 H3
Loches France 47°7N 1°0E 66 C4
Lochgelly U.K. 56°7N 3°19W 25 B9
Lochgilphead U.K. 56°2N 5°26W 24 B5
Lochinver U.K. 58°9N 5°14W 22 F7
Lochmaben U.K. 55°8N 3°27W 25 D9
Lochmaddy U.K. 57°36N 7°10W 22 G3
Lochnagar U.K. 56°57N 3°15W 23 J11
Lochy, L. U.K. 57°0N 4°53W 23 J8
Lock Haven U.S.A. 41°8N 77°28W 112 E9
Lockerbie U.K. 55°7N 3°21W 25 D9
Loddon U.K. 52°32N 1°31E 31 A12
Lodwar Kenya 3°7N 35°36E 96 D7
Łódź Poland 51°45N 19°27E 65 C10
Lofoten Norway 68°30N 13°59E 63 D6
Loftus U.K. 54°34N 0°53W 26 C7
Logan, Ohio, U.S.A. 39°32N 82°25W 112 F6
Logan Utah, U.S.A. 41°44N 111°50W 110 B4
Logan W. Va., U.S.A. 37°51N 81°59W 112 G7
Logan, Mt. Canada 60°34N 140°23W 108 C5
Logansport U.S.A. 40°45N 86°22W 112 E4
Logroño Spain 42°28N 2°27W 67 A4
Lohardaga India 23°27N 84°45E 85 H14
Loir → France 47°33N 0°32W 66 C3
Loire → France 47°16N 2°10W 66 C2
Loja Ecuador 3°59S 79°16W 120 C2
Lomami →
  Dem. Rep. of the Congo 0°46N 24°16E 96 D4
Lombárdia □ Italy 45°40N 9°30E 68 B3
Lomblen Indonesia 8°30S 123°32E 83 F6
Lombok Indonesia 8°45S 116°30E 82 F5
Lomé Togo 6°9N 1°20E 94 G6
Lomela →
  Dem. Rep. of the Congo 0°15S 20°40E 96 E4
Lomond, L. U.K. 56°8N 4°38W 24 B6
Łomża Poland 53°10N 22°2E 65 B12
London Canada 42°59N 81°15W 112 D7
London U.K. 51°30N 0°3W 31 D8
London Gateway U.K. 51°31N 0°29E 31 C10
London Gatwick ✈ (LGW)
  U.K. 51°10N 0°11W 31 D8
London Heathrow ✈ (LHR)
  U.K. 51°28N 0°27W 31 D8
London Stansted ✈ (STN) U.K. 51°54N 0°14E 31 C9
Londonderry U.K. 55°0N 7°20W 18 A7
Londonderry, C. Australia 13°45S 126°55E 98 C4
Londrina Brazil 23°18S 51°10W 121 E4
Long, L. U.K. 56°4N 4°50W 24 B6
Long Beach U.S.A. 33°46N 118°11W 110 D3
Long Bennington U.K. 52°59N 0°44W 27 G7
Long Branch U.S.A. 40°18N 74°0W 113 E11
Long Clawson U.K. 52°51N 0°55W 27 G7
Long Crendon U.K. 51°46N 0°59W 31 C7
Long Eaton U.K. 52°53N 1°15W 27 G6
Long I. Ireland 51°30N 9°34W 20 F3
Long I. The Bahamas 23°20N 75°10W 115 C9
Long I. U.S.A. 40°45N 73°30W 113 E11
Long Itchington U.K. 52°16N 1°22W 30 B6
Long Melford U.K. 52°4N 0°45E 31 B10
Long Mynd, The U.K. 52°35N 2°50W 27 G3
Long Preston U.K. 54°2N 2°14W 27 D4
Long Sutton U.K. 52°48N 0°7E 27 G9
Long Xuyen Vietnam 10°19N 105°28E 82 B3
Longford Ireland 53°43N 7°49W 18 D6
Longford □ Ireland 53°42N 7°45W 18 D6
Longford □ Ireland 53°42N 7°45W 18 D6
Longframlington U.K. 55°18N 1°47W 26 B5
Longhoughton U.K. 55°26N 1°37W 26 B5
Longhua China 22°39N 114°0E 79 a
Longlac Canada 49°45N 86°25W 112 A4
Longreach Australia 23°28S 144°14E 98 E7
Longridge U.K. 53°50N 2°35W 27 E3
Longton U.K. 52°59N 2°48W 27 E3
Longtown Cumb., U.K. 55°1N 2°58W 26 B3
Longtown Hereford, U.K. 51°58N 2°59W 30 C3
Longueuil Canada 45°31N 73°29W 113 C11
Longview Tex., U.S.A. 32°30N 94°44W 111 D8
Longview Wash., U.S.A. 46°8N 122°57W 110 A2
Longyan China 25°10N 117°0E 79 F12
Lons-le-Saunier France 46°40N 5°31E 66 C6
Looe U.K. 50°22N 4°28W 29 G4
Loop Hd. Ireland 52°34N 9°56W 20 D3
Lop Nur China 37°3N 80°11E 78 D5
Lopez, C. Gabon 0°47S 8°40W 96 E1
Lora del Río Spain 37°39N 5°33W 67 D3
Lorain U.S.A. 41°28N 82°11W 112 E6
Loralai Pakistan 30°20N 68°41E 84 D6
Lorca Spain 37°41N 1°42W 67 D5
Lord Howe I. Pac. Oc. 31°33S 159°6E 99 G10
Lord Howe Rise Pac. Oc. 30°0S 162°30E 99 H12
Lordsburg U.S.A. 32°21N 108°43W 110 D5
Lorestān □ Iran 33°30N 48°40E 86 C7
Lorient France 47°45N 3°23W 66 C2
Lorn U.K. 56°26N 5°10W 24 B5
Lorn, Firth of U.K. 56°20N 5°40W 24 B5
Lorraine France 48°53N 6°0E 66 B7
Los Alamos U.S.A. 35°53N 106°19W 110 C5
Los Andes Chile 32°50S 70°40W 121 F2
Los Angeles Chile 37°28S 72°23W 121 F2
Los Angeles U.S.A. 34°3N 118°14W 110 D3
Los Mochis Mexico 25°45N 108°57W 114 B3
Los Roques, Is. Venezuela 11°50N 66°45W 120 A3

Lošinj Croatia 44°30N 14°30E 68 B6
Lossiemouth U.K. 57°42N 3°17W 23 G11
Lostwithiel U.K. 50°24N 4°41W 29 G4
Lot → France 44°18N 0°20E 66 D4
Lota Chile 37°5S 73°10W 121 F2
Loubomo Congo 4°9S 12°47E 96 E2
Loughborough U.K. 52°47N 1°11W 27 G6
Loughed I. Canada 77°26N 105°6W 109 B9
Loughrea Ireland 53°12N 8°33W 20 B5
Loughros More B. Ireland 54°48N 8°32W 18 B4
Louis XIV, Pte. Canada 54°37N 79°45W 109 D12
Louisa U.S.A. 38°7N 82°36W 112 F6
Louisiade Arch. Papua N. G. 11°10S 153°0E 98 C9
Louisiana □ U.S.A. 30°50N 92°0W 111 D8
Louisville U.S.A. 38°15N 85°46W 112 F5
Lourdes France 43°6N 0°3W 66 E3
Louth Ireland 53°58N 6°32W 19 D8
Louth U.K. 53°22N 0°1W 27 F8
Louth □ Ireland 53°56N 6°34W 19 D8
Lovech Bulgaria 43°8N 24°42E 69 C11
Lowell U.S.A. 42°38N 71°19W 113 D12
Lower Beeding U.K. 51°2N 0°15W 31 D8
Lower Saxony = Niedersachsen □
  Germany 52°50N 9°0E 64 B5
Lower Tunguska → Russia 65°48N 88°4E 77 C9
Lowestoft U.K. 52°29N 1°45E 31 B12
Lowick U.K. 55°39N 1°57W 26 A5
Lowther Hills U.K. 55°20N 3°40W 25 D8
Lowville U.S.A. 43°47N 75°29W 113 D10
Loyauté, Îs. N. Cal. 20°50S 166°30E 99 E12
Lu Wo China 22°33N 114°6E 79 a
Lualaba →
  Dem. Rep. of the Congo 0°26N 25°20E 96 D5
Lu'an China 31°45N 116°29E 79 E12
Luanda Angola 8°50S 13°15E 96 F2
Luangwa → Zambia 14°25S 30°25E 97 G6
Luanshya Zambia 13°3S 28°28E 97 G5
Luapula → Africa 9°26S 28°33E 96 F5
Lubango Angola 14°55S 13°30E 97 G2
Lubbock U.S.A. 33°35N 101°51W 110 D6
Lübeck Germany 53°52N 10°40E 64 B6
Lublin Poland 51°12N 22°38E 65 C12
Lubumbashi
  Dem. Rep. of the Congo 11°40S 27°28E 97 G5
Lucan Ireland 53°22N 6°28W 21 B10
Lucania, Mt. Canada 61°1N 140°27W 108 C5
Lucca Italy 43°50N 10°29E 68 C4
Luce Bay U.K. 54°45N 4°48W 24 E6
Lucea Jamaica 18°27N 78°10W 114 a
Lucena Phil. 13°56N 121°37E 83 B6
Lucknow India 26°50N 81°0E 85 F12
Lüda = Dalian China 38°50N 121°40E 79 D13
Lüderitz Namibia 26°41S 15°8E 97 K3
Ludgershall U.K. 51°15N 1°37W 30 D5
Ludgvan U.K. 50°9N 5°30W 29 G2
Ludhiana India 30°57N 75°56E 84 D9
Ludington U.S.A. 43°57N 86°27W 112 D4
Ludlow U.K. 52°22N 2°42W 27 H3
Ludwigsburg Germany 48°53N 9°11E 64 D5
Ludwigshafen Germany 49°29N 8°26E 64 D5
Lufkin U.S.A. 31°21N 94°44W 111 D8
Luga Russia 58°40N 29°55E 70 C4
Lugano Switz. 46°1N 8°57E 64 E5
Lugnaquilla Ireland 52°58N 6°28W 21 C10
Lugo Spain 43°2N 7°35W 67 A2
Lugwardine U.K. 52°4N 2°39W 30 B3
Luhansk Ukraine 48°38N 39°15E 71 E6
Luing U.K. 56°14N 5°39W 24 B4
Luleå Sweden 65°35N 22°10E 63 D8
Luleälven → Sweden 65°35N 22°10E 63 D8
Lundy U.K. 51°10N 4°41W 29 E4
Lune → U.K. 54°0N 2°51W 27 D3
Lüneburger Heide Germany 53°10N 10°12E 64 B6
Lunéville France 48°36N 6°30E 66 B7
Luni → India 24°41N 71°14E 84 G7
Luofu Dem. Rep. of the Congo 0°10S 29°15E 96 E5
Luoyang China 34°40N 112°26E 79 E11
Luray U.S.A. 38°40N 78°28W 112 F8
Lurgan U.K. 54°27N 6°20W 19 B9
Lusaka Zambia 15°28S 28°16E 97 H5
Lüt, Dasht-e Iran 31°30N 58°0E 87 D9
Lutherstadt Wittenberg
  Germany 51°53N 12°39E 64 C7
Luton U.K. 51°53N 0°24W 31 C8
Lutsel K'e Canada 62°24N 110°44W 108 C8
Lutsk Ukraine 50°50N 25°15E 65 C13
Lutterworth U.K. 52°28N 1°12W 27 H6
Luvua → Dem. Rep. of the Congo 6°50S 27°30E 96 F5
Luxembourg Lux. 49°37N 6°9E 64 D4
Luxembourg ■ Europe 49°45N 6°0E 64 D4
Luxor = El Uqsur Egypt 25°41N 32°38E 95 C12
Luzern Switz. 47°3N 8°18E 64 E5
Luzhou China 28°52N 105°20E 78 F10
Luziânia Brazil 16°20S 48°0W 122 C2
Luzon Phil. 16°0N 121°0E 83 A6
Lvov Ukraine 49°50N 24°0E 65 D13
Lyakhov Is. Russia 73°40N 141°0E 77 B15
Lybster U.K. 58°18N 3°15W 23 F11
Lydd U.K. 50°57N 0°55E 31 E10
Lydford U.K. 50°38N 4°8W 29 F5
Lydham U.K. 52°31N 2°58W 27 H3
Lydney U.K. 51°44N 2°33W 30 C4
Lyme B. U.K. 50°42N 2°53W 30 E3
Lyme Regis U.K. 50°43N 2°57W 30 E3
Lyminge U.K. 51°7N 1°6E 31 D11
Lymington U.K. 50°45N 1°32W 30 E5
Lymm U.K. 53°23N 2°29W 27 F4
Lympne U.K. 51°4N 1°2E 31 D11
Lynchburg U.S.A. 37°25N 79°9W 112 G8
Lyndhurst U.K. 50°52N 1°35W 30 E5
Lyneham U.K. 51°30N 1°58W 30 C5
Lynmouth U.K. 51°13N 3°49W 29 E6
Lynn Lake Canada 56°51N 101°3W 108 D9
Lynton U.K. 51°13N 3°50W 29 E6
Lyonnais France 45°45N 4°15E 66 D6
Lyons France 45°46N 4°50E 66 D6
Lysva Russia 58°7N 57°49E 70 C10
Lysychansk Ukraine 48°55N 38°30E 71 E6
Lytchett Minster U.K. 50°44N 2°4W 30 E4
Lytham St. Anne's U.K. 53°45N 3°0W 27 E2
Lythe U.K. 54°30N 0°41W 26 C7
Lyubertsy Russia 55°40N 37°51E 70 C6

174 INDEX

Ma'ān Mexicali

M

Ma'ān *Jordan* 30°12N 35°44E **86** D3
Maas → *Neths.* 51°45N 4°32E **64** C3
Maastricht *Neths.* 50°50N 5°40E **64** C3
Mablethorpe *U.K.* 53°20N 0°15E **27** F9
Macaé *Brazil* 22°20S 41°43W **122** D2
McAlester *U.S.A.* 34°56N 95°46W **111** D7
McAllen *U.S.A.* 26°12N 98°14W **110** E7
MacAlpine L. *Canada* 66°32N 102°45W **108** C9
Macapá *Brazil* 0°5N 51°4W **120** B4
Macau *Brazil* 5°15S 36°40W **120** C6
Macau *China* 22°12N 113°33E **79** a
Macclesfield *U.K.* 53°15N 2°8W **27** F4
M'Clintock Chan. *Canada* 72°0N 102°0W **108** B9
M'Clure Str. *Canada* 75°0N 119°0W **109** B8
McComb *U.S.A.* 31°15N 90°27W **111** D8
McCook *U.S.A.* 40°12N 100°38W **110** B6
McDonald Is. *Ind. Oc.* 53°0S 73°0E **53** G13
MacDonnell Ranges *Australia* 23°40S 133°0E **98** E5
Macduff *U.K.* 57°40N 2°31W **23** G12
Macedonia ☐ *Greece* 40°39N 22°0E **69** D10
Maceió *Brazil* 9°40S 35°41W **122** A3
Macgillycuddy's Reeks *Ireland* 51°58N 9°45W **20** E3
Mach *Pakistan* 29°50N 67°20E **84** E5
Machakos *Kenya* 1°30S 37°15E **96** E7
Machala *Ecuador* 3°20S 79°57W **120** C2
Machars, The *U.K.* 54°46N 4°30W **24** E6
Machias *U.S.A.* 44°43N 67°28W **113** C14
Machilipatnam *India* 16°12N 81°8E **85** L12
Machrihanish *U.K.* 55°25N 5°43W **24** D4
Machu Picchu *Peru* 13°8S 72°30W **120** D2
Machynlleth *U.K.* 52°35N 3°50W **28** B6
Mackay *Australia* 21°8S 149°11E **98** E8
Mackay, L. *Australia* 22°30S 129°0E **98** E4
McKeesport *U.S.A.* 40°20N 79°51W **112** E8
Mackenzie *Canada* 55°20N 123°5W **108** D7
Mackenzie → *Canada* 69°10N 134°20W **108** C6
Mackenzie King I. *Canada* 77°45N 111°0W **109** B8
Mackenzie Mts. *Canada* 64°0N 130°0W **108** B6
Mackinaw City *U.S.A.* 45°47N 84°44W **112** C5
McKinley, Mt. = Denali *U.S.A.* 63°4N 151°0W **108** C4
McKinley Sea *Arctic* 82°0N 0°0 **54** A7
McMinnville *U.S.A.* 45°13N 123°12W **110** A2
McMurdo Sd. *Antarctica* 77°0S 170°0E **55** D11
Macomb *U.S.A.* 40°27N 90°40W **112** E2
Mâcon *France* 46°19N 4°50E **66** C6
Macon *U.S.A.* 32°51N 83°38W **111** D10
McPherson *U.S.A.* 38°22N 97°40W **110** C7
Macquarie I. *Pac. Oc.* 54°36S 158°55E **102** N7
Macroom *Ireland* 51°54N 8°57W **20** E5
Madagascar ■ *Africa* 20°0S 47°0E **97** J9
Madang *Papua N. G.* 5°12S 145°49E **98** B8
Madeira *Atl. Oc.* 32°50N 17°0W **94** B2
Madeira → *Brazil* 3°22S 58°45W **120** C4
Madeleine, Îs. de la *Canada* 47°30N 61°40W **113** B17
Madeley *U.K.* 53°0N 2°20W **27** F4
Madhya Pradesh ☐ *India* 22°50N 78°0E **84** H11
Madison *Ind., U.S.A.* 38°44N 85°23W **112** F5
Madison *S. Dak., U.S.A.* 44°0N 97°7W **111** B7
Madison *Wis., U.S.A.* 43°4N 89°24W **112** D3
Madisonville *U.S.A.* 37°20N 87°30W **112** G4
Madiun *Indonesia* 7°38S 111°32E **82** F4
Madley *U.K.* 52°2N 2°51W **30** B3
Madras = Chennai *India* 13°8N 80°19E **84** N12
Madre de Dios → *Bolivia* 10°59S 66°8W **120** D3
Madre de Dios, I. *Chile* 50°20S 75°10W **121** H2
Madre Occidental, Sierra *Mexico* 27°0N 107°0W **114** B3
Madre Oriental, Sierra *Mexico* 25°0N 100°0W **114** C5
Madrid *Spain* 40°24N 3°42W **67** B4
Madura *Indonesia* 7°30S 114°0E **82** F4
Madurai *India* 9°55N 78°10E **84** Q11
Maebashi *Japan* 36°24N 139°4E **81** E6
Maesteg *U.K.* 51°36N 3°40W **29** D6
Mafeking *S. Africa* 25°50S 25°38E **97** K5
Mafia I. *Tanzania* 7°45S 39°50E **96** F7
Magadan *Russia* 59°38N 150°50E **77** D16
Magallanes, Estrecho de *Chile* 52°30S 75°0W **121** H2
Magangué *Colombia* 9°14N 74°45W **120** B2
Magdalena → *Colombia* 11°6N 74°51W **120** A2
Magdeburg *Germany* 52°7N 11°38E **64** B6
Magee Isle *U.K.* 54°48N 5°43W **19** B10
Magelang *Indonesia* 7°29S 110°13E **82** F4
Magellan's Str. = Magallanes, Estrecho de *Chile* 52°30S 75°0W **121** H2
Maggiore, L. *Italy* 45°57N 8°39E **68** B3
Maggotty *Jamaica* 18°9N 77°46W **114** a
Maghâgha *Egypt* 28°38N 30°50E **95** C12
Magherafelt *U.K.* 54°45N 6°37W **19** B8
Maghreb *N. Afr.* 32°0N 4°0W **90** C3
Maghull *U.K.* 53°31N 2°57W **27** E3
Magnetic Pole (North) *Arctic* 86°25N 157°41W **54** A18
Magnetic Pole (South) *Antarctica* 64°2S 135°43E **55** C9
Magnitogorsk *Russia* 53°27N 59°4E **70** D10
Magog *Canada* 45°18N 72°9W **113** C11
Magway *Myanmar* 20°10N 95°0E **85** J19
Mahābād *Iran* 36°50N 45°45E **86** B6
Mahajanga *Madag.* 15°40S 46°25E **97** H9
Mahakam → *Indonesia* 0°35S 117°17E **82** E5
Mahalapye *Botswana* 23°1S 26°51E **97** J5
Maḥallāt *Iran* 33°55N 50°30E **87** C7
Mahanadi → *India* 20°20N 86°25E **85** J15
Maharashtra ☐ *India* 20°30N 75°30E **84** J9
Mahdia *Tunisia* 35°28N 11°0E **95** A8
Mahesana *India* 23°39N 72°26E **84** H8
Mahilyow *Belarus* 53°55N 30°18E **65** B16
Mai-Ndombe, L. *Dem. Rep. of the Congo* 2°0S 18°20E **96** E3
Maiden Bradley *U.K.* 51°9N 2°17W **30** D4
Maiden Newton *U.K.* 50°46N 2°34W **30** E3
Maidenhead *U.K.* 51°31N 0°42W **31** C7
Maidstone *U.K.* 51°16N 0°32E **31** D10
Maiduguri *Nigeria* 12°0N 13°20E **95** F8
Main → *Germany* 50°0N 8°18E **64** C5
Main → *U.K.* 54°48N 6°18W **19** B9
Maine *France* 48°20N 0°15W **66** C3
Maine ☐ *U.S.A.* 45°20N 69°0W **113** C13
Maine → *Ireland* 52°9N 9°45W **20** D3
Mainland *Orkney, U.K.* 58°59N 3°8W **23** E11
Mainland *Shet., U.K.* 60°15N 1°22W **22** B15
Mainz *Germany* 50°1N 8°14E **64** C5
Maiquetía *Venezuela* 10°36N 66°57W **120** A3
Majorca = Mallorca *Spain* 39°30N 3°0E **67** C7
Majuro *Marshall Is.* 7°9N 171°12E **102** G9
Makale *Indonesia* 3°6S 119°51E **83** E5
Makalu *Nepal* 27°55N 87°8E **78** F6
Makassar *Indonesia* 5°10S 119°20E **83** F5
Makassar, Str. of *Indonesia* 1°0S 118°20E **83** E5
Makgadikgadi Salt Pans *Botswana* 20°40S 25°45E **97** J5
Makhachkala *Russia* 43°0N 47°30E **71** F8
Makhado *S. Africa* 23°1S 29°43E **97** J5
Makhanda *S. Africa* 33°19S 26°31E **97** L5
Makran Coast Range *Pakistan* 25°40N 64°0E **84** G4
Makurdi *Nigeria* 7°43N 8°35E **94** G7
Mal B. *Ireland* 52°50N 9°30W **20** C4
Malabar Coast *India* 11°0N 75°0E **84** P9
Malacca, Straits of *Indonesia* 3°0N 101°0E **82** D2
Málaga *Spain* 36°43N 4°23W **67** D3
Malahide *Ireland* 53°26N 6°9W **21** B10
Malaita *Solomon Is.* 9°0S 161°0E **99** B11
Malakal *South Sudan* 9°33N 31°40E **95** G12
Malakula *Vanuatu* 16°15S 167°30E **99** D12
Malang *Indonesia* 7°59S 112°45E **82** F4
Malanje *Angola* 9°36S 16°17E **96** F3
Mälaren *Sweden* 59°30N 17°10E **63** F7
Malatya *Turkey* 38°25N 38°20E **71** G6
Malawi ■ *Africa* 11°55S 34°0E **97** G6
Malawi, L. *Africa* 12°30S 34°30E **97** G6
Malay Pen. *Asia* 7°25N 100°0E **72** H12
Malāyer *Iran* 34°19N 48°51E **86** C7
Malaysia ■ *Asia* 5°0N 110°0E **82** D4
Malden *U.S.A.* 36°34N 89°57W **112** G3
Malden I. *Kiribati* 4°3S 155°1W **103** H12
Maldives ■ *Ind. Oc.* 5°0N 73°0E **73** H9
Maldon *U.K.* 51°44N 0°42E **31** C10
Maldonado *Uruguay* 34°59S 55°0W **121** F4
Malegaon *India* 20°30N 74°38E **84** J9
Malham Tarn *U.K.* 54°6N 2°10W **26** D4
Malheur L. *U.S.A.* 43°20N 118°48W **110** B3
Mali ■ *Africa* 17°0N 3°0W **94** E5
Malin Hd. *Ireland* 55°23N 7°23W **18** A7
Malin Pen. *Ireland* 55°20N 7°17W **19** A7
Malindi *Kenya* 3°12S 40°5E **96** E8
Mallaig *U.K.* 57°0N 5°50W **22** H6
Mallawi *Egypt* 27°44N 30°44E **95** C12
Mallorca *Spain* 39°30N 3°0E **67** C7
Mallow *Ireland* 52°8N 8°39W **20** D5
Malmesbury *U.K.* 51°35N 2°5W **30** C4
Malmö *Sweden* 55°36N 12°59E **63** F6
Malone *U.S.A.* 44°51N 74°18W **113** C10
Malpas *U.K.* 53°1N 2°45W **27** F3
Malpelo, I. de *Colombia* 4°3N 81°35W **115** G8
Malta ■ *Europe* 35°55N 14°26E **68** a
Maltby *U.K.* 53°25N 1°12W **27** F6
Malton *U.K.* 54°8N 0°49W **26** D7
Malvinas, Is. = Falkland Is. ⧄ *Atl. Oc.* 51°30S 59°0W **121** H4
Mamoré → *Bolivia* 10°23S 65°53W **120** D3
Mamoudzou *Mayotte* 12°48S 45°14E **91** H8
Man *Côte d'Ivoire* 7°30N 7°40W **94** G4
Man, I. of *U.K.* 54°15N 4°30W **19** C12
Manacles, The *U.K.* 50°2N 5°4W **29** G3
Manado *Indonesia* 1°29N 124°51E **83** D6
Managua *Nic.* 12°6N 86°20W **114** E7
Manaus *Brazil* 3°0S 60°0W **120** C3
Manby *U.K.* 53°21N 0°6E **27** F9
Manchester *U.K.* 53°29N 2°12W **27** F4
Manchester *U.S.A.* 42°59N 71°28W **113** D12
Manchester Int. ✈ (MAN) *U.K.* 53°21N 2°17W **27** F4
Manchuria *China* 45°0N 125°0E **79** C14
Manchurian Plain *China* 47°0N 124°0E **72** D14
Mandal *Norway* 58°2N 7°25E **63** F5
Mandalay *Myanmar* 22°0N 96°4E **85** J20
Mandan *U.S.A.* 46°50N 100°54W **110** A6
Mandaue *Phil.* 10°20N 123°56E **83** B6
Mandeville *Jamaica* 18°2N 77°31W **114** a
Mandla *India* 22°39N 80°30E **85** H12
Mandsaur *India* 24°3N 75°8E **84** G9
Mandvi *India* 22°51N 69°22E **84** H6
Manea *U.K.* 52°29N 0°10E **31** B9
Manfalût *Egypt* 27°20N 30°52E **95** C12
Manfredónia *Italy* 41°38N 15°55E **68** D6
Mangabeiras, Chapada das *Brazil* 10°0S 46°30W **122** B1
Mangaluru *India* 12°55N 74°47E **84** N9
Mangnai *China* 37°52N 91°43E **78** D7
Mangole *Indonesia* 1°50S 125°55E **83** E6
Mangotsfield *U.K.* 51°29N 2°30W **30** D4
Manhattan *U.S.A.* 39°11N 96°35W **111** C7
Manhuaçu *Brazil* 20°15S 42°2W **122** D2
Manica *Mozam.* 18°58S 32°59E **97** H6
Manicoré *Brazil* 5°48S 61°16W **120** C3
Manicouagan → *Canada* 49°30N 68°30W **109** E13
Manicouagan, Rés. *Canada* 51°5N 68°40W **109** D13
Manihiki *Cook Is.* 10°24S 161°1W **103** J11
Manila *Phil.* 14°35N 120°58E **83** B6
Manipur ☐ *India* 25°0N 94°0E **85** G19
Manisa *Turkey* 38°38N 27°30E **71** G4
Manistee *U.S.A.* 44°15N 86°19W **112** C4
Manistee → *U.S.A.* 44°15N 86°21W **112** C4
Manistique *U.S.A.* 45°57N 86°15W **112** C4
Manitoba ☐ *Canada* 53°30N 97°0W **108** D10
Manitoba, L. *Canada* 51°0N 98°45W **108** D10
Manitou Is. *U.S.A.* 45°8N 86°0W **112** C4
Manitoulin I. *Canada* 45°40N 82°30W **112** C6
Manitowoc *U.S.A.* 44°5N 87°40W **112** C4
Manizales *Colombia* 5°5N 75°32W **120** B2
Mankato *U.S.A.* 44°10N 94°0W **111** B8
Mannar *Sri Lanka* 9°1N 79°54E **84** Q11
Mannar, G. of *Asia* 8°30N 79°0E **84** Q11
Mannheim *Germany* 49°29N 8°29E **64** D5
Manning *Canada* 56°53N 117°39W **108** D8
Manningtree *U.K.* 51°56N 1°5E **31** C11
Manokwari *Indonesia* 0°54S 134°0E **83** E8
Manosque *France* 43°49N 5°47E **66** E6
Manresa *Spain* 41°48N 1°50E **67** B6
Mansel I. *Canada* 62°0N 80°0W **109** C12
Mansfield *U.K.* 53°9N 1°11W **27** F6
Mansfield *U.S.A.* 40°45N 82°31W **112** E6
Mansfield Woodhouse *U.K.* 53°11N 1°12W **27** F6
Manta *Ecuador* 1°0S 80°40W **120** C1
Mantes-la-Jolie *France* 48°58N 1°41E **66** B4
Mantiqueira, Serra da *Brazil* 22°0S 44°0W **117** F6
Manton *U.K.* 52°38N 0°41W **27** G7
Manton *U.S.A.* 44°25N 85°24W **112** C5
Mántova *Italy* 45°9N 10°48E **68** B4
Manuel Alves → *Brazil* 11°19S 48°28W **122** B1
Manzai *Pakistan* 32°12N 70°15E **84** C7
Manzanillo *Cuba* 20°20N 77°31W **115** C9
Manzanillo *Mexico* 19°3N 104°20W **114** D4
Manzouli *China* 49°35N 117°25E **79** B12
Maó *Spain* 39°53N 4°16E **67** C8
Maoming *China* 21°50N 110°54E **79** G11
Mapam Yumco *China* 30°45N 81°28E **78** E5
Maputo *Mozam.* 25°58S 32°32E **97** K6
Maputo B. *Mozam.* 25°50S 32°45E **90** J7
Maqên *China* 34°24N 100°6E **78** E9
Maqên Gangri *China* 34°55N 99°18E **78** E8
Maquinchao *Argentina* 41°15S 68°50W **121** G3
Maquoketa *U.S.A.* 42°4N 90°40W **112** D2
Mar *U.K.* 57°11N 2°53W **23** H12
Mar, Serra do *Brazil* 25°30S 49°0W **117** F6
Mar Chiquita, L. *Argentina* 30°40S 62°50W **121** F3
Mar del Plata *Argentina* 38°0S 57°30W **121** F4
Mara Rosa *Brazil* 14°1S 49°11W **122** B1
Marabá *Brazil* 5°20S 49°5W **120** C5
Maracá, I. de *Brazil* 2°10N 50°30W **120** B4
Maracaibo *Venezuela* 10°40N 71°37W **120** A2
Maracaibo, L. de *Venezuela* 9°40N 71°30W **120** B2
Maracay *Venezuela* 10°15N 67°28W **120** A3
Maradi *Niger* 13°29N 7°20E **94** F7
Maragogipe *Brazil* 12°46S 38°55W **122** B3
Marajo, I. de *Brazil* 1°0S 49°30W **120** C5
Maranguape *Brazil* 3°55S 38°50W **120** C6
Maranhão ☐ *Brazil* 5°0S 46°0W **120** C5
Marañón → *Peru* 4°30S 73°35W **120** C2
Marazion *U.K.* 50°7N 5°29W **29** G3
Marbella *Spain* 36°30N 4°57W **67** D3
March *U.K.* 52°33N 0°5E **31** A9
Marche *France* 46°5N 1°20E **66** C4
Marcus I. *Pac. Oc.* 24°20N 153°58E **102** E7
Mardan *Pakistan* 34°20N 72°0E **84** B8
Marden *U.K.* 52°7N 2°42W **30** B3
Mardin *Turkey* 37°20N 40°43E **71** G7
Maree, L. *U.K.* 57°40N 5°26W **22** G7
Mareham le Fen *U.K.* 53°8N 0°4W **27** F8
Marfleet *U.K.* 53°45N 0°17W **27** E8
Margarita, I. de *Venezuela* 11°0N 64°0W **120** A3
Margate *U.K.* 51°23N 1°23E **31** D11
Marg'ilon *Uzbekistan* 40°27N 71°42E **87** A12
Māreow, Dasht-e *Afghan.* 30°40N 62°30E **87** D10
Mari El ☐ *Russia* 56°30N 48°0E **70** C8
Mariana Trench *Pac. Oc.* 13°0N 145°0E **102** F6
Marías, Is. *Mexico* 21°25N 106°28W **114** C3
Maribor *Slovenia* 46°36N 15°40E **64** E8
Marie Byrd Land *Antarctica* 79°30S 125°0W **55** D14
Mariental *Namibia* 24°36S 18°0E **97** J3
Marietta *U.S.A.* 39°25N 81°27W **112** F7
Marília *Brazil* 22°13S 50°0W **120** E4
Marinette *U.S.A.* 45°6N 87°38W **112** C4
Maringá *Brazil* 23°26S 52°2W **121** E4
Marion *Ill., U.S.A.* 37°44N 88°56W **112** G3
Marion *Ind., U.S.A.* 40°32N 85°40W **112** E5
Marion *Ohio, U.S.A.* 40°35N 83°8W **112** E6
Mariupol *Ukraine* 47°5N 37°31E **71** E6
Marka *Somalia* 1°48N 44°50E **89** G3
Markam *China* 29°42N 98°38E **78** F8
Market Bosworth *U.K.* 52°38N 1°24W **27** G6
Market Deeping *U.K.* 52°41N 0°19W **27** G8
Market Drayton *U.K.* 52°54N 2°29W **27** G4
Market Harborough *U.K.* 52°29N 0°55W **27** H7
Market Lavington *U.K.* 51°17N 1°58W **30** D5
Market Rasen *U.K.* 53°24N 0°20W **27** F8
Market Warsop *U.K.* 53°12N 1°9W **27** F6
Market Weighton *U.K.* 53°52N 0°40W **27** E7
Markfield *U.K.* 52°42N 1°17W **27** G6
Markham, Mt. *Antarctica* 83°0S 164°0E **55** E11
Marks Tey *U.K.* 51°52N 0°49E **31** C10
Marlborough *U.K.* 51°25N 1°43W **30** D5
Marlborough Downs *U.K.* 51°27N 1°53W **30** D5
Marlow *U.K.* 51°34N 0°46W **31** C7
Marmara, Sea of *Turkey* 40°45N 28°15E **71** F4
Marmaris *Turkey* 36°50N 28°14E **86** B2
Marmora *Canada* 44°28N 77°41W **112** C9
Marne → *France* 48°47N 2°29E **66** B5
Marnhull *U.K.* 50°57N 2°19W **30** E4
Maroua *Cameroon* 10°40N 14°20E **95** F8
Marple *U.K.* 53°24N 2°4W **27** F4
Marquette *U.S.A.* 46°33N 87°24W **112** B4
Marquis *St. Lucia* 14°2N 60°54W **114** b
Marquises, Îs. *French Polynesia* 9°30S 140°0W **103** H14
Marrakesh *Morocco* 31°9N 8°0W **94** B4
Marree *Australia* 29°39S 138°1E **98** F6
Marsá Matrûh *Egypt* 31°19N 27°9E **95** B11
Marsabit *Kenya* 2°18N 38°0E **96** D7
Marsala *Italy* 37°48N 12°26E **68** F5
Marseilles *France* 43°18N 5°23E **66** E6
Marsh I. *U.S.A.* 29°34N 91°53W **111** E8
Marshall *U.S.A.* 32°33N 94°23W **111** D8
Marshall Is. ■ *Pac. Oc.* 9°0N 171°0E **102** G9
Marshfield *U.K.* 51°28N 2°19W **30** D4
Marshfield *U.S.A.* 44°40N 90°10W **112** C2
Marske-by-the-Sea *U.K.* 54°36N 1°0W **26** C7
Marston Moor *U.K.* 53°58N 1°17W **27** E6
Martaban *Myanmar* 16°30N 97°35E **85** L20
Martapura *Indonesia* 3°22S 114°47E **82** E4
Martham *U.K.* 52°42N 1°37E **31** A12
Martha's Vineyard *U.S.A.* 41°25N 70°38W **113** E12
Martigues *France* 43°24N 5°4E **66** E6
Martinique ⧄ *W. Indies* 14°40N 61°0W **115** E12
Martins Bay *Barbados* 13°12N 59°29W **114** c
Martinsburg *U.S.A.* 39°27N 77°58W **112** F9
Martinsville *U.S.A.* 39°26N 86°25W **112** F4
Martley *U.K.* 52°15N 2°21W **30** B4
Martock *U.K.* 50°58N 2°46W **30** E3
Marwar *India* 25°43N 73°45E **84** G8
Mary *Turkmenistan* 37°40N 61°50E **87** B10
Maryborough *Australia* 25°31S 152°37E **98** F9
Maryland ☐ *U.S.A.* 39°0N 76°30W **112** F9
Maryport *U.K.* 54°44N 3°28W **26** C2
Marystown *Canada* 47°10N 55°10W **109** E14
Marytavy *U.K.* 50°36N 4°7W **29** F5
Masai Steppe *Tanzania* 4°30S 36°30E **96** E7
Masan *S. Korea* 35°11N 128°32E **79** D14
Masandam, Ra's *Oman* 26°30N 56°30E **89** B6
Masaya *Nic.* 12°0N 86°7W **114** E7
Masbate *Phil.* 12°21N 123°36E **83** B6
Mascara *Algeria* 35°26N 0°6E **94** A6
Maseru *Lesotho* 29°18S 27°30E **97** K5
Masham *U.K.* 54°14N 1°39W **26** D5
Mashhad *Iran* 36°20N 59°35E **87** B9
Mashonaland *Zimbabwe* 16°30S 31°0E **97** H6
Maşīrah, Jazīrat *Oman* 21°0N 58°50E **89** C6
Masjed Soleyman *Iran* 31°55N 49°18E **86** D7
Mask, L. *Ireland* 53°36N 9°22W **18** D3
Mason City *U.S.A.* 43°9N 93°12W **111** B8
Massa *Italy* 44°1N 10°9E **68** B4
Massachusetts ☐ *U.S.A.* 42°30N 72°0W **113** D11
Massawa *Eritrea* 15°35N 39°25E **89** D2
Massena *U.S.A.* 44°56N 74°54W **113** C10
Massiah Street *Barbados* 13°9N 59°29W **114** c
Massif Central *France* 44°55N 3°0E **66** D5
Massillon *U.S.A.* 40°48N 81°32W **112** E7
Masurian Lakes *Poland* 53°50N 21°0E **65** B11
Masvingo *Zimbabwe* 20°8S 30°49E **97** J6
Mata-Utu *Wall. & F. Is.* 13°17S 176°8W **99** C15
Matabeleland *Zimbabwe* 18°0S 27°0E **97** H5
Matadi *Dem. Rep. of the Congo* 5°52S 13°31E **96** F2
Matagalpa *Nic.* 13°0N 85°58W **114** E7
Matagami *Canada* 49°45N 77°34W **109** E12
Matagami, L. *Canada* 49°50N 77°40W **109** E12
Matagorda I. *U.S.A.* 28°15N 96°30W **111** E7
Matamoros *Coahuila, Mexico* 25°32N 103°15W **114** B5
Matamoros *Tamaulipas, Mexico* 25°53N 97°30W **114** B5
Matane *Canada* 48°50N 67°33W **109** E13
Matanzas *Cuba* 23°0N 81°40W **115** C8
Matara *Sri Lanka* 5°58N 80°30E **84** S12
Mataró *Spain* 41°32N 2°29E **67** B7
Matehuala *Mexico* 23°39N 100°39W **114** C4
Mateke Hills *Zimbabwe* 21°48S 31°0E **97** J6
Matera *Italy* 40°40N 16°36E **68** D7
Mathura *India* 27°30N 77°40E **84** F10
Mati *Phil.* 6°55N 126°15E **83** C7
Matlock *U.K.* 53°9N 1°33W **27** F5
Mato Grosso ☐ *Brazil* 14°0S 55°0W **120** D4
Mato Grosso, Planalto do *Brazil* 15°0S 55°0W **120** D4
Mato Grosso do Sul ☐ *Brazil* 18°0S 55°0W **120** D4
Matola *Mozam.* 25°57S 32°27E **97** K6
Matopo Hills *Zimbabwe* 20°36S 28°20E **97** J5
Maṭruḥ *Oman* 23°37N 58°30E **87** F9
Matsu Tao *Taiwan* 26°8N 119°56E **79** F12
Matsue *Japan* 35°25N 133°10E **81** F3
Matsumoto *Japan* 36°15N 138°0E **81** E6
Matsusaka *Japan* 34°34N 136°32E **81** F5
Matsuyama *Japan* 33°45N 132°45E **81** G3
Mattagami → *Canada* 50°43N 81°29W **109** D11
Mattancheri *India* 9°50N 76°15E **84** Q10
Mattawa *Canada* 46°20N 78°45W **112** B8
Matterhorn *Switz.* 45°58N 7°39E **64** F4
Matthew, Î. *N. Cal.* 22°29S 171°15E **99** E13
Mattoon *U.S.A.* 39°29N 88°23W **112** F3
Maturín *Venezuela* 9°45N 63°11W **120** B3
Maubeuge *France* 50°17N 3°57E **66** A6
Maubin *Myanmar* 16°44N 95°39E **85** L19
Maudin Sun *Myanmar* 16°0N 94°30E **85** M19
Maui *U.S.A.* 20°48N 156°20W **110** H16
Maumee → *U.S.A.* 41°42N 83°28W **112** E6
Maumturk Mts. *Ireland* 53°32N 9°42W **18** D2
Maun *Botswana* 20°0S 23°26E **97** H4
Mauna Kea *U.S.A.* 19°50N 155°28W **110** J17
Mauna Loa *U.S.A.* 19°30N 155°35W **110** J17
Mauritania ■ *Africa* 20°50N 10°0W **94** E3
Mauritius ■ *Ind. Oc.* 20°0S 57°0E **91** J9
Mawgan *U.K.* 50°4N 5°13W **29** G3
Mawlamyine *Myanmar* 16°30N 97°40E **85** L20
Maxixe *Mozam.* 23°54S 35°17E **97** J7
Maxwellheugh *U.K.* 55°35N 2°26W **25** C11
May, I. of *U.K.* 56°11N 2°32W **25** B10
May Pen *Jamaica* 17°58N 77°15W **114** a
Mayaguana *The Bahamas* 22°30N 72°44W **115** C10
Mayagüez *Puerto Rico* 18°12N 67°9W **115** D11
Maybole *U.K.* 55°21N 4°42W **24** D6
Mayfield *E. Sussex, U.K.* 51°1N 0°17E **31** D9
Mayfield *Staffs., U.K.* 53°1N 1°47W **27** F5
Mayfield *U.S.A.* 36°44N 88°38W **112** G3
Maykop *Russia* 44°35N 40°10E **71** F7
Maynooth *Ireland* 53°23N 6°34W **21** B9
Mayo *Canada* 63°38N 135°57W **108** C6
Mayo ☐ *Ireland* 53°53N 9°3W **18** D3
Mayon Volcano *Phil.* 13°15N 123°41E **83** B6
Mayotte ⧄ *Ind. Oc.* 12°50S 45°10E **97** G9
Maysville *U.S.A.* 38°39N 83°46W **112** F6
Māzandarān ☐ *Iran* 36°30N 52°0E **87** B8
Mazar *China* 36°32N 77°1E **78** D4
Mazār-e Sharīf *Afghan.* 36°41N 67°0E **87** B11
Mazaruni → *Guyana* 6°25N 58°35W **120** B4
Mazatlán *Mexico* 23°13N 106°25W **114** C3
Mazyr *Belarus* 51°59N 29°15E **70** D4
Mbabane *Eswatini* 26°18S 31°6E **97** K6
Mbaïki *C.A.R.* 3°53N 18°1E **96** D3
Mbala *Zambia* 8°46S 31°24E **96** F6
Mbale *Uganda* 1°8N 34°12E **96** D6
Mbandaka *Dem. Rep. of the Congo* 0°1N 18°18E **96** D3
Mbanza Ngungu *Dem. Rep. of the Congo* 5°12S 14°53E **96** F2
Mbeya *Tanzania* 8°54S 33°29E **96** F6
Mbour *Senegal* 14°22N 16°54W **94** F2
Mbuji-Mayi *Dem. Rep. of the Congo* 6°9S 23°40E **96** F4
Mdantsane *S. Africa* 32°56S 27°46E **97** L5
Mead, L. *U.S.A.* 36°0N 114°44W **110** C4
Meadow Lake *Canada* 54°10N 108°26W **108** D9
Meadville *U.S.A.* 41°39N 80°9W **112** E7
Meaford *Canada* 44°36N 80°35W **112** C7
Mealsgate *U.K.* 54°47N 3°13W **26** C2
Mearns, Howe of the *U.K.* 56°52N 2°26W **23** J13
Measham *U.K.* 52°43N 1°31W **27** G5
Meath ☐ *Ireland* 53°40N 6°57W **19** D8
Meaux *France* 48°58N 2°50E **66** B5
Mecca *Si. Arabia* 21°30N 39°54E **86** F4
Mechelen *Belgium* 51°2N 4°29E **64** C3
Mecklenburg *Germany* 53°33N 11°40E **64** B7
Mecklenburger Bucht *Germany* 54°20N 11°40E **64** A6
Medan *Indonesia* 3°40N 98°38E **82** D1
Médéa *Algeria* 36°12N 2°50E **94** A6
Medellín *Colombia* 6°15N 75°35W **120** B2
Medford *Oreg., U.S.A.* 42°19N 122°52W **110** B2
Medford *Wis., U.S.A.* 45°9N 90°20W **112** C2
Medicine Hat *Canada* 50°0N 110°45W **108** E8
Medina *Si. Arabia* 24°35N 39°52E **86** E4
Mediterranean Sea *Europe* 35°0N 15°0E **90** C5
Médoc *France* 45°10N 0°50W **66** D3
Medstead *U.K.* 51°8N 1°3W **30** D6
Medvezhyegorsk *Russia* 63°0N 34°25E **70** B5
Medway → *U.K.* 51°27N 0°46E **31** D10
Meekatharra *Australia* 26°32S 118°29E **98** F2
Meerut *India* 29°1N 77°42E **84** E10
Meghalaya ☐ *India* 25°50N 91°0E **85** G17
Meghna → *Bangla.* 22°50N 90°50E **85** H17
Megisti *Greece* 36°8N 29°34E **86** B2
Meharry, Mt. *Australia* 22°59S 118°35E **98** D2
Meighen I. *Canada* 80°0N 99°30W **109** B10
Meiktila *Myanmar* 20°53N 95°54E **85** J19
Meizhou *China* 24°16N 116°6E **79** G12
Mejillones *Chile* 23°10S 70°30W **121** E2
Mekele *Ethiopia* 13°33N 39°30E **89** E2
Mekhtar *Pakistan* 30°30N 69°15E **84** D6
Meknès *Morocco* 33°57N 5°33W **94** B4
Mekong → *Asia* 9°30N 106°15E **82** C3
Melaka *Malaysia* 2°15N 102°15E **82** D2
Melanesia *Pac. Oc.* 4°0S 155°0E **102** H7
Melbourn *U.K.* 52°4N 0°0 **31** B9
Melbourne *Australia* 37°48S 144°58E **98** H8
Melbourne *U.K.* 52°50N 1°25W **27** G6
Mélèzes → *Canada* 57°40N 69°29W **109** D13
Melfort *Canada* 52°50N 104°37W **108** D9
Melilla *N. Afr.* 35°21N 2°57W **67** E4
Melitopol *Ukraine* 46°50N 35°22E **71** E6
Melksham *U.K.* 51°23N 2°8W **30** D4
Melmerby *U.K.* 54°45N 2°35W **26** C3
Melrhir, Chott *Algeria* 34°13N 6°30E **94** B7
Melrose *U.K.* 55°36N 2°43W **25** C10
Melsonby *U.K.* 54°29N 1°42W **26** D5
Melton Constable *U.K.* 52°52N 1°2E **31** A11
Melton Mowbray *U.K.* 52°47N 0°54W **27** G7
Melun *France* 48°32N 2°39E **66** B5
Melville *Canada* 50°55N 102°50W **108** D9
Melville, L. *Canada* 53°30N 60°0W **109** D14
Melville I. *Australia* 11°30S 131°0E **98** C5
Melville I. *Canada* 75°30N 112°0W **109** B8
Melville Pen. *Canada* 68°0N 84°0W **109** C11
Memphis *U.S.A.* 35°8N 90°2W **111** C9
Menai Bridge *U.K.* 53°14N 4°10W **28** A5
Menai Strait *U.K.* 53°11N 4°13W **28** A5
Mende *France* 44°31N 3°30E **66** D5
Mendip Hills *U.K.* 51°17N 2°40W **30** D3
Mendlesham *U.K.* 52°16N 1°6E **31** B11
Mendocino, C. *U.S.A.* 40°26N 124°25W **110** B2
Mendota *U.S.A.* 41°33N 89°7W **112** E3
Mendoza *Argentina* 32°50S 68°52W **121** F3
Menominee *U.S.A.* 45°6N 87°37W **112** C4
Menominee → *U.S.A.* 45°6N 87°35W **112** C4
Menomonie *U.S.A.* 44°53N 91°55W **112** C2
Menorca *Spain* 40°0N 4°0E **67** C8
Mentawai, Kepulauan *Indonesia* 2°0S 99°0E **82** E1
Merced *U.S.A.* 37°18N 120°29W **110** C2
Mercedes *Corrientes, Argentina* 29°10S 58°5W **121** E4
Mercedes *San Luis, Argentina* 33°40S 65°21W **121** F3
Mercedes *Uruguay* 33°12S 58°0W **121** F4
Mercy, C. *Canada* 65°0N 63°30W **109** C13
Mere *U.K.* 51°6N 2°16W **30** D4
Mergui *Myanmar* 12°26N 98°34E **82** B1
Mérida *Mexico* 20°58N 89°37W **114** C7
Mérida *Spain* 38°55N 6°25W **67** C2
Mérida *Venezuela* 8°24N 71°8W **120** B2
Mérida, Cord. de *Venezuela* 9°0N 71°0W **117** C3
Meriden *U.K.* 52°26N 1°38W **27** H5
Meriden *U.S.A.* 41°32N 72°48W **113** E11
Meridian *U.S.A.* 32°22N 88°42W **111** D9
Merowe Dam *Sudan* 18°35N 31°56E **95** E12
Merrick *U.K.* 55°8N 4°28W **24** D7
Merrill *U.S.A.* 45°11N 89°41W **112** C3
Merritt *Canada* 50°10N 120°45W **108** D7
Merse *U.K.* 55°43N 2°16W **25** C11
Mersea I. *U.K.* 51°47N 0°58E **31** C10
Mersey → *U.K.* 53°25N 3°1W **27** F2
Merseyside ☐ *U.K.* 53°31N 3°2W **27** E2
Mersin *Turkey* 36°51N 34°36E **71** G5
Merthyr Tydfil *U.K.* 51°45N 3°22W **28** D7
Merton ☐ *U.K.* 51°25N 0°11W **31** D8
Meru *Kenya* 0°3N 37°40E **96** D7
Meru *Tanzania* 3°15S 36°46E **96** E7
Mesa *U.S.A.* 33°25N 111°50W **110** D4
Mesopotamia *Iraq* 33°30N 44°0E **86** C5
Messina *Italy* 38°11N 15°34E **68** E6
Messina, Str. di *Italy* 38°15N 15°35E **68** F6
Mestre, Espigão *Brazil* 12°30S 46°10W **122** B1
Meta → *S. Amer.* 6°12N 67°28W **120** B3
Meta Incognita Pen. *Canada* 62°45N 68°30W **109** C13
Metheringham *U.K.* 53°9N 0°23W **27** F8
Methwold *U.K.* 52°32N 0°33E **31** A10
Metlakatla *U.S.A.* 55°8N 131°35W **108** D6
Metropolis *U.S.A.* 37°9N 88°44W **112** G3
Metz *France* 49°8N 6°10E **66** B7
Meuse → *Europe* 50°45N 5°41E **64** C3
Mevagissey *U.K.* 50°16N 4°48W **29** G4
Mevagissey B. *U.K.* 50°17N 4°47W **29** G4
Mexborough *U.K.* 53°30N 1°15W **27** E6
Mexiana, I. *Brazil* 0°0 49°30W **120** B5
Mexicali *Mexico* 32°40N 115°30W **114** A1

INDEX 175
México
Needham Market

México *Mexico* 19°24N 99°9W **114** D5
Mexico ■ *Cent. Amer.* 25°0N 105°0W **114** C4
Mexico, G. of *Cent. Amer.* 25°0N 90°0W **114** C7
Meymaneh *Afghan.* 35°53N 64°38E **87** C11
Mezen → *Russia* 65°44N 44°22E **70** A7
Mezhdurechensk *Russia* 53°41N 88°3E **76** D9
Mhonadh, Na h-Eileanan = Monach Is. *U.K.* 57°32N 7°40W **22** G2
Miami *U.S.A.* 25°46N 80°11W **111** E10
Mīāndowāb *Iran* 37°0N 46°5E **86** B6
Mīāneh *Iran* 37°30N 47°40E **86** B6
Mianwali *Pakistan* 32°38N 71°28E **84** C7
Mianyang *China* 31°22N 104°47E **78** E9
Miass *Russia* 54°59N 60°6E **70** D11
Micheldever *U.K.* 51°9N 1°14W **30** D6
Michigan □ *U.S.A.* 44°0N 85°0W **112** B4
Michigan, L. *U.S.A.* 44°0N 87°0W **112** D4
Michipicoten I. *Canada* 47°40N 85°40W **112** B5
Michurinsk *Russia* 52°58N 40°27E **70** D7
Mickle Fell *U.K.* 54°37N 2°18W **26** C4
Mickleover *U.K.* 52°55N 1°33W **27** G5
Mickleton *U.K.* 54°36N 2°2W **26** C4
Micoud *St. Lucia* 13°49N 60°54W **114** b
Micronesia *Pac. Oc.* 11°0N 160°0E **102** G7
Micronesia, Federated States of ■ *Pac. Oc.* 9°0N 150°0E **102** G7
Mid & East Antrim □ *U.K.* 54°52N 6°14W **19** B9
Mid Ulster □ *U.K.* 54°36N 6°45W **19** B8
Middelburg *S. Africa* 31°30S 25°0E **97** L5
Middle East *Asia* 35°0N 40°0E **72** E5
Middleham *U.K.* 54°17N 1°48W **26** D5
Middlemarsh *U.K.* 50°51N 2°28W **30** E4
Middlesbrough *U.K.* 54°35N 1°13W **26** C6
Middleton *Gt. Man., U.K.* 53°33N 2°12W **27** E4
Middleton *Norfolk, U.K.* 52°43N 0°29E **31** A9
Middleton Cheney *U.K.* 52°5N 1°16W **30** B6
Middleton in Teesdale *U.K.* 54°38N 2°4W **26** C4
Middleton on the Wolds *U.K.* 53°56N 0°35W **27** E7
Middletown *U.K.* 54°17N 6°51W **19** C8
Middletown *N.Y., U.S.A.* 41°27N 74°25W **113** E10
Middletown *Ohio, U.S.A.* 39°31N 84°24W **112** F5
Middlewich *U.K.* 53°12N 2°28W **27** F4
Middlezoy *U.K.* 51°5N 2°54W **30** D3
Midhurst *U.K.* 50°59N 0°44W **31** E7
Midi, Canal du → *France* 43°45N 1°21E **66** E4
Midland *Canada* 44°45N 79°50W **112** C8
Midland *Mich., U.S.A.* 43°37N 84°14W **112** D5
Midland *Tex., U.S.A.* 32°0N 102°3W **110** D6
Midleton *Ireland* 51°55N 8°10W **20** E6
Midsomer Norton *U.K.* 51°17N 2°28W **30** D4
Midway Is. *Pac. Oc.* 28°13N 177°22W **102** E10
Midwest *U.S.A.* 42°0N 90°0W **111** C9
Mieres *Spain* 43°18N 5°48W **67** A3
Mikhaylovka *Russia* 50°3N 43°5E **71** D7
Milan *Italy* 45°28N 9°10E **68** B3
Milborne Port *U.K.* 50°58N 2°28W **30** E4
Mildenhall *U.K.* 52°21N 0°32E **31** B10
Mildura *Australia* 34°13S 142°9E **98** G7
Miles City *U.S.A.* 46°25N 105°51W **110** A5
Milford *U.S.A.* 38°55N 75°26W **113** F10
Milford Haven *U.K.* 51°42N 5°7W **28** D3
Milford on Sea *U.K.* 50°43N 1°35W **30** E5
Milḩ, Baḩr al *Iraq* 32°40N 43°35E **86** C5
Milk → *U.S.A.* 48°4N 106°19W **110** A5
Millau *France* 44°8N 3°4E **66** D5
Millbrook *U.K.* 50°20N 4°14W **29** G5
Millet *St. Lucia* 13°55N 60°59W **114** b
Millinocket *U.S.A.* 45°39N 68°43W **113** C13
Millom *U.K.* 54°13N 3°16W **26** D2
Millville *U.S.A.* 39°24N 75°2W **113** F10
Milngavie *U.K.* 55°56N 4°19W **24** C7
Milnthorpe *U.K.* 54°14N 2°45W **26** D3
Milos *Greece* 36°44N 24°25E **69** F11
Milton Abbot *U.K.* 50°35N 4°16W **29** F5
Milton Keynes *U.K.* 52°1N 0°44W **31** B7
Miltown Malbay *Ireland* 52°52N 9°24W **20** C4
Milverton *U.K.* 51°1N 3°16W **30** D2
Milwaukee *U.S.A.* 43°2N 87°54W **112** D4
Milwaukee Deep *Atl. Oc.* 19°50N 68°0W **115** D11
Min Jiang → *Fujian, China* 26°0N 119°35E **79** F12
Min Jiang → *Sichuan, China* 28°45N 104°40E **78** F9
Minas *Uruguay* 34°20S 55°10W **121** F4
Minas Gerais □ *Brazil* 18°50S 46°0W **122** C1
Minatitlán *Mexico* 17°59N 94°31W **114** D6
Minchinhampton *U.K.* 51°42N 2°11W **30** C4
Mindanao *Phil.* 8°0N 125°0E **83** C6
Mindoro *Phil.* 13°0N 121°0E **83** B6
Mindoro Str. *Phil.* 12°30N 120°30E **83** B6
Minehead *U.K.* 51°12N 3°29W **30** D2
Mineral Wells *U.S.A.* 32°48N 98°7W **110** D7
Minfeng *China* 37°4N 82°46E **78** D5
Minginish *U.K.* 57°14N 6°15W **22** H5
Mingulay *U.K.* 56°49N 7°39W **22** J2
Minna *Nigeria* 9°37N 6°30E **94** G7
Minneapolis *U.S.A.* 44°57N 93°16W **111** B8
Minnesota □ *U.S.A.* 46°0N 94°15W **111** A8
Minorca = Menorca *Spain* 40°0N 4°0E **67** C8
Minot *U.S.A.* 48°14N 101°18W **110** A6
Minsk *Belarus* 53°52N 27°30E **65** B14
Minster *Kent, U.K.* 51°20N 1°20E **31** D11
Minster *Kent, U.K.* 51°25N 0°50E **31** D10
Minsterley *U.K.* 52°39N 2°54W **27** G3
Minto, L. *Canada* 57°13N 75°0W **109** D12
Miramichi *Canada* 47°2N 65°28W **109** E13
Miramichi B. *Canada* 47°15N 65°0W **113** B15
Mirim, L. *S. Amer.* 32°45S 52°50W **121** F4
Mirnyy *Russia* 62°33N 113°53E **77** C12
Mirpur Khas *Pakistan* 25°30N 69°0E **84** G6
Mirs Bay *China* 22°33N 114°24E **79** a
Mirzapur *India* 25°10N 82°34E **85** G13
Mishawaka *U.S.A.* 41°40N 86°11W **112** E4
Miskolc *Hungary* 48°7N 20°50E **65** D11
Misool *Indonesia* 1°52S 130°10E **83** E8
Mişrātah *Libya* 32°24N 15°3E **95** B9
Missinaibi → *Canada* 50°43N 81°29W **109** D11
Mississippi □ *U.S.A.* 33°0N 90°0W **111** D9
Mississippi → *U.S.A.* 29°9N 89°15W **111** E9
Mississippi River Delta *U.S.A.* 29°10N 89°15W **111** E9
Missoula *U.S.A.* 46°52N 114°1W **110** A4
Missouri □ *U.S.A.* 38°25N 92°30W **111** C8
Missouri → *U.S.A.* 38°49N 90°7W **111** C8
Mistassini, L. *Canada* 51°0N 73°30W **109** D12
Misterton *Notts., U.K.* 53°27N 0°50W **27** F7
Misterton *Somst., U.K.* 50°52N 2°47W **30** E3
Mitcheldean *U.K.* 51°51N 2°28W **30** C4
Mitchell *U.S.A.* 43°43N 98°2W **110** B7
Mitchell → *Australia* 15°12S 141°35E **98** D7
Mitchelstown *Ireland* 52°15N 8°16W **20** D6
Mito *Japan* 36°20N 140°30E **81** E7
Mitrovicë *Kosovo* 42°54N 20°52E **69** C9
Mitú *Colombia* 1°15N 70°13W **120** B2
Mitumba, Mts. *Dem. Rep. of the Congo* 7°0S 27°30E **96** F5
Miugh Laigh = Mingulay *U.K.* 56°49N 7°39W **22** J2
Miyakonojō *Japan* 31°40N 131°5E **81** H2
Miyazaki *Japan* 31°56N 131°30E **81** H2
Mizen Hd. *Cork, Ireland* 51°27N 9°50W **20** F3
Mizen Hd. *Wicklow, Ireland* 52°51N 6°4W **21** C10
Mizoram □ *India* 23°30N 92°40E **85** H18
Mjøsa *Norway* 60°40N 11°0E **63** E6
Mljet *Croatia* 42°43N 17°30E **68** C7
Mo i Rana *Norway* 66°20N 14°7E **63** D6
Moab *U.S.A.* 38°35N 109°33W **110** C5
Moate *Ireland* 53°24N 7°44W **18** E6
Mobaye *C.A.R.* 4°25N 21°5E **96** D4
Moberly *U.S.A.* 39°25N 92°26W **111** C8
Mobile *U.S.A.* 30°41N 88°3W **111** D9
Mobridge *U.S.A.* 45°32N 100°26W **110** A6
Moçambique *Mozam.* 15°3S 40°42E **97** H8
Mochudi *Botswana* 24°27S 26°7E **97** J5
Mocoa *Colombia* 1°7N 76°35W **120** B2
Mococa *Brazil* 21°28S 47°0W **122** D1
Mocuba *Mozam.* 16°54S 36°57E **97** H7
Modbury *U.K.* 50°21N 3°55W **29** G6
Módena *Italy* 44°40N 10°55E **68** B4
Modesto *U.S.A.* 37°39N 121°0W **110** C2
Moffat *U.K.* 55°21N 3°27W **25** D9
Mogadishu *Somalia* 2°2N 45°25E **89** G4
Mogi-Mirim *Brazil* 22°29S 47°0W **122** D1
Mohammedia *Morocco* 33°44N 7°21W **94** B4
Moher, Cliffs of *Ireland* 52°58N 9°27W **20** C4
Moidart *U.K.* 56°49N 5°41W **22** J6
Moidart, L. *U.K.* 56°47N 5°52W **22** J6
Moisie → *Canada* 50°14N 66°5W **109** D13
Mojave Desert *U.S.A.* 35°0N 116°30W **110** D3
Moji das Cruzes *Brazil* 23°31S 46°11W **122** D1
Mokpo *S. Korea* 34°50N 126°25E **79** E14
Mold *U.K.* 53°9N 3°8W **28** A7
Molde *Norway* 62°45N 7°9E **63** E5
Moldova ■ *Europe* 47°0N 28°0E **65** E15
Mole → *U.K.* 51°24N 0°21W **31** D8
Molepolole *Botswana* 24°28S 25°28E **97** J5
Mollendo *Peru* 17°0S 72°0W **120** D2
Moloka'i *U.S.A.* 21°8N 157°0W **110** H16
Molopo → *Africa* 28°30S 20°12E **97** K4
Molucca Sea *Indonesia* 0°0 125°0E **83** E6
Moluccas *Indonesia* 1°0S 127°0E **83** E7
Mombasa *Kenya* 4°3S 39°40E **96** E7
Mompós *Colombia* 9°14N 74°26W **120** B2
Mon □ *Myanmar* 16°0N 97°30E **85** L20
Mona Passage *W. Indies* 18°30N 67°45W **115** D11
Monach Is. *U.K.* 57°32N 7°40W **22** G2
Monaco ■ *Europe* 43°46N 7°23E **66** E7
Monadhliath Mts. *U.K.* 57°10N 4°4W **23** H9
Monaghan *Ireland* 54°15N 6°57W **19** C8
Monaghan □ *Ireland* 54°11N 6°56W **19** C8
Monar, L. *U.K.* 57°26N 5°8W **22** H7
Monar Forest *U.K.* 57°27N 5°10W **22** H7
Monasterevin *Ireland* 53°8N 7°4W **21** B8
Monavullagh Mts. *Ireland* 52°14N 7°35W **21** D7
Mönchengladbach *Germany* 51°11N 6°27E **64** C4
Monclova *Mexico* 26°54N 101°25W **114** B4
Moncton *Canada* 46°7N 64°51W **113** B15
Moneague *Jamaica* 18°16N 77°7W **114** a
Moneymore *U.K.* 54°41N 6°40W **19** B8
Mongolia ■ *Asia* 47°0N 103°0E **78** B9
Mongolia, Plateau of *Asia* 45°0N 105°0E **72** D12
Mongu *Zambia* 15°16S 23°12E **97** H4
Monifieth *U.K.* 56°30N 2°48W **25** B10
Monmouth *U.K.* 51°48N 2°42W **28** D8
Monmouth *U.S.A.* 40°55N 90°39W **112** E2
Monmouthshire □ *U.K.* 51°48N 2°54W **28** D8
Monnow → *U.K.* 51°49N 2°43W **30** C3
Monroe *La., U.S.A.* 32°30N 92°7W **111** D8
Monroe *Mich., U.S.A.* 41°55N 83°24W **112** E6
Monroe *Wis., U.S.A.* 42°36N 89°38W **112** D3
Monrovia *Liberia* 6°18N 10°47W **94** G3
Mons *Belgium* 50°27N 3°58E **64** C3
Mont-de-Marsan *France* 43°54N 0°31W **66** E3
Mont-Laurier *Canada* 46°35N 75°30W **109** E12
Montana *Bulgaria* 43°27N 23°16E **69** C10
Montaña *Peru* 6°0S 73°0W **120** C2
Montana □ *U.S.A.* 47°0N 110°0W **110** A5
Montargis *France* 47°59N 2°43E **66** C5
Montauban *France* 44°2N 1°21E **66** D4
Montbéliard *France* 47°31N 6°48E **66** C7
Montceau-les-Mines *France* 46°40N 4°23E **66** C6
Monte Azul *Brazil* 15°9S 42°53W **122** C2
Monte-Carlo *Monaco* 43°44N 7°25E **66** E7
Monte Caseros *Argentina* 30°10S 57°50W **121** F4
Monte Cristi *Dom. Rep.* 19°52N 71°39W **115** D10
Montego Bay *Jamaica* 18°28N 77°55W **114** a
Montélimar *France* 44°33N 4°45E **66** D6
Montello *U.S.A.* 43°48N 89°20W **112** D3
Montemorelos *Mexico* 25°12N 99°49W **114** B5
Montenegro ■ *Europe* 42°40N 19°20E **69** C8
Monterey *U.S.A.* 36°37N 121°55W **110** C2
Montería *Colombia* 8°46N 75°53W **120** B2
Monterrey *Mexico* 25°40N 100°19W **114** B4
Montes Claros *Brazil* 16°30S 43°50W **122** C2
Montevideo *Uruguay* 34°50S 56°11W **121** F4
Montgomery *U.K.* 52°34N 3°8W **28** B7
Montgomery *U.S.A.* 32°23N 86°19W **111** D9
Monticello *U.S.A.* 40°45N 86°46W **112** E4
Montluçon *France* 46°22N 2°36E **66** C5
Montmagny *Canada* 46°58N 70°34W **113** B12
Montpelier *Idaho, U.S.A.* 42°19N 111°18W **110** B4
Montpelier *Vt., U.S.A.* 44°16N 72°35W **113** C11
Montpellier *France* 43°37N 3°52E **66** E5
Montréal *Canada* 45°30N 73°33W **113** C11
Montreux *Switz.* 46°26N 6°55E **64** E4
Montrose *U.K.* 56°44N 2°27W **23** J13
Montrose *U.S.A.* 38°29N 107°53W **110** C5
Montserrat ☑ *W. Indies* 16°40N 62°10W **115** D12
Monywa *Myanmar* 22°7N 95°11E **85** H19
Monza *Italy* 45°35N 9°16E **68** B3
Monze, C. *Pakistan* 24°47N 66°37E **84** G5
Moorfoot Hills *U.K.* 55°44N 3°8W **25** C9
Moorhead *U.S.A.* 46°53N 96°45W **111** A7
Moose Jaw *Canada* 50°24N 105°30W **108** D9
Moosehead L. *U.S.A.* 45°38N 69°40W **113** C13
Moosomin *Canada* 50°9N 101°40W **108** D9
Moosonee *Canada* 51°17N 80°39W **109** D11
Mopti *Mali* 14°30N 4°0W **94** F5
Mora *Sweden* 61°2N 14°38E **63** E6
Mora, Na h-Eileanan = Shiant Is. *U.K.* 57°54N 6°22W **22** G5
Moradabad *India* 28°50N 78°50E **84** E11
Morant Bay *Jamaica* 17°53N 76°25W **114** a
Morant Pt. *Jamaica* 17°55N 76°12W **114** a
Morar, L. *U.K.* 56°57N 5°40W **22** J6
Moratuwa *Sri Lanka* 6°45N 79°55E **84** R11
Morava → *Serbia* 44°36N 21°4E **69** B9
Morava → *Slovakia* 48°10N 16°59E **65** D9
Moravian Hts. *Czechia* 49°30N 15°40E **56** F9
Moray □ *U.K.* 57°31N 3°18W **23** G11
Moray Firth *U.K.* 57°40N 3°52W **23** G10
Morden *Canada* 49°15N 98°10W **108** E10
Mordvinia □ *Russia* 54°20N 44°30E **70** D7
Moreau → *U.S.A.* 45°18N 100°43W **110** A6
Morebattle *U.K.* 55°31N 2°22W **25** C11
Morecambe *U.K.* 54°5N 2°52W **26** D3
Morecambe B. *U.K.* 54°7N 3°0W **26** D3
Moree *Australia* 29°28S 149°54E **98** F9
Morehead *U.S.A.* 38°11N 83°26W **112** F6
Morelia *Mexico* 19°42N 101°7W **114** D4
Morena, Sierra *Spain* 38°20N 4°0W **67** C3
Moresby I. *Canada* 52°30N 131°40W **108** D6
Moreton-in-Marsh *U.K.* 51°59N 1°41W **30** C5
Moretonhampstead *U.K.* 50°39N 3°46W **29** F6
Morgan City *U.S.A.* 29°42N 91°12W **111** E8
Morgantown *U.S.A.* 39°38N 79°57W **112** F8
Morioka *Japan* 39°45N 141°8E **81** D7
Morlaix *France* 48°36N 3°52W **66** B2
Morley *U.K.* 53°45N 1°36W **27** E5
Morocco ■ *N. Afr.* 32°0N 5°50W **94** B4
Morogoro *Tanzania* 6°50S 37°40E **96** F7
Morón *Cuba* 22°8N 78°39W **115** C9
Mörön *Mongolia* 49°38N 100°9E **78** B9
Morondava *Madag.* 20°17S 44°17E **97** J8
Moroni *Comoros Is.* 11°40S 43°16E **91** H8
Morotai *Indonesia* 2°10N 128°30E **83** D7
Morpeth *U.K.* 55°10N 1°41W **26** B5
Morphou *Cyprus* 35°12N 32°59E **86** C3
Morrinhos *Brazil* 17°45S 49°10W **122** C1
Morris *U.S.A.* 41°22N 88°26W **112** E3
Morte Bay *U.K.* 51°9N 4°14W **29** E5
Morte Pt. *U.K.* 51°11N 4°14W **29** E5
Mortehoe *U.K.* 51°11N 4°12W **29** E5
Mortimer's Cross *U.K.* 52°16N 2°50W **30** B3
Morton Fen *U.K.* 52°49N 0°20W **27** G8
Morvan *France* 47°5N 4°3E **66** C6
Morwenstow *U.K.* 50°54N 4°33W **29** F4
Moscos Is. *Myanmar* 14°0N 97°30E **85** N20
Moscow *Russia* 55°45N 37°37E **70** C6
Moscow *U.S.A.* 46°44N 117°0W **110** A3
Mosel → *Europe* 50°22N 7°36E **64** C4
Moses Lake *U.S.A.* 47°8N 119°17W **110** A3
Moshi *Tanzania* 3°22S 37°18E **96** E7
Mosjøen *Norway* 65°51N 13°12E **63** D6
Mosselbaai *S. Africa* 34°11S 22°8E **97** L4
Mossley *U.K.* 53°33N 2°1W **27** E4
Mossoró *Brazil* 5°10S 37°15W **120** C6
Most *Czechia* 50°31N 13°38E **64** C7
Mostaganem *Algeria* 35°54N 0°5E **94** A6
Mostar *Bos.-H.* 43°22N 17°50E **69** C7
Mosul *Iraq* 36°15N 43°5E **86** B5
Motcombe *U.K.* 51°1N 2°13W **30** D4
Motherwell *U.K.* 55°47N 3°58W **25** C8
Motihari *India* 26°30N 84°55E **85** F14
Motril *Spain* 36°31N 3°37W **67** D4
Mottama, G. of *Myanmar* 16°5N 96°30E **85** L20
Mottisfont *U.K.* 51°2N 1°32W **30** D5
Mouila *Gabon* 1°50S 11°0E **96** E2
Moule à Chique, C. *St. Lucia* 13°43N 60°57W **114** b
Moulins *France* 46°35N 3°19E **66** C5
Moulouya, O. → *Morocco* 35°5N 2°25W **94** B5
Moulton *U.K.* 52°17N 0°52W **31** B7
Moundou *Chad* 8°40N 16°10E **95** G9
Moundsville *U.S.A.* 39°55N 80°44W **112** F7
Mount Carmel *U.S.A.* 38°25N 87°46W **112** F4
Mount Desert I. *U.S.A.* 44°21N 68°20W **113** C13
Mount Gambier *Australia* 37°50S 140°46E **98** H7
Mount Hagen *Papua N. G.* 5°52S 144°16E **98** B7
Mount Isa *Australia* 20°42S 139°26E **98** E6
Mount Magnet *Australia* 28°2S 117°47E **98** F2
Mount Pleasant *U.S.A.* 43°36N 84°46W **112** D5
Mount Sterling *U.S.A.* 38°4N 83°56W **112** F6
Mount Vernon *Ind., U.S.A.* 37°56N 87°54W **112** F3
Mount Vernon *Ohio, U.S.A.* 40°23N 82°29W **112** E6
Mountain Ash *U.K.* 51°40N 3°23W **28** D7
Mountain Home *U.S.A.* 43°8N 115°41W **110** B3
Mountain View *U.S.A.* 19°33N 155°7W **110** J17
Mountmellick *Ireland* 53°7N 7°20W **21** B8
Mountrath *Ireland* 53°0N 7°28W **21** C8
Mount's Bay *U.K.* 50°5N 5°31W **29** G2
Mountsorrel *U.K.* 52°44N 1°8W **27** G6
Mourne → *U.K.* 54°52N 7°26W **18** B7
Mourne Mts. *U.K.* 54°10N 6°0W **19** C9
Moville *Ireland* 55°11N 7°3W **19** A7
Moy → *Ireland* 54°8N 9°8W **18** C3
Moyen Atlas *Morocco* 33°0N 5°0W **94** B4
Mozambique ■ *Africa* 19°0S 35°0E **97** H7
Mozambique Chan. *Africa* 17°30S 42°30E **90** H8
Mozdok *Russia* 43°45N 44°48E **71** F7
Mpanda *Tanzania* 6°23S 31°1E **96** F6
Mpumalanga *S. Africa* 29°50S 30°33E **97** K6
Msaken *Tunisia* 35°49N 10°33E **95** A8
Mthatha *S. Africa* 31°36S 28°49E **97** L5
Mtwara-Mikindani *Tanzania* 10°20S 40°20E **96** G8
Muar *Malaysia* 2°3N 102°34E **82** D2
Mubi *Nigeria* 10°18N 13°16E **95** F8
Much Dewchurch *U.K.* 51°58N 2°45W **30** C3
Much Marcle *U.K.* 51°59N 2°29W **30** C4
Much Wenlock *U.K.* 52°35N 2°33W **27** G3
Muchinga Mts. *Zambia* 11°30S 31°30E **97** G6
Muck *U.K.* 56°50N 6°15W **22** J5
Muckle Flugga *U.K.* 60°51N 0°54W **22** A16
Muckle Roe *U.K.* 60°23N 1°27W **22** B15
Mucuri *Brazil* 18°0S 39°36W **122** C3
Mudanjiang *China* 44°38N 129°30E **79** C14
Mufulira *Zambia* 12°32S 28°15E **97** G5
Muğla *Turkey* 37°15N 28°22E **71** G4
Muir of Ord *U.K.* 57°32N 4°28W **23** G9
Muktsar *India* 30°30N 74°30E **84** D9
Mulanje, Mt. *Malawi* 16°2S 35°33E **97** H7
Mulde → *Germany* 51°53N 12°15E **64** C7
Mulhacén *Spain* 37°4N 3°20W **67** D4
Mulhouse *France* 47°40N 7°20E **66** C7
Mull *U.K.* 56°25N 5°56W **24** B4
Mull, Sound of *U.K.* 56°30N 5°50W **24** A4
Mullaghareirk Mts. *Ireland* 52°20N 9°10W **20** D4
Mullet Pen. *Ireland* 54°13N 10°2W **18** C1
Mullingar *Ireland* 53°31N 7°21W **18** D7
Mullion *U.K.* 50°1N 5°16W **29** G3
Mulroy B. *Ireland* 55°15N 7°46W **18** A6
Multan *Pakistan* 30°15N 71°36E **84** D7
Mumbai *India* 18°56N 72°50E **84** K8
Mumbles Hd. *U.K.* 51°34N 3°59W **29** D6
Muna *Indonesia* 5°0S 122°30E **83** F6
Muncie *U.S.A.* 40°12N 85°23W **112** E5
Mundesley *U.K.* 52°53N 1°25E **31** A11
Mundo Novo *Brazil* 11°50S 40°29W **122** B2
Munger *India* 25°23N 86°30E **85** G15
Munich *Germany* 48°8N 11°34E **64** D6
Munising *U.S.A.* 46°25N 86°40W **112** B4
Münster *Germany* 51°58N 7°37E **64** C4
Munster □ *Ireland* 52°18N 8°44W **20** D5
Murashi *Russia* 59°30N 49°0E **70** C8
Murat → *Turkey* 38°46N 40°0E **71** G7
Murchison → *Australia* 27°45S 114°0E **98** F1
Murcia *Spain* 38°5N 1°10W **67** D5
Murcia □ *Spain* 37°50N 1°30W **67** D5
Mureş → *Romania* 46°15N 20°13E **65** E11
Murfreesboro *U.S.A.* 35°51N 86°24W **111** C9
Muriaé *Brazil* 21°8S 42°23W **122** D2
Müritz *Germany* 53°25N 12°42E **64** B7
Murmansk *Russia* 68°57N 33°10E **70** A5
Murom *Russia* 55°35N 42°3E **70** C7
Muroran *Japan* 42°25N 141°0E **81** B7
Murray *U.S.A.* 36°37N 88°19W **112** G3
Murray → *Australia* 35°20S 139°22E **98** H6
Murton *U.K.* 54°50N 1°22W **26** C6
Mururoa *French Polynesia* 21°52S 138°55W **103** K14
Murwara *India* 23°46N 80°28E **85** H12
Murzūq *Libya* 25°53N 13°57E **95** C8
Muş *Turkey* 38°45N 41°30E **71** G7
Mûsa, Gebel *Egypt* 28°33N 33°59E **86** D3
Muscat *Oman* 23°37N 58°36E **87** F9
Musgrave Ranges *Australia* 26°0S 132°0E **98** F5
Musina *S. Africa* 22°20S 30°5E **97** J6
Muskegon *U.S.A.* 43°14N 86°16W **112** D4
Muskegon → *U.S.A.* 43°14N 86°21W **112** D4
Muskogee *U.S.A.* 35°45N 95°22W **111** C7
Musselburgh *U.K.* 55°57N 3°2W **25** C9
Musselshell → *U.S.A.* 47°21N 107°57W **110** A5
Mutare *Zimbabwe* 18°58S 32°38E **97** H6
Mutton I. *Ireland* 52°49N 9°32W **20** C3
Mŭynoq *Uzbekistan* 43°44N 59°10E **87** A9
Muz Tag *China* 36°25N 87°25E **78** D6
Muzaffarabad *Pakistan* 34°25N 73°30E **84** B8
Muzaffarnagar *India* 29°26N 77°40E **84** E10
Muztagh-Ata *China* 38°17N 75°7E **78** D4
Mwanza *Tanzania* 2°30S 32°58E **96** E6
Mweelrea *Ireland* 53°39N 9°49W **18** D2
Mwene-Ditu *Dem. Rep. of the Congo* 6°35S 22°27E **96** F4
Mweru, L. *Zambia* 9°0S 28°40E **96** F5
My Tho *Vietnam* 10°29N 106°23E **82** B3
Myanmar ■ *Asia* 21°0N 96°30E **85** J20
Mycenæ *Greece* 37°43N 22°46E **69** F10
Myddle *U.K.* 52°49N 2°47W **27** G3
Myingyan *Myanmar* 21°30N 95°20E **85** J19
Myitkyina *Myanmar* 25°24N 97°26E **85** G20
Mykolaiv *Ukraine* 46°58N 32°0E **71** E5
Mymensingh *Bangla.* 24°45N 90°24E **85** G17
Mynydd Du *U.K.* 51°52N 3°50W **28** D6
Mynydd Preseli *U.K.* 51°57N 4°48W **28** D4
Myrtoan Sea *Greece* 37°0N 23°20E **69** F10
Mysuru *India* 12°17N 76°41E **84** N10
Mytishchi *Russia* 55°50N 37°50E **70** C6

N

Na Hearadh = Harris *U.K.* 57°50N 6°55W **22** G4
Na Hearadh a Deas = South Harris *U.K.* 57°50N 7°0W **22** G4
Na Hearadh a Tuath = North Harris *U.K.* 58°0N 6°55W **22** F4
Naab → *Germany* 49°1N 12°2E **64** D6
Naas *Ireland* 53°12N 6°40W **21** B9
Naberezhnyye Chelny *Russia* 55°42N 52°19E **70** C9
Nabeul *Tunisia* 36°30N 10°44E **95** A8
Nābulus *West Bank* 32°14N 35°15E **86** C3
Nacala *Mozam.* 14°32S 40°34E **97** G8
Nacogdoches *U.S.A.* 31°36N 94°39W **111** D8
Nacozari de García *Mexico* 30°25N 109°38W **114** A3
Nadiad *India* 22°41N 72°56E **84** H8
Nador *Morocco* 35°14N 2°58W **94** B5
Nafferton *U.K.* 54°1N 0°23W **27** D8
Nafud Desert *Si. Arabia* 28°15N 41°0E **86** D5
Naga *Phil.* 13°38N 123°15E **83** B6
Nagaland □ *India* 26°0N 94°30E **85** G19
Nagano *Japan* 36°40N 138°10E **81** E6
Nagaoka *Japan* 37°27N 138°51E **81** E6
Nagappattinam *India* 10°46N 79°51E **84** P11
Nagasaki *Japan* 32°47N 129°50E **81** G1
Nagaur *India* 27°15N 73°45E **84** F8
Nagercoil *India* 8°12N 77°26E **84** Q10
Nagles Mts. *Ireland* 52°8N 8°30W **20** D6
Nagorno-Karabakh □ *Azerbaijan* 39°55N 46°45E **71** F8
Nagoya *Japan* 35°10N 136°50E **81** F5
Nagpur *India* 21°8N 79°10E **84** J11
Nagqu *China* 31°29N 92°3E **78** E7
Naha *Japan* 26°13N 127°42E **79** F14
Nailsea *U.K.* 51°26N 2°44W **30** D3
Nailsworth *U.K.* 51°41N 2°14W **30** C4
Nain *Canada* 56°34N 61°40W **109** D13
Nairn *U.K.* 57°35N 3°53W **23** G10
Nairobi *Kenya* 1°17S 36°48E **96** E7
Naivasha *Kenya* 0°40S 36°30E **96** E7
Najafābād *Iran* 32°40N 51°15E **87** C7
Najd *Si. Arabia* 26°30N 42°0E **86** E5
Najibabad *India* 29°40N 78°20E **84** E11
Najin *N. Korea* 42°12N 130°15E **79** C15
Najrān *Si. Arabia* 17°34N 44°18E **89** D3
Nakhodka *Russia* 42°53N 132°54E **77** E14
Nakhon Ratchasima *Thailand* 14°59N 102°12E **82** B2
Nakhon Sawan *Thailand* 15°35N 100°10E **82** A2
Nakhon Si Thammarat *Thailand* 8°29N 100°0E **82** C2
Nakina *Canada* 50°10N 86°40W **109** D11
Nakuru *Kenya* 0°15S 36°4E **96** E7
Nalchik *Russia* 43°30N 43°33E **71** F7
Nallamalai Hills *India* 15°30N 78°50E **84** M11
Nam Co *China* 30°30N 90°45E **78** E7
Namak, Daryācheh-ye *Iran* 34°30N 52°0E **87** C8
Namaland *Namibia* 26°0S 17°0E **97** K3
Namangan *Uzbekistan* 41°0N 71°40E **87** A12
Namcha Barwa *China* 29°40N 95°10E **78** F8
Namib Desert *Namibia* 22°30S 15°0E **97** J3
Namibe *Angola* 15°7S 12°11E **97** H2
Namibia ■ *Africa* 22°0S 18°9E **97** J3
Nampa *U.S.A.* 43°34N 116°34W **110** B3
Namp'o *N. Korea* 38°52N 125°10E **79** D14
Nampula *Mozam.* 15°6S 39°15E **97** H7
Namumea *Tuvalu* 5°41S 176°9E **99** B14
Namur *Belgium* 50°27N 4°52E **64** C3
Nan Ling *China* 25°0N 112°30E **79** F11
Nanaimo *Canada* 49°10N 124°0W **108** E7
Nanchang *China* 28°42N 115°55E **79** F12
Nanchong *China* 30°43N 106°2E **78** E10
Nancy *France* 48°42N 6°12E **66** B7
Nanda Devi *India* 30°23N 79°59E **84** D11
Nanded *India* 19°10N 77°20E **84** K10
Nandurbar *India* 21°20N 74°15E **84** J9
Nanga Parbat *Pakistan* 35°10N 74°35E **84** B9
Nanjing *China* 32°2N 118°47E **79** E12
Nanning *China* 22°48N 108°20E **78** G10
Nanping *China* 26°38N 118°10E **79** F12
Nansen Sd. *Canada* 81°0N 91°0W **109** A10
Nantes *France* 47°12N 1°33W **66** C3
Nantong *China* 32°1N 120°52E **79** E13
Nantou *China* 22°32N 113°55E **79** a
Nantucket I. *U.S.A.* 41°16N 70°5W **113** E12
Nantwich *U.K.* 53°4N 2°31W **27** F3
Nanuque *Brazil* 17°50S 40°21W **122** C2
Nanyang *China* 33°11N 112°30E **79** E11
Nanyuki *Kenya* 0°2N 37°4E **96** D7
Napa *U.S.A.* 38°18N 122°17W **110** C2
Napier *N.Z.* 39°30S 176°56E **99** H14
Naples *Italy* 40°50N 14°15E **68** D6
Napo → *Peru* 3°20S 72°40W **120** C2
Nappa *U.K.* 53°58N 2°13W **27** E4
Narayanganj *Bangla.* 23°40N 90°33E **85** H17
Narberth *U.K.* 51°47N 4°44W **28** D4
Narbonne *France* 43°11N 3°0E **66** E5
Narborough *U.K.* 52°34N 1°13W **27** G6
Nares Str. *Arctic* 80°0N 70°0W **109** A13
Narmada → *India* 21°38N 72°36E **84** J8
Narodnaya *Russia* 65°5N 59°58E **70** A10
Narva *Estonia* 59°23N 28°12E **63** F9
Narvik *Norway* 68°28N 17°26E **63** D7
Naryan-Mar *Russia* 67°42N 53°12E **70** A9
Nasca *Peru* 14°50S 74°57W **120** D2
Naseby *U.K.* 52°24N 0°59W **31** B7
Nashua *U.S.A.* 42°45N 71°28W **113** D12
Nashville *U.S.A.* 36°10N 86°47W **111** C9
Nasik *India* 19°58N 73°50E **84** K8
Nasirabad *India* 26°15N 74°45E **84** F9
Nasiriyah *Iraq* 31°0N 46°15E **86** D6
Nassau *The Bahamas* 25°5N 77°20W **115** B9
Nasser, L. *Egypt* 23°0N 32°30E **95** D12
Natal *Brazil* 5°47S 35°13W **120** C6
Natashquan *Canada* 50°14N 61°46W **109** D13
Natashquan → *Canada* 50°7N 61°50W **109** D13
Natchez *U.S.A.* 31°34N 91°24W **111** D8
Natchitoches *U.S.A.* 31°46N 93°5W **111** D8
Nathdwara *India* 24°55N 73°50E **84** G8
Natitingou *Benin* 10°20N 1°26E **94** F6
Natron, L. *Tanzania* 2°20S 36°0E **96** E7
Natuna Besar, Kepulauan *Indonesia* 4°0N 108°15E **82** D3
Nauru ■ *Pac. Oc.* 1°0S 166°0E **102** H8
Navan *Ireland* 53°39N 6°41W **19** D8
Navarino, I. *Chile* 55°0S 67°40W **121** H3
Navarra □ *Spain* 42°40N 1°40W **67** A5
Navenby *U.K.* 53°6N 0°31W **27** F7
Naver → *U.K.* 58°32N 4°14W **23** E9
Navoiy *Uzbekistan* 40°9N 65°22E **76** E7
Navojoa *Mexico* 27°6N 109°26W **114** B3
Navsari *India* 20°57N 72°59E **84** J8
Nawabshah *Pakistan* 26°15N 68°25E **84** F6
Naxçıvan □ *Azerbaijan* 39°25N 45°26E **71** G8
Naxos *Greece* 37°8N 25°25E **69** F11
Naypyidaw *Myanmar* 19°44N 96°12E **85** K20
Nazaré *Brazil* 13°2S 39°0W **122** B3
Nazas → *Mexico* 25°12N 104°12W **114** B4
Naze, The *U.K.* 51°53N 1°18E **31** C11
Nazret *Ethiopia* 8°32N 39°22E **89** F2
Ndjamena *Chad* 12°10N 15°0E **95** F8
Ndola *Zambia* 13°0S 28°34E **97** G5
Neagh, Lough *U.K.* 54°37N 6°25W **19** B9
Near Is. *U.S.A.* 52°30N 174°0E **108** D1
Neath *U.K.* 51°39N 3°48W **28** D6
Neblina, Pico da *Brazil* 0°48N 66°2W **120** B3
Nebraska □ *U.S.A.* 41°30N 99°30W **110** B7
Nébrodi, Monti *Italy* 37°54N 14°35E **68** F6
Neckar → *Germany* 49°27N 8°29E **64** D5
Necochea *Argentina* 38°30S 58°50W **121** F4
Needham Market *U.K.* 52°9N 1°4E **31** B11

Needles, The U.K. 50°39N 1°35W 30 E5
Neenah U.S.A. 44°11N 88°28W 112 C3
Neepawa Canada 50°15N 99°30W 108 D10
Neftekumsk Russia 44°46N 44°50E 71 F7
Nefteyugansk Russia 61°5N 72°42E 76 C8
Negaunee U.S.A. 46°30N 87°36W 112 B4
Negele Ethiopia 5°20N 39°36E 89 F2
Negombo Sri Lanka 7°12N 79°50E 84 R11
Negra, Pta. Peru 6°6S 81°10W 117 D2
Negril Jamaica 18°22N 78°20W 114 a
Negro → Argentina 41°2S 62°47W 121 G3
Negro → Brazil 3°0S 60°0W 120 C3
Negros Phil. 9°30N 122°40E 83 C6
Nei Mongol Zizhiqu □ China 42°0N 112°0E 79 C11
Neijiang China 29°35N 104°55E 78 F9
Neisse → Europe 52°4N 14°46E 64 B8
Neiva Colombia 2°56N 75°18W 120 B2
Nellore India 14°27N 79°59E 84 M11
Nelson Canada 49°30N 117°20W 108 E8
Nelson N.Z. 41°18S 173°16E 99 J13
Nelson U.K. 53°50N 2°13W 27 E4
Nelson → Canada 54°33N 98°2W 108 D10
Neman → Lithuania 55°25N 21°10E 63 F8
Nen Jiang → China 45°28N 124°30E 79 B13
Nenagh Ireland 52°52N 8°11W 20 C6
Nene → U.K. 52°49N 0°11E 31 A9
Nenjiang China 49°10N 125°10E 79 B14
Neosho → U.S.A. 36°48N 95°18W 111 C7
Nepal ■ Asia 28°0N 84°30E 85 F14
Nephi U.S.A. 39°43N 111°50W 110 G8
Nephin Ireland 54°1N 9°22W 18 C3
Nephin Beg Range Ireland 54°0N 9°40W 18 C2
Nerastro, Sarīr Libya 24°20N 20°37E 95 D10
Neryungri Russia 57°38N 124°28E 77 D13
Ness, L. U.K. 57°15N 4°32W 23 H8
Neston U.K. 53°17N 3°4W 27 F2
Netherbury U.K. 50°46N 2°45W 30 E3
Netherlands ■ Europe 52°0N 5°30E 64 B3
Netherlands Antilles = ABC Islands
  W. Indies 12°15N 69°0W 115 E11
Netley U.K. 50°52N 1°20W 30 E6
Nettilling L. Canada 66°30N 71°0W 109 C12
Nettlebed U.K. 51°34N 0°59W 31 C7
Nettleham U.K. 53°16N 0°29W 27 F8
Neuchâtel Switz. 47°0N 6°55E 64 E4
Neuchâtel, Lac de Switz. 46°53N 6°50E 64 E4
Neuquén Argentina 38°55S 68°0W 121 F3
Neusiedler See Austria 47°50N 16°47E 65 E9
Neva → Russia 59°56N 30°20E 70 C5
Nevada □ U.S.A. 39°0N 117°0W 110 G5
Nevers France 47°0N 3°9E 66 C5
Nevinnomyssk Russia 44°40N 42°0E 71 F7
New Abbey U.K. 54°59N 3°37W 25 E9
New Alresford U.K. 51°5N 1°8W 30 D6
New Amsterdam Guyana 6°15N 57°36W 120 B4
New Bedford U.S.A. 41°38N 70°56W 113 E12
New Britain Papua N. G. 5°50S 150°20E 98 B9
New Britain U.S.A. 41°40N 72°47W 113 E11
New Brunswick U.S.A. 40°30N 74°27W 113 E10
New Brunswick □ Canada 46°50N 66°30W 113 B14
New Caledonia ☒ Pac. Oc. 21°0S 165°0E 99 E12
New Castle Ind., U.S.A. 39°55N 85°22W 112 F5
New Castle Pa., U.S.A. 41°0N 80°21W 112 E7
New Delhi India 28°36N 77°11E 84 E10
New England U.S.A. 43°0N 71°0W 111 B12
New Forest △ U.K. 50°53N 1°34W 30 E5
New Galloway U.K. 55°5N 4°9W 24 D7
New Georgia Is. Solomon Is. 8°15S 157°30E 99 B10
New Glasgow Canada 45°35N 62°36W 109 E13
New Guinea Oceania 4°0S 136°0E 98 B7
New Hampshire □ U.S.A. 44°0N 71°30W 113 D12
New Haven U.S.A. 41°18N 72°55W 113 E11
New Hebrides = Vanuatu ■
  Pac. Oc. 15°0S 168°0E 99 D12
New Holland U.S.A. 53°42N 0°21W 27 E8
New Iberia U.S.A. 30°1N 91°49W 111 D8
New Ireland Papua N. G. 3°20S 151°50E 98 A9
New Jersey □ U.S.A. 40°0N 74°30W 113 E10
New Lexington U.S.A. 39°43N 82°13W 112 F6
New Liskeard Canada 47°31N 79°41W 109 E12
New London U.S.A. 41°22N 72°6W 113 E11
New Madrid U.S.A. 36°36N 89°32W 112 G3
New Mexico □ U.S.A. 34°30N 106°0W 110 D5
New Mills U.K. 53°23N 2°0W 27 F5
New Milton U.K. 50°45N 1°40W 30 E5
New Orleans U.S.A. 29°57N 90°4W 111 E8
New Philadelphia U.S.A. 40°30N 81°27W 112 E7
New Plymouth N.Z. 39°4S 174°5E 99 H13
New Providence
  The Bahamas 25°25N 77°35W 115 B9
New Quay U.K. 52°13N 4°21W 28 C5
New Radnor U.K. 52°15N 3°9W 28 C7
New Romney U.K. 50°59N 0°57E 31 E10
New Ross Ireland 52°23N 6°57W 21 D9
New Rossington U.K. 53°29N 1°4W 27 F6
New Siberian Is. Russia 75°0N 142°0E 77 B15
New South Wales □ Australia 33°0S 146°0E 98 G8
New York U.S.A. 40°43N 74°0W 113 E11
New York □ U.S.A. 43°0N 75°0W 113 D9
New Zealand ■ Oceania 40°0S 176°0E 99 J14
Newark Del., U.S.A. 39°41N 75°46W 113 F10
Newark N.J., U.S.A. 40°44N 74°10W 113 E10
Newark N.Y., U.S.A. 43°3N 77°6W 112 D9
Newark Ohio, U.S.A. 40°3N 82°24W 112 E6
Newark-on-Trent U.K. 53°5N 0°48W 27 F7
Newberry U.S.A. 46°21N 85°30W 112 B5
Newbiggin-by-the-Sea U.K. 55°11N 1°31W 26 B5
Newbigging U.K. 55°42N 3°34W 25 C8
Newbridge Ireland 53°11N 6°48W 21 B9
Newburgh U.S.A. 41°30N 74°1W 113 E10
Newburn U.K. 54°59N 1°43W 26 C5
Newbury U.K. 51°24N 1°20W 30 D6
Newburyport U.S.A. 42°49N 70°53W 113 D12
Newby Bridge U.K. 54°17N 2°57W 26 D3
Newcastle Australia 33°0S 151°46E 98 G9
Newcastle Canada 47°1N 65°38W 113 B15
Newcastle Ireland 52°27N 9°3W 20 D4
Newcastle S. Africa 27°45S 29°58E 97 K5
Newcastle U.K. 54°13N 5°54W 19 C10
Newcastle Emlyn U.K. 52°2N 4°28W 28 C5
Newcastle-under-Lyme U.K. 53°1N 2°14W 27 F4

Newcastle-upon-Tyne U.K. 54°58N 1°36W 26 C5
Newcastleton U.K. 55°11N 2°49W 25 D10
Newent U.K. 51°56N 2°24W 30 C4
Newfoundland & Labrador □
  Canada 52°0N 58°0W 109 D14
Newham □ U.K. 51°31N 0°3E 31 C9
Newhaven U.K. 50°47N 0°3E 31 E9
Newington Kent, U.K. 51°6N 1°7E 31 D11
Newington Kent, U.K. 51°21N 0°41E 31 D10
Newlyn U.K. 50°6N 5°34W 29 G2
Newlyn East U.K. 50°22N 5°5W 29 G3
Newman Australia 23°18S 119°45E 98 E2
Newmarket Ireland 52°13N 9°0W 20 D5
Newmarket U.K. 52°15N 0°25E 31 B9
Newnham U.K. 51°48N 2°27W 30 C4
Newport Ireland 53°53N 9°33W 18 D2
Newport Essex, U.K. 51°59N 0°14E 31 C9
Newport I. of W., U.K. 50°42N 1°17W 30 E6
Newport Newport, U.K. 51°35N 3°0W 29 D8
Newport Pembs., U.K. 52°1N 4°51W 28 C4
Newport Telford & Wrekin, U.K. 52°46N 2°22W 27 G4
Newport Ark., U.S.A. 35°37N 91°16W 111 C8
Newport Ky., U.S.A. 39°5N 84°29W 112 F5
Newport R.I., U.S.A. 41°29N 71°19W 113 E12
Newport Vt., U.S.A. 44°56N 72°13W 113 C11
Newport News U.S.A. 36°58N 76°25W 111 C11
Newport Pagnell U.K. 52°5N 0°43W 31 B7
Newquay U.K. 50°25N 5°6W 29 G3
Newry U.K. 54°11N 6°21W 19 C9
Newry, Mourne & Down □
  U.K. 54°8N 6°3W 19 C10
Newton Abbot U.K. 50°32N 3°37W 29 F6
Newton Arlosh U.K. 54°53N 3°14W 26 C2
Newton Aycliffe U.K. 54°37N 1°34W 26 C5
Newton Ferrers U.K. 50°19N 4°3W 29 G5
Newton le Willows U.K. 53°28N 2°38W 27 F3
Newton St. Cyres U.K. 50°46N 3°36W 29 F6
Newton Stewart U.K. 54°57N 4°30W 24 E6
Newtonmore U.K. 57°4N 4°8W 23 H9
Newtown U.K. 52°31N 3°19W 28 B7
Newtown St. Boswells U.K. 55°34N 2°39W 25 C10
Newtownabbey U.K. 54°40N 5°56W 19 B10
Newtownards U.K. 54°36N 5°42W 19 B10
Newtownstewart U.K. 54°43N 7°23W 18 B7
Neyshābūr Iran 36°10N 58°50E 87 B9
Ngamring China 29°14N 87°10E 78 F6
Nganglong Kangri China 33°0N 81°0E 78 E5
Ngaoundéré Cameroon 7°15N 13°35E 96 C2
Ngerulmud Palau 7°27N 134°38E 102 G5
Ngoring Hu China 34°55N 97°5E 78 E8
Ngorongoro Tanzania 3°11S 35°32E 96 E7
Nguru Nigeria 12°56N 10°29E 95 F8
Nha Trang Vietnam 12°16N 109°10E 82 B3
Nhamundá → Brazil 2°12S 56°41W 120 C4
Niagara Falls Canada 43°7N 79°5W 109 E12
Niagara Falls U.S.A. 43°5N 79°4W 112 D8
Niamey Niger 13°27N 2°6E 94 F6
Nias Indonesia 1°0N 97°30E 82 D1
Nicaragua ■ Cent. Amer. 11°40N 85°30W 114 E7
Nicaragua, L. de Nic. 12°0N 85°30W 114 E7
Nice France 43°42N 7°14E 66 E7
Nicholasville U.S.A. 37°53N 84°34W 112 G5
Nicobar Is. Ind. Oc. 8°0N 93°30E 53 D14
Nicosia Cyprus 35°10N 33°25E 86 C3
Nicoya, Pen. de Costa Rica 9°45N 85°40W 114 F7
Nidd → U.K. 53°59N 1°23W 27 E6
Nidderdale U.K. 54°5N 1°46W 26 D5
Niedersachsen □ Germany 52°50N 9°0E 64 B5
Nieuw Nickerie Suriname 6°0N 56°59W 120 B4
Niğde Turkey 37°58N 34°40E 86 B3
Niger ■ W. Afr. 17°30N 10°0E 94 E7
Niger → W. Afr. 5°33N 6°33E 94 G7
Nigeria ■ W. Afr. 8°30N 8°0E 94 G7
Niigata Japan 37°58N 139°0E 81 E6
Ni'ihau U.S.A. 21°54N 160°9W 110 H14
Nijmegen Neths. 51°50N 5°52E 64 C3
Nikolayevsk-na-Amur
  Russia 53°8N 140°44E 77 D15
Nikopol Ukraine 47°35N 34°25E 71 E5
Nikšić Montenegro 42°50N 18°57E 69 C8
Nile → Africa 30°10N 31°6E 95 B12
Nimach India 24°30N 74°56E 84 G9
Nîmes France 43°50N 4°23E 66 E6
Nineveh Iraq 36°25N 43°10E 86 B5
Ninfield U.K. 50°53N 0°26E 31 E9
Ningbo China 29°51N 121°28E 79 F13
Ningjing Shan China 31°0N 98°20E 78 E8
Ningxia Hui □ China 38°0N 106°0E 78 D10
Niobrara → U.S.A. 42°46N 98°3W 110 B7
Niort France 46°19N 0°29W 66 C3
Nipawin Canada 53°20N 104°0W 108 D9
Nipigon Canada 49°0N 88°17W 112 A3
Nipigon, L. Canada 49°50N 88°30W 109 E11
Nipissing, L. Canada 46°20N 80°0W 109 E12
Niquelândia Brazil 14°33S 48°23W 122 B1
Niš Serbia 43°19N 21°58E 69 C9
Niterói Brazil 22°53S 43°7W 122 D2
Nith → U.K. 55°14N 3°33W 25 D8
Nitra Slovakia 48°19N 18°4E 65 D10
Nitra → Slovakia 47°46N 18°10E 65 D10
Niuafo'ou Tonga 15°30S 175°58W 99 D15
Niue ☒ Pac. Oc. 19°2S 169°54W 99 D17
Nivernais France 47°15N 3°30E 66 C5
Nizamabad India 18°45N 78°7E 84 K11
Nizhnekamsk Russia 55°38N 51°49E 70 C9
Nizhnevartovsk Russia 60°56N 76°38E 76 C8
Nizhniy Novgorod Russia 56°20N 44°0E 70 C7
Nizhniy Tagil Russia 57°55N 59°57E 70 C10
Nizhyn Ukraine 51°5N 31°55E 71 D5
Nizwá Oman 22°56N 57°32E 89 C6
Nkawkaw Ghana 6°36N 0°49W 94 G5
Nkongsamba Cameroon 4°55N 9°55E 96 D1
Noakhali Bangla. 22°48N 91°10E 85 H17
Nobeoka Japan 32°36N 131°41E 81 G2
Noblesville U.S.A. 40°3N 86°1W 112 E5
Nogales Mexico 31°19N 110°56W 114 A2
Nogales U.S.A. 31°21N 110°56W 110 D4
Noirmoutier, Î. de France 46°58N 2°10W 66 C2
Nola C.A.R. 3°35N 16°4E 96 D3
Nome U.S.A. 64°30N 165°25W 108 C3

Nord-Ostsee-Kanal Germany 54°12N 9°32E 64 A5
Nordelph U.K. 52°35N 0°17E 31 A9
Norderstedt Germany 53°42N 10°1E 64 B5
Nordfriesische Inseln Germany 54°40N 8°20E 64 A5
Nordkapp Norway 71°10N 25°50E 63 C9
Nordrhein-Westfalen □
  Germany 51°45N 7°30E 64 C4
Nordvik Russia 74°2N 111°32E 77 B12
Nore → Ireland 52°25N 6°58W 21 D9
Norfolk Nebr., U.S.A. 42°2N 97°25W 111 B7
Norfolk Va., U.S.A. 36°50N 76°17W 111 C11
Norfolk □ U.K. 52°39N 0°54E 31 A10
Norfolk Broads △ U.K. 52°45N 1°30E 31 A11
Norfolk I. Pac. Oc. 28°58S 168°3E 99 F12
Norham U.K. 55°43N 2°9W 26 A4
Norilsk Russia 69°20N 88°6E 77 C9
Normal U.S.A. 40°31N 88°59W 112 E3
Norman U.S.A. 35°13N 97°26W 110 C7
Norman Wells Canada 65°17N 126°51W 108 C7
Normandie France 48°45N 0°10E 66 B4
Normanton Australia 17°40S 141°10E 98 D7
Normanton U.K. 53°42N 1°24W 27 E6
Norristown U.S.A. 40°7N 75°21W 113 E10
Norrköping Sweden 58°37N 16°11E 63 F7
Norrland Sweden 62°15N 15°45E 63 E7
Norseman Australia 32°8S 121°43E 98 G3
Norte, Serra do Brazil 11°20S 59°0W 120 D4
North, C. Canada 47°2N 60°20W 113 B17
North Ayrshire □ U.K. 55°45N 4°44W 24 C6
North Battleford Canada 52°50N 108°17W 108 D9
North Bay Canada 46°20N 79°30W 109 E12
North Berwick U.K. 56°4N 2°42W 25 B10
North C. Canada 47°5N 64°0W 113 B15
North C. N.Z. 34°23S 173°4E 99 G13
North Canadian → U.S.A. 35°22N 95°37W 110 C7
North Carolina □ U.S.A. 35°30N 80°0W 111 C11
North Cerney U.K. 51°45N 1°57W 30 C5
North Channel Canada 46°0N 83°0W 112 B6
North Channel U.K. 55°13N 5°52W 24 D4
North Dakota □ U.S.A. 47°30N 100°15W 110 A7
North Dorset Downs U.K. 50°51N 2°30W 30 E4
North Downs U.K. 51°19N 0°21E 31 D9
North Esk → U.K. 56°46N 2°24W 23 J13
North European Plain Europe 55°0N 25°0E 56 E10
North Foreland U.K. 51°22N 1°28E 31 D11
North Harris U.K. 58°0N 6°55W 22 F4
North Hill U.K. 50°33N 4°27W 29 F5
North Hykeham U.K. 53°11N 0°35W 27 F7
North I. N.Z. 38°0S 175°0E 99 H14
North Korea ■ Asia 40°0N 127°0E 79 D14
North Macedonia ■ Europe 41°53N 21°40E 69 D9
North Magnetic Pole Arctic 86°29.5N 157°41W 54 A13
North Minch U.K. 58°5N 5°55W 22 F6
North Molton U.K. 51°3N 3°49W 29 E6
North Northamptonshire □
  U.K. 52°24N 0°43W 31 B7
North Ossetia-Alaniya □
  Russia 43°30N 44°30E 71 F7
North Petherton U.K. 51°5N 3°1W 30 D2
North Platte U.S.A. 41°8N 100°46W 110 B6
North Platte → U.S.A. 41°7N 100°42W 110 B6
North Pole Arctic 90°0N 0°0W 54 A
North Pt. Barbados 13°20N 59°37W 114 c
North Ronaldsay U.K. 59°22N 2°26W 23 D13
North Saskatchewan →
  Canada 53°15N 105°5W 108 D9
North Sea Europe 56°0N 4°0E 56 D6
North Sea Canal = Nord-Ostsee-Kanal
  Germany 54°12N 9°32E 64 A5
North Somercotes U.K. 53°27N 0°8E 27 F9
North Sunderland U.K. 55°34N 1°40W 26 A5
North Tawton U.K. 50°48N 3°54W 29 F6
North Thompson →
  Canada 50°40N 120°20W 108 D7
North Thoresby U.K. 53°28N 0°4W 27 F8
North Tidworth U.K. 51°15N 1°40W 30 D5
North Tyne → U.K. 55°0N 2°8W 26 C4
North Uist U.K. 57°40N 7°15W 22 G3
North Vernon U.S.A. 39°0N 85°38W 112 F5
North Walsham U.K. 52°50N 1°22E 31 A11
North West C. Australia 21°45S 114°9E 98 E1
North West Highlands U.K. 57°33N 4°58W 23 G8
North West River Canada 53°30N 60°10W 109 D13
North York Moors △ U.K. 54°27N 0°51W 26 D7
North Yorkshire □ U.K. 54°15N 1°25W 26 D6
Northallerton U.K. 54°20N 1°26W 26 D6
Northam Australia 31°35S 116°42E 98 G2
Northam U.K. 51°2N 4°13W 29 E5
Northampton U.K. 52°15N 0°53W 31 B7
Northampton U.S.A. 42°19N 72°38W 113 D11
Northamptonshire □ U.K. 52°16N 0°55W 31 B7
Northern Circars India 17°30N 82°30E 85 L13
Northern Ireland □ U.K. 54°45N 7°0W 19 B8
Northern Marianas ☒ Pac. Oc. 17°0N 145°0E 102 F6
Northern Sporades Greece 39°15N 23°30E 69 E10
Northern Territory □ Australia 20°0S 133°0E 98 E5
Northfleet U.K. 51°26N 0°20E 31 D9
Northiam U.K. 50°59N 0°36E 31 E10
Northleach U.K. 51°49N 1°50W 30 C5
Northrepps U.K. 52°54N 1°21E 31 A11
Northumberland □ U.K. 55°12N 2°0W 26 B4
Northumberland △ Northumberland,
  U.K. 55°15N 2°20W 26 B4
Northumberland Str.
  Canada 46°20N 64°0W 109 E13
Northwich U.K. 53°15N 2°31W 27 F3
Northwold U.K. 52°33N 0°36E 31 A10
Norton N. Yorks., U.K. 54°8N 0°47W 26 D7
Norton Suffolk, U.K. 52°16N 0°52E 31 B10
Norton Fitzwarren U.K. 51°1N 3°8W 30 D2
Norton Sd. U.S.A. 63°50N 164°0W 108 C3
Norwalk U.S.A. 41°15N 82°37W 112 E6
Norway ■ Europe 63°0N 11°0E 63 E6
Norway House Canada 53°59N 97°50W 108 D10
Norwegian B. Canada 77°30N 90°0W 109 B11
Norwegian Sea Atl. Oc. 66°0N 1°0E 56 B6
Norwich U.K. 52°38N 1°18E 31 A11
Norwich U.S.A. 42°32N 75°32W 113 D10
Noss Hd. U.K. 58°28N 3°3W 23 F11

Nossa Senhora do Socorro
  Brazil 10°52S 37°7W 122 B3
Nossob → S. Africa 26°55S 20°45E 97 K4
Notre Dame B. Canada 49°45N 55°30W 109 E14
Nottaway → Canada 51°22N 78°55W 109 D12
Nottingham U.K. 52°58N 1°10W 27 G6
Nottingham I. Canada 63°20N 77°55W 109 C12
Nottinghamshire □ U.K. 53°10N 1°3W 27 F6
Nouâdhibou Mauritania 20°54N 17°0W 94 D2
Nouâdhibou, Râs Mauritania 20°50N 17°0W 94 D2
Nouakchott Mauritania 18°9N 15°58W 94 E2
Nouméa N. Cal. 22°17S 166°30E 99 E12
Nova Friburgo Brazil 22°16S 42°30W 122 D2
Nova Iguaçu Brazil 22°45S 43°28W 122 D2
Nova Scotia □ Canada 45°10N 63°0W 113 C16
Nova Venécia Brazil 18°45S 40°24W 122 C2
Novara Italy 45°28N 8°38E 68 B3
Novaya Zemlya Russia 75°0N 56°0E 76 B6
Novi Pazar Serbia 43°12N 20°28E 69 C9
Novi Sad Serbia 45°18N 19°52E 69 B8
Novocherkassk Russia 47°27N 40°15E 71 E7
Novokuybyshevsk Russia 53°7N 49°58E 70 D8
Novokuznetsk Russia 53°45N 87°10E 76 D9
Novomoskovsk Russia 54°5N 38°15E 70 D6
Novorossiysk Russia 44°43N 37°46E 71 F6
Novoshakhtinsk Russia 47°46N 39°58E 71 E6
Novosibirsk Russia 55°0N 83°5E 76 D9
Novotroitsk Russia 51°10N 58°15E 70 D10
Novyy Urengoy Russia 65°48N 76°52E 76 C8
Nowy Sącz Poland 49°40N 20°41E 65 D11
Noyabrsk Russia 64°34N 76°21E 76 C8
Nu Jiang → China 29°58N 97°25E 78 F8
Nu Shan China 26°0N 99°20E 78 F8
Nubia Africa 21°0N 32°0E 90 D7
Nubian Desert Sudan 21°30N 33°30E 95 D12
Nueces → U.S.A. 27°51N 97°30W 110 E7
Nueltin L. Canada 60°30N 99°30W 108 C10
Nueva Rosita Mexico 27°57N 101°13W 114 B4
Nuevitas Cuba 21°30N 77°20W 115 C9
Nuevo Laredo Mexico 27°30N 99°31W 114 B5
Nuku'alofa Tonga 21°10S 175°12W 99 E16
Nukulaelae Tuvalu 9°23S 179°52E 99 B14
Nukus Uzbekistan 42°27N 59°41E 87 A9
Nullarbor Plain Australia 31°10S 129°0E 98 G4
Numan Nigeria 9°29N 12°3E 95 G8
Numazu Japan 35°7N 138°51E 81 F6
Nunavut □ Canada 66°0N 85°0W 109 C11
Nuneaton U.K. 52°32N 1°27W 27 G6
Nunivak I. U.S.A. 60°10N 166°30W 108 B3
Nunney U.K. 51°12N 2°22W 30 D4
Núoro Italy 40°20N 9°20E 68 D3
Nur-Sultan = Astana
  Kazakhstan 51°10N 71°30E 76 D8
Nuremberg Germany 49°27N 11°3E 64 D6
Nusantara Indonesia 0°58S 116°43E 82 E5
Nusaybin Turkey 37°3N 41°10E 71 G7
Nuuk Greenland 64°10N 51°35W 54 C5
Nuuveldberge S. Africa 32°10S 21°45E 97 L4
Nyagan Russia 62°30N 65°38E 76 C7
Nyahururu Kenya 0°2N 36°27E 96 D7
Nyainqêntanglha Shan China 30°0N 90°0E 78 E7
Nyâlâ Sudan 12°2N 24°58E 95 F10
Nyalam China 28°32N 86°4E 78 F6
Nyíregyháza Hungary 47°58N 21°47E 65 E11
Nysa Poland 50°30N 17°22E 65 C9
Nzérékoré Guinea 7°49N 8°48W 94 G4

O

Oa, Mull of U.K. 55°35N 6°20W 24 C3
Oadby U.K. 52°36N 1°5W 27 G6
Oahe, L. U.S.A. 44°27N 100°24W 110 A6
O'ahu U.S.A. 21°28N 157°58W 110 H16
Oak Hill U.S.A. 37°59N 81°9W 112 G7
Oak Ridge U.S.A. 36°1N 84°16W 111 C10
Oakengates U.K. 52°41N 2°26W 27 G4
Oakham U.K. 52°40N 0°43W 27 G7
Oakland U.S.A. 37°48N 122°18W 110 C2
Oates Land Antarctica 69°0S 160°0E 55 C11
Oaxaca Mexico 17°3N 96°43W 114 D5
Ob → Russia 66°45N 69°30E 76 C7
Ob, G. of Russia 69°0N 73°0E 76 C8
Oba Canada 49°4N 84°7W 109 E11
Oban U.K. 56°25N 5°29W 24 B5
Oberhausen Germany 51°28N 6°51E 64 C4
Obi, Kepulauan Indonesia 1°23S 127°45E 83 E7
Óbidos Brazil 1°50S 55°30W 120 C4
Obihiro Japan 42°56N 143°12E 81 B8
Obozerskiy Russia 63°34N 40°21E 70 B7
Obshchi Syrt Russia 52°0N 53°0E 56 E16
Ocala U.S.A. 29°11N 82°8W 111 E10
Occidental, Cordillera Colombia 5°0N 76°0W 117 C3
Occidental, Grand Erg Algeria 30°20N 1°0E 94 B6
Ocean City U.S.A. 39°17N 74°35W 113 F10
Oceanside U.S.A. 33°12N 117°23W 110 D3
Ochil Hills U.K. 56°14N 3°40W 25 B8
Ocho Rios Jamaica 18°24N 77°6W 114 a
Oconto U.S.A. 44°53N 87°52W 112 C4
Odawara Japan 35°20N 139°6E 81 F6
Odense Denmark 55°22N 10°23E 63 F6
Oder → Europe 53°33N 14°38E 64 B8
Odesa Ukraine 46°30N 30°45E 71 E5
Odessa U.S.A. 31°52N 102°23W 110 D6
Odiham U.K. 51°15N 0°55W 31 D7
Odintsovo Russia 55°40N 37°16E 70 C6
Odisha □ India 20°0N 84°0E 85 K14
Odra → Europe 53°33N 14°38E 64 B8
Offa Nigeria 8°13N 4°42E 94 G6
Offaly □ Ireland 53°15N 7°30W 21 B8
Offenbach Germany 50°6N 8°44E 64 C5
Ogaden Ethiopia 7°30N 45°30E 89 F3
Ōgaki Japan 35°21N 136°37E 81 F5
Ogasawara Gunto Pac. Oc. 27°0N 142°0E 102 E6
Ogbomosho Nigeria 8°1N 4°11E 94 G6
Ogden U.S.A. 41°13N 111°58W 110 B4
Ogdensburg U.S.A. 44°42N 75°30W 113 C10
Ogooué → Gabon 1°0S 9°0E 96 E1
Ohio □ U.S.A. 40°15N 82°45W 112 E5
Ohio → U.S.A. 36°59N 89°8W 112 G3
Ohře → Czechia 50°30N 14°10E 64 C8
Ohrid, L. N. Macedonia 41°8N 20°52E 69 D9

Oil City U.S.A. 41°26N 79°42W 112 E8
Oise → France 49°0N 2°4E 66 B5
Oistins Barbados 13°4N 59°33W 114 c
Oistins B. Barbados 13°4N 59°33W 114 c
Ōita Japan 33°14N 131°36E 81 G2
Ojos del Salado, Cerro
  Argentina 27°0S 68°40W 121 E3
Oka → Russia 56°20N 43°59E 70 C7
Okara Pakistan 30°50N 73°31E 84 D8
Okavango Delta Botswana 18°45S 22°45E 97 H4
Okayama Japan 34°40N 133°54E 81 F3
Okazaki Japan 34°57N 137°10E 81 F5
Okeechobee, L. U.S.A. 27°0N 80°50W 111 E10
Okehampton U.K. 50°44N 4°0W 29 F5
Okhotsk Russia 59°20N 143°10E 77 D15
Okhotsk, Sea of Asia 55°0N 145°0E 77 D15
Oki-Shotō Japan 36°5N 133°15E 81 E3
Okinawa-Jima Japan 26°32N 128°0E 79 F14
Oklahoma □ U.S.A. 35°20N 97°30W 110 C7
Oklahoma City U.S.A. 35°30N 97°30W 110 C7
Öland Sweden 56°45N 16°38E 63 F7
Olavarría Argentina 36°55S 60°20W 121 F3
Ólbia Italy 40°55N 9°31E 68 D3
Old Basing U.K. 51°16N 1°3W 30 D6
Old Crow Canada 67°30N 139°55W 108 C6
Old Fletton U.K. 52°33N 0°14W 31 A8
Old Leake U.K. 53°2N 0°5E 27 F9
Old Town U.S.A. 44°56N 68°39W 113 C13
Oldbury U.K. 51°38N 2°33W 30 C3
Oldcastle Ireland 53°46N 7°10W 19 D7
Oldenburg Germany 53°9N 8°13E 64 B5
Oldham U.K. 53°33N 2°7W 27 F4
Oldmeldrum U.K. 57°20N 2°19W 23 H13
Olean U.S.A. 42°5N 78°26W 112 D8
Olekminsk Russia 60°25N 120°30E 77 C13
Olenek → Russia 73°0N 120°10E 77 B13
Oléron, Î. d' France 45°55N 1°15W 66 D3
Ólgiy Mongolia 48°56N 89°57E 78 B6
Olímpia Brazil 20°44S 48°54W 122 D1
Oliveira Brazil 20°39S 44°50W 122 D2
Ollagüe Chile 21°15S 68°10W 120 E3
Ollerton U.K. 53°12N 1°1W 27 F6
Olmaliq Uzbekistan 40°50N 69°35E 76 E7
Olney U.K. 52°10N 0°41W 31 B7
Olney U.S.A. 38°44N 88°5W 112 F3
Olomouc Czechia 49°38N 17°12E 65 D9
Olsztyn Poland 53°48N 20°29E 65 B11
Olt → Romania 43°43N 24°51E 65 G13
Olympia Greece 37°39N 21°39E 69 F9
Olympia U.S.A. 47°3N 122°53W 110 A2
Olympus, Mt. Greece 40°6N 22°23E 69 D10
Olympus, Mt. U.S.A. 47°48N 123°43W 110 A2
Omagh U.K. 54°36N 7°19W 18 B7
Omaha U.S.A. 41°17N 95°58W 111 B7
Oman ■ Asia 23°0N 58°0E 89 C6
Oman, G. of Asia 24°30N 58°30E 87 E9
Ombersley U.K. 52°16N 2°13W 30 B4
Omdurmân Sudan 15°40N 32°28E 95 E12
Ometepec Mexico 16°41N 98°25W 114 D5
Omsk Russia 55°0N 73°12E 76 D8
Ōmuta Japan 33°5N 130°26E 81 G2
Ondangwa Namibia 17°57S 16°4E 97 H3
Öndörhaan Mongolia 47°19N 110°39E 79 B11
Onega → Russia 63°58N 38°2E 70 B6
Onega, L. Russia 61°44N 35°22E 70 B6
Onega B. Russia 64°24N 36°38E 70 B6
Oneida U.S.A. 43°6N 75°39W 113 D10
O'Neill U.S.A. 42°27N 98°39W 110 B7
Oneonta U.S.A. 42°27N 75°4W 113 D10
Onitsha Nigeria 6°6N 6°42E 94 G7
Onny → U.K. 52°24N 2°47W 27 H3
Onslow B. U.S.A. 34°20N 77°15W 111 D11
Ontario U.S.A. 44°2N 116°58W 110 B3
Ontario □ Canada 48°0N 83°0W 109 E11
Ontario, L. N. Amer. 43°20N 78°0W 112 D8
Ontonagon U.S.A. 46°52N 89°19W 112 B3
Oostende Belgium 51°15N 2°54E 64 C2
Opava Czechia 49°57N 17°58E 65 D9
Opole Poland 50°42N 17°58E 65 C9
Oradea Romania 47°2N 21°58E 65 E11
Orai India 25°58N 79°30E 84 G11
Öræfajökull Iceland 64°2N 16°39W 63 B2
Oral Kazakhstan 51°20N 51°20E 71 D9
Oran Algeria 35°45N 0°39W 94 A5
Orange Australia 33°15S 149°7E 98 G8
Orange France 44°8N 4°47E 66 D6
Orange → S. Africa 28°41S 16°28E 97 K3
Orange, C. Brazil 4°20N 51°30W 120 B4
Orange Walk Belize 18°6N 88°33W 114 D7
Orangeville Canada 43°55N 80°5W 112 D7
Ordos China 39°50N 110°0E 79 D10
Ordos Desert China 39°50N 109°0E 79 D10
Ordu Turkey 40°55N 37°53E 71 F6
Örebro Sweden 59°20N 15°18E 63 F7
Oregon □ U.S.A. 44°0N 121°0W 110 B2
Orekhovo-Zuyevo Russia 55°50N 38°55E 70 C6
Orel Russia 52°57N 36°3E 70 D6
Orem U.S.A. 40°19N 111°42W 110 B4
Orenburg Russia 51°45N 55°6E 70 D10
Orford U.K. 52°6N 1°33E 31 B12
Orford Ness U.K. 52°5N 1°35E 31 B12
Oriental, Cordillera Colombia 6°0N 73°0W 117 C3
Oriental, Grand Erg Algeria 30°0N 6°30E 94 B7
Orihuela Spain 38°7N 0°55W 67 C5
Orinoco → Venezuela 9°15N 61°30W 120 B3
Oristano Italy 39°54N 8°36E 68 E3
Orizaba Mexico 18°51N 97°6W 114 D5
Orizaba, Pico de Mexico 18°58N 97°15W 114 D5
Orkhon → Mongolia 50°21N 106°0E 78 A10
Orkney □ U.K. 59°2N 3°13W 23 D11
Orkney Is. U.K. 59°0N 3°0W 23 E12
Orlando U.S.A. 28°32N 81°22W 111 E10
Orléanais France 48°0N 2°0E 66 C5
Orléans France 47°54N 1°52E 66 C4
Orléans, Î. d' Canada 46°54N 70°58W 113 B12
Ormara Pakistan 25°16N 64°33E 84 G4
Ormesby St. Margaret U.K. 52°41N 1°41E 31 A12
Ormoc Phil. 11°0N 124°37E 83 B6
Ormskirk U.K. 53°35N 2°54W 27 E3
Örnsköldsvik Sweden 63°17N 18°40E 63 E7

Oronsay — Port Carlisle

Oronsay U.K. 56°1N 6°15W 24 B3
Orsha Belarus 54°30N 30°25E 70 D5
Ortegal, C. Spain 43°43N 7°52W 67 A2
Oruro Bolivia 18°0S 67°9W 120 D3
Orwell → U.K. 51°59N 1°18E 31 C11
Ōsaka Japan 34°42N 135°30E 81 F4
Osh Kyrgyzstan 40°37N 72°49E 76 E8
Oshakati Namibia 17°45S 15°40E 97 H3
Oshawa Canada 43°50N 78°50W 109 E12
Oshkosh U.S.A. 44°1N 88°33W 112 C3
Oshogbo Nigeria 7°48N 4°37E 94 G6
Osijek Croatia 45°34N 18°41E 69 B8
Osizweni S. Africa 27°49S 30°7E 97 K6
Oskaloosa U.S.A. 41°18N 92°39W 111 B8
Oskarshamn Sweden 57°15N 16°27E 63 F7
Öskemen Kazakhstan 50°0N 82°36E 76 E9
Oslo Norway 59°54N 10°43E 63 F6
Oslofjorden Norway 59°20N 10°35E 63 F6
Osmaniye Turkey 37°5N 36°10E 71 G6
Osmotherley U.K. 54°22N 1°18W 26 D6
Osnabrück Germany 52°17N 8°3E 64 B5
Osorno Chile 40°25S 73°0W 121 G2
Ossa, Mt. Australia 41°52S 146°3E 98 J8
Ossett U.K. 53°41N 1°34W 27 E5
Ostend = Oostende Belgium 51°15N 2°54E 64 C2
Österdalälven → Sweden 60°30N 15°7E 63 F7
Östersund Sweden 63°10N 14°38E 63 E6
Ostfriesische Inseln Germany 53°42N 7°0E 64 B4
Ostrava Czechia 49°51N 18°18E 65 D10
Ostrołęka Poland 53°4N 21°32E 65 B11
Ostrów Wielkopolski Poland 51°36N 17°44E 65 C9
Ostrowiec-Świętokrzyski Poland 50°55N 21°22E 65 C11
Oswaldtwistle U.K. 53°43N 2°26W 27 E4
Oswego U.S.A. 43°27N 76°31W 112 D9
Oswestry U.K. 52°52N 3°3W 27 G2
Otaru Japan 43°10N 141°0E 81 B7
Otjiwarongo Namibia 20°30S 16°33E 97 J3
Otley U.K. 53°54N 1°41W 27 E5
Otranto Italy 40°9N 18°28E 69 D8
Otranto, Str. of Italy 40°15N 18°40E 69 D8
Ōtsu Japan 35°0N 135°50E 81 F4
Ottawa Canada 45°26N 75°42W 113 C10
Ottawa U.S.A. 41°21N 88°51W 112 E3
Ottawa Is. Canada 59°35N 80°10W 109 D11
Otter → U.K. 50°38N 3°19W 29 F7
Otterburn U.K. 55°14N 2°11W 26 B4
Ottery St. Mary U.K. 50°44N 3°17W 29 F7
Ottumwa U.S.A. 41°1N 92°25W 111 B8
Ouachita → U.S.A. 31°38N 91°49W 111 D8
Ouachita Mts. U.S.A. 34°30N 94°30W 111 D8
Ouagadougou Burkina Faso 12°25N 1°30W 94 F5
Oubangi → Dem. Rep. of the Congo 0°30S 17°50E 96 E3
Oudtshoorn S. Africa 33°35S 22°14E 97 L4
Ouezzane Morocco 34°51N 5°35W 94 B4
Oughterard Ireland 53°26N 9°18W 20 B4
Oujda Morocco 34°41N 1°55W 94 B5
Oulton U.K. 52°30N 1°43E 31 B12
Oulton Broad U.K. 52°28N 1°42E 31 B12
Oulu Finland 65°1N 25°29E 63 D9
Oulujärvi Finland 64°25N 27°15E 63 E9
Oulujoki → Finland 65°1N 25°30E 63 D9
Oundle U.K. 52°29N 0°28W 31 B8
Ourense Spain 42°19N 7°55W 67 A2
Ouro Fino Brazil 22°16S 46°25W 122 D1
Ouro Prêto Brazil 20°20S 43°30W 122 D2
Ouse → E. Sussex, U.K. 50°47N 0°4E 31 E9
Ouse → N. Yorks., U.K. 53°44N 0°55W 27 E7
Outaouais → Canada 45°27N 74°8W 109 E12
Outer Hebrides U.K. 57°30N 7°15W 22 H2
Outjo Namibia 20°5S 16°7E 97 J3
Outwell U.K. 52°37N 0°14E 31 A9
Ovalle Chile 30°33S 71°18W 121 F2
Ovamboland Namibia 18°30S 16°0E 97 H3
Over Wallop U.K. 51°9N 1°36W 30 D5
Overton U.K. 51°15N 1°15W 30 D6
Oviedo Spain 43°25N 5°50W 67 A3
Owatonna U.S.A. 44°5N 93°14W 111 B8
Owen Sound Canada 44°35N 80°55W 109 E11
Owen Stanley Ra. Papua N. G. 8°30S 147°0E 98 B8
Owens L. U.S.A. 36°26N 117°57W 110 C3
Owensboro U.S.A. 37°46N 87°7W 112 G4
Owo Nigeria 7°10N 5°39E 94 G7
Owosso U.S.A. 43°0N 84°10W 112 D5
Owston Ferry U.K. 53°29N 0°47W 27 F7
Owyhee → U.S.A. 43°49N 117°2W 110 B3
Oxford U.K. 51°46N 1°15W 30 C6
Oxfordshire □ U.K. 51°48N 1°16W 30 C6
Oxnard U.S.A. 34°12N 119°11W 110 D3
Oyama Japan 36°18N 139°48E 81 E6
Oyem Gabon 1°34N 11°31E 96 D2
Oykel → U.K. 57°56N 4°26W 23 G9
Oyo Nigeria 7°46N 3°56E 94 G6
Ozark Plateau U.S.A. 37°20N 91°40W 111 C8
Ozarks, L. of the U.S.A. 38°12N 92°38W 111 C8

P

Paarl S. Africa 33°45S 18°56E 97 L3
Pab Hills Pakistan 26°30N 66°45E 84 F5
Pabaidh = Pabbay U.K. 57°46N 7°14W 22 G3
Pabbay U.K. 57°46N 7°14W 22 G3
Pabna Bangla. 24°1N 89°18E 85 G16
Pacaraima, Sa. S. Amer. 4°0N 62°30W 120 B3
Pacasmayo Peru 7°20S 79°35W 120 C2
Pachuca Mexico 20°7N 98°44W 114 C5
Pacific Ocean 10°0N 140°0W 103 G14
Padang Indonesia 1°0S 100°20E 82 E2
Padangsidempuan Indonesia 1°30N 99°15E 82 D1
Paddock Wood U.K. 51°11N 0°24E 31 D9
Paderborn Germany 51°42N 8°45E 64 C5
Padiham U.K. 53°48N 2°18W 27 E4
Padre I. U.S.A. 27°10N 97°25N 111 E7
Padstow U.K. 50°33N 4°58W 29 F4
Padstow B. U.K. 50°34N 4°57W 29 F4
Padua Italy 45°25N 11°53E 68 B4
Paducah U.S.A. 37°5N 88°37W 112 G3
Pag Croatia 44°25N 15°3E 68 B6
Pagadian Phil. 7°55N 123°30E 83 C6
Page U.S.A. 36°57N 111°27W 110 C4

Pāhala U.S.A. 19°12N 155°29W 110 J17
Paignton U.K. 50°26N 3°35W 29 G6
Paine Grande, Cerro Chile 50°59S 73°4W 121 H2
Painesville U.S.A. 41°43N 81°15W 112 E7
Painswick U.K. 51°47N 2°10W 30 C4
Painted Desert U.S.A. 36°0N 111°0W 110 C4
Paintsville U.S.A. 37°49N 82°48W 112 G6
País Vasco □ Spain 42°50N 2°45W 67 A4
Paisley U.K. 55°50N 4°25W 24 C7
Paita Peru 5°11S 81°9W 120 C1
Pakistan ■ Asia 30°0N 70°0E 84 E7
Pakxe Laos 15°5N 105°52E 82 A3
Palagruža Croatia 42°24N 16°15E 68 C7
Palakkad India 10°46N 76°42E 84 P10
Palani Hills India 10°14N 77°33E 84 P10
Palanpur India 24°10N 72°25E 84 G8
Palapye Botswana 22°30S 27°7E 97 J5
Palau ■ Palau 7°30N 134°30E 102 G5
Palawan Phil. 9°30N 118°30E 82 C5
Palembang Indonesia 3°0S 104°50E 82 E2
Palencia Spain 42°1N 4°34W 67 A3
Palermo Italy 38°7N 13°22E 68 E5
Palestine U.S.A. 31°46N 95°38W 111 D7
Palgrave U.K. 52°22N 1°6E 31 B11
Pali India 25°50N 73°20E 84 G8
Palikir Micronesia 6°55N 158°9E 102 G7
Palk Strait Asia 10°0N 79°45E 84 Q11
Palm Springs U.S.A. 33°50N 116°33W 110 D3
Palma de Mallorca Spain 39°35N 2°39E 67 C7
Palmares Brazil 8°41S 35°28W 122 A3
Palmas Brazil 10°12S 48°21W 122 B1
Palmas, C. Liberia 4°27N 7°46W 94 H4
Palmeira dos Índios Brazil 9°25S 36°37W 122 A3
Palmer U.S.A. 61°36N 149°7W 108 C5
Palmer Land Antarctica 73°0S 63°0W 55 D18
Palmerston North N.Z. 40°21S 175°39E 99 J14
Palmira Colombia 3°32N 76°16W 120 B2
Palmyra Syria 34°36N 38°15E 86 C4
Palmyra Is. Pac. Oc. 5°52N 162°5W 103 G11
Palopo Indonesia 3°0S 120°16E 83 E6
Palu Indonesia 1°0S 119°52E 83 E5
Palu Turkey 38°45N 40°0E 71 G7
Pamiers France 43°7N 1°39E 66 E4
Pamir Tajikistan 37°40N 73°0E 87 B13
Pamlico Sd. U.S.A. 35°20N 76°0W 111 C11
Pampa U.S.A. 35°32N 100°58W 110 C6
Pampas Argentina 35°0S 63°0W 121 F3
Pamplona-Iruña Spain 42°48N 1°38W 67 A5
Pana U.S.A. 39°23N 89°5W 112 F3
Panaji India 15°25N 73°50E 84 M8
Panamá Panama 9°0N 79°25W 115 F9
Panama ■ Cent. Amer. 8°48N 79°55W 115 F9
Panamá, G. de Panama 8°4N 79°20W 115 F9
Panama, Isthmus of Cent. Amer. 9°0N 79°0W 115 F9
Panama Canal Panama 9°10N 79°37W 115 F9
Panama City U.S.A. 30°10N 85°40W 111 D9
Panay Phil. 11°10N 122°30E 83 B6
Pančevo Serbia 44°52N 20°41E 69 B9
Panevėžys Lithuania 55°42N 24°25E 63 F8
Pangani Tanzania 5°25S 38°58E 96 F7
Pangbourne U.K. 51°29N 1°6W 30 D6
Pangkalpinang Indonesia 2°10S 106°10E 82 E3
Pangnirtung Canada 66°8N 65°43W 109 C13
Pantar Indonesia 8°28S 124°10E 83 F6
Pante Macassar Timor-Leste 9°30S 123°58E 83 F6
Pantelleria Italy 36°50N 11°57E 68 F4
Panzhihua China 26°33N 101°44E 78 D9
Papa Stour U.K. 60°20N 1°42W 22 B14
Papa Westray U.K. 59°20N 2°55W 23 D12
Papantla Mexico 20°27N 97°19W 114 C5
Papeete Tahiti 17°32S 149°34W 103 J13
Paphos Cyprus 34°46N 32°25E 86 C3
Papua □ Indonesia 4°0S 137°0E 83 E9
Papua, G. of Papua N. G. 9°0S 144°50E 98 B7
Papua New Guinea ■ Oceania 8°0S 145°0E 98 B8
Pará □ Brazil 3°20S 52°0W 120 C4
Paracatu Brazil 17°10S 46°50W 122 C1
Paracel Is. S. China Sea 15°50N 112°0E 82 A4
Paragould U.S.A. 36°3N 90°29W 111 C8
Paraguaçu → Brazil 12°45S 38°54W 122 B3
Paraguaná, Pen. de Venezuela 12°0N 70°0W 120 A3
Paraguarí Paraguay 25°36S 57°0W 121 E4
Paraguay ■ S. Amer. 23°0S 57°0W 121 E4
Paraguay → Paraguay 27°18S 58°38W 121 E4
Paraíba □ Brazil 7°0S 36°0W 120 C6
Parakou Benin 9°25N 2°40E 94 G6
Paramaribo Suriname 5°50N 55°10W 120 B4
Paraná Argentina 31°45S 60°30W 121 F3
Paraná □ Brazil 12°30S 47°48W 122 B1
Paraná → Argentina 24°30S 51°0W 121 F4
Paraná → Argentina 33°43S 59°15W 121 F4
Paranaguá Brazil 25°30S 48°30W 122 E1
Paranaíba Brazil 20°6S 51°4W 120 E4
Paranaíba → Brazil 20°6S 51°4W 120 E4
Paranapanema → Brazil 22°40S 53°9W 121 E4
Parbhani India 19°8N 76°52E 84 K10
Pardo → Brazil 15°40S 39°0W 122 C3
Pardubice Czechia 50°3N 15°45E 64 C8
Parecis, Serra dos Brazil 13°0S 60°0W 120 D4
Parepare Indonesia 4°0S 119°40E 83 E5
Parima, Serra Brazil 2°30N 64°0W 120 B3
Pariñas, Pta. Peru 4°30S 82°0W 117 D2
Parintins Brazil 2°40S 56°50W 120 C4
Pariparit Kyun Myanmar 14°52N 93°41E 85 M18
Paris France 48°53N 2°20E 66 B5
Paris U.S.A. 33°40N 95°33W 111 D7
Park Falls U.S.A. 45°56N 90°27W 112 C2
Parla Spain 40°14N 3°46W 67 B4
Parma Italy 44°48N 10°20E 68 B4
Parnaíba Brazil 10°10S 44°38W 122 B2
Parnaíba → Brazil 2°54S 41°47W 120 C5
Pärnu Estonia 58°28N 24°33E 63 F8
Paros Greece 37°5N 25°12E 69 F11
Parracombe U.K. 51°11N 3°55W 29 E6
Parrett → U.K. 51°12N 3°1W 30 D2
Parry Is. Canada 77°0N 110°0W 109 B9
Parry Sound Canada 45°20N 80°0W 109 E12
Parsons U.S.A. 37°20N 95°16W 111 C7
Parton U.K. 54°35N 3°33W 26 C1

Partry Mts. Ireland 53°40N 9°28W 18 D3
Paru → Brazil 1°33S 52°38W 120 C4
Pasadena Calif., U.S.A. 34°9N 118°8W 110 D3
Pasadena Tex., U.S.A. 29°43N 95°13W 111 E7
Paschimbanga □ India 23°0N 88°0E 85 H16
Pascua, I. de Chile 27°7S 109°23W 103 K17
Paso Robles U.S.A. 35°38N 120°41W 110 C2
Passage West Ireland 51°52N 8°21W 20 E6
Passau Germany 48°34N 13°28E 64 D7
Passo Fundo Brazil 28°10S 52°20W 121 E4
Passos Brazil 20°45S 46°37W 122 D1
Pastaza → Peru 4°50S 76°52W 120 C2
Pasto Colombia 1°13N 77°17W 120 B2
Patagonia Argentina 45°0S 69°0W 121 G3
Paterson U.S.A. 40°54N 74°9W 113 E10
Pathankot India 32°18N 75°45E 84 C9
Pathein Myanmar 16°45N 94°30E 85 L19
Pathfinder Res. U.S.A. 42°28N 106°51W 110 B5
Patiala India 30°23N 76°26E 84 D10
Patkai Bum India 27°0N 95°30E 85 F19
Patmos Greece 37°21N 26°36E 69 F12
Patna India 25°35N 85°12E 85 G14
Patos Brazil 6°55S 37°16W 120 C6
Patos, L. dos Brazil 31°20S 51°0W 121 F4
Patos de Minas Brazil 18°35S 46°32W 122 C1
Patra Greece 38°14N 21°47E 69 E9
Patrington U.K. 53°41N 0°1W 27 E8
Patrocínio Brazil 18°57S 47°0W 122 C1
Patten U.S.A. 46°0N 68°38W 113 C13
Patterdale U.K. 54°32N 2°56W 26 C5
Pau France 43°19N 0°25W 66 E3
Paulatuk Canada 69°25N 124°0W 108 C7
Paulistana Brazil 8°9S 41°9W 122 A2
Paull U.K. 53°44N 0°14W 27 E8
Paulo Afonso Brazil 9°21S 38°15W 122 A3
Pavia Italy 45°7N 9°8E 68 B3
Pavlodar Kazakhstan 52°33N 77°0E 76 D8
Pavlohrad Ukraine 48°30N 35°52E 71 E6
Pavlovo Russia 55°58N 43°5E 70 C7
Pawtucket U.S.A. 41°53N 71°23W 113 E12
Paxton U.S.A. 40°27N 88°6W 112 E3
Payakumbuh Indonesia 0°20S 100°35E 82 E2
Payette U.S.A. 44°5N 116°56W 110 B3
Payne L. Canada 59°30N 74°30W 109 D12
Paysandú Uruguay 32°19S 58°8W 121 F4
Payson U.S.A. 34°14N 111°20W 110 D4
Paz, B. de la Mexico 24°9N 110°25W 114 C2
Pazardzhik Bulgaria 42°12N 24°20E 69 C11
Peace → Canada 59°0N 111°25W 108 D8
Peace River Canada 56°15N 117°18W 108 D8
Peacehaven U.K. 50°48N 0°0 31 E8
Peak District △ U.K. 53°24N 1°46W 27 F5
Peak City U.S.A. 21°24N 157°59W 110 H16
Pearl → U.S.A. 30°11N 89°32W 111 D9
Pearl Harbor U.S.A. 21°21N 157°57W 110 H16
Pearl River Bridge China 22°15N 113°48E 79 a
Peasenhall U.K. 52°16N 1°27E 31 B11
Peawanuck Canada 55°15N 85°12W 109 D11
Pechora Russia 65°10N 57°11E 70 A10
Pechora → Russia 68°13N 54°15E 70 A9
Pechora B. Russia 68°40N 54°0E 70 A9
Pecos U.S.A. 31°26N 103°30W 110 D6
Pecos → U.S.A. 29°42N 101°22W 110 E6
Pécs Hungary 46°5N 18°15E 65 E10
Pedra Azul Brazil 16°2S 41°17W 122 C2
Pedro Afonso Brazil 9°0S 48°10W 122 A1
Peebles U.K. 55°40N 3°11W 25 D9
Peel I. of Man 54°13N 4°40W 19 C12
Peel → Canada 67°0N 135°0W 108 C6
Peel Fell U.K. 55°18N 2°34W 26 B3
Peel Sd. Canada 73°0N 96°0W 108 B10
Pegswood U.K. 55°11N 1°39W 26 B5
Pegu Myanmar 19°0N 96°0E 85 K20
Pegwell Bay U.K. 51°18N 1°24E 31 D11
Peixe Brazil 12°0S 48°40W 122 B1
Pejë Kosovo 42°40N 20°17E 69 C9
Pekalongan Indonesia 6°53S 109°40E 82 F3
Pekanbaru Indonesia 0°30N 101°15E 82 D2
Pekin U.S.A. 40°35N 89°40W 112 E3
Peking = Beijing China 39°53N 116°21E 79 D12
Pelagie, Is. Italy 35°39N 12°33E 68 G5
Pelée, Mt. Martinique 14°48N 61°10W 115 D12
Peleng Indonesia 1°20S 123°30E 83 E6
Pelješac Croatia 42°55N 17°25E 68 C7
Pelly → Canada 62°47N 137°19W 108 C6
Pelly Bay Canada 68°38N 89°50W 109 C11
Peloponnesos □ Greece 37°10N 22°0W 69 F10
Pelotas Brazil 31°42S 52°23W 121 F4
Pelvoux, Massif du France 44°52N 6°20E 66 D7
Pematangsiantar Indonesia 2°57N 99°5E 82 D1
Pemba Mozam. 12°58S 40°30E 96 G8
Pemba I. Tanzania 5°0S 39°45E 96 F7
Pembridge U.K. 52°13N 2°52W 30 B3
Pembroke Canada 45°50N 77°7W 109 E12
Pembroke U.K. 51°41N 4°55W 28 D4
Pembrokeshire □ U.K. 51°52N 4°56W 28 D3
Pembrokeshire Coast △ U.K. 51°50N 5°2W 28 D3
Pembury U.K. 51°8N 0°20E 31 D9
Pen-y-bont ar Ogwr = Bridgend U.K. 51°30N 3°34W 29 D6
Pen-y-Ghent U.K. 54°10N 2°14W 26 D4
Peñas, C. de Spain 43°42N 5°52W 67 A3
Peñas, G. de Chile 47°0S 75°0W 121 G2
Pend Oreille, L. U.S.A. 48°10N 116°21W 110 A3
Pendeen U.K. 50°9N 5°41W 29 G2
Pendle Hill U.K. 53°52N 2°19W 27 E4
Pendleton U.S.A. 45°40N 118°47W 110 A3
Penedo Brazil 10°15S 36°36W 122 B3
Penetanguishene Canada 44°50N 79°55W 112 C8
Penfro = Pembroke U.K. 51°41N 4°55W 28 D4
Penicuik U.K. 55°50N 3°13W 25 D9
Peninsular Malaysia □ Malaysia 4°0N 102°0E 82 D2
Penistone U.K. 53°31N 1°37W 27 E5
Penkridge U.K. 52°44N 2°6W 27 G4
Penn Yan U.S.A. 42°40N 77°3W 112 D9
Pennines U.K. 54°45N 2°27W 26 C4
Pennsylvania □ U.S.A. 40°45N 77°30W 112 E8
Penong Australia 31°56S 133°1E 98 G5

Penrith U.K. 54°40N 2°45W 26 C3
Penryn U.K. 50°9N 5°7W 29 G3
Pensacola U.S.A. 30°25N 87°13W 111 D9
Pensacola Mts. Antarctica 84°0S 40°0W 55 E1
Penshurst U.K. 51°10N 0°12E 31 D9
Penticton Canada 49°30N 119°38W 108 E8
Pentire Pt. U.K. 50°35N 4°56W 29 F4
Pentland Firth U.K. 58°43N 3°10W 23 E11
Pentland Hills U.K. 55°48N 3°25W 25 C9
Penwortham U.K. 53°45N 2°46W 27 E3
Penygroes U.K. 53°3N 4°17W 28 A5
Penza Russia 53°15N 45°5E 70 D8
Penzance U.K. 50°7N 5°33W 29 G2
Peoria U.S.A. 40°42N 89°36W 112 E3
Perabumulih Indonesia 3°27S 104°15E 82 E2
Perdido, Mte. Spain 42°40N 0°5E 67 A6
Pereira Colombia 4°49N 75°43W 120 B2
Pergamino Argentina 33°52S 60°30W 121 F3
Péribonka → Canada 48°45N 72°5W 109 E12
Périgueux France 45°10N 0°42E 66 D4
Perm Russia 58°0N 56°10E 70 C10
Pernambuco □ Brazil 8°0S 37°0W 120 C6
Pernik Bulgaria 42°35N 23°2E 69 C10
Perpignan France 42°42N 2°53E 66 E5
Perranporth U.K. 50°20N 5°11W 29 G3
Perranzabuloe U.K. 50°19N 5°9W 29 G3
Perryton U.S.A. 36°24N 100°48W 110 C6
Perryville U.S.A. 37°43N 89°52W 112 G3
Persepolis Iran 29°55N 52°50E 87 D8
Pershore U.K. 52°7N 2°4W 30 B4
Persian Gulf Asia 27°0N 50°0E 87 E7
Perth Australia 31°57S 115°52E 98 G2
Perth Canada 44°55N 76°15W 112 C9
Perth U.K. 56°24N 3°26W 25 B9
Perth & Kinross □ U.K. 56°45N 3°55W 23 J9
Peru Illinois 40°45N 86°4W 112 E4
Peru ■ S. Amer. 4°0S 75°0W 120 C2
Peru-Chile Trench Pac. Oc. 20°0S 72°0W 103 K20
Perugia Italy 43°7N 12°23E 68 C5
Pervomaysk Ukraine 48°10N 30°46E 71 E5
Pervouralsk Russia 56°59N 59°59E 70 C10
Pésaro Italy 43°54N 12°55E 68 C5
Pescara Italy 42°28N 14°13E 68 C6
Peshawar Pakistan 34°2N 71°37E 84 B7
Pesqueira Brazil 8°20S 36°42W 122 A3
Petah Tiqwa Israel 32°6N 34°53E 86 C3
Peterborough Canada 44°20N 78°20W 109 E12
Peterborough U.K. 52°35N 0°15W 31 A8
Peterchurch U.K. 52°2N 2°56W 30 B3
Peterculter U.K. 57°6N 2°16W 23 H13
Peterhead U.K. 57°31N 1°48W 23 G14
Peterlee U.K. 54°47N 1°20W 26 C6
Petersburg Alaska, U.S.A. 56°48N 132°58W 108 D6
Petersburg Va., U.S.A. 37°14N 77°24W 112 G9
Petersfield U.K. 51°1N 0°56W 31 D7
Petit Piton St. Lucia 13°51N 61°5W 114 b
Petitot → Canada 60°14N 123°29W 108 C7
Petitsikapau L. Canada 54°37N 66°25W 109 D13
Peto Mexico 20°8N 88°55W 114 C7
Petoskey U.S.A. 45°22N 84°57W 112 C5
Petra Jordan 30°20N 35°22E 86 D3
Petrolândia Brazil 9°5S 38°20W 122 A3
Petrolina Brazil 9°24S 40°30W 122 A2
Petropavl Kazakhstan 54°53N 69°13E 76 D7
Petropavlovsk-Kamchatskiy Russia 53°3N 158°43E 77 D16
Petrópolis Brazil 22°33S 43°9W 122 D2
Petrozavodsk Russia 61°41N 34°20E 70 B5
Petworth U.K. 51°0N 0°36W 31 E7
Pevensey U.K. 50°49N 0°23E 31 E9
Pevensey Levels U.K. 50°50N 0°20E 31 E9
Pewsey U.K. 51°20N 1°45W 30 D5
Pewsey, Vale of U.K. 51°22N 1°40W 30 D5
Pforzheim Germany 48°52N 8°41E 64 D5
Phalodi India 27°12N 72°24E 84 F8
Phan Rang -Thap Cham Vietnam 11°34N 109°0E 82 B3
Phan Thiet Vietnam 11°1N 108°9E 82 B3
Phi Phi, Ko Thailand 7°45N 98°46E 82 C1
Philadelphia U.S.A. 39°57N 75°9W 113 E10
Philippine Sea Pac. Oc. 18°0N 125°0E 72 G14
Philippine Trench Pac. Oc. 12°0N 126°6E 83 B7
Philippines ■ Asia 12°0N 123°0E 83 B6
Phillips U.S.A. 45°42N 90°24W 112 C2
Phitsanulok Thailand 16°50N 100°12E 82 A2
Phnom Penh Cambodia 11°33N 104°55E 82 B2
Phoenix U.S.A. 33°26N 112°4W 110 D4
Phoenix Is. Kiribati 3°30S 172°0W 99 A16
Phuket Thailand 7°53N 98°24E 82 C1
Piacenza Italy 45°1N 9°40E 68 B3
Piatra Neamț Romania 46°56N 26°21E 65 E14
Piauí □ Brazil 7°0S 43°0W 120 C5
Piauí → Brazil 6°38S 42°42W 120 C5
Piave → Italy 45°32N 12°44E 68 B5
Picardie France 49°50N 3°0E 66 B5
Pichilemu Chile 34°22S 72°0W 121 F2
Pickering U.K. 54°15N 0°46W 26 D7
Pickering, Vale of U.K. 54°14N 0°45W 26 D7
Picos Brazil 7°5S 41°28W 120 C5
Picton Canada 44°1N 77°9W 112 C9
Pidley U.K. 52°33N 0°4W 31 B8
Pidurutalagala Sri Lanka 7°10N 80°50E 84 R12
Piedmont U.S.A. 34°42N 82°28W 111 D10
Piedras Negras Mexico 28°42N 100°31W 114 B4
Piemonte □ Italy 45°0N 8°0E 68 B2
Pierre U.S.A. 44°22N 100°21W 110 C6
Pietermaritzburg S. Africa 29°35S 30°25E 97 K6
Pikes Peak U.S.A. 38°50N 105°3W 110 C6
Pikeville U.S.A. 37°29N 82°31W 112 G6
Pilar Paraguay 26°50S 58°20W 121 E4
Pilcomayo → Paraguay 25°21S 57°42W 121 E4
Pilibhit India 28°40N 79°50E 84 E11
Pilica → Poland 51°52N 21°17E 65 C11
Pilling U.K. 53°56N 2°54W 27 E3
Pilton U.K. 51°10N 2°36W 30 D3
Pimentel Peru 6°45S 79°55W 120 C2
Pinar del Rio Cuba 22°26N 83°40W 115 C8
Pinchbeck U.K. 52°50N 0°9W 27 G8
Pinckneyville U.S.A. 38°5N 89°23W 112 F3
Pindus Mts. Greece 40°0N 21°0E 69 E9

Pine Bluff U.S.A. 34°13N 92°1W 111 D8
Pinega → Russia 64°30N 44°19E 70 B8
Pingdingshan China 33°43N 113°27E 79 E11
P'ingtung Taiwan 22°38N 120°30E 79 G13
Pingxiang Guangxi Zhuangzu, China 22°6N 106°46E 78 G10
Pingxiang Jiangxi, China 27°43N 113°48E 79 F11
Pinheiro Brazil 2°31S 45°5W 120 C5
Pinhoe U.K. 50°44N 3°28W 29 F7
Pinsk Belarus 52°10N 26°1E 70 D4
Piombino Italy 42°55N 10°32E 68 C4
Piotrków Trybunalski Poland 51°23N 19°43E 65 C10
Pipmuacan, Rés. Canada 49°45N 70°30W 113 A12
Piracicaba Brazil 22°45S 47°40W 122 D1
Pirapora Brazil 17°20S 44°56W 122 C2
Pireas Greece 37°57N 23°42E 69 F10
Pirmasens Germany 49°12N 7°36E 64 D4
Pisa Italy 43°43N 10°23E 68 C4
Pisagua Chile 19°40S 70°15W 120 D2
Pishan China 37°30N 78°33E 78 D4
Pistóia Italy 43°55N 10°54E 68 C4
Pit → U.S.A. 40°47N 122°6W 110 B2
Pitcairn I. Pac. Oc. 25°5S 130°5W 103 K14
Piteå Sweden 65°20N 21°25E 63 D8
Pitești Romania 44°52N 24°54E 65 F13
Pitlochry U.K. 56°42N 3°44W 23 J10
Pittsburg U.S.A. 37°25N 94°42W 111 C8
Pittsburgh U.S.A. 40°26N 79°58W 112 E8
Pittsfield U.S.A. 42°27N 73°15W 113 D11
Piura Peru 5°15S 80°38W 120 C1
Placentia Canada 47°20N 54°0W 109 E14
Placentia B. Canada 47°0N 54°40W 109 E14
Placetas Cuba 22°15N 79°44W 115 C9
Plainview U.S.A. 34°11N 101°43W 110 D6
Plata, Río de la → S. Amer. 34°45S 57°30W 121 F4
Platte → U.S.A. 39°16N 94°50W 111 C8
Plattsburgh U.S.A. 44°42N 73°28W 113 C11
Plauen Germany 50°30N 12°8E 64 C7
Playa del Carmen Mexico 20°37N 87°4W 114 C7
Plenty, B. of N.Z. 37°45S 177°0E 99 H14
Plessisville Canada 46°14N 71°47W 113 B12
Pleven Bulgaria 43°26N 24°37E 69 C11
Plock Poland 52°32N 19°40E 65 B10
Ploiești Romania 44°57N 26°5E 65 F14
Plovdiv Bulgaria 42°8N 24°44E 69 C11
Plymouth U.K. 50°22N 4°10W 29 G5
Plymouth Ind., U.S.A. 41°21N 86°19W 112 E4
Plymouth Wis., U.S.A. 43°45N 87°59W 112 D4
Plympton U.K. 50°23N 4°5W 29 G5
Plymstock U.K. 50°21N 4°7W 29 G5
Plynlimon = Pumlumon Fawr U.K. 52°28N 3°46W 28 C6
Plzeň Czechia 49°45N 13°22E 64 D7
Po → Italy 44°57N 12°4E 68 B5
Pocatello U.S.A. 42°52N 112°27W 110 B4
Pocklington U.K. 53°56N 0°46W 27 E7
Poços de Caldas Brazil 21°50S 46°33W 122 D1
Podgorica Montenegro 42°30N 19°19E 69 C8
Podolsk Russia 55°25N 37°30E 70 C6
Pohang S. Korea 36°1N 129°23E 79 D14
Pohnpei Micronesia 6°55N 158°10E 102 G7
Point Hope U.S.A. 68°21N 166°47W 108 C3
Point L. Canada 65°15N 113°4W 108 C8
Point Pleasant U.S.A. 38°51N 82°8W 112 F6
Pointe-à-Pitre Guadeloupe 16°15N 61°32W 115 D12
Pointe-Noire Congo 4°48S 11°53E 96 E2
Poitiers France 46°35N 0°20E 66 C4
Poitou France 46°40N 0°10W 66 C3
Pokhara Nepal 28°14N 83°58E 85 E13
Poland ■ Europe 52°0N 20°0E 65 C10
Polatsk Belarus 55°30N 28°50E 70 C4
Polden Hills U.K. 51°7N 2°50W 30 D3
Polegate U.K. 50°49N 0°16E 31 E9
Polesworth U.K. 52°37N 1°36W 27 G5
Polevskoy Russia 56°26N 60°11E 70 C11
Polokwane S. Africa 23°54S 29°25E 97 J5
Polperro U.K. 50°20N 4°32W 29 G4
Polruan U.K. 50°19N 4°38W 29 G4
Poltava Ukraine 49°35N 34°35E 71 E5
Polynesia Pac. Oc. 10°0S 162°0W 103 F11
Pomeranian Lakes Poland 53°40N 16°37E 65 B9
Ponca City U.S.A. 36°42N 97°5W 111 C7
Ponce Puerto Rico 18°1N 66°37W 115 D11
Pond Inlet Canada 72°40N 77°0W 109 B12
Ponferrada Spain 42°32N 6°35W 67 A2
Ponta Grossa Brazil 25°7S 50°10W 121 E4
Pontardawe U.K. 51°43N 3°51W 28 D6
Pontardulais U.K. 51°43N 4°3W 28 D5
Pontarlier France 46°54N 6°20E 66 C7
Pontchartrain, L. U.S.A. 30°5N 90°5W 111 D9
Pontefract U.K. 53°42N 1°18W 27 E6
Ponteland U.K. 55°3N 1°45W 26 B5
Pontevedra Spain 42°26N 8°40W 67 A1
Pontiac Ill., U.S.A. 40°53N 88°38W 112 E3
Pontiac Mich., U.S.A. 42°38N 83°18W 112 D6
Pontianak Indonesia 0°3S 109°15E 82 E3
Pontine Mts. Turkey 41°0N 36°45E 73 B6
Pontivy France 48°5N 2°58W 66 B2
Pontrilas U.K. 51°56N 2°52W 30 C3
Pontypool U.K. 51°42N 3°2W 28 D7
Pontypridd U.K. 51°36N 3°20W 28 D7
Ponziane, Ísole Italy 40°55N 12°57E 68 D5
Poole U.K. 50°43N 1°59W 30 E5
Poole Harbour U.K. 50°41N 2°0W 30 E5
Pooley Bridge U.K. 54°37N 2°48W 26 C3
Poopó, L. de Bolivia 18°30S 67°35W 120 D3
Popayán Colombia 2°27N 76°36W 120 B2
Poplar Bluff U.S.A. 36°46N 90°24W 111 C8
Popocatépetl, Volcán Mexico 19°2N 98°38W 114 D5
Porbandar India 21°44N 69°43E 84 J6
Porcupine → U.S.A. 66°34N 145°19W 108 C5
Pori Finland 61°29N 21°48E 63 E8
Porlock U.K. 51°13N 3°35W 29 E6
Port Alberni Canada 49°14N 124°50W 108 E7
Port Antonio Jamaica 18°10N 76°26W 114 a
Port Arthur Australia 43°7S 147°50E 98 J8
Port Arthur U.S.A. 29°54N 93°56W 111 E8
Port Augusta Australia 32°30S 137°50E 98 G6
Port-au-Prince Haiti 18°40N 72°20W 115 D10
Port Carlisle U.K. 54°57N 3°11W 26 C2

Port-Cartier Canada 50°2N 66°50W 109 D13
Port-de-Paix Haiti 19°50N 72°50W 115 D10
Port Elgin Canada 44°25N 81°25W 112 C7
Port Elizabeth = Gqeberha
  S. Africa 33°58S 25°40E 97 L5
Port Ellen U.K. 55°38N 6°11W 24 C3
Port Erin I. of Man 54°5N 4°45W 19 C12
Port-Gentil Gabon 0°40S 8°50E 96 E1
Port Glasgow U.K. 55°56N 4°41W 24 C6
Port Harcourt Nigeria 4°40N 7°10E 94 H7
Port Hawkesbury Canada 45°36N 61°22W 109 E13
Port Hedland Australia 20°25S 118°35E 98 E2
Port Hope Simpson Canada 52°33N 56°18W 109 D14
Port Huron U.S.A. 42°58N 82°26W 112 D6
Port Isaac U.K. 50°35N 4°50W 29 F4
Port Isaac B. U.K. 50°36N 4°50W 29 F4
Port Lincoln Australia 34°42S 135°52E 98 G6
Port Louis Mauritius 20°10S 57°30E 91 H9
Port McNeill Canada 50°35N 127°6W 108 D7
Port Macquarie Australia 31°25S 152°25E 98 G9
Port Maria Jamaica 18°22N 76°54W 114 a
Port Morant Jamaica 17°54N 76°19W 114 a
Port Moresby Papua N. G. 9°24S 147°8E 98 B8
Port Nolloth S. Africa 29°17S 16°52E 97 K3
Port of Spain Trin. & Tob. 10°40N 61°31W 120 A3
Port Pirie Australia 33°10S 138°1E 98 G6
Port Said Egypt 31°16N 32°18E 95 B12
Port St. Lucie U.S.A. 27°18N 80°21W 111 E10
Port St. Mary U.K. 54°5N 4°44W 19 C12
Port Shepstone S. Africa 30°44S 30°28E 97 L6
Port Sudan Sudan 19°32N 37°9E 95 E13
Port Talbot U.K. 51°35N 3°47W 29 D6
Port Vila Vanuatu 17°45S 168°18E 99 D12
Port Washington U.S.A. 43°23N 87°53W 112 D4
Port William U.K. 54°46N 4°35W 24 E6
Portadown U.K. 54°25N 6°27W 19 C9
Portaferry U.K. 54°23N 5°33W 19 C10
Portage U.S.A. 43°33N 89°28W 112 D3
Portage la Prairie Canada 49°58N 98°18W 108 E10
Portarlington Ireland 53°9N 7°14W 21 B8
Porth Tywyn = Burry Port
  U.K. 51°41N 4°15W 28 D5
Porthcawl U.K. 51°29N 3°42W 29 E6
Porthleven U.K. 50°4N 5°19W 29 G3
Porthmadog U.K. 52°55N 4°8W 28 B5
Portishead U.K. 51°29N 2°46W 30 D3
Portknockie U.K. 57°42N 2°51W 23 G12
Portland Maine, U.S.A. 43°39N 70°16W 113 D12
Portland Oreg., U.S.A. 45°32N 122°37W 110 A2
Portland, I. of U.K. 50°33N 2°26W 30 E4
Portland Bight Jamaica 17°52N 77°5W 114 a
Portland Bill U.K. 50°31N 2°28W 29 F9
Portland Pt. Jamaica 17°42N 77°11W 114 a
Portlaoise Ireland 53°2N 7°18W 21 B8
Portmarnock Ireland 53°26N 6°8W 21 B10
Portmore Jamaica 17°53N 76°53W 114 a
Porto Portugal 41°8N 8°40W 67 B1
Pôrto Alegre Brazil 30°5S 51°10W 121 F4
Porto Esperança Brazil 19°37S 57°29W 120 D4
Porto Nacional Brazil 10°40S 48°30W 122 B1
Porto-Novo Benin 6°23N 2°42E 94 G6
Porto Seguro Brazil 16°26S 39°5W 122 C3
Porto Tórres Italy 40°50N 8°24E 68 D3
Porto-Vecchio France 41°35N 9°16E 66 F8
Porto Velho Brazil 8°46S 63°54W 120 C3
Porton U.K. 51°8N 1°43W 30 D5
Portpatrick U.K. 54°51N 5°7W 24 E5
Portree U.K. 57°25N 6°12W 22 H5
Portrush U.K. 55°12N 6°40W 19 A8
Portslade U.K. 50°50N 0°12W 31 E8
Portsmouth U.K. 50°48N 1°6W 30 E6
Portsmouth N.H., U.S.A. 43°5N 70°45W 113 D12
Portsmouth Ohio, U.S.A. 38°44N 82°57W 112 F6
Portsmouth Va., U.S.A. 36°58N 76°23W 111 C11
Portsoy U.K. 57°41N 2°41W 23 G12
Portstewart U.K. 55°11N 6°43W 19 A8
Porttipahdan tekojärvi Finland 68°5N 26°40E 63 D9
Portugal ■ Europe 40°0N 8°0W 67 C1
Portumna Ireland 53°6N 8°14W 20 B6
Posadas Argentina 27°30S 55°50W 121 E4
Posse Brazil 14°4S 46°18W 122 B1
Postmasburg S. Africa 28°18S 23°5E 97 K4
Potchefstroom S. Africa 26°41S 27°7E 97 K5
Potenza Italy 40°38N 15°48E 68 D6
Poti Georgia 42°10N 41°38E 71 F7
Potiskum Nigeria 11°39N 11°2E 95 F8
Potomac → U.S.A. 38°0N 76°23W 112 F9
Potosí Bolivia 19°38S 65°50W 120 D3
Potsdam Germany 52°23N 13°3E 64 B7
Potsdam U.S.A. 44°40N 74°59W 113 C10
Potter Heigham U.K. 52°42N 1°34E 31 A12
Potterne U.K. 51°20N 2°0W 30 D4
Potters Bar U.K. 51°42N 0°11W 31 C8
Potterspury U.K. 52°5N 0°52W 31 B7
Pottstown U.S.A. 40°15N 75°39W 113 E10
Pottsville U.S.A. 40°41N 76°12W 113 E9
Pottuvil Sri Lanka 6°55N 81°50E 84 R12
Poughkeepsie U.S.A. 41°42N 73°56W 113 E11
Poulaphouca Res. Ireland 53°8N 6°30W 21 B10
Poulton-le-Fylde U.K. 53°51N 2°58W 27 E3
Poundstock U.K. 50°44N 4°36W 29 F4
Pouso Alegre Brazil 22°14S 45°57W 122 D1
Powder → U.S.A. 46°45N 105°26W 110 A5
Powell, L. U.S.A. 36°57N 111°29W 110 C4
Powell River Canada 49°50N 124°35W 108 E7
Powers U.S.A. 45°41N 87°32W 112 C4
Powick U.K. 52°10N 2°14W 30 B4
Powys □ U.K. 52°20N 3°20W 28 E7
Poyang Hu China 29°5N 116°20E 79 F12
Poza Rica Mexico 20°33N 97°27W 114 C5
Poznań Poland 52°25N 16°55E 65 B9
Pozzuoli Italy 40°49N 14°7E 68 D6
Prado Brazil 17°20S 39°13W 122 C3
Prague Czechia 50°4N 14°25E 64 C8
Praia Cabo Verde 15°2N 23°34W 91 E1
Praia Grande Brazil 24°0S 46°24W 122 D1
Prairie du Chien U.S.A. 43°3N 91°9W 112 D2
Prata Brazil 19°25S 48°54W 122 C1
Prato Italy 43°53N 11°6E 68 C4
Pratt U.S.A. 37°39N 98°44W 110 C7
Prawle Pt. U.K. 50°12N 3°44W 29 G6

Praya Indonesia 8°39S 116°17E 82 F5
Prayagraj India 25°25N 81°58E 85 G12
Prees U.K. 52°54N 2°40W 27 G3
Preesall U.K. 53°55N 2°57W 27 E3
Prescott Canada 44°45N 75°30W 113 C10
Prescott U.S.A. 34°33N 112°28W 110 D4
Presidencia Roque Sáenz Peña
  Argentina 26°45S 60°30W 121 E3
Presidente Prudente Brazil 22°5S 51°25W 120 E4
Presidio U.S.A. 29°34N 104°22W 110 E6
Prespa, L. N. Macedonia 40°55N 21°0E 69 D9
Presque Isle U.S.A. 46°41N 68°1W 113 B13
Prestatyn U.K. 53°20N 3°24W 28 A7
Prestbury U.K. 51°54N 2°2W 30 C4
Presteigne U.K. 52°17N 3°0W 28 C7
Preston Borders, U.K. 55°49N 2°19W 25 C11
Preston Dorset, U.K. 50°38N 2°26W 30 E4
Preston Lancs., U.K. 53°46N 2°42W 27 E3
Preston U.S.A. 42°6N 111°53W 110 B4
Prestonpans U.K. 55°58N 2°58W 25 C10
Prestwich U.K. 53°32N 2°17W 27 E4
Prestwick U.K. 55°29N 4°37W 24 D6
Pretoria S. Africa 25°44S 28°12E 97 K5
Pribilof Is. U.S.A. 57°0N 170°0W 108 D2
Price U.S.A. 39°36N 110°49W 110 C4
Prieska S. Africa 29°40S 22°42E 97 K4
Prilep N. Macedonia 41°21N 21°32E 69 D9
Prince Albert Canada 53°15N 105°50W 108 D9
Prince Albert Pen. Canada 72°30N 116°0W 108 B8
Prince Albert Sd. Canada 70°25N 115°0W 108 B8
Prince Alfred, C. Canada 74°20N 124°40W 109 B7
Prince Charles I. Canada 67°47N 76°12W 109 C12
Prince Charles Mts. Antarctica 72°0S 67°0E 55 D6
Prince Edward I. □ Canada 46°20N 63°20W 113 B16
Prince Edward Is. Ind. Oc. 46°35S 38°0E 53 G11
Prince George Canada 53°55N 122°50W 108 D7
Prince Gustaf Adolf Sea
  Canada 78°30N 107°0W 109 B9
Prince of Wales I. Canada 73°0N 99°0W 108 B10
Prince of Wales I. U.S.A. 55°47N 132°50W 108 D6
Prince Patrick I. Canada 77°0N 120°0W 109 B8
Prince Rupert Canada 54°20N 130°20W 108 D6
Prince William Sd. U.S.A. 60°40N 147°0W 108 C5
Princes Risborough U.K. 51°43N 0°49W 31 C7
Princeton Ill., U.S.A. 41°23N 89°28W 112 E3
Princeton Ind., U.S.A. 38°21N 87°34W 112 F4
Princeton Ky., U.S.A. 37°7N 87°53W 112 G4
Princeton W. Va., U.S.A. 37°22N 81°6W 112 G7
Princetown U.K. 50°33N 4°0W 29 F5
Príncipe São Tomé & Príncipe 1°37N 7°25E 90 F4
Pripet → Europe 51°20N 30°15E 65 C16
Pripet Marshes Europe 52°10N 27°10E 65 B15
Prishtinë Kosovo 42°40N 21°13E 69 C9
Privas France 44°45N 4°37E 66 D6
Prizren Kosovo 42°13N 20°45E 69 C9
Probolinggo Indonesia 7°46S 113°13E 82 F4
Probus U.K. 50°17N 4°58W 29 G4
Progreso Mexico 21°20N 89°40W 114 C7
Proprià Brazil 10°13S 36°51W 122 B3
Provence France 43°40N 5°46E 66 E6
Providence U.S.A. 41°49N 71°24W 113 E12
Providencia, I. de Caribbean 13°25N 81°26W 115 E8
Provins France 48°33N 3°15E 66 B5
Provo U.S.A. 40°14N 111°39W 110 B4
Prudhoe U.K. 54°57N 1°52W 26 C5
Prudhoe Bay U.S.A. 70°18N 148°22W 108 B5
Pruszków Poland 52°9N 20°49E 65 B11
Prut → Romania 45°28N 28°10E 65 F15
Pryluky Ukraine 50°30N 32°24E 71 D5
Przemyśl Poland 49°50N 22°45E 65 D12
Pskov Russia 57°50N 28°25E 70 C4
Puddletown U.K. 50°44N 2°20W 30 E4
Pudsey U.K. 53°47N 1°40W 27 E5
Puducherry India 11°59N 79°50E 84 P11
Puebla Mexico 19°3N 98°12W 114 D5
Pueblo U.S.A. 38°16N 104°37W 110 C6
Puerto Aisén Chile 45°27S 73°0W 121 G2
Puerto Barrios Guatemala 15°40N 88°32W 114 D7
Puerto Cabello Venezuela 10°28N 68°1W 120 A3
Puerto Cabezas Nic. 14°0N 83°30W 115 E8
Puerto Carreño Colombia 6°12N 67°22W 120 B3
Puerto Cortés Honduras 15°51N 88°0W 114 D7
Puerto Deseado Argentina 47°55S 66°0W 121 G3
Puerto La Cruz Venezuela 10°13N 64°38W 120 A3
Puerto Madryn Argentina 42°48S 65°4W 121 G3
Puerto Maldonado Peru 12°30S 69°10W 120 D3
Puerto Montt Chile 41°28S 73°0W 121 G2
Puerto Plata Dom. Rep. 19°48N 70°45W 115 D10
Puerto Princesa Phil. 9°46N 118°45E 83 C5
Puerto Rico ☑ W. Indies 18°15N 66°45W 115 D11
Puerto Rico Trench Atl. Oc. 19°50N 66°0W 115 D11
Puerto San Julián Argentina 49°18S 67°43W 121 G3
Puerto Suárez Bolivia 18°58S 57°52W 120 D4
Puerto Wilches Colombia 7°21N 73°54W 120 B2
Puertollano Spain 38°43N 4°7W 67 C3
Puffin I. Ireland 51°50N 10°24W 20 E2
Puget Sound U.S.A. 47°50N 122°30W 110 A2
Pukapuka Cook Is. 10°53S 165°49W 103 J11
Pula Croatia 44°54N 13°57E 68 B5
Pulacayo Bolivia 20°25S 66°41W 120 E3
Pulaski U.S.A. 37°3N 80°47W 111 C10
Pulborough U.K. 50°58N 0°30W 31 E8
Pulham Market U.K. 52°26N 1°13E 31 B11
Pulham St. Mary U.K. 52°26N 1°16E 31 B11
Pullman U.S.A. 46°44N 117°10W 110 A3
Pumlumon Fawr U.K. 52°28N 3°46W 28 C6
Pune India 18°29N 73°57E 84 K8
Punjab □ India 31°0N 76°0E 84 D10
Punjab □ Pakistan 32°0N 72°30E 84 E9
Puno Peru 15°55S 70°3W 120 D2
Punta Arenas Chile 53°10S 71°0W 121 H2
Puntland Somalia 9°0N 50°0E 89 F4
Punxsutawney U.S.A. 40°57N 78°59W 112 E8
Purbeck, Isle of U.K. 50°39N 1°59W 30 E5
Purfleet U.K. 51°29N 0°16E 31 D9
Puri India 19°50N 85°58E 85 K14
Purley on Thames U.K. 51°29N 1°3W 30 D6
Purnia India 25°45N 87°31E 85 G15
Puruliya India 23°17N 86°24E 85 H15
Purus → Brazil 3°42S 61°28W 120 C3
Putian China 25°23N 119°0E 79 F12

Putorana, Gory Russia 69°0N 95°0E 77 C10
Puttalam Sri Lanka 8°1N 79°55E 84 Q11
Putumayo → S. Amer. 3°7S 67°58W 120 C3
Puvirnituq Canada 60°2N 77°10W 109 C12
Puy-de-Dôme France 45°46N 2°57E 66 D5
Puyehue Chile 40°40S 72°37W 121 G2
Pwllheli U.K. 52°53N 4°25W 28 B5
Pyinmana Myanmar 19°45N 96°12E 85 K20
P'yŏngyang N. Korea 39°0N 125°30E 79 D14
Pyramid L. U.S.A. 40°1N 119°35W 110 C3
Pyrénées Europe 42°45N 0°18E 66 E4

Q
Qaanaaq Greenland 77°30N 69°10W 54 B4
Qā'emshahr Iran 36°30N 52°53E 87 B8
Qaidam Basin China 37°0N 95°0E 78 D8
Qamdo China 31°15N 97°6E 78 E8
Qandyaghash Kazakhstan 49°28N 57°25E 71 E10
Qaqortoq Greenland 60°43N 46°0W 54 C5
Qarqan He → China 39°30N 88°30E 78 C6
Qarshi Uzbekistan 38°53N 65°48E 87 B11
Qatar ■ Asia 25°30N 51°15E 87 E7
Qattâra Depression Egypt 29°30N 27°30E 95 C11
Qazvin Iran 36°15N 50°0E 86 B7
Qena Egypt 26°10N 32°43E 95 C12
Qeqertarsuaq Greenland 69°15N 53°38W 54 C5
Qeshm Iran 26°55N 56°10E 87 E9
Qianshan China 22°15N 113°31E 79 a
Qiemo China 38°8N 85°32E 78 C6
Qijiaojing China 43°28N 91°36E 78 C7
Qikiqtarjuaq Canada 67°33N 63°0W 109 C13
Qilian Shan China 38°30N 96°0E 78 D8
Qingdao China 36°5N 120°20E 79 D13
Qinghai □ China 36°0N 98°0E 78 D8
Qinhuangdao China 39°56N 119°30E 79 D12
Qinling Shandi China 33°50N 108°10E 79 E10
Qinzhou China 21°58N 108°38E 78 G10
Qiqihar China 47°26N 124°0E 79 B13
Qira China 37°0N 80°48E 78 D5
Qitai China 44°2N 89°35E 78 C6
Qitaihe China 45°48N 130°51E 79 B15
Qom Iran 34°40N 51°0E 87 C7
Qo'qon Uzbekistan 40°31N 70°56E 87 A12
Qostanay Kazakhstan 53°10N 63°35E 76 D7
Quadring U.K. 52°54N 0°10W 27 G8
Quang Ngai Vietnam 15°13N 108°58E 82 A3
Quantock Hills U.K. 51°8N 3°10W 30 D2
Quanzhou China 24°55N 118°34E 79 G12
Quaqtaq Canada 60°55N 69°40W 109 C13
Quartu Sant'Élena Italy 39°15N 9°10E 68 E3
Québec Canada 46°52N 71°13W 113 B12
Québec □ Canada 48°0N 74°0W 109 E12
Queen Charlotte Sd. Canada 51°0N 128°0W 108 D7
Queen Elizabeth Is. Canada 76°0N 95°0W 109 B10
Queen Elizabeth Land
  Antarctica 85°0S 60°0W 55 E18
Queen Maud G. Canada 68°15N 102°30W 108 C9
Queenborough U.K. 51°25N 0°46E 31 D10
Queensbury U.K. 53°46N 1°50W 27 E5
Queensferry U.K. 55°59N 3°23W 25 C9
Queensland □ Australia 22°0S 142°0E 98 E7
Queenstown N.Z. 45°1S 168°40E 99 K12
Queenstown S. Africa 31°52S 26°52E 97 L5
Queimadas Brazil 11°0S 39°38W 122 B3
Quelimane Mozam. 17°53S 36°58E 97 H7
Quendale, B. of U.K. 59°53N 1°20W 22 C15
Querétaro Mexico 20°36N 100°23W 114 C4
Quesnel Canada 53°0N 122°30W 108 D7
Quesnel L. Canada 52°30N 121°20W 108 D7
Quetta Pakistan 30°15N 66°55E 84 D5
Quetzaltenango Guatemala 14°50N 91°30W 114 E6
Quezon City Phil. 14°37N 121°2E 83 B6
Qui Nhon Vietnam 13°40N 109°13E 82 B3
Quibdó Colombia 5°42N 76°40W 120 B2
Quilán, C. Chile 43°15S 74°30W 121 G2
Quilpie Australia 26°35S 144°11E 98 F7
Quimper France 48°0N 4°9W 66 B1
Quincy Ill., U.S.A. 39°56N 91°23W 111 C8
Quincy Mass., U.S.A. 42°14N 71°0W 113 D12
Quito Ecuador 0°15S 78°35W 120 C2
Qujing China 25°32N 103°41E 78 F9
Qulsary Kazakhstan 46°59N 54°1E 71 E9
Qŭnghirot Uzbekistan 43°2N 58°50E 87 A9
Quorndon U.K. 52°46N 1°10W 27 G6
Quseir Egypt 26°7N 34°16E 95 C12
Quzhou China 28°57N 118°54E 79 F12

R
Raahe Finland 64°40N 24°28E 63 E8
Raasay U.K. 57°25N 6°4W 22 H5
Raasay, Sd. of U.K. 57°30N 6°8W 22 H5
Raba Indonesia 8°36S 118°55E 83 F5
Rabat Morocco 34°2N 6°48W 94 B4
Rabaul Papua N. G. 4°24S 152°18E 98 A9
Rābigh Si. Arabia 22°50N 39°5E 89 C2
Race, C. Canada 46°40N 53°5W 109 E14
Rach Gia Vietnam 10°5N 105°5E 82 B3
Racine U.S.A. 42°44N 87°47W 112 D4
Rackheath U.K. 52°40N 1°22E 31 A11
Radcliffe U.K. 53°34N 2°18W 27 E4
Radcliffe on Trent U.K. 52°57N 1°2W 27 G6
Radford U.S.A. 37°8N 80°34W 112 G7
Radley U.K. 51°41N 1°14W 30 C6
Radnor Forest U.K. 52°17N 3°10W 28 C7
Radom Poland 51°23N 21°12E 65 C11
Radstock U.K. 51°17N 2°26W 30 D4
Rae Bareli India 26°18N 81°20E 85 F12
Rae Isthmus Canada 66°40N 87°30W 109 C11
Rafaela Argentina 31°10S 61°30W 121 F3
Rafsanjān Iran 30°30N 56°5E 87 D9
Ragusa Italy 36°55N 14°44E 68 F6
Rahimyar Khan Pakistan 28°30N 70°25E 84 E7
Raichur India 16°10N 77°20E 84 L10
Raigarh India 21°56N 83°25E 85 J13
Rainbow Lake Canada 58°30N 119°23W 108 D8

Rainham U.K. 51°22N 0°37E 31 D10
Rainier, Mt. U.S.A. 46°52N 121°46W 110 A2
Rainworth U.K. 53°7N 1°7W 27 F6
Rainy L. Canada 48°42N 93°10W 108 E10
Raipur India 21°17N 81°45E 85 J12
Raj Nandgaon India 21°5N 81°5E 85 J12
Rajahmahendravaram India 17°1N 81°48E 85 L12
Rajapalaiyam India 9°25N 77°35E 84 Q10
Rajasthan □ India 26°45N 73°30E 84 F8
Rajkot India 22°15N 70°56E 84 H7
Rajshahi Bangla. 24°22N 88°39E 85 G16
Rakhine □ Myanmar 19°0N 94°15E 85 K18
Rakiura = Stewart I. N.Z. 46°58S 167°54E 99 K12
Raleigh U.S.A. 35°47N 78°39W 111 C11
Rame Head U.K. 50°19N 4°13W 29 G5
Ramelton Ireland 55°2N 7°39W 18 A6
Ramgarh India 23°40N 85°35E 85 H14
Ramna Stacks U.K. 60°35N 1°24W 22 A15
Râmnicu Vâlcea Romania 45°9N 24°21E 65 F13
Rampside U.K. 54°6N 3°9W 26 D2
Rampur India 28°50N 79°5E 84 E11
Ramree I. Myanmar 19°0N 93°40E 85 K19
Ramsbottom U.K. 53°38N 2°19W 27 E4
Ramsey I. of Man 54°20N 4°22W 19 C13
Ramsey Cambs., U.K. 52°27N 0°7W 31 B8
Ramsey Essex, U.K. 51°55N 1°13E 31 C11
Ramsgate U.K. 51°20N 1°25E 31 D11
Rancagua Chile 34°10S 70°50W 121 F2
Ranchi India 23°19N 85°27E 85 H14
Randalstown U.K. 54°45N 6°19W 19 B9
Randers Denmark 56°29N 10°1E 63 F6
Rangpur Bangla. 25°42N 89°22E 85 G16
Rankin Inlet Canada 62°30N 93°0W 108 C10
Rannoch U.K. 56°40N 4°20W 23 J9
Rannoch, L. U.K. 56°41N 4°20W 23 J9
Rannoch Moor U.K. 56°38N 4°48W 23 J8
Rantoul U.S.A. 40°19N 88°9W 112 E3
Rapa French Polynesia 27°35S 144°20W 103 K13
Rapallo Italy 44°21N 9°14E 68 B3
Raper, C. Canada 69°44N 67°6W 109 C13
Rapid City U.S.A. 44°5N 103°14W 110 B6
Rarotonga Cook Is. 21°30S 160°0W 103 K12
Ra's al Khaymah U.A.E. 25°50N 55°59E 87 E9
Rasht Iran 37°20N 49°40E 86 B7
Rat Islands U.S.A. 52°0N 178°0E 108 D1
Ratangarh India 28°5N 74°35E 84 E9
Rathcoole Ireland 53°17N 6°29W 21 B10
Rathdrum Ireland 52°56N 6°14W 21 C10
Rathkeale Ireland 52°32N 8°56W 20 C5
Rathlin I. U.K. 55°18N 6°14W 19 A9
Ratlam India 23°20N 75°0E 84 H9
Ratnagiri India 16°57N 73°18E 84 L8
Raton U.S.A. 36°54N 104°24W 110 C6
Rattray Hd. U.K. 57°38N 1°50W 23 G14
Rauma Finland 61°10N 21°30E 63 E8
Raunds U.K. 52°21N 0°32W 31 B7
Raurkela India 22°14N 84°50E 85 H14
Ravenglass U.K. 54°22N 3°24W 26 D2
Ravenna Italy 44°25N 12°12E 68 B5
Ravenstonedale U.K. 54°26N 2°25W 26 D4
Ravi → Pakistan 30°35N 71°49E 84 D7
Rawalpindi Pakistan 33°38N 73°8E 84 C8
Rawlins U.S.A. 41°47N 107°14W 110 B5
Rawmarsh U.K. 53°27N 1°21W 27 F6
Rawson Argentina 43°15S 65°5W 121 G3
Rawtenstall U.K. 53°42N 2°17W 27 E4
Ray, C. Canada 47°33N 59°15W 109 E14
Rayleigh U.K. 51°36N 0°37E 31 C10
Rayong Thailand 12°40N 101°20E 82 B2
Raz, Pte. du France 48°2N 4°47W 66 C1
Ré, Î. de France 46°12N 1°30W 66 C3
Reading U.K. 51°27N 0°58W 30 D7
Reading U.S.A. 40°20N 75°56W 113 E10
Reay Forest U.K. 58°22N 4°55W 23 F8
Rebiana Desert Libya 24°30N 21°0E 95 D10
Recife Brazil 8°0S 35°0W 122 A4
Reconquista Argentina 29°10S 59°45W 121 E4
Red → U.S.A. 31°1N 91°45W 111 D8
Red Bluff U.S.A. 40°11N 122°15W 110 B2
Red Deer Canada 52°20N 113°50W 108 D8
Red Dial U.K. 54°49N 3°10W 26 C2
Red L. U.S.A. 48°8N 94°45W 111 A8
Red Lake Canada 51°3N 93°49W 108 D10
Red Oak U.S.A. 41°1N 95°14W 111 B7
Red River of the North →
  N. Amer. 49°0N 97°15W 108 D10
Red Sea Asia 25°0N 36°0E 89 C2
Red Wing U.S.A. 44°34N 92°31W 111 B8
Redbridge □ U.K. 51°35N 0°7E 31 C9
Redcar U.K. 54°37N 1°4W 26 D6
Redding U.S.A. 40°35N 122°24W 110 B2
Redditch U.K. 52°18N 1°55W 30 B5
Rede → U.K. 55°9N 2°13W 26 B4
Redesmouth U.K. 55°8N 2°13W 26 B4
Redhill U.K. 51°14N 0°9W 31 D8
Redlynch U.K. 50°59N 1°41W 30 E5
Redmile U.K. 52°55N 0°48W 27 G7
Redmire U.K. 54°19N 1°55W 26 D5
Redon France 47°40N 2°6W 66 C2
Redruth U.K. 50°14N 5°14W 29 G3
Ree, L. Ireland 53°35N 8°0W 18 D6
Reedham U.K. 52°34N 1°34E 31 A12
Reepham U.K. 52°46N 1°6E 31 A11
Reese → U.S.A. 40°48N 117°4W 110 B3
Reeth U.K. 54°23N 1°56W 26 D5
Regensburg Germany 49°1N 12°6E 64 D7
Réggio di Calábria Italy 38°6N 15°39E 68 F6
Réggio nell'Emília Italy 44°43N 10°36E 68 B4
Regina Canada 50°27N 104°35W 108 D9
Reichenbach Germany 50°37N 12°17E 64 C7
Reigate U.K. 51°14N 0°12W 31 D8
Reims France 49°15N 4°1E 66 B6
Reina Adelaida, Arch. Chile 52°20S 74°0W 121 H2
Reindeer L. Canada 57°15N 102°15W 108 D9
Remanso Brazil 9°41S 42°4W 122 A2
Remscheid Germany 51°11N 7°12E 64 C4
Renfrew Canada 45°30N 76°40W 112 C9
Renfrew U.K. 55°52N 4°24W 24 C7
Rennell Solomon Is. 11°40S 160°10E 99 C11
Rennes France 48°7N 1°41W 66 B3
Reno U.S.A. 39°31N 119°48W 110 C3

Repton U.K. 52°50N 1°33W 27 G5
Republican → U.S.A. 39°4N 96°48W 111 C7
Repulse Bay Canada 66°30N 86°30W 109 C11
Resistencia Argentina 27°30S 59°0W 121 E4
Resolute Canada 74°42N 94°54W 109 B10
Resolution I. Canada 61°30N 65°0W 109 C13
Reston U.K. 55°51N 2°10W 25 C11
Retford U.K. 53°19N 0°56W 27 F7
Rethimno Greece 35°18N 24°30E 69 G11
Réunion ☑ Ind. Oc. 21°0S 56°0E 91 J9
Reus Spain 41°10N 1°5E 67 B6
Reutlingen Germany 48°29N 9°12E 64 D5
Revda Russia 56°48N 59°57E 70 C10
Revelstoke Canada 51°0N 118°10W 108 D8
Revillagigedo, Is. de Pac. Oc. 18°40N 112°0W 114 D2
Rewa India 24°33N 81°25E 85 G12
Rewari India 28°15N 76°40E 84 E10
Rexburg U.S.A. 43°49N 111°47W 110 B4
Rey Malabo Eq. Guin. 3°45N 8°50E 96 D1
Reykjavík Iceland 64°10N 21°57W 63 B1
Reynosa Mexico 26°7N 98°18W 114 B5
Rēzekne Latvia 56°30N 27°17E 63 F9
Rhayader U.K. 52°18N 3°29W 28 C7
Rheidol → U.K. 52°25N 4°5W 28 C5
Rheine Germany 52°17N 7°26E 64 B4
Rheinland-Pfalz □ Germany 50°0N 7°0E 64 C4
Rhine → Europe 51°52N 6°2E 64 C4
Rhinelander U.S.A. 45°38N 89°25W 112 C3
Rhinns Pt. U.K. 55°40N 6°29W 24 C3
Rhins, The U.K. 54°52N 5°3W 24 E5
Rhode Island □ U.S.A. 41°40N 71°30W 113 E12
Rhodes Greece 36°15N 28°10E 69 F13
Rhodope Mts. Bulgaria 41°40N 24°20E 69 D11
Rhondda U.K. 51°39N 3°31W 28 D6
Rhône → France 43°28N 4°42E 66 E6
Rhosllanerchrugog U.K. 53°1N 3°3W 28 A7
Rhossili U.K. 51°34N 4°17W 29 D5
Rhossili B. U.K. 51°32N 4°14W 29 D5
Rhum = Rùm U.K. 57°0N 6°20W 22 J5
Rhydaman = Ammanford
  U.K. 51°48N 3°59W 28 D6
Rhyl U.K. 53°20N 3°29W 28 A7
Rhymney U.K. 51°46N 3°17W 28 D7
Riau, Kepulauan □ Indonesia 0°30N 104°20E 82 D2
Ribble → U.K. 53°52N 2°25W 27 E4
Ribeirão Prêto Brazil 21°10S 47°50W 122 D1
Riberalta Bolivia 11°0S 66°0W 120 D3
Riccall U.K. 53°50N 1°3W 27 E6
Rice Lake U.S.A. 45°30N 91°44W 112 C2
Richards Bay S. Africa 28°48S 32°6E 97 K6
Richfield U.S.A. 38°46N 112°5W 110 C4
Richland U.S.A. 46°17N 119°18W 110 A3
Richland Center U.S.A. 43°21N 90°23W 112 D2
Richlands U.S.A. 37°6N 81°48W 112 G7
Richmond U.K. 54°25N 1°43W 26 D5
Richmond Ind., U.S.A. 39°50N 84°53W 112 F5
Richmond Ky., U.S.A. 37°45N 84°18W 112 G5
Richmond Va., U.S.A. 37°33N 77°27W 112 G9
Richmond-upon-Thames □
  U.K. 51°27N 0°17W 31 D8
Rickmansworth U.K. 51°38N 0°29W 31 C8
Ridgecrest U.S.A. 35°38N 117°40W 110 C3
Ridgway U.S.A. 41°25N 78°44W 112 E8
Ridsdale U.K. 55°9N 2°9W 26 B4
Rievaulx U.K. 54°16N 1°7W 26 D6
Rift Valley Africa 7°0N 30°0E 90 G7
Rīga Latvia 56°53N 24°8E 63 F8
Riga, G. of Latvia 57°40N 23°45E 63 F8
Rīgestān Afghan. 30°15N 65°0E 87 D11
Rigolet Canada 54°10N 58°23W 109 D14
Rijeka Croatia 45°20N 14°21E 68 B6
Rillington U.K. 54°9N 0°42W 26 D7
Rímini Italy 44°3N 12°33E 68 B5
Rimouski Canada 48°27N 68°30W 109 E13
Ringmer U.K. 50°53N 0°5E 31 E9
Ringwood U.K. 50°50N 1°47W 30 E5
Rio Branco Brazil 9°58S 67°49W 120 C3
Río Claro Brazil 22°19S 47°35W 122 D1
Rio Cuarto Argentina 33°10S 64°25W 121 F3
Rio de Janeiro Brazil 22°54S 43°12W 122 D2
Rio de Janeiro □ Brazil 22°50S 43°0W 122 D2
Río Gallegos Argentina 51°35S 69°15W 121 H3
Rio Grande Brazil 32°0S 52°20W 121 F4
Rio Grande de Santiago →
  Mexico 21°36N 105°26W 114 C3
Rio Grande do Norte □ Brazil 5°40S 36°0W 120 C6
Rio Grande do Sul □ Brazil 30°0S 53°0W 121 E4
Rio Largo Brazil 9°28S 35°50W 122 A4
Ríohacha Colombia 11°33N 72°55W 120 A2
Ripley Derby, U.K. 53°3N 1°24W 27 F6
Ripley N. Yorks., U.K. 54°3N 1°34W 26 D5
Ripon U.K. 54°9N 1°31W 26 D6
Ripon U.S.A. 43°51N 88°50W 112 D3
Risca U.K. 51°37N 3°5W 29 D7
Rishton U.K. 53°46N 2°26W 27 E4
Rivera Uruguay 31°0S 55°50W 121 F4
Riverhead U.S.A. 40°55N 72°40W 113 E11
Riverside U.S.A. 33°59N 117°22W 110 D3
Riverton U.S.A. 43°2N 108°23W 110 B5
Riviera = Côte d'Azur France 43°25N 7°10E 66 E7
Rivière-du-Loup Canada 47°50N 69°30W 109 E13
Riyadh Si. Arabia 24°41N 46°42E 86 E6
Rize Turkey 41°0N 40°30E 71 F7
Rizhao China 35°25N 119°30E 79 D12
Roade U.K. 52°9N 0°53W 31 B7
Roanne France 46°3N 4°4E 66 C6
Roanoke → U.S.A. 37°16N 79°56W 112 G8
Roanoke → U.S.A. 35°57N 76°42W 111 C11
Roberton U.K. 55°25N 2°54W 25 D10
Roberval Canada 48°32N 72°15W 109 E12
Robin Hood's Bay U.K. 54°27N 0°32W 26 D7
Robstown U.S.A. 27°47N 97°40W 110 E7
Roca, C. da Portugal 38°40N 9°31W 67 C1
Rocester U.K. 52°57N 1°50W 27 G5
Rocha Uruguay 34°30S 54°25W 121 F4
Rochdale U.K. 53°38N 2°9W 27 E4
Roche U.K. 50°24N 4°50W 29 G4
Rochefort France 45°56N 0°57W 66 D3
Rochester Medway, U.K. 51°23N 0°31E 31 D10
Rochester Northumberland,
  U.K. 55°17N 2°17W 26 B4

Rochester

São Gonçalo

Rochester Ind., U.S.A. 41°4N 86°13W **112 E4**
Rochester Minn., U.S.A. 44°1N 92°28W **111 B8**
Rochester N.H., U.S.A. 43°18N 70°59W **113 D12**
Rochester N.Y., U.S.A. 43°10N 77°37W **112 D9**
Rochford U.K. 51°34N 0°43E **31 C10**
Rock Hill U.S.A. 34°56N 81°1W **111 D10**
Rock Island U.S.A. 41°30N 90°34W **112 E2**
Rock Springs U.S.A. 41°35N 109°14W **110 B5**
Rockall Atl. Oc. 57°37N 13°42W **56 D3**
Rockcliffe U.K. 54°57N 3°0W **26 C3**
Rockford U.S.A. 42°16N 89°6W **112 D3**
Rockhampton Australia 23°22S 150°32E **98 E9**
Rockingham U.K. 52°31N 0°43W **31 A7**
Rockingham Forest U.K. 52°29N 0°42W **31 B7**
Rockland U.S.A. 44°6N 69°7W **113 C13**
Rocky Mount U.S.A. 35°57N 77°48W **111 C11**
Rocky Mts. N. Amer. 49°0N 115°0W **108 D7**
Rodez France 44°21N 2°33E **66 D5**
Roding → U.K. 51°31N 0°6E **31 C9**
Rodrigues Ind. Oc. 19°45S 63°20E **53 E13**
Roe → U.K. 55°6N 6°59W **19 A8**
Roes Welcome Sd. Canada 65°0N 87°0W **109 C11**
Rogans Seat U.K. 54°26N 2°7W **26 D4**
Rogate U.K. 51°0N 0°50W **31 D7**
Rogers City U.S.A. 45°25N 83°49W **112 C6**
Rohri Pakistan 27°45N 68°51E **84 F6**
Rojo, C. Mexico 21°33N 97°20W **114 C5**
Rolla U.S.A. 37°57N 91°46W **111 C8**
Roma Australia 26°32S 148°49E **98 F8**
Romaine → Canada 50°18N 63°47W **109 D13**
Romania ■ Europe 46°0N 25°0E **65 F12**
Romans-sur-Isère France 45°3N 5°3E **66 D6**
Rome Italy 41°54N 12°28E **68 D5**
Rome Ga., U.S.A. 34°15N 85°10W **111 D9**
Rome N.Y., U.S.A. 43°13N 75°27W **113 D10**
Romney U.K. 39°21N 78°45W **112 F8**
Romney Marsh U.K. 51°2N 0°54E **31 D10**
Romorantin-Lanthenay France 47°21N 1°45E **66 C4**
Romsey U.K. 51°0N 1°29W **30 D5**
Rona U.K. 57°34N 5°59W **22 G6**
Roncador, Serra do Brazil 12°30S 52°30W **120 D4**
Rondônia □ Brazil 11°0S 63°0W **120 D3**
Rondonópolis Brazil 16°28S 54°38W **120 D4**
Ronge, L. la Canada 55°6N 105°17W **108 D9**
Ronne Ice Shelf Antarctica 77°30S 60°0W **55 D18**
Roosevelt → Brazil 7°35S 60°20W **120 C3**
Roosevelt I. Antarctica 79°30S 162°0W **55 D12**
Ropsley U.K. 52°54N 0°30W **27 F8**
Roquetas de Mar Spain 36°46N 2°36W **67 D4**
Roraima □ Brazil 2°0N 61°30W **120 B3**
Roraima, Mt. Venezuela 5°10N 60°40W **120 B3**
Rosario Argentina 33°0S 60°40W **121 F3**
Rosario Mexico 22°58N 105°53W **114 C3**
Rosario de la Frontera Argentina 25°50S 65°0W **121 E3**
Roscommon Ireland 53°38N 8°11W **18 D5**
Roscommon □ Ireland 53°49N 8°23W **18 D5**
Roscrea Ireland 52°57N 7°49W **20 C7**
Roseau Dominica 15°17N 61°24W **115 D12**
Roseburg U.S.A. 43°13N 123°20W **110 B2**
Rosedale Abbey U.K. 54°21N 0°52W **26 D7**
Rosehearty U.K. 57°42N 2°7W **23 G13**
Rosenheim Germany 47°51N 12°7E **64 E7**
Rosetown Canada 51°35N 107°59W **108 D9**
Roseville U.S.A. 38°45N 121°17W **110 C2**
Roslavl Russia 53°57N 32°55E **70 D5**
Ross Ice Shelf Antarctica 80°0S 180°0E **55 E12**
Ross-on-Wye U.K. 51°54N 2°34W **30 C3**
Ross River Canada 62°30N 131°30W **108 C6**
Ross Sea Antarctica 74°0S 178°0E **55 D11**
Rossall Pt. U.K. 53°55N 3°3W **27 E2**
Rossan Pt. Ireland 54°42N 8°47W **18 B4**
Rosses, The Ireland 55°2N 8°20W **18 A5**
Rossignol L. Canada 44°12N 65°10W **113 C15**
Rosslare Ireland 52°17N 6°24W **21 D10**
Rosslare Harbour Ireland 52°15N 6°20W **21 D10**
Rossosh Russia 50°15N 39°28E **71 D6**
Rostock Germany 54°5N 12°8E **64 A7**
Rostov Russia 47°15N 39°45E **71 E6**
Roswell Ga., U.S.A. 34°2N 84°22W **111 D10**
Roswell N. Mex., U.S.A. 33°24N 104°32W **110 D6**
Rote Indonesia 10°50S 123°0E **83 F6**
Rothbury U.K. 55°19N 1°58W **26 B5**
Rothbury Forest U.K. 55°19N 1°50W **26 B5**
Rother → U.K. 50°59N 0°45E **31 E10**
Rotherham U.K. 53°26N 1°20W **27 F6**
Rothes U.K. 57°32N 3°13W **23 G11**
Rothesay U.K. 55°50N 5°3W **24 C5**
Rothwell N. Northants., U.K. 52°25N 0°48W **31 B7**
Rothwell W. Yorks., U.K. 53°45N 1°28W **27 E6**
Rotorua N.Z. 38°9S 176°16E **99 H14**
Rotterdam Neths. 51°55N 4°30E **64 C3**
Rottingdean U.K. 50°48N 0°4W **31 E8**
Rotuma Fiji 12°25S 177°5E **99 C14**
Roubaix France 50°40N 3°10E **66 A5**
Rouen France 49°27N 1°4E **66 B4**
Round Mt. Australia 30°26S 152°16E **98 G9**
Rousay U.K. 59°10N 3°2W **23 D11**
Roussillon France 42°30N 2°35E **66 E5**
Rouyn-Noranda Canada 48°20N 79°0W **109 E12**
Rovaniemi Finland 66°29N 25°41E **63 D9**
Rovigo Italy 45°4N 11°47E **68 B4**
Rowanburn U.K. 55°5N 2°55W **25 D10**
Roxas Phil. 11°36N 122°49E **83 B6**
Roxburgh U.K. 55°35N 2°28W **25 C11**
Roxby U.K. 53°38N 0°38W **27 E7**
Royal Canal Ireland 53°30N 7°13W **21 B8**
Royal Leamington Spa U.K. 52°18N 1°31W **30 B5**
Royal Tunbridge Wells U.K. 51°7N 0°16E **31 D9**
Royal Wootton Bassett U.K. 51°32N 1°54W **30 C5**
Royale, Isle U.S.A. 48°0N 88°54W **112 B3**
Royan France 45°37N 1°2W **66 D3**
Royston U.K. 52°3N 0°0 **31 B8**
Royton U.K. 53°34N 2°8W **27 E4**
Rub' al Khālī Si. Arabia 19°0N 48°0E **89 D4**
Rubery U.K. 52°24N 2°1W **30 B4**
Rubh a' Mhail U.K. 55°56N 6°8W **24 C3**
Rubha Hunish U.K. 57°42N 6°20E **22 G5**
Rubtsovsk Russia 51°30N 81°10E **78 D10**
Ruby L. U.S.A. 40°10N 115°28W **110 B3**

Rudston U.K. 54°6N 0°20W **26 D8**
Rufford U.K. 53°38N 2°50W **27 E3**
Rufiji → Tanzania 7°50S 39°15E **96 F7**
Rugby U.K. 52°23N 1°16W **30 B6**
Rugeley U.K. 52°46N 1°55W **27 G5**
Rügen Germany 54°22N 13°24E **64 A7**
Ruhr → Germany 51°27N 6°43E **64 C4**
Ruki → Dem. Rep. of the Congo 0°5N 18°17E **96 E3**
Rukwa, L. Tanzania 8°0S 32°20E **96 F6**
Rùm U.K. 57°0N 6°20W **22 J5**
Rùm, Sound of U.K. 56°55N 6°14W **22 J5**
Rumford U.S.A. 44°33N 70°33W **113 C12**
Runaway Bay Jamaica 18°27N 77°20W **114 a**
Runcorn U.K. 53°21N 2°44W **27 F3**
Rundu Namibia 17°52S 19°43E **97 H3**
Rungwe Tanzania 9°11S 33°32E **90 G7**
Ruo Shui → China 41°0N 100°16E **78 D6**
Ruoqiang China 38°55N 88°10E **78 D6**
Rupert U.S.A. 42°37N 113°41W **110 B4**
Rupert → Canada 51°29N 78°45W **109 D12**
Ruse Bulgaria 43°48N 25°59E **69 C12**
Rush Ireland 53°31N 6°6W **21 A10**
Rushden U.K. 52°18N 0°35W **31 B7**
Rushville Ill., U.S.A. 40°7N 90°34W **112 E1**
Rushville Ind., U.S.A. 39°37N 85°27W **112 F5**
Ruskington U.K. 53°3N 0°22W **27 F8**
Russellville U.S.A. 35°17N 93°8W **111 C8**
Russia ■ Eurasia 62°0N 105°0E **77 C11**
Rustavi Georgia 41°30N 45°0E **71 F8**
Rustenburg S. Africa 25°41S 27°14E **97 K5**
Rutherglen U.K. 55°49N 4°13W **24 C7**
Ruthin U.K. 53°6N 3°19W **28 A7**
Ruthwell U.K. 55°0N 3°25W **25 E9**
Rutog China 33°27N 79°42E **78 E4**
Ruvuma → Tanzania 10°29S 40°28E **96 G8**
Ruwenzori Africa 0°30N 29°55E **96 D5**
Rwanda ■ Africa 2°0S 30°0E **96 E5**
Ryan, L. U.K. 55°0N 5°2W **24 E5**
Ryazan Russia 54°40N 39°40E **70 D6**
Rybachi Pen. Russia 69°43N 32°0E **70 A5**
Rybinsk Russia 58°5N 38°50E **70 C6**
Rybinsk Res. Russia 58°30N 38°25E **70 C6**
Rydal U.K. 54°27N 2°59W **26 D3**
Ryde U.K. 50°43N 1°9W **30 E6**
Rye U.K. 50°57N 0°45E **31 E10**
Rye → U.K. 54°11N 0°44W **26 D7**
Rye Bay U.K. 50°52N 0°49E **31 E10**
Ryhope U.K. 54°53N 1°21W **26 C6**
Ryton U.K. 52°22N 1°25W **30 B6**
Ryukyu Is. Japan 26°0N 126°0E **79 F14**
Rzeszów Poland 50°5N 21°58E **65 C11**
Rzhev Russia 56°20N 34°20E **70 C5**

S

Saale → Germany 51°56N 11°54E **64 C6**
Saar → Europe 49°41N 6°32E **64 D4**
Saarbrücken Germany 49°14N 6°59E **64 D4**
Saaremaa Estonia 58°30N 22°30E **63 F8**
Sabadell Spain 41°28N 2°7E **67 B7**
Sabah □ Malaysia 6°0N 117°0E **82 C5**
Sabhā Libya 27°9N 14°29E **95 C8**
Sabinas Mexico 27°51N 101°7W **114 B4**
Sabinas Hidalgo Mexico 26°30N 100°10W **114 B4**
Sabine → U.S.A. 29°59N 93°47W **111 E8**
Sable, C. Canada 43°29N 65°38W **113 D15**
Sable, C. U.S.A. 25°9N 81°8W **111 E10**
Sable I. Canada 44°0N 60°0W **109 E14**
Sachsen □ Germany 50°55N 13°10E **64 C7**
Sachsen-Anhalt □ Germany 52°0N 12°0E **64 C7**
Saco U.S.A. 43°30N 70°27W **113 D12**
Sacramento U.S.A. 38°35N 121°29W **110 C2**
Sacramento → U.S.A. 38°3N 121°56W **110 C2**
Sacramento Mts. U.S.A. 32°30N 105°30W **110 D5**
Sado Japan 38°0N 138°25E **81 D6**
Safford U.S.A. 32°50N 109°43W **110 D5**
Saffron Walden U.K. 52°1N 0°16E **31 B9**
Safi Morocco 32°18N 9°20W **94 B4**
Saga Japan 33°15N 130°16E **81 C2**
Sagaing Myanmar 21°52N 95°59E **85 J19**
Sagar India 23°50N 78°44E **84 H11**
Saginaw U.S.A. 43°26N 83°56W **112 D6**
Saginaw B. U.S.A. 43°50N 83°40W **112 D6**
Sagua la Grande Cuba 22°50N 80°10W **115 C8**
Saguenay → Canada 48°22N 71°0W **113 A12**
Sagunt Spain 39°42N 0°18W **67 C5**
Sahara Africa 23°0N 5°0E **94 D6**
Saharanpur India 29°58N 77°33E **84 E10**
Sahel Africa 16°0N 5°0E **94 E5**
Sahiwal Pakistan 30°45N 73°8E **84 D8**
Saidpur Bangla. 25°48N 89°0E **85 G16**
St. Abb's Head U.K. 55°55N 2°8W **25 C11**
St. Agnes Corn., U.K. 50°19N 5°13W **29 G3**
St. Agnes Corn., U.K. 49°54N 6°21W **29 H1**
St. Agnes Hd. U.K. 50°19N 5°15W **29 G3**
St. Albans U.K. 51°45N 0°19W **31 C8**
St. Albans Vt., U.S.A. 44°49N 73°5W **113 C11**
St. Albans W. Va., U.S.A. 38°23N 81°50W **112 F7**
St. Alban's Head U.K. 50°34N 2°4W **30 E4**
St. Andrews U.K. 56°20N 2°47W **25 B10**
St. Ann's U.K. 55°14N 3°28W **25 D9**
St. Ann's Bay Jamaica 18°26N 77°12W **114 a**
St. Anthony Canada 51°22N 55°35W **109 D14**
St. Asaph U.K. 53°15N 3°27W **28 A7**
St-Augustin Canada 51°13N 58°38W **109 D14**
St. Augustine U.S.A. 29°54N 81°19W **111 E10**
St. Austell U.K. 50°20N 4°47W **29 G4**
St. Bees U.K. 54°30N 3°35W **26 C1**
St. Bees Hd. U.K. 54°31N 3°38W **26 C1**
St. Blazey U.K. 50°22N 4°43W **29 G4**
St. Brides B. U.K. 51°49N 5°9W **28 D3**
St-Brieuc France 48°30N 2°46W **66 B2**
St. Buryan U.K. 50°4N 5°37W **29 G2**
St. Catharines Canada 43°10N 79°15W **112 D8**
St. Catherine's Pt. U.K. 50°34N 1°18W **30 E6**
St. Charles U.S.A. 38°47N 90°29W **112 F2**
St. Clair, L. N. Amer. 42°27N 82°39W **112 D6**
St. Clears U.K. 51°49N 4°31W **28 D4**
St. Cloud U.S.A. 45°34N 94°10W **111 A8**
St. Columb Major U.K. 50°26N 4°58W **29 G4**
St. Croix U.S. Virgin Is. 17°45N 64°45W **115 D12**

St. David's U.K. 51°53N 5°16W **28 D3**
St. David's Head U.K. 51°54N 5°19W **28 D3**
St-Denis France 48°56N 2°20E **66 B5**
St-Dizier France 48°38N 4°56E **66 B6**
St. Dominick U.K. 50°29N 4°16W **29 G3**
St. Elias, Mt. U.S.A. 60°18N 140°56W **108 C5**
St. Elias Mts. N. Amer. 60°33N 139°28W **108 C6**
St. Enoder U.K. 50°22N 4°59W **29 G4**
St. Erth U.K. 50°9N 5°26W **29 G3**
St-Étienne France 45°27N 4°22E **66 D6**
St-Félicien Canada 48°40N 72°25W **113 A11**
St-Flour France 45°2N 3°6E **66 D5**
St. Gallen Switz. 47°26N 9°22E **64 E5**
St-Gaudens France 43°6N 0°44E **66 E4**
St. George U.S.A. 37°6N 113°35W **110 C4**
St-Georges Canada 46°8N 70°40W **113 B12**
St. George's Grenada 12°5N 61°43W **115 E12**
St. George's Channel Europe 52°0N 6°0W **21 E11**
St. Germans U.K. 50°23N 4°19W **29 G5**
St. Helena Atl. Oc. 15°58S 5°42W **52 E9**
St. Helens U.K. 53°27N 2°44W **27 F3**
St. Helens, Mt. U.S.A. 46°12N 122°12W **110 A2**
St. Helier U.K. 49°10N 2°7W **29 J9**
St-Hyacinthe Canada 45°40N 72°58W **109 E12**
St. Ignace U.S.A. 45°52N 84°44W **112 C5**
St. Issey U.K. 50°30N 4°57W **29 G4**
St. Ives Cambs., U.K. 52°20N 0°4W **31 B8**
St. Ives Corn., U.K. 50°12N 5°30W **29 G3**
St. Ives B. U.K. 50°13N 5°27W **29 G3**
St-Jean, L. Canada 48°40N 72°0W **113 A12**
St-Jérôme Canada 45°47N 74°0W **113 C11**
St. John Canada 45°20N 66°8W **113 C12**
St. John's Antigua & B. 17°6N 61°51W **115 D12**
St. John's Canada 47°35N 52°40W **109 E14**
St. Johns U.S.A. 43°0N 84°33W **112 D5**
St. Johns → U.S.A. 30°24N 81°24W **111 D10**
St. Johns Chapel U.K. 54°44N 2°10W **26 C4**
St. John's Pt. Ireland 54°34N 8°27W **18 B5**
St. Johnsbury U.S.A. 44°25N 72°1W **113 C11**
St. Joseph Mich., U.S.A. 42°6N 86°29W **112 D4**
St. Joseph Mo., U.S.A. 39°46N 94°50W **111 C8**
St. Joseph, L. Canada 51°10N 90°35W **109 D10**
St. Just U.K. 50°7N 5°42W **29 G2**
St. Keverne U.K. 50°3N 5°6W **29 G3**
St. Kilda U.K. 57°49N 8°34W **22 b**
St. Kitts & Nevis ■ W. Indies 17°20N 62°40W **115 D12**
St. Lawrence → Canada 49°30N 66°0W **109 E13**
St. Lawrence, Gulf of Canada 48°25N 62°0W **109 E13**
St. Lawrence I. U.S.A. 63°30N 170°30W **108 C3**
St. Levan U.K. 50°2N 5°41W **29 G2**
St-Lô France 49°7N 1°5W **66 B3**
St-Louis Senegal 16°8N 16°27W **94 E2**
St. Louis U.S.A. 38°37N 90°11W **112 F2**
St. Lucia ■ W. Indies 14°0N 60°57W **114 b**
St. Mabyn U.K. 50°35N 4°47W **29 F4**
St. Magnus B. U.K. 60°25N 1°35W **22 B14**
St-Malo France 48°39N 2°1W **66 B2**
St-Marc Haiti 19°10N 72°41W **115 D10**
St. Margaret's-at-Cliffe U.K. 51°9N 1°23E **31 D11**
St-Martin □ W. Indies 18°5N 63°5W **115 D12**
St. Martins Barbados 13°5N 59°28W **114 c**
St. Martin's U.K. 49°58N 6°17W **29 H1**
St. Mary Bourne U.K. 51°15N 1°24W **30 D6**
St. Mary's Corn., U.K. 49°55N 6°18W **29 H1**
St. Mary's Orkney, U.K. 58°54N 2°54W **23 E12**
St. Marys U.S.A. 41°26N 78°34W **112 E8**
St. Mary's Sd. U.K. 49°54N 6°20W **29 H1**
St. Matthew I. U.S.A. 60°24N 172°42W **108 C2**
St. Mawes U.K. 50°10N 5°2W **29 G3**
St. Merryn U.K. 50°32N 5°1W **29 F3**
St. Michael's Mount U.K. 50°7N 5°29W **29 G3**
St. Minver U.K. 50°33N 4°53W **29 F4**
St. Moritz Switz. 46°30N 9°51E **64 E5**
St-Nazaire France 47°17N 2°12W **66 C2**
St. Neots U.K. 52°14N 0°15W **31 B8**
St-Omer France 50°45N 2°15E **66 A5**
St. Osyth U.K. 51°47N 1°5E **31 C11**
St. Paul U.S.A. 44°56N 93°5W **111 B8**
St. Paul, Î. Ind. Oc. 38°55S 77°34E **53 F13**
St. Peter Port U.K. 49°26N 2°33W **29 J8**
St. Petersburg Russia 59°55N 30°20E **70 C5**
St. Petersburg U.S.A. 27°46N 82°40W **111 E10**
St-Pierre-et-Miquelon ☑ N. Amer. 46°55N 56°10W **109 E14**
St-Quentin France 49°50N 3°16E **66 B5**
St. Stephen Canada 45°16N 67°17W **113 C14**
St. Stephen U.K. 50°21N 4°53W **29 G4**
St. Teath U.K. 50°35N 4°45W **29 F4**
St. Thomas Canada 42°45N 81°10W **112 D7**
St-Tropez France 43°17N 6°38E **66 E7**
St. Tudy U.K. 50°33N 4°45W **29 F4**
St. Vincent, G. Australia 35°0S 138°0E **98 G6**
St. Vincent & the Grenadines ■ W. Indies 13°0N 61°10W **115 E12**
Ste. Genevieve U.S.A. 37°59N 90°2W **112 G2**
Ste-Marie Canada 46°26N 71°0W **113 B12**
Saintes France 45°45N 0°37W **66 D3**
Saintfield U.K. 54°28N 5°49W **19 C10**
Saintonge France 45°40N 0°50W **66 D3**
Saipan N. Marianas 15°12N 145°45E **102 F6**
Saitama Japan 35°54N 139°38E **81 F7**
Sajama Bolivia 18°7S 69°0W **120 D3**
Sakākah Si. Arabia 30°0N 40°8E **86 D5**
Sakakawea, L. U.S.A. 47°30N 101°25W **110 A6**
Sakarya Turkey 40°48N 30°25E **71 F5**
Sakata Japan 38°55N 139°50E **81 D6**
Sakha □ Russia 66°0N 130°0E **77 C13**
Sakhalin Russia 51°0N 143°0E **77 D15**
Sakurajima Japan 31°35N 130°39E **81 H2**
Sala Sweden 59°58N 16°35E **63 F7**
Sala-y-Gómez Pac. Oc. 26°28S 105°28W **103 K17**
Salado → La Pampa, Argentina 37°30S 67°0W **121 F3**
Salado → Santa Fe, Argentina 31°40S 60°41W **121 F3**
Salālah Oman 16°56N 53°59E **89 D5**
Salamanca Spain 40°58N 5°39W **67 B3**
Salamanca U.S.A. 42°10N 78°43W **112 D8**
Salar de Uyuni Bolivia 20°30S 67°45W **120 E3**
Salavat Russia 53°21N 55°55E **70 D10**
Salaverry Peru 8°15S 79°0W **120 C2**

Salayar Indonesia 6°7S 120°30E **83 F6**
Salcombe U.K. 50°14N 3°47W **29 G6**
Saldanha S. Africa 33°0S 17°58E **97 L3**
Sale Australia 38°6S 147°6E **98 H8**
Sale U.K. 53°26N 2°19W **27 F4**
Salekhard Russia 66°30N 66°35E **76 C7**
Salem India 11°40N 78°11E **84 P11**
Salem Ind., U.S.A. 38°36N 86°6W **112 F4**
Salem Mass., U.S.A. 42°31N 70°53W **113 D12**
Salem Ohio, U.S.A. 40°54N 80°52W **112 E7**
Salem Oreg., U.S.A. 44°56N 123°2W **110 B2**
Salem Va., U.S.A. 37°18N 80°3W **112 G7**
Salerno Italy 40°41N 14°47E **68 D6**
Salford U.K. 53°30N 2°18W **27 F4**
Salford Priors U.K. 52°10N 1°53W **30 B5**
Salida U.S.A. 38°32N 106°0W **110 C5**
Salina U.S.A. 38°50N 97°37W **110 C7**
Salina Cruz Mexico 16°10N 95°12W **114 D5**
Salinas Ecuador 2°10S 80°58W **120 C1**
Salinas U.S.A. 36°40N 121°39W **110 C2**
Salinas → U.S.A. 36°45N 121°48W **110 C2**
Salinas Grandes Argentina 30°0S 65°0W **121 E3**
Salisbury U.K. 51°4N 1°47W **30 D5**
Salisbury U.S.A. 38°22N 75°36W **113 F10**
Salisbury I. Canada 63°30N 77°0W **109 C12**
Salisbury Plain U.K. 51°14N 1°55W **30 D5**
Salmon U.S.A. 45°11N 113°54W **110 A4**
Salmon → U.S.A. 45°51N 116°47W **110 A3**
Salmon Arm Canada 50°40N 119°15W **108 D8**
Salmon River Mts. U.S.A. 45°0N 114°30W **110 B4**
Salon-de-Provence France 43°39N 5°6E **66 E6**
Salsk Russia 46°28N 41°30E **71 E7**
Salt → U.S.A. 33°23N 112°19W **110 D4**
Salt Lake City U.S.A. 40°45N 111°53W **110 B4**
Salta Argentina 24°57S 65°25W **121 E3**
Saltash U.K. 50°24N 4°14W **29 G5**
Saltburn-by-the-Sea U.K. 54°35N 0°58W **26 C7**
Saltcoats U.K. 55°38N 4°47W **24 D6**
Saltee Is. Ireland 52°7N 6°37W **21 D9**
Saltfleet U.K. 53°25N 0°11E **27 F9**
Saltfleetby U.K. 53°23N 0°10E **27 F9**
Saltillo Mexico 25°25N 101°0W **114 B4**
Salton Sea U.S.A. 33°15N 115°45W **110 D3**
Saltwood U.K. 51°4N 1°2E **31 D11**
Salvador Brazil 13°0S 38°30E **122 B3**
Salween → Myanmar 16°31N 97°37E **78 G8**
Salyan Azerbaijan 39°33N 48°59E **71 G8**
Salzburg Austria 47°48N 13°2E **64 E7**
Salzgitter Germany 52°9N 10°19E **64 B6**
Samar Phil. 12°0N 125°0E **83 B7**
Samara Russia 53°8N 50°6E **70 D9**
Samarinda Indonesia 0°30S 117°9E **82 E5**
Samarqand Uzbekistan 39°40N 66°55E **87 B11**
Sambalpur India 21°28N 84°4E **85 J14**
Sambhal India 28°35N 78°37E **84 E11**
Sambhar India 26°52N 75°6E **84 F9**
Samoa ■ Pac. Oc. 14°0S 172°0W **99 C16**
Samos Greece 37°45N 26°50E **69 F12**
Samothraki Greece 40°28N 25°28E **69 D11**
Sampford Courtenay U.K. 50°47N 3°58W **29 F6**
Samsun Turkey 41°15N 36°22E **71 F6**
Samui, Ko Thailand 9°30N 100°0E **82 C2**
San → Poland 50°45N 21°51E **65 C11**
San Ambrosio Pac. Oc. 26°28S 79°53W **103 K20**
San Andrés, I. de Caribbean 12°42N 81°46W **115 E8**
San Andres Mts. U.S.A. 33°0N 106°30W **110 D5**
San Andrés Tuxtla Mexico 18°27N 95°13W **114 D5**
San Angelo U.S.A. 31°28N 100°26W **110 D6**
San Antonio Chile 33°40S 71°40W **121 F2**
San Antonio U.S.A. 29°25N 98°29W **110 E7**
San Antonio → U.S.A. 28°30N 96°54W **111 E7**
San Antonio Oeste Argentina 40°40S 65°0W **121 G3**
San Bernardino U.S.A. 34°7N 117°19W **110 D3**
San Bernardino Str. Phil. 13°0N 124°10E **83 B6**
San Bernardo Chile 33°40S 70°50W **121 F2**
San Blas, C. U.S.A. 29°40N 85°21W **111 E9**
San Carlos Phil. 10°29N 123°25E **83 B6**
San Carlos de Bariloche Argentina 41°10S 71°25W **121 G2**
San Carlos de Bolívar Argentina 36°15S 61°6W **121 F3**
San Cristóbal Argentina 30°20S 61°10W **121 F3**
San Cristóbal Solomon Is. 10°30S 161°0E **99 C12**
San Cristóbal Venezuela 7°46N 72°14W **120 B2**
San Cristóbal de las Casas Mexico 16°45N 92°38W **114 D6**
San Diego U.S.A. 32°42N 117°9W **110 D3**
San Felipe Venezuela 10°20N 68°44W **120 A3**
San Félix Pac. Oc. 26°23S 80°0W **103 K20**
San Fernando Chile 34°30S 71°0W **121 F2**
San Fernando Spain 36°28N 6°17W **67 D2**
San Fernando de Apure Venezuela 7°54N 67°15W **120 B3**
San Francisco U.S.A. 37°46N 122°23W **110 C2**
San Francisco, C. de Colombia 6°18N 77°29W **117 C3**
San Francisco de Macorís Dom. Rep. 19°19N 70°15W **115 D10**
San Gottardo, P. del Switz. 46°33N 8°33E **64 E5**
San Ignacio Bolivia 16°20S 60°55W **120 D3**
San Joaquín → U.S.A. 38°4N 121°51W **110 C2**
San Jorge, G. Argentina 46°0S 66°0W **121 G3**
San José Costa Rica 9°55N 84°2W **115 F8**
San Jose Phil. 12°27N 121°4E **83 B6**
San Jose U.S.A. 37°20N 121°53W **110 C2**
San José de Chiquitos Bolivia 17°53S 60°50W **120 D3**
San José de Jáchal Argentina 30°15S 68°46W **121 F3**
San José del Cabo Mexico 23°3N 109°41W **114 C3**
San Juan Argentina 31°30S 68°30W **121 F3**
San Juan Puerto Rico 18°28N 66°7W **115 D11**
San Juan → Nic. 10°56N 83°42W **115 E8**
San Juan → U.S.A. 37°16N 110°26W **110 C4**
San Juan de la Maguana Dom. Rep. 18°49N 71°12W **115 D10**
San Juan de los Morros Venezuela 9°55N 67°21W **120 B3**
San Juan Mts. U.S.A. 37°30N 107°0W **110 C5**
San Lorenzo, Mte. Argentina 47°40S 72°20W **121 G2**
San Lucas, C. Mexico 22°52N 109°53W **114 C3**

San Luis Argentina 33°20S 66°20W **121 F3**
San Luis Obispo U.S.A. 35°17N 120°40W **110 C2**
San Luis Potosí Mexico 22°9N 100°59W **114 C4**
San Marcos U.S.A. 29°53N 97°56W **110 E7**
San Marino ■ Europe 43°56N 12°25E **68 C5**
San Matías, G. Argentina 41°30S 64°0W **121 G3**
San Miguel El Salv. 13°30N 88°12W **114 E7**
San Miguel de Tucumán Argentina 26°50S 65°20W **121 E3**
San Nicolás Argentina 33°25S 60°10W **121 F3**
San Pedro Côte d'Ivoire 4°50N 6°33W **94 H4**
San Pedro de las Colonias Mexico 25°45N 102°59W **114 B4**
San Pedro de Macoris Dom. Rep. 18°30N 69°18W **115 D11**
San Pedro Sula Honduras 15°30N 88°0W **114 D7**
San Pietro Italy 39°8N 8°17E **68 E3**
San Rafael Argentina 34°40S 68°21W **121 F3**
San Remo Italy 43°49N 7°46E **68 C2**
San Salvador El Salv. 13°40N 89°10W **114 E7**
San Salvador The Bahamas 24°0N 74°30W **115 C10**
San Salvador de Jujuy Argentina 24°10S 64°48W **121 E3**
San Severo Italy 41°41N 15°23E **68 D6**
San Valentin, Mte. Chile 46°30S 73°30W **121 G2**
Sana' = Sanaa Yemen 15°27N 44°12E **89 D3**
Sanaa Yemen 15°27N 44°12E **89 D3**
Sanaga → Cameroon 3°35N 9°38E **96 D1**
Sanandaj Iran 35°18N 47°1E **86 C6**
Sancti Spíritus Cuba 21°52N 79°33W **115 C9**
Sancy, Puy de France 45°32N 2°50E **66 D5**
Sandakan Malaysia 5°53N 118°4E **82 C5**
Sanday U.K. 59°16N 2°31W **23 D12**
Sandbach U.K. 53°9N 2°21W **27 F4**
Sandgate U.K. 51°4N 1°10E **31 D11**
Sandhurst U.K. 51°21N 0°48W **31 D7**
Sandown U.K. 50°40N 1°10W **30 E6**
Sandpoint U.S.A. 48°17N 116°33W **110 A3**
Sandray U.K. 56°53N 7°31W **22 J2**
Sandringham U.K. 52°51N 0°31E **31 A10**
Sandusky U.S.A. 41°27N 82°42W **112 E6**
Sandwich U.K. 51°16N 1°21E **31 D11**
Sandy U.K. 52°8N 0°17W **31 B8**
Sandy U.S.A. 40°32N 111°50W **110 B4**
Sandy L. Canada 53°2N 93°0W **108 D10**
Sanford, Mt. U.S.A. 62°13N 144°8W **108 C5**
Sangihe, Pulau Indonesia 3°35N 125°30E **83 D7**
Sangli India 16°55N 74°33E **84 L9**
Sangre de Cristo Mts. U.S.A. 37°30N 105°20W **110 C5**
Sanikiluaq Canada 56°32N 79°14W **109 D12**
Sankt Pölten Austria 48°12N 15°38E **64 D8**
Sankuru → Dem. Rep. of the Congo 4°17S 20°25E **96 E4**
Sanliurfa Turkey 37°12N 38°50E **71 G6**
Sanlúcar de Barrameda Spain 36°46N 6°21W **67 D2**
Sanmenxia China 34°47N 111°12E **79 E11**
Sanming China 26°15N 117°40E **79 F12**
Sanndraigh = Sandray U.K. 56°53N 7°31W **22 J2**
Sanquhar U.K. 55°22N 3°54W **25 D8**
Sant Feliu de Guíxols Spain 41°45N 3°1E **67 B7**
Santa Ana El Salv. 14°0N 89°31W **114 E7**
Santa Ana U.S.A. 33°46N 117°52W **110 D3**
Santa Barbara U.S.A. 34°25N 119°42W **110 D3**
Santa Clara Cuba 22°20N 80°0W **115 C9**
Santa Clarita U.S.A. 34°24N 118°33W **110 D3**
Santa Coloma de Gramenet Spain 41°27N 2°13E **67 B7**
Santa Cruz Bolivia 17°43S 63°10W **120 D3**
Santa Cruz U.S.A. 36°58N 122°1W **110 C2**
Santa Cruz de Tenerife Canary Is. 28°28N 16°15W **94 C2**
Santa Cruz Is. Solomon Is. 10°30S 166°0E **99 C12**
Santa Cruz Mts. Jamaica 17°58N 77°43W **114 a**
Santa Fé Argentina 31°35S 60°41W **121 F3**
Santa Fe U.S.A. 35°41N 105°57W **110 C5**
Santa Inés, I. Chile 54°0S 73°0W **121 H2**
Santa Isabel Solomon Is. 8°0S 159°0E **99 B10**
Santa Maria Brazil 29°40S 53°48W **121 E4**
Santa Maria U.S.A. 34°57N 120°26W **110 D2**
Santa Maria → Mexico 31°0N 107°14W **114 A3**
Santa Marta Colombia 11°15N 74°13W **120 A2**
Santa Marta, Sierra Nevada de Colombia 10°55N 73°50W **120 A2**
Santa Rosa Argentina 36°40S 64°17W **121 F3**
Santa Rosa U.S.A. 38°26N 122°43W **110 C2**
Santai China 31°5N 104°58E **78 E9**
Santana do Livramento Brazil 30°55S 55°30W **121 F4**
Santander Spain 43°27N 3°51W **67 A4**
Santanilla, Is. Honduras 17°22N 83°57W **115 D8**
Santarém Brazil 2°25S 54°42W **120 C4**
Santarém Portugal 39°12N 8°42W **67 C1**
Santiago Chile 33°26S 70°40W **121 F2**
Santiago de Compostela Spain 42°52N 8°37W **67 A1**
Santiago de Cuba Cuba 20°0N 75°49W **115 D9**
Santiago de los Caballeros Dom. Rep. 19°30N 70°40W **115 D10**
Santiago del Estero Argentina 27°50S 64°15W **121 E3**
Santo Amaro Brazil 12°30S 38°43W **122 B3**
Santo André Brazil 23°39S 46°29W **122 D1**
Sant' Antioco Italy 39°4N 8°27E **68 E3**
Santo Antônio de Jesus Brazil 12°58S 39°16W **122 B3**
Santo Domingo Dom. Rep. 18°30N 69°59W **115 D11**
Santo Domingo de los Colorados Ecuador 0°15S 79°9W **120 C2**
Santorini Greece 36°23N 25°27E **69 F11**
Santos Brazil 24°0S 46°20W **122 D1**
Santos Dumont Brazil 22°55S 43°10W **122 D2**
Sanxiang China 22°21N 113°25E **79 a**
Sanya China 18°14N 109°29E **79 H10**
São Bernardo do Campo Brazil 23°45S 46°34W **122 D1**
São Borja Brazil 28°39S 56°0W **121 E4**
São Caitano Brazil 8°21S 36°6W **122 A3**
São Carlos Brazil 22°0S 47°50W **122 D1**
São Francisco → Brazil 10°30S 36°24W **122 A3**
São Gonçalo Brazil 22°48S 43°5W **122 D2**

São João da Boa Vista

São João da Boa Vista Brazil 22°0S 46°52W 122 D1
São João de Meriti Brazil 22°48S 43°22W 122 D2
São João del Rei Brazil 21°8S 44°15W 122 D2
São João do Piauí Brazil 8°21S 42°15W 122 A2
São José do Rio Preto Brazil 20°50S 49°20W 122 D1
São José dos Campos Brazil 23°7S 45°52W 122 D1
São Lourenço Brazil 22°7S 45°3W 122 D1
São Luís Brazil 2°39S 44°15W 120 C5
São Marcos → Brazil 18°15S 47°37W 122 C1
São Marcos, B. de Brazil 2°0S 44°0W 120 C5
São Mateus Brazil 18°44S 39°50W 122 C3
São Paulo Brazil 23°32S 46°38W 122 D1
São Paulo □ Brazil 22°0S 49°0W 120 E5
São Roque, C. de Brazil 5°30S 35°16W 120 C6
São Sebastião do Paraíso Brazil 20°54S 46°59W 122 D1
São Tomé São Tomé & Príncipe 0°10N 6°39E 90 F4
São Tomé & Príncipe ■ Africa 0°12N 6°39E 91 F4
São Vicente Brazil 23°57S 46°23W 122 D1
São Vicente, C. de Portugal 37°0N 9°0W 67 D1
Saône → France 45°44N 4°50E 66 D6
Sapele Nigeria 5°50N 5°40E 94 G7
Sapporo Japan 43°0N 141°21E 81 B7
Saqqez Iran 36°15N 46°20E 86 B6
Sar-e Pol Afghan. 36°10N 66°0E 87 B11
Sarāburī Thailand 14°30N 100°55E 82 B2
Sarajevo Bos.-H. 43°52N 18°26E 69 C8
Saranac Lakes U.S.A. 44°20N 74°28W 113 C10
Saransk Russia 54°10N 45°10E 70 D8
Sarapul Russia 56°28N 53°48E 70 C9
Sarasota U.S.A. 27°20N 82°32W 111 E10
Saratoga Springs U.S.A. 43°5N 73°47W 113 D11
Saratov Russia 51°30N 46°2E 71 D8
Sarawak □ Malaysia 2°0N 113°0E 82 D4
Sarda → India 27°21N 81°23E 85 F12
Sardinia □ Italy 40°0N 9°0E 68 D3
Sargasso Sea Atl. Oc. 27°0N 72°0W 104 G13
Sargodha Pakistan 32°10N 72°40E 84 C8
Sarh Chad 9°5N 18°23E 95 G9
Sārī Iran 36°30N 53°4E 87 B8
Sariwon N. Korea 38°31N 125°46E 79 D14
Sark U.K. 49°25N 2°22W 29 J9
Sarlat-la-Canéda France 44°54N 1°13E 66 D4
Sarmiento Argentina 45°35S 69°5W 121 G3
Sarnia Canada 42°58N 82°23W 109 E11
Sarqan Kazakhstan 45°24N 79°55E 78 B4
Sarreguemines France 49°5N 7°4E 66 B7
Sarthe → France 47°33N 0°31W 66 C3
Sasebo Japan 33°10N 129°43E 81 G1
Saskatchewan □ Canada 54°40N 106°0W 108 D9
Saskatchewan → Canada 53°37N 100°40W 108 D9
Saskatoon Canada 52°10N 106°38W 108 D9
Sássari Italy 40°43N 8°34E 68 D3
Sassnitz Germany 54°29N 13°39E 64 A7
Satmala Hills Maharashtra, India 20°15N 74°40E 84 J9
Satmala Hills Telangana, India 19°45N 78°45E 84 K11
Satna India 24°35N 80°50E 85 G12
Satpura Ra. India 21°25N 76°10E 84 J10
Satu Mare Romania 47°46N 22°55E 65 E12
Saudi Arabia ■ Asia 26°0N 44°0E 89 B3
Sault Ste. Marie Canada 46°30N 84°20W 112 B5
Saumur France 47°15N 0°5W 66 C3
Saundersfoot U.K. 51°43N 4°42W 28 D4
Saurimo Angola 9°40S 20°12E 96 F4
Sava → Serbia 44°50N 20°26E 69 B9
Savai'i Samoa 13°28S 172°24W 99 C16
Savanna-la-Mar Jamaica 18°10N 78°10W 114 a
Savannah U.S.A. 32°5N 81°6W 111 D10
Savannah → U.S.A. 32°2N 80°53W 111 D10
Savannakhet Laos 16°30N 104°49E 82 A2
Savoie □ France 45°26N 6°25E 66 D7
Savona Italy 44°17N 8°30E 68 B3
Sawatch Range U.S.A. 39°0N 106°30W 110 C5
Sawbridgeworth U.K. 51°48N 0°9E 31 C9
Sawel Mt. U.K. 54°50N 7°2W 19 B7
Sawston U.K. 52°8N 0°10E 31 B9
Sawtry U.K. 52°27N 0°17W 31 B8
Sawu Indonesia 10°35S 121°50E 83 F6
Sawu Sea Indonesia 9°30S 121°50E 83 F6
Saxilby U.K. 53°16N 0°38W 27 F7
Saxlingham Nethergate U.K. 52°32N 1°18E 31 A11
Saxmundham U.K. 52°13N 1°30E 31 B12
Saxony = Sachsen □ Germany 50°55N 13°10E 64 C7
Sayan Mts. Russia 54°0N 96°0E 77 D10
Saydā Lebanon 33°35N 35°25E 86 C3
Sayre U.S.A. 41°59N 76°32W 112 E9
Sázava → Czechia 49°53N 14°24E 64 D8
Scafell Pike U.K. 54°27N 3°14W 26 D2
Scalby U.K. 54°18N 0°26W 26 D8
Scalloway U.K. 60°9N 1°17W 22 B15
Scalpay Highl., U.K. 57°18N 6°0W 22 H6
Scalpay W. Isles, U.K. 57°52N 6°40W 22 H4
Scamblesby U.K. 53°17N 0°5W 27 F8
Scandicci Italy 43°45N 11°11E 68 C4
Scandinavia Europe 64°0N 12°0E 56 C8
Scapa Flow U.K. 58°53N 3°3W 23 E11
Scarba U.K. 56°11N 5°43W 24 B4
Scarborough U.K. 54°17N 0°24W 26 D8
Scariff I. Ireland 51°44N 10°15W 20 E2
Scarning U.K. 52°41N 0°54E 31 A10
Scarp U.K. 58°1N 7°8W 22 F3
Schaffhausen Switz. 47°42N 8°39E 64 E5
Schelde → Belgium 51°15N 4°16E 64 C3
Schenectady U.S.A. 42°49N 73°57W 113 D11
Schiehallion U.K. 56°40N 4°6W 24 A7
Schleswig Germany 54°31N 9°34E 64 A5
Schleswig-Holstein □ Germany 54°30N 9°30E 64 A5
Schreiber Canada 48°45N 87°20W 112 A4
Schwäbische Alb Germany 48°20N 9°30E 64 D5
Schwarzwald Germany 48°30N 8°20E 64 D5
Schwerin Germany 53°36N 11°22E 64 B6
Schwyz Switz. 47°2N 8°39E 64 E5
Scilly Is. U.K. 49°56N 6°22W 29 H1
Scioto → U.S.A. 38°44N 83°1W 112 F6
Scole U.K. 52°22N 1°10E 31 B11
Scone U.K. 56°25N 3°24W 25 B9
Scopwick U.K. 53°8N 0°24W 27 F8
Scotia Sea Antarctica 56°5S 56°0W 55 B18
Scotland □ U.K. 57°0N 0°0W 62 C5
Scott I. Antarctica 67°0S 179°0W 55 C11

Scottish Borders □ U.K. 55°35N 2°50W 25 C10
Scottsbluff U.S.A. 41°52N 103°40W 110 B6
Scottsburg U.S.A. 38°41N 85°47W 112 F5
Scrabster U.K. 58°36N 3°33W 23 E10
Scranton U.S.A. 41°25N 75°40W 113 E10
Scremerston U.K. 55°44N 2°0W 26 A5
Scunthorpe U.K. 53°36N 0°39W 27 E7
Scutari Albania 42°4N 19°32E 69 C8
Scutari Turkey 41°1N 29°0E 86 A2
Seaford U.K. 50°47N 0°7E 31 E9
Seaford U.S.A. 38°39N 75°37W 113 F10
Seaforth, L. U.K. 57°52N 6°36W 22 G4
Seaham U.K. 54°50N 1°20W 26 C6
Seahouses U.K. 55°34N 1°39W 26 A5
Seal → Canada 59°4N 94°48W 108 D10
Seamer U.K. 54°15N 0°26W 26 D8
Seascale U.K. 54°24N 3°29W 26 D2
Seaton Cumb., U.K. 54°40N 3°31W 26 C1
Seaton Devon, U.K. 50°42N 3°5W 29 F7
Seaton Delaval U.K. 55°5N 1°33W 26 B5
Seattle U.S.A. 47°36N 122°19W 110 A2
Sebastián Vizcaíno, B. Mexico 28°0N 114°30W 114 B2
Şebinkarahisar Turkey 40°22N 38°28E 71 F6
Sedalia U.S.A. 38°42N 93°14W 111 C8
Sedan France 49°43N 4°57E 66 B6
Sedbergh U.K. 54°20N 2°31W 26 D3
Sedgefield U.K. 54°40N 1°26W 26 C6
Seend U.K. 51°21N 2°4W 30 D4
Segesta Italy 37°56N 12°50E 68 F5
Ségou Mali 13°30N 6°16W 94 F4
Segovia Spain 40°57N 4°10W 67 B3
Séguéla Côte d'Ivoire 7°55N 6°40W 94 G4
Sehore India 23°10N 77°5E 84 H10
Seil U.K. 56°18N 5°38W 24 B4
Seine → France 49°26N 0°26E 66 B4
Sekondi-Takoradi Ghana 4°58N 1°45W 94 H5
Selborne U.K. 51°6N 0°56W 31 D7
Selby U.K. 53°47N 1°5W 27 E6
Selebi-Phikwe Botswana 21°58S 27°48E 97 J5
Selenge Mörön → Asia 52°16N 106°16E 78 A10
Selkirk Canada 50°10N 96°55W 108 D10
Selkirk U.K. 55°33N 2°50W 25 C10
Selkirk Mts. Canada 51°15N 117°40W 108 D8
Sellafield U.K. 54°25N 3°29W 26 D2
Selma U.S.A. 32°25N 87°1W 111 D9
Selsey U.K. 50°44N 0°47W 31 E7
Selsey Bill U.K. 50°43N 0°47W 31 E7
Selvas Brazil 6°30S 67°0W 120 C3
Selwyn L. Canada 60°0N 104°30W 108 C9
Selwyn Mts. Canada 63°0N 130°0W 108 C6
Semarang Indonesia 7°0S 110°26E 82 F4
Semey Kazakhstan 50°30N 80°10E 76 D9
Semnān Iran 35°40N 53°23E 87 C8
Sena Madureira Brazil 9°5S 68°45W 120 C3
Sendai Japan 38°15N 140°53E 81 D7
Seneca L. U.S.A. 42°40N 76°54W 112 D9
Senegal ■ W. Afr. 14°30N 14°30W 94 F3
Sénégal → W. Afr. 15°48N 16°32W 94 E2
Senegambia Africa 12°45N 12°0W 90 E2
Senhor-do-Bonfim Brazil 10°30S 40°10W 122 B2
Senja Norway 69°25N 17°30E 63 D7
Senkaku Is. E. China Sea 25°45N 123°30E 79 F13
Senlis France 49°13N 2°35E 66 B5
Sennen U.K. 50°4N 5°42W 29 G2
Sens France 48°11N 3°15E 66 B5
Seoul S. Korea 37°31N 126°58E 79 D14
Seph → U.K. 54°18N 1°9W 26 D6
Sept-Îles Canada 50°13N 66°22W 109 D13
Seram Indonesia 3°10S 129°0E 83 E7
Seram Sea Indonesia 2°30S 128°30E 83 E7
Serang Indonesia 6°8S 106°10E 82 F3
Serbia ■ Europe 43°20N 20°0E 69 B9
Serdar Turkmenistan 39°4N 56°23E 87 B9
Seremban Malaysia 2°43N 101°53E 82 D2
Serengeti Plain Tanzania 2°40S 35°0E 96 E7
Sergipe □ Brazil 10°30S 37°30W 122 B3
Sergiyev Posad Russia 56°20N 38°10E 70 C6
Serhetabat Turkmenistan 35°20N 62°18E 87 C10
Serifos Greece 37°9N 24°30E 69 F11
Serov Russia 59°29N 60°35E 76 C11
Serowe Botswana 22°25S 26°43E 97 J5
Serpukhov Russia 54°55N 37°28E 70 D6
Serra Brazil 20°7S 40°18W 122 D2
Serra de Mesa, Barragem de Brazil 14°30S 48°30W 122 B1
Serrinha Brazil 11°39S 39°0W 122 B3
Sète France 43°25N 3°42E 66 E5
Sete Lagoas Brazil 19°27S 44°16W 122 C2
Sétif Algeria 36°9N 5°26E 94 A7
Settat Morocco 33°0N 7°40W 94 B4
Settle U.K. 54°5N 2°16W 26 D4
Setúbal Portugal 38°30N 8°58W 67 C1
Setúbal, B. de Portugal 38°40N 8°56W 67 C1
Seul, Lac Canada 50°20N 92°30W 108 D10
Seul, L. Armenia 40°30N 45°20E 71 F8
Sevastopol Ukraine 44°35N 33°30E 71 F5
Sevenoaks U.K. 51°16N 0°11E 31 D9
Severn → Canada 56°2N 87°36W 109 D11
Severn → U.K. 51°35N 2°40W 30 C3
Severn Beach U.K. 51°33N 2°39W 30 C3
Severn Stoke U.K. 52°6N 2°12W 30 B4
Severnaya Zemlya Russia 79°0N 100°0E 77 B10
Severodvinsk Russia 64°27N 39°58E 70 B6
Severomorsk Russia 69°5N 33°27E 70 A5
Sevier → U.S.A. 39°4N 113°6W 110 C4
Sevier L. U.S.A. 38°54N 113°9W 110 C4
Seville Spain 37°23N 5°58W 67 D2
Seward U.S.A. 60°7N 149°27W 108 C5
Seward Peninsula U.S.A. 65°30N 166°0W 108 C3
Seychelles ■ Ind. Oc. 5°0S 56°0E 91 G9
Seyðisfjörður Iceland 65°16N 13°57W 63 A3
Seydişehir Turkey 37°25N 31°51E 71 G5
Seymour U.S.A. 38°58N 85°53W 112 F5
Sfântu Gheorghe Romania 45°52N 25°48E 65 F13
Sfax Tunisia 34°49N 10°48E 95 B8
Sha Tin China 22°23N 114°12E 79 a
Shaanxi □ China 35°0N 109°0E 79 D10
Shabeelle → Somalia 2°0N 44°0E 89 G3
Shache China 38°20N 77°10E 78 D4
Shaftesbury U.K. 51°0N 2°11W 30 D4

Shahjahanpur India 27°54N 79°57E 84 F11
Shajing China 22°44N 113°48E 79 a
Shakhty Russia 47°40N 40°16E 71 E7
Shaki Nigeria 8°41N 3°21E 94 G6
Shaldon U.K. 50°32N 3°31W 29 F6
Shaluli Shan China 30°40N 99°55E 78 E8
Shamo, L. Ethiopia 5°45N 37°30E 89 F2
Shan □ Myanmar 21°30N 98°30E 85 J21
Shandong □ China 36°0N 118°0E 79 D12
Shandong Pen. China 37°0N 121°0E 79 D13
Shanghai China 31°15N 121°26E 79 E13
Shangqiu China 34°26N 115°36E 79 E12
Shangrao China 28°25N 117°59E 79 F12
Shanklin U.K. 50°38N 1°11W 30 E6
Shannon → Ireland 52°35N 9°30W 20 C4
Shannon ✈ (SNN) Ireland 52°42N 8°57W 20 C5
Shannon, Mouth of the Ireland 52°30N 9°55W 20 D3
Shantou China 23°18N 116°40E 79 G12
Shanxi □ China 37°0N 112°0E 79 D11
Shaoguan China 24°48N 113°35E 79 G11
Shaoxing China 30°0N 120°35E 79 E13
Shaoyang China 27°14N 111°25E 79 F11
Shap U.K. 54°32N 2°40W 26 C3
Shapinsay U.K. 59°3N 2°51W 23 D12
Shaqra' Si. Arabia 25°15N 45°16E 86 E6
Sharjah U.A.E. 25°23N 55°26E 87 E8
Shark B. Australia 25°30S 113°32E 98 F1
Sharm el Sheikh Egypt 27°53N 34°18E 86 E3
Sharon U.S.A. 41°14N 80°31W 112 E7
Sharpness U.K. 51°43N 2°28W 30 C4
Sharya Russia 58°22N 45°20E 70 C8
Shasta, Mt. U.S.A. 41°25N 122°12W 110 B2
Shawano U.S.A. 44°47N 88°36W 112 C3
Shawbury U.K. 52°48N 2°39W 27 G3
Shawinigan Canada 46°35N 72°50W 109 E12
Shawnee U.S.A. 35°20N 96°55W 111 C7
Shebbear U.K. 50°51N 4°15W 29 F5
Sheboygan U.S.A. 43°46N 87°45W 112 D4
Sheelin, L. Ireland 53°48N 7°20W 18 D7
Sheep Haven Ireland 55°11N 7°52W 18 A6
Sheerness U.K. 51°26N 0°47E 31 D10
Sheffield U.K. 53°23N 1°28W 27 F6
Shefford U.K. 52°2N 0°20W 31 B8
Shehy Mts. Ireland 51°47N 9°15W 20 E4
Shekou China 22°30N 113°55E 79 a
Shelburne Canada 43°47N 65°20W 113 D15
Shelby U.S.A. 48°30N 111°51W 110 A4
Shelbyville Ill., U.S.A. 39°24N 88°48W 112 F3
Shelbyville Ind., U.S.A. 39°31N 85°47W 112 F5
Shelikhov G. Russia 59°30N 157°0E 77 D16
Shenandoah U.S.A. 40°49N 76°12W 113 E9
Shenandoah → U.S.A. 39°19N 77°44W 112 F9
Shendi Sudan 16°46N 33°22E 95 E12
Shenfield U.K. 51°38N 0°22E 31 C9
Shenyang China 41°48N 123°27E 79 C13
Shenzhen China 22°32N 114°5E 79 a
Shenzhen Bao'an Int. ✈ (SZX) China 22°41N 113°49E 79 a
Shenzhen Wan China 22°27N 113°55E 79 a
Shepparton Australia 36°23S 145°26E 98 H8
Sheppey, I. of U.K. 51°25N 0°48E 31 D10
Shepshed U.K. 52°47N 1°18W 27 G6
Shepton Mallet U.K. 51°11N 2°33W 30 D3
Sherborne U.K. 50°57N 2°31W 30 E3
Sherborne St. John U.K. 51°17N 1°7W 30 D6
Sherbrooke Canada 45°28N 71°57W 113 C12
Sherburn U.K. 54°11N 0°32W 26 D7
Sherburn in Elmet U.K. 53°48N 1°15W 27 E6
Shere U.K. 51°13N 0°27W 31 D8
Sherfield English U.K. 51°1N 1°34W 30 D5
Sheridan U.S.A. 44°48N 106°58W 110 B5
Sheriff Hutton U.K. 54°5N 1°0W 26 D7
Sheringham U.K. 52°56N 1°13E 31 A11
Sherkin I. Ireland 51°28N 9°26W 20 F4
Sherman U.S.A. 33°38N 96°36W 111 D7
Sherston U.K. 51°34N 2°14W 30 C4
Sherwood Forest U.K. 53°6N 1°7W 27 F6
Shetland □ U.K. 60°30N 1°30W 22 B15
Shetland Is. U.K. 60°30N 1°30W 22 B15
Sheung Shui China 22°31N 114°7E 79 a
Sheyenne → U.S.A. 47°2N 96°50W 111 A7
Shiant Is. U.K. 57°54N 6°22E 22 G3
Shibām Yemen 15°59N 48°36E 89 D4
Shiel, L. U.K. 56°48N 5°34W 22 J8
Shifnal U.K. 52°39N 2°23W 27 G4
Shihezi China 44°15N 86°2E 78 C6
Shijiazhuang China 38°2N 114°28E 79 D11
Shikarpur Pakistan 27°57N 68°39E 84 F6
Shikoku □ Japan 33°30N 133°30E 81 G3
Shilbottle U.K. 55°22N 1°40W 26 B5
Shildon U.K. 54°38N 1°38W 26 C5
Shiliguri India 26°45N 88°25E 85 F16
Shillelagh Ireland 52°45N 6°32W 21 C9
Shillingstone U.K. 50°53N 2°15W 30 E4
Shillong India 25°35N 91°53E 85 G17
Shimla India 31°2N 77°9E 84 D10
Shimonoseki Japan 33°58N 130°55E 81 G2
Shin, L. U.K. 58°5N 4°30W 23 F8
Shinyanga Tanzania 3°45S 33°27E 96 E6
Shipdham U.K. 52°38N 0°54E 31 A10
Shiphoirt, L. = Seaforth, L. U.K. 57°52N 6°36W 22 G4
Shipley U.K. 53°50N 1°47W 27 E5
Shipston-on-Stour U.K. 52°3N 1°36W 30 B5
Shipton under Wychwood U.K. 51°51N 1°36W 30 C5
Shiraz Iran 29°42N 52°30E 87 D8
Shire → Africa 17°42S 35°19E 97 H7
Shirebrook U.K. 53°12N 1°13W 27 F6
Shivamogga India 13°57N 75°32E 84 N9
Shivpuri India 25°26N 77°42E 84 G10
Shizuishan China 39°15N 106°50E 78 D10
Shizuoka Japan 34°57N 138°24E 81 F6
Shoeburyness U.K. 51°31N 0°49E 31 C10
Shoreham-by-Sea U.K. 50°50N 0°16W 31 E8
Shreveport U.S.A. 32°31N 93°45W 111 D8
Shrewsbury U.K. 52°43N 2°45W 27 G3
Shrewton U.K. 51°12N 1°54W 30 D5
Shrirampur India 22°44N 88°21E 85 H16
Shrivenham U.K. 51°36N 1°38W 30 C5
Shropshire □ U.K. 52°36N 2°45W 27 G3

Shuangliao China 43°29N 123°30E 79 C13
Shuangyashan China 46°28N 131°5E 79 B15
Shule China 39°25N 76°3E 78 D4
Shule He → China 40°20N 92°50E 78 C7
Shumagin Is. U.S.A. 55°7N 160°30W 108 D4
Shumen Bulgaria 43°18N 26°55E 69 C12
Shunan Japan 34°3N 131°50E 81 F2
Shuqrā' Yemen 13°22N 45°44E 89 E4
Shwebo Myanmar 22°30N 95°45E 85 H19
Shymkent Kazakhstan 42°18N 69°36E 87 A12
Si Kiang = Xi Jiang → China 22°5N 113°20E 79 G11
Siahan Range Pakistan 27°30N 64°40E 84 F4
Sialkot Pakistan 32°32N 74°30E 84 C9
Šiauliai Lithuania 55°56N 23°15E 63 F8
Šibenik Croatia 43°48N 15°54E 68 C6
Siberia Russia 60°0N 100°0E 72 B11
Siberut Indonesia 1°30S 99°0E 82 E1
Sibi Pakistan 29°30N 67°54E 84 E5
Sibiu Romania 45°45N 24°9E 65 F13
Sible Hedingham U.K. 51°59N 0°37E 31 C10
Sibolga Indonesia 1°42N 98°45E 82 D1
Sibsey U.K. 53°2N 0°1E 27 F9
Sibu Malaysia 2°18N 111°49E 82 D4
Sibuyan Sea Phil. 12°30N 122°20E 83 B6
Sichuan □ China 30°30N 103°0E 78 E9
Sicily Italy 37°30N 14°30E 68 F6
Sicily, Str. of Medit. S. 37°35N 11°56E 68 F4
Sicuani Peru 14°21S 71°10W 120 D2
Sidbury U.K. 50°42N 3°14W 29 F7
Sidi-bel-Abbès Algeria 35°13N 0°39W 94 A5
Sidlaw Hills U.K. 56°32N 3°2W 25 B9
Sidlesham U.K. 50°47N 0°47W 31 E7
Sidmouth U.K. 50°40N 3°15W 29 F7
Sidney Nebr., U.S.A. 41°8N 102°59W 110 B6
Sidney Ohio, U.S.A. 40°17N 84°9W 112 E5
Sidra = Surt Libya 31°11N 16°39E 95 B9
Siedlce Poland 52°10N 22°20E 65 B12
Siegen Germany 50°51N 8°0E 64 C5
Siena Italy 43°19N 11°21E 68 C4
Sierra Blanca Peak U.S.A. 33°23N 105°49W 110 D5
Sierra Leone ■ W. Afr. 9°0N 12°0W 94 G3
Sierra Nevada Spain 37°3N 3°15W 67 D4
Sierra Nevada U.S.A. 39°0N 120°30W 110 C3
Sierra Vista U.S.A. 31°33N 110°18W 110 D4
Sifnos Greece 37°0N 24°45E 69 F11
Sighty Crag U.K. 55°7N 2°38W 26 B3
Sikar India 27°33N 75°10E 84 F9
Sikasso Mali 11°18N 5°35W 94 F4
Sikeston U.S.A. 36°53N 89°35W 112 G3
Sikhote Alin Ra. Russia 45°0N 136°0E 77 E14
Sikkim □ India 27°50N 88°30E 85 F16
Silesia Poland 51°0N 16°30E 64 C9
Silifke Turkey 36°22N 33°58E 71 G5
Siling Co China 31°50N 89°20E 78 E6
Silloth U.K. 54°52N 3°23W 26 C2
Silsden U.K. 53°55N 1°55W 27 E5
Silver City U.S.A. 32°46N 108°17W 110 D5
Silvermine Mts. Ireland 52°47N 8°15W 20 C6
Silverstone U.K. 52°5N 1°2W 30 B6
Silverton U.K. 50°49N 3°29W 29 F7
Simao China 22°47N 101°5E 78 G9
Simcoe, L. Canada 44°25N 79°20W 112 C8
Simeulue Indonesia 2°45N 95°45E 82 D1
Simferopol Ukraine 44°55N 34°3E 71 F5
Simi Greece 36°35N 27°50E 69 F12
Simonsbath U.K. 51°8N 3°46W 29 E6
Simonside U.K. 55°17N 1°59W 26 B5
Simplonpass Switz. 46°15N 8°3E 64 E5
Simpson Desert Australia 25°0S 137°0E 98 F6
Simpson Pen. Canada 68°34N 88°45W 109 C11
Sinai Egypt 29°0N 34°0E 95 C12
Sincelejo Colombia 9°18N 75°24W 120 B2
Sinclair's B. U.K. 58°31N 3°5W 23 F11
Sind Sagar Doab Pakistan 32°0N 71°30E 84 D7
Sindh □ Pakistan 26°0N 69°0E 84 G6
Sines Portugal 37°56N 8°51W 67 D1
Singapore ■ Asia 1°17N 103°51E 82 D2
Singaraja Indonesia 8°7S 115°6E 82 F5
Singida Tanzania 4°49S 34°48E 96 E6
Singkawang Indonesia 1°0N 108°57E 82 D3
Singleton U.K. 50°55N 0°46W 31 E7
Sinkiang □ China 42°0N 86°0E 78 C6
Sinop Turkey 42°1N 35°11E 71 F6
Sintra Portugal 38°47N 9°25W 67 C1
Sion Switz. 46°14N 7°20E 64 E4
Sion Mills U.K. 54°48N 7°29W 18 B7
Sioux City U.S.A. 42°30N 96°24W 111 B7
Sioux Falls U.S.A. 43°33N 96°44W 111 B7
Sioux Lookout Canada 50°10N 91°50W 108 D10
Siping China 43°8N 124°21E 79 C13
Sir James MacBrien, Mt. Canada 62°7N 127°41W 108 C7
Siracusa Italy 37°4N 15°17E 68 F6
Sirajganj Bangla. 24°25N 89°47E 85 G16
Sīrjān Iran 29°30N 55°45E 87 D8
Sirsa India 29°33N 75°4E 84 E9
Sirte = Surt Libya 31°11N 16°39E 95 B9
Sīstān Asia 30°50N 61°0E 87 D10
Sitapur India 27°38N 80°45E 85 F12
Sitges Spain 41°17N 1°47E 67 B6
Sitka U.S.A. 57°3N 135°20W 108 D6
Sittingbourne U.K. 51°21N 0°45E 31 D10
Sittwe Myanmar 20°18N 92°45E 85 J18
Sivas Turkey 39°43N 36°58E 71 G6
Sivrihisar Turkey 39°30N 31°58E 71 G5
Siwa Egypt 29°11N 25°31E 95 C11
Siwalik Range Nepal 28°0N 83°0E 85 F13
Siwan India 26°13N 84°21E 85 F14
Six Cross Roads Barbados 13°7N 59°28W 114 c
Sixmilebridge Ireland 52°44N 8°46W 20 C5
Sizewell U.K. 52°12N 1°37E 31 B12
Sjælland Denmark 55°30N 11°30E 63 F6
Skagerrak Denmark 57°30N 9°0E 63 F5
Skagway U.S.A. 59°28N 135°19W 108 D6
Skeena → Canada 54°9N 130°5W 108 D6
Skegness U.K. 53°9N 0°20E 27 F9
Skeleton Coast Namibia 20°0S 13°0E 97 J2
Skellefteå Sweden 64°45N 20°50E 63 E8
Skellefteälven → Sweden 64°45N 21°10E 63 E8
Skellingthorpe U.K. 53°15N 0°37W 27 F7
Skelmersdale U.K. 53°33N 2°48W 27 E3
Skelmorlie U.K. 55°52N 4°53W 24 C6

Skelton Cleve., U.K. 54°34N 0°58W 26 C7
Skelton Cumb., U.K. 54°43N 2°51W 26 C3
Skerries, The U.K. 53°25N 4°36W 28 A4
Skiathos Greece 39°12N 23°30E 69 E10
Skibbereen Ireland 51°33N 9°16W 20 E4
Skiddaw U.K. 54°39N 3°9W 26 C2
Skikda Algeria 36°50N 6°58E 94 A7
Skipsea U.K. 53°58N 0°13W 27 E8
Skipton U.K. 53°58N 2°3W 27 E4
Skiros Greece 38°55N 24°34E 69 E11
Skopelos Greece 39°9N 23°47E 69 E10
Skopje N. Macedonia 42°1N 21°26E 69 C9
Skovorodino Russia 54°0N 124°0E 77 D13
Skowhegan U.S.A. 44°46N 69°43W 113 C13
Skull Ireland 51°32N 9°34W 20 E3
Skye U.K. 57°15N 6°10W 22 H5
Slaidburn U.K. 53°58N 2°26W 27 E4
Slaney → Ireland 52°26N 6°33W 21 D9
Slatina Romania 44°28N 24°22E 65 F13
Slave → Canada 61°18N 113°39W 108 C8
Slave Coast W. Afr. 6°0N 2°30E 94 G6
Slave Lake Canada 55°17N 114°43W 108 D8
Sleaford U.K. 53°0N 0°24W 27 F7
Sleat, Sd. of U.K. 57°5N 5°47W 22 H6
Sledmere U.K. 54°4N 0°35W 26 D7
Sleeper Is. Canada 58°30N 81°0W 109 D11
Sleights U.K. 54°27N 0°40W 26 D7
Slieve Aughty Ireland 53°4N 8°30W 20 B5
Slieve Bloom Ireland 53°4N 7°40W 21 B7
Slieve Donard U.K. 54°11N 5°55W 19 C10
Slieve Gamph Ireland 54°6N 9°0W 18 C4
Slieve Gullion U.K. 54°7N 6°26W 19 C9
Slieve League Ireland 54°40N 8°42W 18 B4
Slieve Mish Ireland 52°12N 9°50W 20 D3
Slievenamon Ireland 52°25N 7°34W 21 D7
Sligo Ireland 54°16N 8°28W 18 C5
Sligo □ Ireland 54°8N 8°42W 18 C4
Sligo B. Ireland 54°18N 8°40W 18 C4
Sliven Bulgaria 42°42N 26°19E 69 C12
Slough U.K. 51°30N 0°36W 31 C7
Slovak Rep. = Slovakia ■ Europe 48°30N 20°0E 65 D10
Slovakia ■ Europe 48°30N 20°0E 65 D10
Slovenia ■ Europe 45°58N 14°30E 64 F8
Slovyansk Ukraine 48°55N 37°36E 71 E6
Słupsk Poland 54°30N 17°3E 65 A9
Slutsk Belarus 53°2N 27°31E 70 D4
Slyne Hd. Ireland 53°25N 10°10W 18 E1
Smallwood Res. Canada 54°5N 64°30W 109 D13
Smederevo Serbia 44°40N 20°57E 69 B9
Smerwick Harbour Ireland 52°12N 10°23W 20 D2
Smethwick U.K. 52°30N 1°57W 27 G5
Smithfield U.K. 54°59N 2°51W 26 C3
Smiths Falls Canada 44°55N 76°0W 113 C9
Smoky → Canada 56°10N 117°21W 108 D8
Smoky Hill → U.S.A. 39°4N 96°48W 111 C7
Smolensk Russia 54°45N 32°5E 70 D5
Snaefell I. of Man 54°16N 4°27W 19 C13
Snainton U.K. 54°14N 0°33W 26 D7
Snaith U.K. 53°42N 1°1W 27 E6
Snake → U.S.A. 46°12N 119°2W 110 A3
Snape U.K. 52°10N 1°30E 31 B12
Snettisham U.K. 52°53N 0°31E 31 A10
Snizort, L. U.K. 57°33N 6°28W 22 H5
Snøhetta Norway 62°19N 9°16E 63 E5
Snow Hill U.S.A. 38°11N 75°24W 113 F10
Snowdon U.K. 53°4N 4°5W 28 A5
Snowdonia △ U.K. 53°7N 3°59W 28 A6
Snowy Mts. Australia 36°30S 148°20E 98 H8
Sobat → South Sudan 9°22N 31°33E 95 G12
Sobradinho, Represa de Brazil 9°30S 42°0W 122 A2
Sobral Brazil 3°50S 40°20W 120 C5
Soc Trang Vietnam 9°37N 105°50E 82 D3
Sochi Russia 43°35N 39°40E 71 F6
Société, Îs. de la French Polynesia 17°0S 151°0W 103 J12
Socorro U.S.A. 34°4N 106°54W 110 D5
Socotra Yemen 12°30N 54°0E 89 E5
Söderhamn Sweden 61°18N 17°10E 63 E7
Sofia Bulgaria 42°45N 23°20E 69 C10
Sognefjorden Norway 61°10N 5°50E 63 E5
Sohâg Egypt 26°33N 31°43E 95 C12
Soham U.K. 52°21N 0°21E 31 B9
Soissons France 49°25N 3°19E 66 B5
Sokhumi Georgia 43°0N 41°0E 71 F7
Sokodé Togo 9°0N 1°11E 94 G6
Sokoto Nigeria 13°2N 5°16E 94 F7
Sol, Costa del Spain 36°30N 4°30W 67 D3
Solapur India 17°43N 75°56E 84 L9
Soldotna U.S.A. 60°29N 151°3W 108 C4
Soledad Colombia 10°55N 74°46W 120 A2
Solent, The U.K. 50°45N 1°25W 30 E6
Solihull U.K. 52°26N 1°47W 27 H5
Solikamsk Russia 59°38N 56°50E 70 C10
Solingen Germany 51°10N 7°5E 64 C4
Sollefteå Sweden 63°12N 17°20E 63 E7
Sóller Spain 39°46N 2°43E 67 C7
Sologne France 47°40N 1°45E 66 C4
Solomon Is. ■ Pac. Oc. 6°0S 155°0E 99 B10
Solomon Sea Papua N. G. 7°0S 150°0E 98 B9
Solon China 46°32N 121°10E 79 B13
Solothurn Switz. 47°13N 7°32E 64 E4
Solway Firth U.K. 54°49N 3°35W 26 C1
Somali Pen. Africa 7°0N 46°0E 90 F8
Somalia ■ Africa 7°0N 47°0E 89 F4
Somaliland □ Somalia 10°0N 46°0E 89 E4
Sombrerete Mexico 23°38N 103°39W 114 C4
Somerset U.S.A. 37°5N 84°36W 112 G5
Somerset □ U.K. 51°9N 3°0W 30 D2
Somerset I. Canada 73°30N 93°0W 108 B10
Somersham U.K. 52°24N 0°1W 31 B8
Somerton U.K. 51°2N 2°43W 30 D3
Somme → France 50°11N 1°38E 66 A4
Songhua Hu China 43°35N 126°50E 79 C14
Songhua Jiang → China 47°45N 132°30E 79 B15
Songkhla Thailand 7°13N 100°37E 82 C2
Sonid Youqi China 42°45N 112°48E 79 C11
Sonning U.K. 51°28N 0°54W 31 D7
Sonora → Mexico 28°50N 111°33W 114 B2
Sonoran Desert U.S.A. 33°40N 113°30W 110 D4
Sonoyta Mexico 31°51N 112°50W 114 A2

Sonoyta

Sopot Poland 54°27′N 18°31′E 65 A10
Sorel-Tracy Canada 46°0′N 73°10′W 113 C11
Soria Spain 41°43′N 2°32′W 67 B4
Sorocaba Brazil 23°31′S 47°27′W 122 D1
Sørøya Norway 70°40′N 22°30′E 63 C8
Sosnowiec Poland 50°20′N 19°10′E 65 C10
Soufrière St. Lucia 13°51′N 61°3′W 114 b
Soufrière Bay St. Lucia 13°51′N 61°4′W 114 b
Sound, The U.K. 50°20′N 4°10′W 29 G5
Souris → N. Amer. 49°40′N 99°34′W 108 E9
Sousse Tunisia 35°50′N 10°38E 95 A8
South Africa ■ Africa 32°0′S 23°0′E 97 L4
South America 10°0′S 60°0′W 117 E5
South Australia □ Australia 32°0′S 139°0′E 98 G6
South Ayrshire □ U.K. 55°18′N 4°41′W 24 D6
South Bend U.S.A. 41°41′N 86°15′W 112 E4
South Benfleet U.K. 51°33′N 0°36E 31 C10
South Brent U.K. 50°25′N 3°51′W 29 G6
South Carolina □ U.S.A. 34°0′N 81°0′W 111 D10
South Cave U.K. 53°47′N 0°37′W 27 E7
South Charleston U.S.A. 38°22′N 81°44′W 112 F7
South China Sea Asia 10°0′N 113°0′E 82 C4
South Dakota □ U.S.A. 44°15′N 100°0′W 110 B7
South Dorset Downs U.K. 50°40′N 2°26′W 30 E4
South Downs △ U.K. 50°50′N 0°50′W 31 E7
South East C. Australia 43°40′S 146°50′E 98 J8
South Elkington U.K. 53°23′N 0°4′W 27 F8
South Esk → U.K. 56°43′N 2°31′W 23 J12
South Foreland U.K. 51°8′N 1°24′E 31 D11
South Georgia Antarctica 54°30′S 37°0′W 55 B1
South Harris U.K. 57°50′N 7°0′W 22 G4
South Hayling U.K. 50°47′N 0°58′W 31 E7
South I. N.Z. 44°0′S 170°0′E 99 J13
South Korea ■ Asia 36°0′N 128°0′E 79 D14
South Lanarkshire □ U.K. 55°37′N 3°53′W 25 C8
South Magnetic Pole
  Antarctica 64°2′S 135°43E 55 C9
South Molton U.K. 51°1′N 3°51′W 29 E6
South Nahanni → Canada 61°3′N 123°21′W 108 C7
South Negril Pt. Jamaica 18°16′N 78°22′W 114 a
South Orkney Is. Antarctica 63°0′S 45°0′W 55 C18
South Ossetia □ Georgia 42°21′N 44°2′E 71 F7
South Petherton U.K. 50°57′N 2°46′W 30 E5
South Petherwin U.K. 50°36′N 4°24′W 29 F5
South Platte → U.S.A. 41°7′N 100°42′W 110 B6
South Pole Antarctica 90°0′S 0°0′E 55 E
South Pt. Barbados 13°2′N 59°32′W 114 c
South Ronaldsay U.K. 58°48′N 2°58′W 23 E12
South Sandwich Is. Antarctica 57°0′S 27°0′W 55 B1
South Saskatchewan →
  Canada 53°15′N 105°5′W 108 D9
South Shetland Is. Antarctica 62°0′S 59°0′W 55 C18
South Shields U.K. 55°0′N 1°25′W 26 C6
South Sudan ■ Africa 8°0′N 30°0′E 95 G11
South Tawton U.K. 50°44′N 3°55′W 29 F6
South Tyne → U.K. 54°59′N 2°8′W 26 C4
South Uist U.K. 57°20′N 7°15′W 22 H3
South Woodham Ferrers U.K. 51°39′N 0°37′E 31 C10
South Yorkshire □ U.K. 53°27′N 1°36′W 27 F5
Southam U.K. 52°18′N 1°23′W 30 B6
Southampton U.K. 50°54′N 1°23′W 30 E6
Southampton I. Canada 64°30′N 84°0′W 109 C11
Southborough U.K. 51°9′N 0°16E 31 D9
Southend-on-Sea U.K. 51°32′N 0°44E 31 C10
Southern Alps N.Z. 43°41′S 170°11′E 99 J13
Southern Indian L. Canada 57°10′N 98°30′W 108 D10
Southern Ocean 62°0′S 60°0′E 53 H13
Southern Uplands U.K. 55°28′N 3°52′W 25 D8
Southery U.K. 52°31′N 0°24E 31 A9
Southminster U.K. 51°40′N 0°51′E 31 C10
Southport U.K. 53°39′N 3°0′W 27 E2
Southwark □ U.K. 51°29′N 0°6′W 31 D8
Southwell U.K. 53°4′N 0°57′W 27 F7
Southwick U.K. 50°50′N 0°13′W 31 E8
Southwold U.K. 52°20′N 1°41′E 31 B12
Sovetsk Russia 55°6′N 21°50E 63 F8
Sowerby U.K. 54°14′N 1°21′W 26 D6
Soweto S. Africa 26°14′S 27°52′E 97 K5
Spain ■ Europe 39°0′N 4°0′W 67 B4
Spalding U.K. 52°48′N 0°9′W 27 G8
Spanish Canada 46°12′N 82°20′W 112 B6
Spanish Town Jamaica 18°0′N 76°57′W 114 a
Sparkford U.K. 51°2′N 2°33′W 30 D3
Sparks U.S.A. 39°32′N 119°45′W 110 C3
Sparta Greece 37°5′N 22°25E 69 F10
Sparta U.S.A. 43°56′N 90°49′W 112 D2
Spartanburg U.S.A. 34°56′N 81°57′W 111 D10
Spartivento, C. Italy 37°55′N 16°4E 68 F7
Speightstown Barbados 13°15′N 59°39′W 114 c
Speke U.K. 53°21′N 2°52′W 27 F3
Spencer U.S.A. 43°9′N 95°9′W 111 B7
Spencer G. Australia 34°0′S 137°20E 98 G6
Spennymoor U.K. 54°42′N 1°36′W 26 C5
Sperrin Mts. U.K. 54°50′N 7°0′W 19 B7
Spey → U.K. 57°40′N 3°6′W 23 G11
Spilsby U.K. 53°10′N 0°6E 27 F9
Spithead U.K. 50°45′N 1°10′W 30 E6
Split Croatia 43°31′N 16°26E 68 C7
Spofforth U.K. 53°57′N 1°27′W 27 E6
Spokane U.S.A. 47°40′N 117°24′W 110 A3
Spooner U.S.A. 45°50′N 91°53′W 112 C2
Spratly Is. S. China Sea 8°20′N 112°0′E 82 C4
Spree → Germany 52°32′N 13°12E 64 B7
Spring Hall Barbados 13°18′N 59°36′W 114 c
Springbok S. Africa 29°42′S 17°54′E 97 K3
Springfield Ill., U.S.A. 39°48′N 89°39′W 112 F3
Springfield Mass., U.S.A. 42°6′N 72°35′W 113 D11
Springfield Mo., U.S.A. 37°13′N 93°17′W 111 C8
Springfield Ohio, U.S.A. 39°55′N 83°49′W 112 F6
Springfield Oreg., U.S.A. 44°3′N 123°1′W 110 B2
Springhill Canada 45°40′N 64°4′W 113 C15
Springs S. Africa 26°13′S 28°25′E 97 K5
Sproatley U.K. 53°47′N 0°11′W 27 E8
Spurn Hd. U.K. 53°35′N 0°8E 27 E9
Srebrenica Bos.-H. 44°6′N 19°18E 69 B8
Sredinnyy Ra. Russia 57°0′N 160°0′E 77 D16
Sri Lanka ■ Asia 7°30′N 80°50′E 84 R12
Srikakulam India 18°14′N 83°58E 85 K13
Srinagar India 34°5′N 74°50E 84 B9
Stacks Mts. Ireland 52°20′N 9°34′W 20 D3
Staffa U.K. 56°27′N 6°21′W 24 B3
Stafford U.K. 52°49′N 2°7′W 27 G4

Staffordshire □ U.K. 52°53′N 2°10′W 27 G4
Staindrop U.K. 54°36′N 1°47′W 26 C5
Staines-upon-Thames U.K. 51°26′N 0°29′W 31 D8
Stainforth U.K. 53°37′N 1°0′W 27 E7
Stainmore Forest U.K. 54°29′N 2°5′W 26 D4
Stainton U.K. 53°18′N 0°24′W 27 F8
Staithes U.K. 54°34′N 0°46′W 26 C7
Stakhanov Ukraine 48°35′N 38°40E 71 E6
Stalbridge U.K. 50°57′N 2°23′W 30 E4
Stalham U.K. 52°47′N 1°31E 31 A12
Stallingborough U.K. 53°35′N 0°12′W 27 E8
Stalybridge U.K. 53°28′N 2°3′W 27 F4
Stamford U.K. 52°39′N 0°29′W 27 G8
Stamford U.S.A. 41°3′N 73°32′W 113 E11
Stamford Bridge U.K. 54°0′N 0°54′W 27 E7
Stamfordham U.K. 55°3′N 1°53′W 26 B5
Standish U.K. 53°35′N 2°41′W 27 E3
Standish U.S.A. 43°59′N 83°57′W 112 D6
Stanford on Teme U.K. 52°18′N 2°25′W 30 B4
Stanhope U.K. 54°45′N 2°1′W 26 C4
Stanley Falk. Is. 51°40′S 59°51′W 121 H4
Stanley U.K. 54°53′N 1°41′W 26 C5
Stannington U.K. 55°7′N 1°40′W 26 B5
Stanovoy Ra. Russia 55°0′N 130°0′E 77 D13
Stansted Mountfitchet U.K. 51°52′N 0°11E 31 C9
Stanwix U.K. 54°55′N 2°56′W 26 C3
Stapleford U.K. 52°57′N 1°16′W 27 G6
Staplehurst U.K. 51°9′N 0°34E 31 D10
Stara Zagora Bulgaria 42°26′N 25°39E 69 C11
Staraya Russa Russia 57°58′N 31°23E 70 C5
Starbuck I. Kiribati 5°37′S 155°55′W 103 H12
Start B. U.K. 50°15′N 3°39′W 29 G6
Start Pt. U.K. 50°13′N 3°39′W 29 G6
Staryy Oskol Russia 51°19′N 37°55E 71 D6
State College U.S.A. 40°48′N 77°52′W 112 E9
Staten, I. = Estados, I. de Los
  Argentina 54°40′S 64°30′W 121 H3
Staunton U.K. 51°57′N 2°17′W 30 C4
Staunton U.S.A. 38°9′N 79°4′W 112 F8
Stavanger Norway 58°57′N 5°40E 63 F5
Staveley Cumb., U.K. 54°23′N 2°48′W 26 D5
Staveley Derby., U.K. 53°16′N 1°21′W 27 F6
Stavropol Russia 45°5′N 42°0′E 71 E7
Steiermark □ Austria 47°26′N 15°0E 64 E8
Steinkjer Norway 64°1′N 11°31E 63 E6
Stellarton Canada 45°32′N 62°30′W 113 C16
Stellenbosch S. Africa 33°58′S 18°50E 97 L3
Stenhousemuir U.K. 56°2′N 3°48′W 25 B8
Steornabhaigh = Stornoway
  U.K. 58°13′N 6°23′W 22 F5
Stephenville Canada 48°31′N 58°35′W 109 E14
Steppe Asia 50°0′N 50°0′E 72 C7
Sterling Colo., U.S.A. 40°37′N 103°13′W 110 B6
Sterling Ill., U.S.A. 41°48′N 89°42′W 112 E3
Sterlitamak Russia 53°40′N 56°0′E 70 D10
Stettiner Haff Germany 53°47′N 14°15E 64 B8
Stettler Canada 52°19′N 112°40′W 108 D8
Steubenville U.S.A. 40°22′N 80°37′W 112 E7
Stevenage U.K. 51°55′N 0°13′W 31 C8
Stevens Point U.S.A. 44°31′N 89°34′W 112 C3
Stevenston U.K. 55°39′N 4°45′W 24 C6
Stewart Canada 55°56′N 129°57′W 108 D7
Stewart → Canada 63°19′N 139°26′W 108 C6
Stewart I. N.Z. 46°58′S 167°54E 99 K12
Stewarton U.K. 55°40′N 4°32′W 24 C6
Steyning U.K. 50°53′N 0°18′W 31 E8
Steyr Austria 48°3′N 14°25E 64 D8
Stikine → Canada 56°40′N 132°30′W 108 D6
Stillington U.K. 54°6′N 1°6′W 26 D6
Stillwater U.S.A. 36°7′N 97°4′W 111 A8
Stiperstones U.K. 52°36′N 2°55′W 27 G3
Stirling U.K. 56°8′N 3°57′W 25 B8
Stirling □ U.K. 56°12′N 4°18′W 24 B7
Stobo U.K. 55°38′N 3°17′W 25 C9
Stockbridge U.K. 51°7′N 1°29′W 30 D6
Stockholm Sweden 59°19′N 18°4E 63 F7
Stockport U.K. 53°25′N 2°9′W 27 F4
Stocksbridge U.K. 53°29′N 1°35′W 27 F5
Stockton U.S.A. 37°58′N 121°17′W 110 C2
Stockton-on-Tees U.K. 54°35′N 1°19′W 26 C6
Stoer, Pt. of U.K. 58°16′N 5°23′W 22 F7
Stoke U.K. 51°26′N 0°41E 31 D10
Stoke Ferry U.K. 52°34′N 0°31E 31 A10
Stoke Fleming U.K. 50°19′N 3°37′W 29 G6
Stoke Mandeville U.K. 51°47′N 0°47′W 31 C7
Stoke-on-Trent U.K. 53°1′N 2°11′W 27 F4
Stoke Prior U.K. 52°19′N 2°4′W 30 B4
Stokesley U.K. 54°28′N 1°12′W 26 D6
Stone Bucks., U.K. 51°48′N 0°52′W 31 C7
Stone Staffs., U.K. 52°55′N 2°9′W 27 G4
Stonehaven U.K. 56°59′N 2°12′W 23 J13
Stonehouse U.K. 51°45′N 2°16′W 30 C4
Stoneham Aspal U.K. 52°12′N 1°8E 31 B11
Stony Stratford U.K. 52°3′N 0°50′W 31 B7
Stony Tunguska → Russia 61°50′N 90°13E 77 C10
Stora Lulevatten Sweden 67°10′N 19°30E 63 D7
Storavan Sweden 65°45′N 18°10E 63 D7
Store Bælt Denmark 55°20′N 11°0E 63 F6
Stormberge S. Africa 31°16′S 26°17′E 97 L5
Stornoway U.K. 58°13′N 6°23′W 22 F5
Storsjön Sweden 63°9′N 14°30E 63 E6
Stort → U.K. 51°46′N 0°2E 31 C9
Storuman Sweden 65°5′N 17°10E 63 D7
Stotfold U.K. 52°1′N 0°13′W 31 B8
Stour → Dorset, U.K. 50°43′N 1°47′W 30 E5
Stour → Kent, U.K. 51°18′N 1°22E 31 D11
Stour → Suffolk, U.K. 51°57′N 1°4E 31 C11
Stour → Worcs., U.K. 52°21′N 2°17′W 30 B4
Stourbridge U.K. 52°28′N 2°8′W 27 H4
Stourport-on-Severn U.K. 52°21′N 2°17′W 30 B4
Stow U.K. 55°42′N 2°50′W 25 C10
Stow Bardolph U.K. 52°38′N 0°24E 31 A9
Stow-on-the-Wold U.K. 51°56′N 1°42′W 30 C5
Stowmarket U.K. 52°12′N 1°0E 31 B10
Stradbroke U.K. 52°19′N 1°16E 31 B11
Stralsund Germany 54°18′N 13°4E 64 A7
Strangford L. U.K. 54°30′N 5°37′W 19 C10
Stranraer U.K. 54°54′N 5°1′W 24 E5
Strasbourg France 48°35′N 7°42E 66 B7
Stratford Canada 43°23′N 81°0′W 112 D7
Stratford St. Mary U.K. 51°58′N 1°0E 31 C10

Stratford-upon-Avon U.K. 52°12′N 1°42′W 30 B5
Strath Avon U.K. 57°18′N 3°23′W 23 H11
Strath Dearn U.K. 57°20′N 4°0′W 23 H9
Strath Glass U.K. 57°22′N 4°42′W 23 H8
Strath Halladale U.K. 58°30′N 3°51′W 23 F10
Strath Naver U.K. 58°24′N 4°12′W 23 F9
Strath of Kildonan U.K. 58°14′N 3°56′W 23 F10
Strath Spey U.K. 57°9′N 3°49′W 23 H10
Strath Tay U.K. 56°40′N 3°48′W 25 A8
Strathaven U.K. 55°40′N 4°5′W 24 C7
Strathbogie U.K. 57°25′N 2°45′W 23 H12
Strathmore Angus, U.K. 56°37′N 3°7′W 23 J11
Strathmore Highl., U.K. 58°22′N 4°40′W 23 F8
Strathpeffer U.K. 57°35′N 4°32′W 23 G8
Strathroy Canada 42°58′N 81°38′W 112 D7
Strathy Pt. U.K. 58°36′N 4°1′W 23 E9
Stratton U.K. 50°49′N 4°32′W 29 F4
Stratton St. Margaret U.K. 51°35′N 1°44′W 30 C5
Streatley U.K. 51°31′N 1°8′W 30 C6
Street U.K. 51°8′N 2°44′W 30 D3
Strensall U.K. 54°3′N 1°4′W 26 D6
Stretford U.K. 53°28′N 2°17′W 27 F4
Stroma U.K. 58°41′N 3°7′W 23 E11
Strómboli Italy 38°47′N 15°13E 68 E6
Stromeferry U.K. 57°21′N 5°33′W 22 H6
Stromness U.K. 58°58′N 3°17′W 23 E11
Stronsay U.K. 59°7′N 2°35′W 23 D12
Stroud U.K. 51°45′N 2°13′W 30 C4
Stuart L. Canada 54°30′N 124°30′W 108 D7
Studland U.K. 50°39′N 1°58′W 30 E5
Studley U.K. 52°16′N 1°53′W 30 B5
Sturgeon Bay U.S.A. 44°50′N 87°23′W 112 C4
Sturgeon Falls Canada 46°25′N 79°57′W 112 B8
Sturminster Marshall U.K. 50°47′N 2°5′W 30 E4
Sturminster Newton U.K. 50°55′N 2°18′W 30 E4
Sturt Stony Desert Australia 28°30′S 141°0′E 98 F6
Sturton U.K. 53°19′N 0°39′W 27 F7
Stuttgart Germany 48°48′N 9°11E 64 D5
Stuttgart U.S.A. 34°30′N 91°33′W 111 D8
Suakin Sudan 19°8′N 37°20E 95 E13
Subā Si. Arabia 27°10′N 35°40E 86 E3
Subotica Serbia 46°6′N 19°39E 69 A8
Suceava Romania 47°38′N 26°16E 65 E14
Suck → Ireland 53°17′N 8°3′W 20 B6
Sucre Bolivia 19°0′S 65°15′W 120 D3
Sudan ■ Africa 15°0′N 30°0′E 95 E11
Sudbury Canada 52°54′N 1°45′W 27 G5
Sudbury Suffolk, U.K. 52°2′N 0°45E 31 B10
Sudd South Sudan 8°20′N 30°0′E 95 G12
Sudeten Europe 50°20′N 16°45E 65 C9
Suez Egypt 29°58′N 32°31E 95 C12
Suez, G. of Egypt 28°40′N 33°0E 95 C12
Suez Canal Egypt 31°0′N 32°20E 95 B12
Suffolk □ U.K. 52°16′N 1°0E 31 B11
Sugluk Canada 62°14′N 75°38′W 109 C12
Suḩār Oman 24°20′N 56°40E 87 E9
Suihua China 46°32′N 126°55E 79 B14
Suining China 30°26′N 105°35E 78 E10
Suir → Ireland 52°16′N 7°9′W 21 D8
Sukabumi Indonesia 6°56′S 106°50E 82 F3
Sukhona → Russia 61°15′N 46°39E 70 C8
Sukkur Pakistan 27°42′N 68°54E 84 F6
Sulaiman Range Pakistan 30°30′N 69°50E 84 D6
Sulawesi Indonesia 2°0′S 120°0′E 83 E6
Sullana Peru 4°52′S 80°39′W 120 C1
Sullom Voe U.K. 60°27′N 1°20′W 22 B15
Sulu Arch. Phil. 6°0′N 121°0′E 83 C6
Sulu Sea E. Indies 8°0′N 120°0′E 83 C6
Sumare Brazil 22°49′S 47°16′W 122 D1
Sumatra Indonesia 0°40′N 100°20E 82 D2
Sumba Indonesia 9°45′S 119°35E 83 F5
Sumbawa Indonesia 8°26′S 117°30E 82 F5
Sumburgh Hd. U.K. 59°52′N 1°17′W 22 C15
Summer L. U.S.A. 42°50′N 120°45′W 110 B3
Summerside Canada 46°24′N 63°47′W 109 E13
Sumqayit Azerbaijan 40°34′N 49°38E 71 F8
Sumter U.S.A. 33°55′N 80°21′W 111 D10
Sumy Ukraine 50°57′N 34°50E 71 D5
Sun Valley U.S.A. 43°42′N 114°21′W 110 B4
Sunart, L. U.K. 56°43′S 5°42′W 22 J6
Sunart, L. U.K. 56°42′N 5°43′W 22 J6
Sunbury U.S.A. 40°52′N 76°48′W 112 E9
Sunda, Selat Indonesia 6°20′S 105°30E 82 F3
Sunda Is. Indonesia 5°0′S 105°0E 102 H2
Sundarbans Asia 22°0′N 89°0E 85 J16
Sunderland U.K. 54°55′N 1°23′W 26 C6
Sundsvall Sweden 62°23′N 17°17E 63 E7
Sungaipenuh Indonesia 2°1′S 101°20E 82 E2
Sunk Island U.K. 53°39′N 0°6′W 27 E8
Sunninghill U.K. 51°24′N 0°39′W 31 D7
Sunshine Coast Australia 26°30′S 153°0E 98 F9
Superior U.S.A. 46°44′N 92°6′W 112 B1
Superior, L. N. Amer. 47°0′N 87°0′W 112 B4
Sûr Lebanon 33°19′N 35°16E 86 C3
Sura → Russia 56°6′N 46°0E 70 C8
Surabaya Indonesia 7°17′S 112°45E 82 F4
Surakarta Indonesia 7°35′S 110°48E 82 F4
Surat India 21°12′N 72°55E 84 J8
Surgut Russia 61°14′N 73°20E 76 C8
Surigao Phil. 9°47′N 125°29E 83 C7
Suriname ■ S. Amer. 4°0′N 56°0′W 120 B4
Surrey □ U.K. 51°15′N 0°31′W 31 D8
Surt Libya 31°11′N 16°39E 95 B9
Surt, Khalīj Libya 31°40′N 18°30E 95 B9
Surtsey Iceland 63°20′N 20°30′W 63 B1
Susquehanna → U.S.A. 39°33′N 76°5′W 113 F9
Sussex Canada 45°45′N 65°37′W 113 C15
Sutherland U.K. 58°12′N 4°50′W 23 F8
Sutlej → Pakistan 29°23′N 71°3E 84 E7
Sutterton U.K. 52°55′N 0°6′W 27 G8
Sutton □ U.K. 51°21′N 0°11′W 31 D8
Sutton Bridge U.K. 52°46′N 0°11E 27 G9
Sutton Coldfield U.K. 52°35′N 1°49′W 27 G6
Sutton Courtenay U.K. 51°39′N 1°16′W 30 C6
Sutton in Ashfield U.K. 53°8′N 1°16′W 27 F6
Sutton-on-Sea U.K. 53°18′N 0°16E 27 F9
Sutton Scotney U.K. 51°9′N 1°20′W 30 D6
Suva Fiji 18°6′S 178°30E 99 D14
Suwałki Poland 54°8′N 22°59E 65 A12
Suwarrow Is. Cook Is. 13°15′S 163°5′W 103 J11
Suzhou China 31°19′N 120°38E 79 E13
Svalbard Arctic 78°0′N 17°0E 54 B8

Svealand Sweden 60°20′N 15°0E 63 E7
Sverdrup Chan. Canada 79°56′N 96°25′W 109 B10
Sverdrup Is. Canada 79°0′N 97°0′W 109 B10
Svir → Russia 60°30′N 32°48E 70 B5
Swadlincote U.K. 52°47′N 1°33′W 27 G5
Swaffham U.K. 52°39′N 0°42E 31 A10
Swakopmund Namibia 22°37′S 14°30E 97 J2
Swan Hill Australia 35°20′S 143°33E 98 H7
Swan River Canada 52°10′N 101°16′W 108 D9
Swanage U.K. 50°36′N 1°58′W 30 E5
Swansea U.K. 51°37′N 3°57′W 29 D6
Swansea B. U.K. 51°32′N 3°57′W 29 D6
Swartberge S. Africa 33°20′S 22°0′E 90 K6
Swaziland = Eswatini ■
  Africa 26°30′S 31°30E 97 K6
Sweden ■ Europe 57°0′N 15°0E 63 F7
Sweetwater U.S.A. 32°28′N 100°25′W 110 D6
Swellendam S. Africa 34°1′S 20°26E 97 L4
Swift Current Canada 50°20′N 107°45′W 108 D9
Swilly, L. Ireland 55°12′N 7°33′W 18 A6
Swindon U.K. 51°34′N 1°46′W 30 C5
Swineshead U.K. 52°57′N 0°10′W 27 G8
Swinford Ireland 53°57′N 8°58′W 18 D4
Swinton Borders, U.K. 55°43′N 2°15′W 25 C11
Swinton Gt. Man., U.K. 53°31′N 2°20′W 27 E4
Swinton S. Yorks., U.K. 53°29′N 1°20′W 27 F6
Switzerland ■ Europe 46°30′N 8°0E 64 E5
Swords Ireland 53°28′N 6°13′W 21 B10
Sydney Australia 33°52′S 151°12E 98 G9
Sydney Canada 46°7′N 60°7′W 113 B17
Syktyvkar Russia 61°45′N 50°40E 70 B9
Sylhet Bangla. 24°54′N 91°52E 85 G17
Symington U.K. 55°36′N 3°36′W 25 C8
Symonds Yat U.K. 51°51′N 2°38′W 30 C3
Syracuse U.S.A. 43°3′N 76°9′W 113 D9
Syrdarya → Kazakhstan 46°3′N 61°0E 76 E7
Syria ■ Asia 35°0′N 38°0E 86 C4
Syrian Desert Asia 32°0′N 40°0E 86 C4
Syston U.K. 52°42′N 1°3′W 27 G6
Syzran Russia 53°12′N 48°30E 70 D8
Szczecin Poland 53°27′N 14°27E 64 B8
Szechwan = Sichuan □ China 30°30′N 103°0E 78 E9
Szeged Hungary 46°16′N 20°10E 65 E11
Székesfehérvár Hungary 47°15′N 18°25E 65 E10
Szekszárd Hungary 46°22′N 18°42E 65 E10
Szolnok Hungary 47°10′N 20°15E 65 E11
Szombathely Hungary 47°14′N 16°38E 65 E9

T
Tabas Iran 33°35′N 56°55E 87 C9
Tablas I. Phil. 12°25′N 122°2E 83 B6
Table B. S. Africa 33°35′S 18°25E 97 L3
Table Mt. S. Africa 33°58′S 18°26E 97 L3
Tabora Tanzania 5°2′S 32°50E 96 F6
Tabrīz Iran 38°7′N 46°20E 86 B6
Tabuaeran Kiribati 3°51′N 159°22′W 103 G12
Tabūk Si. Arabia 28°23′N 36°36E 86 D4
Tacheng China 46°40′N 82°58E 78 B5
Tacloban Phil. 11°15′N 124°58E 83 B6
Tacna Peru 18°0′S 70°20′W 120 D2
Tacoma U.S.A. 47°14′N 122°26′W 110 A2
Tacuarembó Uruguay 31°45′S 56°0′W 121 F4
Tadcaster U.K. 53°53′N 1°16′W 27 E6
Tademaït, Plateau du Algeria 28°30′N 2°30E 94 C6
Tadley U.K. 51°21′N 1°7′W 30 D6
Taganrog Russia 47°12′N 38°50E 71 E6
Taguatinga Brazil 12°27′S 46°22′W 122 B1
Tagus → Europe 38°40′N 9°24′W 67 C1
Tahiti French Polynesia 17°37′S 149°27′W 103 J13
Tahoe, L. U.S.A. 39°6′N 120°2′W 110 C2
Tahoua Niger 14°57′N 5°16E 94 F7
Tahta Egypt 26°44′N 31°32E 95 C12
Tai Hu China 31°5′N 120°10E 79 E13
Tai Po China 22°27′N 114°10E 79 a
Tai'an China 36°12′N 117°8E 79 D12
Taiyuan China 37°52′N 112°33E 79 D11
Taizhou China 32°28′N 119°55E 79 E12
Ta'izz Yemen 13°35′N 44°2E 89 E3
Tajikistan ■ Asia 38°30′N 70°0E 87 B12
Tak Thailand 16°52′N 99°8E 82 A1
Takamatsu Japan 34°20′N 134°5E 81 F4
Takaoka Japan 36°47′N 137°0E 81 E5
Takasaki Japan 36°20′N 139°0E 81 E6
Takeshima = Liancourt Rocks
  Asia 37°15′N 131°52E 81 E2
Taklamakan Desert China 38°0′N 83°0E 78 D5
Talara Peru 4°38′S 81°18′W 120 C1
Talaud, Kepulauan Indonesia 4°30′N 126°50E 83 D7
Talavera de la Reina Spain 39°55′N 4°46′W 67 C3
Talca Chile 35°28′S 71°40′W 121 F2
Talcahuano Chile 36°40′S 73°10′W 121 F2
Taldyqorghan Kazakhstan 45°10′N 78°45E 76 E8
Talgarth U.K. 52°0′N 3°14′W 28 D7
Taliabu Indonesia 1°50′S 125°0E 83 E6
Tallaght Ireland 53°17′N 6°22′W 21 B10
Tallahassee U.S.A. 30°27′N 84°17′W 111 D10
Tallinn Estonia 59°22′N 24°48E 63 F8
Taloyoak Canada 69°32′N 93°32′W 108 C10
Taltal Chile 25°23′S 70°33′W 121 E2
Tamale Ghana 9°22′N 0°50′W 94 G5
Tamana Kiribati 2°30′S 175°59E 99 A13
Tamanrasset Algeria 22°50′N 5°30E 94 D7
Tamar → U.K. 50°27′N 4°15′W 29 G5
Tambov Russia 52°45′N 41°28E 70 D7
Tame → U.K. 52°44′N 1°43′W 27 G5
Tamerton Foliot U.K. 50°25′N 4°11′W 29 G5
Tamil Nadu □ India 11°0′N 77°0E 84 P10
Tampa U.S.A. 27°56′N 82°27′W 111 E10
Tampa B. U.S.A. 27°50′N 82°30′W 111 E10
Tampere Finland 61°30′N 23°50E 63 E8
Tampico Mexico 22°13′N 97°51′W 114 C5

Tamworth Australia 31°7′S 150°58E 98 G9
Tamworth U.K. 52°39′N 1°41′W 27 G5
Tana → Kenya 2°32′S 40°31E 96 E8
Tana → Norway 70°30′N 28°14E 63 C9
Tana, L. Ethiopia 13°5′N 37°30E 89 E2
Tanami Desert Australia 18°50′S 132°0E 98 D5
Tanana → U.S.A. 65°10′N 151°58′W 108 C4
Tandil Argentina 37°15′S 59°6′W 121 F4
Tandragee U.K. 54°21′N 6°24′W 19 C9
Tanezrouft Algeria 23°9′N 0°11E 94 D6
Tanga Tanzania 5°5′S 39°2E 96 F7
Tanganyika, L. Africa 6°40′S 30°0E 96 F6
Tanggula Shan China 32°40′N 92°10E 78 E7
Tanggula Shankou China 32°42′N 92°27E 78 E7
Tangier Morocco 35°50′N 5°49′W 94 A4
Tangjia China 22°22′N 113°35E 79 a
Tangra Yumco China 31°0′N 86°38E 78 E6
Tangshan China 39°38′N 118°10E 79 D12
Tanimbar, Kepulauan
  Indonesia 7°30′S 131°30E 83 F8
Tanjungbalai Indonesia 2°55′N 99°44E 82 D1
Tanjungpandan Indonesia 2°43′S 107°38E 82 E3
Tanjungredeb Indonesia 2°9′N 117°29E 82 D5
Tanna Vanuatu 19°30′S 169°20E 99 D12
Tannu Ola Asia 51°0′N 94°0E 77 D10
Tanta Egypt 30°45′N 30°57E 95 B12
Tanworth U.K. 52°20′N 1°50′W 30 B5
Tanzania ■ Africa 6°0′S 34°0E 96 F6
Tanzhou China 22°16′N 113°28E 79 a
Taolanaro Madag. 25°2′S 47°0E 97 K9
Taonan China 45°22′N 122°40E 79 B13
Taos U.S.A. 36°24′N 105°35′W 110 C5
Tapachula Mexico 14°54′N 92°17′W 114 E6
Tapajós → Brazil 2°24′S 54°41′W 120 C4
Tapti → India 21°8′N 72°41E 84 J8
Taquaritinga Brazil 21°24′S 48°30′W 122 D1
Tarakan Indonesia 3°20′N 117°35E 82 D5
Taransay U.K. 57°54′N 7°0′W 22 G3
Táranto Italy 40°28′N 17°14E 68 D7
Táranto, G. di Italy 40°8′N 17°20E 68 D7
Tarasaigh = Taransay U.K. 57°54′N 7°0′W 22 G3
Tarawa Kiribati 1°30′N 173°0E 102 G9
Taraz Kazakhstan 42°54′N 71°22E 87 A12
Tarbagatay, Khrebet Kazakhstan 48°0′N 83°0E 76 E9
Tarbat Ness U.K. 57°52′N 3°47′W 23 G10
Tarbela Dam Pakistan 34°8′N 72°52E 84 B8
Tarbert Argyll & Bute, U.K. 55°52′N 5°25′W 24 C5
Tarbert W. Isles, U.K. 57°54′N 6°49′W 22 G4
Tarbes France 43°15′N 0°3E 66 E4
Tarcoola Australia 30°44′S 134°36E 98 G5
Taree Australia 31°50′S 152°30E 98 G9
Tarfaya Morocco 27°55′N 12°55′W 94 C3
Târgovişte Romania 44°55′N 25°27E 65 F13
Târgu Jiu Romania 45°5′N 23°19E 65 F12
Târgu Mureş Romania 46°31′N 24°38E 65 E13
Tarija Bolivia 21°30′S 64°40′W 120 E3
Tarim Basin China 40°0′N 84°0E 78 C5
Tarim He → China 39°30′N 88°30E 78 D6
Tarleton U.K. 53°41′N 2°50′W 27 E3
Tarn → France 44°5′N 1°6E 66 E4
Tarnów Poland 50°3′N 21°0E 65 C11
Taroudannt Morocco 30°30′N 8°52′W 94 B4
Tarporley U.K. 53°10′N 2°40′W 27 F3
Tarragona Spain 41°5′N 1°17E 67 B6
Tarsus Turkey 36°58′N 34°55E 71 G5
Tartu Estonia 58°20′N 26°44E 63 F9
Tartūs Syria 34°55′N 35°55E 86 C3
Tashkent Uzbekistan 41°20′N 69°10E 87 A12
Tasiilaq Greenland 65°40′N 37°20′W 54 C6
Tasikmalaya Indonesia 7°18′S 108°12E 82 F3
Tasman Sea Pac. Oc. 36°0′S 160°0E 99 H10
Tasmania □ Australia 42°0′S 146°30E 98 J8
Tassili n' Ajjer Algeria 25°47′N 8°1E 94 C7
Tatar Str. Russia 50°0′N 141°0E 77 E14
Tatarstan □ Russia 55°30′N 51°30E 70 C9
Tatnam, C. Canada 57°16′N 91°0′W 109 D10
Tatra Slovakia 49°20′N 20°0E 65 D11
Tattenhall U.K. 53°7′N 2°46′W 27 F3
Tatuí Brazil 23°25′S 47°53′W 122 D1
Tatvan Turkey 38°31′N 42°15E 71 G7
Taubaté Brazil 23°0′S 45°36′W 122 D1
Tauern Austria 47°15′N 12°40E 64 E7
Taunggyi Myanmar 20°50′N 97°0E 85 J20
Taunton U.K. 51°1′N 3°5′W 30 D2
Taunton U.S.A. 41°54′N 71°6′W 113 E12
Taunus Germany 50°13′N 8°34E 64 C5
Taurus Mts. Turkey 37°0′N 32°30E 71 G5
Tavan Bogd Uul Mongolia 49°10′N 87°49E 78 B6
Tavistock U.K. 50°33′N 4°9′W 29 F5
Taw → U.K. 51°4′N 4°4′W 29 E5
Tawas City U.S.A. 44°16′N 83°31′W 112 C6
Tawau Malaysia 4°20′N 117°55E 82 D5
Taxkorgan Tajik Zizhixian
  China 37°49′N 75°14E 78 D4
Tay → U.K. 56°37′N 3°38′W 25 A8
Tay, Firth of U.K. 56°25′N 3°8′W 25 B9
Tay, L. U.K. 56°32′N 4°8′W 24 A7
Taylor, Mt. U.S.A. 35°14′N 107°37′W 110 C5
Taylorville U.S.A. 39°33′N 89°18′W 112 F3
Tayport U.K. 56°27′N 2°52′W 25 B10
Taz → Russia 67°32′N 78°40E 76 C8
Taza Morocco 34°16′N 4°6′W 94 B5
Tbilisi Georgia 41°43′N 44°50E 71 F7
Te Ika-a-Māui = North I. N.Z. 38°0′S 175°0E 99 H14
Te Waipounamu = South I.
  N.Z. 44°0′S 170°0E 99 J13
Tebay U.K. 54°26′N 2°35′W 26 D3
Tébessa Algeria 35°22′N 8°8E 94 A7
Tees → U.K. 54°37′N 1°10′W 26 C6
Teesdale U.K. 54°37′N 2°10′W 26 C4
Teesside U.K. 54°36′N 1°15′W 26 C6
Tegal Indonesia 6°52′S 109°8E 82 F3
Tegid, L. = Bala, L. U.K. 52°53′N 3°37′W 28 B6
Tegucigalpa Honduras 14°5′N 87°14′W 114 E7
Tehrān Iran 35°41′N 51°25E 87 C7
Tehuantepec Mexico 16°21′N 95°13′W 114 D5
Tehuantepec, G. de Mexico 15°50′N 95°12′W 114 D5
Tehuantepec, Istmo de
  Mexico 17°15′N 94°30′W 114 D6
Teifi → U.K. 52°5′N 4°41′W 28 C4
Teign → U.K. 50°32′N 3°32′W 29 F6
Teignmouth U.K. 50°33′N 3°31′W 29 F6

Tejen ... Urmia

Tejen *Turkmenistan*	37°23N 60°31E	87 B10
Tekirdağ *Turkey*	40°58N 27°30E	71 F4
Tel Aviv-Jaffa *Israel*	32°4N 34°48E	86 C3
Tela *Honduras*	15°40N 87°28W	114 D7
Telangana □ *India*	17°30N 78°30E	84 K11
Telegraph Creek *Canada*	58°0N 131°10W	108 D6
Teles Pires → *Brazil*	7°21S 58°33W	120 C4
Telford *U.K.*	52°40N 2°27W	27 G4
Tell City *U.S.A.*	37°57N 86°46W	112 G4
Telpos Iz *Russia*	63°16N 59°13E	70 B10
Teluk Intan *Malaysia*	4°3N 101°0E	82 D2
Tema *Ghana*	5°41N 0°0	94 G5
Teme → *U.K.*	52°11N 2°13W	30 B4
Temirtau *Kazakhstan*	50°5N 72°56E	76 D8
Témiscaming *Canada*	46°44N 79°5W	112 B8
Temple *U.S.A.*	31°6N 97°21W	111 D7
Temple Combe *U.K.*	51°0N 2°24W	30 D4
Temple Ewell *U.K.*	51°8N 1°17E	31 D11
Temple Sowerby *U.K.*	54°38N 2°36W	26 C3
Templemore *Ireland*	52°47N 7°51W	20 C7
Temuco *Chile*	38°45S 72°40W	121 F2
Tenali *India*	16°15N 80°35E	85 L12
Tenbury Wells *U.K.*	52°19N 2°35W	30 B3
Tenby *U.K.*	51°40N 4°42W	28 D4
Tenerife *Canary Is.*	28°15N 16°35W	94 C2
Tengchong *China*	25°0N 98°28E	78 G8
Tengger Desert *China*	38°0N 104°10E	78 D9
Tennant Creek *Australia*	19°30S 134°15E	98 E5
Tennessee □ *U.S.A.*	36°0N 86°30W	111 C9
Tennessee → *U.S.A.*	37°4N 88°34W	111 C9
Tenterden *U.K.*	51°4N 0°42E	31 D10
Teófilo Otoni *Brazil*	17°50S 41°30W	122 C2
Tepic *Mexico*	21°30N 104°54W	114 C4
Teraina *Kiribati*	4°43N 160°25W	103 G12
Téramo *Italy*	42°39N 13°42E	68 C5
Teresina *Brazil*	5°9S 42°45W	120 C5
Termiz *Uzbekistan*	37°15N 67°15E	87 B11
Terni *Italy*	42°34N 12°37E	68 C5
Ternopil *Ukraine*	49°30N 25°40E	65 D13
Terrace *Canada*	54°30N 128°35W	108 D7
Terrassa *Spain*	41°34N 2°1E	67 B7
Terre Haute *U.S.A.*	39°28N 87°25W	112 F4
Terschelling *Neths.*	53°25N 5°20E	64 B3
Teruel *Spain*	40°22N 1°8W	67 B5
Tesiyn Gol → *Mongolia*	50°40N 93°20E	78 A7
Teslin *Canada*	60°10N 132°43W	108 C6
Test → *U.K.*	50°56N 1°29W	30 E6
Tetbury *U.K.*	51°38N 2°10W	30 C4
Tete *Mozam.*	16°13S 33°33E	97 H6
Tetney *U.K.*	53°29N 0°1W	27 F8
Tétouan *Morocco*	35°35N 5°21W	94 A4
Tetovo *N. Macedonia*	42°1N 20°59E	69 C9
Teuco → *Argentina*	25°35S 60°11W	121 E3
Teutoburger Wald *Germany*	52°5N 8°22E	64 B5
Teviot → *U.K.*	55°29N 2°38W	25 D10
Teviotdale *U.K.*	55°25N 2°50W	25 D10
Teviothead *U.K.*	55°20N 2°56W	25 D10
Tewkesbury *U.K.*	51°59N 2°9W	30 C4
Texarkana *U.S.A.*	33°26N 94°3W	111 D8
Texas □ *U.S.A.*	31°40N 98°30W	111 D7
Texel *Neths.*	53°5N 4°50E	64 B3
Teynham *U.K.*	51°20N 0°50E	31 D10
Tezpur *India*	26°40N 92°45E	85 F18
Thabana Ntlenyana *Lesotho*	29°30S 29°16E	97 K5
Thabazimbi *S. Africa*	24°40S 27°21E	97 J5
Thailand ■ *Asia*	16°0N 102°0E	82 A2
Thailand, G. of *Asia*	11°30N 101°0E	82 B2
Thal Desert *Pakistan*	31°10N 71°30E	84 D7
Thalassery *India*	11°45N 75°30E	84 P9
Thame *U.K.*	51°45N 0°58W	31 C7
Thame → *U.K.*	51°39N 1°9W	30 C6
Thane *India*	19°12N 72°59E	84 K8
Thanet, I. of *U.K.*	51°21N 1°20E	31 D11
Thanjavur *India*	10°48N 79°12E	84 P11
Thar Desert *Pakistan*	28°0N 72°0E	84 F8
Thargomindah *Australia*	27°58S 143°46E	98 F7
Thasos *Greece*	40°40N 24°40E	69 D11
Thatcham *U.K.*	51°24N 1°15W	30 D6
Thatta *Pakistan*	24°42N 67°55E	84 G5
Thaxted *U.K.*	51°57N 0°22E	31 C9
The Pas *Canada*	53°45N 101°15W	108 D9
Theale *U.K.*	51°26N 1°5W	30 D6
Thebes *Egypt*	25°40N 32°35E	95 C12
Thelon → *Canada*	64°16N 96°4W	108 C9
Thermopolis *U.S.A.*	43°39N 108°13W	110 B5
Thermopylæ *Greece*	38°48N 22°35E	69 E10
Thessalon *Canada*	46°20N 83°30W	112 B6
Thessaloniki *Greece*	40°38N 22°58E	69 D10
Thetford *U.K.*	52°25N 0°45E	31 B10
Thetford Mines *Canada*	46°8N 71°18W	109 E12
Thiers *France*	45°52N 3°33E	66 D5
Thiès *Senegal*	14°50N 16°51W	94 F2
Thika *Kenya*	1°1S 37°5E	96 E7
Thimphu *Bhutan*	27°31N 89°45E	85 F16
Thionville *France*	49°20N 6°10E	66 B7
Thira = Santorini *Greece*	36°23N 25°27E	69 F11
Thirlmere *U.K.*	54°32N 3°4W	26 C2
Thirsk *U.K.*	54°14N 1°19W	26 D6
Thiruvananthapuram *India*	8°41N 77°0E	84 Q10
Thlewiaza → *Canada*	60°29N 94°40W	108 D9
Thomasville *U.S.A.*	30°50N 83°59W	111 D10
Thompson *Canada*	55°45N 97°52W	108 D10
Thornaby on Tees *U.K.*	54°33N 1°18W	26 C6
Thornbury *U.K.*	51°36N 2°31W	30 C3
Thorndon *U.K.*	52°17N 1°9E	31 B11
Thorne *U.K.*	53°37N 0°57W	27 E7
Thornham *U.K.*	52°58N 0°35E	31 A10
Thornthwaite *U.K.*	54°37N 3°13W	26 C2
Thornton *U.K.*	53°52N 3°0W	26 D2
Thornton Dale *U.K.*	54°15N 0°42W	26 D7
Thorpe *U.K.*	52°38N 1°22E	31 A11
Thorpe le Soken *U.K.*	51°51N 1°11E	31 C11
Thrace *Europe*	41°0N 27°0E	69 D11
Thrace, Sea of *Greece*	40°30N 25°0E	69 D11
Thrapston *U.K.*	52°24N 0°32W	31 B7
Three Gorges Dam *China*	30°45N 111°15E	79 C11
Threlkeld *U.K.*	54°37N 3°3W	26 C2
Threshfield *U.K.*	54°4N 2°1W	26 D4
Thrissur *India*	10°30N 76°18E	84 P10
Thunder B. *U.S.A.*	45°0N 83°20W	112 C6
Thunder Bay *Canada*	48°20N 89°15W	112 A3
Thüringer Wald *Germany*	50°35N 11°0E	64 C6
Thurlby *U.K.*	52°45N 0°22W	27 G8
Thurles *Ireland*	52°41N 7°49W	20 C7
Thurmaston *U.K.*	52°40N 1°5W	27 G6
Thursby *U.K.*	54°51N 3°2W	26 C2
Thurso → *Italy*	41°44N 12°14E	68 D5
Thurso *U.K.*	58°36N 3°32W	23 E10
Thurso → *U.K.*	58°36N 3°32W	23 E10
Thurston I. *Antarctica*	72°0S 100°0W	55 D16
Tian Shan *Asia*	40°30N 76°0E	78 C4
Tianjin *China*	39°7N 117°12E	79 D12
Tianjun *China*	38°0N 98°30E	78 D8
Tianmen *China*	30°39N 113°9E	79 E11
Tianshui *China*	34°32N 105°40E	78 E10
Tiaret *Algeria*	35°20N 1°21E	94 A6
Tibasti, Sarīr *Libya*	22°50N 18°30E	95 D9
Tiber → *Italy*	41°44N 12°14E	68 D5
Tiberias, L. = Galilee, Sea of *Israel*	32°45N 35°35E	86 C3
Tibesti *Chad*	21°0N 17°30E	95 D9
Tibet = Xizang Zizhiqu □ *China*	32°0N 88°0E	78 E6
Tibet, Plateau of *Asia*	32°0N 86°0E	72 E10
Tiburón, I. *Mexico*	29°0N 112°25W	114 B2
Ticehurst *U.K.*	51°3N 0°25E	31 D9
Ticino → *Italy*	45°9N 9°14E	68 B3
Tickhill *U.K.*	53°26N 1°6W	27 F6
Ticonderoga *U.S.A.*	43°51N 73°26W	113 D11
Tideswell *U.K.*	53°17N 1°47W	27 F5
Tieling *China*	42°20N 123°55E	79 C13
Tierra de Campos *Spain*	42°10N 4°50W	67 A3
Tierra del Fuego, I. Grande de *Argentina*	54°0S 69°0W	121 H3
Tiffin *U.S.A.*	41°7N 83°11W	112 E6
Tignish *Canada*	46°58N 64°2W	113 B15
Tigris → *Asia*	31°0N 47°25E	86 D6
Tijuana *Mexico*	32°32N 117°1W	114 A1
Tikhoretsk *Russia*	45°56N 40°5E	71 E7
Tikhvin *Russia*	59°35N 33°30E	70 C5
Tikrīt *Iraq*	34°35N 43°37E	86 C5
Tiksi *Russia*	71°40N 128°45E	77 B13
Tilburg *Neths.*	51°31N 5°6E	64 C3
Tilbury *U.K.*	51°27N 0°22E	31 D9
Till → *U.K.*	55°41N 2°13W	26 A4
Tillicoultry *U.K.*	56°9N 3°45W	25 B8
Tilmanstone *U.K.*	51°12N 1°18E	31 D11
Tilt → *U.K.*	56°46N 3°51W	23 J10
Timaru *N.Z.*	44°23S 171°14E	99 J13
Timișoara *Romania*	45°43N 21°15E	65 F11
Timmins *Canada*	48°28N 81°25W	109 E11
Timor *Asia*	9°0S 125°0E	83 F7
Timor-Leste ■ *Asia*	8°50S 126°0E	83 F7
Timor Sea *Ind. Oc.*	12°0S 127°0E	72 K14
Tingewick *U.K.*	51°59N 1°2W	30 C6
Tingri *China*	28°34N 86°38E	78 F6
Tinogasta *Argentina*	28°5S 67°32W	121 E3
Tinos *Greece*	37°33N 25°8E	69 F11
Tintagel *U.K.*	50°39N 4°46W	29 F4
Tintagel Hd. *U.K.*	50°40N 4°47W	29 F4
Tipperary *Ireland*	52°28N 8°10W	20 D6
Tipperary □ *Ireland*	52°37N 7°55W	20 C7
Tipton *U.K.*	52°32N 2°4W	27 G4
Tipton *U.S.A.*	41°46N 91°8W	112 E2
Tiptree *U.K.*	51°48N 0°46E	31 C9
Tiranë *Albania*	41°18N 19°49E	69 D8
Tiraspol *Moldova*	46°55N 29°35E	65 E15
Tirebolu *Turkey*	40°58N 38°45E	71 F6
Tiree *U.K.*	56°31N 6°55W	24 A2
Tiree, Passage of *U.K.*	56°30N 6°30W	24 B2
Tirich Mir *Pakistan*	36°15N 71°55E	84 A7
Tirol □ *Austria*	47°3N 10°43E	64 E6
Tiruchchirappalli *India*	10°45N 78°45E	84 P11
Tirunelveli *India*	8°45N 77°45E	84 Q10
Tiruppur *India*	11°5N 77°22E	84 P10
Tisa → *Serbia*	45°15N 20°17E	69 B9
Tisbury *U.K.*	51°4N 2°5W	30 D4
Tisdale *Canada*	52°50N 104°0W	108 D9
Titchfield *U.K.*	50°50N 1°15W	30 E6
Titicaca, L. *S. Amer.*	15°30S 69°30W	120 D3
Titusville *U.S.A.*	41°38N 79°41W	112 E8
Tiverton *U.K.*	50°54N 3°29W	29 F7
Tivoli *Italy*	41°58N 12°45E	68 D5
Tizi-Ouzou *Algeria*	36°42N 4°3E	94 A6
Tlaxiaco *Mexico*	17°25N 97°35W	114 D5
Tlemcen *Algeria*	34°52N 1°21W	94 B3
Toamasina *Madag.*	18°10S 49°25E	97 H9
Toba, Danau *Indonesia*	2°30N 98°30E	82 D1
Toba Kakar *Pakistan*	31°30N 69°0E	84 D6
Tobago *Trin. & Tob.*	11°10N 60°30W	120 A3
Tobermory *Canada*	45°12N 81°40W	112 C7
Tobermory *U.K.*	56°38N 6°5W	24 A3
Tobol → *Russia*	58°10N 68°12E	76 D7
Tobolsk *Russia*	58°15N 68°10E	76 D7
Tocantins → *Brazil*	1°45S 49°10W	120 C5
Toddington *U.K.*	51°57N 0°32W	31 C7
Todmorden *U.K.*	53°43N 2°6W	27 E4
Todos os Santos, B. de *Brazil*	12°48S 38°38W	122 B3
Toe Hd. *U.K.*	57°50N 7°8W	22 G3
Togliatti *Russia*	53°32N 49°24E	70 D8
Togo ■ *W. Afr.*	8°30N 1°35E	94 G6
Tok *U.S.A.*	63°20N 142°59W	108 C5
Tokachi-Dake *Japan*	43°17N 142°5E	81 B8
Tokat *Turkey*	40°22N 36°35E	71 F6
Tokelau Is. ☑ *Pac. Oc.*	9°0S 171°45W	99 B16
Tokushima *Japan*	34°4N 134°34E	81 F4
Tōkyō *Japan*	35°43N 139°45E	81 F6
Toledo *Spain*	39°50N 4°2W	67 C3
Toledo *U.S.A.*	41°39N 83°33W	112 E6
Toledo, Montes de *Spain*	39°33N 4°20W	67 C3
Toliara *Madag.*	23°21S 43°40E	97 J8
Tolima *Colombia*	4°40N 75°19W	120 B2
Toluca *Mexico*	19°17N 99°40W	114 D5
Tomah *U.S.A.*	43°59N 90°30W	112 D2
Tomakomai *Japan*	42°38N 141°36E	81 B7
Tomaszów Mazowiecki *Poland*	51°30N 20°2E	65 C10
Tombador, Serra do *Brazil*	12°0S 58°0W	120 D4
Tombigbee → *U.S.A.*	31°8N 87°57W	111 D9
Tombouctou *Mali*	16°50N 3°0W	94 E5
Tomini, Teluk *Indonesia*	0°10S 121°0E	83 E6
Tomintoul *U.K.*	57°15N 3°23W	23 H11
Tomsk *Russia*	56°30N 85°5E	76 D9
Tonbridge *U.K.*	51°11N 0°17E	31 D9
Tone → *U.K.*	50°58N 3°20W	29 F7
Tonga ■ *Pac. Oc.*	19°50S 174°30W	99 D16
Tonga Trench *Pac. Oc.*	18°0S 173°0W	99 D16
Tongareva *Cook Is.*	9°0S 158°0W	103 H12
Tongatapu Group *Tonga*	21°0S 175°0W	99 E16
Tongchuan *China*	41°42N 125°58E	79 C14
Tongliao *China*	43°38N 122°18E	79 C13
Tongling *China*	30°55N 117°48E	79 E12
Tongue → *U.S.A.*	46°25N 105°52W	110 A5
Tongue *U.K.*	58°29N 4°25W	23 F9
Tonk *India*	26°6N 75°54E	84 F9
Tonkin, G. of *Asia*	20°0N 108°0E	78 G10
Tonlé Sap *Cambodia*	13°0N 104°0E	82 B2
Tonopah *U.S.A.*	38°4N 117°14W	110 C3
Toowoomba *Australia*	27°32S 151°56E	98 F9
Topeka *U.S.A.*	39°3N 95°40W	111 C7
Topolobampo *Mexico*	25°36N 109°3W	114 B3
Topsham *U.K.*	50°41N 3°28W	29 F7
Tor B. *U.K.*	50°25N 3°33W	29 G6
Torbay □ *U.K.*	50°26N 3°31W	29 G6
Tornealven → *Europe*	65°50N 24°12E	63 D8
Torneträsk *Sweden*	68°24N 19°15E	63 D7
Tornio *Finland*	65°50N 24°12E	63 D8
Toro, Cerro del *Chile*	29°10S 69°50W	121 E3
Toronto *Canada*	43°39N 79°20W	112 D8
Torpoint *U.K.*	50°23N 4°13W	29 G5
Torquay *U.K.*	50°27N 3°32W	29 G6
Torre del Greco *Italy*	40°47N 14°22E	68 D6
Torrejón de Ardoz *Spain*	40°27N 3°29W	67 B4
Torrelavega *Spain*	43°20N 4°5W	67 A3
Torremolinos *Spain*	36°38N 4°30W	67 D3
Torrens, L. *Australia*	31°0S 137°50E	98 G6
Torrent *Spain*	39°27N 0°28W	67 C5
Torreón *Mexico*	25°33N 103°26W	114 B4
Torres Strait *Australia*	9°50S 142°20E	98 C7
Torridge → *U.K.*	51°0N 4°13W	29 E5
Torridon, L. *U.K.*	57°35N 5°50W	22 G6
Torthorwald *U.K.*	55°6N 3°32W	25 D8
Tortosa *Spain*	40°49N 0°31E	67 B6
Toruń *Poland*	53°2N 18°39E	65 B10
Torver *U.K.*	54°20N 3°6W	26 D2
Tory I. *Ireland*	55°16N 8°13W	18 A6
Toscana □ *Italy*	43°25N 11°0E	68 C4
Toshka, Buheirat en *Egypt*	22°50N 31°0E	95 D12
Totland *U.K.*	50°41N 1°32W	30 E5
Totley *U.K.*	53°20N 1°32W	27 F5
Totnes *U.K.*	50°26N 3°42W	29 G6
Totton *U.K.*	50°55N 1°29W	30 E6
Tottori *Japan*	35°30N 134°15E	81 F4
Toubkal, Djebel *Morocco*	31°0N 8°0W	94 B4
Touggourt *Algeria*	33°6N 6°4E	94 B7
Toul *France*	48°40N 5°53E	66 B6
Toulon *France*	43°10N 5°55E	66 E6
Toulouse *France*	43°37N 1°27E	66 E4
Touraine *France*	47°20N 0°30E	66 C4
Tournai *Belgium*	50°35N 3°25E	64 C2
Tournon-sur-Rhône *France*	45°4N 4°50E	66 D6
Tours *France*	47°22N 0°40E	66 C4
Towanda *U.S.A.*	41°46N 76°27W	112 E9
Towcester *U.K.*	52°8N 0°59W	31 B7
Town Yetholm *U.K.*	55°33N 2°17W	25 C11
Townsville *Australia*	19°15S 146°45E	98 D8
Towraghondi *Afghan.*	35°13N 62°16E	84 B3
Towson *U.S.A.*	39°24N 76°36W	112 F9
Toyama *Japan*	36°40N 137°15E	81 E5
Toyohashi *Japan*	34°45N 137°25E	81 F5
Toyota *Japan*	35°3N 137°7E	81 F5
Trabzon *Turkey*	41°0N 39°45E	71 F6
Trafalgar, C. *Spain*	36°10N 6°2W	67 D2
Trail *Canada*	49°5N 117°40W	108 E8
Tralee *Ireland*	52°16N 9°42W	20 D3
Tralee B. *Ireland*	52°17N 9°55W	20 D3
Tramore *Ireland*	52°10N 7°10W	21 D8
Tramore B. *Ireland*	52°9N 7°10W	21 D8
Tranent *U.K.*	55°57N 2°57W	25 C10
Trang *Thailand*	7°33N 99°38E	82 C1
Transantarctic Mts. *Antarctica*	85°0S 170°0W	55 E12
Transnistria □ *Moldova*	47°20N 29°15E	65 E15
Transylvania *Romania*	46°30N 24°0E	65 E12
Transylvanian Alps *Romania*	45°30N 25°0E	65 F12
Trápani *Italy*	38°1N 12°29E	68 E5
Trasimeno, L. *Italy*	43°8N 12°6E	68 C5
Traverse City *U.S.A.*	44°46N 85°38W	112 C5
Trawbreaga B. *Ireland*	55°20N 7°25W	18 A7
Trawsfynydd *U.K.*	52°54N 3°55W	28 B6
Tredegar *U.K.*	51°47N 3°14W	28 D7
Trefaldwyn = Montgomery *U.K.*	52°34N 3°8W	28 B7
Trefynwy = Monmouth *U.K.*	51°48N 2°42W	28 D8
Tregaron *U.K.*	52°14N 3°56W	28 C6
Treinta y Tres *Uruguay*	33°16S 54°17W	121 F4
Trelew *Argentina*	43°10S 65°20W	121 E3
Trent → *U.K.*	53°41N 0°42W	27 E7
Trentham *U.K.*	52°58N 2°11W	27 G4
Trento *Italy*	46°4N 11°8E	68 A4
Trenton *Canada*	44°10N 77°34W	112 C9
Trenton *U.S.A.*	40°14N 74°46W	113 E10
Tres Arroyos *Argentina*	38°26S 60°20W	121 F3
Três Corações *Brazil*	21°44S 45°15W	122 D1
Três Lagoas *Brazil*	20°50S 51°43W	120 E4
Três Pontas *Brazil*	21°23S 45°29W	122 D1
Três Puntas, C. *Argentina*	47°0S 66°0W	121 G3
Três Rios *Brazil*	22°20S 43°30W	122 D2
Tresco *U.K.*	49°57N 6°20W	29 H1
Treviso *Italy*	45°40N 12°15E	68 B5
Trevose Hd. *U.K.*	50°32N 5°3W	29 F3
Tribal Areas □ *Pakistan*	33°0N 70°0E	84 C7
Trier *Germany*	49°45N 6°38E	64 D4
Trieste *Italy*	45°40N 13°46E	68 B5
Trim *Ireland*	53°33N 6°48W	19 D8
Trimdon *U.K.*	54°42N 1°24W	26 C6
Trimley *U.K.*	51°59N 1°20E	31 C11
Trincomalee *Sri Lanka*	8°38N 81°15E	84 Q12
Trindade *Atl. Oc.*	20°20S 29°50W	52 F8
Trinidad *Bolivia*	14°46S 64°50W	120 D3
Trinidad *Cuba*	21°48N 80°0W	115 C9
Trinidad *U.S.A.*	37°10N 104°31W	110 C6
Trinidad & Tobago ■ *W. Indies*	10°30N 61°20W	115 E12
Trinity → *U.S.A.*	29°45N 94°43W	111 E8
Trinity B. *Canada*	48°20N 53°10W	109 E14
Trinity Is. *U.S.A.*	56°33N 154°25W	108 D4
Tripoli *Lebanon*	34°31N 35°50E	86 C3
Tripoli *Libya*	32°49N 13°7E	95 B8
Tripolitania *Libya*	31°0N 13°0E	95 B8
Tripura □ *India*	24°0N 92°0E	85 H18
Tristan da Cunha *Atl. Oc.*	37°6S 12°20W	52 F9
Trnava *Slovakia*	48°23N 17°35E	65 D9
Trois-Rivières *Canada*	46°25N 72°34W	109 E12
Trollhättan *Sweden*	58°17N 12°20E	63 F6
Trombetas → *Brazil*	1°55S 55°35W	120 C4
Tromsø *Norway*	69°40N 18°56E	63 D7
Tronador *Argentina*	41°10S 71°50W	121 G2
Trondheim *Norway*	63°36N 10°25E	63 E6
Trondheimsfjorden *Norway*	63°35N 10°30E	63 E6
Troon *U.K.*	55°33N 4°39W	24 C6
Trossachs, The *U.K.*	56°14N 4°24W	24 B7
Trostan *U.K.*	55°3N 6°10W	19 A9
Trotternish *U.K.*	57°32N 6°15W	22 G5
Trou Gras Pt. *St. Lucia*	13°51N 60°53W	114 b
Trout L. *N.W.T., Canada*	60°40N 121°14W	108 C7
Trout L. *Ont., Canada*	51°20N 93°15W	108 D10
Trowbridge *U.K.*	51°18N 2°12W	30 D4
Troy *Turkey*	39°57N 26°12E	71 E4
Troy *Ala., U.S.A.*	31°48N 85°58W	111 D9
Troy *N.Y., U.S.A.*	42°44N 73°41W	113 D11
Troy *Ohio, U.S.A.*	40°2N 84°12W	112 E5
Troyes *France*	48°19N 4°3E	66 B6
Trujillo *Honduras*	16°0N 86°0W	114 D7
Trujillo *Peru*	8°6S 79°0W	120 C2
Trujillo *Venezuela*	9°22N 70°38W	120 B2
Truk *Micronesia*	7°25N 151°46E	102 G7
Trull *U.K.*	51°0N 3°6W	30 E2
Trumpington *U.K.*	52°10N 0°7E	31 B9
Truro *Canada*	45°21N 63°14W	109 E13
Truro *U.K.*	50°16N 5°4W	29 G3
Tsavo *Kenya*	2°59S 38°28E	96 E7
Tseung Kwan *China*	22°19N 114°15E	79 a
Tshikapa *Dem. Rep. of the Congo*	6°28S 20°48E	96 F4
Tsiigehtchic *Canada*	67°15N 134°0W	108 C6
Tsimlyansk Res. *Russia*	48°0N 43°0E	71 E7
Tskhinvali *Georgia*	42°14N 44°1E	71 F7
Tsuchiura *Japan*	36°5N 140°15E	81 E7
Tsuen Wan *China*	22°22N 114°6E	79 a
Tsugaru Str. *Japan*	41°35N 141°0E	81 C7
Tsumeb *Namibia*	19°9S 17°44E	97 H3
Tsuruoka *Japan*	38°44N 139°50E	81 D6
Tsushima *Japan*	34°20N 129°20E	81 F1
Tuam *Ireland*	53°31N 8°51W	18 D4
Tuamotu, Îs. *French Polynesia*	17°0S 144°0W	103 J13
Tuapse *Russia*	44°5N 39°10E	71 F6
Tubarão *Brazil*	28°30S 49°0W	121 E5
Tübingen *Germany*	48°31N 9°4E	64 D5
Tubruq *Libya*	32°7N 23°55E	95 B10
Tubuaï, Îs. *French Polynesia*	25°0S 150°0W	103 K13
Tucson *U.S.A.*	32°13N 110°58W	110 D4
Tucumcari *U.S.A.*	35°10N 103°44W	110 C6
Tucupita *Venezuela*	9°2N 62°3W	120 B3
Tucuruí *Brazil*	3°42S 49°44W	120 C5
Tucuruí, Represa de *Brazil*	4°0S 49°30W	120 C5
Tuen Mun *China*	22°23N 113°57E	79 a
Tuguegarao *Phil.*	17°35N 121°42E	83 A4
Tuktoyaktuk *Canada*	69°27N 133°2W	108 C6
Tula *Russia*	54°13N 37°38E	70 D6
Tulancingo *Mexico*	20°5N 98°22W	114 C5
Tulare *U.S.A.*	36°13N 119°21W	110 C3
Tulcán *Ecuador*	0°48N 77°43W	120 B2
Tulcea *Romania*	45°13N 28°46E	65 F15
Tulita *Canada*	64°57N 125°30W	108 C7
Tulla *Ireland*	52°53N 8°46W	20 C5
Tullamore *Ireland*	53°16N 7°31W	21 B7
Tulle *France*	45°16N 1°46E	66 D4
Tullow *Ireland*	52°49N 6°45W	21 C9
Tulsa *U.S.A.*	36°10N 95°55W	111 C7
Tumaco *Colombia*	1°50N 78°45W	120 B2
Tumbes *Peru*	3°37S 80°27W	120 C1
Tummel → *U.K.*	56°42N 3°59W	23 J9
Tummel, L. *U.K.*	56°43N 3°55W	23 J10
Tumucumaque, Serra *Brazil*	2°0N 55°0W	120 B4
Tunis *Tunisia*	36°50N 10°11E	95 A8
Tunisia ■ *Africa*	33°30N 9°10E	95 A7
Tunja *Colombia*	5°33N 73°25W	120 B2
Tunstall *U.K.*	52°9N 1°27E	31 B11
Tupaciguara *Brazil*	18°35S 48°42W	122 C1
Tupelo *U.S.A.*	34°16N 88°43W	111 D9
Tupiza *Bolivia*	21°30S 65°40W	120 E3
Turfan Basin *China*	42°40N 89°25E	78 C6
Turgutlu *Turkey*	38°30N 27°43E	71 G4
Turin *Italy*	45°3N 7°40E	68 B2
Turkana, L. *Africa*	3°30N 36°5E	96 D7
Turkey ■ *Eurasia*	39°0N 36°0E	71 G6
Türkmenbashi *Turkmenistan*	40°5N 53°5E	87 A8
Turkmenistan ■ *Asia*	39°0N 59°0E	87 B9
Turks & Caicos Is. ☑ *W. Indies*	21°20N 71°20W	115 C10
Turku *Finland*	60°30N 22°19E	63 E8
Turnberry *U.K.*	55°18N 4°49W	24 D6
Turneffe Is. *Belize*	17°20N 87°50W	114 D7
Turpan *China*	43°58N 89°10E	78 C6
Turriff *U.K.*	57°32N 2°27W	23 H13
Tuticorin *India*	8°50N 78°12E	84 Q11
Tutuila *Amer. Samoa*	14°19S 170°50W	99 C16
Tutume *Botswana*	20°30S 27°5E	97 J5
Tuul Gol → *Mongolia*	48°30N 104°25E	78 B9
Tuva □ *Russia*	51°30N 95°0E	77 D10
Tuvalu ■ *Pac. Oc.*	8°0S 178°0E	99 B14
Tuxford *U.K.*	53°14N 0°54W	27 F7
Tuxpan *Mexico*	20°57N 97°24W	114 C5
Tuxtla Gutiérrez *Mexico*	16°45N 93°7W	114 D6
Tuz Gölü *Turkey*	38°42N 33°18E	71 G5
Tuzla *Bos.-H.*	44°34N 18°41E	69 B8
Tver *Russia*	56°55N 35°59E	70 C6
Tweed → *U.K.*	55°45N 2°0W	25 C11
Tweedmouth *U.K.*	55°45N 2°0W	26 A5
Tweedshaws *U.K.*	55°27N 3°29W	25 D9
Twenty *U.K.*	52°47N 0°17W	27 G8
Twin Falls *U.S.A.*	42°34N 114°28W	110 B4
Two Harbors *U.S.A.*	47°2N 91°40W	112 B2
Two Rivers *U.S.A.*	44°9N 87°34W	112 C4
Twyford *Hants., U.K.*	51°1N 1°19W	30 D6
Twyford *Wokingham, U.K.*	51°28N 0°51W	31 D7
Tychy *Poland*	50°9N 18°59E	65 C10
Tydd St. Mary *U.K.*	52°45N 0°7E	27 G9
Tyler *U.S.A.*	32°21N 95°18W	111 D7
Tyndrum *U.K.*	56°26N 4°42W	24 B6
Tyne → *U.K.*	54°59N 1°32W	26 C5
Tyne & Wear □ *U.K.*	55°6N 1°17W	26 B6
Tynemouth *U.K.*	55°1N 1°26W	26 B6
Tyrol = Tirol □ *Austria*	47°3N 10°43E	64 E6
Tyrrhenian Sea *Medit. S.*	40°0N 12°30E	68 E5
Tyumen *Russia*	57°11N 65°29E	76 D7
Tywardreath *U.K.*	50°21N 4°42W	29 G4
Tywi → *U.K.*	51°48N 4°21W	28 D5
Tywyn *U.K.*	52°35N 4°5W	28 B5
Tzaneen *S. Africa*	23°47S 30°9E	97 J6

U

U.S.A. = United States of America ■ *N. Amer.*	37°0N 96°0W	110 C7
U.S. Virgin Is. ☑ *W. Indies*	18°20N 65°0W	115 D12
Uaupés → *Brazil*	0°2N 67°16W	120 B3
Ubá *Brazil*	21°8S 43°0W	122 D2
Ubaitaba *Brazil*	14°18S 39°20W	122 B3
Ube *Japan*	33°56N 131°15E	81 G2
Uberaba *Brazil*	19°50S 47°55W	122 C1
Uberlândia *Brazil*	19°0S 48°20W	122 C1
Ubon Ratchathani *Thailand*	15°15N 104°50E	82 A2
Ucayali → *Peru*	4°30S 73°30W	120 C2
Uckfield *U.K.*	50°58N 0°7E	31 E9
Udagamandalam *India*	11°30N 76°44E	84 P10
Udaipur *India*	24°36N 73°44E	84 G8
Uddingston *U.K.*	55°49N 4°5W	24 C7
Údine *Italy*	46°3N 13°14E	68 A5
Udmurtia □ *Russia*	57°30N 52°30E	70 C9
Udon Thani *Thailand*	17°29N 102°46E	82 A2
Udupi *India*	13°25N 74°42E	84 N9
Uele → *Dem. Rep. of the Congo*	3°45N 24°45E	96 D4
Ufa *Russia*	54°45N 55°55E	70 D10
Uffculme *U.K.*	50°54N 3°20W	29 F7
Ufford *U.K.*	52°8N 1°23E	31 B11
Uganda ■ *Africa*	2°0N 32°0E	96 D6
Ugborough *U.K.*	50°22N 3°53W	29 G6
Uibhist a Deas = South Uist *U.K.*	57°20N 7°15W	22 H3
Uibhist a Tuath = North Uist *U.K.*	57°40N 7°15W	22 G3
Uig *U.K.*	57°35N 6°21W	22 G5
Uinta Mts. *U.S.A.*	40°45N 110°30W	110 B4
Ujjain *India*	23°9N 75°43E	84 H9
Ukhta *Russia*	63°34N 53°41E	70 B9
Ukiah *U.S.A.*	39°9N 123°13W	110 C2
Ukraine ■ *Europe*	49°0N 32°0E	71 E5
Ulaan-Uul *Mongolia*	46°4N 100°49E	78 B9
Ulaangom *Mongolia*	50°5N 92°10E	78 A7
Ulan Bator *Mongolia*	47°55N 106°53E	78 B10
Ulan Ude *Russia*	51°45N 107°40E	77 D11
Ulceby Cross *U.K.*	53°15N 0°7E	27 F9
Ulhasnagar *India*	19°15N 73°10E	84 K8
Uliastay *Mongolia*	47°56N 97°28E	78 B8
Ullapool *U.K.*	57°54N 5°9W	22 G7
Ulleungdo *S. Korea*	37°30N 130°30E	81 E2
Ullswater *U.K.*	54°34N 2°52W	26 C3
Ulm *Germany*	48°23N 9°58E	64 D5
Ulsan *S. Korea*	35°20N 129°15E	79 D14
Ulster □ *U.K.*	54°35N 6°30W	19 B9
Ulukhaktok *Canada*	70°44N 117°44W	108 B8
Ulungur He → *China*	47°1N 87°24E	78 B6
Uluru *Australia*	25°23S 131°5E	98 F5
Ulva *U.K.*	56°29N 6°13W	24 B3
Ulverston *U.K.*	54°13N 3°5W	26 D2
Ulyanovsk *Russia*	54°20N 48°25E	70 D8
Uman *Ukraine*	48°40N 30°12E	71 E5
Umeå *Sweden*	63°45N 20°20E	63 E8
Umeälven → *Sweden*	63°45N 20°20E	63 E8
Umlazi *S. Africa*	29°59S 30°54E	97 L6
Umm al Qaywayn *U.A.E.*	25°30N 55°35E	87 E8
Umnak I. *U.S.A.*	53°15N 168°20W	108 D3
Umuahia *Nigeria*	5°31N 7°26E	94 G7
Unalakleet *U.S.A.*	63°52N 160°47W	108 C3
Unalaska *U.S.A.*	53°53N 166°32W	108 D3
Unalaska I. *U.S.A.*	53°35N 166°50W	108 D3
'Unayzah *Si. Arabia*	26°6N 43°58E	86 E5
Uncía *Bolivia*	18°25S 66°40W	120 D3
Ungava, Pén. d' *Canada*	60°0N 74°0W	109 D12
Ungava B. *Canada*	59°30N 67°30W	109 D13
União dos Palmares *Brazil*	9°10S 36°2W	122 A3
Unimak I. *U.S.A.*	54°45N 164°0W	108 D3
Union City *U.S.A.*	36°26N 89°3W	112 G3
Uniontown *U.S.A.*	39°54N 79°44W	112 F8
United Arab Emirates ■ *Asia*	23°50N 54°0E	87 F8
United Kingdom ■ *Europe*	53°0N 2°0W	62 E6
United States of America ■ *N. Amer.*	37°0N 96°0W	110 C7
Unst *U.K.*	60°44N 0°53W	22 A16
Unzen-Dake *Japan*	32°45N 130°17E	81 G2
Upavon *U.K.*	51°18N 1°48W	30 D5
Upington *S. Africa*	28°25S 21°15E	97 K4
'Upolu *Samoa*	13°58S 172°0W	99 C16
Upper Heyford *U.K.*	51°56N 1°15W	30 C6
Upper Klamath L. *U.S.A.*	42°25N 121°55W	110 B2
Uppingham *U.K.*	52°36N 0°43W	27 G7
Uppsala *Sweden*	59°53N 17°38E	63 F7
Upton *U.K.*	53°13N 2°53W	27 F3
Upton-upon-Severn *U.K.*	52°3N 2°12W	30 B4
Upwey *U.K.*	50°39N 2°29W	30 E4
Ur *Iraq*	30°55N 46°25E	86 D6
Ural → *Kazakhstan*	47°0N 51°48E	71 E9
Ural Mts. *Eurasia*	60°0N 59°0E	70 C10
Uranium City *Canada*	59°34N 108°37W	108 D9
Uraricoera → *Brazil*	3°2N 60°30W	120 B3
Urbana *Ill., U.S.A.*	40°7N 88°12W	112 E3
Urbana *Ohio, U.S.A.*	40°7N 83°45W	112 E6
Urganch *Uzbekistan*	41°40N 60°41E	87 A10
Urmia *Iran*	37°40N 45°0E	86 B6

INDEX 183

Urmia, L. — Whittlesford

Urmia, L. *Iran* 37°50N 45°30E **86 B6**
Urmston *U.K.* 53°27N 2°21W **27 F4**
Uruaçu *Brazil* 14°30S 49°10W **122 B1**
Uruapan *Mexico* 19°24N 102°3W **114 D4**
Urubamba → *Peru* 10°43S 73°48W **120 D2**
Uruguai → *Brazil* 26°0S 53°30W **121 E4**
Uruguaiana *Brazil* 29°50S 57°0W **121 E4**
Uruguay ■ *S. Amer.* 32°30S 56°30W **121 F4**
Uruguay → *S. Amer.* 34°12S 58°18W **117 G5**
Ürümqi *China* 43°45N 87°45E **78 C6**
Usa → *Russia* 66°16N 59°49E **70 A10**
Uşak *Turkey* 38°43N 29°28E **71 G4**
Usakos *Namibia* 21°54S 15°31E **97 J3**
Usedom *Germany* 53°55N 14°2E **64 B8**
Ushant *France* 48°28N 5°6W **66 B1**
Ushuaia *Argentina* 54°50S 68°23W **121 H3**
Usk → *U.K.* 51°33N 2°58W **29 D8**
Usolye Sibirskoye *Russia* 52°48N 103°40E **77 D11**
Uspallata, P. de *Argentina* 32°37S 69°22W **121 F3**
Usselby *U.K.* 53°26N 0°21W **27 F8**
Ussuriysk *Russia* 43°48N 131°59E **81 B2**
Ust-Ilimsk *Russia* 58°3N 102°39E **77 D11**
Ust-Kut *Russia* 56°50N 105°42E **77 D11**
Ústí nad Labem *Czechia* 50°41N 14°3E **64 C8**
Ústica *Italy* 38°42N 13°11E **68 E5**
Usu *China* 44°27N 84°40E **78 C5**
Usumacinta → *Mexico* 18°24N 92°38W **114 D6**
Utah □ *U.S.A.* 39°20N 111°30W **110 C4**
Utah L. *U.S.A.* 40°12N 111°48W **110 B4**
Utica *U.S.A.* 43°6N 75°14W **113 D10**
Utrecht *Neths.* 52°5N 5°8E **64 B3**
Utsunomiya *Japan* 36°30N 139°50E **81 E6**
Uttar Pradesh □ *India* 27°0N 80°0E **84 F12**
Uttaradit *Thailand* 17°36N 100°5E **82 A2**
Uttarakhand □ *India* 30°0N 79°30E **84 D11**
Uttoxeter *U.K.* 52°54N 1°52W **27 G5**
Uusikaupunki *Finland* 60°47N 21°25E **63 E8**
Uvalde *U.S.A.* 29°13N 99°47W **110 E7**
Uvira *Dem. Rep. of the Congo* 3°22S 29°3E **96 E5**
Uvs Nuur *Mongolia* 50°20N 92°30E **78 A7**
Uyuni *Bolivia* 20°28S 66°47W **120 E3**
Uzbekistan ■ *Asia* 41°30N 65°0E **87 A10**
Uzhhorod *Ukraine* 48°36N 22°18E **65 D12**

V

Vaal → *S. Africa* 29°4S 23°38E **97 K4**
Vaasa *Finland* 63°6N 21°38E **63 E8**
Vadakara *India* 11°35N 75°40E **84 P9**
Vadodara *India* 22°20N 73°10E **84 H8**
Vadsø *Norway* 70°3N 29°50E **63 C9**
Vaduz *Liech.* 47°8N 9°31E **64 E5**
Váh → *Slovakia* 47°43N 18°7E **65 D9**
Vail *U.S.A.* 39°40N 106°20W **110 C5**
Vaila *U.K.* 60°12N 1°36W **22 B14**
Val-d'Or *Canada* 48°7N 77°47W **109 E12**
Valdai Hills *Russia* 57°0N 33°30E **70 C5**
Valdés, Pen. *Argentina* 42°30S 63°45W **121 G3**
Valdez *U.S.A.* 61°7N 146°16W **108 C5**
Valdivia *Chile* 39°50S 73°14W **121 F2**
Valdosta *U.S.A.* 30°50N 83°17W **111 D10**
Vale of Glamorgan □ *U.K.* 51°28N 3°25W **29 E7**
Valença *Brazil* 13°20S 39°5W **122 B3**
Valence *France* 44°57N 4°54E **66 D6**
Valencia *Spain* 39°27N 0°23W **67 C5**
Valencia *Venezuela* 10°11N 68°0W **120 A3**
Valencia □ *Spain* 39°20N 0°40W **67 C5**
Valencia, G. de *Spain* 39°30N 0°20E **67 C6**
Valencia I. *Ireland* 51°54N 10°22W **20 E2**
Valenciennes *France* 50°20N 3°34E **66 A5**
Valera *Venezuela* 9°19N 70°37W **120 B2**
Valladolid *Mexico* 20°41N 88°12W **114 C7**
Valladolid *Spain* 41°38N 4°43W **67 B3**
Valledupar *Colombia* 10°29N 73°15W **120 A2**
Vallejo *U.S.A.* 38°7N 122°14W **110 C2**
Vallenar *Chile* 28°30S 70°50W **121 E2**
Valletta *Malta* 35°54N 14°31E **68 G6**
Valley *U.K.* 53°16N 4°34W **28 A4**
Valley City *U.S.A.* 46°55N 98°0W **110 A7**
Valparaíso *Chile* 33°2S 71°40W **121 F2**
Van *Turkey* 38°30N 43°20E **71 G7**
Van, L. *Turkey* 38°30N 43°0E **71 G7**
Van Buren *U.S.A.* 47°10N 67°58W **113 B13**
Van Wert *U.S.A.* 40°52N 84°35W **112 E5**
Vanadzor *Armenia* 40°48N 44°30E **71 F7**
Vancouver *Canada* 49°15N 123°7W **108 E7**
Vancouver *U.S.A.* 45°38N 122°40W **110 A2**
Vancouver I. *Canada* 49°50N 126°0W **108 E7**
Vandalia *U.S.A.* 38°58N 89°6W **112 F3**
Vanderhoof *Canada* 54°0N 124°0W **108 D7**
Vänern *Sweden* 58°47N 13°30E **63 F6**
Vännäs *Sweden* 63°58N 19°48E **63 E7**
Vannes *France* 47°40N 2°47W **66 C2**
Vanrhynsdorp *S. Africa* 31°36S 18°44E **97 L3**
Vantaa *Finland* 60°18N 24°56E **63 E8**
Vanua Levu *Fiji* 16°33S 179°15E **99 D14**
Vanuatu ■ *Pac. Oc.* 15°0S 168°0E **99 D12**
Varanasi *India* 25°22N 83°0E **85 G13**
Varangerfjorden *Norway* 70°3N 29°25E **63 C9**
Varberg *Sweden* 57°6N 12°20E **63 F6**
Vardø *Norway* 70°23N 31°5E **63 C10**
Varese *Italy* 45°48N 8°50E **68 B3**
Varginha *Brazil* 21°33S 45°25W **122 D1**
Varna *Bulgaria* 43°13N 27°56E **69 C12**
Vasa Barris → *Brazil* 11°10S 37°10W **122 B3**
Västerås *Sweden* 59°37N 16°38E **63 F7**
Västervik *Sweden* 57°43N 16°33E **63 F7**
Vaté *Vanuatu* 17°40S 168°25E **99 D12**
Vatersay *U.K.* 56°55N 7°32W **22 J2**
Vatican City ■ *Europe* 41°54N 12°27E **68 D5**
Vatnajökull *Iceland* 64°30N 16°48W **63 B2**
Vättern *Sweden* 58°25N 14°30E **63 F6**
Vaughn *U.S.A.* 34°36N 105°13W **110 D5**
Vava'u Group *Tonga* 18°40S 174°0W **99 D16**
Vega *Norway* 65°40N 11°55E **63 D6**
Vegreville *Canada* 53°30N 112°5W **108 D8**
Vélez-Málaga *Spain* 36°48N 4°5W **67 D3**
Velhas → *Brazil* 17°13S 44°49W **122 C2**
Velikiy Novgorod *Russia* 58°30N 31°25E **70 C5**
Velikiye Luki *Russia* 56°25N 30°32E **70 C5**
Veliko Tarnovo *Bulgaria* 43°5N 25°41E **69 C11**
Velikonda Range *India* 14°45N 79°10E **84 M11**
Vellore *India* 12°57N 79°10E **84 N11**
Velsk *Russia* 61°10N 42°0E **70 B7**
Vendée □ *France* 46°50N 1°35W **66 C3**
Vendôme *France* 47°47N 1°3E **66 C4**
Venézia, G. di *Italy* 45°15N 13°0E **68 B5**
Venezuela ■ *S. Amer.* 8°0N 66°0W **120 B3**
Venezuela, G. de *Venezuela* 11°30N 71°0W **120 A2**
Vengurla *India* 15°53N 73°45E **84 M8**
Venice *Italy* 45°27N 12°21E **68 B5**
Ventnor *U.K.* 50°36N 1°12W **30 E6**
Ventoux, Mt. *France* 44°10N 5°17E **66 D6**
Ventspils *Latvia* 57°25N 21°32E **63 F8**
Veracruz *Mexico* 19°11N 96°8W **114 D5**
Veraval *India* 20°53N 70°27E **84 J7**
Vercelli *Italy* 45°19N 8°25E **68 B3**
Verde → *U.S.A.* 33°33N 111°40W **110 D4**
Verdun *France* 49°9N 5°24E **66 B6**
Vereeniging *S. Africa* 26°38S 27°57E **97 K5**
Verkhoyansk *Russia* 67°35N 133°25E **77 C14**
Verkhoyansk Ra. *Russia* 66°0N 129°0E **77 C13**
Vermont □ *U.S.A.* 44°0N 73°0W **113 D11**
Vernal *U.S.A.* 40°27N 109°32W **110 B5**
Vernon *Canada* 50°20N 119°15W **108 D8**
Vernon *U.S.A.* 34°9N 99°17W **110 D7**
Verona *Italy* 45°27N 10°59E **68 B4**
Versailles *France* 48°48N 2°7E **66 B5**
Vert, C. *Senegal* 14°45N 17°30W **94 F2**
Verviers *Belgium* 50°37N 5°52E **64 C3**
Verwood *U.K.* 50°52N 1°52W **30 E5**
Veryan *U.K.* 50°13N 4°56W **29 G4**
Veryan B. *U.K.* 50°13N 4°51W **29 G4**
Vesoul *France* 47°40N 6°11E **66 C7**
Vesterålen *Norway* 68°45N 15°0E **63 D7**
Vestfjorden *Norway* 67°55N 14°0E **63 D6**
Vesuvio *Italy* 40°49N 14°26E **68 D6**
Veszprém *Hungary* 47°8N 17°57E **65 E9**
Vianópolis *Brazil* 16°40S 48°35W **122 C1**
Viaréggio *Italy* 43°52N 10°14E **68 C4**
Vicenza *Italy* 45°33N 11°33E **68 B4**
Vichada → *Colombia* 4°55N 67°50W **120 B3**
Vichy *France* 46°9N 3°26E **66 C5**
Vickerstown *U.K.* 54°6N 3°15W **26 D2**
Vicksburg *U.S.A.* 32°21N 90°53W **111 D8**
Victoria *Canada* 48°30N 123°25W **108 E7**
Victoria *China* 22°17N 114°11E **79 a**
Victoria *U.S.A.* 28°48N 97°0W **111 E7**
Victoria □ *Australia* 37°0S 144°0E **98 H7**
Victoria, L. *Africa* 1°0S 33°0E **96 E6**
Victoria Falls *Zimbabwe* 17°58S 25°52E **97 H5**
Victoria I. *Canada* 71°0N 111°0W **108 B8**
Victoria Ld. *Antarctica* 75°0S 160°0E **55 D11**
Victoria Str. *Canada* 69°31N 100°30W **108 C9**
Victoriaville *Canada* 46°4N 71°56W **113 B12**
Vidin *Bulgaria* 43°59N 22°50E **69 C10**
Viedma, L. *Argentina* 49°30S 72°30W **121 G2**
Vienna *Austria* 48°12N 16°22E **64 D9**
Vienne *France* 45°31N 4°53E **66 D6**
Vienne → *France* 47°13N 0°5E **66 C4**
Vientiane *Laos* 17°58N 102°36E **82 A2**
Vierge Pt. *St. Lucia* 13°49N 60°53W **114 b**
Vierzon *France* 47°13N 2°5E **66 C5**
Vietnam ■ *Asia* 19°0N 106°0E **82 A3**
Vieux Fort *St. Lucia* 13°46N 60°58W **114 b**
Vigévano *Italy* 45°19N 8°51E **68 B3**
Vigo *Spain* 42°12N 8°41W **67 A1**
Vijayapura *India* 16°50N 75°55E **84 L9**
Vijayawada *India* 16°31N 80°39E **85 L12**
Vikna *Norway* 64°55N 10°58E **63 E6**
Vila Nova de Gaia *Portugal* 41°8N 8°37W **67 B1**
Vila Velha *Brazil* 20°20S 40°17W **122 D2**
Vilaine → *France* 47°30N 2°27W **66 C2**
Vilhelmina *Sweden* 64°35N 16°39E **63 E7**
Vilhena *Brazil* 12°40S 60°5W **120 D3**
Vilkitski Str. *Russia* 78°0N 103°0E **77 B11**
Villa Bella *Bolivia* 10°25S 65°22W **120 D3**
Villa María *Argentina* 32°20S 63°10W **121 F3**
Villach *Austria* 46°37N 13°51E **64 E7**
Villahermosa *Mexico* 17°59N 92°55W **114 D6**
Villajoyosa *Spain* 38°30N 0°12W **67 C5**
Villarrica *Paraguay* 25°40S 56°30W **121 E4**
Villavicencio *Colombia* 4°9N 73°37W **120 B2**
Ville-Marie *Canada* 47°20N 79°30W **112 B8**
Villeneuve-sur-Lot *France* 44°24N 0°42E **66 D4**
Vilnius *Lithuania* 54°38N 25°19E **63 G9**
Vilyuy → *Russia* 64°24N 126°26E **77 C13**
Vilyuysk *Russia* 63°40N 121°35E **77 C13**
Viña del Mar *Chile* 33°0S 71°30W **121 F2**
Vincennes *U.S.A.* 38°41N 87°32W **112 F4**
Vindhya Ra. *India* 22°50N 77°0E **84 H10**
Vineland *U.S.A.* 39°29N 75°2W **113 F10**
Vinnytsya *Ukraine* 49°15N 28°30E **65 D15**
Virden *Canada* 49°50N 100°56W **108 E9**
Vire *France* 48°50N 0°53W **66 B3**
Virgenes, C. *Argentina* 52°19S 68°21W **121 H3**
Virgin → *U.S.A.* 36°28N 114°21W **110 C4**
Virgin Is. (British) ⊠ *W. Indies* 18°30N 64°30W **115 D12**
Virgin Is. (U.S.) ⊠ *W. Indies* 18°20N 65°0W **115 D12**
Virginia *S. Africa* 28°8S 26°55E **97 K5**
Virginia *U.S.A.* 47°31N 92°32W **111 A8**
Virginia □ *U.S.A.* 37°30N 78°45W **112 G8**
Virginia Beach *U.S.A.* 36°49N 76°9W **111 C11**
Viroqua *U.S.A.* 43°34N 90°53W **112 D2**
Vis *Croatia* 43°4N 16°10E **68 C7**
Visalia *U.S.A.* 36°20N 119°18W **110 C3**
Visby *Sweden* 57°37N 18°18E **63 F7**
Viscount Melville Sd. *Canada* 74°10N 108°0W **109 B9**
Vishakhapatnam *India* 17°45N 83°20E **85 L13**
Vistula → *Poland* 54°22N 18°55E **65 A10**
Viterbo *Italy* 42°25N 12°6E **68 C5**
Viti Levu *Fiji* 17°30S 177°30E **99 D14**
Vitim → *Russia* 59°26N 112°34E **77 D12**
Vitória *Brazil* 20°20S 40°22W **122 D2**
Vitória da Conquista *Brazil* 14°51S 40°51W **122 B2**
Vitória-Gasteiz *Spain* 42°50N 2°41W **67 A4**
Vitsyebsk *Belarus* 55°10N 30°15E **70 C5**
Vittória *Italy* 36°57N 14°32E **68 F6**
Vizianagaram *India* 18°6N 83°30E **85 K13**
Vladikavkaz *Russia* 43°0N 44°35E **71 F7**
Vladimir *Russia* 56°15N 40°30E **70 C7**
Vladivostok *Russia* 43°10N 131°53E **77 E14**
Vlissingen *Neths.* 51°26N 3°34E **64 C2**
Vlorë *Albania* 40°32N 19°28E **69 D8**
Vltava → *Czechia* 50°21N 14°30E **64 D8**
Voe *U.K.* 60°21N 1°16W **22 B15**
Vogelsberg *Germany* 50°31N 9°12E **64 C5**
Vohimena, Tanjon' i *Madag.* 25°36S 45°8E **97 K9**
Voi *Kenya* 3°25S 38°32E **96 E7**
Vojvodina □ *Serbia* 45°20N 20°0E **69 B9**
Volga → *Russia* 46°0N 48°30E **71 E8**
Volga Hts. *Russia* 51°0N 46°0E **71 D8**
Volgodonsk *Russia* 47°33N 42°5E **71 E7**
Volgograd *Russia* 48°40N 44°25E **71 E7**
Volgograd Res. *Russia* 50°0N 45°20E **71 D8**
Vologda *Russia* 59°10N 39°45E **70 C6**
Volos *Greece* 39°24N 22°59E **69 E10**
Volsk *Russia* 52°5N 47°22E **70 D8**
Volta → *Ghana* 5°46N 0°41E **94 G6**
Volta, L. *Ghana* 7°30N 0°0 **94 G6**
Volta Redonda *Brazil* 22°31S 44°5W **122 D2**
Volzhskiy *Russia* 48°56N 44°46E **71 E7**
Vorkuta *Russia* 67°48N 64°20E **70 A11**
Voronezh *Russia* 51°40N 39°10E **71 D6**
Vosges *France* 48°20N 7°10E **66 B7**
Vostok I. *Kiribati* 10°5S 152°23W **103 J12**
Votkinsk *Russia* 57°0N 53°55E **70 C9**
Vratsa *Bulgaria* 43°15N 23°30E **69 C10**
Vryburg *S. Africa* 26°55S 24°45E **97 K4**
Vryheid *S. Africa* 27°45S 30°47E **97 K6**
Vulcano *Italy* 38°24N 14°58E **68 E6**
Vung Tau *Vietnam* 10°21N 107°4E **82 B3**
Vyazma *Russia* 55°10N 34°15E **70 C5**
Vyborg *Russia* 60°43N 28°47E **70 B4**
Vychegda → *Russia* 61°18N 46°36E **70 B8**
Vyrnwy, L. *U.K.* 52°48N 3°31W **28 B6**
Vyshniy Volochek *Russia* 57°30N 34°30E **70 C5**

W

Waal → *Neths.* 51°37N 5°0E **64 C3**
Wabasca → *Canada* 58°22N 115°20W **108 D8**
Wabash *U.S.A.* 40°48N 85°49W **112 E5**
Wabash → *U.S.A.* 37°48N 88°2W **112 G3**
Waco *U.S.A.* 31°33N 97°9W **111 D7**
Wad Medani *Sudan* 14°28N 33°30E **95 F12**
Waddesdon *U.K.* 51°51N 0°55W **31 C7**
Waddingham *U.K.* 53°27N 0°32W **27 F7**
Waddington *U.K.* 53°10N 0°32W **27 F7**
Waddington, Mt. *Canada* 51°23N 125°15W **108 D7**
Wadebridge *U.K.* 50°31N 4°51W **29 F4**
Wadhurst *U.K.* 51°3N 0°20E **31 D9**
Wadi Halfa *Sudan* 21°53N 31°19E **95 D12**
Wager B. *Canada* 65°26N 88°40W **109 C11**
Wagga Wagga *Australia* 35°7S 147°24E **98 H8**
Wah *Pakistan* 33°45N 72°40E **84 C8**
Wahiawā *U.S.A.* 21°30N 158°2W **110 H15**
Waigeo *Indonesia* 0°20S 130°40E **83 E8**
Wailuku *U.S.A.* 20°53N 156°30W **110 H16**
Wainfleet All Saints *U.K.* 53°7N 0°15E **27 F9**
Wakayama *Japan* 34°15N 135°15E **81 F4**
Wake I. *Pac. Oc.* 19°18N 166°36E **102 F8**
Wakefield *Jamaica* 18°26N 77°42W **114 a**
Wakefield *U.K.* 53°41N 1°29W **27 E6**
Wakkanai *Japan* 45°28N 141°35E **81 A7**
Walberswick *U.K.* 52°19N 1°40E **31 B12**
Wałbrzych *Poland* 50°45N 16°18E **64 C9**
Walbury Hill *U.K.* 51°21N 1°28W **30 D6**
Waldron *U.K.* 50°56N 0°13E **31 E9**
Wales □ *U.K.* 52°19N 4°43W **28 C4**
Walgett *Australia* 30°0S 148°5E **98 G8**
Walker L. *U.S.A.* 38°42N 118°43W **110 C3**
Walla Walla *U.S.A.* 46°4N 118°20W **110 A3**
Wallaceburg *Canada* 42°34N 82°23W **112 D6**
Wallachia *Romania* 44°35N 25°0E **65 F13**
Wallasey *U.K.* 53°25N 3°2W **27 F2**
Wallingford *U.K.* 51°35N 1°8W **30 C6**
Wallis & Futuna, Îs. ⊠ *Pac. Oc.* 13°18S 176°10W **99 C15**
Walls *U.K.* 60°14N 1°33W **22 B14**
Wallsend *U.K.* 54°59N 1°31W **26 C5**
Walmer *U.K.* 51°11N 1°25E **31 D11**
Walney, I. of *U.K.* 54°6N 3°15W **26 D2**
Walpole *U.K.* 52°45N 0°13E **31 A9**
Walsall *U.K.* 52°35N 1°58W **27 G5**
Walsenburg *U.S.A.* 37°38N 104°47W **110 C6**
Walsoken *U.K.* 52°41N 0°11E **31 A9**
Waltham *U.K.* 53°31N 0°7W **27 E8**
Waltham Abbey *U.K.* 51°41N 0°1E **31 C9**
Waltham Forest □ *U.K.* 51°35N 0°0 **31 C9**
Waltham on the Wolds *U.K.* 52°50N 0°48W **27 G7**
Walton-on-the-Naze *U.K.* 51°51N 1°17E **31 C11**
Walvis Bay *Namibia* 23°0S 14°28E **97 J2**
Wamba *Dem. Rep. of the Congo* 2°10N 27°57E **96 D5**
Wanborough *U.K.* 51°33N 1°42W **30 C5**
Wandsworth □ *U.K.* 51°27N 0°11W **31 D8**
Wanganui *N.Z.* 39°56S 175°3E **99 H14**
Wanleweyne *Somalia* 2°37N 44°54E **89 G3**
Wansbeck → *U.K.* 55°10N 1°32W **26 B5**
Wantage *U.K.* 51°35N 1°25W **30 C6**
Wanxian *China* 30°42N 108°20E **78 E10**
Wanzai *China* 22°12N 113°31E **79 a**
Wapakoneta *U.S.A.* 40°34N 84°12W **112 E5**
Warangal *India* 17°58N 79°35E **84 L11**
Warboys *U.K.* 52°24N 0°4W **31 B8**
Ward *Ireland* 53°26N 6°20W **21 B10**
Wardha *India* 20°45N 78°39E **84 J11**
Wardington *U.K.* 52°7N 1°17W **30 B6**
Wardle *U.K.* 53°7N 2°35W **27 F3**
Ward's Stone *U.K.* 54°1N 2°36W **27 D3**
Ware *U.K.* 51°49N 0°1W **31 C8**
Wareham *U.K.* 50°42N 2°7W **30 E4**
Wark *U.K.* 55°6N 2°14W **26 B4**
Warkworth *U.K.* 55°21N 1°37W **26 B5**
Warley *U.K.* 52°30N 1°59W **27 H5**
Warminster *U.K.* 51°12N 2°10W **30 D4**
Warrego → *Australia* 30°24S 145°21E **98 G8**
Warren *Mich., U.S.A.* 42°28N 83°1W **112 D6**
Warren *Ohio, U.S.A.* 41°14N 80°49W **112 E7**
Warren *Pa., U.S.A.* 41°51N 79°9W **112 E8**
Warrenpoint *U.K.* 54°6N 6°15W **19 C9**
Warri *Nigeria* 5°30N 5°41E **94 G7**
Warrington *U.K.* 53°24N 2°35W **27 F3**
Warrnambool *Australia* 38°25S 142°30E **98 H7**
Warsaw *Poland* 52°14N 21°0E **65 B11**
Warsaw *U.S.A.* 41°14N 85°51W **112 E5**
Warta → *Poland* 52°35N 14°39E **64 B8**
Warwick *U.K.* 52°18N 1°35W **30 B5**
Warwick *U.S.A.* 41°42N 71°28W **113 E12**
Warwickshire □ *U.K.* 52°14N 1°38W **30 B5**
Wasatch Ra. *U.S.A.* 40°0N 111°30W **110 B4**
Wash, The *U.K.* 52°58N 0°20E **31 A9**
Washburn *U.S.A.* 46°40N 90°54W **112 B2**
Washford *U.K.* 51°9N 3°21W **30 D2**
Washington *U.K.* 54°55N 1°30W **26 C6**
Washington *D.C., U.S.A.* 38°53N 77°2W **112 F9**
Washington *Ind., U.S.A.* 38°40N 87°10W **112 F4**
Washington *Pa., U.S.A.* 40°10N 80°15W **112 E7**
Washington □ *U.S.A.* 47°30N 120°30W **110 A2**
Washington, Mt. *U.S.A.* 44°16N 71°18W **113 C12**
Washington I. *U.S.A.* 45°23N 86°54W **112 C4**
Wasilla *U.S.A.* 61°35N 149°26W **108 C5**
Waskaganish *Canada* 51°30N 78°40W **109 D12**
Wast Water *U.K.* 54°26N 3°18W **26 D2**
Watampone *Indonesia* 4°29S 120°25E **83 E6**
Watchet *U.K.* 51°10N 3°19W **30 D2**
Waterbeach *U.K.* 52°16N 0°12E **31 B9**
Waterbury *U.S.A.* 41°33N 73°3W **113 E11**
Waterford *Ireland* 52°15N 7°8W **21 D8**
Waterford □ *Ireland* 52°10N 7°40W **21 D7**
Waterford Harbour *Ireland* 52°8N 6°58W **21 D9**
Watergate B. *U.K.* 50°26N 5°4W **29 G3**
Waterloo *Canada* 43°30N 80°32W **112 D7**
Waterloo *Ill., U.S.A.* 38°20N 90°9W **112 F2**
Waterloo *Iowa, U.S.A.* 42°30N 92°21W **111 B8**
Watersmeet *U.S.A.* 46°16N 89°11W **112 B3**
Watertown *N.Y., U.S.A.* 43°59N 75°55W **113 D10**
Watertown *S. Dak., U.S.A.* 44°54N 97°7W **111 B7**
Watertown *Wis., U.S.A.* 43°12N 88°43W **112 D3**
Waterville *U.S.A.* 44°33N 69°38W **113 C13**
Watford *U.K.* 51°40N 0°24W **31 C8**
Watlington *Norfolk, U.K.* 52°40N 0°24E **31 A9**
Watlington *Oxon., U.K.* 51°38N 1°0W **30 C6**
Watrous *Canada* 51°40N 105°25W **108 D9**
Watsa *Dem. Rep. of the Congo* 3°4N 29°30E **96 D5**
Watseka *U.S.A.* 40°47N 87°44W **112 E4**
Watson Lake *Canada* 60°6N 128°49W **108 C7**
Watton *U.K.* 52°34N 0°51E **31 A10**
Wau *South Sudan* 7°45N 28°1E **95 G11**
Waukegan *U.S.A.* 42°22N 87°50W **112 D4**
Waukesha *U.S.A.* 43°1N 88°14W **112 D3**
Waupaca *U.S.A.* 44°21N 89°5W **112 C3**
Waupun *U.S.A.* 43°38N 88°44W **112 D3**
Wausau *U.S.A.* 44°58N 89°38W **112 C3**
Wautoma *U.S.A.* 44°4N 89°18W **112 C3**
Wauwatosa *U.S.A.* 43°2N 88°0W **112 D4**
Waveney → *U.K.* 52°35N 1°39E **31 A12**
Waver → *U.K.* 54°50N 3°15W **26 C2**
Wawa *Canada* 47°59N 84°47W **112 B5**
Waycross *U.S.A.* 31°13N 82°21W **111 D10**
Wayne *U.S.A.* 38°13N 82°27W **112 F6**
Waynesboro *U.S.A.* 38°4N 78°53W **112 F8**
Waynesburg *U.S.A.* 39°54N 80°11W **112 F7**
Wazirabad *Pakistan* 32°30N 74°8E **84 C9**
Weald, The *U.K.* 51°4N 0°20E **31 D9**
Wear → *U.K.* 54°55N 1°23W **26 C6**
Weardale *U.K.* 54°44N 2°5W **26 C4**
Wearhead *U.K.* 54°45N 2°13W **26 C4**
Weaver → *U.K.* 53°17N 2°35W **27 F3**
Weaverham *U.K.* 53°16N 2°35W **27 F3**
Webster Springs *U.S.A.* 38°29N 80°25W **112 F7**
Weddell Sea *Antarctica* 72°30S 40°0W **55 D1**
Wedmore *U.K.* 51°13N 2°48W **30 D3**
Wednesbury *U.K.* 52°34N 2°1W **27 G4**
Wednesfield *U.K.* 52°37N 2°2W **27 G4**
Weedon Bec *U.K.* 52°15N 1°5W **30 B6**
Weifang *China* 36°44N 119°7E **79 D12**
Weihai *China* 37°30N 122°6E **79 D13**
Weipa *Australia* 12°40S 141°50E **98 C7**
Welch *U.S.A.* 37°26N 81°35W **112 G7**
Weldon *U.K.* 55°17N 1°45W **26 B5**
Welford *W. Berkshire, U.K.* 51°27N 1°24W **30 D6**
Welford *W. Northants., U.K.* 52°25N 1°3W **30 B6**
Welkom *S. Africa* 28°0S 26°46E **97 K5**
Welland *Canada* 43°0N 79°15W **112 D8**
Welland → *U.K.* 52°51N 0°5W **27 G8**
Wellesley Is. *Australia* 16°42S 139°30E **98 D6**
Wellingborough *U.K.* 52°19N 0°41W **31 B7**
Wellington *N.Z.* 41°19S 174°46E **99 J13**
Wellington *Somst., U.K.* 50°58N 3°13W **30 E2**
Wellington *Telford & Wrekin, U.K.* 52°42N 2°30W **27 G3**
Wellington, I. *Chile* 49°30S 75°0W **121 G2**
Wellington Chan. *Canada* 75°0N 93°0W **109 B10**
Wells *U.K.* 51°13N 2°39W **30 D3**
Wells-next-the-Sea *U.K.* 52°57N 0°51E **31 A10**
Wellsboro *U.S.A.* 41°45N 77°18W **112 E9**
Wellsville *U.S.A.* 42°7N 77°57W **112 D9**
Welney *U.K.* 52°31N 0°15E **31 A9**
Wels *Austria* 48°9N 14°1E **64 D8**
Welshpool *U.K.* 52°39N 3°8W **28 B7**
Welton *U.K.* 53°18N 0°29W **27 F8**
Welwyn Garden City *U.K.* 51°48N 0°12W **31 C8**
Wem *U.K.* 52°52N 2°44W **27 G3**
Wembury *U.K.* 50°19N 4°6W **29 G5**
Wemindji *Canada* 53°0N 78°49W **109 D12**
Wemyss Bay *U.K.* 55°53N 4°53W **24 C6**
Wenatchee *U.S.A.* 47°25N 120°19W **110 A2**
Wendover *U.K.* 51°45N 0°44W **31 C7**
Wenlock Edge *U.K.* 52°30N 2°43W **27 H3**
Wensleydale *U.K.* 54°17N 2°0W **26 D4**
Wensu *China* 41°15N 80°10E **78 C5**
Wensum → *U.K.* 52°40N 1°15E **31 A11**
Wenzhou *China* 28°0N 120°38E **79 F13**
Weobley *U.K.* 52°11N 2°50W **30 B3**
Werrington *U.K.* 50°39N 4°23W **29 F5**
Weser → *Germany* 53°36N 8°28E **64 B5**
West Antarctica *Antarctica* 80°0S 90°0W **55 D15**
West Auckland *U.K.* 54°38N 1°43W **26 C5**
West Bank □ *Asia* 32°6N 35°13E **86 C3**
West Bend *U.S.A.* 43°25N 88°11W **112 D3**
West Bengal = Paschimbanga □ *India* 23°0N 88°0E **85 H16**
West Berkshire □ *U.K.* 51°25N 1°17W **30 D6**
West Beskids *Europe* 49°30N 19°0E **65 D10**
West Bridgford *U.K.* 52°55N 1°8W **27 G6**
West Bromwich *U.K.* 52°32N 1°59W **27 G5**
West Burra *U.K.* 60°5N 1°21W **22 B15**
West Calder *U.K.* 55°51N 3°33W **25 C8**
West Coker *U.K.* 50°55N 2°40W **30 E3**
West Falkland *Falk. Is.* 51°40S 60°0W **121 H3**
West Fen *U.K.* 53°5N 0°5W **27 F8**
West Frankfort *U.S.A.* 37°54N 88°55W **111 C9**
West Grinstead *U.K.* 50°58N 0°19W **31 E8**
West Haddon *U.K.* 52°20N 1°3W **30 B6**
West Kirby *U.K.* 53°23N 3°11W **27 F2**
West Linton *U.K.* 55°46N 3°21W **25 C9**
West Lulworth *U.K.* 50°37N 2°14W **30 E4**
West Malling *U.K.* 51°17N 0°26E **31 D9**
West Meon *U.K.* 51°1N 1°5W **30 D6**
West Mersea *U.K.* 51°46N 0°56E **31 C10**
West Midlands □ *U.K.* 52°26N 2°0W **27 H5**
West Moors *U.K.* 50°49N 1°53W **30 E5**
West Northamptonshire □ *U.K.* 52°8N 0°59W **30 B6**
West Palm Beach *U.S.A.* 26°43N 80°3W **111 E10**
West Point *U.S.A.* 37°32N 76°48W **112 G9**
West Rasen *U.K.* 53°23N 0°24W **27 F8**
West Seneca *U.S.A.* 42°51N 78°48W **112 D8**
West Siberian Plain *Russia* 62°0N 75°0E **72 B9**
West Sussex □ *U.K.* 50°55N 0°30W **31 E8**
West Virginia □ *U.S.A.* 38°45N 80°30W **112 F7**
West Yorkshire □ *U.K.* 53°45N 1°40W **27 E5**
Westbourne *U.K.* 50°52N 0°55W **31 E7**
Westbrook *U.S.A.* 43°41N 70°22W **113 D12**
Westbury *Shrops., U.K.* 52°41N 2°55W **27 G3**
Westbury *Wilts., U.K.* 51°15N 2°11W **30 D4**
Westbury-on-Severn *U.K.* 51°50N 2°25W **30 C4**
Wester Ross *U.K.* 57°37N 4°51W **22 G6**
Westerham *U.K.* 51°16N 0°5E **31 D9**
Western Australia □ *Australia* 25°0S 118°0E **98 F2**
Western Ghats *India* 14°0N 75°0E **84 N9**
Western Isles = Eilean Siar □ *U.K.* 57°30N 7°10W **22 G3**
Western Sahara ■ *Africa* 25°0N 13°0W **94 D3**
Westerwald *Germany* 50°38N 7°56E **64 C4**
Westfield *U.K.* 50°55N 0°35E **31 E10**
Westhill *U.K.* 57°9N 2°19W **23 H13**
Westhoughton *U.K.* 53°33N 2°31W **27 E3**
Westmeath □ *Ireland* 53°33N 7°34W **18 D6**
Westminster *U.S.A.* 39°34N 76°59W **112 F9**
Westmoreland *Barbados* 13°13N 59°37W **114 c**
Westmorland & Furness *U.K.* 54°28N 2°40W **26 C3**
Weston *U.K.* 52°51N 2°1W **27 G4**
Weston *U.S.A.* 39°2N 80°28W **112 F7**
Weston-super-Mare *U.K.* 51°21N 2°58W **30 D3**
Westport *Ireland* 53°48N 9°31W **18 D2**
Westray *U.K.* 59°18N 3°0W **23 D11**
Westruther *U.K.* 55°45N 2°35W **25 C10**
Westward Ho! *U.K.* 51°2N 4°15W **29 E5**
Wetar *Indonesia* 7°48S 126°30E **83 F7**
Wetaskiwin *Canada* 52°55N 113°24W **108 D8**
Wetherby *U.K.* 53°56N 1°23W **27 E6**
Wetwang *U.K.* 54°1N 0°35W **27 D7**
Wewak *Papua N. G.* 3°38S 143°41E **98 A7**
Wexford *Ireland* 52°20N 6°28W **21 D10**
Wexford □ *Ireland* 52°20N 6°25W **21 D10**
Wexford Harbour *Ireland* 52°20N 6°25W **21 D10**
Wey → *U.K.* 51°22N 0°27W **31 D8**
Weybourne *U.K.* 52°57N 1°9E **31 A11**
Weybridge *U.K.* 51°22N 0°27W **31 D8**
Weyburn *Canada* 49°40N 103°50W **108 E9**
Weymouth *U.K.* 50°37N 2°28W **30 E4**
Wha Ti *Canada* 63°8N 117°16W **108 C8**
Whale Cove *Canada* 62°10N 92°34W **108 C10**
Whales, B. of *Antarctica* 78°0S 160°0W **55 D12**
Whalley *U.K.* 53°49N 2°24W **27 E4**
Whalsay *U.K.* 60°22N 0°59W **22 B16**
Whalton *U.K.* 55°8N 1°46W **26 B5**
Whangarei *N.Z.* 35°43S 174°21E **99 H13**
Whaplode *U.K.* 52°42N 0°3W **27 G8**
Wharekauri = Chatham Is. *Pac. Oc.* 44°0S 176°40W **99 J15**
Wharfe → *U.K.* 53°51N 1°9W **27 E6**
Wharfedale *U.K.* 54°6N 2°1W **26 D4**
Wheatley Hill *U.K.* 54°45N 1°23W **26 C6**
Wheeler Pk. *U.S.A.* 38°57N 114°15W **110 C4**
Wheeling *U.S.A.* 40°4N 80°43W **112 E7**
Whernside *U.K.* 54°14N 2°24W **26 D4**
Whicham *U.K.* 54°15N 3°21W **26 D2**
Whimple *U.K.* 50°46N 3°20W **29 F7**
Whipsnade *U.K.* 51°51N 0°32W **31 C7**
Whissendine *U.K.* 52°43N 0°46W **27 G7**
Whitburn *U.K.* 55°52N 3°40W **25 C8**
Whitby *U.K.* 54°29N 0°37W **26 D7**
Whitchurch *Devon, U.K.* 50°32N 4°9W **29 F5**
Whitchurch *Hants., U.K.* 51°14N 1°20W **30 D6**
Whitchurch *Hereford, U.K.* 51°51N 2°39W **30 C3**
Whitchurch *Shrops., U.K.* 52°59N 2°40W **27 G3**
White → *Ark., U.S.A.* 33°57N 91°5W **111 D8**
White → *Ind., U.S.A.* 38°25N 87°45W **112 F4**
White → *Utah, U.S.A.* 40°4N 109°41W **110 B5**
White Esk → *U.K.* 55°13N 3°11W **25 D9**
White Horse, Vale of *U.K.* 51°37N 1°30W **30 C5**
White Horse Hill *U.K.* 51°34N 1°33W **30 C5**
White Mts. *Calif., U.S.A.* 37°30N 118°15W **110 C3**
White Mts. *N.H., U.S.A.* 44°15N 71°15W **111 B12**
White Nile → *Sudan* 15°38N 32°31E **95 E12**
White Sea *Russia* 66°30N 38°0E **70 A6**
Whiteadder Water → *U.K.* 55°51N 2°25W **25 C11**
Whitecourt *Canada* 54°10N 115°45W **108 D8**
Whitefish Pt. *U.S.A.* 46°45N 84°59W **112 B5**
Whitehall *U.S.A.* 44°22N 91°19W **112 C2**
Whitehaven *U.K.* 54°33N 3°35W **26 C1**
Whitehorse *Canada* 60°43N 135°3W **108 C6**
Whitesand B. *U.K.* 50°21N 4°18W **29 G5**
Whitewater *U.S.A.* 42°50N 88°44W **112 D3**
Whithorn *U.K.* 54°44N 4°26W **24 E7**
Whitley Bay *U.K.* 55°3N 1°27W **26 B6**
Whitney, Mt. *U.S.A.* 36°35N 118°18W **110 C3**
Whitstable *U.K.* 51°21N 1°3E **31 D11**
Whittington *Derby, U.K.* 53°16N 1°26W **27 F6**
Whittington *Shrops., U.K.* 52°52N 3°0W **27 G3**
Whittlesey *U.K.* 52°33N 0°8W **31 A8**
Whittlesford *U.K.* 52°7N 0°9E **31 B9**

Whitwell

Zwolle

Whitwell Derby, U.K. 53°17N 1°12W 27 F6
Whitwell I. of W., U.K. 50°36N 1°15W 30 E6
Whitwick U.K. 52°45N 1°22W 27 G6
Whitworth U.K. 53°39N 2°11W 27 E4
Wholdaia L. Canada 60°43N 104°20W 108 C9
Whyalla Australia 33°2S 137°30E 98 G6
Wiarton Canada 44°40N 81°10W 112 C7
Wiay U.K. 57°24N 7°13W 22 H3
Wichita U.S.A. 37°42N 97°20W 111 C7
Wichita Falls U.S.A. 33°54N 98°30W 110 D7
Wick U.K. 58°26N 3°5W 23 F11
Wickford U.K. 51°36N 0°33E 31 C10
Wickham U.K. 50°54N 1°11W 30 E6
Wickham Market U.K. 52°9N 1°23E 31 B11
Wicklow Ireland 52°59N 6°3W 21 C10
Wicklow Hd. Ireland 52°58N 6°0W 21 C10
Wicklow Mts. △ Ireland 53°6N 6°21W 21 B11
Wickwar U.K. 51°36N 2°23W 30 C4
Widdrington U.K. 55°15N 1°35W 26 B5
Widecombe U.K. 50°34N 3°49W 29 F6
Widemouth U.K. 50°47N 4°34W 29 F4
Widnes U.K. 53°23N 2°45W 27 F3
Wiener Neustadt Austria 47°49N 16°16E 64 E9
Wiesbaden Germany 50°4N 8°14E 64 C5
Wigan U.K. 53°33N 2°38W 27 E3
Wight, Isle of □ U.K. 50°41N 1°17W 30 E6
Wigmore U.K. 52°19N 2°51W 30 B3
Wigston U.K. 52°35N 1°6W 27 G6
Wigton U.K. 54°50N 3°10W 26 C2
Wigtown U.K. 54°53N 4°27W 24 E7
Wigtown B. U.K. 54°46N 4°15W 24 E7
Wilhelm, Mt. Papua N. G. 5°50S 145°1E 98 B8
Wilhelmshaven Germany 53°31N 8°7E 64 B5
Wilkes-Barre U.S.A. 41°15N 75°53W 113 E10
Wilkes Land Antarctica 69°0S 120°0E 55 D9
Wilkins Ice Shelf Antarctica 70°30S 72°0W 55 D17
Willemstad Curaçao 12°5N 68°55W 115 E11
Willenhall U.K. 52°36N 2°2W 27 G4
Willesborough U.K. 51°8N 0°56E 31 D10
Williams Lake Canada 52°10N 122°10W 108 D7
Williamsburg U.S.A. 37°16N 76°43W 112 G9
Williamson U.S.A. 37°41N 82°17W 112 G6
Williamsport U.S.A. 41°15N 77°1W 112 E9
Willingdon U.K. 50°47N 0°17E 31 E9
Williston U.S.A. 48°9N 103°37W 110 A6
Williston L. Canada 56°0N 124°0W 108 D7
Williton U.K. 51°9N 3°19W 30 D2
Willmar U.S.A. 45°7N 95°3W 111 A7
Willoughby U.K. 53°13N 0°12E 27 F9
Wilmington U.K. 50°47N 3°7W 29 F7
Wilmington Del., U.S.A. 39°45N 75°33W 113 F10
Wilmington N.C., U.S.A. 34°14N 77°55W 111 D11
Wilmslow U.K. 53°19N 2°13W 27 F4
Wilnecote U.K. 52°36N 1°39W 27 G5
Wilton U.K. 51°5N 1°51W 30 D5
Wiltshire □ U.K. 51°18N 1°53W 30 D5
Wimblington U.K. 52°31N 0°4E 31 A9
Wimborne Minster U.K. 50°48N 1°59W 30 E5
Wincanton U.K. 51°3N 2°24W 30 D4
Winchelsea U.K. 50°55N 0°43E 31 E10
Winchester U.K. 51°4N 1°18W 30 D6
Winchester Ky., U.S.A. 37°59N 84°11W 112 G6
Winchester Va., U.S.A. 39°11N 78°10W 112 F8
Wind → U.S.A. 43°12N 108°12W 110 B5
Wind River Range U.S.A. 43°0N 109°30W 110 B5
Windermere U.K. 54°23N 2°55W 26 D3
Windhoek Namibia 22°35S 17°4E 97 J3
Windrush → U.K. 51°43N 1°24W 30 C6
Windsor Canada 42°18N 83°0W 109 E11
Windsor U.K. 51°29N 0°36W 31 D7
Windward Is. W. Indies 13°0N 61°0W 115 E12
Windward Passage Caribbean 20°0N 74°0W 115 D10
Wing U.K. 51°53N 0°43W 31 C7
Wingham U.K. 51°16N 1°13E 31 D11
Winisk → Canada 55°17N 85°5W 109 D11
Winkleigh U.K. 50°50N 3°58W 29 F6
Winkler Canada 49°10N 97°56W 108 E10
Winneba Ghana 5°25N 0°36W 94 G5
Winnebago, L. U.S.A. 44°0N 88°26W 112 D3
Winnemucca U.S.A. 40°58N 117°44W 110 B3
Winnipeg Canada 49°54N 97°9W 108 E10
Winnipeg, L. Canada 52°0N 97°0W 108 D10
Winnipegosis L. Canada 52°30N 100°0W 108 C9
Winona U.S.A. 44°3N 91°39W 111 B8
Winooski → U.S.A. 44°29N 73°11W 113 C11
Winsford U.K. 53°12N 2°31W 27 F3
Winslow U.K. 51°57N 0°52W 31 C7
Winslow U.S.A. 35°2N 110°42W 110 C4
Winster U.K. 53°9N 1°39W 27 F5
Winston-Salem U.S.A. 36°6N 80°15W 111 C10
Winterborne Abbas U.K. 50°42N 2°33W 30 E3
Winterthur Switz. 47°30N 8°44E 64 E5
Winterton N. Lincs., U.K. 53°39N 0°37W 27 E7
Winterton Norfolk, U.K. 52°43N 1°41E 31 A12
Winton Australia 22°24S 143°3E 98 E7

Wirksworth U.K. 53°6N 1°35W 27 F5
Wirral U.K. 53°25N 3°0W 27 F2
Wisbech U.K. 52°41N 0°9E 31 A9
Wisborough Green U.K. 51°2N 0°30W 31 D7
Wisconsin □ U.S.A. 44°45N 89°30W 111 B9
Wisconsin Rapids U.S.A. 44°23N 89°49W 112 C3
Wishaw U.K. 55°46N 3°54W 25 C8
Wiske → U.K. 54°19N 1°27W 26 D6
Witham U.K. 51°48N 0°40E 31 C10
Witham → U.K. 52°59N 0°2W 27 F8
Withern U.K. 53°18N 0°8E 27 F9
Withernsea U.K. 53°44N 0°1E 27 E9
Witley U.K. 51°9N 0°39W 31 D7
Witney U.K. 51°48N 1°28W 30 C6
Wittersham U.K. 51°0N 0°43E 31 D10
Wiveliscombe U.K. 51°2N 3°19W 30 D2
Wivenhoe U.K. 51°51N 0°59E 31 C10
Wkra → Poland 52°27N 20°44E 65 B11
Włocławek Poland 52°40N 19°3E 65 B10
Woburn U.K. 51°59N 0°36W 31 C7
Woburn Sands U.K. 52°1N 0°39W 31 B7
Wodonga Australia 36°5S 146°50E 98 H8
Woking U.K. 51°19N 0°34W 31 D7
Wokingham U.K. 51°24N 0°49W 31 D7
Wolf Rock U.K. 49°57N 5°49W 29 H2
Wolfsburg Germany 52°25N 10°48E 64 B6
Wolin Poland 53°50N 14°37E 64 B8
Wollaston L. Canada 58°7N 103°10W 108 D9
Wollaston Pen. Canada 69°30N 115°0W 108 C8
Wollongong Australia 34°25S 150°54E 98 G9
Wolsingham U.K. 54°44N 1°52W 26 C5
Wolverhampton U.K. 52°35N 2°7W 27 G4
Wolverton U.K. 52°3N 0°47W 31 B7
Wolviston U.K. 54°38N 1°18W 26 C6
Wombwell U.K. 53°32N 1°25W 27 E6
Woodroffe, Mt. Australia 26°20S 131°45E 98 F5
Wônsan N. Korea 39°11N 127°27E 79 D14
Wonston U.K. 51°8N 1°18W 30 D6
Woodbridge U.K. 52°6N 1°20E 31 B11
Woodbury U.K. 50°41N 3°24W 29 F7
Woodhall Spa U.K. 53°10N 0°12W 27 F8
Woodhouse U.K. 53°22N 1°21W 27 F6
Woodley U.K. 51°27N 0°53W 31 D7
Woods, L. of the N. Amer. 49°15N 94°45W 108 E10
Woodstock N.B., Canada 46°11N 67°37W 109 E13
Woodstock Ont., Canada 43°10N 80°45W 112 D7
Woodstock U.K. 51°51N 1°20W 30 C6
Wookey U.K. 51°13N 2°41W 30 D3
Wookey Hole U.K. 51°14N 2°40W 30 D3
Wool U.K. 50°40N 2°12W 30 E4
Woolacombe U.K. 51°10N 4°13W 29 E5
Wooler U.K. 55°33N 2°1W 26 A4
Woonsocket U.S.A. 42°0N 71°31W 113 E11
Wootton Wawen U.K. 52°16N 1°47W 30 B5
Worcester S. Africa 33°39S 19°27E 97 L3
Worcester U.K. 52°11N 2°12W 30 B4
Worcester U.S.A. 42°16N 71°48W 113 D12
Worcestershire □ U.K. 52°13N 2°10W 30 B4
Worfield U.K. 52°34N 2°21W 27 G4
Workington U.K. 54°39N 3°33W 26 C1
Worksop U.K. 53°18N 1°7W 27 F6
Worms Germany 49°37N 8°21E 64 D5
Wortham U.K. 52°21N 1°3E 31 B11
Worthing Barbados 13°5N 59°35W 114 c
Worthing U.K. 50°49N 0°21W 31 E8
Worthington U.S.A. 43°37N 95°36W 111 B7
Wotton under Edge U.K. 51°37N 2°20W 30 C4
Wragby U.K. 53°18N 0°17W 27 F8
Wrangel I. Russia 71°0N 180°0E 77 B19
Wrangell U.S.A. 56°28N 132°23W 108 D6
Wrangell Mts. U.S.A. 61°30N 142°0W 108 C5
Wrangle U.K. 53°3N 0°7E 27 F9
Wrath, C. U.K. 58°38N 5°1W 22 E7
Wrekin, The U.K. 52°41N 2°32W 27 G3
Wrentham U.K. 52°23N 1°40E 31 B12
Wrexham U.K. 53°3N 3°0W 28 A8
Wrexham □ U.K. 53°1N 3°0W 28 D7
Wrigley Canada 63°16N 123°37W 108 C7
Writtle U.K. 51°44N 0°27E 31 C9
Wrocław Poland 51°5N 17°5E 65 C9
Wroughton U.K. 51°31N 1°47W 30 C5
Wroxham U.K. 52°42N 1°24E 31 A11
Wu Jiang → China 29°40N 107°20E 78 F10
Wuhai China 39°39N 106°48E 78 D10
Wuhan China 30°31N 114°18E 79 E11
Wuhu China 31°22N 118°21E 79 E12
Wuppertal Germany 51°16N 7°12E 64 C4
Würzburg Germany 49°46N 9°55E 64 D5
Wushi China 41°9N 79°13E 78 C4
Wutongqiao China 29°22N 103°50E 78 F9
Wuwei China 37°57N 102°34E 78 D9
Wuxi China 31°33N 120°18E 79 E13
Wuyi Shan China 27°0N 117°0E 79 F12
Wuzhong China 38°2N 106°12E 78 D10
Wuzhou China 23°30N 111°18E 79 G11

Wye U.K. 51°10N 0°57E 31 D10
Wye → U.K. 51°38N 2°40W 30 C3
Wylye → U.K. 51°5N 1°51W 30 D5
Wymondham Leics., U.K. 52°35N 1°7E 31 A11
Wymondham Norfolk, U.K. 52°35N 1°7E 31 A11
Wyndham Australia 15°33S 128°3E 98 D4
Wyoming □ U.S.A. 43°0N 107°30W 110 B5
Wyre → U.K. 53°52N 2°57W 27 E3
Wyre Forest U.K. 52°24N 2°24W 27 H4

X

Xaçmaz Azerbaijan 41°31N 48°42E 71 F8
Xai-Xai Mozam. 25°6S 33°31E 97 J6
Xalapa Mexico 19°32N 96°55W 114 D5
Xankándi Azerbaijan 39°52N 46°49E 71 G8
Xenia U.S.A. 39°41N 83°56W 112 F6
Xi Jiang → China 22°5N 113°20E 79 G11
Xiaguan China 25°32N 100°16E 78 F9
Xiamen China 24°25N 118°4E 79 G12
Xi'an China 34°15N 109°0E 79 E10
Xiang Jiang → China 28°55N 112°50E 79 F11
Xiangfan China 32°2N 112°8E 79 E11
Xianggang = Hong Kong □ China 22°11N 114°14E 79 a
Xiangtan China 27°51N 112°54E 79 F11
Xiantao China 30°25N 113°25E 79 E11
Xianyang China 34°20N 108°40E 79 E10
Xichang China 27°51N 102°19E 78 F9
Xigazê China 29°5N 88°45E 78 F6
Xilinhot China 43°52N 116°2E 79 C12
Ximiao China 40°59N 100°12E 78 C9
Xinghua China 32°58N 119°48E 79 E12
Xingu → Brazil 1°30S 51°53W 120 C4
Xingyi China 25°3N 104°59E 78 F9
Xining China 36°34N 101°40E 78 D9
Xinwan China 22°47N 113°40E 79 a
Xinxiang China 35°18N 113°50E 79 D11
Xinyang China 32°6N 114°3E 79 E11
Xinyi China 34°23N 118°21E 79 E12
Xique-Xique Brazil 10°50S 42°40W 122 B2
Xixiang China 22°34N 113°52E 79 a
Xizang Zizhiqu □ China 32°0N 88°0E 78 E6
Xuanhua China 40°40N 115°2E 79 C12
Xuwen China 20°20N 110°10E 79 G11
Xuzhou China 34°18N 117°10E 79 E12

Y

Y Drenewydd = Newtown U.K. 52°31N 3°19W 28 B7
Y Fenni = Abergavenny U.K. 51°49N 3°1W 28 D7
Y Gelli Gandryll = Hay-on-Wye U.K. 52°5N 3°8W 28 C7
Y Trallwng = Welshpool U.K. 52°39N 3°8W 28 B7
Ya'an China 29°58N 103°5E 78 F9
Yablonovyy Ra. Russia 53°0N 114°0E 77 D12
Yacuiba Bolivia 22°0S 63°43W 120 E3
Yakeshi China 49°17N 120°44E 79 B13
Yakima U.S.A. 46°36N 120°31W 110 A2
Yakutat U.S.A. 59°33N 139°44W 108 D6
Yakutsk Russia 62°5N 129°50E 77 C13
Yala Thailand 6°33N 101°18E 82 C2
Yalong Jiang → China 26°40N 101°55E 78 F9
Yalta Ukraine 44°30N 34°10E 71 F5
Yalu Jiang → China 39°55N 124°19E 79 D13
Yamagata Japan 38°15N 140°15E 81 D7
Yamaguchi Japan 34°10N 131°32E 81 F2
Yamal Pen. Russia 71°0N 70°0E 76 B7
Yambol Bulgaria 42°30N 26°30E 69 C12
Yamethin Myanmar 20°29N 96°18E 85 J20
Yamoussoukro Côte d'Ivoire 6°49N 5°17W 94 G4
Yampa → U.S.A. 40°32N 108°59W 110 B5
Yamuna → India 25°30N 81°53E 85 G12
Yamzho Yumco China 28°48N 90°35E 78 F7
Yan'an China 36°35N 109°26E 79 D10
Yanbu 'al Baḥr Si. Arabia 24°5N 38°5E 86 E4
Yancheng China 33°23N 120°8E 79 E13
Yangambi Dem. Rep. of the Congo 0°47N 24°24E 96 D4
Yangjiang China 21°50N 111°59E 79 G11
Yangôn Myanmar 16°45N 96°20E 85 L20
Yangquan China 37°58N 113°31E 79 D11
Yangtse = China 31°48N 121°10E 79 E13
Yangzhou China 32°21N 119°26E 79 E12
Yanji China 42°59N 129°30E 79 C14
Yankton U.S.A. 42°53N 97°23W 111 B7
Yanqi China 42°5N 86°35E 78 C6
Yantai China 37°34N 121°22E 79 D13
Yantian China 22°35N 114°16E 79 a
Yaoundé Cameroon 3°50N 11°35E 96 D2
Yap Pac. Oc. 9°30N 138°10E 102 G5
Yapen Indonesia 1°50S 136°0E 83 E9
Yaqui → Mexico 27°37N 110°39W 114 B2

Yaraka Australia 24°53S 144°3E 98 E7
Yarcombe U.K. 50°51N 3°5W 29 F7
Yare → U.K. 52°35N 1°38E 31 A12
Yaren Nauru 0°33S 166°55E 102 H8
Yarkant He → China 40°26N 80°59E 78 C5
Yarkhun → Pakistan 36°17N 72°30E 84 A8
Yarm U.K. 54°31N 1°21W 26 C6
Yarmouth Canada 43°50N 66°7W 109 E13
Yarmouth U.K. 50°42N 1°29W 30 E6
Yaroslavl Russia 57°35N 39°55E 70 C6
Yarrow U.K. 55°33N 3°1W 25 C9
Yarumal Colombia 6°58N 75°24W 120 B2
Yāsūj Iran 30°31N 51°31E 87 D7
Yate U.K. 51°32N 2°25W 30 C4
Yathkyed L. Canada 62°40N 98°0W 108 C10
Yatsushiro Japan 32°30N 130°40E 81 G2
Yatton U.K. 51°23N 2°49W 30 D3
Yavari → Peru 4°21S 70°2W 120 C2
Yaxley U.K. 52°31N 0°16W 31 A8
Yazd Iran 31°55N 54°27E 87 D8
Yazoo → U.S.A. 32°22N 90°54W 111 D8
Yazoo City U.S.A. 32°51N 90°25W 111 D8
Yealmpton U.K. 50°21N 4°1W 29 G5
Yecheng China 37°54N 77°26E 78 D4
Yelets Russia 52°40N 38°30E 70 D6
Yell U.K. 60°35N 1°5W 22 A15
Yell Sd. U.K. 60°33N 1°15W 22 A15
Yellow = Huang He → China 37°55N 118°50E 79 D12
Yellow Sea China 35°0N 123°0E 79 D13
Yellowhead Pass Canada 52°53N 118°25W 108 D8
Yellowknife Canada 62°27N 114°29W 108 C8
Yellowstone → U.S.A. 47°59N 103°59W 110 A6
Yellowstone Nat. Park △ U.S.A. 44°40N 110°30W 110 B5
Yemen ■ Asia 15°0N 44°0E 89 E3
Yenisey → Russia 71°50N 82°40E 76 B9
Yeo → U.K. 51°2N 2°54W 30 D3
Yeola India 20°2N 74°30E 84 J9
Yeovil U.K. 50°57N 2°38W 30 E3
Yerevan Armenia 40°10N 44°31E 71 F7
Yes Tor U.K. 50°41N 4°0W 29 F5
Yeu, Î. d' France 46°42N 2°20W 66 C2
Yevpatoriya Ukraine 45°15N 33°20E 71 E5
Yeysk Russia 46°40N 38°12E 71 E6
Yibin China 28°45N 104°32E 78 F9
Yichang China 30°40N 111°20E 79 E11
Yichun China 47°44N 128°52E 79 B14
Yilehuli Shan China 51°20N 124°20E 79 A13
Yinchuan China 38°30N 106°15E 78 D10
Yingkou China 40°37N 122°18E 79 C13
Yining China 43°58N 81°10E 78 C5
Yixing China 31°21N 119°48E 79 E12
Yiyang China 28°35N 112°18E 79 F11
Yogyakarta Indonesia 7°49S 110°22E 82 F4
Yokkaichi Japan 34°55N 136°38E 81 F5
Yokohama Japan 35°27N 139°28E 81 F6
Yokosuka Japan 35°20N 139°40E 81 F6
Yonago Japan 35°25N 133°19E 81 F3
Yong'an China 25°59N 117°25E 79 F12
Yongzhou China 26°17N 111°37E 79 F11
Yonkers U.S.A. 40°56N 73°52W 113 E11
Yonne → France 48°23N 2°58E 66 B5
York U.K. 53°58N 1°6W 27 E6
York U.S.A. 39°58N 76°44W 112 F9
York, C. Australia 10°42S 142°31E 98 C7
York, Vale of U.K. 54°15N 1°25W 26 D6
Yorkshire Dales △ U.K. 54°12N 2°10W 26 D4
Yorkshire Wolds U.K. 54°8N 0°31W 26 D7
Yorkton Canada 51°11N 102°28W 108 D9
Yosemite Nat. Park △ U.S.A. 37°45N 119°40W 110 C3
Yoshkar Ola Russia 56°38N 47°55E 70 C8
Youghal Ireland 51°56N 7°52W 20 E7
Youghal B. Ireland 51°55N 7°49W 20 E7
Youlgreave U.K. 53°11N 1°40W 27 F5
Youngstown U.S.A. 41°6N 80°39W 112 E7
Yoxall U.K. 52°46N 1°47W 27 G5
Yoxford U.K. 52°16N 1°31E 31 B12
Yozgat Turkey 39°51N 34°47E 71 G5
Yr Wyddgrug = Mold U.K. 53°9N 3°8W 28 A7
Yreka U.S.A. 41°44N 122°38W 110 B2
Ystalyfera U.K. 51°46N 3°48W 28 D5
Ythan → U.K. 57°19N 1°59W 23 H14
Yu Jiang → China 23°22N 110°3E 79 G11
Yuan Jiang → China 28°55N 111°50E 79 F11
Yuanping China 38°42N 112°46E 79 D11
Yuba City U.S.A. 39°8N 121°37W 110 C2
Yucatán Mexico 19°30N 89°0W 114 D7
Yucatan Channel Caribbean 22°0N 86°30W 114 C7
Yuen Long China 22°26N 114°2E 79 a
Yueyang China 29°21N 113°5E 79 F11
Yukon □ Canada 63°0N 135°0W 108 C6
Yukon → U.S.A. 62°32N 163°54W 108 C3
Yulin China 38°20N 109°30E 79 D10
Yuma U.S.A. 32°43N 114°37W 110 D4

Yumen China 39°50N 97°30E 78 D8
Yungas Bolivia 17°0S 66°0W 120 D3
Yunling Shan China 28°30N 98°50E 78 F8
Yunnan □ China 25°0N 102°0E 78 F9
Yurimaguas Peru 5°55S 76°7W 120 C2
Yushu China 33°5N 96°55E 78 E8
Yutian China 36°52N 81°42E 78 D5
Yuxi China 24°30N 102°35E 78 G9
Yuzhno-Sakhalinsk Russia 46°58N 142°45E 77 E15
Yuzhou China 34°10N 113°28E 79 E11
Yvetot France 49°37N 0°44E 66 B4

Z

Zāb al Kabīr → Iraq 36°1N 43°24E 86 B5
Zābol Iran 32°0N 67°0E 87 D10
Zabrze Poland 50°18N 18°50E 65 C10
Zacatecas Mexico 22°47N 102°35W 114 C4
Zadar Croatia 44°8N 15°14E 68 B6
Zagaoua Chad 15°30N 22°24E 95 E10
Zagazig Egypt 30°40N 31°30E 95 B12
Zagreb Croatia 45°50N 15°58E 68 B7
Zagros Mts. Iran 33°45N 48°5E 86 C7
Zāhedān Iran 29°30N 60°50E 87 D10
Zahlah Lebanon 33°52N 35°50E 86 C3
Zakynthos Greece 37°47N 20°54E 69 F9
Zalantun China 48°0N 122°43E 79 B13
Zambezi → Africa 18°35S 36°20E 97 H7
Zambia ■ Africa 15°0S 28°0E 97 G5
Zamboanga Phil. 6°59N 122°3E 83 C6
Zamora Mexico 19°59N 102°16W 114 D4
Zamora Spain 41°30N 5°45W 67 B3
Zamość Poland 50°43N 23°15E 65 C12
Zanda China 31°32N 79°50E 78 E4
Zanesville U.S.A. 39°56N 82°1W 112 F6
Zanjān Iran 36°40N 48°35E 86 B7
Zanzibar Tanzania 6°12S 39°12E 96 F7
Zaouiet Reggâne Algeria 26°32N 0°3E 94 C6
Zaoyang China 32°10N 112°45E 79 E11
Zaozhuang China 34°50N 117°35E 79 E12
Zapala Argentina 39°0S 70°5W 121 F2
Zaporizhzhia Ukraine 47°50N 35°10E 71 E6
Zaragoza Spain 41°39N 0°53W 67 B5
Zaranj Afghan. 30°55N 61°55E 87 D10
Zárate Argentina 34°7S 59°0W 121 F4
Zaria Nigeria 11°0N 7°40E 94 F7
Zarzis Tunisia 33°31N 11°2E 95 B8
Zaskar Mts. India 33°15N 77°30E 84 C10
Zaysan, L. Kazakhstan 48°0N 83°0E 76 E9
Zayü China 28°48N 97°27E 78 F8
Zeebrugge Belgium 51°19N 3°12E 64 C2
Zeil, Mt. Australia 23°30S 132°23E 98 E5
Zelenograd Russia 56°1N 37°12E 70 C6
Zenica Bos.-H. 44°10N 17°57E 69 B7
Zhangjiabian China 22°33N 113°28E 79 a
Zhangjiakou China 40°48N 114°55E 79 C11
Zhangye China 38°50N 100°23E 78 D9
Zhangzhou China 24°30N 117°35E 79 G12
Zhanjiang China 21°15N 110°20E 79 G11
Zhaoqing China 23°0N 112°20E 79 G11
Zhaotong China 27°20N 103°44E 78 F9
Zhejiang □ China 29°0N 120°0E 79 F13
Zhengzhou China 34°45N 113°34E 79 E11
Zhezqazghan Kazakhstan 47°44N 67°40E 76 E7
Zhigansk Russia 66°48N 123°27E 77 C13
Zhlobin Belarus 52°55N 30°0E 70 D5
Zhob Pakistan 31°20N 69°31E 84 D6
Zhongdian China 27°48N 99°42E 78 F8
Zhongshan China 22°26N 113°20E 79 a
Zhuhai China 22°17N 113°34E 79 a
Zhumadian China 32°59N 114°2E 79 E11
Zhuzhou China 27°49N 113°12E 79 F11
Zhytomyr Ukraine 50°20N 28°40E 65 C15
Zibo China 36°47N 118°3E 79 D12
Zielona Góra Poland 51°57N 15°31E 64 C8
Zigong China 29°15N 104°48E 78 F9
Ziguinchor Senegal 12°35N 16°20W 94 F2
Žilina Slovakia 49°12N 18°42E 65 D10
Zimbabwe ■ Africa 19°0S 30°0E 97 H5
Zinder Niger 13°48N 9°0E 94 F7
Ziway, L. Ethiopia 8°0N 38°50E 89 F2
Zlatoust Russia 55°10N 59°40E 70 C10
Zlín Czechia 49°14N 17°40E 65 D9
Zonguldak Turkey 41°28N 31°50E 71 F5
Zrenjanin Serbia 45°22N 20°23E 69 B9
Zug Switz. 47°10N 8°31E 64 E5
Zunyi China 27°42N 106°53E 78 F10
Zürich Switz. 47°22N 8°32E 64 E5
Zvishavane Zimbabwe 20°17S 30°2E 97 J6
Zwelitsha S. Africa 32°55S 27°22E 97 L5
Zwickau Germany 50°44N 12°30E 64 C7
Zwolle Neths. 52°31N 6°6E 64 B4

Published in Great Britain in 2024 by Philip's,
a division of Octopus Publishing Group Limited
(www.octopusbooks.co.uk)
Carmelite House
50 Victoria Embankment
London EC4Y 0DZ

An Hachette UK Company (www.hachette.co.uk)

101st edition

ISBN 978-1-84907-696-8 (HARDBACK EDITION)
ISBN 978-1-84907-697-5 (PAPERBACK EDITION)

Printed in Dubai

Philip's World Atlases are published in association with The Royal Geographical
Society (with The Institute of British Geographers).
The Society was founded in 1830 and given a Royal Charter in 1859 for
'the advancement of geographical science'. Today it is a leading world centre for
geographical learning – supporting education, teaching, research and expeditions,
and promoting public understanding of the subject.
Further information about the Society and how to join may be found on its
website at: www.rgs.org

Royal Geographical Society
with IBG
Advancing geography and geographical learning

PHOTOGRAPHIC ACKNOWLEDGEMENTS
Alamy Stock Photo /Denys Bilytskyi p.139l, /Eduardo Blanco p. 37c, /Maxim
Burkovskiy p. 139r, /Derek Croucher p. 37t, /Ian Dagnall p. 43, /noah Emad p. 131,
/Peter Reynolds/LGPL p.36, /Kevin Schafer p. 85 ian woolcock p. 37b; China RSGS
p. 16tl; Digital Globe p. 11; Lavizzara/Dreamstime using data supplied by NASA
p.116; Horvath Zoltan/Dreamstime.com pp. 9, 17, 49, 123, NASA pp. 13, 13c,
13bc; NPA Satellite Mapping, CGG Services (UK) Ltd Front cover, pp. 10, 16tr,
14b, 88, 130; Shutterstock/Steve Meese p. 41; /r.nagy p141; Tower Hamlets Local
History Library and Archives p. 14t; USGS pp. 12, 13b, 16b, 16br.

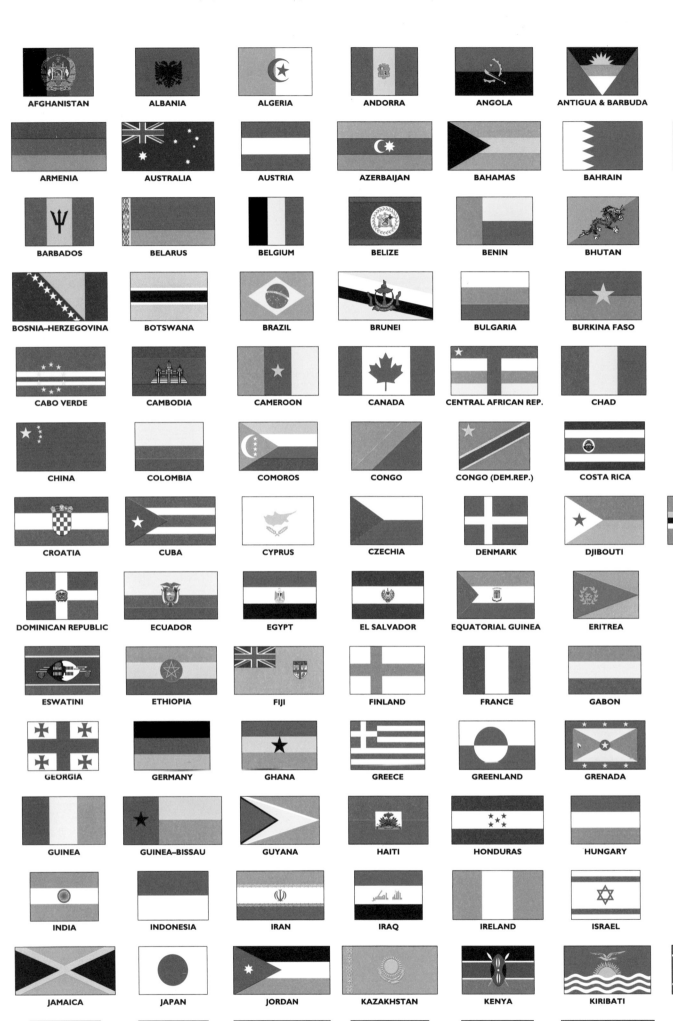

AFGHANISTAN	ALBANIA	ALGERIA	ANDORRA	ANGOLA	ANTIGUA & BARBUDA	ARGENTINA
ARMENIA	AUSTRALIA	AUSTRIA	AZERBAIJAN	BAHAMAS	BAHRAIN	BANGLADESH
BARBADOS	BELARUS	BELGIUM	BELIZE	BENIN	BHUTAN	BOLIVIA
BOSNIA–HERZEGOVINA	BOTSWANA	BRAZIL	BRUNEI	BULGARIA	BURKINA FASO	BURUNDI
CABO VERDE	CAMBODIA	CAMEROON	CANADA	CENTRAL AFRICAN REP.	CHAD	CHILE
CHINA	COLOMBIA	COMOROS	CONGO	CONGO (DEM.REP.)	COSTA RICA	CÔTE D'IVOIRE
CROATIA	CUBA	CYPRUS	CZECHIA	DENMARK	DJIBOUTI	DOMINICA
DOMINICAN REPUBLIC	ECUADOR	EGYPT	EL SALVADOR	EQUATORIAL GUINEA	ERITREA	ESTONIA
ESWATINI	ETHIOPIA	FIJI	FINLAND	FRANCE	GABON	GAMBIA
GEORGIA	GERMANY	GHANA	GREECE	GREENLAND	GRENADA	GUATEMALA
GUINEA	GUINEA–BISSAU	GUYANA	HAITI	HONDURAS	HUNGARY	ICELAND
INDIA	INDONESIA	IRAN	IRAQ	IRELAND	ISRAEL	ITALY
JAMAICA	JAPAN	JORDAN	KAZAKHSTAN	KENYA	KIRIBATI	KOREA, NORTH
KOREA, SOUTH	KOSOVO	KUWAIT	KYRGYZSTAN	LAOS	LATVIA	LEBANON